The Alden Amos Big Book of Handspinning

Illustrations by Stephenie Gaustad

INTERWEAVE PRESS

The Alden Amos Big Book of Handspinning
By Alden Amos

Editor: Deborah Robson
Managing Editor: Marilyn Murphy
Proofreaders: Judy Berndt, Doree Pitkin
Editorial & Production Assistant: Nancy Arndt
Print Manager: Kathé Hayden

Cover Illustrations: Stephenie Gaustad, Susan Strawn Bailey
Cover Design: Dean Howes
Back Cover Photo: Joe Coca
Interior Illustrations: Stephenie Gaustad
Page Design: Dean Howes
Production: Dean Howes

Text copyright © 2001, Alden Amos
Illustration copyright © 2001, Stephenie Gaustad

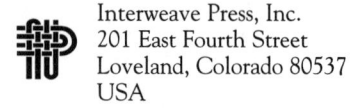

Interweave Press, Inc.
201 East Fourth Street
Loveland, Colorado 80537
USA

Printed in the United States.

Library of Congress Cataloging-in-Publication

Amos, Alden.
   [Big book of handspinning]
   The Alden Amos big book of handspinning : being a compendium of information, advice, and opinions on the noble art & craft / illustrations by Stephenie Gaustad.
      p. cm.
   1.Hand spinning. I.Title: Big book of handspinning. II. Title.

TT847 .A46 2001
746.1'2-dc21   2001016898

First printing: IWP-5M:201:RRD

Contents

Preface 9
Acknowledgments 10

INTRODUCTION 12
WHERE WE ARE, AND HOW WE GOT HERE
On the subject of *time*, and having enough of it 13
Notes to the novice, the proficient, and the general reader 14
On equipment: guidance, and a caveat to builders 15
Why you may want to read further 16

CHAPTER 1 17
IN WHICH WE EXAMINE THE ORIGINS OF SPINNING, DISCOVER THE POWER OF TWIST, ENCOUNTER THE THREE DEFINING QUALITIES OF ANY YARN, AND ASK "WHY SPIN TODAY?"
Spinning at its most basic: drafting and twisting, grist and fiber 18
Why does anybody spin today? 23

CHAPTER 2 26
INTRODUCTIONS TO THE BASIC CONCEPTS BEHIND FIBER, THE BIG FOUR FIBERS FOR HANDSPINNERS (WOOL, COTTON, FLAX, AND SILK), FIBER PREPARATION (CARDING AND COMBING), AND SPINNING METHODS (WOOLEN AND WORSTED)
Fibers in general 26
Introduction to wool ◆ *Introduction to cotton* ◆ *Introduction to silk* ◆ *Introduction to flax and linen*
Fiber preparation in general 35
Preparing wool ◆ *Preparing cotton* ◆ *Preparing flax* ◆ *Preparing silk*
An introduction to woolen and worsted spinning methods 41

CHAPTER 3 43
FIRST ENCOUNTERS: WOOL AND THE SPINNING WHEEL
Grease wool, and why you want to wash before spinning 44
The path to clean wool 46
Better living through chemistry? ◆ *Soft and hard water* ◆ *Wool in the wash*

Wool-scouring teaches basic principles 62
Arranging for orderly fibers: Start with carding 63
The actions of carding ◆ *The purposes of carding* ◆ *A lesson in carding*
Almost-worsted yarns 72
Spinning tools 73
Manual and driven spindles, including simple spinning wheels ◆ *Flyer-and-bobbin spinning wheels*
Spinning your first yarn on a wheel 77

CHAPTER 4 87
DETERMINING THE CHARACTER OF YARN: GRIST, TWIST, FIBER, AND SPINNING METHOD
Grist 88
Determining grist by direct measurement ◆ *Grist and the metric system* ◆ *Determining grist from yarn diameter (wraps per inch)* ◆ *Determining grist with a McMorran Yarn Balance*
Amount of twist 101
The power of friction ◆ *"Yarns" without twist* ◆ *The effects of different amounts of twist* ◆ *Counting twist with tracer fibers* ◆ *Determining twist in a fresh single by self-plying* ◆ *The limitations of the self-ply method* ◆ *Determining twist amounts by untwisting* ◆ *Determining twist angles* ◆ *How much twist is enough?*
Fiber 118
Spinning method 123

CHAPTER 5 126
ACCURATE MEASUREMENTS AND SOME PHYSICAL PROPERTIES OF THE BIG FOUR FIBERS: IN WHICH WE LOOK AT HOW FIBERS STRETCH WHEN MEASURED, FIGURE MOISTURE CONTENT AND REGAIN, AND LEARN A BIT MORE ABOUT THE BIG FOUR'S PHYSICAL PROPERTIES AND CULTURAL REQUIREMENTS
Accuracy and length measurements 129
Accuracy and weight measurements 132
**Some physical properties and growing requirements of
the Big Four fibers** 136

CHAPTER 6 139
SINKAGE AND SHRINKAGE: A DISCOURSE ON FIBER AND OTHER STUFF THAT COMES WITH IT, ON FIBER PREPARATION (WITH PARTICULAR ATTENTION TO WOOL AND FLAX), ON THE LOSS AND GAIN OF TIME, ON VARIOUS TYPES OF COMBING, AND ON THE VALUE OF PRODUCTIVITY

Figuring wool's moisture content 139
Figuring wool's clean yield 142
The value of scouring and carding 143
The cost of doing it yourself 145
Raw or commercially prepared fiber? 147
Contaminants and chemical damage 149
An overview of types of wool combing 151
Rough-combing ◆ *Lock combing* ◆ *Full worsted combing* ◆ *Spinning semi-worsted yarn*
Flax 167
Processing flax ◆ *Spinning flax*
How fast can a person spin? 172

CHAPTER 7 174
SPINNERS' TOOLS AND SAVVY: TYPES OF DISTAVES, SPINDLES, AND WHEELS; HIRING OUT FIBER PREPARATION; ISSUES WITH STORAGE AND CRITTERS; MAKING ROPE FROM LEFTOVERS; AND DISASSEMBLING YARN

Distaves 174
Refining your spindle skills 176
Princess Twinkle versus the Egyptians ◆ *Spindle proficiency*
Spinning wheels 181
What kind of wheel is it? ◆ *Tensioning systems* ◆ *Using the classification information* ◆ *Tensioning notes* ◆ *Motor spinners*
Hiring out your fiber preparation 193
Storage, and contending with critters 196
Moths and carpet beetles: How they work ◆ *Getting rid of bugs*
Setting twist and storing yarn 199
Records 201

The luxury of handspun rope 202
Making rope ◆ *Using rope*

Disassembling yarn 206

CHAPTER 8 208
WHEEL MECHANICS: IN WHICH ARE DISCLOSED AN ASTOUNDING NUMBER OF THINGS, SOME OF WHICH WILL MAKE YOU A FASTER SPINNER

Continuous and discontinuous spinning devices 209

The flyer-and-bobbin assembly 210
 Single-drive, bobbin-lead wheels ◆ Single-drive, flyer-lead wheels ◆ Double-drive wheels ◆ Slippage saves the day ◆ Double-drive wheel adjustments ◆ Solving a double-drive equation by operating the wheel as single-drive, flyer-lead ◆ Changes in twist amounts during winding-off ◆ Additional notes on flyer-and-bobbin wheels

Driven spindles 236

CHAPTER 9 242
THE PURPOSEFUL YARN: PROJECTS AND CALCULATIONS, AND YARN FOR ALL REASONS

Fiber through history 243
The relationship between the yarn and the textile technique 244
General considerations for all yarns 248
How much yarn? 249
Educated guesses 254

CHAPTER 10 263
YARN HANDLING AND PROCESSING FROM BOBBIN TO HANK: IN WHICH WE LEARN TO MANAGE SKEINS WITH SPEED AND ACCURACY WHILE REMAINING PERSONALLY UNSNARLED

Equipment for winding skeins 264
Equipment for unwinding skeins 266
Skein construction 271
Skein handling 277

CHAPTER 11 284
PLYING: AN INTRODUCTION TO A HIGH-LEVEL SKILL OFTEN TAKEN FOR GRANTED

Why ply? 285
Simple, complex, and the matter of strength 288
Twist: S and Z, up and down 290
The four great principles of plying 291
First principle: Tension ◆ Second principle: Distance ◆ Third principle: Ply from re-wound bobbins ◆ Digression on yarn packages ◆ Fourth principle: Constant motion
Plying methods 297
Jerk-it and tromp-and-hope plying ◆ Hand-over-hand plying
Imperfect yarns, improved yarns, and novelty yarns 306
Plying and twist 310
Approaching the "ideal" plied yarn ◆ A flirtation with novelty yarns ◆ Complex yarns

CHAPTER 12 332
TOOLS AND EQUIPMENT

1: Scutching sword and base 333
2: Beetling mallet and log 335
3: Nøstepinne or winding stick (ball winder) 337
4: Hooked stick (twisty-stick) and crochet hook 339
5: Niddy-noddy, two forms 341
6: Coin spindle or tahkli 344
7: Drop spindles: low- and high-whorl 346
8: Thai spindle 348
9: Southwestern spindle 349
10: Storage bobbins and rack 350
11: Simple combs, ripples, and hackles 351
12: Distaves: hand-held, belt, and freestanding 358
13: Skirders 362
14: Blocking reel and stand 363
Additional comments on building equipment 368

Chapter 13 369
Noils, linters, and thrums: Recipes, tips, charts, calculations, and miscellanea

Mixtures 369
Carding-and-spinning oil emulsion ◆ Drive-band dressing ◆ Special wheel polish ◆ A good soap recipe ◆ Saxon blue, oleum, or acid indigo ◆ Rob Gunter's soap quench, or super-quench ◆ Sizing recipes

The art of the drive-band 377
Bumpless drive-bands ◆ Double-drive drive-bands: "Why are they saying those terrible things about my drive-band crossing?" ◆ How to put on a plain old drive-band

Factors and calculations: yarns and fabrics 383
Twist factors ◆ A method for estimating yarn grist from the thread count of a plain-weave cloth ◆ A method for estimating yarn grist from the thickness of a textile ◆ Conversion table, wraps-to-grist ◆ Fiber burn chart ◆ Maximum yarn capacities for common bobbin sizes ◆ Standard yarn capacity of various spindle copps ◆ How to calculate requirements for making ropes and cords

Calculating drive ratios and take-up 389
How to calculate single-drive ratios ◆ How to calculate double-drive, bobbin-lead ratios ◆ Differential rotational speed (DRS)

Special treats 398
Punis, and how to make them ◆ A short discussion of fine spinning ◆ Real homemade ginger beer ◆ Flax crackers

An Idiosyncratic Glossary 404

An Opinionated, Annotated Bibliography 474

PREFACE

No one person can claim to "write" a book such as this. The theme has been stated time and again, by those better spoken than I. You know, along the lines of "No man is an island" or "I owe it all to Miss Gorkum, my third-grade English teacher, who forced me to read," and so forth.

Fact is, I didn't "write" any of this. These aren't my words. These are everyone's words: your words, her words, his words, their words.

What I have done is to borrow these words, our words, and attempt to arrange them in a way that represents the concepts, principles, and experiences of handspinning.

The facts, opinions, observations, mistakes, victories, achievements, images, and anecdotes have all been gained in the company of other handspinners, other people. Producing this work is not and never has been a solo experience.

I am humbly grateful to all who have let me see, listen, participate, and, above all, to learn.

Acknowledgments

To everyone who bought a wheel, a fiber-flogger, or other equipment, thereby helping to pay the rent. . . .

To everyone who suffered through our classes, being used as test subjects or demonstrators, or having to beat the clock, or to count humps, turns and twists. . . .

To all of you who keep the faith, who follow and forward "the ancient and honorable craft". . . .

To all of you who turn out for contests, meetings, demonstrations, fairs, spin-ins, sheep-to-shawls, workshops, bring-and-brags, and retreats. . . .

To all of you who sponsor such affairs. . . .

Thank you, one and all.

And thanks to the giants, the heroic figures, the stellar beings who have let me look over their shoulders, who have supported me with meals, materials, money, space, time, and encouragement, who have furnished example, challenge, and goal. I can do no less than to list them (in no significant order, you guys): Susan Claire Druding, Bette and Bernie Hochberg, Celia Quinn, Paula Simmons, Bertie Williams, Andy MacEwan, Candace Crockett, Bob Harris, Lee Raven, Kate Obenour, Maggie Broznan, Barbara Pendergast, Glory Dale Koehler, Norman Russell, Rachel Brown, Rita Jean Stochoski, Elsie Davenport, Allen Fannin, Jane Patrick, Tui Hedstrom, Richard and Walter and the ladies Ashford, Rick Reeves, Ann Bliss, Mabel Ross, Jan Louet, Mary Black, the "other" Mary Black, Ted Carson, Lynn Teague, Henry Clemes, Helen Canzonari, Peter Collingwood, Alice Tulloch, Brucie Connell, Kathy MacPherson, Becky Norton, C. Norman and Dorothy Hicks, Ann Blinks, Ginny Thorsen, Dale Pettigrew, Bill and Liz Taylor, Nan Miller, Cece Paape, Phyllis Patterson, Barry and Dan Schacht, Pat Slaven, Marie Masuda, Jerri Bissel, Peter Teal, Naomi Towner Whiting, Sara Lamb, John and Karen McNary, Judith Buxton, Iris Kitagawa, Betty Amos (Mom), Art and Evelyn Cozens, Salli Rasberry, Erma Green, Esther McKinley, Helen Pope, Doc Ward, Sarah Swett, Lolli Jacobson, Karen Alessandro, Lew and Katie Turner, Jean Case, Cheryl Kolander, Gisela and Bill Evitt, Terry Tinkham, Deirdre Wallace, Doug Olsen and Alice Wood, Francis Siminoff, Jay Gaynor, Priscilla Gibson-Roberts, Kate Peck Kent, Olive and Harry Linder, Persis Grayson, Tony Cardarelle,

Karen Pauli, Martha Stanley, Marilyn Wetton, Rosemary Brock, Bruce and Debra Matz, Laura Wynholds, Jim and Michel Williams . . . for what you have done for me, no, for what you have done for us all: thank you.

Particular and special thanks to the following people, for making this book a reality:

Deborah Robson who has prevailed through the years as both my editor and the editor of *Spin-Off* magazine;

Linda Ligon, publisher and friend, who has kept this project afloat with kindness, calm wit, encouragement, and an occasional dinner;

Elaine Benfatto who, with her style, humor, and expertise, has greatly aided in preparation of this manuscript;

Marilyn Murphy and Dean Howes of Interweave Press who have taken my proddings, mumblings, and queries with good humor and grace, thereby aiding and abetting this work in becoming a "real" book. Thank you.

And to my life's light, my illumination, the wind beneath my wings, the gentle soul who has had to put up with this book business for so many years, my wife and boon companion, Stephenie Gaustad.

Thank you, Stephenie.

INTRODUCTION

Where We Are, and How We Got Here

WAY BACK IN THE 1960S, most handspinning occurred at craft schools and historic sites, or as an activity to supplement family incomes in rural Appalachia.

With advent of the 1970s, handspinning became both avant garde and popular: it presented just the right mix of back-to-nature commitment, rebellion, self-reliance, and other swell qualities. Handspinning was "good," and best when done in the grease.

At the close of the decade, a new direction was taken, involving vast amounts of strange yarn assembled under the aegis of Originality, Individuality, Creativity, and that giant-killer of criticism, Self-Expression. The Artiste, the Atelier, and peculiar yarn ruled supreme.

Along came the 1980s and a new wave of handspinners. This group discovered that, with a little care, they could produce something approaching "real" yarn, useful for knitting, weaving, crocheting, tatting, needlepoint—just everything! As the possibilities presented by this mind-boggling notion blossomed forth, handspinners became critical of their yarns' suitability and embraced textile crafts beyond the spinning process.

At the beginning of the twenty-first century, yesterday's handspinner is likely to be today's weaver, knitter, needleworker, et cetera. Likewise, yesterday's weaver or knitter may have become a handspinner. By either avenue, we have craft workers who produce yarn as well as textiles and who recognize the advantages of handspun yarns.

ON THE SUBJECT OF *TIME*, AND HAVING ENOUGH OF IT

One result of this is an historical repeat from most of the preceding centuries: the supply of handspun yarn falls short of the demand. Today's handspinner has commitments to knitting, weaving, and other textile crafts, as well as to the wheel. To make matters worse, the more time spent in weaving, for example, the more yarn is needed; but what of the time in which to spin it?

The word *time* has many meanings. We "time" a departure, ask "What is the time?" say "Time is of the essence," and "Now is the time for all good persons to come to the aid of their geopolitical unit." Time remains ambiguous and ubiquitous and not easily defined, even when placed securely in context.

Our concern here is with *time* as stated in the handworker's cantata, the textile version of which is sung in three parts:

The handspinner's lament: "Where will I find the time?"

The knitter's harmonic: "It takes too much time."

And *the weaver's contrapuntal:* "I have no time for that."

In years gone by, spinning was a necessary, daily part of life. The question of having enough "time," if it came up at all, was either rhetorical or in response to local crisis. The textile arts might be temporarily halted by harvest home, roof fire, or High Holy day. Otherwise, spinning (and its many related tasks) continued at every opportunity.

Atomic clocks and acts of parliament notwithstanding, *today* still contains as much time as days always have. Yet nowadays only the most fortunate handspinner can find more than a few hours in a week for spinning. Surrounded as we are by labor-saving devices, many of the demands on our time must be self-imposed. We budget and spend disposable hours according to a priority system. Bluntly stated, to warrant the expenditure of time, spinning must be high enough on the list.

Spinning, like every other skill, develops from a mixture of knowledge and experience. The knowledge is won through study; the experience through application. Knowledge may be found in books, but experience comes only through practice. Both study and practice take time, time, and more time. Thus, to become accomplished at handspinning, you must spend time; to get the time, you may have to re-evaluate other elements of your days.

NOTES TO THE NOVICE, THE PROFICIENT, AND THE GENERAL READER

Do not feel that you have to be an experienced, dedicated handspinner to understand and use this book, which is intended to benefit anyone interested in the ancient and honorable craft of handspinning. In fact, the novice may gain more than the old hand. Veteran handspinners (your author included) tend to be insulated from reality by layers of opinion, glowing self-esteem, and preconceived notions.

Handspinning's heritage extends over thousands of years. Much of the information presented here bears the credential of centuries of usage. This alone does not remove it from critical examination; the worth of a design or a technique cannot be judged solely on how long it has been around. Yet the long-term survival of a particular operation or specific tool shape indicates that it may be practical and effective. At the least, it warrants a proper trial.

By the same token, new and unusual procedures should be examined carefully before being adopted whole-heartedly. The "old ways" may not be best, but they carry their own proof of worth: enough archaic fabrics and artifacts remain to bear this out. The results are not yet in for modern textile tricks and shortcuts. Consider the use of the family microwave for dyeing. Setting aside for a moment the unresolved human health issues, it will be years before we have conclusive evidence about the long-range effects of this practice on fibers and dyestuffs.

This book was written with one main premise in mind: the more you learn about a craft, the better you are at that craft. (At the same time, the better you are at something, such as handspinning, the more you realize how much there is yet to learn.) The purpose of this work is to increase your self-confidence, and thereby expand your skill base. We intend to accomplish this by addressing three major topics:

Procedure, or *what you do,*

Technique, or *how you do it,* and

Equipment, or *what you do it on.*

As you read, two things will become apparent. First, in handspinning there is almost always more than one correct answer. Second, 99 percent of what's here is probably something you thought about, but did not explore because no one else seemed to be doing it. The remaining 1 percent will cause you to clap your hand to your forehead and exclaim, "Of course! Why didn't I think of that?!"

You'll find that the footnotes contain a wealth of subjective and semi-relevant theoretical matter. We couldn't resist the asides (which we find fascinating), but this format removes diversions from the path of the reader who is after results and not small lectures.

As an example, consider the following statement, which I lifted from an old high-school Latin grammar: *Flavius Secundus gave Galba Agricolas three silver pennies for a prize sheep.* A typical footnote might go on about the probable breed of sheep, Flavius' political affiliations, the twentieth-century monetary equivalent of three silver pennies, the changing state of the Roman wool market, and so forth. Interesting reading, but Flavius still paid three silver pennies to Galba for a prize sheep.

If you like to digress, enjoy these forays. If not, ignore them.

ON EQUIPMENT: GUIDANCE, AND A CAVEAT TO BUILDERS

This book contains information about the design and construction of useful devices. All of the equipment may be built with hand tools. General instructions and notes are included, written under the assumption that the reader has a working relationship with simple joinery skills. While none of the projects requires secret dovetails or teahouse joinery, none falls into the "Plywood Fun for Everyone" category either.

If you plan to build some of the equipment, or have it built for you, keep in mind that there will be a strong tendency to modify the designs and their dimensions. Such changes are most often made to speed manufacture, to reduce material costs, to make construction easier, or to incorporate untried ideas—not to increase the tool's performance or useful life.

Plans are frequently changed because the builder (who is seldom the end user) decides that the designer has (1) no experience with the real world or (2) included troublesome, unnecessary, time-consuming details simply to complicate life. So the builder modifies. Unfortunately, once the structure enters active service, the purpose of the missing features becomes painfully obvious.

At other times, the builder takes a notion to improve on a design without a firm grasp of what is involved. Speaking of his first owner-built loom, James Scarlett writes: "Unwisely, especially for a beginner, I built one or two improvements of my own devising into this loom; but they were easy enough to remove and I eventually got it working well enough to do the job for which it was intended." [1]

WHY YOU MAY WANT TO READ FURTHER

What good things will happen to you as a result of this book? Well, it should answer a lot of questions about handspinning in general, show you ways to solve more specialized problems, and serve as a convenient reference. (An added benefit will accrue if you study the footnotes: material contained in them is guaranteed to make you either a very knowledgeable handspinner or a crashing bore, depending on who you are talking to at the time.) And, all other things being equal, you will about double your output of handspun yarn.

It is the author's sincere wish that you find the book readable, enjoyable, and—above all—useful.

---

[1] James D. Scarlett, How to Weave Fine Cloth (Reston, Virginia: Reston Publishing Company, 1981), page 180.

Chapter 1

In which we examine the origins of spinning, discover the power of twist, encounter the three defining qualities of any yarn, and ask "Why spin today?"

Humans have been handspinning for many thousands of years. How long ago spinning became a craft is anyone's guess, but conservative estimates place the event well before recorded history. All ancient civilizations practiced handspinning. Most of us are aware of the fabrics found in King Tutankhamen's tomb,[1] but many sources show that handspinning existed long before Tut.

To open a pharaoh's well-preserved tomb and find evidence of textile work is one thing; the contents will be (we hope!) in good condition and can be dated. Unfortunately, archaeological finds more often take place in conditions where any textiles have long since perished. How then can we determine that ancient peoples were handspinners?

Even when no thread, yarn, or textile is found, circumstantial evidence may indicate the presence of spinning. A pictograph may illustrate the process, or a fragment of text may describe yarns and textiles. More dramatic and positive evidence comes from impressions of textiles on long-buried pottery shards; these are the "fingerprints" of cloth, yarns, or cords that perhaps were wrapped around new pots or vessels soft enough to mold to their contours.

---

[1] Ca. 1370–1352 B.C., and king of Egypt 1361–1352 B.C.

In any case, based on the direct evidence of surviving textiles, we can say that handspinning has been a going business for at least seventy centuries.[2]

We don't really need to know who first invented spinning, or when. Still, it is interesting to ponder these topics. An equally absorbing question concerns which came first, the spinner or the weaver? There is reason to believe that the two crafts coexisted for a time during which neither depended on the other. The weaver used nonspun elements, and the spinner constructed cords and ropes. It is fairly safe to say that baskets, mats, hunting nets, and bowstrings—all woven without spinning, or spun but not woven—appeared long before tweeds and satins, which required the combination of skills. Eventually, both warp and weft came to consist of spun yarns and threads, resulting in woven cloth as we understand it today.

SPINNING AT ITS MOST BASIC: DRAFTING AND TWISTING, GRIST AND FIBER

Spinning is a simple process. A loose mass of fiber is gradually drawn out, while twist introduced into the lengthening strand turns it into yarn. To illustrate this, obtain a little fiber and start spinning. The wad of filler from the top of a pill bottle will do for the fiber, and your fingers will substitute for a spinning wheel or spindle. Hold the fiber in one hand and with your other hand tweak out a little tuft, rolling it between your fingers as you pull. Continue rolling or twisting in the same direction and keep pulling, or *drafting*, to use the spinning term. Congratulations! You are now handspinning.

Spinning consists of drawing out plus twisting.

---

[2] *Those who are really interested in handspinning and textiles have to get their feet wet with a little textile history. Because handspinning is no longer an everyday craft, and is not passed down from parent to child, we must go to other sources to get our "tradition," or background material. A word of caution when you read ponderous historical tomes: few of the authors are handspinners. Their remarks should be considered those of an onlooker, not a practitioner.*

You would probably not choose to use the finger-rolling method to spin yarn for a sweater. There are faster ways to put in the twist. Even so, the basic procedure is the same whether you twist the fiber with your fingers, a spindle, or a wheel. You draft the fiber and you introduce twist.

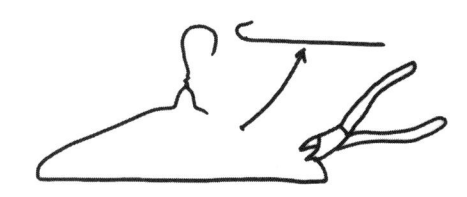

Here's how to make a twisty-stick from a section of coat-hanger wire.

When you first draft the fiber, little or no twist is present. For this reason, the fibers slide past each other without much resistance. This makes drafting easy and smooth. As twist is added, the new length of yarn becomes firmer and stronger, soon reaching a point where the fibers no longer slide past each other and the yarn will break before it will draft any more. On the other hand, if not enough twist is put into the yarn, the fibers continue to slip easily, and the yarn has no strength.

As an experiment in elementary spindle spinning, obtain a piece of coat-hanger or similar wire and cut a length of about 8 inches. Smooth the rough and jagged ends, and then bend one end into a simple hook about ½ inch long. This item is known in handspinning circles as a *twisty-stick*.[3]

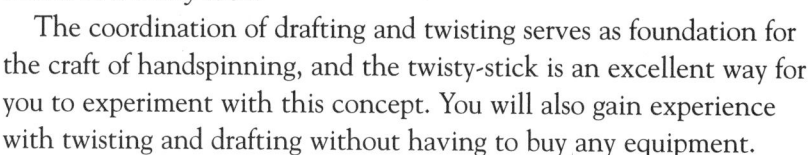

A Scandinavian twisty-stick.

The coordination of drafting and twisting serves as foundation for the craft of handspinning, and the twisty-stick is an excellent way for you to experiment with this concept. You will also gain experience with twisting and drafting without having to buy any equipment.

Twisty-stick in hand, hook a few fibers from the supply, pull gently,

---

[3] *Bette Hochberg and Celia Quinn have made the twisty-stick a popular item. In the simple wire version, it is an excellent, low-cost, effective teaching aid. It also provides a handy and convenient way to check out the "spinnability" of fibers. It is easy, and worthwhile, to cut out a little cardboard or plywood disk and turn your twisty-stick into a supported or drop spindle. For an 8-inch twisty-stick, cut a disk about 1½ inches in diameter. Punch or drill a tight-fitting hole in the center. When you want to change from stick to spindle, force the disk onto the shaft, positioning it about 5 inches from the hook. A word of caution: where young spinners are concerned, twisty-sticks are not a good idea, unless closely supervised. Scholar's note: the same device is known and used in Scandinavia, where it is made of wood, usually carved and decorated in a folk motif, and fitted with an iron or brass hook.*

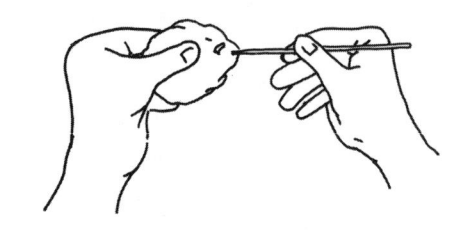

Start by hooking the twisty-stick into the fiber.

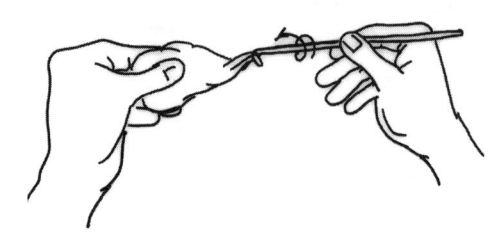

Then pull the twisty-stick away from the fiber mass while twisting the stick and the pulled-out bit of fiber.

and roll the wire between your fingers. Continue to draft and twist. You will begin to experience the interplay between the rate of drafting and the rate of twisting. If you draft a little too fast for the twist rate, the thread will get thinner and thinner, then fall apart. If you draft too slowly for the twist rate, the yarn will get firm, then lumpy and unpleasant, and finally you will not be able to draft any more.

The trick is to draft smoothly and slowly while rolling in enough twist to keep the yarn together, but not so much that it becomes difficult or impossible to continue drafting. The main thing to practice in handspinning is coordinating your twisting and drafting rates so that the process of turning fiber into yarn becomes smooth and easy.

It doesn't matter if you are using a twisty-stick, a spinning wheel, or a drop spindle: the two elements you pay attention to are twisting rate and drafting rate. As long as these are coordinated, you will have little trouble spinning a good yarn.

Drafting rate is nothing more than a measurement of the length of yarn that you draft out in a given amount of time. For example, if you draft 10 inches of yarn in one minute, your drafting rate is 10 inches per minute. The amount of time and the unit of measurement can be anything convenient to think about; what's important is the relationship between the yarn and time. When spinning with a drop spindle or spinning wheel, your drafting rate will be easier to express as yards (not inches) per minute because it is lots faster to spin on a spindle or wheel than with fingers or a twisty-stick.

Twist rate is equally simple. It consists of the number of twists or turns put into a length of yarn in a given amount of time. If you roll or twist the yarn 20 times in one minute, your twist rate is 20 turns per minute. Twist rate is usually expressed in RPM, or revolutions per minute. Using your fingers, a twist rate of 30 to 50 RPM is pretty good; on some wheel-driven spindles, the twist rate may approach 10,000 RPM.

The next useful concept is *twists per inch,* one common way of beginning to describe a yarn. Suppose you have rolled a twisty-stick between your fingers 30 times. Let's also suppose that during those turns you drafted 10 inches of yarn. You have a yarn 10 inches long with 30 turns in it. The average number of twists per inch is 3 (30 turns divided by 10 inches).

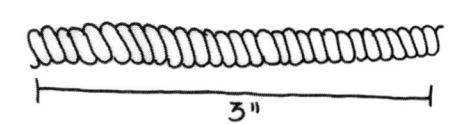

There are 30 twists in this 3-inch piece of yarn, so there are 10 twists per inch.

Here's an important point to remember: the main thing that makes yarn strong is the amount of twist. Even when a yarn is spun from very strong and long fibers, such as silk, flax, or ramie, if there is not enough twist, the yarn will be weak.

Imagine what will happen if you roll the twisty-stick 10 more times, using the same 10 inches of yarn. Obviously your yarn has more twist in it—specifically 4 turns per inch instead of 3. Several other things also change. If you measured the yarn length very carefully before you added more twist, you might notice that it is now shorter. All in all, this 4-turn-per-inch yarn is firmer, stronger, and shorter than the 3-turn-per-inch yarn.

The amount of twist is only one of several factors to be considered when measuring or discussing yarn. Another important factor is the *grist,* or the relationship between a yarn's weight and its length. Grist is expressed by weighing a length of yarn and then stating its weight and length together.

For example, suppose you have 10 yards of yarn that weigh 1 ounce. Grist is usually stated as so many units of length per unit of weight. In this case the unit of weight is ounces and the unit of length is yards; the grist is 10 yards per ounce.

In common practice, grist is stated in yards per pound. Since there are 16 ounces in 1 pound, we could also say that our sample yarn, at 10 yards per ounce, has a grist of 160 yards per pound. How did we arrive at that? Simple: if 1 ounce of yarn is 10 yards long, how long would 16 ounces (1 pound) of the same yarn be? Answer: 10 yards times 16, or 160 yards.

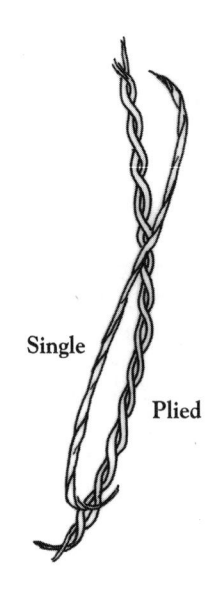

Single yarn (left) and plied yarn (right).

Grist and twist are related. You already know that if you change the twist amount in a yarn, you will change its length. This means that if the yarn gets a little shorter but still weighs the same, there are fewer yards to the ounce or pound. Use the 160 yard-per-pound yarn as an example. Take a 10-yard length of that yarn (which weighs 1 ounce), and add enough twist to shorten it to 9 yards. It still weighs 1 ounce, but now it is shorter. Since 9 yards weigh 1 ounce, how many yards of this yarn are in 16 ounces, or 1 pound? Answer: 16 times 9, or 144 yards per pound.

You do not need to remember any of these grist or twist amounts, which don't represent any particular yarn. The purpose of the figures is to show the importance of twist amounts. Twist profoundly affects a yarn's strength, grist, and feel.

The choice of fiber is also important. Obviously, different fibers produce different yarns. A silk yarn is very different from a cotton yarn, and wool is not a substitute for flax; yet there are other considerations.

Consider our example yarn, and assume it is a single yarn. To a handspinner, *single* means that the yarn is a single strand and is not twisted together (or *plied*) with another yarn. If spun from long, coarse wool or hair, a single with a grist of 160 yards per pound would be practical for use in a rug. If spun from cotton, a single of the same grist would be fragile and useless.

The reasons for this are complex, but they relate to the lengths and diameters of the individual fibers. Relatively short and small-diameter fibers, such as cotton, can be spun into a thick single, but the result will be a yarn with little tensile strength or abrasion resistance. Long and coarse fibers, such as camel hair or jute, cannot be spun into fine singles.

The fiber you choose thus to some extent determines the possible grists of your single yarns. To make a strong and durable cotton yarn with a grist of 160 yards per pound, you need to spin many fine cotton singles and ply them together.

The three important qualities of twist, grist, and fiber are used to describe all yarns. When you can control twist, grist, and fiber content, you are in a position to spin yarns to fit specific needs: yarns that are just the right size, with just the right amount of twist, and from just the right fiber.

To restate the basics: handspinning consists of drafting a fiber mass and introducing twist. The critical factor in yarn strength is the amount of twist. With too little twist, the yarn has no strength. With too much twist, you cannot draft and control the yarn. The three terms used to describe a yarn are grist (usually measured in yards per pound), twist amounts (usually measured in turns per inch), and the fiber from which the yarn is spun. During spinning, the two primary factors are the twisting rate (measured in revolutions per minute) and the drafting rate (measured in yards per minute).

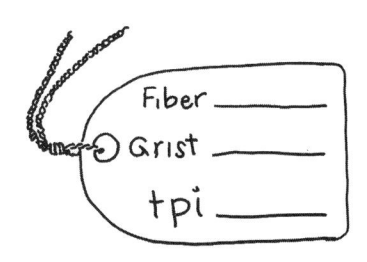

A skein tag records essential data.

WHY DOES ANYBODY SPIN TODAY?

Now you know something about handspinning. The next question may be why anyone today wants to do it. Of numerous possible answers, the best is the one most personal to you.

Maybe you have always been fascinated by handcrafts, or you have wanted to try handspinning for years. Maybe spinning wheels and the associated tools delight you, or perhaps you feel something like love at first sight. Maybe you are a knitter or a weaver who wants to be able to produce any yarn you want, when you want it. You could be a specialist in archaic textiles who needs handspun yarns for authenticity, or you may just like handspun yarn. Maybe you want to sell your yarn to make money, or you want to spin yarns you could not otherwise afford.

Whatever your interest in handspinning, you will always find a warm welcome from other handspinners, and you will find pleasure, challenge, satisfaction, and wide horizons in this ancient and honorable craft.

Contemporary handspinners enjoy great variety in what they spin and how they go about it. Silk, cotton, cashmere, fine wools, linen, ramie, mohair, angora, hemp—all the fibers of the world are available to us, often as close as our local spinning shop. Even when you are isolated, the mail will bring catalogs filled with wonderful fibers and equipment you may obtain from sources around the world.

Being a contemporary handspinner is exciting and interesting. You can attend conferences at the local, regional, state, national, and even international levels. You may participate in handspinners' study trips, retreats, workshops, tours, guilds, and art council events. County fairs, state fairs, craft or historical theme fairs, school displays, public demonstrations, and historical sites all have a place, a need, even a demand for handspinners and their craft.

IMAGINE YOUR KEEN SENSE OF ACHIEVEMENT AND SATISFACTION WHEN YOU HANDLE THE FIRST GARMENT OR PIECE OF CLOTH YOU HAVE MADE IN ITS ENTIRETY.

Handspinning can be a highly visible activity, full of color and movement, or it can be the peace and comfort of quiet industry at home. You can spin by yourself, with just a few friends, with dozens of other handspinners, or for an audience of thousands.

Handspinning is an open-ended craft. You may enter it with a handful of fiber and a simple spindle. You can start from the very beginning, raising your own flax or sheep, and perform every process involved in converting yarn to cloth to a coat. You can also obtain fully prepared fiber, spin yarn, and do no more. There is nothing wrong with that. But wouldn't it be interesting and fun to make something from your own yarn? Selecting materials, applying color, spinning yarn, and making a garment or project offers an exciting opportunity to learn skills, experiment with ideas, and control every step from raw fiber to fabric of warmth and beauty.

Making good fabric or a garment from scratch is not quick or easy. It requires planning, attention to detail, commitment, and a certain degree of self-discipline. Is it worth it? Without question, yes.

Imagine your keen sense of achievement and satisfaction when you handle the first garment or piece of cloth you have made in its entirety. That pleasure and pride never fade, and in addition you have the garment or cloth to use in any way you want. Not only that—if your public persona calls for you to be in historic costume, what better way to show authenticity than to wear the real thing?

A famous musician once remarked that there is more to playing the flute than "just moving the fingers and blowing." The same sort of thing may be said about handspinning: there's more to it than "just twisting and drafting." In this case, that "more" is, in large part, made up of what are called "related tasks," things a handspinner needs to do in order to make the yarn and finish the job—like applying dyestuff; cleansing and arranging fiber; washing, conditioning, and packaging yarn; designing and planning the project; and working on marketing strategy.

Skills in related tasks are not reserved for the accomplished handspinner. You need to gather these skills to become an accomplished spinner. The more you know about the spinning process and its related tasks, the more proficient a handspinner you will be.

One thing is for certain: the more you learn about handspinning and all the wonderful things that go with it, the more you will enjoy it.

CHAPTER 2

INTRODUCTIONS TO THE BASIC CONCEPTS BEHIND FIBER, THE "BIG FOUR" FIBERS FOR HANDSPINNERS (WOOL, COTTON, FLAX, AND SILK), FIBER PREPARATION (CARDING AND COMBING), AND SPINNING METHODS (WOOLEN AND WORSTED)

FIBERS IN GENERAL

The handspinner's working material consists of various strands, hairs, tendrils, and filaments, all lumped together under the generic title *fibers*. Because the production, preparation, and characteristics of fibers strongly affect the yarns spun from them, an understanding of these factors is of considerable value.

In theory, a yarn can be spun out of anything that has two ends. In theory, we could spin up telephone poles as well as the wadding from the tops of pill bottles. Still, most of us choose more traditional and easily manipulated fibers.

It is difficult to say how many spinnable fibers exist. Humans have discovered a great many, but probably not all, usable fibers.[1] The

---

[1] *Most likely to have been overlooked are vegetable fibers. For example, the discovery of flax eliminated the need to seek additional flax-like fibers. They probably exist, but there has not been enough demand (read "profit opportunity") to support more discovery and development of flax alternatives. For a specific listing of fibers important enough to have drawn commercial attention, read "Standard Definitions of Terms Relating to Textile Materials" (including tentative revisions), American Society for Testing Materials. The particular part germane to our topic is "List of Man-Made and Natural Fibers." Not that you need to know all that stuff to spin. You don't. Just some of it.*

discovery of one satisfactory fiber tends to remove any pressing reason to search further for similar materials.

Every fiber and fiber blend humans have encountered has been spun into yarn, at one time or another, although the fact that a fiber can be spun into yarn does not mean that the results will warrant the effort. After 7,000 years of testing, relatively few fibers have met widespread acceptance and been put to general use.

A discussion of man-made and synthetic fibers exceeds the scope of this work. To forestall raised eyebrows, it is the author's premise that we should begin with the basics and study those fibers that the man-mades and synthetics have yet to satisfactorily replace. So we will limit our discussion to fibers that are (1) readily available to handspinners, (2) of natural origin, and (3) usable.

Readily available means the fiber can be obtained from more than one commercial source and that the sources can be located by the general spinning audience.

Of natural origin means fibers that grew as plants, were directly produced by animals, or resulted from geologic activity. The geologic, or mineral, fiber (asbestos) is hazardous, of limited use, and will not be considered further, leaving us with vegetable and animal fibers.

What does *usable* mean? This arbitrary classification gives us a place to start. Let's say that a usable fiber's technical advantages cause it to be favored over others of similar character, and that several cultures appreciate and use this fiber.

Some plant sources of fibers.

Both vegetable and animal fibers are divided into subgroups according to their sources and types. Vegetable sources produce from seed, fruit, leaf, stem, and root fibers. Animals generate wool, hair, filaments, and sinew. The subgroups can be organized in further divisions, tabulating fiber characteristics which help you select fiber and convert it into appropriate end products.

Angora rabbit silk moth

sheep Angora goat

llama camel

Some animal sources of fibers.

We could select a fiber simply on the basis of its source: vegetable or animal. The fibers in each of these groups share general qualities. For example, when wetted, vegetable fibers tend to become stronger, and animal fibers tend to become weaker. Vegetable fibers are generally stronger (wet or dry) than animal fibers. Vegetable fibers ignite and burn rather easily, while animal fibers seem to have some natural "fireproofing."

While these statements offer rough guidance, you need to understand all characteristics of a fiber, not just its generalities. Not all vegetable fibers become stronger when wet, and some are weaker than animal fibers. To choose well, you need more precise information.

Besides, there are factors to consider other than wet-strength and fire-resistance, especially when we intend to make clothing. Wear and comfort requirements then become important—how warm or cool the fabric will be, how resistant to light and abrasion, how strong and resilient, how well it will take dyes or absorb moisture, and so forth. All these things are largely determined by the fiber's inherent qualities.[2]

The major fibers in use for handspinning are wool, cotton, silk, and flax. These fibers have played such an important part in human events that, in a sense, their stories parallel that of civilization. These four provided the foundations for textile development. We'll discuss secondary and luxury fibers in good time; but for now, ladies and gentlemen, the "Big Four."

---

[2] *Obviously the system of fabric construction (knitting, weaving, crochet, and so forth) affects a textile's performance, as do finishing methods and the amount of twist in the yarn. We'll get to those later. No matter what the fiber, the most critical factor affecting yarn strength is twist, yet no amount of twist will turn wool into silk, or cotton into cashmere. You need to understand the fibers themselves in order to choose between tussah and bombyx silk, between luster wool and the Downs, between Sea Island cotton and flax line. Will you choose by the price tag, or the romantic sound of the name? No. We suggest a reading of* Fibre Facts *by Bette Hochberg, a compact and practical guide to fiber characteristics.*

Introduction to wool

In English-speaking nations, handspinners most often use wool, for several reasons. It is readily available, supported by tradition (when the general public thinks about handspinning, they think of wool), simple to prepare, and easy to spin.

Wool is an animal fiber, and by general agreement *wool* means the fleece or hairy coat of animals commonly called sheep.[3] The differences between wool and hair, wool and fur, and so forth, can be argued. From a non-technical perspective, these differences are matters of degree, and more or less in the eye of the beholder.[4]

Wool is composed of a complex protein compound called *keratin*, which contains carbon, oxygen, nitrogen, hydrogen, and sulphur.[5] (Make a mental note about the sulphur; we'll come back to it quite a bit later.) Wool is elastic, resilient, makes good insulation, and is damaged by alkalis. Wool will absorb a lot of moisture without feeling wet. Wool also has the ability to felt, or to form a solid, matted sort of fabric, like the felt in a hat.

Felting can be either good or bad. Felting can produce thick, soft, and warm fabrics, as found in blankets. Felting can also shrink and harden a favorite sweater or shirt so badly that it can no longer be worn. You can

---

[3] *Family Bovidae, genus Ovis, and so forth. O. aries is the domesticated species.*

[4] *Often a single fiber will have both hair-like and wool-like characteristics. The problem of "What is wool, what is hair?" has been with us for many years. The following statement was written nearly two centuries ago: "It is not easy to point out the precise difference between wool and hair, for though, in general when both are presented to us, we decide without hesitation, yet in so many instances, their properties so blend with each other, as to oblige the best judges to determine differently. In fact, it is not very uncommon to find filaments which in different part of their lengths exhibit both substances too visible to be mistaken." This quote comes from Werner Von Bergen, reflecting remarks made by a British wool-stapler named Luccock circa 1805. Von Bergen's own view on the matter was that "[I]t is extremely difficult to draw a clear line of demarcation between wool and hair, or to state definitely that one is hair and another is wool." As far as a practical difference between hair and fur goes, there isn't any.*

[5] *Because keratin also makes up the hair on human heads and bodies, people who feel that they are sensitive or allergic to wool may really react to something else, such as the many chemical finishes applied by industry.*

control or avoid felting by adjusting the conditions that cause it: heat, moisture, and movement. Of the three, movement is the most critical. We'll discuss this more later, under "Fiber Preparation."

Wool is the only major fiber that is readily available in a raw state. Unless you raise your own flax, cotton, or silk, you will generally buy these other fibers in a semi-prepared or completely prepared form. While wool is often purchased one step removed from the source, the other fibers have usually gone through several processes.

Introduction to cotton

Look at cotton, for example. Unless you can buy directly from the field, you'll have difficulty finding raw cotton—that is, fiber still in the boll. Cotton more often appears as a finished preparation, already ginned, cleaned, and carded.

Cotton, a vegetable material, is further type-classed as a seed-covering fiber of the cotton plant, family Malvaceae, genus *Gossypium*. Raw cotton fiber or *lint* is about 94 percent cellulose. The remaining approximately 6 percent shows up as protein, pectin, waxes, sugars, ash, and other substances, including traces of organic acids. When thoroughly scoured, clean lint consists of 98 to 99 percent cellulose.

Cotton is strong and becomes stronger when wet. It can withstand boiling, soapy water, and hot pressing. Laundry soaps and washing soda do not harm cotton, which makes it easy to launder. Because cotton will not felt; rubbing, scrubbing, and general agitation only help in getting it clean.

Cotton is comfortable: it absorbs moisture quickly, yet dries quickly. Cotton fabrics do not develop static electricity and so have little tendency to cling. Cotton resists abrasion and may be spun into very fine yarns.

Cotton is versatile, inexpensive, and fascinating. Unlike wool, cotton doesn't need to be washed before spinning, and cotton will not attract moths.

Cotton does not handle the same way as wool during the spinning, but that does not mean that cotton is harder to spin. It's just different. Part of the reason for this comes from its staple length. *Staple* refers to the average length of a particular fiber. Wools average roughly 3 inches, and cottons average perhaps 1 inch or less. Staple lengths of cotton range from 5/8 inch (G. *herbaceum*) to 2 1/4 inches (G. *barbadense*). Wool staples may run from less than 2 inches (Suffolk) to more than 15 inches (Cotswold).

The staple length of any fiber is based on what is considered typical growth for a season. With cotton, the staple length represents how much a particular variety grows in a year. With wool, the staple length represents the amount of fiber a given sheep or breed of sheep grows between shearings.[6]

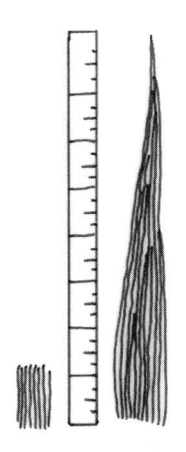

Cotton and wool have very different staple lengths.

Introduction to silk

Another animal fiber has a staple length measured not in inches or feet, but in yards or even miles: silk. Silk has been called the queen of textile fibers and at one time was worth its weight in gold. The secret details of silk production, or sericulture, were carefully guarded.

A filament fiber, silk comes from the cocoons of several insects of the order Lepidoptera, suborder Glossata, and two different families, Bombycidae and Saturniidae. The species *Bombyx mori* (one of the Bombycidae) produces *cultivated* silk, and *wild* or tussah silk generally derives from the effort of *Antheraea paphia* (one of the Saturniidae).

Other filament silks exist (for example, spider silks), but have never been in general use for textiles.[7] Handspinners seldom see the best

---

[6] *Some sheep may be sheared more than once a year, but if you shear a critter every three months, the wool would tend to be short staple, now wouldn't it? So if you had a Cotswold or Leicester (pronounced lester, rhymes with Chester) that supposedly had a staple of 12 inches or more, four shearings a year would give you wool about 3 inches long. Looks like a job for common sense. With shearing twice yearly, the total wool produced per animal will tend to be greater, on the order of a pound per year per animal (grease weight). But the shearing crews will have to get paid twice. General practice, with a few exceptions, is to shear once a year. North American sheep-shearing season runs from about the last week of February until about the last week in July.*

grades of silk, which become threads and yarns at their points of origin.

To harvest silk, soften the cocoons in hot water and then unwind them. A cocoon is nothing more than a center-wound ball of filament yarn, and if the beginning (outside) end can be found, you can simply unwind the whole thing. A number of cocoons are unwound at the same time, and the filaments are combined and wound together onto reels. This reeled silk is then twisted or, to use the technical term, *thrown*. The operation essentially resembles plying. The thrown silk can then be used directly as yarn for weaving.

Working with silk filament produces a certain amount of waste. The waste, called *schappe* (pronounced *SHOP-ee*), contains fibers of high quality, except that they are relatively short stuff. While the filament unwound from a perfect cocoon may be over a thousand yards long, schappe consists of broken strands and bits from a foot or less to several yards in length. After being cut to a uniform length, the schappe is carded or combed. Handspinners most often see and use silk in this form, although they can also obtain the fiber as cocoons (complete with worm within), as *mawata* (cocoons opened and spread out as a form of wadding), as *caps* (roughly reeled cocoons), and in other intriguing arrangements.

Silk is elastic, smooth, and very lustrous when clean. Silk does not felt or attract moths. It conducts heat poorly, so silk fabrics feel warm to the touch. Pure silk possesses an aura of elegance, a luster, and degree of luxury matched by no other fiber.

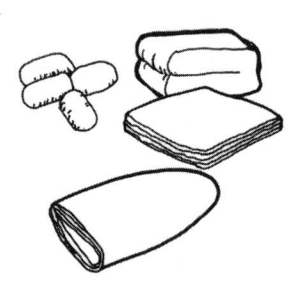

Silk forms, clockwise from left side: cocoons, silk brick, stacked hankies, silk bells, or mawata.

---

7 Except by spiders, ha, ha. Little joke there. Until after the Second World War, spider silk was used to make the cross-hairs in binoculars, optical sights, and telescopes. We all know that a spider "spins" her web, but in reality she extrudes the strands and glues them together. No weaving or spinning takes place, although a successful spider becomes very good at wrapping silk around strangers. Numerous wild silk moths live on the North American continent, including the polyphemus, the ceanothus, and the cecropia. A rough count of silk-producing moths that have been used commercially is an eye-opener; there are about twenty, half-a-dozen of which remain valuable today.

Bombyx silk is white, or nearly so, and takes dyes well. Tussah silks come in warm hues, from tans to dark browns. Tussah does not dye well and is tougher and coarser than cultivated silk.

Raw silk is contaminated with a natural glue called sericin, which amounts to roughly 25 percent of its weight. Sericin is an albuminous substance; a well-known example of albumin is egg white. Sericin, which holds the cocoon together, is softened, but not removed, before reeling takes place. This does not cause any particular difficulty during spinning, and the sericin is better removed from finished yarns and fabric than from unspun fiber.

Eventually, however, the sericin should be removed. Its presence dulls or eliminates silk's luster, and it causes the fabric to feel clammy or sticky under some circumstances, stiff and uncomfortable under others. Sericin makes it difficult to achieve consistent dye penetration, uniform or *level* colors, and reproducible work. To clean silk when you're ready, simmer the material in a strong soapy solution, or, to use the commercial term, *boil it off*. When the fiber is dry, pick out the junk as you would when working with any other fiber.

Silk, often called the strongest of the natural fibers, is occasionally compared favorably in strength to steel wire. While this makes good advertising copy, it isn't quite true.

Introduction to flax and linen

At least three other natural fibers are stronger than silk, and one belongs to the "Big Four": flax. A vegetable fiber, flax also falls under the classification of *bast* fibers, which means that the fiber comes from the inner bark tissue of stems of the source plant, in this case family Linaceae, genus *Linum*, species *usitatissimum*.[8] Flax fiber is made up of many bundles of tiny fiberlets, called *ultimates*, which are attached and

---

[8] Other bast fibers in commercial use include hemp (Cannabis sativa . . . right), jute (Corchorus spp.), kenaf (Hibiscus cannabinus), and ramie (Boehmeria nivea). The other common vegetable fibers that are stronger than silk are ramie and hemp. In case you wondered, sisal, henequen, abaca, and such are leaf fibers. They are not often available to, or used by, contemporary handspinners.

bound to other ultimates by a pectin substance. These bundles of ultimates constitute what we see as the flax fiber.

The full length of the plant stem determines the overall length of the fiber. Because the longest fiber commands the best price, flax harvesters pull up the plants, roots and all, instead of cutting them.

Flax fiber is about 70 percent cellulose and about 30 percent pectin substances, lignin, and ash. During washing, the pectin slowly breaks down and the fiber bundles split into finer and finer divisions, so linen fabrics become softer and "nicer" with extended use.

Notice the term *linen*. The subject of flax is riddled with tradition, and this is an example of a traditional oddity: the moment flax becomes yarn, its name changes to linen. This can be confusing, because the word *linen* itself is misleading; for example, we speak of *table linens* or *bed linens* even when the items are made of cotton or cotton/synthetic blends. To clear things up: *linen* as a generic term often describes intended use rather than fiber content. When applied to yarn, *linen* means that the fiber ingredient is flax.

The flax fiber is glossy, smooth, and, as we've noted, very strong. As with most other vegetable fibers, flax becomes stronger when wet. Flax (like cotton) is quickly affected by acids, tolerates alkalis, and launders well. Flax is a *cool* fiber: it conducts heat better than cotton. Flax absorbs moisture more quickly than cotton, and it dries faster too.

Linen yarns are spun from either *line flax* or *tow*. Both line and tow are flax: the difference between the two takes place during the last steps in fiber preparation. Line is long, carefully hackled (combed) flax, and in some grades looks like blonde human hair. Line spins into the finest and smoothest linen yarn possible. Tow, a byproduct of the line-flax preparation process, is the short, fuzzy stuff removed during hackling or combing. It is frequently carded and handled in the same manner as wool. Yarns spun from tow are rough and "hairy."

Line flax comes in a form known as a *strick*. A strick (rhymes with *stick*) is an industrial-sized bundle, too large and bulky for handspinning. So a handspinner divides the strick into convenient amounts called *fingers*. A strick of line flax may weigh a

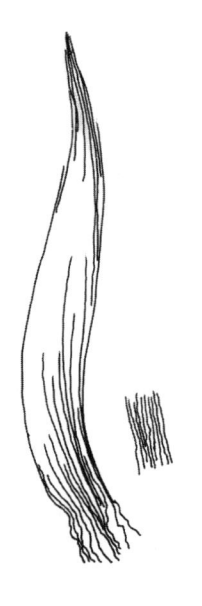

Line flax (left) and tow flax (right).

pound or more, and a finger might weigh about an ounce. Tow is available commercially in two carded forms, one a bulk mass and the other a linear, rope-like preparation known as *sliver*.

A word of caution: flax fiber, whether line or tow, is very flammable. Once converted into yarns and fabrics, it catches fire about as readily as cotton. As fiber, however, it can all too easily be ignited when conditions are wrong. In fact, flax tow was the preferred tinder material in flint-and-steel tinder boxes, the precursors of kitchen matches. As picturesque as it seems, don't spin flax beside an open fireplace, and stay away from other open flames or intense heat sources.

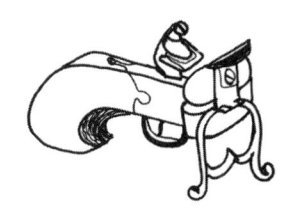

Flax tow served as the tinder material in flint-and-steel days.

Getting flax from plant to spinning-ready fiber requires involved, long-term processing. Before describing flax preparation in detail, we will outline the general principles of fiber preparation.

Fiber preparation in general

In its simplest form, fiber preparation consists of three steps: (1) gathering the raw fiber, (2) cleaning the fiber, and (3) arranging the fiber in an orderly manner. Each of these steps may contain various sub-steps, distinct tasks in their own right.

Preparing wool

1. Gathering the fiber. Wool generally gets removed from the sheep by shearing, rather like giving the animal a haircut. Wool from a few sheep breeds can be plucked or *rooed*.[9] Then the wool, bundled and packaged in various ways, comes to the hand of the spinner.

---

[9] *There are also several methods for harvesting with what is called* pulled *or* pelt *wool, harvested from sheep slaughtered for market purposes. To separate the wool from the hides, you can use a lime treatment or a depilatory treatment, or can let the hides get "ripe" enough that the wool comes off easily. It might interest you to learn that what we know as Hudson's Bay blankets are made from pulled wool and have been for hundreds of years.*

Once sheared, the fleece is *tagged* and *skirted* to remove the dirtiest parts. Tagging and skirting differ only in degree. Tagging often takes place right on the shearing-shed floor when the most obviously clumped or stained portions of the fleece get thrown out. Skirting is usually left up to you. Next comes grading, which means deciding what the fleece as a whole will be best suited for: rugs? stockings? a sturdy tweed skirt?

After grading comes *sorting,* or dividing a fleece into categories by quality, color, or other criteria. For example, the pile of wool might be sorted into three grades by fineness: coarse, general-purpose, and best. Or it could be sorted with the darkest parts in one pile, the grays in another, the red-browns in a third, and so on.

Gather wool by shearing.

2. Cleaning the fiber. Good working practice at this point requires *picking* or *teasing* the wool. This means literally picking and teasing apart the lumps, mats, and stuck-together locks and wads of wool to open them up—rather like unwadding the socks and underwear before doing a family wash.

Once the wool is picked, it is wash-time, traditionally called *scouring*. Scouring involves exposing the wool to quantities of soap and water (scouring proper), quantities of water alone (rinsing), and a period of no water at all (drying).

In its raw form, or *in the grease,* wool contains, by weight, about 60 percent fiber and 40 percent foreign matter. The foreign matter is composed of countryside, barnyard, grease, and vegetable junk, plus sheep dip, field chemicals, marking fluids, and other things. That list makes a good argument for washing raw wool before spinning it. While numerous legendary and emotional reasons support spinning in the grease, few realistic ones do.

Begin to prepare fleece by washing it.

When wool is washed, the conditions for felting

36   The Alden Amos Big Book of Handspinning

(mentioned in the introduction to wool) exist. The wash water provides moisture and should provide the heat. All that is left is movement. If you control movement, you control the felting. In short, don't agitate wet wool any more than necessary.[10]

Washing raw wool requires large amounts of water. The wash vessel should be of generous capacity because wool fibers with lots of room to move don't felt as readily as fibers which are packed closely together. Having plenty of tub-room also gets the wool cleaner. As a frame of reference, a family bathtub will handle raw wool in one-pound lots. The scouring and rinsing of each pound will require perhaps three half-full tubs of warm-to-hot water.

Scouring wool is a craft in its own right, just one of the many commanded by the complete handspinner. For now, remember that clean wool is better to work with than dirty wool, and you must wash wool carefully to avoid felting it.

3. Arranging the fiber in an orderly form. The clean, dried wool now will be combed or carded into orderly forms for spinning.

Preparing cotton

1. Gathering the fiber. Cotton is picked, like fruit. Until fairly recent times, cotton was hand-picked but the mechanical picker now rules supreme.
2. Cleaning the fiber. Once picked, cotton is transported to the next step, invariably the *gin*, a machine that removes the fiber, or lint, from the seeds. Gins also use dryers and mechanical cleaners that shake, blow, and otherwise remove grit, sand, and bits of vegetable matter from the de-seeded cotton. In the normal course of things, the clean, dry fiber is then baled for shipment.
3. Arranging the fiber in an orderly form. Cotton can be carded, combed, or bowed. Carding cotton is virtually the same as for wool. Hand-combing of cotton is not practiced much by handspinners, but

---

[10] *For purposes of cleanliness, hot water washes wool much better than cold water. "Hot" in wool-scouring means 110–120°F or hotter. Cold water does not prevent felting; it just requires you to poke the wool around while you try to make it clean the wool. Tempus fugit.*

resembles the combing of wool. Combs used for cotton are quite small.

Bowing is a simple, although subtle, process. A tight bow-string is vibrated close to a mass of ginned cotton, causing the fibers to be thoroughly flicked about and opened up. This method works well where labor is cheap, demands are modest, and time is plentiful.

Bowing cotton is a labor-intensive but effective method of opening out the fiber.

Preparing flax

1. Gathering the fiber. The flax plants are pulled when ready and temporarily bundled together. In an operation called rippling, the seed pods are raked or combed off.
2. Cleaning the fiber. The useful portions of flax fiber must be separated from the plant stem. There are numerous steps and variations to this process; we'll describe a generic traditional method.

The dried bundles of flax plants undergo a controlled form of rotting, called *retting*, which breaks down the non-fiber parts of the plant. In some places, retting occurs when plants are soaked under water. In others, the bundles are laid in open fields, where dew, rain, and general damp accomplish the same end.

After retting, the bundles are dried, both to stop the retting process and to make the woody stems brittle. Then the bundles are crushed in an operation called *breaking*. Flax can be broken by being pounded, passed through a device called a flax *break*, run over by a heavy wheel, or passed through fluted rollers.

Once broken, the flax is *scutched* or *swingled*. This separates out the broken bits of woody matter that still cling to the fiber. Scutching consists of holding a bundle of broken flax, usually draped over a convenient log or other work surface or laid in a notch cut into an upright board, and slicing, scraping, and striking it with a wooden sword.

Finally the flax fiber can be arranged for spinning.

Flax is pulled, stacked to dry, rippled, and then retted.

3. Arranging the fiber in an orderly form. Flax can be combed, although not in the same way as wool. In wool combing, the comb moves through the fiber. With flax, the fiber moves through the combing device, called a *hackle*, which is fixed in place. The flax is dragged through the hackle teeth, which separate the fiber bundles and align them in parallel fashion. The process of hackling occurs through the use of several sets of hackles, progressively finer. On each pass, short, coarse, and broken fibers catch in the hackle teeth; the short material—the tow—is removed and saved. Flax, combed to satisfaction, becomes a 20- to 30-inch-long bundle of fibers, tapered at both ends. This is line flax.
Sounds pretty involved, doesn't it?

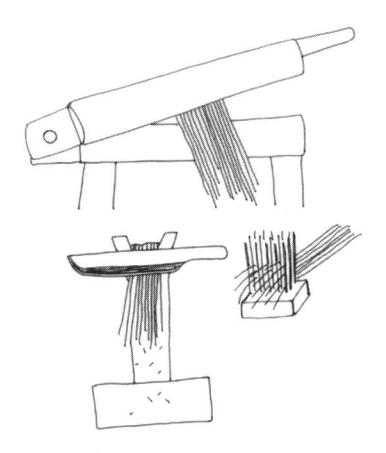

After it has been retted, flax is broken, scutched, and hackled.

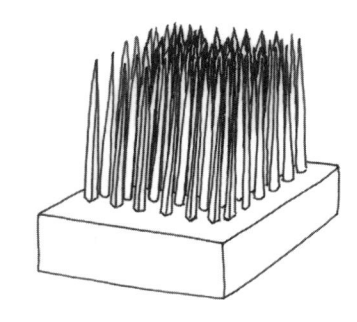

Preparing silk

We have saved silk for last, not because it is so special but because it can get so complicated. Maybe *involved* is a better word.

1. Gathering the fiber. Silk is gathered by collecting great quantities of cocoons. In the normal course of events, a silkworm spins a cocoon, turns into a moth, breaks out of the cocoon, and sets about moth-like duties. In getting out of the cocoon, the moth breaks through the continuous filament of the cocoon in many places, making it impossible for humans to unwind the fiber. Standard practice requires that the silkworm be terminated before this happens. The cocoons are then dried and stored until a convenient time for reeling.

   For reeling, the cocoons are placed in a basin of almost-boiling water and allowed to soften somewhat. The reeling-operative (I dug that term out of a Victorian text) finds the beginning of the filament, connects it to a slowly turning reel, and

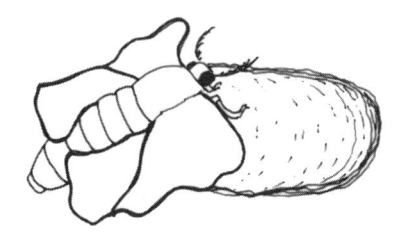

This is a hackle. It is used to separate the long flax fibers (line) from the short material (tow).

Silk moth and cocoon.

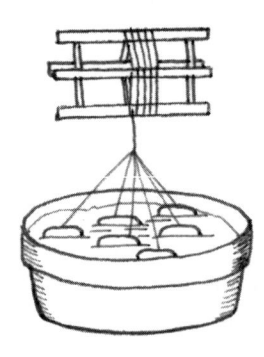

Reeling silk involves unwinding cocoons, several at a time.

unwinds the cocoon. Because a single filament is too fine to be of any textile use, groups of cocoons are unwound simultaneously, and their individual filaments combined into one multifilament strand. Once reeled, the silk is *thrown*, which is a fancy name for twisting.

Reeling (and to a lesser degree throwing) produces a certain amount of waste silk and there are always cocoons that cannot be reeled for various reasons. All of this waste silk is consigned to the schappe category. Schappe becomes spun silk, as opposed to reeled silk, and schappe represents the major silk source for handspinners. Schappe is opened (picked), cut to uniform length, and then carded or combed, like cotton or wool.

2. Cleaning the fiber. Silk fiber, once gathered, is generally clean enough to spin. Silk is not normally cleaned until after it has been spun into yarn or converted into fabric.[11] About the only time you have to clean silk before spinning is when you have raised, purchased, or fallen heir to a quantity of mangled, semi-occupied cocoons. In which case you have my sympathy.

3. Arranging the fiber in an orderly form. Simplicity itself. Treat it like wool: card it or comb it. Silk should be combed, if possible, to emphasize its distinctive qualities, which include luster, sleekness, and sheer luxury.

These qualities don't show to best advantage in yarn spun from carded fiber, but they are accented by being spun from combed fibers, for simple reasons. When the fibers are parallel, neat, and orderly, the sleek, smooth surface of the yarn reflects light in an orderly way. With random fibers running every which way, the soft, fuzzy surface of the yarn breaks up the light's reflection.

---

[11] *Reasons for this are complex, but there is one underlying principle: whoever boils it off, loses money. Silk, sold by weight, is expensive. Boiling-off reduces the weight by about 20 percent. Most schemes to "maximize" financial returns on silk involve adulteration; leaving the sericin on the fiber is positively benign compared to what modern chemistry can do.*

For comparison, consider a sheet of aluminum foil. A freshly rolled-out length, bright and shiny, makes a pretty fair mirror. Now, crumple it up. Even after you flatten it out again, the foil has an entirely different way of reflecting light. Why? Because the surface's creases and wrinkles break up the light, reflecting it in random directions. This corresponds to the random orientation of carded fibers and of the yarns spun from them. The unwrinkled foil, of course, represents a yarn spun from lustrous, parallel, combed fibers.

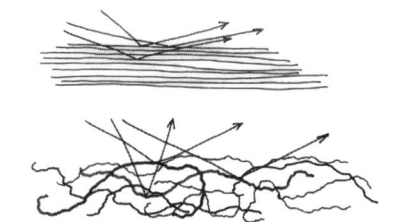

Light reflects differently off a worsted preparation (above) than it does off a woolen preparation (below).

AN INTRODUCTION TO WOOLEN AND WORSTED SPINNING METHODS

That brings us to a discussion of spinning methods, which have a lot to do with how fibers are arranged in the yarn. The most reflective (lustrous) and sleekest (smooth) yarns are spun from combed fibers, using the *worsted* method of spinning, and the softest, warmest, fuzziest yarns are spun from carded fibers, using the *woolen* spinning method.

To review quickly, spinning occurs when you draft out fiber and twist it. Without twist, the lengthening strand of fibers falls apart; with too much twist, drafting cannot be controlled, and the yarn makes lumps and bumps, or else drafting stops completely. Take your twisty-stick and fiber in hand (if you can't find these items, follow along in spirit), hook a few fibers from the supply, draw them out, and roll the twisty-stick between your fingers. Continue drawing and twisting, drawing and twisting. See, there's nothing hard about handspinning. It seems easy, actually. . . .

Well, it is, but we just encountered two new concepts, *woolen* spinning and *worsted* spinning. Despite their names, these two spinning methods have nothing to do with wool. You can use either method with wool, cotton, flax, silk, or any other fiber. The woolen method, also called *drafting-against-twist*, works best with carded fibers. The worsted method, *drafting-without-twist*, suits combed fibers. Those alternate names describe the processes and offer help in understanding them.

Let's look first at the woolen method, or *drafting-against-twist*. When you used the twisty-stick, you spun with the woolen method. You drafted a little, twisted a little; drafted a little more, twisted a little more; and so on. To draft out more fiber from the mass in your hand, you pulled on the yarn, right? The twist in the yarn ran up into the fiber mass and caused more fiber to be pulled out. Well, that is called drafting-against-twist.

The worsted method, or drafting-without-twist, does not work well on a twisty-stick, but for the sake of demonstration we'll give it a try. In worsted spinning, you need to remember to keep the twist out of the drafting area, the work zone between the yarn and the fiber mass where drafting takes place. Try this: hook a few fibers onto the twisty-stick, as before. Start to pull just a bit, but do not twist. Of course, if you pull too much, the strand of unspun fiber will come apart. Just before this happens, disconnect the twisty-stick and put it down somewhere. You should have a short, untwisted strand of yarn sticking out of the main fiber mass. Reach up with your finger tips and gently tweak and tease out more fiber. Keep that untwisted section growing, but do not twist! Congratulations! You are drafting-without-twist.

Drafting-without-twist (worsted technique).

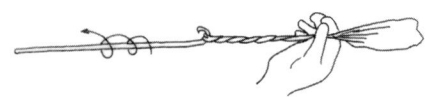

Drafting-against-twist (woolen technique).

Big deal . . . this so-called yarn has no virtue, strength, or character whatsoever. What can we do to improve it? Correct. Put in twist.

Either hook up the twisty-stick to the far end and start rolling, or twist one end of the yarn between your fingers. Whatever works. But do not allow *any* twist to get into the drafting area. If you want to draft more, put down the twisty-stick and pull out the fiber with your fingertips—without rolling it, without twisting it, and without pulling on the section of yarn that you have already spun. That's worsted spinning. Makes woolen spinning seem simple, doesn't it?

But now you should understand the difference between the two, and that is what we're after. Worsted-method spinning works best with combed fibers, and woolen-method spinning is just the thing for carded fibers. And don't worry: you will have plenty of opportunities to practice both methods in the next few chapters.

Chapter 3

First encounters:
Wool and the spinning wheel

Wool is a good fiber to start your spinning career with, if only because wool is easy to obtain. In fact, pass the word that you are looking for some wool and sooner or later someone will present you with a bunch.

But if you don't want to wait, do this: (1) Get a stamp, an envelope, a blank check, a piece of paper, and a ballpoint pen. (2) Get a copy of *Spin-Off* magazine and turn to the advertisements. (3) Select an outfit that sells various sorts of wool. (4) Write the company's name and address on the envelope and their name on your check. (5) Make out the check for thirty dollars; sign and date it. (6) On the piece of paper, clearly print your name, your parcel-delivery address including zip code, and your phone number. Add the following statement: "Dear people: Please send me as much clean, white, Romney-type wool as you can for thirty dollars, including shipping. Thank you." (7) Put the check and note in the envelope, seal it, apply the stamp, and mail the envelope. Now wait for the delivery truck or your postal person to bring you wool.

Simple, isn't it? Please, no complaints about how difficult it is to find wool. Mail-order businesses can place the world's fibers, from abaca to zebra hair, at your fingertips. Even flax or cotton may be in short supply at your local store. But you can get almost anything you might want to spin through the mail. In fact, mail order may be the only way to obtain exotic items such as pineapple, nettle, wolf, and buffalo.

Back to our opening premise, that of using wool to launch your spinning career—and not just because you can obtain it easily. Wool also produces a yarn that is welcomed and enjoyed by many people. With wool yarn, you can knit, crochet, weave, hook rugs, do needlepoint. . . .

There's a strong possibility that if you don't practice one or more of these crafts, you are close to someone who does.

In a sense, people are waiting for you to start spinning.

GREASE WOOL, AND WHY YOU WANT TO WASH BEFORE SPINNING

Several traditions surround the use of wool, and one is the concept of spinning *in the grease*, which means making yarn from unwashed wool. Aside from being a grand occasion to whomp on a sacred cow, a discussion of spinning in the grease serves to introduce more advanced aspects of fiber preparation.

In honor of those who champion spinning in the grease, we list three reasons for doing so: (1) You do not know any better. (2) You do not have any water. (3) Your customer demands it.[1]

Here are reasons for not spinning in the grease: (1) Clean wool is easier to card. (2) Grease wool is impossible to comb. (3) Unwashed wool may be contaminated with all sorts of unpleasant things.

Some argue that mechanical picking and shaking adequately remove dirt and vegetable matter from grease wool. Sure, the sticks and clods come out, which is good. But the fine grit and chaff stay stuck to the grease. The grease and dirt have to come out eventually. It is far easier to clean wool while it's still fiber than to get stuff out of yarn. Grease does not facilitate spinning, or, to be more specific, does not aid in spinning a strong, uniform, and evenly twisted yarn.

Scour that wool.

---

[1] *A customer may commission you to produce yarns for knitting, and grease-spun yarns enjoy a minor recurring popularity for use in making "waterproof" fishermen's sweaters and the like. Advertisements notwithstanding, natural grease does not make yarns or fabrics waterproof. There is one legitimate reason for spinning in the grease, and that is for the production of specific traditional or archaic woolen fabrics, such as Welsh-style blankets. In this case, the yarn spun in the grease permits maximum collapse (take-up and shrinkage) to occur during scouring, piece-dyeing, and fulling of the fabric.*

While it is possible to spin beautiful yarn from grease wool, it's easier to spin good yarn from clean wool. The essential problem is that you are taking a random, dirty, and disorganized sheep fleece and turning it into dependable, predictable, and uniform yarn. The grease and dirt get in the way of this transformation. Raw fleece ages quickly. Among other things, the waxes and fats of the grease oxidize. As a result, resistance to drafting increases and the wool becomes physically harder to draft. Not only harder to draft, but inconsistent as well, because the exposed surfaces oxidize more than the fibers inside the mass of wool. On top of that, the amount and character of the grease vary throughout the fleece.

Wool grease softens when warm and hardens when cold, so grease wool must be spun when warm. A temperature of 110°F or higher is about right, since that's where grease melts. Makes for pretty warm work.

> WOOL GREASE SOFTENS WHEN WARM AND HARDENS WHEN COLD, SO GREASE WOOL MUST BE SPUN WHEN WARM.

By weight, yarn spun from grease wool is about 60 to 80 percent wool and 20 to 40 percent something else. As a result, the diameter of the yarn and how much a length of the yarn weighs both depend on the grease and dirt content. This raises hob with trying to spin matching yarn from another fleece, or even from another part of the same fleece, because the grease and dirt are never distributed evenly. Even if a handspinner produces look-alike skeins of grease yarn, there is no way to be sure the skeins contain the same amount of wool.

To avoid all grease-related problems, scour the wool before carding, combing, or spinning. *Scouring* is the textile synonym for washing, especially in the sense of getting something thoroughly clean. Actually, we advocate scouring often: first the wool, then the yarns, fabrics, and finished articles.

Consider what a sheep comes in contact with while wearing its "working clothes:" sheep dip, field sprays for weed and insect control, medications, manure, and great quantities of dust, sand, and dirt. Finished textiles require none of these items, and all of them are especially undesirable for clothing. Here's a basic principle by which we live:

If you do not, will not, or cannot wash an item in soap and water, you have no business wearing it.[2]

By now you are screaming, "All right, I'll scour it! Gimme a break!," so we will discuss the scouring process.

THE PATH TO CLEAN WOOL

We want to remove everything that is not wool or chemically bound to the wool (like dye). This includes discrete junk, such as twigs, bits of grass, and seeds; grit, which involves dirt, sand, and dust; contaminants,

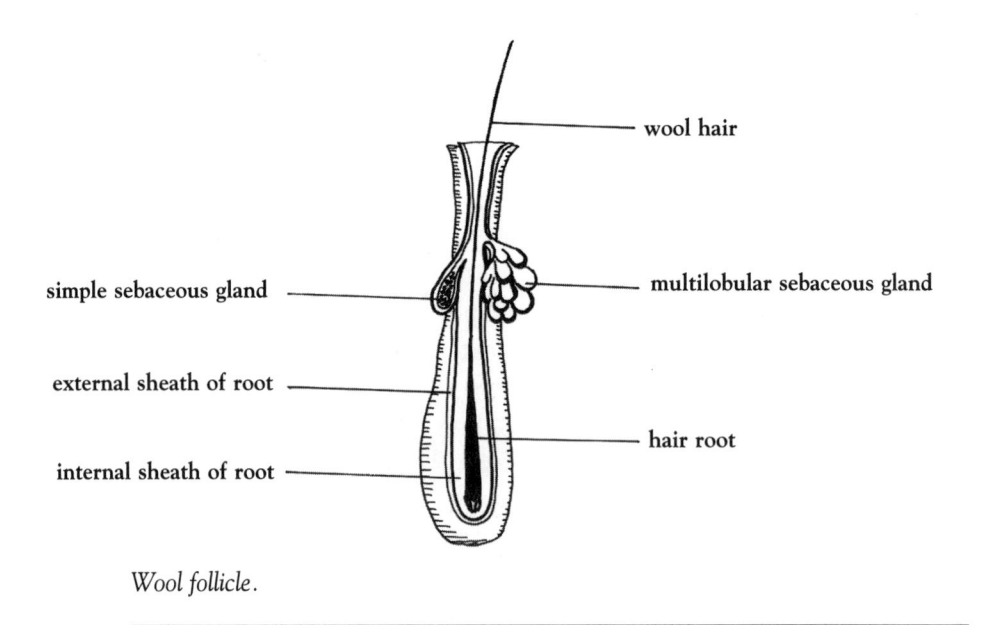

Wool follicle.

---

[2] *This applies to all textiles and fabrics. Cotton and flax are not usually scoured before spinning unless they have been dyed in fiber form, but both should be scoured as soon as possible afterward. Silk may have been degummed, or boiled-off, but it needs to be scoured again. Aside from the wonderful effects of scouring on fabric structure, textile fibers get filthy, unsanitary, and contaminated before they reach your hands. Worse, actually; at some point in the life of a field crop (like flax and cotton), the plants are almost certain to get sprayed or dusted with something really bad that kills weeds or bugs. Fiber is also stored in warehouses, where it may encounter spray for roaches, gas for moths, or rat poison. I could go on, but for now I rest my case for soap and water.*

like sheep dip, branding fluids, and field-spray residue; and the ubiquitous and infamous grease.

Wool grease is not a single substance, and it is not technically "grease." Wool workers call this substance *yolk*, and it is composed of oil, fat, wax, and *suint*.[3] The hair follicles proper secrete the oil in the mix. *Suint*, pronounced *soo-INT*, is the general name for the potassium-related salts of fatty acids secreted by the suint glands. It roughly corresponds to dried sweat. The sebaceous (pronounced *seh-BAY-shuss*) glands exude the wool fat itself.

Suint washes out with plain water. Not so with the fatty, waxy material, the so-called grease or yolk. The grease may be (and commercially has been) removed with volatile solvents, such as naphtha or gasoline. But such solvents are dangerous, and it is best not to use them at home. Fortunately, proper water-based scouring works fine.

Because water-based scouring became the standard technique many centuries before solvents came on the scene, most wool-scouring details have a very long track record. In water-based scouring, waxes and oils must be *emulsified* and/or *saponified* (two key words in the coming discussion) to be separated from the wool. Water alone does eventually reduce the grease, although most of us speed up the process by adding agents to the water (soap, for example).

Better living through chemistry?

Most of us take soap for granted. While we know what it does, few know how it works. Pay attention and you will find out, and also gain a couple of words that you can wave about if conversation lags.

Soap works in a remarkably simple way. A soap-and-water solution, as in your scouring tub, consists of little soap molecules and water. Each of the soap molecules has an oil- or fat-loving end and a water-loving end. Technically we say that each molecule has an *oleophilic* end, balanced by

---

[3] *Suint is essentially concentrated sheep sweat and consists largely of potassium-based (as in potash, or potassium carbonate) salts of fatty acids, combined with sulfate, phosphate, and nitrogen compounds. The "grease" part is a form of wax. In the trade, this stuff is referred to as wool fat. As extracted from the scouring process it is called degras, and in a refined form comes to market as* lanolin.

a *hydrophilic* end. In the scouring bath, the soap molecules surround the dirty, greasy bits. The oil-loving ends of the soap molecules attach to the greasy bits. Their water-loving ends support the greasy bits in the bath water, keeping them from settling back on the fiber.

That basic concept sets the stage for a discussion of *emulsification* and *saponification,* the two key words when it comes to scouring wool.

Emulsification describes the division of fats and oils into minute particles and their concurrent dispersion into the surrounding medium—in this case, the scouring bath. Consider a familiar example: a tall, cold glass of homogenized milk. Milk is homogenized (emulsified) through mechanical means. Some of us are old enough to remember when one had to shake the milk bottle before pouring; those who skipped this step were deemed subhuman by their relatives (those who later drank "skim milk," not by choice).

Along came the emulsification process known as *homogenization,* and our worries were over. Today, milk experiences an industrial-strength mega-shake before being jugged, no doubt eliminating one form of maternal and sibling wrath from human culture. Homogenization breaks up the cream (butterfat) into particles or droplets so fine that they cannot collect together again. The fluid subjected to this treatment becomes a milk-and-cream emulsion. The milk turns homogenous, or uniform in cream content. While we call it homogenized, you and I both know it's just emulsified.

The grease on wool might be emulsified if we shook it up like milk, but wool agitated in such a manner would felt up as hard as a turnip. Instead, we use soap: as we mentioned above, soap breaks wool fat and dirt into tiny globules and suspends them in the wash-water, producing an emulsion of soapy water, wool fat, and dirt.

Saponification means something else entirely. Where emulsification results from mechanical mixture, saponification requires chemical changes at the molecular level.

Saponification describes the chemical reaction between fats (and/or oils) and

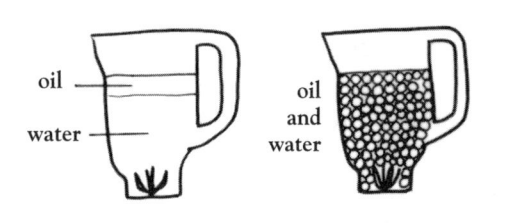

In emulsification, oils or fats are broken up into small particles that cannot collect together again.

certain alkaline materials. When strong alkaline forms of sodium or potassium react with fats, they produce a water-soluble soap. In fact, very good homemade soap can be made by combining common lye (sodium hydroxide) with scrap fats, oils, and shortening from the kitchen.[4] Soaps made this way, called *natural* soaps, have a lot going for them. Unfortunately, they share one primary disadvantage: they work poorly in hard water because they react with calcium and magnesium (the "hard" part of hard water) to produce insoluble soap compounds known as *scum*. These insoluble compounds cause bathtub rings and are the reason that you don't want to scour wool in hard water. The calcium/magnesium salts form a hard-to-remove scum on fiber that strongly affects the way that fiber feels, spins, dyes, and finishes.

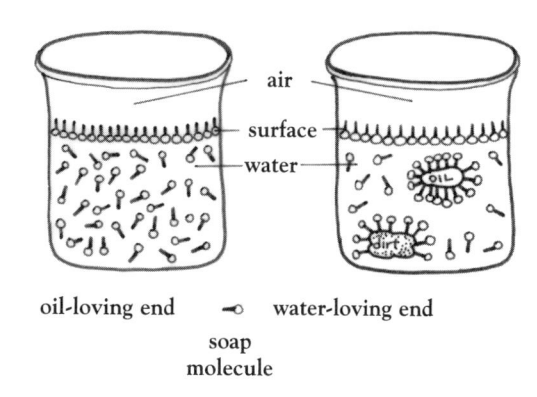

Each soap molecule has an oil-loving end and a water-loving end. The molecules surround bits of dirt and oil and suspend them in the wash water, producing an emulsion of soapy water, wool fat, and dirt.

So if you have a choice, scour in soft water. For reasons that will become clear, you can use hard water if you have to. Water from wells and springs generally falls into the hard-water category. Surface water (from lakes, rivers, streams, and creeks) stands a better chance of being soft.

Because suint is composed mostly of potassium salts, it dissolves readily

---

[4] *Just follow the directions on the side of a can of Lewis' Red Devil Lye. It will make about 9 pounds of pretty good soap. One thing about soap-making: always follow the instructions exactly. Stephenie Gaustad, who has made hundreds of pounds of soap, says this: "Pay attention to details, follow instructions, and don't make soap when you're tired." Homemade soap differs a lot from what you obtain at retail. For one thing, it still contains all the glycerin, which has been removed from the commercial variety. For another, you know exactly what went into your soap, which you can't say about store-bought. Finally, homemade soap contains no perfume, no packaging aids, and no fillers or magic extenders. This becomes obvious in the tub or shower, because homemade soap lasts, and lasts, and lasts. The Red Devil people will send you a booklet on soap-making if you ask: Red Devil Booklet, PO Box 814, Riverton, NJ 08077.*

in water. These potassium salts are "on our side," so to speak, because they tend to form valuable soaps.

Scouring benefits from the introduction of additional alkali. These additions promote the partial saponification of the wool fat and act as a detergent in their own right. Much more important, however, is that alkali "protects" the soap.

Soap protection requires explanation. You will remember that soap is made by reacting alkali with fats and oils. Fats, including wool fat or grease, are composed mainly of fatty acids. Wool itself falls on the acidic side of the scale. Add some vegetal matter (tannic acid) and you have a collection of acidic elements in the scouring bath. Under acidic conditions, soap starts to revert, breaks down into fatty acids, and quits acting like soap. It changes into greasy stuff with no detergent value and zero cleaning power. To keep this from happening, we add alkali to the scouring liquid. We'll use washing soda as our alkali and will talk about how much in a short while.

Our next concern is temperature. Wool fat melts between 105 and 110°F, a fact which establishes the minimum effective temperature for the scouring liquid, or *liquor*, to use the technical term, a combination of soap, water, and alkali. It is much more efficient to emulsify and saponify melted wool fat than solid fat. Heating the scouring liquor to at least 110°F is the easiest way to accomplish this. Still, the bath should not be too hot: above 125°F, even mild alkalis damage wool. This places the optimum scouring temperature between 110 and 120°F.

This narrow temperature range provides one of several good reasons to use a *high liquor ratio*—lots of liquid in relation to the amount of fiber (measured by weight when you get official about it). The bigger the bath, the more stable the temperature, even when you dump in a mass of dirty wool. Lots of liquid also allows more room for moving the fiber around.

Here's an example. If you put 1 pound of wool into a tub containing 10 pounds of scouring liquor, the liquor ratio is stated as *10-to-1*. The practical numbers end

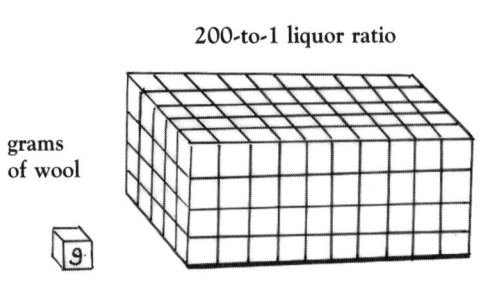

200-to-1 liquor ratio

grams of wool

9

Weight comparison of wool to scouring liquor.

up being much more dramatically spaced. For scouring lightly soiled wool, you want a minimum liquor ratio on the order of 150-to-1, or 150 pounds of liquor for each pound of wool. For heavily soiled wools, you'll need a ratio of at least 250-to-1. For general scouring, start with a ratio of 200-to-1.

In plain English, this means *use a lot of water*. Water weighs about 8.33 pounds per gallon. To scour 1 pound of wool at a liquor ratio of 150-to-1, you need 150 pounds or about 18 gallons of water. For a ratio of 200-to-1, you need about 24 gallons (199.92 pounds), and at 250-to-1, about 30 gallons (249.9 pounds).

In case you wonder how we arrived at our figures, they're based on the dimensions of family bathtubs.[5] For those who set up dedicated scouring equipment, a 24-gallon bath also fits nicely into a 55-gallon steel drum that has been sliced in half lengthwise.[6]

How much soap should you use? You can tell by observing the scour. If you don't have enough, there will be no suds, and the wool will not get clean. In general, about 2 ounces of soap for each 100 pounds (12 gallons) of water will get the process going.

Alkali must be added in accurate amounts. Always keep in mind that too much alkali, or even the right amount at a temperature that's too

---

[5] *The actual calculations are based on more accurate factors than are stated in the text, but then we rounded them off, since less precise numbers are more memorable and useful. Here is what we did. Water weighs 8.33 pounds per gallon, or 62.4 pounds per cubic foot. Of course water expands as you heat it, so a gallon of hot water weighs less than a gallon of cold, but we don't care. We then took various industrial standards for scouring liquors and scaled them down to usable amounts, using a bathtub as a default size of scouring bowl. We measured numerous bathtubs and established an average: 48 inches long by 20 inches wide by 10 inches deep (9,600 cubic inches or 5.56 cubic feet). We took nominal width and length dimensions at a waterline of 1 inch, and determined depth by the position of the overflow spout. Old claw-footed tubs hold more than modern tubs. A tub filled to maximum capacity at the overflow spout contains about 42 gallons or 350 pounds of water. A little over half-full, it holds about 24 gallons or 200 pounds of water. About right for a pound of dirty wool.*

[6] *Do not become alarmed at the amount of water involved. It's not as bad as it sounds, because we intend to use each batch of water for more than 1 pound of wool. Just not more than a pound at a time.*

high, will damage wool. The preferred form of alkali is *washing soda*, otherwise known as *sodium carbonate*. (Do not use baking soda, or sodium bicarbonate, which is too weak.) The maximum recommended amount is 6 ounces of washing soda per 200 pounds (24 gallons) of water, and this is for temperatures of less than 120°F and exposure of five minutes or less (that means the wool is kept in the liquor for no more than five minutes).

There is no advantage to soaking wool for hours, or overnight. If raw wool has been picked and opened reasonably well, a two- or three-minute sojourn in a proper scouring environment will do more toward cleaning it than a weekend soak in a magic potion.

Anything you add to water to make up the scouring liquor is called an *assist*. Both soap and washing soda qualify as assists. Another assist that you may use instead of the soap/soda combination is *detergent*. Strictly speaking, soap is a detergent, but we will make a distinction here between soap and the consumer-packaged, synthetic substances called laundry detergents—Tyde, Bellow, New Blu Smear, Mytee-Cleen, and the like.[7] The chief advantage of synthetic detergents over natural soaps is that the synthetics work in hard water, so you can scour wool with hard water if you use synthetic detergents.

---

[7] Detergent *comes from a form of the Latin verb meaning to* wipe *or* cleanse. *Synthetic detergents of the consumer-pack variety are generally made from alkyl benzene sulfonates or alkyl sulfates, derived from petrochemicals. Synthetic detergents were in use by the late 1930s but did not become big supermarket items until after World War II. The aftermath of the Korean War increased the availability of detergents even further. Part of the reason for this was GI loans. Lots of folks used these funds to buy homes, so developers built many houses, most with hot-and-cold running* hard *water. Synthetic detergents were invented to work with hard water. About this time, synthetic fibers also became generally available. Natural soap does not work well with fake fibers, for involved reasons that we will not cover. Synthetic detergents could be tailored toward the new fibers. As a result, contemporary consumer-pack detergents function best on synthetic fibers and blends but don't work as well on straight natural fibers. Actually, they don't work too well with the synthetics, either. Enter the optical brighteners, complex agents designed to offset the dingy grays that synthetic fibers develop over time. The theory behind optical brighteners: if you can't make it clean, make it look clean. There you have it: bad water plus fake fibers equals plastic soap. The good life. For an interesting overview of the situation, read* Textile Laundering Technology *by C. L. Riggs and J. C. Sherrill.*

Synthetic detergents come in many forms. Those that are both useful for wool scouring and readily available are marketed for use in the home laundry. Liquid dishwashing detergents don't work as well, because any substance touted as being sweet and lotion-like to your pinkies tends to fall flat on its precious face when *mano-a-mano* with raw ram fleece. Machine (dishwasher) detergents make your stemware glitter; they're not intended to scrub out grease, goo, and barnyard.

Although we will end up using synthetic laundry detergents to scour wool in hard water, keep in mind that they weren't made to scour raw wool. They were made to achieve the following goals: cleanse synthetic/natural fiber blends (mainly cotton-polyester), biodegrade to specification, add optical brighteners, control foaming, deliver perfume, apply softening agents and enzymes, address bacteria and chocolate and blood stains, protect your washing machine from corrosion, contain some distinctive "new" and advertisable ingredient, and be easy to package, stable in storage, and cheap to produce. Their retail containers or package units will have visual appeal and won't become grubby or unattractive during dispensing and use of the product.

However, all we want to do is scour some wool.

To avoid a long technical discussion, your wool will benefit from the most generic, least added-to, most old-fashioned synthetic detergent you can find.

Test-scour a lock.

Because all detergents are different and there are so many of them, we can't tell you how much detergent to use. However, we can offer some guidelines for figuring out the right amount. You will need to try out your detergent with samples of the wool you want to clean.

Some detergents contain alkali compounds, among other things. Some don't. The detergent's alkalinity carries its greatest risk to your wool. A good practical test is to mix 1 teaspoon of the detergent into 1 quart of water, introduce a lock of wool, and simmer it for a few minutes. If an active alkali is present, the wool will be seriously damaged, and that damage will be visible.

Does the detergent need to be *protected* with an alkali, as soaps do? Several detergents designed to perform well on synthetic fibers and blends behave like natural soap if the scouring liquor becomes acidic—they break down into fatty goo and lose their cleaning ability. To check for this, make up a test bath containing a quart of water, a quarter-teaspoon of detergent, and a cup of vinegar. Warm it to 110°F and add a small lock of greasy wool. Swish the wool around, then remove it. It should be clean. If it is not, make up another test bath without the vinegar (just water and detergent). Introduce another small lock of greasy wool, swish it around, and check it. It should be clean. If not, try a third bath made of water, detergent, and a generous pinch of washing soda. If this doesn't do the trick, change detergents.

Here's another guideline. How much does the package say to use for a large load of heavily soiled wash? Use double that amount for each 200 pounds (24 gallons) of scouring liquor.

With most consumer detergents, three-fourths of the stuff in the measuring cup is politely called *processing and packaging aids,* or filler, so don't be put off by sheer bulk. Just make sure to dissolve the stuff completely in the scouring liquor before you introduce the wool.

Water temperature still matters. Wool fat still melts at 110°F, no matter what the side of the detergent package claims about cold-water washes. If you are using a non-built detergent (one without additional alkalis), you could take the temperature higher than 120°F, but just because you can doesn't mean you should. A tub full of damaged or felted wool is not funny.

Soft and hard water

The facts of life about hard water are just that: facts of life. Hard water contains minerals—such as calcium, magnesium, and iron—that react with natural soaps, forming insoluble scums that will not rinse out. You know the stuff that makes bathtub rings? Not something you want on your prize fiber.

The softer the water, the better the cleaning action of all detergents, synthetic or natural. Local and municipal authorities usually take the official attitude that water at 5.8 grains per gallon (100 parts per million) or less qualifies as "soft." That is not soft enough. If your water is harder than 3 grains per gallon, it does not matter what the bureaucrats say; what you think, feel, or hope; what your neighbors swear by; or what optimistic blurb has been engraved on your new water-softener.

Soap won't give good results, synthetic detergents don't work as well as they should, and that's it. Commercial laundry operations usually soften water to less than 2 grains per gallon (34.2 parts per million), and they don't do it for the fun of it. They do it so they can get stuff clean.

If your water is much harder than 3 grains per gallon, you need to look to synthetic detergents for good results. If your water is acidic, you already know it because your pipes corrode. Acid water is bad news for drinking and plumbing but easy to control in the scour. Just add washing soda.

Softened water (water that has been treated by a water softener) gives good scouring results as long as the treated water measures around 3 grains/gallon (or about 50 parts per million) or less. Natural soaps work well enough at this level.

It is possible, but no longer practical, to soften water by adding assists directly to the scour liquor. The necessary agents are costly and hard to find. They are also complex phosphates, and many locations restrict or ban the use of phosphates. These additives work as *sequestering agents*, in this case combining with (or sequestering) the calcium and magnesium ions of the hard water so they can't react with anything else, like the soap. In days before phosphates were banned, two commonly used items were sodium tripolyphosphate and sodium hexametaphosphate, better known as Calgon.[8]

If you do live in an area where phosphates can be obtained and used, you will run into the *ingredient dependence effect*, or what happens if you think you put the stuff in the scouring bath but didn't: a tub full of sticky, weird wool.

Wool in the wash

With all of this applied chemistry at hand, you are ready to scour some greasy wool, right? Not if you expect this book to tell you to stuff a third of a fleece into a dishpan, sprinkle it with mysterious pink fluid that

---

[8] *The word Calgon came about by condensing the phrase CALcium be GONe, and the material has been around since the Victorian era as a sort of laboratory curiosity. By the 1930s, it was being used as a water conditioner for steam-heating plants. During World War II, it was an important strategic material because of its use in ships' boilers. Calgon is still with us, although not available in all stores in all areas.*

smells like cinnamon candy, and wait for the wool to jump out—all clean, soft, and the envy of your peers. Sorry, no can do. Wool is wool, soap is soap, water is water. We're talking basics.

Imagine that a proper scouring bath has been made up, with either soap or natural detergent, and brought to temperature. Also imagine that you have 5 pounds of fleece (raw weight). Do you need five times 200 pounds of water? Not exactly. To be on the safe side, think in terms of *more*. In any situation other than survival, water is lots cheaper than wool.

If everything goes right, you can scour each pound of wool with three tubs' worth of water. These include a *first scour* tub, a *second scour* tub, and a *rinse* tub. By "everything goes right," we mean you work no more than a pound of wool at a time and can correctly make up your scouring liquors and the wool isn't too dreadfully dirty.

Each tub contains about 24 gallons of water, or a liquor ratio of about 200-to-1. When in doubt, add water. You can't use too much water, although you can easily use too little. The dirtier the wool, and/or the harder the water, the more hot water and detergent you will need, and, no matter what this book says, if the wool isn't clean when you are done, it isn't clean. So repeat with fresh suds, as required.

Willowing scoured wool after it has dried removes a lot of junk from the fleece.

You can economize on water (and heat) by using the *rinse* tub of the first batch to make up the *first scour* tub for the second batch, and so forth. If you have more than one tub, you can invent all sorts of thrifty stunts. For example, the *second scour* tub of the first run can become the *first scour* tub of the second, while the last *rinse* tub becomes the new *second scour*. In this case, the only water dumped comes from the old *first scour*.

Of course you make up each tub using hot water. It makes sense to have your hot-water heater do as much of the work as possible, but you will need to fine-tune the tub water temperature from time to time, preferably without using a great deal of water or time.[9] While making up the bath, put a few gallons of water on the stove and heat them to a boil. Then you can easily "touch up" the bath temperature.

Be sure to open up the wool before you get it wet. No tight lumps or matted wads; no sticks, twigs, or clumps of barnyard. The more stuff you can get out of it at each step, the better your spinning will be.

It is worth your while to *willow* the wool before scouring. It is also worthwhile to willow scoured wool after it has dried. Willowing is nothing more than spreading the picked, loose wool out on a coarse screen or lattice and flogging the hell out of it with a couple of smooth, limber sticks or switches. Hold one stick in each hand and whip away, right-left-right-left, and so on. You can work off petty frustrations while removing an amazing amount of junk from your fleece.

For scouring, do not try to handle more than a pound of wool at a time. This is a fairly large amount, even when raw and dirty. We're going to discuss scouring a 5-pound *lot* of wool, about the quantity in a moderate-sized, well-skirted fleece. For ease of handling and description, imagine that you begin by dividing your 5 pounds of fleece into six equal amounts (each will contain about 14 ounces of wool). In the instructions following, these batches get identifying numbers during the first scour which become useful during later scours.

Ideally, your set-up will involve three or four (or five!) separate tubs, lined up end to end, with water and heat controls. Such arrangements are possible and even useful. They are called *scouring trains* and have been around for many, many years. But realistically, your first exercises in wool-scouring will be limited to a single family bathtub. So we'll start there.

---

[9] *If you can raise the heat setting on your water heater, you will find it worthwhile to do so when you are scouring wool. Most domestic water heaters have adjustable heat controls (if you can get to them), and most controls have been set for a maximum temperature of around 120°F. This is done to keep careless types and people with sensitive hides from scalding themselves. It is not hot enough for your purposes. Each scour tub requires about two-thirds of an average tank's capacity, since domestic water heaters usually handle about 35 gallons. It might be helpful to know what your own hot water heater's top temperature is, along with its capacity and recovery rate. Meanwhile, crank the unit up to 150°F or above (hot!), and remember to set it back down when you are through scouring.*

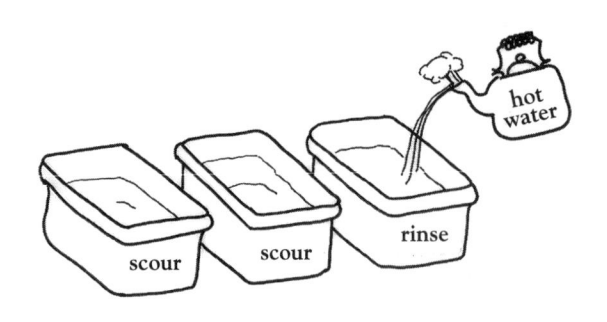

A small-scale scouring train.

Home scouring of wool requires an impressive collection of pots, pans, buckets, dishpans, measuring cups, tongs, rakes, spoons, mops, and rubber gloves (if you have dainty hands). Gather this paraphernalia before you start, because you shouldn't take time for container quests once you expose the wool to alkali.

First scour. Enter the first of your six batches at the far end of the tub and gently pat it down until it is good and wet. Now start moving the soggy mess slowly toward the other end of the tub. Kind of herd it along, as if you were a giant and the wool was 235 third-graders on a field trip. Keep it moving, at a speed that takes you about a minute to get it to the other end of the tub. Turn around and go back. Make three or four trips. You want to flow the hot scouring liquor through every part of the wool.

At 120°F the water is *not* going to be scalding hot, but it will be warmer than you will care to keep your hands in. As a matter of fact, if it is not uncomfortably warm for your hands, it is not hot enough. To direct traffic and to fish the wool out after its last trip, use a wooden stick or a small garden rake. Do not agitate the wool or stir it around like pudding. Just keep it moving, nice and easy.

If the tub has a sloping end, drag the wool (batch 1) up the slope and let it drain. If this doesn't work, you need an old colander, a bike basket, or a dish tub with holes punched in it. Arrange this container so the scouring liquid can drain back into the bath; you can't just sit there and hold it because you have to get the next batch of wool going. Lift the wool into the container and let it drain while you continue working.

Check the liquor temperature. If it is not at least 118°F, dump in a couple of gallons of boiling water, stir, and check the temperature again. You want the liquor to hover around 120°F.

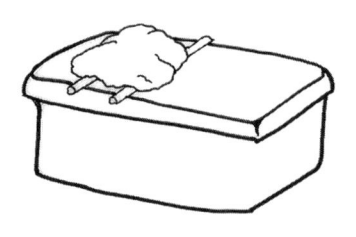

Draining the scoured wool.

Take this opportunity to add another ounce of detergent or soap to the liquor (plus, if you're using natural soap, an ounce of washing soda). Be sure these things dissolve fully before you put in any wool.

Start the next batch of wool on its slow three or four laps through the suds, same as the first batch. When done, drag it out and drain it (batch 2).

By now the scouring liquor looks awful. You could go on, but exercise discretion and pull the plug. Drain and rinse the tub, then make a fresh scour bath, same as the first.

With the liquor up to temperature and your assists added, run batch 3 just like the first two. Then check the temperature, bring it up, and add make-up detergent (and soda, if required). Run batch 4. Drag it out of harm's way, then drain and rinse the tub again.

Set up one more first-scour bath. Run batch 5. Check and correct the temperature, add detergent and necessary assist, and run batch 6, the final one. Drain and rinse the tub again.

You cannot take all afternoon to do this. Your wool has alkali on it (if you're using soap, it had better have alkali on it!) and don't let the fact that it is out of the tub lull you into a false sense of security. The wool shouldn't be agitated, but you should be.

Second scour. Make up a second-scour bath. It will contain the same amount of detergent or soap as a first-scour bath, but only half as much soda, if you are using soda. The temperature can also be a little lower, but not below 115°F. This time you may be able to run three batches through one bath, but it is best to play it safe. Therefore, we will describe the second scour as moving two batches through each tub of water.

Select the last batch you ran through the first first-scour bath (batch 2), be sure it is well drained, and start it through as before. Check the temperature, adjust as needed (115°F or above), then run the first batch you ran through the first first-scour bath (batch 1).

Drain, rinse, and refill the tub, making up another second-scour bath. Run as above, with batch 4 and then batch 3.

Drain, rinse, and refill again, making up the third second-scour bath. Run batch 6, then batch 5. This *first-last, last-first* drill gives each batch a chance to be first through a fresh scour bath.

Wuzzing. This refinement will increase the effectiveness of your

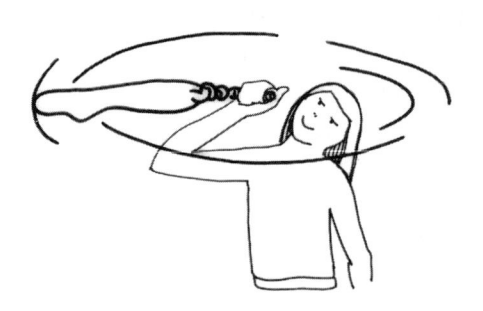

Wuzzing gets more scouring liquor out of the wool and increases scouring efficiency.

scouring: instead of merely draining the batches between tubs, *wuzz* them. Wuzzing means spinning out the water, and it operates on the same principle as the spin cycle of your washing machine. The industrial name for this process is *hydroextraction*. It is nothing more than centrifugal extraction of liquid. Wuzzing has a few drawbacks. It is more work, you cannot save the wuzzed liquor, and it is messy. The advantage is that you can produce clean wool with smaller amounts of soap and water.

A safe, low-tech way to wuzz wool is to gently stuff it into one foot-and-calf section of old panty hose, get a firm grip, and swing it around overhead, pretending you are a helicopter or the world's mightiest swordsperson. Water will fly everywhere. If you care, do this outside.

Whiz the wool around until (1) you fall over, (2) you become exhausted, or (3) no more water flies out. Levels one and two usually arrive long before level three. If you stuff the whole 5 pounds in there, you may get to level one on your first or second swing.

Don't worry about level three. While the radioactive decay of plutonium is measured in *half-lives*, wuzzing is measured in *half-water*. The first ten swings remove half the water, the next ten swings remove half of what remains, the third ten swings remove half of that, and so on. The more you wuzz your wool, the more water you will remove, but you'll never finish. Wuzz for a while, then quit.

Some folks use a washing machine's spin cycle to do the wuzzing. Before trying this, sit down and think about all the things that can go wrong. Provide for them, and then take your chances.

Rinsing. Drain and rinse the tub, then refill it with plain water at about 110°F. Be sure the scoured wool is well-drained (preferably wuzzed). Then enter two batches at a time into the tub. Move the wool from end to end several times, then remove it and drain or wuzz it. If you can still see the bottom of the tub, enter two more batches and treat as you did the first two.

Acid-rinse only if you insist. Several authorities state that you should add lemon juice or vinegar to your final rinse. If you think that you must rinse with acid, vinegar is the better of the two. It consists of acetic acid and water, plus insignificant traces of other things. Lemon juice contains all sorts of things, and it's expensive. The only purpose of an acid rinse is to neutralize residual alkali. It does not cut any remaining soap film, whatever that is; quite the opposite. Remember what acid does to soap?

Acid-rinsing is okay, as long as (1) it really is the final rinse, (2) you have made sure that all, repeat all, detergents (especially natural soaps!) have been removed first, and (3) you have used so much alkali that you need to neutralize it to prevent fiber damage.

If you do acid-rinse, or *sour*, as the process is called in the textile trades, do not be stingy. Use at least a quart of store vinegar for each pound of wool, based on the weight you started with. Our 5-pound lot would get 5 quarts (a gallon *and* a quart) of white vinegar. Do not just add vinegar to your third, or rinse, tub. Make up a fourth tub containing nothing but water and vinegar. This tub needs to be about 105°F. Enter all the goods at one time, move them around a little, and then you can let them sit for a few minutes. Not a few hours. Let them sit for a little, move them around again, then remove and drain, wuzz as you see fit, and look toward drying.

If you have measured your assists with any care, rinsed with plenty of hot, plain water, and not rushed things along, you have no need for an acid rinse. Yet if you feel you must, go ahead. Just be sure all traces of soap are gone first.

Drying. There are many schemes for drying wool. They all seem to work, eventually. Two things help in a big way, no matter which system you use: wuzzing and spreading the wool out in thin layers.

After the flood, drought. The safest way to dry wool is to locate a warm, dry room with reasonable air circulation. Find lattices, grates, or coarse-mesh, rustproof screens and arrange them on sawhorses in the room. Gently spread out the wool on the screens, then go away and leave everything alone for three days.

It is often stated that you shouldn't dry wool in sunlight, because sunlight degrades the fiber. This is true. Sunlight degrades all fibers. However, a little common sense gives you some latitude in how you treat your wool. Wool fabric shows significant surface damage after 2,000 hours of direct sunlight exposure. That's equivalent to 5.5 hours of sunlight every day for a full year. Moral: don't leave your wool to dry in the sun for a year.

On the other hand, what is to be gained by drying wool in the sun? As far as drying itself goes, there's no real advantage. But you may want the sunlight to do something else for you, such as kill moth larvae or zap germs and mildew.

Wool dries best in moving air. That's the main thing. With plenty of air movement, it dries quickly. This doesn't mean it will dry in a hurricane. It does mean you can dry wool on rainy days, as long as you keep it under cover and air moves through it.

Do not try to dry wool fiber in a clothes dryer. You will likely get felt, mats, and mess.

A good way to store dry, scoured wool is in big muslin bags, tied tightly around their necks with heavy string and hung from rafters. Get wide unbleached muslin, wash and shrink it, then make big, flat bags. Cut strips about 2 feet wide across the goods, so the selvedges lie along the open top edges of the bag. Our resident bag-maker sews these up with flat-felled or French seams, all neat and tidy.

WOOL SCOURING TEACHES BASIC PRINCIPLES

An understanding of the wool-scouring process provides solid groundwork for other textile-scouring activities, in fact for any process involving wet fiber or fabric. Wool scouring sets the standard against which other activities are measured. To coin a phrase, "If you can scour wool, you can scour anything."

Proficiency in wool washing gives you a working command of washday chemistry, which can be put to good use with other fibers. For example, in learning to wash wool, you discover how soap and alkali interact. This chemical principle also holds true in the washing machine. So do the interactions between soap and acid. If these chemical actions matter when you are scouring fleece, they matter when you are scouring cotton sheets. In some respects, perhaps they matter more.

Take the subject of hard water. Hard water has the problems described in the text even if you choose to ignore them, or pretend to know nothing about them, or have never heard of them.

There is no pressing reason to restate all that stuff about soaps, synthetic detergents, and water quality when these subjects come up again. The concepts apply to all fibers, but for literary convenience we will now assume that you know what we are talking about and we will send you to this section to refresh your memory.[10]

Arranging for orderly fibers: Start with carding

The next area of fiber preparation involves arranging the fibers in some orderly manner. There are two general methods of doing this, namely *carding*, which results in a *woolen* preparation, and *combing*, which results in a *worsted* preparation. Each method comes with numerous and minor variations.

Contemporary hand workers strongly favor carding as a means of preparing wool. This is not because carding is *better* than combing, any more than apples are *better* than mittens. It is, however, easier to manage a set of hand cards than to wield a pair of wool combs.

There is more to it than that, of course. Carding arranges wool fibers in an *orderly but random* way, the ideal form from which to spin lofty,

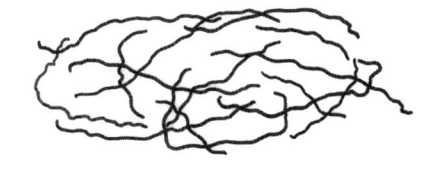

Carded fiber ends up arranged like this.

soft yarns. These yarns emphasize wool's more popular qualities: warmth, softness, and "wooliness." Woolen yarns function well for knitting and weaving.

---

[10] *The concept of* literary convenience *is closely related to* literary device, *although the two do not share the same root. Literary device is usually a stylistic scheme. In using a literary device, we might imagine (and require you to imagine) that the washing soda speaks to the calcium ions, or that we are traveling in a tiny submarine through hot scouring liquor. Literary convenience is common in Amos' work. After addressing a subject once, additional coverage is avoided through use of pomposities, such as this footnote. The root or source of literary convenience is the English phrase lazy author. The source of literary device is, of course, cutesie author, or its archaic form, precious scrivener.*

Combing is considered a specialized system of preparation. If expressly done in order to produce worsted-spun yarns, the process requires a lot of time and many steps. In general, combing results in fiber arrangements (and yarns) that play down the fact that the fiber is wool.

There is considerable difference between the two methods of preparation—enough, in fact, that we will save our explanation of combing for later. For the present we will explore, as they say in Berkeley, the world of carding.

The actions of carding

It makes no difference what tools you use for carding, the process involves just two actions. Doesn't matter if you work with hand cards, a bench or drum carder, a miniature carding machine, or some great greasy hulk of a commercial carding machine, the principles are the same. So we will explain with reference to hand cards, the equipment most readily available for experimentation.

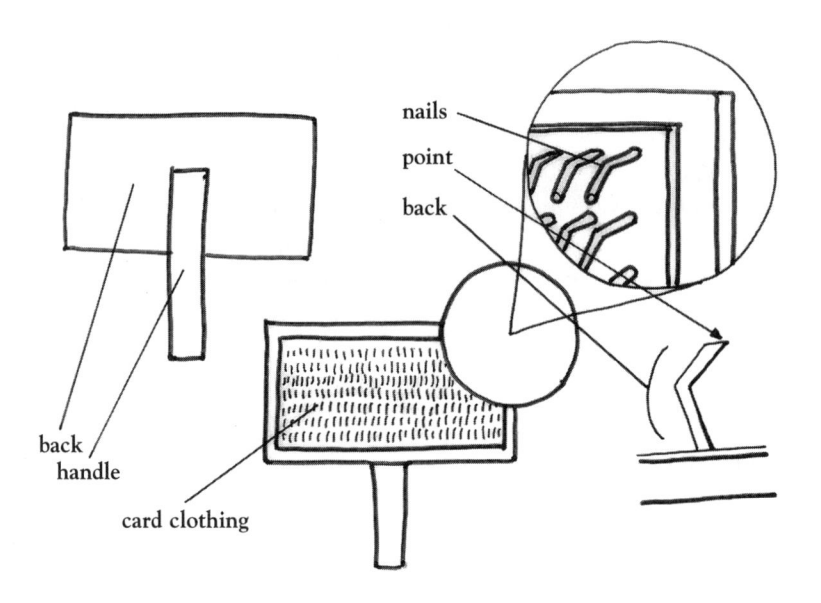

The parts of a hand card.

Card structure. Hand cards come in pairs, rather like shoes, and, like shoes, having one is normally not as good as having a pair. Take a look at a pair of cards.[11] Each card consists of a paddle-like structure with a handle sticking out of one wide edge. One side of the paddle is plain, except that it may have trademarks and sheep pictures applied to it. The paddle-board may be flat or may display a gentle curve. The non-plain side is covered with a sort of steel fur called *card clothing*. The card clothing interests us, particularly the wire teeth.

Hold a card up at eye level as if it were a frying pan and you wanted to glance at the bottom without spilling any of the contents. Now sight along the rows of teeth. Each tooth goes straight for a little way, then bends toward the edge of the card where the handle is mounted. The bend is called the *knee*, and in machine applications both the knee angle and wire angle (with respect to the foundation material) are important. They matter with hand cards too, but not as much. Anyway, the knee side of the wire is the *back*.

If we take a little fiber in hand and drag it across the card toward the handle, not much happens: the teeth bend down out of the way and the fiber slides over their tips.

Now drag the fiber in the other direction, away from the handle edge. Well, well. The teeth *bend up and into the way*, hooking and catching fiber on their *points*. Interesting.

Get the other hand card and hold it up with the first, with both clothing sides flat against each other and the handles sticking in opposite directions. Once again sight down the rows of teeth. Each card's *knees* face in the same direction as the other card's points. This is called *point-to-point*. Hold the cards with the clothing sides together and the handles going in the same

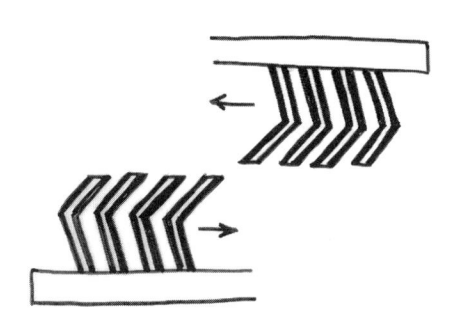

Carding is done point-to-point.

---

[11] *Dog-grooming tools called slickers look a lot like hand cards, although they're much smaller and very lightweight. If you have two slickers around, you can go through this exercise with them. However, you will need to invest in a real pair of hand cards to process more than a few wool fibers.*

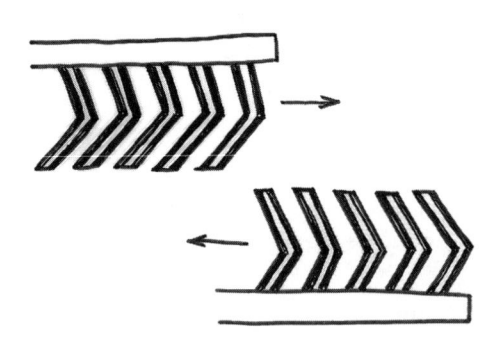

Stripping is done point-to-back.

direction. Sight down the teeth. This is called *point-to-back*.

By passing wool between the cards in a particular sequence, you can open up the fiber and create a uniform mass of even density. The more uniform this mass, the easier your spinning will be later.

The two actions. Two things happen when you pass wool between the cards. (1) *Carding* occurs when the teeth of the carding cloth pass point-to-point with wool between them. (2) *Stripping* occurs when the teeth of the carding cloth pass point-to-back with wool between them.

To reiterate in shorthand, carding is point-to-point and stripping is point-to-back.[12]

Return to your examination of the hand cards and the bit of wool.

Carding. If you stick some fiber between the two cards held with handles going in opposite directions, and slide them away from each other, moving each card toward its handle direction, what happens? Simple. The fiber catches on the points of each card and the fiber mass pulls apart. Some of the fiber snags on one card, some on the other.

When the teeth pass point-to-point, the basic carding action occurs. One card can be stationary while the other one moves, both cards can move away from each other, or both can move in the same direction at different speeds; the effect is the same. If two layers of card clothing are working point-to-point, carding is being done.

Stripping. Turn one card around, so the handles of both cards stick out on the same side. In this position, the teeth will work point-to-back. This produces the stripping action. As in carding, one card may move

---

[12] *One other direction of movement is possible. What about back-to-back? It's easy enough to try with hand cards. Hold them in point-to-point position (handles opposite), then move either one or both of the cards toward the handle(s). Push them together, so to speak. What happens? Not much. The back-to-back motion doesn't offer any benefits for hand carding. A sort of back-to-back motion takes place on big wool carding machines, where it is called raising, but that's another story.*

while one is stationary, both may move in opposition, or both may move in the same direction at different speeds. When the teeth pass point-to-back, stripping occurs.

The purposes of carding

The primary objective of carding is to disentangle each individual fiber from the surrounding fibers. Secondary objectives are to blend the fibers so they become a more homogeneous mass, to package the fibers in a way that facilitates smooth and uniform drafting, and to mechanically clean the fiber. Let's look at each objective separately.

Disentangling. If we disentangle and free the fibers, they will draft as individuals rather than indiscriminate tangled clumps. This means we can ultimately spin a uniform yarn.[13]

Blending. Carding is the premier method for blending fibers, whether you want to combine two colors to get a third, or to smoothly mix several grades of fiber to aid in spinning a uniform yarn.

Packaging. The basic fiber package produced by hand carding is called the *rolag* (pronounced *ROLL-ahhg*),[14] although several other forms are both practical and possible.

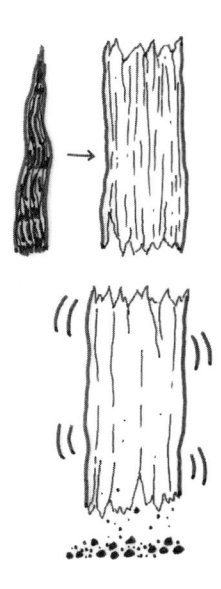

The purposes of carding are to open, clean, and blend fibers.

---

[13] *Yes, you can spin a uniform yarn from wool that has been removed directly from the sheep, and you will avoid a lot of preparation time. However, it will take you forever to spin a significant quantity of decent yarn. The time it will cost you to employ this "short-cut" can't be recovered. The more time you spend preparing your fiber, the faster, easier, and better your spinning will go. There really are no exceptions.*

[14] *The oldest English-language precursor to rolags that your author has personally seen is* rowyls *(1568), followed by* rowans *(1635) and* rowes *or* roves *(1683). By the end of the eighteenth century,* rowls, rowlls, rolls, rowves, roves, rowans, *and* rowens *abound, but not one rolag has been sighted. Alice Morse Earle uses* roll *in 1898; M. M. Atwater knew nothing of rolags, but named these fiber units* rolls *as recently as 1928; Fannin avoids using* rolag; *Hochberg encloses the word in quotes; Burnham et al. in 1980 say* roll . . . *so whence cometh* rolag? *The word seems to be Celtic, probably from the highland Scots, and means* rowl, rowyl, rowve, roll, *and so forth. The word* rolag *appears to have been placed into contemporary handspinning use by Elsie Davenport in her great work,* Your Handspinning, *first published in 1953.*

Mechanical cleaning. Carding, as a process, has considerable cleaning power. To illustrate the point, do a little carding over a clean tabletop. Ye gods, where did all that junk come from?

The junk (*swarf*) consists of seed bits, dust, topsoil, sand, dehydrated bug parts, sheep dandruff, and what-not. Carding opens the fibers and exposes all sorts of hidden things. It's like turning pants pockets inside out. Scoured wool drops more junk than greasy wool, because grease wool glues the small stuff to the fiber.

Each operation in the process of carding gives you an opportunity to pick garbage out of the wool. As the cards are being loaded, as they are worked, and then as you form the rolags or laps, you have chance after chance to pick out straw, sticks, seeds, burrs, second cuts, kemp, and so on.

Pick out everything you don't want in the yarn! Develop the habit of doing so, automatically, without thinking. Every time you see something that doesn't need to be there, pick it out. At times when there seems to be too much stuff to pick out all at once, go for the biggest and most obnoxious bits.

A lesson in carding

With the wool clean, dry, and open, you can card it up for spinning. We mentioned willowing earlier. If you willow scoured wool before carding, the thrashing opens it up and fluffs it, shaking loose even more vegetable matter.

You will need a set of hand cards to learn how to card. There are no substitutes, and a pair of reasonable cards will cost about the same as a nice night-out dinner for two.

One tradition suggests (sometimes strongly) that you mark your hand cards *right* and *left*, and thereafter use them that way, with the one marked *right* in your right hand and the one marked *left* in your left hand. In decades of hand carding, your author has yet to see justification for this. In fact, like rotating tires on the family car, changing positions on cards will give you uniform (maximum) wear.

In the following directions, there will be no right or left hand. Rather, your *master* hand holds the master card and your *other* hand holds the other card. Don't go into a swivit about being ambidextrous. Which hand do you write with? Which hand do you open doors with? Which is your main eating hand? Which hand fumbles with the keys while the other holds the packages? Which hand fumbles with the keys on the second attempt? That's your master hand. The other hand is, well, the other hand.

To card some wool, first sit down. Then grasp a small handful of wool with your master hand. With the other hand, grab a card by the handle as if it were a skillet. Lay the skillet . . . sorry, lay the card on your thigh, prickle-side up, still grasping the handle. With your master hand, gently rub the wad of wool across the card, always rubbing away from the handle. This is *charging* or *loading* the card. Do not try to see how much wool you can cram on there. A few rubs across should suffice.

Put down the wad of wool and pick up the remaining card with your master hand. Hold it skillet-fashion, but with the teeth pointing down. Gently place it on top of the charged card, with the two card handles on opposite edges of the card "sandwich." Slowly pull or slide the top card (in your master hand) across the bottom card (in your other hand), moving in the point-to-point direction. In this case, the top card moves in the direction its own handle points to.

Do not force the two cards together by pressing down with the top card. The surfaces of the cards should barely touch each other.

Drag the top card clear across the bottom card. Once the top card passes the edge of the bottom card, raise the top card to give a little clearance, then swing it over and down, back to the starting, "sandwich" position.

Repeat these operations between four and six times, dragging the top card across the bottom card, always in the point-to-point direction.

There you are . . . you're carding. Fun, isn't it?

But wait. There's more.

You need to learn the stripping action, the point-to-back movement. Bring both cards up in front of you, holding them as if you wanted to clap them together, face-to-face. The card in your other hand should be holding most of the wool, although there will also be wool on the card in your master hand. The handles of both cards will point down. Now raise the card in your master hand a little higher than the card in your other hand. You want the bottom (handle) edge of the master card even with the top edge of the other card. Sight along the teeth to be sure, but now you are in the point-to-back position, ready to begin stripping.

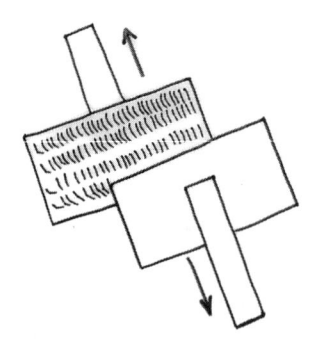

Carding. 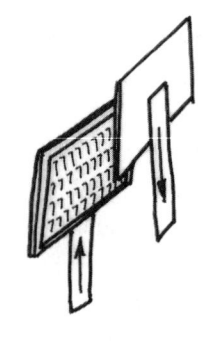   *Stripping motion 1.* 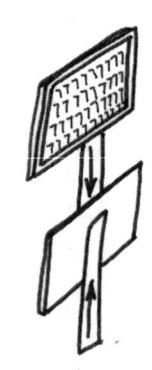   *Stripping motion 2.*

Here we go. Hold the other card firm and slide the master card down the face of the other card. Once. Amazing! With very little effort (compared to carding), all the wool came off one of the cards. That is the stripping action, which takes place whenever the cards move point-to-back.

Lay both cards down on a table, face-up, and gently pick and pry the wool off of the cards. Roll it up longways, that is, from or toward the long edges of the cards. If you roll toward the handle edge, the wool will peel off quite easily. This will not be the world's finest rolag; we left out several of the more sophisticated procedures. But it's a rolag and you can spin from it.

Did you take this opportunity to remove any annoying bits of seed? Hardened wads and tufts of second-cuts? Now that your wool has been carded, are you really happy with your scouring job?

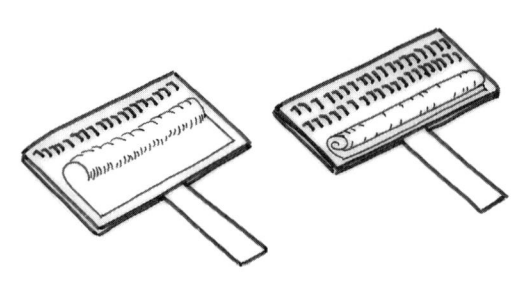

Form a rolag by rolling the wool toward the handle.

Once the wool is in spinning form, you can't really improve it. If the fiber is not clear, clean, lofty, and uniform, no amount of technology or expertise can make it so. Just like computers: garbage in, garbage out.

Make a few more rolags, and we will move on to spinning.

70   The Alden Amos Big Book of Handspinning

carding

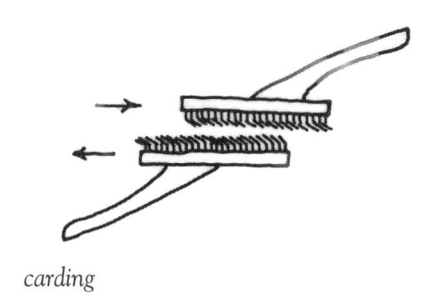

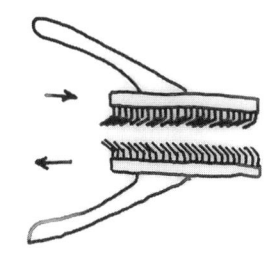

stripping top card

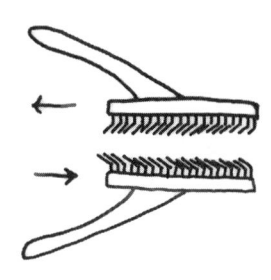

stripping bottom card

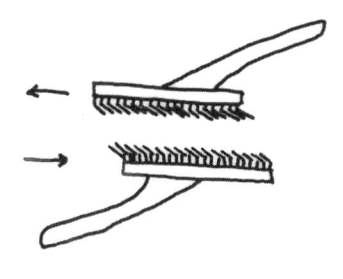

not carding (only available on rotary carder)

Here are the four carding and stripping motions.

ALMOST-WORSTED YARNS

You were introduced earlier to the concepts of woolen-system spinning and worsted-system spinning. Although *true* worsted yarns are produced by drafting-without-twist from combed fibers, a pretty good worsted-like yarn may be spun from a carded rolag, although you'll prepare the rolags a little differently.

After carding, strip the layer of wool off the cards and lay this flat batt or lap on the table. Now roll it up side-to-side, opposite the way you rolled when you were introduced to carding. Before, you rolled the fiber from long edge to long edge, making a roll as long as the cards are wide. This time, roll the wool from one end to the other, making a shorter, plumper package.

When you card, the fibers end up randomly arranged, pointing every which way, right? Not exactly. In reality, most of the fibers end up parallel to the direction of carding.

If you roll a rolag edge-to-edge, you make a tube with the fibers wrapped around it. When you spin this arrangement from either end, most of the fibers lie (before drafting) at right angles to the yarn. That makes fuzzy, lofty yarns.

When you roll a rolag from side-to-side, most of the fibers lie parallel to the sides of the roll. When you spin from the end of this roll, most of the fibers line up with the axis of the yarn. That makes leaner, denser, less fuzzy yarns.

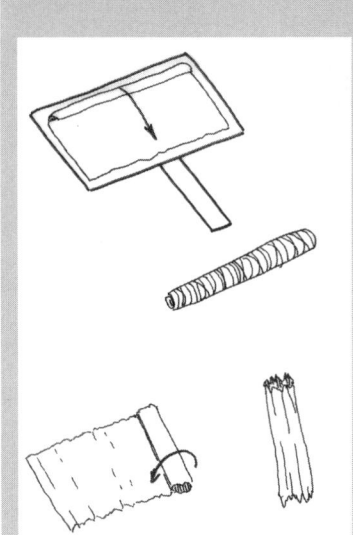

So if you prepare this type of *mostly parallel* rolag and keep the twist out of the drafting zone, you will encourage the fibers to stay parallel to each other. You will spin an *almost*-worsted yarn.

It should be noted that the drafting of fibers forces them to become more aligned with each other (parallel to the direction of draft). You could also say that if *any* drafting takes place, the result cannot be *true* woolen yarn, since drafting forces a number of the individual fibers to align with each other. In a *true* woolen yarn, the fibers are completely random. By this reasoning, anything that reduces randomness causes the yarn to be less woolen.

You can roll a rolag lengthwise or crosswise. The direction you choose will affect the yarn you spin.

In practice, most of this discussion offers only theoretical value. Still, the handspinner can put it to good use. For now, it's just something to think about.

SPINNING TOOLS

Draft we must, and spin we will, and right now we do not care whether the yarn we make is woolen or worsted. So we will spin woolen, right after we review a few things and learn something about spinning tools.

As you remember, woolen-system spinning works with drafting-against-twist. The twist nibbles away at the fiber mass, right up there in the drafting zone, and you as a handspinner must keep the twist from grabbing too much fiber (and interfering with a smooth, even draft) or falling behind (causing the yarn to thin out and drift to nothingness).

At the same time, you have to keep the wheel or spindle going, monitor the amount of twist in the new yarn (enough? too much?), make joins, keep everything neat and tidy, answer questions, and look picturesque. Pretty tall order, isn't it?

You can accomplish all this most efficiently by drafting, twisting, and winding-on at a constant rate. The amount of yarn you produce for each of these cycles is called a *make*. In other words, a *make* is the amount of yarn you produce for each complete set of drafting, spinning, and winding-on operations. So all you have to do is draft the same length of yarn, take the same amount of time for twisting and winding-on, and keep a constant speed on the wheel or spindle. Repeat this, make after make, and you will have consistent yarn.

This brings up the subject of spinning tools. Besides your hands, the most important tools are the spindle and the wheel. In later chapters we will get very technical about these pieces of equipment, calling them *twist-insertion devices* and worse. For now, we can stay very basic.

Manual and driven spindles, including the simplest spinning wheels

A spindle is a glorified version of our friend the twisty-stick. A *drop spindle* is a twisty-stick with a fairly heavy disk, or *whorl*, stuck on its shaft that adds weight and acts as a flywheel. A *supported spindle* also has a whorl, which it uses for its flywheel effect alone. All of these tools, including the twisty-stick, fall into a category called *manual spindles*.

Drop spindles hang from the yarn during spinning, and the whole weight of the spindle dangles from the spinner's hands. Drop spindles come in two major types: low-whorl and high-whorl. If the whorl is at the bottom of the shaft when the spindle is in use, you have a low-whorl spindle. If it's at the top, you have a high-whorl type.

Supported spindles are designed to have most, or all, of the spindle's weight supported by the ground, a special holder, the spinner's leg, or a table, instead of by the yarn. Supported spindles also fall into two major types: large and small.

If a spindle is mounted on a framework and driven indirectly (that is, not by your hand's direct contact with its shaft), it is called a *driven spindle*. Examples of driven spindles include the great wheel, the box charkha, the banjo charkha, and various treadle-wheel arrangements.

On a spindle, you tie or fasten one end of a piece of yarn (the *starter yarn*) to the spindle shaft, lead the loose end of that yarn parallel to the spindle and past its tip, and place that loose end adjacent to a mass of fiber. Begin to rotate the spindle by hand, by turning the wheel, or by pushing the treadle. Each revolution of the spindle will put one turn or twist into the starter yarn. Eventually enough twist will be transmitted along the yarn to cause the free end to rotate. Because the free end of the yarn is in contact with the fiber mass, the loose fibers in the mass will start wrapping around it, making a sort of connection, or *join*.

Slowly move the fiber mass away from the spindle, while continuing to rotate the spindle. The twist moves up the fiber mass and a length of new yarn forms. If you keep putting in twist, you can keep drafting, until you can reach no further.

You now have to do something with the newly spun yarn. Swing the fiber mass over so that your new yarn no longer extends parallel to the spindle shaft but extends at right angles to it, and then wind it up on the spindle shaft.

A little experimentation shows that when you spin,

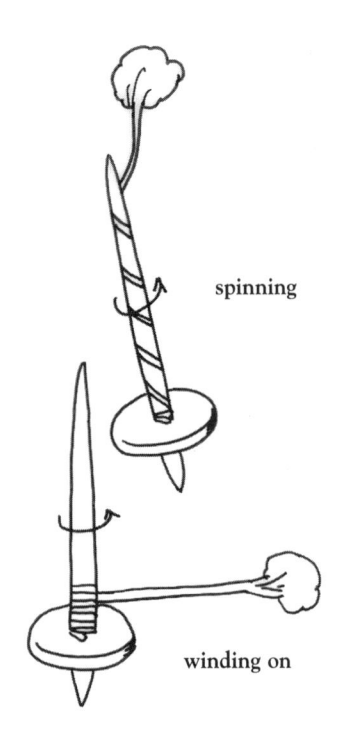

When using spindle, you twist with the yarn coming off the tip at about a 30-degree angle. You wind on with the yarn at a 90-degree angle to the shaft.

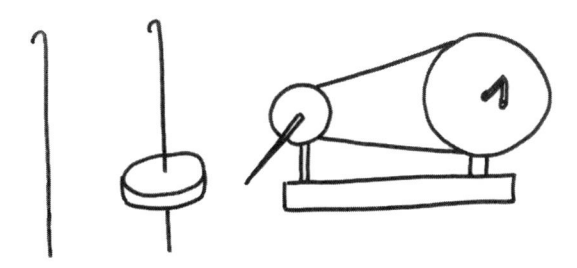

The spindle wheel, also called a driven spindle, *mechanizes rotation. This is how it developed: first there was a hooked stick, which then acquired a weight to make it spin longer, and then the drive wheel arrived to keep it turning smoothly and quickly.*

the yarn doesn't have to be in a parallel line with the spindle, but can be at any angle less than a right angle, or 90 degrees. For those of you who like precision, a good angle is about 30 degrees. As long as the angle is less than 90 degrees, the yarn keeps falling over the spindle tip as the spindle rotates and adds twist. When the angle approaches 90 degrees, the yarn can't fall over the spindle tip, so it winds onto the spindle shaft.

Good spindle technique requires that you keep the spindle tip clear of wound-on yarn, so after each make of yarn, stop the spindle, back it up a bit to unwind the yarn that has spiraled out to the spindle tip, and then

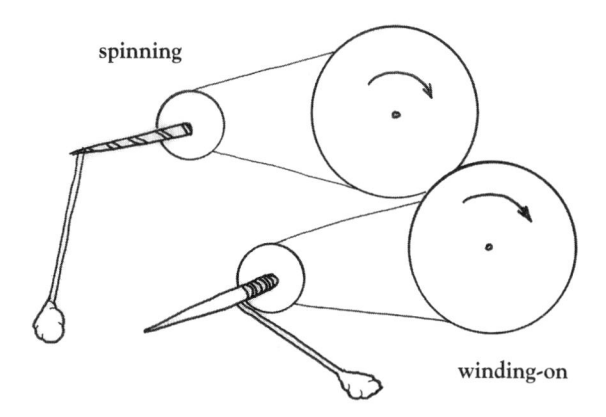

Spinning and winding-on with a driven spindle resemble the same processes on the hand spindle, with similar angles for each action.

wind on. This builds up the yarn package in the central part of the spindle, away from the tip.

Notice that you have to stop the spindle to do this. The sequence of stopping the spindle, backing it up a little, winding-on, and then spinning again is called *discontinuous spinning*. This is the chief characteristic of spindle systems, and also their main disadvantage.

Flyer-and-bobbin spinning wheels

Where there is a problem, someone will devise a solution. By the end of the fifteenth century, a system known as the flyer-and-bobbin came into use. The flyer-and-bobbin combination permits *continuous spinning*. Newly spun yarn feeds directly onto a *bobbin* that is part of the wheel, eliminating the steps of stopping, backing off, and winding-on after each make of yarn.

The main difficulty of the flyer-and-bobbin system is complexity. The apparatus requires several components, the design, fit, and function of which are critical to good operation. Modern wheel builders are slowly learning *how* critical these aspects are.[15]

---

[15] It has been said that "[a] spinning wheel is a remarkably simple, yet subtle device." I think this paraphrases a statement by Elsie Davenport, who said, "Although apparently so simple in construction, the action of the spinning wheel is extremely subtle and, to make it function really well, a thorough understanding and a nice adjustment of all its parts is essential." (This comes from Your Handspinning, Elsie G. Davenport, page 59). Remarks concerning the subtleties of the flyer-and-bobbin system were not new in Elsie's time (1953). In 1724, a gentleman named Richard Hall complained that his efforts to find out the "true geometrical proportions" of the various elements in a flyer-and-bobbin wheel were "all in vain," and none of "the ablest wheelwrights" could or would explain "this mystery in the trade" to his satisfaction. Mr. Hall wanted to bring all the dimensions, ratios, and proportions "to a more mechanick regulation then [sic] at present it is under" (quoted by Bette Hochberg in Spin Span Spun: Fact and Folklore for Spinners, page 37). As a student wheelbuilder, the author sincerely wishes that Mr. Hall had accomplished his desire, and had kindly furnished the author with his notes. Patricia Baines, in her great scholarly work, Spinning Wheels, Spinners and Spinning (page 69), quotes Denis Diderot, who assembled a detailed overview of eighteenth-century spinning technology in 1765: "Le rouât est une machine qui nous paroit simple et qui, exposé par-tout á nos yeux, n'arrâte pas un instant notre attention, mais qui n'en est pas moins ingénieuse." Work on that, all you Francophiles.

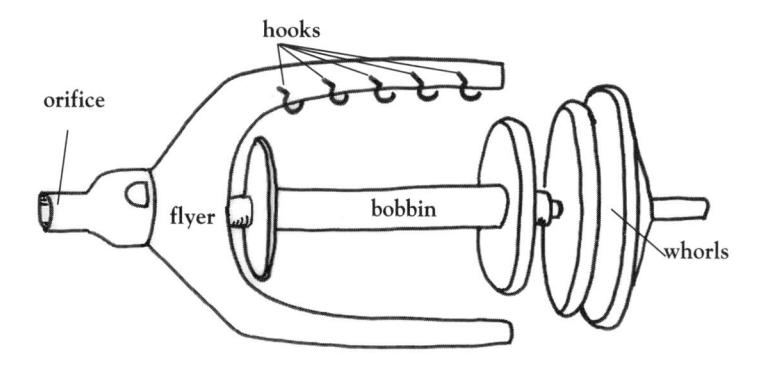

A basic flyer.

In the most common design for this type of spinning tool, a drive wheel, set in motion by a treadle, propels the flyer and/or the bobbin. Occasionally, the drive wheel receives its power by being hand-turned or motor-driven. Still, the overwhelming favorite for the past 400 years or so has been the treadled, wheel-driven, flyer-and-bobbin assemblage generally known as a spinning wheel.

Spinning wheels come in many shapes and regional styles, with various types of flyer-and-bobbin arrangements. But they all do the same thing, and they do it in the same way.

A flyer-and-bobbin system consists of the *flyer* itself, which is that U-shaped affair with a shaft stuck through its middle, and the *bobbin*, a glorified spool for holding yarn.

The flyer usually includes a series of hooks, which guide the yarn onto the bobbin. The hooks do what your hands do when you wind yarn onto a spindle shaft.

The bobbin stores the yarn. With a spindle, you normally wind newly spun yarn directly onto the spindle shaft, or *blade*, to use the technical term. That won't work on the flyer-and-bobbin system, for reasons that will become obvious.

SPINNING YOUR FIRST YARN ON A WHEEL

Suppose that we have a flyer-and-bobbin wheel and we want to start spinning. We will start with a yard-long length of ready-made yarn, called the *leader*. We firmly attach one end of the leader to the middle, or *core*, of the bobbin, and lead its other end from the bobbin core up and across one or more flyer hooks, then out through the flyer eye, barrel, and orifice.

The bobbin can rotate independently on the flyer shaft. That is, the flyer can rotate at one speed while the bobbin rotates at a different speed. The flyer shaft serves as an *axle* for the bobbin. This whole affair hangs between two supports, so that the flyer and flyer shaft can rotate as required. The axle itself (the flyer and flyer shaft) can rotate freely, and the bobbin can rotate independently of that.

Suppose we tie the outboard end of the leader to a post or a chair back, or just hold it firmly, and then start rotating either the flyer or the bobbin, with a hand or by treadling. What happens? If you hold the leader taut (and you make sure the yarn can't slip around the bobbin core), the bobbin and flyer must turn together. If one turns, the other turns, because the flyer is *tied* to the bobbin (or the bobbin is *tied* to the flyer, depending on your point of view). At the same time, one twist gets put into the leader with each rotation of the flyer-and-bobbin assembly.

Now suppose you hold the free end of the leader in contact with a nice, fat rolag. After a while, the twist builds up to the point where the free end of the leader begins to rotate, wrapping up some of the loose fiber. Just as with the spindle, you have a join between the leader and the fiber mass and you can start drafting the fiber into new yarn. And again, you draft as far as you can reach, letting the twist nibble away at the fiber. When you have drafted as long a make of yarn as you can, the yarn again needs to be wound-up out of the way.

This is where the flyer-and-bobbin arrangement earns its keep.

Relax your pull against the yarn, continue to rotate the flyer with your hand or the treadle, and the yarn winds through the flyer orifice and eye, over the hooks, and onto the bobbin.

You don't have to stop the wheel, back up, or anything. Just keep treadling, relax your pull, and let the yarn wind on.

Here's a nice side effect, too. While you wind on, everything still turns and still puts in twist, so you don't lose any twisting time, as you do when winding-on with a spindle.

The flyer-and-bobbin system does this winding-on-but-still-twisting stunt by having the flyer turn a little faster or slower than the bobbin. This feature of *differential speed* is built into the system. The system *wants* to wind-on, and it will, any time you let the bobbin and flyer turn at different speeds.

A good system allows us to defeat this winding-on action whenever we want to; otherwise, the wheel will wind on before we have put in enough twist. So the system lets us make the flyer and bobbin turn at the same speed whenever we want, simply by hanging on to the yarn. We can do this easily because we can pull a lot harder than the flyer-and-bobbin system can.

But the moment we relax our pull on the yarn, the system takes over. It wants the flyer to turn faster or slower than the bobbin, and it wants to wind-on the new yarn, and if everything is working properly, it will do those things.

There are three major ways of arranging for the bobbin and flyer to turn at different speeds: (1) drive the flyer with a single drive-band and put a braking device on the bobbin; (2) drive the bobbin with a single drive-band and put a braking device on the flyer; (3) drive both flyer and bobbin with a doubled drive-band, but have different *pulley* or *whorl diameters* on the two parts.

At this stage in your handspinning career, it doesn't matter which system you have. Several makes of wheel build in provisions which allow you to change from one system to another.

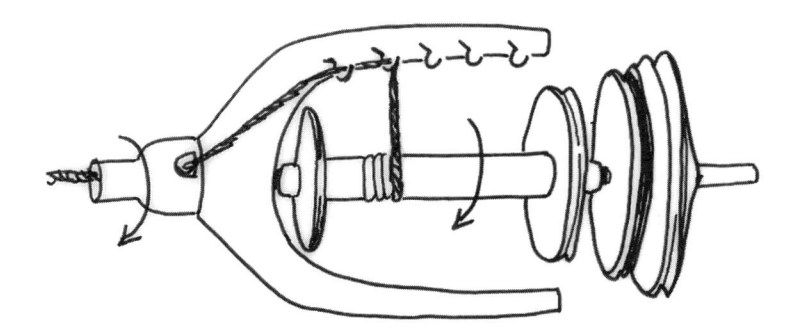

When twisting is taking place, the bobbin and the flyer rotate in phase.

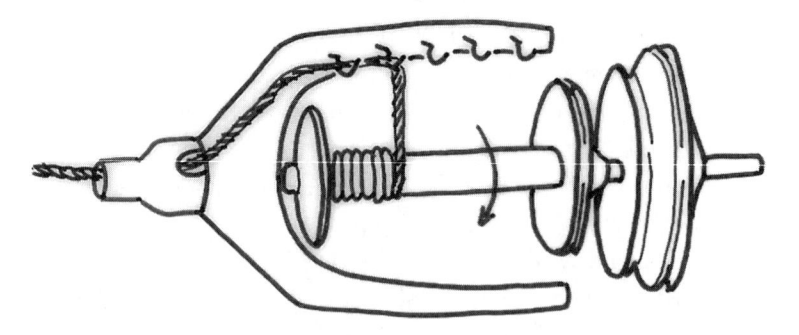

When the bobbin draws in yarn, the flyer and bobbin rotate at different rates.

The main thing to remember is that if the wheel will not wind on, one of the two elements—the flyer or the bobbin—cannot rotate faster or slower than the other element. This is important. If the flyer cannot rotate faster or slower than the bobbin (or the bobbin cannot rotate faster or slower than the flyer), winding-on of the newly spun yarn will not happen. The system will keep right on twisting, because it does that whenever it turns at all. It will twist until your yarn turns into harsh, kinked-up wire, and then it will keep twisting until the yarn finally breaks.

So what do you do when the yarn won't wind on?

Answer: *stop treadling*. You cannot treadle your way out of trouble. Stop. Then find and correct the problem. You know that the wheel won't wind on because the flyer and bobbin can't turn at different speeds. You need to find out why.

Sad but true: the main reason flyers and bobbins can't turn at different speeds is because we don't let them. For some reason, many handspinners develop the idea that the wheel shouldn't pull much when they are drafting, but it should pull like *anything* when they are ready to wind-on. Conventional wheels don't work that way.[16] So don't wait for the wheel to tug the yarn out of your hand; instead, gently relax your pull against the wheel. *Let* the wheel have the yarn, and most of the time it will take it away with a minimum of muss and fuss.

However, there will be times when nothing you do in a gentle, peaceful way will get the idiotic thing to wind-on. Here are other reasons why the two elements cannot turn at different speeds:

1. A few fibers are caught on a flyer hook, or the yarn itself has either split or looped over a hook.
2. The yarn is kinked, and the kink cannot get past a flyer hook.
3. The yarn is too big to slide easily through the eye, barrel, orifice, or hooks.
4. The bobbin is so full that yarn is rubbing on the flyer arms and stalling the bobbin.
5. The yarn has fallen over the end of the bobbin and wound on to the flyer shaft.
6. The yarn is routed from flyer eye to bobbin in an unusual way.
7. The brake system has self-adjusted or gone kaput.
8. The drive cords need adjustment, replacement, or overhaul.
9. You are exceeding the design potential of the system, which means you are trying to do something that neither you nor the system was designed to do.
10. Your wheel contains mismatched, ill-fitting, or incorrect parts.
11. You need to clean and thoroughly lubricate the wheel.
12. All of the above, plus about a hundred other little things that experience will help with.

Suppose the opposite is true: the wheel winds on too forcefully, or has too much *take-up*, as this quality is called. One solution is to adjust the bobbin and flyer so they are not so fiercely independent, and consequently so willing to rotate at different speeds.

This is accomplished in various ways, according to the system and

---

[16] *In the middle 1970s, the author collaborated with Susan C. Druding on engineering and assembling a spinning device that did pull very little during drafting and pull a lot while winding-on. Powered by a half-horsepower electric motor, it weighed 100 pounds and was ugly as sin. But the monster performed as advertised, swiftly turning great quantities of greasy fleece into "art" yarn (maybe yarn isn't the word, but never mind) which got thrown into assorted dye pots. We sold a lot of that stuff to the Southwest, as I recollect. The machine had an accelerator and a brake. You stomped the gas for twisting, then hit the brake to wind-on. A 2-pound weight on the brake-band gave it enough incumbent pull to wind-on the thin sections of the so-called yarn, but for the nasty parts the brake pedal did the job; it would haul you out of the chair and into the flyer if you didn't let go of the yarn or get off the brake. You could spin pretty fast on it too. I think we could go through 20 pounds or so of fiber between trips to the bagel shop.*

your ingenuity, but each flyer-and-bobbin system has a *best* range of operation, and you cannot deviate too far from that and expect the system to work. Here are things to try:

1. On a single-drive wheel, reduce the brake-band tension.
2. On a double-drive wheel, reduce the drive-band tension.
3. On a double-drive wheel, reposition the drive-band to reduce the difference in diameter between the flyer whorl and the bobbin whorl.
4. On a double-drive wheel, change to a thin, hard, slippery drive-band.
5. Route the yarn through the flyer in convoluted ways.
6. Build up the diameter of the bobbin core.
7. Clean and thoroughly lubricate the wheel.
8. Face the fact that you cannot reduce the take-up any more and use this wheel to spin heavier yarn.[17]

Focus on drafting. You've been treadling a bit while you explored winding-on, but let's back up a minute. For this next exercise, don't treadle the wheel. Just because there's a treadle doesn't mean you have to start tromping away; you have to learn to draft before you can treadle with confidence. Just turn the wheel over by hand.

Once you have joined a rolag onto the leader and everything seems to be in order, try drafting a bit, then put in more twist, then draft a bit, then put in more twist, until you have about a yard of your own yarn between your hand and the orifice. Whenever you need more twist, turn the wheel again, always going in the same direction. You need more twist when drafting gets scary and thin. When this happens, stop drafting, hang on to the yarn so it can't wind on, turn the wheel over a turn or two to put in more twist, then stop. When the wheel isn't turning, you don't have to worry that it's putting in too much twist or taking the yarn away from you. You can concentrate on drafting.

Each time you turn the wheel over, you rotate the flyer and bobbin. If you don't hold back on the yarn, whenever those two turn they will also wind on the yarn, and you're not ready for that yet. Even when you

---

[17] *Despite advertisements to the contrary, no one wheel will do it all. A number of wheels out there barely do any of it, although you would not gather that impression from reading about them. Learn to spin well. Then judge for yourself what a piece of equipment can handle.*

don't let them turn at different speeds, but make them turn together, you store up more twist in the yarn that you are holding. When you have stored up more twist, you can draft more new yarn.

Continue to turn and draft until you have about 4 feet of yarn hanging out there and can't reach any farther. This is when you start treadling. Be sure the wheel turns in the same direction as when you moved it by hand.

Treadling is easy. Stick your foot in there (either one, it doesn't matter), resting most of its weight right above the treadle bar, or, to be more specific, the treadle pivot axis. With your foot in place, reach out with your free hand and flip the wheel to start it turning. If a single flip of your hand doesn't set the wheel in motion, turn the wheel with your hand until the crank goes just past the top center and the treadle is up but just starting to go down. As the treadle goes down, push down with your toes. Give another push with your toes each time the crank comes over center. Don't expect the wheel to be able to lift the weight of your whole foot when the treadle starts to rise again. If your heel is back far enough, this won't be a problem.

Some authorities state that you should be able to start and stop the wheel with your foot alone, at any time and with the wheel and crank in any position. How delightful and charming. We haven't the time for such niceties just now, so use your hand to start and stop the wheel.

Once the wheel is going, treadle along so your foot goes down (and up) about once a second or faster. Do not go too slowly; if you do, the wheel will stall, you will decide you need to treadle harder (causing the wheel to reverse out of its stalled position), and off you will go, merrily unspinning and unwinding everything.

It does not really matter which direction you go, but it matters a whole lot if you change your mind once you have started. So even when we tell you there is no wrong way, that's a lie . . . the wrong way is the opposite of the way you were going.

> IT DOES NOT REALLY MATTER WHICH DIRECTION YOU GO, BUT IT MATTERS A WHOLE LOT IF YOU CHANGE YOUR MIND ONCE YOU HAVE STARTED.

As you treadle, three things will come to your immediate attention. First, there should be a pull against the yarn that didn't exist when the equipment stood still. If there isn't, don't worry about it yet. Second, you will find that treadling is not hard. Third, it will dawn upon you that you are building up a lot of twist, rather quickly. Holy cow, stop treadling!

Kind of exciting, isn't it?

By now, you may have 4 feet or so of well-twisted yarn. Let's wind on manually this time. With your free hand, reach over and rotate the bobbin in the winding-on direction, to make sure the yarn wraps correctly onto the bobbin. Let the rotation of the bobbin pull your other hand toward the flyer as the yarn feeds through the orifice. It will be slow going. If you feel daring, start the wheel and treadle it along. Whether you wind on by hand or with the treadle assisting, stop when the fiber mass and your drafting hand arrive at a point about a foot away from the orifice.

Now for a real spinner's secret. Using your non-drafting hand, reach up and grab the yarn about 2 inches away from the death-grip being exercised by your drafting hand. The hand that holds the fiber is officially the *drafting hand,* and the other hand, the one you just put to work by grabbing the yarn, is your *pull hand.* Remember that: drafting hand and pull hand.

Your pull hand is the heroic hand. It does all the dirty work. It starts and stops the wheel, changes the yarn's position on the flyer hooks, makes drive-band adjustments, and transfers liquid refreshments from table to handspinner's lips and back again. The drafting hand performs only three duties: it controls the drafting zone, keeps tension on the yarn, and holds the fiber supply.

Now your pull hand is grasping or pinching the yarn 2 inches from the drafting hand. Here's the handspinner's secret, in two simple parts. (1) You draft against your pull hand, not against the wheel. (2) The wheel pulls against your pull hand, not against the drafting zone.

Here's the explanation for part 1. When you draft, you often have to pull fairly hard—at least, it is to your advantage to be able to do so. If your drafting hand pulls against your pull hand, you can put a lot more tension between your two hands than you can between your drafting hand and the wheel.

Here's the explanation for part 2. When you draft, sometimes you want very little tension or pull against the drafting zone; in fact, sometimes you want so little tension that the normal take-up pull from the wheel exceeds your requirements. You can control this by letting the wheel tug against your pull hand, instead of against the drafting zone.

Give it a try. Start that wheel going at a fair pace. It's as hard to spin slowly as it is to spin quickly. Sometimes harder. Get that drafting moving along, and watch the twist. Remember that you can't treadle your way out of trouble.

All you have to do now is open and close your pull-hand fingers from time to time and allow a little twist to get into the newly drafted section. Not much twist, only enough to keep the draft going.

Once you have drafted your full make, open and close your pull-hand fingers a few times to let a little more twist through, and then let go completely with your pull hand, while continuing to treadle at your established rate.

Hang the full make out there, letting it soak up twist until you think it has enough, then run the yarn in; let the wheel have it. Stop about a foot from the flyer, pinch the yarn with your pull hand, and start the cycle again.

Remember to keep your pull hand at least a foot away from the orifice. There is no advantage whatsoever in crowding the flyer. Work your pull hand a foot or more away from the orifice. Likewise, keep your drafting hand away from your pull hand, except at the very beginning of a draw and at the end of a wind-on.

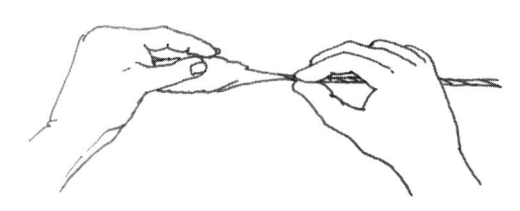

The left hand is the drafting hand and the right is the pull hand.

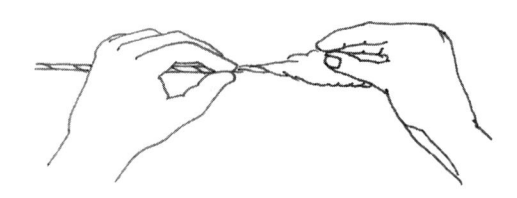

You can also work so that the right hand is the drafting hand and the left is the pull hand.

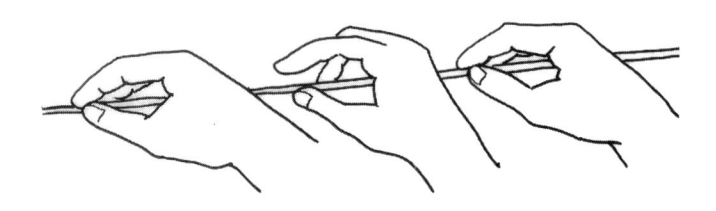

Open and close the pull hand to control how much twist moves up into the fiber.

The farther apart your hands are, and the farther your hands are from the flyer, the more control you have over the yarn. We don't mean that you must spread your wings for each draw, but don't sit there hunched up like you're wearing handcuffs. At the end of a good draw, your drafting hand and your pull hand should be about a yard apart.

Until you have had more practice, do not expect your yarn to win prizes. The chances are that this first yarn contains plenty of twist, and is less uniform in diameter than you might like. Spend a moment considering these things, but not more.

Control comes with practice, but not just spinning practice. Remember your first attempts with the twisty-stick? With hand cards? With scouring? With buying fiber?

What about color and dye work? What are the best ways to handle yarn, to skein it, to package and sell it? What about plying, and novelty yarns? Other fibers?

There is still a lot to explore and learn, and all of it will help you make more and better yarn. If you could become an accomplished, knowledgeable handspinner by learning about drafting and twisting alone, you would be a grand master in a week.

Once upon a time, so a story goes, knowledgeable weavers lusted after beginners' yarns because such yarns were reputed to have wonderful qualities. These yarns were scarce, even rare, because spinners, becoming ever more skilled, could never duplicate them. Contrary to old legends, today's handweavers don't care much about your first spinning efforts, unless you are giving them away. Most weavers will take any yarn, if it is free.

So what are you going to do with your first yarn? Your first yarn should turn into something useful and ceremonial, such as a tea-pot divot. I'm serious. Give yourself a rite of passage by making something durable and useful from your first yarn.

Of course, you will decide to make an item that requires lots more yarn than you have. That part is good, but it contains a bittersweet element. Your skills will rapidly improve—so rapidly that in a few days or weeks you will be tempted to discard the yarn that you are so proud of now. Don't.

It is not good to forget how we began. Save that yarn. Use it. Move on, and remember where you started from.

Chapter 4

Determining the character of yarn: Grist, twist, fiber, and spinning method

As a handspinner, you have complete control over the yarn you produce. Fiber content, methods of preparation, the manner in which it is spun: all of these and more are not only up to your discretion, they are your responsibility. You therefore need to understand the physical structure of yarn and be able to describe the factors that give a yarn its identity.

What makes yarn coarse? What makes warp yarn different from knitting yarn? What makes one yarn soft and lofty, and another yarn lean, firm, and smooth? A series of yarns answering these descriptions may be spun from the same fiber, on the same wheel, by the same handspinner. What makes them different?

Four major factors determine the physical structure of a single yarn: (1) grist, (2) amount of twist, (3) fiber, and (4) method of spinning. Three additional major factors characterize yarns constructed of more than one strand (plied, cabled, and so forth): (1) twist direction, (2) number of elements, and (3) ply direction.

These qualify as major factors because any change in these qualities produces a significant difference in the finished yarn. To control these factors, we must be able to measure and describe each in a practical, objective manner. To say that a yarn is "high-twist," "fine," or "heavy" provides only general information. None of these words offers a useful statement.

This chapter will consider the first four factors: grist, twist, fiber, and spinning method. Later chapters will examine twist direction, number of elements, and ply direction.

Grist

Grist is the one universal factor shared by all yarns. Whether bulky, heavy, coarse, extra-fine, high-twist, low-twist, no-twist, four-ply, single, or an amazing novelty, yarn always has grist.

Grist describes the relationship between yarn weight and yarn length. Grist is a composite value, like *feet per second* or *miles per gallon*.

"Feet per second," a distance/time statement, notes how many feet an object—like a golf ball, or an escalator—travels in one second. "Miles

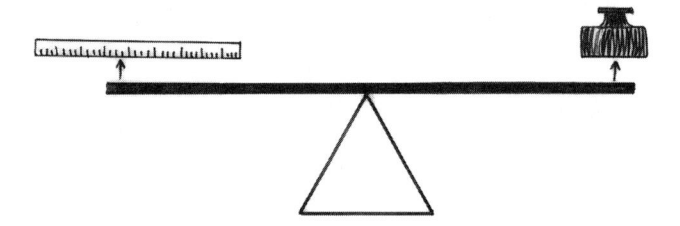

Grist reflects the relationship between length and weight.

per gallon," a distance/quantity statement, often reflects the number of miles an automobile may travel on a gallon of fuel.

Grist is a length/weight statement. It describes the length of a given or fixed weight of yarn. Because all yarns have length and weight, all yarns may be described by grist statements,[1] which usually occur in one

---

[1] *Interplanetary and stellar travelers among us know that grist is actually a mass/length statement, and the faster you go, the heavier your yarn. In a relative weigh, of course. . . . Sorry. . . . While on the subject of space travel and zero-gravity, let's think about handspinning with a drop-spindle in a zero-G environment. Without gravity, the spindle cannot "drop." But what if we gently swing the spindle in a circle, making rotational forces act in gravity's place? We can control the apparent "weight" by increasing or decreasing the diameter of the spindle orbit and/or the speed with which the spindle travels around that orbit. Then we need to deal with a few other little problems: the rotational center of the handspinner/drop-spindle combination, the amusing effects of rapidly changing the diameter of the spindle orbit as yarn is drafted and then wound on, the interesting ballistic results of yarn failure, the disposition of fly waste (dust, dirt, and broken fibers) released by the spinning process, and so on. . . .*

of two forms: indirect (as a *count value*) or direct (as a ratio between units of length and units of weight).

Indirect or count systems are somewhat complicated and are usually based on how many skeins of a specific length it takes to weigh 1 pound. Basically, thicker or "heavier" yarns produce fewer "standard-length" skeins per pound than finer or "lighter" yarns. For example, cotton yarn counts are based on skeins (or *hanks*) 840 yards long. Thus a 1-count cotton has a grist of 840 yards per pound, a 2-count cotton is 1,680 yards per pound (2 × 840), a 5-count cotton is 4,200 yards per pound (5 × 840), and so forth. Many other count systems exist. Because you can never be quite certain which system is being used and what its values are, you end up translating everything into yards per pound. So why not start there?

For clarity, handspinners should use a direct method of stating grist. The one favored in this work is *yards per pound*.

For example, if you spin a yarn so thick and heavy that you make only 100 yards (length) of yarn from a pound (weight) of fiber, then that yarn's grist is 100 yards per pound. Spin the same pound of fiber into a yarn 1000 yards long and that yarn's grist is 1000 yards per pound. While both yarns weigh 1 pound, one has less length and one has more length.

How can we "stretch" a pound of fiber during the spinning to produce more yards from a given weight? While the answer may not be obvious, it is simple: attenuate or draft the fiber supply to a greater degree. In short, spin a "finer" yarn, one with fewer fibers in each unit of length.

The following should illustrate why the grist

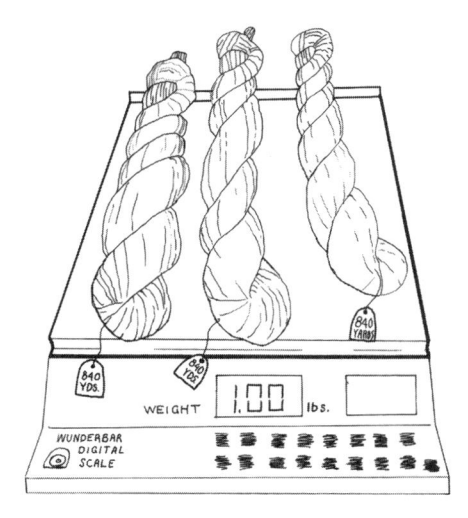

When cotton is called "3-count," that means 1 pound of fiber has been spun into three skeins of 840 yards each.

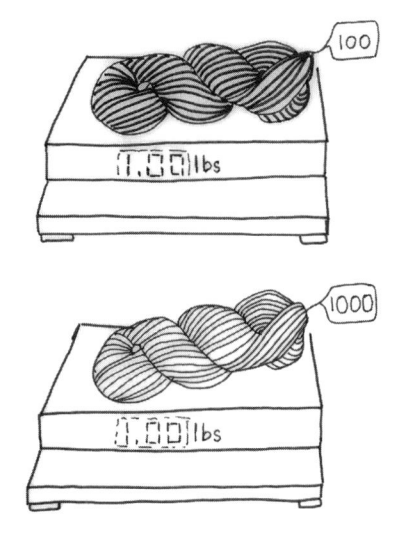

For yarn with a grist of 100 yards per pound, a 100-yard skein weighs 1 pound. For yarn with a grist of 1000 yards per pound, a 1000-yard skein weighs the same amount.

The Alden Amos Big Book of Handspinning

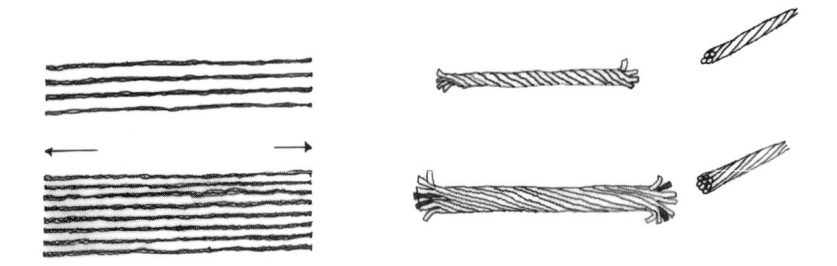

Grist changes when you use fewer fibers in a given length. Assuming that the fibers are the same size, four fibers make a finer yarn than eight fibers do.

changes when you use fewer fibers in a given length. Imagine that you have a dozen foot-long pieces of string, each of which represents a giant strand of fiber. Now suppose that you lay four of them side by side and twist them together. You are making a model "yarn" about 1 foot long, with four "fibers" in it. Now do the same with the other eight pieces. Lay them side by side and twist them together. This new model "yarn" is the same length as the first model, but contains twice as many "fibers." Because it consists of twice as many "fibers," it also weighs twice as much as the first model. It is a coarser, or "heavier," yarn.[2]

Our conclusion? Yarns with small diameters ("fine" yarns) have less weight per unit of length than yarns with large diameters ("coarse" yarns). Stated simply, 1,000 yards of fine yarn weigh less than 1,000 yards of coarse yarn.

Let's suppose that you have mail-ordered two skeins of yarn, which we will call A and B. The yarn in skein A appears thicker and firmer to you

---

[2] *The astute reader will observe that the yarn diameter must also change. However, in case you wonder, doubling the fiber amount per unit of length does not double the yarn's diameter. A yarn with 800 yards per pound is not twice as big as a yarn with 1,600 yard per pound; doubling the grist increases the diameter by about 41.5 percent. To get a yarn twice the diameter of our 1,600 yard-per-pound example, we need one with a grist of about 400 yards per pound. This relationship information comes from calculations based on finding the area of a circle and such. Remember that stuff? You may also remember that as you double the diameter of a circle, you quadruple its area. For the handspinner, this means that as you double the diameter of the yarn, you have room to fit in four times as much fiber. We go into this at some length later; you readers of footnotes will be less surprised than other readers when that time comes.*

When you have two skeins of the same length but different grist, the finer yarn weighs less.

than the yarn in skein B. When you put skein A on your scale, it weighs 1 pound. Skein B weighs ⅓ pound. "Well," you say to yourself, "let's see how long these skeins are." Both are the same length, say 1000 yards. Because skein A weighs 1 pound for 1000 yards, its grist is 1000 yards per pound, abbreviated YPP (or y.p.p.). Skein B also contains 1000 yards, but only weighs ⅓ pound, right? You already know the answer.... Because you would need three 1000-yard skeins of yarn B to come up with 1 pound, its grist is 3000 YPP.

Fine yarns have higher grist numbers, and coarse yarns have lower grist numbers. We saw this in the example, because 3000 YPP is a higher number than 1000 YPP.

Determining grist by direct measurement

You can calculate grist in several ways. For the most definitive method, measure a yarn's length and weight and then do a little math. This technique works—no ifs, ands, or buts. A typical formula follows:

$$G = \left(\frac{M}{W}\right)L$$

G is grist, M is the primary weight unit, W is the weight of the sample, and L is the length of the sample.

The values of M, W, and L depend on the weight/length system being used: metric (meters, kilograms) or English (feet, pounds). For grist in yards per pound, M is 16, W is the sample weight in ounces, and L is the sample length in yards. For grist in meters per kilogram, M is 1000, W is the sample weight in grams, and L is the sample length in meters.

Example 1: 20 yards of yarn weigh ½ ounce. What is the grist in yards

Grist and the Metric System

The metric system is upon us. Therefore, we include the grist calculations for metric-system yarns. For you, as a handspinner, the metric system is neither essential nor critical. On the other hand, there is no reason whatsoever not to become conversant with metric measurements, as they have the very real advantage of straightforward decimal conversion. In addition, most accurate, reasonably priced scales (for weighing yarn samples, dye, letters, and so forth) measure metric units, and for practical chemistry, metric (decimal) increments are a lot easier to use than pints, pounds, grains, ounces, drachmas, and the like.

Still, many of today's handspinners grew up with non-metric literature, syntax, and usage, as well as artistry. We all know Denver, Colorado, as the Mile-High City. Who would recognize it as the "1.6093 km-high" city? What of those famous songs, "1.5748 meter, eyes of blue" and "You load 14,515.2 kilograms, what do you get?" and "1.8288 meter, 2.1336 meter, 2.4384 meter bunch, daylight come, and I wan' go home . . . "? Consider Shylock and his .4536 kg of flesh, and Moon River, wider than 1.6093 kilometer, and the certainty that 28.35 grams of prevention are worth more than 453.6 grams of cure.

We will show you, as required, how the metric system fits into the scheme of things . . . but you will not find in this book the almost obligatory, inane use of parenthetical, equivalent values.[3]

---

[3] *Among other things, parenthetical values confuse and distract readers. Also, everyone who puts in conversions nobly rounds off numbers, to make reading "easier." The following instructions, extracted from a set of plans for a spinning wheel, suggest that you "cut the 2.25 cm/sq. (⅞") sticks to length, with 10 of them 24 cm (9½") and the remaining 2 to 22 cm (8⅝") in length." Aside from the fact that these are not very good plans, this quote indicates a basic and serious problem: the metric and English foot-pound systems are not interchangeable; 2.25 cm is not ⅞ inch, 24 cm is not 9½ inches, and 22 cm is not 8⅝ inches. Instead, 2.25 cm is equal to .8858267 inch (⅞ in. = .875), 24 cm is equal to 9.4488188 inches (9½ in. = 9.50), and 22 cm is equal to 8.6614173 inches (8⅝ in. = 8.625). Consider what happens when you go the other way: ⅞ inch = 2.2225 cm, 9½ inches = 24.13 cm, and 8⅝ inches = 21.9075 cm. There is nothing wrong with either system, but they do not "mix and match."*

per pound? M = 16 ounces, W = .5 ounce, L = 20 yards. M/W is 16 divided by .5, which is 32. 32 times L (20 yards) is 640 yards per pound.

Example 2: 117 yards of yarn weigh 1¼ ounces. What is the grist in yards per pound? M = 16 ounces, W = 1.25 ounces, L = 117 yards. M/W is 16 divided by 1.25, which is 12.8. 12.8 times L (117 yards) is 1,497.6 yards per pound.

Example 3: 20 meters of yarn weigh 14 grams. What is the grist in meters per kilogram? M = 1000 grams, W = 14 grams, L = 20 meters. M/W is 1,000 divided by 14, or 71.428. 71.428 times L (20 meters) is 1,428.57 meters per kilogram.

To convert yards per pound into meters per kilogram, multiply yards per pound by 2.1. To convert meters per kilogram into yards per pound, multiply meters per kilogram by .496.

That wasn't so hard, was it?

Determining grist from yarn diameter (wraps per inch)

You can also measure grist by finding the yarn's diameter and then calculating the weight/length aspect. This method depends upon the close relationship between grist and yarn diameter. Grist, in yards per pound, equals the product of the yarn diameter (measured in fractions of an inch) squared, and then multiplied by an appropriate factor, which is determined by twist component and fiber quality.

This means that as the diameter of the yarn changes, so does the grist. It also means that this change may be calculated, with reasonable accuracy, as long as proper factor numbers are used.[4] In order to use this

---

[4] *Finding appropriate factor numbers is a study in its own right. One might say that it borders on the obscure and arcane. Be that as it may, you will find factor numbers in Chapter 13, and their function and application are discussed in Chapter 5. To give you a preview, the factor numbers are based on many conditions: fiber source, type, length, diameter, straightness, and specific gravity; spinning method, fiber preparation method, incumbent twist, and use of assists. With the rough edges filed off, we are looking at this: a yarn spun worsted-method (drafted without twist) to a given diameter contains more weight of fiber per length than yarn spun woolen-method to the same diameter, all other things being equal. Not only that, the worsted-spun yarn will compress less, which means that the measured diameter of a worsted yarn is closer to reality than that of a woolen yarn. There is more to it, of course . . . which is why we return to the topic later.*

method, it is handy, but not obligatory, to know how to do the math. A table in Chapter 13 lets you look up the yarn diameter and find the grist. You will still have to find the diameter of your yarn, and in a moment we'll talk about how to obtain a workable approximation. But first we'll give you the basic formula.

The math. In proper notation, the formula looks like this:

$$G = (D^2)F$$

G is grist, D is the yarn diameter (in fractions of an inch), and F is a factor number, assigned according to the yarn characteristics.

Example 1: Let's work a quick example using a factor of .87, which is about right for a "medium-firm" woolen (and woolen-spun) yarn. Yarn diameter is 1/40 inch. 40 times 40 equals 1,600, and that times .87 gives us 1,392 yards per pound.

Example 2: Now for a tough one. The yarn diameter is 1/60 inch, and it is a "firm" worsted so we'll use a factor of .90. 60 times 60 equals 3,600, and that times .90 gives us 3,240 yards per pound.

Finding the diameter of your yarn. You can very conveniently measure yarn diameter with an inch gauge. One common form of inch gauge consists of a small, flat piece of wood, bone, horn, ivory, plastic, metal, or composition board, perhaps 2 inches long, 3/4 inch wide, and 1/8 inch thick, with a shallow (1/8-inch) notch exactly 1 inch long cut in the center of one long side. For another form of inch gauge, called a round gauge, you can cut a shallow recess around a rod, stick, or tool handle—for example, the handle of a wheel-threading hook. The recess may be 1/4 inch smaller in diameter than the diameter of the handle, and 1 inch long. This type works the same as the flat gauge.

With either type, wrap yarn around the gauge, filling the notch from end to end. The number of turns required to fill the 1-inch notch represents the yarn diameter in fractions of an inch. For exam-

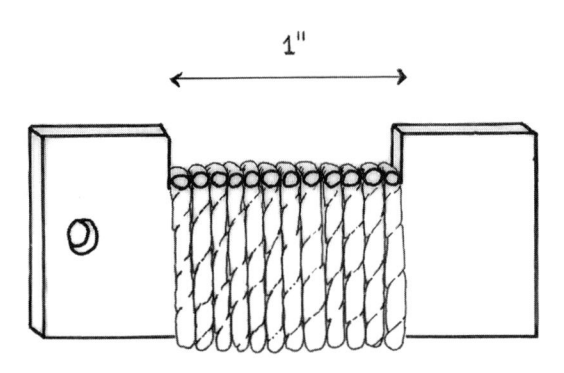

An inch gauge is a simple device which lets you measure the diameter of a yarn.

ple, if twenty turns fill the gauge end to end, then the yarn diameter is 1/20 inch.

What you are doing, of course, is finding out how many strands of the yarn may be laid side by side in a 1-inch space. This is a sort of reverse measurement; instead of measuring the diameter of a single strand with a calibrated device, you measure the calibrated device (notch) with diameters of yarn. In the preceding example, you can say that the notch is twenty diameters wide. Because we know that the notch is 1 inch wide and also 20 diameters wide, each diameter is 1/20 inch.

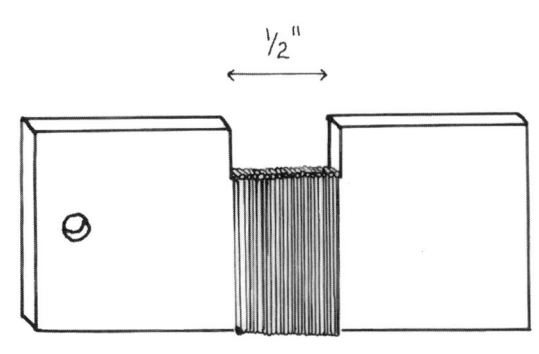

The notch in an "inch" gauge need not be 1 inch long. For fine yarns, you will find a 1/2-inch notch easier to use.

The notch does not have to be 1 inch wide. It may be 2 inches wide, or 1/2 inch wide, or whatever. With a 1-inch notch, we don't need to make conversions. The wrap count is the yarn diameter in fractions of an inch.

However, the 1-inch notch doesn't work particularly well for fine yarns. You think you will never stop winding and you risk losing track of the number of wraps. For example, a cotton yarn with a grist of 5,500 yards per pound will require at least 80 turns on a 1-inch gauge. Although that's not an especially fine yarn (as cottons go), it is still a lot of wraps. In this case, a shorter notch, say 1/2 inch long, will give good results. A yarn that wraps 80 to 84 in a 1-inch notch will wrap 40 to 42 in a 1/2-inch notch. Fewer wraps and less trouble.

On the other hand, if you have a thick yarn that packs approximately 17 1/2 wraps onto the 1-inch gauge, you will get a more accurate count by using a 2-inch gauge.

Keep in mind a simple rule for making measurements and taking samples: *the larger and/or more frequent the sample(s), the more realistic the results.* You will see variations on this statement throughout this book.

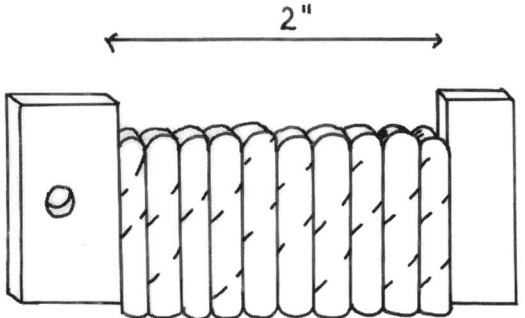

For coarse yarns, a 2-inch notch will give you more accurate measurements.

The Alden Amos Big Book of Handspinning 95

A yarn gauge is only as good as the person using it. When making diameter measurements, you must follow two procedures to obtain accurate, reproducible results: (1) when wrapping yarn onto the gauge, do not wind the yarn on tightly, that is, under high tension, and (2) always pack the turns to refusal.[5]

Wind under low or moderate tension to prevent the yarn from flattening out. The tighter you wrap yarn, the flatter and wider it gets. This raises hob with the diameter measurement. Still, you must wind with enough tension to keep the wraps from overlapping or riding up over one another.

Packing the turns to refusal means that you will slide each turn firmly toward one end of the gauge notch. If you wind yarn onto an inch gauge without packing the turns, you will not obtain an accurate measurement. For this reason, simply wrapping yarn around a ruler cannot produce consistent or accurate results. The notch gives you a surface to pack the yarn against.

Starting at one end of the notch, wrap between three and five turns onto the gauge, using moderate tension so the wraps are snug, not tight. Stop winding and slide or pack the turns firmly against one end of the notch. Wind on between three and five more wraps, and then pack these firmly against the first few turns. Keeping track of the number of

---

[5] *Strictly speaking, a measurement must be repeatable (or demonstrable on demand, which is the same thing) to be considered accurate. There is also a difference between what a thing is supposed to be and what it actually is. An anecdote from your author's dim past will serve as an example. We were in machine-shop, learning about micrometers. The instructor observed that no two people would get the same measurement, nor would a single individual get consistent measurements without considerable experience, and announced that he would demonstrate the truth of his statement. He passed around a little block of glassy material and had each of us measure its length and width with the shop-standard micrometer. He was right. We all got different measurements. Only after eight weeks of practice could we consistently measure that little thing, which he finally told us was an industrial diamond, ground to .25000 square by .31250 long. That's nothing but plain ¼ inch by 5⁄16 inch, right? Also, I never managed to measure the block "right," even after he told us what it was "supposed" to be; however, I could measure it and get the same reading each time. So don't worry about what the answer is "supposed to be," as long as you get consistent and repeatable results. Besides, you don't need to carry grist measurements and yarn diameters out to five decimal places.*

wraps, continue this process until you are unable to get another wrap into the notch. There should be no wraps riding above any other wraps. If there are, unwind and start again.

Count as you wrap, because turns become hard to count after they are packed into the gauge; for fine yarns and soft, fuzzy ones, counting after packing becomes almost impossible. Still, it is possible to recount, and this is one advantage of the flat gauge over the round gauge. The sides of the flat gauge allow you to sit there and, using a needle or pin to separate the yarns, laboriously count the turns. The round gauge does not allow you to do this; so if you lose count on a round gauge, unwind and start again.

How accurate, overall, *are* yarn gauges? In theory, very accurate; the reality is something else. If all yarns were perfectly round, were made of identical materials with identical degrees of twist, and did not compress, stretch, or absorb moisture, then yarn gauges could work with close-to-theoretical accuracy. But because yarns are not perfectly round, are made of different materials with varying degrees of twist, and do compress, stretch, absorb (and lose) moisture, the numbers we obtain by simply wrapping require adjustment. This is where the factors come in.

The factors. The problem comes in determining the proper factor to use. Factor numbers in this context adjust for variances in moisture content, twist, fiber

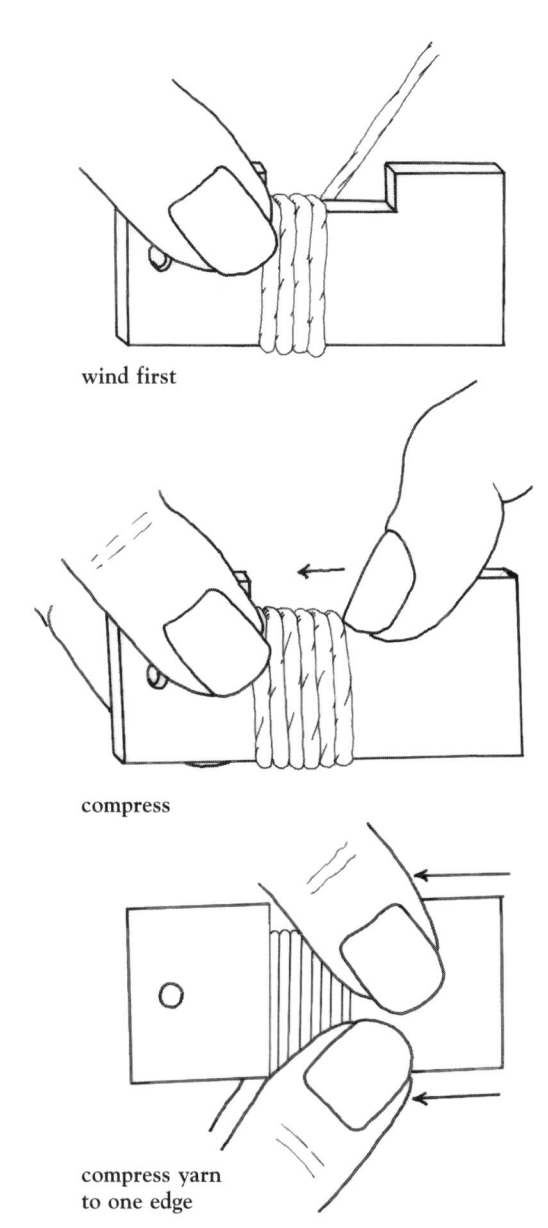

wind first

compress

compress yarn to one edge

For consistency in using an inch gauge, wind the yarn first, then compress the wraps together. Be sure you fit as many wraps into the notch as you can without having them overlap.

diameter, compression characteristics, and so on. Ideally, each yarn would have its own custom-tailored factor number. You can calculate custom numbers through a process which, like casting a horoscope or preparing a tax return, requires many variables and puts them through convoluted manipulations. Faced with this prospect, you may think, "Why bother with this grist business at all?"

There's no question that you need to know what grist is and how to measure it. Why? For the same reasons that you need to know the time, how much gas is in the car, whether today is Friday, or how much you weigh. Which is to say that most of the time you don't need to know those things, but sometimes this information becomes exceedingly important.

Much of the time, grist is a number waiting for a place to be useful. But there will be times when you need to know the grist; then you will discover that there is no substitute for the real thing. Terms like medium-fine, lightweight, sportweight, and bulky, while convenient and comfortable, aren't good enough.[6]

Determining grist with a McMorran Yarn Balance

There is a shortcut method of grist determination that uses both the weight and the length of a sample and requires only simple math. It depends on the use of a fixed-weight balancing scale, known to handspinners and weavers as the McMorran Yarn Balance.

The McMorran is easy to use. Take it out of its box, set it up so the box sits on the edge of a table or counter, put the arm in position with its notched end overhanging the table or counter edge, and loop a sample of yarn over the notch. With shears, lop off little bits of the yarn ends until the balance arm becomes level. What you are doing is adjusting

---

[6] *Specific occasions when the grist is important include: when you want to sell your yarn, whether at retail or wholesale; when you need to calculate yarn quantities and sizes for weaving, knitting, and other projects; when you want to reproduce a specific yarn, or otherwise spin to a standard; or whenever someone asks you what the grist is, for whatever reason. When you know the grist in yards per pound, you can state the bottom line; from that point, another person can convert that figure into other terms. A yarn with a grist of 2,000 yards per pound measures 2,000 yards per pound, whether you call it bulky fingering, fisherman's single weight, or ranch-spun blanket weight.*

the sample weight and finding out how long a piece weighs a fixed (predetermined) amount.

Remove the trimmed yarn, lay it out straight next to a tape measure or ruler and measure its length in inches. The McMorran is calibrated so that each inch of your sample length represents 100 yards per pound. Thus a 4-inch length that weighs enough to level the arm has a grist of 400 yards per pound, a 5-inch length measures 500 yards per pound, a 22½-inch length measures 22½ (2,250) hundred yards per pound, and so on.[7]

Clip off the sample until the arm balances, measure its length, and you have your grist. The system works as well with multiple strands as it does with singles, and this can be a definite advantage when you are checking the grist of fine or twist-active yarns.

Fine yarn samples will be so long that they hit the floor. If you are spinning to a standard of 10,000 yards per pound, the sample yarn you hang over the McMorran will have to be at least 100 inches long, right? The top of your kitchen table is not 100 inches (or even 50 inches) above the floor. How do you keep the ends of the sample from dragging? Make a skein of the sample yarn,

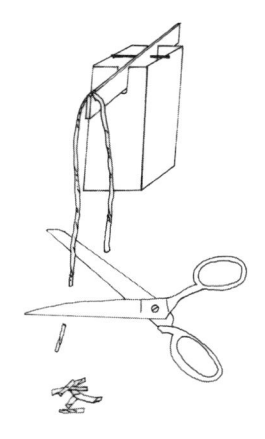

To use a McMorran Balance, drape a strand of your yarn over the arm and snip bits of both ends until the arm hangs level. Make sure the arm moves freely before you start.

When you have trimmed your sample yarn so the McMorran's arm balances, measure the resulting piece.

---

[7] According to information furnished with the units, the McMorran Balance was designed by H. McMorran, B.Sc., formerly lecturer in Textile Testing at the Scottish College of Textiles, Galashiels, Scotland. The device works on the fixed-weight principle and balances level when you hang $1/3600$ pound ($1/225$ ounce) of yarn on the notched arm. If it balances with a piece of yarn 1 inch long, weighing $1/3600$ pound, what does that tell you? If 1 inch weighs $1/3600$ pound, 3,600 times 1 inch will weigh 1 pound; 3,600 inches divided by 36 (the number of inches in a yard) gives you 100, the number of yards per pound. Suppose 15 inches of sample yarn balance the scale; what then? We say to ourselves, "If 15 inches weigh $1/3600$ pound, how many 15-inch lengths will it take to weigh 1 pound?" The answer is 3,600 of them, and 15 inches times 3,600 gives 54,000 inches. Divide by 36 inches (the yard) and discover that 1,500 yards of that yarn weigh 1 pound. Well, that's the grist, isn't it?

with between four and six turns in it, and treat it as if it were one yarn. Lay the small skein over the balance notch and trim its ends until the arm is level. Measure as you would for a single yarn, then multiply the measurement by the number of yarns in the sample.

For example, you hang four strands over the scale and trim and clip until the arm balances. Measure the length of all four strands together, if they are the same length, or the length of each, if you trimmed them individually. Let's imagine that each length is 8½ inches; 8½ inches times 4 gives 34, so your total sample length is 34 inches, and your grist is 3,400 yards per pound.

Yarn that is twist-active wants to self-ply, given a chance. If you are using the McMorran, let it. When you want to check up on yourself during a stint at the wheel, you will be measuring twist-active yarn. Stop spinning, haul a few yards back out of the orifice, break off the yarn, fold it in half, and let it ply on itself. Drape it over the McMorran and trim to balance. Since there are two strands of yarn, double the length measurement and you have the grist.

The McMorran will give you an accurate grist, but only for the sample that you hang over it. Suppose that you are spinning skeins of thick-and-thin yarn at a grist of about 800 yards per pound. Your measured sample will only be 8 inches long. The accuracy of your McMorran measurement will depend on how representative your sample is. Does that 8 inches contain an average number of thick and thin places? Probably not, unless your yarn is remarkably uniform.[8]

Neither the McMorran nor the inch gauge can accurately measure grist for textured or uneven yarns, especially heavyweight ones. Of course, uniform grist usually is not of prime importance in these yarns, anyway. Which is a good thing.

---

[8] *Every "thick" must be balanced with a "thin"; it is impossible to produce a yarn that has twice as many of one element as it does of the other, unless the whole yarn is only three elements long. You can produce a yarn where the "thins" are half the length of the "thicks" (or the reverse), but that is not the same thing. In any length of thick-and-thin yarn, you may have one more "thick" than you do "thins," or one more "thin" than you have "thicks," or you may have equal numbers of each. But you cannot have twice as many "thicks" as "thins," or vice versa.*

Amount of Twist

Another major influence on yarn character is the twist amount, which often has more to do with the way a yarn feels and behaves than any other single factor.

Twist is funny stuff. Everyone knows what it is, but it's hard to describe. You can consider twist to be stored energy. For practical purposes, that's exactly what it is. Basketmakers have a saying that the more energy you "store up" in a basket, the longer it will last. Potters make similar claims. In a general way, yarns and items made from yarn follow this pattern. All else being equal (it seldom is, but never mind), the more twist you put into a yarn, the stronger and more durable it becomes. Of course, you can carry this to excess; you can put in so much twist that the yarn becomes weaker, more brittle, and unmanageable.

Yet we will not be much concerned with measuring twist as stored energy. We will put our efforts into measuring the number of twists in a known length of yarn. [9]

As with grist, there are several ways to measure twist; that is, the drawer contains more than one ruler. Generally, twist is stated as *turns per inch* (the protocol used in this book) or *turns per centimeter*, or occasionally as what is known as *twist*

The amount of twist in a yarn can vary tremendously. Here are low-, medium-, and very high-twist yarns of the same grist (top to bottom).

---

[9] Unlike handspinners, the textile industry pays a great deal of attention to twist as energy. In industry, twist represents energy "consumed." Energy, or power, costs money. When you reduce the amount of twist, yarn costs less to produce. That does not mean the yarn costs less to buy; it means the producer has a greater profit margin. As a result, the twist amounts in many commercially produced yarns are predicated not upon an end use but upon the amount of twist that will hold the yarn together long enough to get out of the mill. This factor forces synthetics upon us in ever-increasing amounts: mills include high-strength synthetics so that yarns have enough tensile integrity to go through winding, packaging, and other essential operations without consuming the energy and time needed to add lots of twist. Of course, we handspinners can put in as much twist as we like.

angle. (Less often, twist may be measured as *turns per yard* or *turns per meter.*)

Twist is important. Why? To answer that, we will discuss basic yarn structure.

The power of friction

If you lay a number of fibers side by side, more or less parallel, you have a sort of yarn. This yarn will not contain twist, and it will be short. Its length will roughly equal the staple length of the fibers. If you grip all the fibers at both their ends and place a lengthwise strain or pull on this "yarn," its tensile strength will equal the sum of the individual fibers' strength.

This yarn has several obvious limitations. Imagine it is made of Lincoln wool, with a typical staple length of 12 inches. First, our yarn length faces a limit of 12 inches, right? We could tie bundles together, end to end, although that would be both tedious and, in terms of yarn strength, unsatisfactory. A yarn is no stronger than its weakest spot, and each knot acts as a weak spot.[10] Our yarn would also have plenty of texture, with a knot every 9 or 10 inches.

How else might we make greater lengths of yarn? Simple: by using twist, instead of knots. Twist and knots function similarly, because they press fibers together by friction.

In a knot, that friction results from what is called the *nip* of the knot. Different knots have greater or lesser amounts of nip, but the point to

---

[10] *The knot itself is not the weak link, although its presence weakens the yarn. Failure occurs in the area where yarn or thread enters and leaves a knot. Yarn seldom if ever breaks within a knot, but most often right outside one. The rigidity of the knot makes the entrance/exit areas act as strain raisers. One also faces the question of which knot to use. Knots are much akin to other ancient and honorable crafts, in that we contemporary folks do not use knots in daily life. Aside from scouting adventures or an excursion into macramé, how many knots do you know? As an example, how many "weaver's knots" are there? Some contemporary weavers may know two, although at least a half a dozen "weaver's knots" have been devised for use in mohair weaving alone. Knots warrant study in their own right. The author recommends his favorite work on the topic,* The Ashley Book of Knots, *for both for its comprehensive treatment of knots and related material and for its readable style.*

remember is that friction makes knots work. The nip presses the fibers together, and their collective friction keeps the join secure.

Twisting a fiber bundle does much the same thing. It presses individual fibers together. When you pull on the fibers, the friction between each fiber and its fellows keeps the yarn together. In general, the more twist you put into a fiber bundle (yarn), the more compactly the fibers are arranged, and the greater the friction. Thus, more twist, more strength.

Twisting allows us to introduce new fibers without having to tie knots. It would be possible for us to tie individual fibers together as we made our yarn, tying in a new length of fiber as each individual fiber ran out, and to stagger our knots so as to distribute them evenly through the fiber bundle. Twisting lets us achieve the same effect without using knots, as long as we arrange our fibers so that they overlap smoothly, gradually, and continuously. We must also use enough twist to compress the fibers, forcing them into contact with each other.

"Yarns" without twist

The whole purpose of this is to let us construct a long yarn from a short fiber.[11] A fiber mass, such as a simple lock of wool or a rolag, may be

---

[11] *Bette Hochberg has an interesting anecdote relating to the working methods of ancient Egyptian handspinners (the folks responsible for those remarkable linen cloths). Contrary to general opinion, the standing maidens shown in Egyptian art working two spindles at once are not spinning. They are twisting. The drafting has already been done and they are simply twisting the roving. Enough of that, on with the story. In the late 1970s, a prestigious museum contacted Bette to see if she could explain a curious item observed in certain ancient Egyptian yarns: a slight thickening at regular intervals in an otherwise superfine flax yarn. This subtle effect could only be observed with magnification. After viewing the examples, it came to Bette that this was caused by the fiber-preparation methods, not the spinning techniques. The fiber-processor had done a superlative job of retting, scutching, hackling, and so forth, and had then laboriously made roving by laying three-fiber bundles together, overlapping a new fiber onto the end of each single component as it ran out, and securing the join with a tiny dab of spit, paste, or similar adhesive. When this roving was finally twisted to give it strength, the resulting yarn was nowhere thicker than four fibers. Shows the results you can get when you are the pharaoh. For lots of good reading and illustrations, including material on early Egyptian textile work, see the reprinted* Hand Spinning and Woolcombing *by Grace M. Crowfoot and H. Ling Roth. Elizabeth Barber also cites this procedure in* Prehistoric Textiles.

drawn out, or attenuated, without twisting into a "yarn" of some length. Unfortunately, this arrangement has little coherence, since nothing presses the fibers together. Without twist-induced pressure to increase fiber-to-fiber friction, such a "yarn" is of minor practical use. It has no resistance to abrasion, no elasticity, and little tensile strength when spanning a distance greater than its average staple length.

Traditionally, such material has a number of names, like *slubbing*, *rove*, *roving*, and *roping*. In commercial practice, this attenuated mass comes from the last preparation step prior to spinning.

Various techniques can increase the strength of roving. One involves the introduction of a small amount of twist, although the trick is to use so little twist that the rove may be further drafted, yet enough twist that the material hangs together while being handled. Another method is to "rub" the roving as it is made; this is by far the method of choice in commercial woolen operations. In machine preparations, the rovings pass between "rubbers" that simply move back and forth, back and forth, across the material as it passes through the machinery. Handspinners perform the same service by rolling drafted fibers between hand and thigh.

The point? These methods increase the strength of the unspun fiber masses so they may be more easily spun, not so that they will serve as replacements for proper yarn.[12]

Imagine that you have a mass of fiber in one hand, and you pull out a little tuft with the other . . . as long as the individual fibers overlap and

---

[12] *Several popular textile techniques, like kiwi knitting and locker hooking, use unspun fibers. The yarn industry also finds the notion of non-spun yarns intriguing, because twist costs money. In theory, the method of fabric construction supplies the necessary compression, making areas which nip the fibers together and generate fiber-to-fiber friction. The theory also assumes that the staple length is greater than the distance between these nip points. Great faith is placed on the fact that if there are two or three stitches to the inch and the staple length is between 5 and 7 inches, then each fiber spans numerous stitches. That should be enough, right? Of course, such projects have greater long-term durability if they are vigorously fulled, or if the back of the finished cloth is coated with adhesives or binders. Even so, materials made by these techniques are ephemeral compared to their counterparts constructed from twisted yarns. The reason? A "yarn" without twist has no abrasion resistance. This quality will be discussed shortly, if you will get back to the text.*

you put in some twist, you are able to draft a little bit, then put in some more twist, and then draft a little more, and so on.

Just like the twisty-stick, right? On a good wheel, and up to tempo, the whole operation has the aura of a magic trick, as anyone observing the long draw will testify.

But no matter if the tool is a twisty-stick or a high-speed industrial machine: friction makes the fibers hold together, and twist aligns and increases that friction.

The effects of different amounts of twist

So there is the "secret key" to yarn construction: twist forces the fibers to press together, and friction between the fibers gives the yarn tensile strength.

Twist does a bit more than make the yarn "strong." Because twist represents stored energy, it follows that we may store lesser or greater amounts of it within a yarn. We are able to produce yarns with "high twist," "low twist," or any degree of twist that we desire. And the reason we want to do that? Because by changing the amount of twist in the yarn we also change the way that the yarn behaves, appears, and feels.

As we increase the twist in a yarn, that yarn (1) increases in tensile strength, (2) becomes more elastic, (3) improves its ability to withstand abrasion (surface wear and tear), (4) changes the way it reflects light, and (5) becomes firmer (harder) and smaller in apparent diameter.

But we cannot keep adding twist and causing these changes to progress. Eventually the positive values swing the other way. For example, tensile strength increases with the twist . . . until a certain point, beyond which additional twist actually weakens the yarn. Eventually the yarn becomes brittle and easily broken. The same applies to elasticity and abrasion resistance. These qualities increase, to a point, and then nosedive as twist continues to accumulate.

But up to that point, twist does do these things. So if we control the twist amounts, we can control, even fine-tune, a major determinant of how the yarn behaves in service.

To control the twist amount, we must be able to measure it. While there are various ways to measure twist amounts, there's only one easy, practical, and universally understandable way to state the results of such measurements: in *turns per unit of length*, which usually means *turns per inch* or *turns per centimeter*.

The most straightforward way to measure a twist amount is to lay a ruler or measuring tape alongside the yarn and count the number of turns in a convenient length, say 1 inch. If the yarn appears to have 3 twists or turns in it, then that is the apparent twist count: 3 turns per inch.

Yet appearances (and apparent twist counts) may be misleading. It takes practice to measure twist accurately. For example, you may be looking at a single yarn, spun from a fine, one-color fiber stock (such as cotton or fine white wool). You will not find clear visual clues to the number of turns in a given length.

Counting twist with tracer fibers

If you included one or two contrasting fibers in the yarn, you *would* have these visual clues and could easily observe the twist direction, number of twists per inch, twist angle, and all that stuff. You can get this effect—that is, provide yourself with highly visible tracer elements—by touching the yarn with a felt-tip pen. Color will wick along a few fibers. If you do not want the color to linger, mix 1 part food coloring with 3 parts tap water and apply the dilute dye with a cotton swab.

Determining twist in a fresh single by self-plying

Another method of determining twist is based on the premise that when freshly spun yarn doubles back on itself, the resulting two-ply accurately indicates the amount of twist contained in the single. This is the most practical way to check twist amounts during a spinning session.

Stop spinning and pull several feet of yarn back out of or off of whatever you are spinning on. You want a long enough piece of yarn to provide a representative sample. Do not cut or break the yarn unless you want to check it on the McMorran

Freshly spun single yarn will twist back on itself.

or to save the length as a sample. Stretch the length out, fold it in half, and let it ply back on itself. Generally, it will ply back on itself if you just let go of the doubled end.

Lay the resulting two-ply next to a measuring device (ruler, inch gauge, or whatever) and count the number of turns per inch in the yarn.

Once you have your count, grasp the end of the yarn, pull gently, and unply the test section. Wind it back onto the wheel and commence spinning again. No waste, no muss, no fuss.

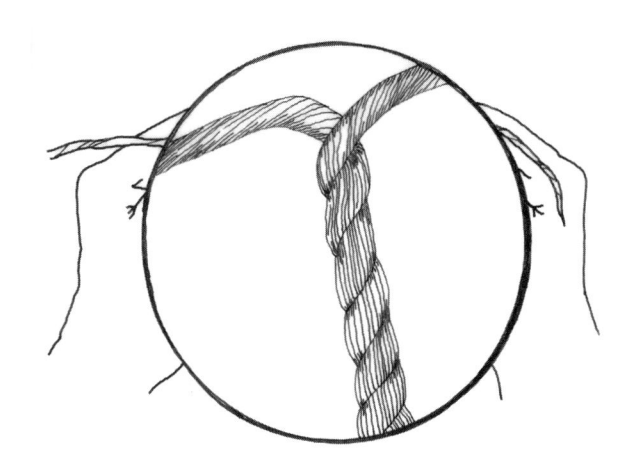

When freshly spun single twists back on itself, it reaches an equilibrium point where the component fibers lie parallel to each other and to the axis of the yarn.

When you first look at a length of two-ply, you may not know what, exactly, you are supposed to count. Which physical feature denotes one twist or turn? Common practice and convenience favor using the "humps." Swell. What are the humps? Imagine a short length of two-ply yarn lying on a piece of paper. Next, pretend that you have pressed the yarn flat with a very heavy iron. Now imagine that you trace along one side of this yarn with a sharp pencil. Your line will record a series of shallow curves, connected end to end, looking like low hills along the horizon. These are the humps.

Back to reality. If a freshly-spun single yarn plies back on itself without hindrance, it produces a two-ply yarn that is said to be "naturally plied." The countertwist in the ply pretty well balances out the twist in the single yarns, and the plied yarn has little tendency to twist further. A two-ply yarn of this type displays about half the twist component of the single. If you count the number of humps in an inch, you have a close approximation of the twist in the single yarn.

Let's see how this works. Imagine that you want to spin up a single at 5 turns per inch, and you

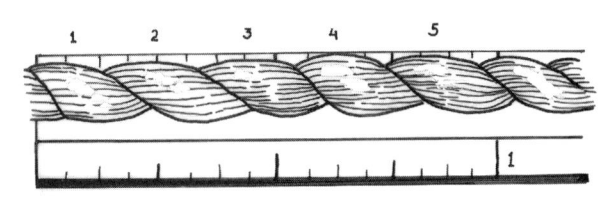

Counting "humps."

decide to check the twist. Stop spinning, pull out a few feet, fold the yarn in half, and let it ply itself. When you lay it beside a ruler, you see five complete humps and about half of a sixth hump in an inch of yarn. According to what you have just read, the twist count of the single is about 5½ turns per inch. You want 5 turns per inch. What do you do?

Spin a few more yards, putting in a little less twist. You do that by (1) running the yarn in just a little faster each time, (2) increasing the length of each draw a little, or (3) not waiting quite as long between draw and wind-on. As a last resort, (4) slow down your treadling slightly.

A word of advice: *do not do all of these things at once,* unless you want a dramatic change in the yarn. Change one thing at a time and see what happens. Otherwise, you may arrive where you want to be, with absolutely no idea how you got there. In itself, that's not so bad. But you may want to arrive at the same place again without having to wander around along the way. So change one thing at a time, observe the results, and remember what you did.

Now check your twist again. Pull some yarn out, let it self-ply, and measure. This time you find four full humps, and maybe just a little more, in one inch. To get a more accurate count, you hit on the wonderful idea of counting the number of turns in a 5-inch length and dividing by five. Well, phooey, even with optimistic fudging, you still get 4¼ turns per inch. You need a bit more twist.

Reverse the procedure you used to get less twist: (1) run the yarn in a little slower, (2) shorten the length of each draw, or (3) wait longer between each draw and wind-on. As a last resort, (4) speed up your treadling slightly.

Once again: do not change everything all at once. When you have established a set of spinning conditions that produces the yarn you want, keep going until you have all the yarn required.

The limitations of the self-ply method

This is all very fine, but we are supposed to be talking about checking twist, not making it. What about checking twist under other conditions, such as three-ply yarn, or single yarns that have been steamed, scoured, blocked, or otherwise set so they no longer ply themselves to the natural-ply amount? The "self-ply, count the humps" method works only with freshly spun yarn, for reasons that we will now make clear.

Generally, twist amounts indicated by the self-ply method are less than accurate if the twist is more than five minutes old. Yarn begins to set itself the moment it is spun or plied. The accuracy of the self-ply method decreases rapidly when yarn is stored.[13] For example, wool yarn spun during a humid Saturday demonstration may set itself completely on the bobbin, a fact you will discover Monday morning when showing a friend how to check the twist. This tendency to self-set may mislead you, especially where ply twists are concerned. Don't assume that a yarn has been plied to a balanced amount of twist just because it shows no immediate desire to twist or untwist itself.

Let's take a moment and clear up this business of *natural ply*, also called *balanced ply*, *balanced twist*, or *ply twist stabilization point*. All of these terms mean that the amount of stored energy (as twist) present in the plied yarn is evenly divided: the tendency of the individual strands to untwist themselves is countered by their tendency to ply themselves together. The opposite is true, as well: the tendency of the individual

---

[13] *The degree of self-set depends on the fiber, relative degree of twist, grist, yarn tension, temperature, amount of moisture present, and amount of time these conditions have been in effect. Any yarn that self-sets will also dynamically respond to certain environmental changes, such as the natural cycle of relative humidity. As an example of this effect, consider weather gauges of the "Black Forest Cuckoo" genre. On bright and sunny days, a little Alpine maiden is in view, waving her milk bucket about. When wet weather threatens, an old man with cape, hat, and staff makes his debut, chasing Heidi back into the clockwork. The mechanical principle behind these events is torsional rotation (twisting or untwisting) of a fiber bundle in response to changes in relative humidity. To demonstrate the action, and to gain a simple humidity indicator, suspend a small weight from a short length of your plied yarn. Let things settle down so the weight stops twirling. Now breathe upon the yarn, as you would to clean a pair of eyeglasses. The weight will rotate. Sure, it may be slow, but then Heidi and the Old Man of the Storm don't exactly scoot in and out, either. You could set this experiment up as a bookshelf or sconce sort of thing. Arrange a pointer (a pencil line or a scratch) on the weight. Install a little shelf underneath your pendant, complete with a paper dial showing calibrations like dry, 50/50, and wet. If your personality changes along with the humidity, have the label read jolly, moody, vicious, or whatever is appropriate. You may have to shorten or lengthen the yarn to adjust rotation and sensitivity of the instrument. By the way, this assemblage works better with wool or hair yarns than with cotton. It doesn't work well at all with synthetics, but who cares? Mr. Science would be proud.*

strands to ply themselves together is countered by their tendency to untwist themselves.

This principle applies only to conventionally plied yarns, where plying occurs in the direction opposite to the twist direction of the elements. (We will speak of unconventionally plied yarns later.) When two or more strands of yarn are plied in such a way that the ply twist exactly counteracts the strand twists, then the yarn is no longer *twist-active*, and in the normal course of events will cause no twist-related problems.

Twist-active means that a yarn attempts to rotate or twist whenever one end is free to turn. Simply stated, a twist-active yarn will kink, snarl, twist, and gyrate if you let go of it. A high-twist cotton single is a classic example of a twist-active yarn. As a rule of thumb, consider all single yarns as inherently twist-active, even when they have been "set."

A single yarn will always lose twist, given time and opportunity.[14] A yarn plied to the balanced-ply point will remain static. Yarns that are not plied to the balanced-ply point may gain or lose ply twist, depending upon the directions and amounts of twist in the individual (and collective) strands.

When we mention plied yarns and speak of natural ply, balanced ply, or balanced twist, this means a plied yarn that has been made twist-stable by means of opposing twist. The twist introduced in one operation is exactly countered by twist introduced in a later operation.

There are other methods of making a yarn twist-stable, however, so you should not assume that a particular plied yarn is a balanced ply simply because it is twist-stable. Why should you care? In a balanced ply, the ply twist tells you about all you need to know concerning the component yarns and their individual twist amounts. When a yarn is

---

[14] *If one end of the yarn is free to rotate about its own long axis, the question is not whether it will untwist but when. As a further Ms./Mr. Science project, obtain a length of single yarn that has been "set." Suspend a weight from this yarn so that the weighted end is free to rotate; in other words, tie a moderate weight on one end and tie the other end to a ceiling hook, rafter, clothesline, or whatever. The yarn may untwist itself the moment you let go of the weight, or it may not start untwisting for many hours. But it will untwist. Exceptions might be heat-set synthetics or yarns that have received chemical treatments for sizing, wrinkle-proofing, and so forth.*

twist-stable, the ply twist amount and direction may have no relationship to the strand twist, and you will have to disassemble the yarn to find the values of the components.

Determining twist amounts by untwisting

There are alternate methods of checking twist amounts. For example, imagine that you have several ounces of a single yarn that you spun up six months ago. You want to check the twist. It will not ply back upon itself accurately. Essentially, you have four options.

Option 1: Ignore the whole question, and skip to the back of the book to look at equipment plans. For shame.

Option 2: Lay the yarn beside a ruler and, armed with a magnifying glass, attempt to follow a single fiber around the yarn enough times to get a twist count. It helps if the fibers are of contrasting colors. A touch with a felt tip pen, or a drop of coffee (or tea, or chocolate, or crème de menthe . . . beer doesn't work, but red wine does) may stain and wick along a few fibers, making the task easier.

Option 3: Untwist a specific length of the yarn, counting the number of untwists it takes to get the yarn back to the no-twist state. This is the "no ifs, no buts, no whens" system, with direct, demonstrable, and absolute results. This method provides the standard to which all other twist-counting techniques are compared.

Untwisting is fairly simple. Collect a shoe box, some paper clips, and a rubber band. Bend one paper clip into a crank shape. Punch a small hole in one end of the shoe box and push the crank through it. Keep the "handle" end of the crank on the outside of the box, and bend the end inside the box into a hook. Snap the rubber band around the box's midpoint, about 4 to 6 inches away from the paper-clip crank. Hook the remaining paper clip over the rubber band.

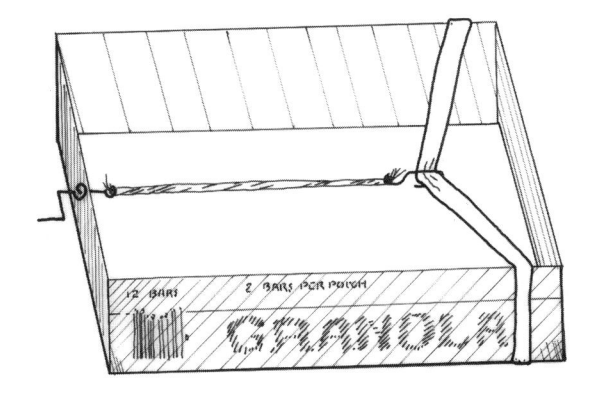

You can also determine how much twist a yarn contains by untwisting a strand and counting the number of turns as you do so. You can construct a simple device to make this easy.

The Alden Amos Big Book of Handspinning   111

Next, prepare a yarn sample. Suppose that it is a two-ply knitting yarn, and you want to find the amount of ply twist. Preparing the sample consists of tying two overhand knots in the yarn, about 3 to 4 inches apart. Clip off any extra yarn. Carefully measure the length of yarn between the two knots. You need to know exactly what the length is before you start messing around with the twist.

Next, catch one knot in the crank's hook and the other knot in the paper-clip/rubber-band arrangement. The rubber band puts a little tension on the sample, keeping it all neat and tidy.[15]

Once you have gotten this stuff arranged, start cranking. Unply the yarn, counting every turn of the crank.

How do you know when you are done? You are done when the strands that were plied lie side by side in a straight line, like railroad tracks. You can easily separate them, from end to end, with the point of a pencil or pen.

You know the length of the sample before untwisting and you know the number of turns required to untwist it. Divide the number of turns by the length of the sample. If the sample is 3 inches long and 6 turns untwisted it, the ply twist is 6 turns divided by 3 inches, or 2 turns per inch.

Simple and straightforward. In the case of a single yarn, proceed along the same lines, except that you will not have separate strands lying side by side. You will have a single strand of soft, untwisted fiber, and you will determine that it is untwisted by visual examination. If you do not see any twist, there isn't any. A magnifying glass helps a lot.

---

[15] *The tension is necessary for several reasons, including the fact that twist (and "untwist") will not travel along yarn that is not under some degree of tension. Also, as you unply a conventional yarn, the strand twist increases, making each strand prone to kink up, snarl, grab other strands, and raise hob with accurate measurement. Keeping the sample under tension prevents this unpleasantness. Last but not least, good twist-checking practice involves retwisting the sample to its original amounts, and again checking the sample length's, twist angle. To get useful results at this stage, you need the same tension throughout the process. When checking a single yarn, we run into a bit of a sticky wicket: the yarn gets weaker (and longer, of course) as the twist is removed. Use too much tension and the yarn will drift apart, perhaps before all of the twist has been removed. Yet if you do not maintain some tension, the twist will not distribute or "undistribute" evenly. Problems, problems.*

Determining twist angles

Option 4 is the *twist-angle* system of measurement, which has the virtue of extreme simplicity. You just measure the twist angle of the subject yarn. The twist angle is the apparent angle described by the fibers or strands as they spiral around the yarn.

To illustrate this, imagine that you are holding a piece of two-ply yarn by one end, allowing the other end to hang straight down. Now look at the yarn closely, and observe that the individual strands spiral about the yarn. The angle of that spiral concerns us. The closer the spiral angle is to the long axis of the yarn, the lower the twist; and the farther the spiral angle is from the long yarn axis, the higher the twist.

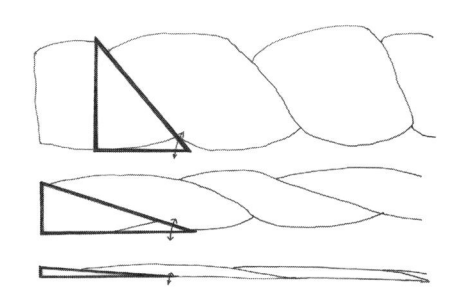

Here's what the twist angles look like in yarns of various grists.

Suppose we have a yarn in which the spiral angle is very small, perhaps 3 to 5 degrees. The fibers (or strands, for plied yarn) will be barely twisted together. Now imagine that we put more and more twist into this same yarn. As we twist, the twist angle increases and the character of the yarn also changes. By the time we put in enough twist to approach a 45-degree angle, the yarn has become quite hard.[16]

The twist-angle system has one aspect that may seem confusing. Yarns of 2,000 and 4,000 yards per pound may have exactly the same twist angle (let's say 30 degrees) yet have entirely different amounts of twist.

---

[16] *Astute Reader will observe that this might have something to do with a yarn getting "shorter" as the twist increases (the yarn doesn't normally get "thicker," because fiber compression increases with twist). Where a low-twist yarn has the fibers aligned closely to the yarn direction, a high-twist yarn has the fibers aligned more or less across the yarn direction. The fibers themselves don't change length (in this context, anyway), so something else has to change. It does, and the "it" is the yarn, which gets "shorter" as the twist increases. Now, connecting twist amounts and angles in an orderly, readable way is simple and involves a few calculations based on essential trigonometry. If a triangle is considered to have six parts (three sides and three angles), we can find values for the unknown parts if we have values for any three of the other parts, if at least one of the known parts is a side.*

The Alden Amos Big Book of Handspinning

The confusion can be explained away, because twist angle relates closely to yarn diameter.

Broken down into major parts, the twist-angle/diameter (grist) relationship can be stated as follows:

1. For a given diameter, different twist amounts produce different twist angles.
2. For a given twist angle, different diameters must have different twist amounts.
3. For a given twist amount, different diameters must have different twist angles.

That isn't clear and understandable? Let's use an illustration.

Imagine that the yarn is a big wood screw or a machine bolt—anything with screw threads. Suppose that there are 6 screw threads per inch of bolt. This is called the *pitch*. If the bolt is ½ inch in diameter, the screw threads describe a certain angle (it is about 57½ degrees).

Next, imagine that we have another bolt with 6 screw threads per inch, but it is 1 inch in diameter. While the diameter has increased, the pitch, or number of screw threads per inch, has stayed the same. The screw-thread angle is much steeper (about 87 degrees).

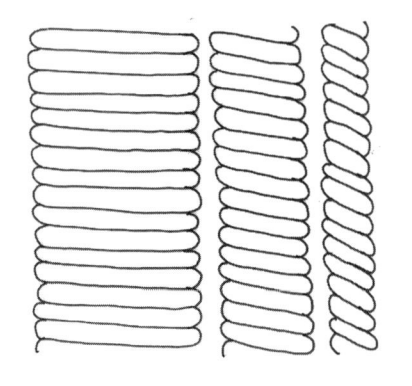

Pretending that our threaded bolts are yarn and that the screw pitch represents the twist angle, it should be clear that for a given number of turns per inch, the angle changes with the diameter.

Twist-angle values are often used to indicate a relative "hardness" or "softness" of a yarn. Essentially, the higher the angle, the harder the yarn; the lower the angle, the softer the yarn.[17]

This is all elegant and wonderful, with considerable value in theoretical and laboratory applications. In real life, several major drawbacks impede the twist-angle system.

First, it is tricky, difficult, and impractical to accurately measure the twist angle of any but the coarsest of single yarns. It is easy enough to measure

Even when the number of twists per inch stays the same, the twist angle changes as the yarn's diameter changes.

the angle on plied yarns, but the measurement is not necessarily accurate, as described below.

Second, you need to obtain more than one angle measurement per sample. To do the job with any accuracy, you should measure half a dozen sample angles and average the results.

Third, there is no convenient way to translate twist-angle adjustments into consistent spinning procedure. To do so means that you must obtain an average twist angle, find the grist, and convert these measurements into turns per inch; compare that with calculations derived from your drive ratio, length of make, and drafting/plying speed; adjust your spinning procedure accordingly; and study the results.

Observation of twist angle allows you to make a rough evaluation of a mass of yarn, or of yarn already converted into fabric. Of course, about all you can say concerning such yarn is what degree of twist it has—if it is "high twist," "low twist," or somewhere in between. Still, that information alone can be helpful.

How much twist is enough?

You already know that friction holds together the fibers in yarn, and that increasing the twist increases the pressure or nip of the fibers. This increased fiber-to-fiber pressure results in more friction and thus a stronger yarn.

---

[17] *The subjects of "how much twist?" and twist angles have been treated by various contemporary writers (including this author). Mabel Ross devotes an interesting part of Chapter 8 in* The Essentials of Yarn Design for Handspinners *to the topic, and she furnishes supplementary data and remarks. An added feature is the inclusion of a removable "angle gauge." Peter Teal's* Hand Woolcombing and Spinning *takes quite a different approach—understandably, considering his stated attitude concerning "woolen" yarns. He avows that "worsted yarns are the elite" and that his book intends to encourage the reader "to investigate and adopt worsted spinning." He goes on to state that by embracing his methodology you (the reader) will, among other things, "lift your spinning out of the rut in which common or garden woolen-spun yarns have lain. . . ." My, goodness. In any case, his chapter on twist (Chapter 8, fancy that!) includes interesting material on twist angle; he also provides supplemental information, along with calculations to play with. Your current writer is breaking with tradition: this is Chapter 4, not Chapter 8.*

Yet you cannot keep putting in twist, making the yarn ever stronger. Eventually the yarn stops increasing in tensile strength and begins to weaken, and ultimately breaks. Why?

Excessive twist places great strain on the individual fibers. The outer fibers may be under such a load that they reach their tensile limit, and any further strain on the yarn causes wholesale fiber breakage.

In addition, increased twist beyond a certain point doesn't provide any usable increase in fiber-to-fiber pressure; we have already arrived at the maximum friction/strength level. Once that level has been reached, any increase in twist quickly becomes damaging. After this point, increased twist will strain (or "pre-load," if you will) the surface layers of fiber. When such a yarn is placed under tension, even slight additional strain exceeds the stress parameters of the individual fibers and they break.[18] With enough additional twist, the strains induced by the twist alone will exceed the breaking strength of the fibers and the yarn will "break" itself.

It is worthwhile to note what happens when a yarn breaks. Breaks come in a variety of types, four of which are of general interest to handspinners: the *normal* break, the *kink* break, the *attrition* break, and the *excessive-twist* break.

Here's a typical sequence of events in the excessive-twist break. A few over-strained fibers rupture, and in doing so reduce the diameter of the yarn at that point. Twist always runs to the thinnest part of the yarn, and that is what happens. Because there is already an excess of twist, the increase causes more fibers to break, again reducing the diameter of the yarn. Twist runs to the thinnest part of the yarn, and adding more causes fibers to break, reducing the diameter further . . . and so forth. Placing the slightest tension strain on the yarn only speeds up the sequence,

---

[18] *In engineering parlance,* strain *is the external force or load that tends to distort or change the shape of the material and* stress *is the internal force by which material resists change or distortion. The primary stress for yarn is called* tensile stress. *When dealing with normal yarns of appropriate twist, tensile stress is virtually the only stress of concern, but with excessively twisted yarns, a form of shearing stress called* torsion *raises its calculating head. We're going to give you some mathematical respite and not go into the workings of this process, as long as you promise not to use excessive twist.*

since tension helps twist travel, right? The only escape from this type of break, once started, is the kink break.

The kink break is fairly complex. It can occur whenever a kink appears, and kinks easily develop in yarn with excessive twist. In a kink, the outer fibers are under great strain and a slight additional load breaks them. This places the next layer under strain, and it also ruptures, and so forth. Kink breaks are not limited to excessively twisted yarns, however, and in many ways resemble the breaks associated with knots.

The attrition break is simple, and is not a break in the sense of ruptured fibers. Attrition breaks produce the typical failure pattern of thick-and-thin yarns or yarns abraded in one area. The yarn must be under tension, as in a loom warp. Since twist attempts to redistribute itself when yarn is under tension, twist runs from the thick parts into the thin parts. The thin parts may be a design feature of the yarn, the result of a mistake on the spinner's part, or caused by external abrasion. The thick parts now do not have enough twist and the yarn "drafts" itself, slimming out the thick portions. In so doing, more "thin" places are made and the yarn becomes longer. A thinner yarn requires more overall twist, but none is available. Instead, the new thin places rob more twist from the remaining thick places, which lose strength and draft even more. The cycle repeats itself quickly, ending only when the yarn "drifts" apart instead of snapping.

The normal break combines fiber breakage and fiber slippage. This is the break you get when you grasp yarn between your hands and pull. First a few fibers break and the rest slip a tiny bit, then a few more break and the rest slip a little, and so on. The entire sequence ends very quickly.[19]

---

[19] *With some fibers, notably cotton, several authorities feel that the individual fibers do not actually break, but that the yarn "slips" apart, that is, the fibers slip past each other. This might be true as a general observation, but in this author's experience individual fibers do break. A strong bit of evidence to back this up is that when a piece of yarn is broken in this manner, the frayed fibers sticking out of each end are almost always much shorter then the fiber's dominant staple length. In addition, a microscopic examination of the broken yarn ends usually reveals ruptured fibers.*

Fiber

It may cross your mind that some fibers are stronger than others, and that yarns made from these fibers will be "stronger" yarns. That is a valid general observation. In tests on equal yarns made from the major fibers, wool fails first, generally followed by cotton, then silk, and finally flax.

Yet yarn strength involves more than raw tensile strength, and yarns are seldom equal. For example, a combed cotton yarn is at least as strong as an equivalent yarn spun from silk noils, and a mohair worsted is often stronger than a similar carded flax (tow) yarn. Cotton spun into a picturesque thick-and-thin silhouette produces about the most failure-prone yarn you can make, even though cotton is a "strong" fiber. Not only that, such a yarn has little resistance to abrasion, although cotton is often the fiber of choice for abrasion-resistant yarns.

Why this is so does not depend simply on grist and twist. The two factors of grist and twist apply, but both the fiber and the spinning method also contribute much to the yarn's character.

This brings us to a short discussion of the third major factor, fiber. The information presented next is not comprehensive. We want to consider several major concepts concerning fibers without cluttering the literary landscape with charts, graphs, superlatives, wool-breed listings, and little animal pictures.

Each fiber has specific mechanical features. These features do not indicate any fiber's "superiority" over another, but they do point the way to suitable uses. In other words, fibers don't compete with each other. Each should be used in ways that benefit from its strengths.

Each individual tendril or filament of fiber is a three-dimensional object, with length, width, and height. The width and height are contained in the term *diameter*, because for convenience we treat all fibers as round, even though they may not be. In addition, fibers are seldom straight, although silk and flax (of the Big Four) tend in that direction.

Wool, of course, offers the classic example of being anything but straight. Most wool fibers show waves and wrinkles (crimp), along with a strong desire to remain waved and wrinkled even after being spun into yarn. This tendency is one reason why wool yarns and fabrics have excellent insulating qualities. Simply stated, even a tightly spun woolen yarn contains a lot of air spaces.

Cotton fibers are convoluted, which is to say that they, too, deviate from the straight and narrow. Each cotton fibril is a flattened tube, bending first in one direction, then in the other.

Flax, essentially straight, shows little variance from a long, straight, and thread-like form, although its fiber structure demonstrates an inherent left-handed (S-twist) spiral. The traditional spinning direction takes account of this last feature; flax singles have customarily been spun in the S direction, although most singles of other fibers are spun Z. There may be no demonstrable gain obtained by spinning flax with an S twist, but by the same token, what advantage is gained by spinning the oppo-

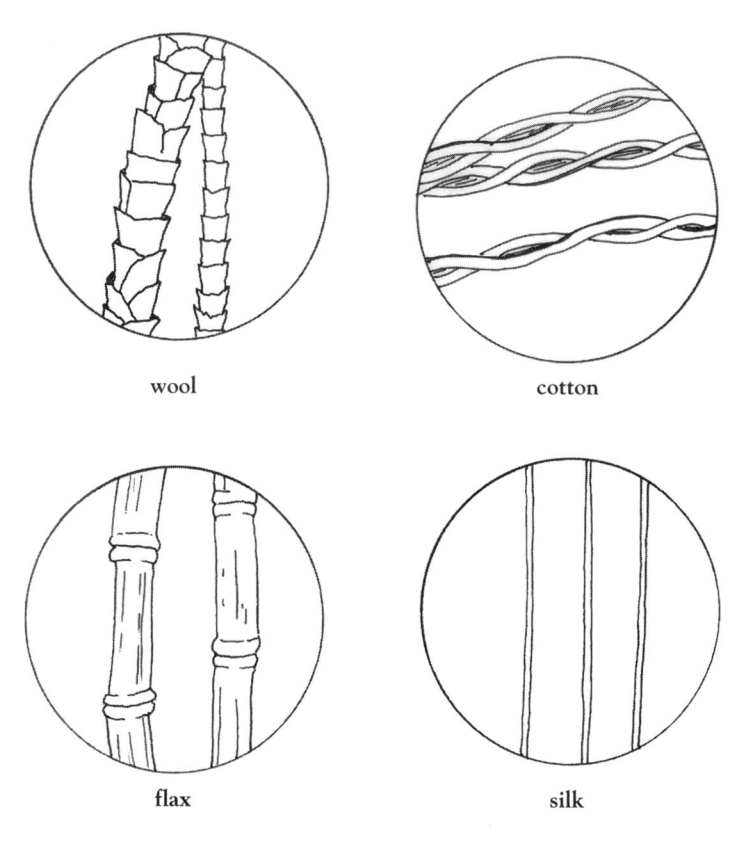

wool

cotton

flax

silk

Looked at closely, individual Big Four fibers show different three-dimensional qualities.

sheep

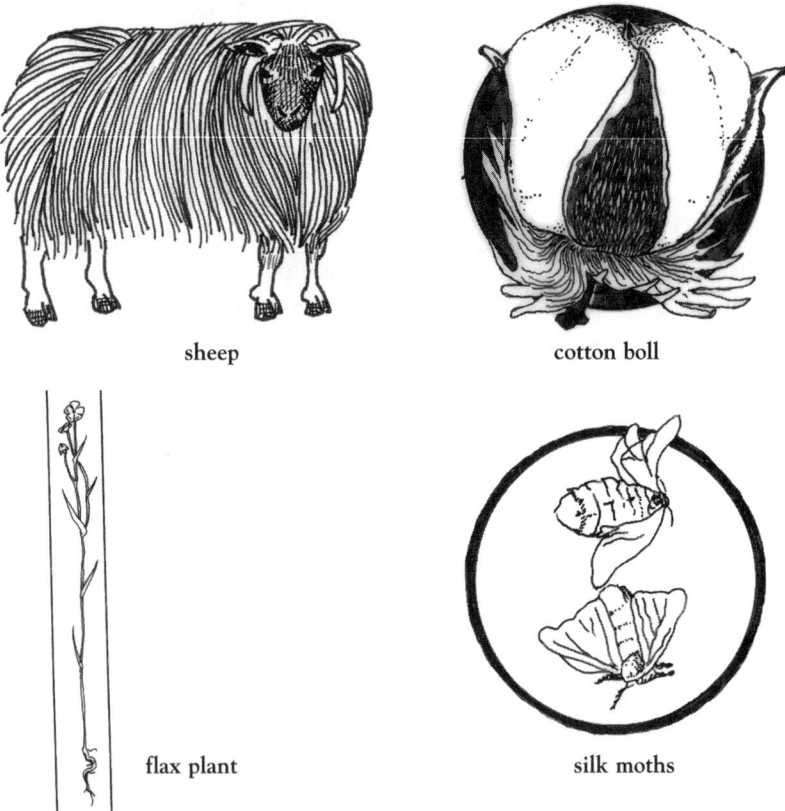

cotton boll

flax plant

silk moths

The Big Four fiber sources.

site way? Several hundred generations of handspinners spun flax S twist, largely by choice; to spin it Z for no other reason than to exercise the option is neither good sense nor good practice.

Silk, an extruded filament, for all practical purposes is considered the straightest and smoothest of the four major fibers.

Flax and cotton are what are called *inextensible fibers*, a fancy way of saying they do not stretch. The term also means that the fiber does not have a useful amount of elasticity. *Elasticity* describes a substance's ability to return to its original shape and dimensions after being deformed or distorted by an applied load. Because cotton and flax do not stretch to any appreciable degree under handspinning circumstances, their elasticity is a moot point.

It is possible to construct *extensible fabrics* that have good elastic qualities from *inextensible fibers*. Examples include cotton crepe and linen seersucker. The "stretch" and elasticity occur as a result of fabric structure and yarn twist, not the inherent qualities of the fibers. We commonly convert cotton into elastic, extensible fabrics (consider the ubiquitous T-shirt), although cotton fiber stretches about as much as a piece of railroad track.

Flax (as linen) does not lend itself to the production of similar knitted fabrics, primarily because the flax fiber available for manufacture is stiffer, less flexible, and coarser than cotton.[20] Linen fabrics and textiles can be quite soft and luxurious, but that results from having been converted into cloth and then exposed to much careful abuse. You will remember (from Chapter 2) that flax is about 70 percent cellulose, with the remaining percentage composed of lignin, pectin, gums, and so forth. Washing, beating, wearing, and boiling the cloth gradually remove the extra 30 percent, leaving nothing but cellulose. After this treatment, the flax fiber may be as fine and flexible as cotton, but spinners aren't likely to want to disassemble cloth simply to obtain flexible spinning fiber.[21]

Wool is extensible, elastic, and resilient—more so than any other natural fiber. Wool can also be *blocked*, a quality not possessed by cotton, silk, or flax. This means that the wool fiber may be shortened or lengthened by the application of heat, moisture, and external force. This process affects the actual fiber, right down at the molecular level. Proper blocking—blocking not carried to excess—does not significantly degrade the fiber. Unfortunately, blocking is an option; and vast numbers of

---

[20] *Flax also costs considerably more than cotton does.*

[21] *Papermakers do just that, more or less. The fiber source for traditional papermaking has been cellulosic rags. Today's hand papermaker often buys specially made, fluffy, felt-like blocks of cotton linters. Until the price of cotton dropped (in the middle-to-late eighteenth century), European papermakers used linen rags exclusively. Today when a major papermaker puts a small percentage of cotton into a paper, the action results in pompous ad copy and a high price. In 1700, poor people wore linen and rich people wore cotton. In 2000, poor people wear synthetics and rich people wear "100-percent Natural Fiber," when they can get it.*

people are often eager to abuse or redefine the limits of an option. Blocking is a remedial process, useful for correcting mistakes. As a further charity, blocking is reversible.

While flax and cotton cannot be blocked, they can be *mercerized,* a process that shortens and enlarges the fiber. Mercerization consists of wet treatment with strong caustic solutions, and its effects are permanent.

Resiliency, as it applies to the wool fiber, means in practical terms that the material does not wrinkle readily; actually, it means that it won't stay wrinkled long. Simply hang a piece of wrinkled, rumpled, folded, or creased woolen fabric over a support for a time and all but the most stubborn of wrinkles will vanish.

That points up the difference between elasticity and resilience, by the way. *Elasticity* refers to immediate recovery from deformation. *Resilience* (also a recovery from deformation) requires time. In textile use, elasticity generally means recovery from tensile loads, or stretching a yarn. Resilience usually means recovery from compression loads, or what happens when you stuff your sweater into a lunchbox. Flax notoriously lacks resilience. Linen fabrics wrinkle easily, and the wrinkles stay until you approach them with something hot and heavy, like an iron.

Silk is neither as elastic nor as resilient as wool. However, no other natural fiber matches silk's combination of tensile strength, elasticity, and resilience. Silk is so extensible that this quality can be troublesome, because silk will stretch more than it will recover, and it stretches without great strain.[22]

---

[22] *We seem to be edging into the realm of Fiber Science. What we are talking about now is called recovery. A yarn or fiber is stretched some nominal amount, say 3 percent of its length; it is then allowed to relax, and the length is again measured. With 100-percent recovery, the length is exactly the same as before stretching. At 3 percent elongation, silk has a recovery figure of about 90 percent, wool about 97 percent, cotton about 70 percent, and flax is down about 60 percent. But before you think that these figures are terribly significant, consider the forces involved. The load required to elongate a linen yarn 3 percent is about 1½ times greater than an equivalent silk yarn can survive. In fact, that load will stretch the silk yarn about 25 percent and then break it. The same load is about five times greater than the load required to break wool, after stretching it 40 percent. The same load will stretch cotton about 6 percent, and just barely break it. The bottom line? Cotton and flax don't stretch.*

That should be enough about fiber for now. It certainly gives reason enough for you to agree that fiber influences yarn character. By the same token, you can see that choosing and using fiber involves much more than meets the casual eye.

Spinning method

Spinning method, or how the yarn is spun, is the fourth major factor that affects yarn character. There are only two basic ways to spin a yarn: the woolen method (drafting-against-twist) and the worsted method (drafting-without-twist).

Of course, the above statement is simplistic. Each method includes several logical and more or less obvious variations. For example, spinning prepared top *over the knuckle* or *out of the fold* can be cited as a good example of *semi-worsted* spinning, yet the spinning method is "pure woolen," and long draw at that. Twisting a cheese roving without drafting could qualify as worsted-method spinning, although the yarn is anything but worsted.

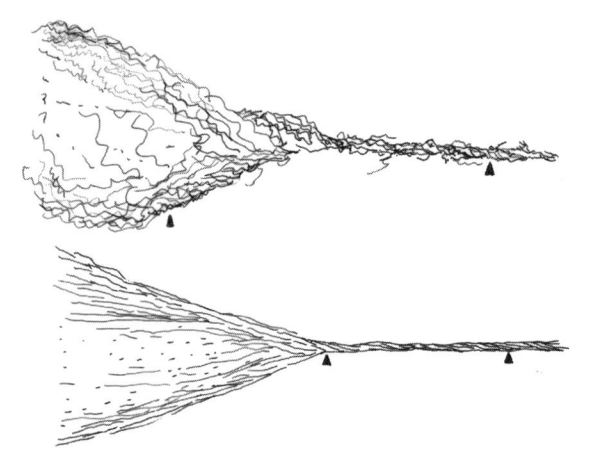

Woolen and worsted drafts, compared. The triangles show where the fingers of each hand are placed. In woolen spinning (above), fibers are as random as possible and the woolen draft works against the twist. Worsted spinning involves fibers arranged as close to parallel as possible, and the worsted draft requires that there be no twist in the drafting area.

Because this chapter deals with the character of yarn, we will consider the way in which spinning method determines the type of yarn that is produced. That is easy enough. Only three basic types of yarn can be spun from any fiber: (1) *worsted-type yarn*, in which the fibers are of uniform length, the fibers have been arranged parallel to the spinning direction, and the yarn is drafted without twist; (2) *woolen-type yarn*, in which the fibers are of mixed lengths, the fibers have been arranged at right angles to the spinning direction, and the yarn is drafted against twist; and (3) *everything else*.

Each yarn type has positive and negative qualities, which include not just yarn characteristics but also methods of production. We will deal with the negative aspects later. Here is the positive stuff.

The worsted-type yarn is characterized by high fiber density, a clear surface with little or no fuzz, good tensile strength relative to diameter, not much tendency to felt (if wool), and good abrasion resistance. Worsted yarns enhance fiber luster if luster is present.

The woolen-type yarn is characterized by low fiber density, a soft and fuzzy surface, good fulling qualities (if wool), excellent insulating abilities, and delightful loft and handle.

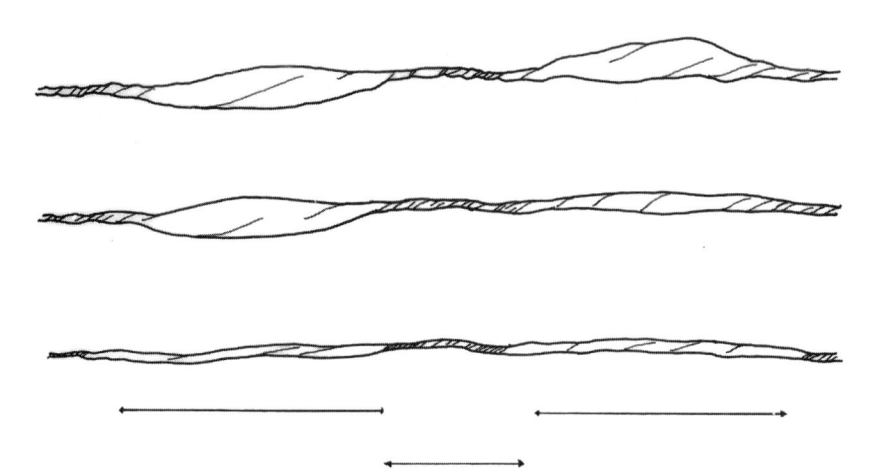

In the woolen drafting technique, larger slubs which form early in the draw (top) become skinnier as the drafting proceeds (middle, moving to bottom). The twist redistributes itself as the thick areas are drawn out.

To obtain a worsted-type yarn, you must use the worsted spinning method, which involves drafting-without-twist. But to gain the full package of worsted effects, you must also spin worsted-style from fibers that have been combed. Not carded, not teased, not flicked: combed, and with all the noils removed.

Why would you want a worsted-type yarn? Because you need a yarn that is lean, strong, and solid, with a clear and visible surface. Or because you need a yarn that has high resistance to abrasion and showcases the fiber's luster.

To obtain a woolen-type yarn, you must spin using the woolen system, which involves drafting-against-twist. Specifically, you must draft a carded preparation against the twist. In some ways, woolen-type spinning is not as clear-cut or simple as worsted-type spinning.

For the purist, there is only one way to spin "true worsted," as we described. If the purist deigns to think about woolen spinning, then said purist feels that the only way to spin "true woolen" is at right angles to the fiber direction of a carded preparation, and without any draft. The thinking behind this no-draft woolen is that drafting forces fibers to become less randomly arranged and more oriented along the yarn direction, thus making the yarn less "woolen-like" and more "worsted-like." Well, golly whillikers.

Everything else (which is the third type of yarn) consists of yarns that are neither true worsted nor true woolen. This group includes about 98 percent of handspinners' yarns. It surely deserves a chapter of its own.

Chapter 5

Accurate measurements and some physical properties of the Big Four fibers: In which we look at how fibers stretch when measured, figure moisture content and regain, and learn a bit more about the Big Four's physical properties and cultural requirements

Yarn is interesting. Some things about it are easy to measure or otherwise evaluate. Grist can be quickly determined, as can the degree or amount of twist. The direction of twist and number of plies (if any) may be found through simple visual means—that is, by looking at the yarn.

Yet other qualities seem to escape convenient measurement. The actual diameter of a yarn (which we broached in Chapter 4), its hardness (or softness), its strength—these items remain elusive. And what of the essentially subjective yet delicious qualities of loft, hand, and halo? There is no doubt that these properties interest the end-user of the yarn, and should, therefore, concern its maker.

Other areas will be of particular interest if you anticipate selling handspun yarn, or products made from handspun yarn. These include economic and time-related matters, such as how long it takes to spin or ply a quantity of warp, what yield of clean yarn can be expected from raw fleece, or what, if any, time/cost benefits come from using commercially prepared fibers.[1]

---

[1] *In light of Federal Trade Commission regulations and general public concern for truth in labeling, if you decide to sell your work it is worth your while to know all you can about your yarn and products made from it. If you anticipate giving everything away—no trade, no barter, just giving it away—then you don't have to worry.*

The purpose for any measurement scheme is to enable a better description or definition of the subject. Suppose you have some yarn. Is it wool? Cotton? Is it a single? What color? How much of it do you have? How much of it are you willing to sell? All? Some? What does it cost? Is the yarn thick or thin? Firm, soft, or what? Can it be washed, or does it have to go to the dry cleaner? Is it strong?

These questions are not silly or whimsical, and they are not all of the questions that are asked. To answer even the least question, you must make an evaluation or measurement. Folk wisdom of many cultures tells us that to name a thing is to control it. The more accurately a thing (or person) is described (named), the greater the power of invocation or dominion.[2]

So it is with yarn. The better we are able to describe it, the more control we have over it. And to describe it, we have to measure it, or take someone else's word for the measurements. We don't need to measure everything about the yarn we spin—only the things that we can reasonably change. We want to measure and describe the major parameters and, for the present, let the minor ones take care of themselves.

For our purposes, a *major parameter* is any parameter that, when altered, results in a readily observed change in yarn structure and/or visual characteristics. Obvious major parameters include fiber type, color, number of plies, amount of twist, and grist. Less obvious major parameters include direction of element twist, fiber preparation, method of spinning, and fiber condition.

Now for a quiz. There's no pass or fail on this one, just some questions to start the thoughts flowing. If you could only measure and describe one

---

[2] *Should you feel that the concept of naming-as-power is limited to primitive tribal cultures, secret spirit societies, quaint superstition, and costumed superheroes, pause for a moment and reflect upon your driver's license and Social Security number. Consider the telephone, bar-coded addresses, draft laws, health plans, insurance policies, and automatic tellers. Possibly other examples will cross your mind.*

[3] *We posed this question to a number of yarn makers and users. No one gave what the author considered the obvious and concise answer to the second question ("enough twist"), which indicates that the author is something of a fuddy-duddy. Responses ranged from "nice color" to "being silk." The winners were "softness" and "warmth." A few respondents considered "strength" worthwhile, and a very few felt "price" was important.*

thing (parameter) about a yarn, what should it be? And what do you consider the most important characteristic or quality of a yarn?[3]

This is a good place to review two words—*subjective* and *objective*. Very simply stated, *subjective* refers to relational judgment, opinion based upon comparison. *Objective* refers to demonstrable, non-relative, physical values. Subjectively, we may say that a yarn is fine, medium, or heavy. Objectively, we say that the yarn measures a specific grist. Objective observations always contain specific values; subjective observations replace those values with adjectives, adverbs, and other slippery items. Enough of semantics—suffice it to say that the greater portion of this book is dedicated to objective observations and measurements.

Measurements concerning yarn dimensions and yarn qualities are not all that hard to make, although the process is not the same as whipping out a tape measure and checking the dimensions of a stove.

The most basic yarn measure, the one most useful to a handspinner, is yarn length. Why?

First, it tells you if you have "enough." If you are a weaver, you know that warps are primarily measured in yards times number of warp ends. When a warp requires 600 warp ends, each 5 yards long, you need 3,000 yards; 2,900 yards are not enough, no matter how you feel about the matter.

Second, knowing a yarn's length allows you to make the next basic measurement: the length/weight relationship, or grist. The measurement of grist has been well discussed in Chapter 4. Should you feel an urge to refresh your memory, by all means return there and refresh away.

Grist is important in its own right, yet establishing a yarn's grist enables us to determine other values as well, including its diameter. When we know the diameter, we can make various advance evaluations of how the yarn should be arranged in the loom; appropriate knitting gauges; weight and character of the resulting fabric; what to expect when the yarn is plied or further twisted in various ways; and so forth.

As you discovered in Chapter 4, we have several ways to figure grist. By using more than one method on the same yarn, we can describe that yarn more precisely. For example, when we calculate diameter on the basis of grist (mathematically) and compare that information to the actual diameter (physically), we are in a position to make an objective evaluation of yarn "hardness" or "softness." Further, knowing the diame-

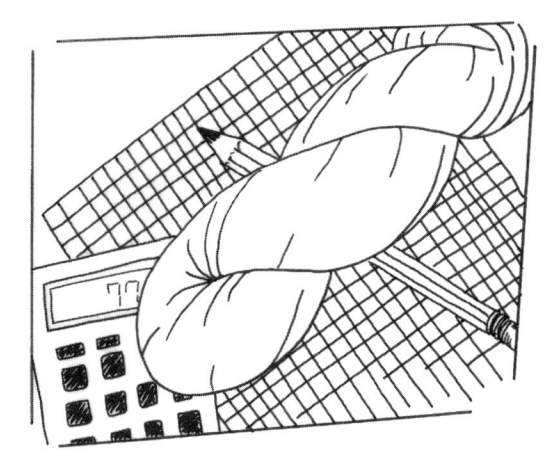

The designer's point of view.

ter of a yarn enables us to predict maximum, minimum, or purpose-appropriate amounts of twist, and so on.

It is possible to calculate an entire project from fiber to fabric—and then to do nothing but sit around and talk about how wonderful it is going to be. While this exercise generates a certain amount of satisfaction, it does not produce a worthwhile substitute for real yarn or fabric.[4] The calculation process offers real and particular value to the designer. Because you are both producer and designer, why not outfit yourself with a full set of the "tools of the trade?"

ACCURACY AND LENGTH MEASUREMENTS

The topic of accuracy raises its head. How accurate do you need to be? What is "accurate?" As mentioned elsewhere, accurate measurements

---

[4] *In theory, if you can obtain any two mechanical parameters of a yarn, you will then be able to determine all the other dimensions or mechanical parameters of that yarn. The process requires assumptions and a fair amount of math; the assumptions fall into the realm of skilled guesses and the math consists mainly of extracting square roots, adjusting them in various ways, and then flogging triangular relationships with same. Aside from the mathematics, the process is roughly similar to calculating a dinosaur's caloric intake from a single fossil tooth.*

are consistent and repeatable. Otherwise, use common sense. Most examples and measurement procedures contained in this work are based on two-decimal accuracy, which considers only the first two decimal places as significant. The exceptions are contained in various mathematical calculations and in critical weight measurements, as found in dyestuff application.[5]

For an illustration, consider our basic measurement, from which all others spring: yarn length.

You are normally concerned with the length in yards and will have no difficulty observing the differences between ¼, ½, and ¾ of a yard. That level of accuracy is acceptable when a skein contains more than, say, 30 yards. For smaller skeins, measure in feet. In this case, you will need to observe the differences between ¼, ½, and ¾ of a foot.

Suppose you are using a McMorran yarn balance to find the weight/length ratio (grist) directly. You are dealing with two observations: (1) whether the arm is level or not and (2) the length of a sample, measured in inches. The McMorran's construction makes a decision about when the arm is level simple. You can easily observe ¼-inch differences in sample length. That is accurate enough; but if you find that you can observe ⅛-inch differences in sample length, why not do so?

There is a big difference between measuring the length of a McMorran sample and measuring the length of yarn contained in a typical skein.

First, the skein often contains hundreds of yards and the McMorran sample is unlikely to be more than 3 or 4 yards long; most McMorran samples range between 10 and 50 inches.

---

[5] *Your author has been faulted over the number of decimal places used in certain published material. The complaint seems based upon the premise that such level of accuracy defies ready observation, and is thus invalid. Perhaps. Are you able to tell the difference between ½, ¼, and ⅛ of an inch? If you are, you are observing one-, two-, and three-decimal accuracy: .5, .25, and .125, respectively. The human eye is well able to determine parallel (width or thickness) variations of less than .005 of an inch, and the author has yet to meet a handspinner who is not sharp at abstract, two-decimal math. Look at the following everyday problem. You can obtain BubbaKreme Yum-dums, 6 oz. size for $.99, or Big, Big Familypounder Yum-dums in Wrink-o-fresh Pak, full pound (16 oz.) for only $2.99. Assuming that you are in the market for Yum-dums, did you have any problem determining the better buy? Well, that's two-decimal math.*

Second, you measure the McMorran sample under a minimum amount of tension (good practice being to use only enough tension to cause the yarn to lie straight next to or on top of a ruler). Skeins, by nature of their construction, are wound under greater tension, which causes yarn to stretch. How much? Under any practical level of tension, some yarns stretch a little and some stretch a lot. But they all stretch. The greater the length being measured, the more this matters.

Imagine that you have a piece of yarn "about" 2 feet long and you want to measure its length to the nearest ½ inch. Simple. Lay the yarn on top of or next to a yardstick, straighten the yarn out, and measure it. Suppose that it measures 22½ inches. Now suppose that you stretch the yarn as tightly as you can, perhaps between two pins: how long is it? Depending on the yarn, it could be 23½ inches, 26 inches, 28 inches, or even more.

Let's carry the example a step further and imagine we are winding a 100-yard skein, under a lot of tension. We wind 100 yards carefully, tightly, and exactly, remove them from the skeiner, place them upon a swift, and then re-wind to another measured skein, using as little tension as possible.

Imagine our surprise when the new skein measures only 89 yards. How did we lose 11 yards? We didn't. We stretched and measured the yarn in the first winding, and measured it under less-stretched conditions in the second winding.

Unrealistic? Not at all. Winding stretch for most yarns may average 10 percent, although you will have to work to get linen or cotton singles to stretch that much. Even so, remember that yarn length is dependent upon yarn tension.

Since it is impractical to directly measure the length of large amounts of yarn without a degree of tension, it follows that you need to notice yarn stretch. You don't have to make an issue of it; just be aware of it and allow for it. There are two simple ways to deal with the problem.

First method. When winding skeins for the purpose of measuring yarn length, attempt to keep the yarn tension moderate and constant from skein to skein. In general, use enough tension to make a neat and tidy skein, and no more.

Second method. When winding yarn for specific projects, allow a few extra turns "for Grandma." That is, always wind a little more than you need. How much more? At least 10 percent.[6]

ACCURACY AND WEIGHT MEASUREMENTS

To find the grist of a yarn, we either weigh a known length or we measure the length of a known weight. The first method (preferable) is the standard against which all other grist evaluations are compared. The second method is the modus operandi of the McMorran yarn balance.

Handy as the McMorran is, more representative ("accurate") values come from weighing greater quantities of yarn, such as large skeins of known length. Here at the home place, we use several scales and weighing devices. For heavy, nasty, cumbersome items (large amounts of raw wool), we employ a steelyard, using the 0–40-pound range in ⅛-pound (2-ounce) increments.

Our general-purpose scale is also our commercial sales scale, calibrated in 100ths of a pound (1 ounce = .0625 pound). For dye work and precise measurement, we use a triple-beam lab (metric) scale, accurate to $1/100$ gram (.00238 ounce).

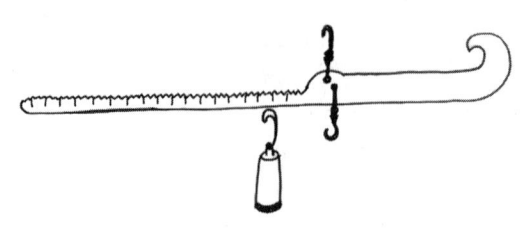

A steelyard works well for weighing large amounts of fiber.

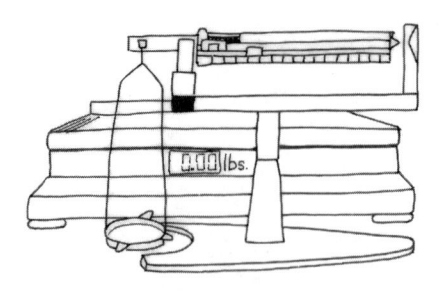

Other types of scales, with finer measurement gradations, can measure working amounts of fiber, dyestuffs, and other materials. In the foreground is a triple-beam scale; in the background, a digital platform scale, often used for commercial sales.

---

[6] *It is impractical to wind or re-wind yarn (for any reason, not just measuring length) with any speed, vigor, and efficiency unless tension is introduced. In fact, it is well-nigh impossible. Because tension-induced stretch is a necessary evil, it might be worthwhile to experience the scope of its influence. Simply wind and measure a skein as you normally do, then very gently, slowly, and carefully (with as little tension as possible) rewind and re-measure. Gives you a good idea of what the percentage is or will be. Once you have that in hand, go ahead and wind everything in your normal fashion—and allow the appropriate extra "for Grandma."*

Moisture affects grist.

We do not use the steelyard for grist measurements. For skeins too large to weigh on the gram scale, we use the commercial sales scale. Of course, this reduces our accuracy, as the commercial scale only determines increments of $1/100$ pound. Yet it is still workable because we measure substantial quantities of yarn, from 6 ounces to 7 pounds or more.

In other words, the smaller your samples, the more accurate your measuring devices need to be. But before you rush out and score a crystal-cased wonder-scale that will weigh your signature, consider the effect that moisture (in the form of relative humidity) has upon the Big Four fibers.

Just as tension changes yarn length, moisture changes yarn weight. How much? Quite a bit. Enough to make the grist figures you work out on a bright summer day appear to be in serious error, should you recheck them on a foggy fall afternoon when drizzle polishes the sill and a kettle sings on the hob.

The preceding statement is subjective, right? It has no values that you can sink your teeth into. Evocative and qualitative, perhaps, but not objective. Let's look objectively at the effect of moisture content on grist.

Laboratory practice is to bring sample yarns to a specific moisture content, or *condition* them, before any test or measurement (not just grist). This makes the tests repeatable, under a given and standard set of parameters. Conditioning consists of exposing the yarn to a standard humidity/temperature environment until no further weight change is observed. Textile standard conditions exist at a temperature of 70°F and a relative humidity value of 65 percent.

After being conditioned to the above standard, a given quantity of clean wool will weigh between 12 and 16 percent more than it weighs when oven-dry. Oven-dry means the fiber is baked in an oven until no further weight loss is observed. A typical laboratory schedule involves two hours at 220°F.

This makes an interesting and informative kitchen-table experiment, if you are so inclined. Select a skein of wool yarn that weighs at least several ounces and for which you know the length. Weigh it as accurately as your equipment allows, record the weight, then pop the skein into a very slow oven (225°F) for a few hours. When you can wait no longer, haul out the sample and weigh it while still piping hot—as soon as possible.[7] The difference between the first weight and the second weight represents water. To calculate this change as a percentage of moisture content, use the following formula.

$$\left(\frac{A-B}{A}\right)100=M$$

A is the sample weight before drying, B is the sample weight after drying, and M is the moisture content.

As an example, imagine that we have a skein of clean, dry wool yarn that weighs 3 ounces, or about 85 grams. This is roughly the capacity of the bobbin on an Ashford Traditional wheel. After recording its weight, we oven-dry the skein for three hours at 225°F. At the end of three hours, we snatch out the skein and weigh it again. Let's suppose that the oven-dry weight is 73 grams.

Obviously, the sample has lost weight—12 grams (about $\frac{7}{16}$ ounce). But to find the percentage of moisture, we must use the formula. It works out as follows:

$$\left(\frac{85-73}{85}\right)100=14.117\%$$

That 14.117 percent represents the moisture content of our sample. To

---

[7] *Immediately might be a better word. One standard test procedure specifies that this operation must take place within 25 seconds. Remember that all of the Big Four fibers take up and release atmospheric moisture quickly. Lay a bit of yarn across the McMorran and trim to balance point. Then bring a boiling kettle over and let the steam blow on your sample, which will pick up enough weight within seconds to unbalance the McMorran.*

place all this in everyday terms, imagine that we have 100 pounds of this yarn. At a moisture content of 14.117 percent, more than 14 pounds of the yarn's weight is water.

That's life. For natural fibers, a moisture content of between 10 and 16 percent by weight is reasonable and appropriate. So why do we bother calculating? Because the information may be very useful (even money-saving) and because we are able to obtain the measurements with simple procedures and equipment.

The amount of moisture that a given fiber (or yarn) takes on while going from "oven-dry" to ambient conditions is called *moisture regain*, and it varies from fiber to fiber.[8] Just for fun, let's calculate the grists of this skein, and how they change. Say the skein is 50-yards long. If 50 yards of this yarn weigh 85 grams at field weight and 73 grams when oven-dry, what are the two grists? Answers: 283 YPP and 310 YPP, respectively.

Calculating the regain on your yarn is hardly worthwhile unless you are (1) just curious, (2) selling a lot of yarn and playing safe with the weight-and-measure folks, (3) reproducing authentic material for museum display, (4) writing a grant proposal to reproduce authentic material, or (5) an instructor/mentor who wants to expand your skill base.

Since you know something of regain, here's a setup where you use the knowledge. A friend hands you a sweater and says, "Oh, help . . . what fiber is it?" You have only a drying oven and a good scale with which to solve the mystery and comfort your friend (the fiber label has been removed, causing this sordid episode to occur in the first place).

What to do? Here is a clue: You know what wool's regain is. A further clue: Acrylic fibers have a regain of about 1.8 percent.

Aha! You weigh the sweater, pop it into the drying oven (a very slow oven, because plastic melts, don't you know!), haul it out and weigh it again. Suppose that it weighed 12 ounces before it went into the oven and 11¾ ounces when it came out. Using the math we picked up earlier, we calculate as follows.

The original weight was 12 ounces; let's call that OW. Oven-dry

---

[8] *Technically, ambient conditions call for 65 percent relative humidity at 70°F.*

weight was 11¾ ounces; let's call that DW. The difference between these two is .25 ounces, and that is the "moisture loss," or ML.

Now we find the "moisture content," or MC, which is (ML × 100) divided by OW.

$$\frac{ML \times 100}{OW} = MC$$

$$\frac{.25 \times 100}{12} = 2.08\%$$

But that is not want we want. We want the "moisture regain," or MR, which equals (ML × 100) divided by DW.

$$\frac{ML \times 100}{DW} = MR$$

$$\frac{.25 \times 100}{11.75} = 2.128\%$$

Our moisture regain equals 2.128 percent.

Well, well, isn't that interesting? Just a little over 2 percent regain. The sweater is not wool. Probably an acrylic or modacrylic.[9]

Remember there are two values here: *moisture content* is expressed as a percentage of the field weight, and *moisture regain* is expressed as a percentage of the oven-dry weight.

While all natural textile fibers are physically affected by moisture content, they also change in response to other physical factors.

SOME PHYSICAL PROPERTIES AND GROWING REQUIREMENTS OF THE BIG FOUR FIBERS

Wool qualities. Wool fiber conducts heat poorly, so it is a good insulator. Thus, wool is "warm." Wool is also the most absorbent of the

---

[9] *There are a number of stovetop tests for fiber identification, and the reader who is so inclined will find useful and convenient material in Chapter 13. But the fact that wool's regain is 12+ percent provides sufficient evidence that this sweater is not wool—or mohair, angora, cashmere, or silk, because all protein fibers have at least a 10 percent regain.*

fibers, holding up to 30 percent moisture (by weight) without feeling wet. The standard moisture regain for wool ranges between 12 and 16 percent.[10] Wool felts, is the weakest of the four fibers, and gets weaker when wet. Wool takes dyestuffs well and resists mild and dilute acids. Wool is destroyed by exposure to alkaline substances and is attacked by the larvae of moths and carpet beetles.

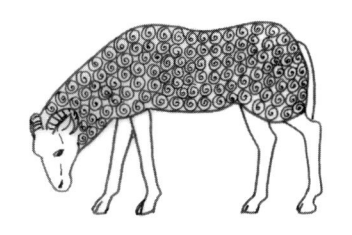

Wool.

Silk qualities. The regain for silk is about 2 percent lower than for wool under standard conditions. Silk does not have wool's ability to absorb large quantities of moisture and still feel dry, but silk dries much more rapidly than wool. It weakens somewhat when wet. Like wool, silk does not conduct heat well. That means that it "feels warm" to the touch. Silk is attacked by weak inorganic acids, by oxygen in the atmosphere, and by carpet-beetle larvae. Sunlight is not good for silk. Static electricity buildup causes problems, especially when it is cold and dry.

Flax qualities. Flax conducts heat much better than wool or silk. As a result, it is a "cooler" fiber. Flax readily absorbs moisture, has a regain of about 1 percent less than wool, and is the fastest drying of the Big Four fibers. It becomes stronger when wet and is unharmed by harsh alkalis. Long exposure to sunlight weakens it somewhat. It is the strongest of the four fibers, about four times stronger than wool.

Cotton qualities. Cotton's regain is about 8.5 percent. Cotton absorbs moisture quickly but does not dry nearly as swiftly as flax. Cotton becomes stronger when wet, and resists alkali damage. Even dilute acids will attack cotton. Sunlight slowly degrades cotton and the effect is accelerated when certain dyestuffs are present. Cotton is not subject to moth or beetle attack, but will mildew unless it is stored in a clean and dry condition.

All of the Big Four fibers may be homegrown in the United States. Wool and flax will grow just about anywhere south of the Arctic Circle. The two that have limitations are cotton and silk.

Silk.

---

[10] *The difference between fine and coarse wools causes this difference of a few percentage points. Fine wools display the greater fluctuation.*

Flax.

Growing cotton. As a general rule, cotton must have a lot of heat and sunlight, but not too much—95°F during the days, 60°F each night, with frequent but light sprinkles of rain. It wants all these conditions for at least four or five months in a row.

If you are north of the 35th parallel, this means your cotton needs to grow as a hothouse crop or as a houseplant. A good planter-box yield would be about ⅛ ounce of lint (and ⅜ ounce of seed) for each square foot of planting.

Growing silk. Silkworms can be raised anywhere; geographic location, however, is limited by proximity to food. Cultivated silkworms eat fresh leaves of the mulberry tree. If you do not have access to many, many mulberry trees with fresh young leaves, you will have problems raising silk. And, unless you have a separate "silk house," the silkworms (actually caterpillars), mulberry leaves, and other paraphernalia will be right there in your living (dining, family, spare) room.

And not just for the weekend. It takes about seven weeks to move from egg to usable cocoon. The critters demand constant attention and vast quantities of food. There are other details.

To top all this off, the yield of fiber will be modest, considering all the labor and space you have devoted to the enterprise. A pound of silk requires between 600 and 800 cocoons, and you will only be able to fit about four silkworms into 1 square foot of your raising area. You will need about 200 square feet to raise a pound of fiber.

Be that as it may, raising silk is an interesting process, a glorified ant-farm, science-class sort of thing. It has been, is being, and can be done.

Raising wool. Of course, there are difficulties surrounding shepherding: This enterprise will not fit into the front room. You need room and facility to raise a sheep or two, and nowadays it seems that your neighbors have more of a say in the matter than you do. Still, there are many smallholders in the wool business.

Growing flax. Flax will grow about anywhere. You can actually raise a useful amount in a small space: a reasonable return is about ¼ ounce of fiber per square foot of flax patch. A 4-foot by 8-foot plot will produce about ½ pound of usable flax fiber, both line and tow.

Cotton.

CHAPTER 6

SINKAGE AND SHRINKAGE: A DISCOURSE ON FIBER AND OTHER STUFF THAT COMES WITH IT, ON FIBER PREPARATION (WITH PARTICULAR ATTENTION TO WOOL AND FLAX), ON THE LOSS AND GAIN OF TIME, ON VARIOUS TYPES OF COMBING, AND ON THE VALUE OF PRODUCTIVITY

Let us imagine we have been offered a large quantity of fleece wool for a reasonable price.[1] Out of curiosity, we run a moisture test before we make our purchasing decision. We weigh out 8 ounces of the stuff, then pop it into a slow oven for a couple of hours. Then we weigh it again. Great Aunt Woolweena! It only weighs 5¾ ounces. Where did the other 2¼ ounces go?

Most of it went up as water vapor. A small portion, perhaps a third of a percent, was lost as volatile oils, which we will disregard for now. Let's figure out the moisture percentage.

FIGURING WOOL'S MOISTURE CONTENT

We'll use the formulas for moisture and regain introduced in Chapter 5 (page 134).

$$\left(\frac{A-B}{A}\right)100 = M$$

---

[1] All dollar amounts in this book have been selected for demonstration purposes only and do not reflect real market conditions.

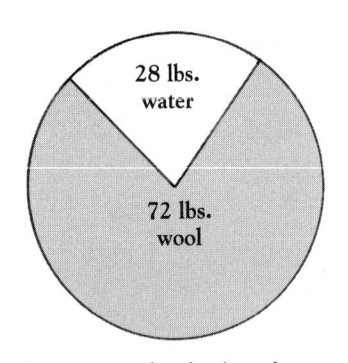

In any given batch of wool fleece, part of the weight consists of moisture.

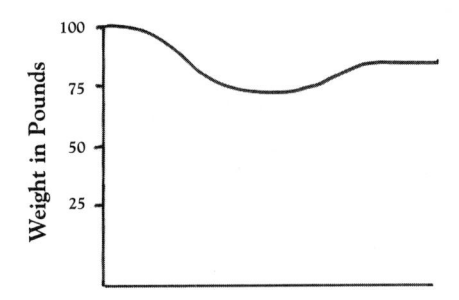

To obtain accurate measurements, the fiber is dried and then allowed to reach a standardized level of moisture content before it is weighed.

A is the sample weight before drying, B is the sample weight after drying, and M is the moisture content.

Here is the formula with numbers, although we have converted the fractions to decimals.

$$\left(\frac{8-5.75}{8}\right)100=28.125\%$$

This means that for every 100 pounds of that wool, about 28 pounds is H_2O. Should the asking price be $3 per pound, we would spend $84.38 for water. We would be wise to follow commercial practice: to quote, buy, and sell at *standard conditions*.[2] As we explained in Chapter 5, that means an oven-dried sample has been exposed to 65 percent relative humidity at 70°F for long enough to achieve stable weight.

The procedure is simple. Representative samples from the bulk lot are weighed, oven-dried until no further weight loss is observed, weighed again, and allowed to regain to the standard condition of moisture content. Equilibrium with the standard environment can be determined when the samples gain no further weight.[3]

Back to that bargain wool. It weighed 8 ounces from the fleece and 5¾ ounces when oven-dry; what can we expect after regain? We let it lie around in the open for a while, weighing it now and again. Eventually, it gains no further weight and seems stable at 6 7/16 ounces. Back to the calculator and

---

[2] We don't have to buy fleece wool with all this hurrah and math. Often we just look at the item and decide if we gotta have it or not. Still, there is no reason not to develop the skills of an experienced, knowledgeable, canny, shrewd, formidable fleece buyer, is there?

[3] Wool, flax, and silk naturally contain about 12 to 15 percent moisture under standard conditions. Cotton contains about 9 percent.

the regain formula from Chapter 5. We shift our measurements from fractions to decimals.

$$\left(\frac{C-O}{O}\right)100 = R$$

$$\left(\frac{6.44-5.75}{5.75}\right)100 = 12\%$$

C is the conditioned weight, O is the oven-dry weight, and R is the regain percent.

The gain of .69 ounces (derived from 6.44–5.75) indicates a regain of 12 percent, pretty normal. We are now ready to find out the actual amount of water we don't need to buy.

We are looking at a 100-pound lot, that is, 100 pounds on the woolshed floor, not from the conditioning house. The price of $3 per pound is okay, but that's figured at normal (say 12 percent) regain. Supposing the seller will bargain, how much should we pay for wool with 28.125 percent moisture on board?

Here's one approach to figuring that out. Suppose we oven-dried the whole lot. The 100-pound weight would be reduced by 28.125 pounds, leaving us with 71.875 pounds. Then we let it regain 12 percent moisture, increasing its weight by 12 percent of 71.875 pounds. This adds 8.625 pounds and gives us a regain weight of 80.5 pounds. We offer a price based on $3 per pound for 80.5 pounds, or a total of $241.50.

Here's another approach. Because we have a sample, we don't oven-dry anything else. We work the formula using the regain, or conditioned, weight of the sample, this way:

$$\left(\frac{F-C}{F}\right)100 = M$$

$$\left(\frac{8-6.44}{8}\right)100 = 19.5\%$$

F is the field weight, C is the conditioned weight, and M is the moisture percent—in this case, extra moisture.

That 19.5 percent represents the difference between regain moisture and field moisture, moisture we don't choose to pay for. Since 19.5 percent of 100 pounds is 19.5 pounds, we subtract those pounds of water from the field weight total of 100 pounds. We arrive at 80.5 pounds, for which we pay $3 per pound, the same total as before: $241.50.

That is how the big people do it: they buy and sell according to the *condition price*. If we didn't calculate the condition, we would pay $300 for 100 pounds. After the extra moisture evaporated, we would have paid the equivalent of $3.73 per pound for the 80.5 pounds of now-conditioned wool.

FIGURING WOOL'S CLEAN YIELD

Not only does fleece take up moisture readily, it is also loaded with grease, dirt, junk, and other extras. These additions contribute between 20 and 80 percent of total fleece weight.

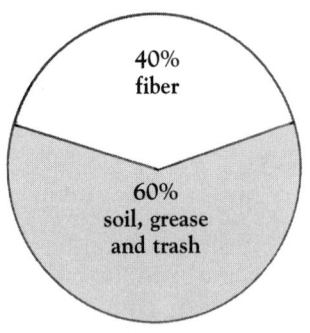

Commercial buyers are concerned with *clean wool price* or *clean wool yield*. The industry figures on about a 60-percent loss, or *shrinkage*, between raw wool and clean. A 60-percent loss equals a 40-percent yield. The buyers perform various yield or "clean-wool" calculations to figure what the scoured wool price will be.

Here's a clean-wool calculation that works for the small-scale buyer.

$$\left(\frac{\text{Raw}}{\text{Yield}}\right)110 = \text{clean}$$

Raw is the raw price per pound, *yield* is the estimated yield, and *clean* is the estimated clean value (price per pound).[4]

Grease wool yields a smaller quantity of scoured wool.

Let's try this with our sample wool purchase. Remember that we are talking $3 a pound for this stuff, woolshed price. Let's further imagine shrinkage at 55 percent, which means we expect a 45-percent yield.

$$\left(\frac{3.00}{45}\right)110 = 7.33$$

The estimated clean value of this lot is $7.33 per pound.

---

[4] A note on the multiplier: Around 1950, when the wool industry still bought wool in small clips from select breeders, the accepted multiplier was 115. Our experience has been that a lower number is more realistic, so we've used 110. Actually, when dealing with a couple of fleece, the stuff that falls off on the way to the car probably skews the whole thing out of that level of accuracy anyway.

THE VALUE OF SCOURING AND CARDING

Imagine that you know someone over at the Sudzncard Co-op who will scour wool for $1 per pound, raw weight, and will also card it for $1 per pound, feed weight. Does this mean you get clean, carded wool for $2 per pound?

Wrong. The $1 per pound for scouring is based on what you walk in the door with—100 pounds of dirty wool. The people doing the scouring care nothing for regain or conditioned values, so that is $100, right off the top, for scouring. Of the 100 pounds scoured, you will end up with about 45 pounds of dry, clean wool.

At this point, let's compare with the clean value we worked on earlier. We have 45 pounds of clean wool, which cost us $241.50 + $100, or $341.50. That is $7.59 per pound. Our calculated clean value was $7.33 per pound. That's pretty close, but not right on. Why? Too many variables.[5]

Carding operators charge by *feed weight*, or the weight of wool fed into the machine. In this case 45 pounds go in, but 45 pounds do not come out. Every carding operation has *sinkage*, which means operational fiber loss. Some of the fiber goes on the floor, some of it is lost as fly waste, some gets contaminated with grease or oil. Even a squeaky-clean carding operation will run at least 5 percent fiber loss, by weight. At the same time, every carding operation adds at

> CARDING OPERATORS CHARGE BY FEED WEIGHT, OR THE WEIGHT OF WOOL FED INTO THE MACHINE. IN THIS CASE 45 POUNDS GO IN, BUT 45 POUNDS DO NOT COME OUT.

---

[5] *In the clean-wool price calculation there is no specific allowance for regain, field moisture content, or exact scouring cost. The wool buyer has to estimate, based on experience, and then verify shrinkage by scouring. According to the American Wool Handbook (1948), a good wool buyer is expected to estimate yield within a percent or so. Most of us will never have the chance to develop such expertise. Still, the calculation gives us a place to start.*

least 5 to 10 percent to the carded mass, by weight, in conditioners, carding oils, and assists.[6]

Carding oil is necessary for two reasons: (1) it lubricates and protects the card clothing, and (2) it gives lubricity to the individual fibers.

Moisture is needed because wool is difficult (if not impossible) to handle unless it contains at least 16 percent moisture. Moisture makes the fiber more elastic and less liable to break, thereby reducing noils.

At the end of Sudzncard's scouring and carding, we get back 42 pounds of ready-to-spin wool. How much did it cost? Let's do the addition.

Raw wool	$241.50	(80.5 pounds at $3)
Scouring	100.00	(100 pounds at $1)
Carding	45.00	(45 pounds at $1)

Our 42 pounds of clean wool cost $386.50. That works out to about $9.20 per pound.

---

[6] *Losses during carding are influenced by various factors: condition and cleanliness of stock, machine settings, feed speeds, amount and nature of assists and conditioners, and type of fiber being carded. Sinkage (fiber loss) can run as high as 30 percent. Add-ons (carding oils, moisture, anti-stats) are necessary and seldom exceed 15 percent of standard regain weight. Now and then, a carding service might offer a package deal (scouring and carding), with a per-pound price based on yield. If you estimate your clean yield carefully, know what your moisture overhead is, and have an idea of competitive carding costs, you will be in a position to tell if a package price is a good deal. But never lose sight of shipping costs: they often contribute a major part of any fiber price.*

By the way, we are paying all this attention to wool because wool is the only fiber that can be contract-processed in small lots. Cotton? Unlikely. Cotton gins deal in multiple bales of 500 pounds each. Flax? Outside of historical sites and private parties, no flax processing is being done. Silk? Not in the U.S.A.

THE COST OF DOING IT YOURSELF

Suppose you did all the work on this lot yourself. How long would it take you to obtain just 1 pound of clean, carded wool? We are not speaking of a quick swish through the suds and a lick'n'promise with the cards. We want 1 pound of clean, clear, well-carded material, formed into rolags and ready to spin. Answer: In eight hours you can pick, scour, and hand-card enough Romney-cross domestic U.S. fleece wool to net 1 pound of rolags.

This does not include the drying time. The amount of wool that you have to dry is not important, as long as you arrange it in thin layers. In general, it takes as long to dry 1 pound as it does to dry 50—if you have the space.

Drying times vary a lot. The movement of air and relative humidity regulate drying. Whenever the relative humidity is low and there is good air movement, wool dries quickly. On hot, windy days, fleece wool will dry to ambient regain in as little as four hours. In still, cool, misty weather, the same process may require four days.

Wool should always be opened or *picked* before you card it. Don't misunderstand: wool is never picked when it is wet. Picking is tedious yet essential. Fleece wool may have to be picked several times. In commercial service, wool is picked before scouring, after scouring and/or dyeing, or after long storage. Picking opens the fiber and breaks up clots, tangles, and mats. As hand workers, we should pick the wool whenever its condition warrants.

Devices that aid this work are called *pickers*. Isn't that amazing? *Swing* or *cradle pickers* are good, as are the rotating-drum types. *Pick combs (stub combs)* and *hackle blocks* also work well. Still, the best pickers of all are *human hands*. They are portable, capable of fine adjustment, powered by a renewable energy source, computer-directed, judgmental, and often capable of being talked into volunteer service.

After scouring and picking comes the carding. Use of a hand-turned drum carder will speed things up, although not as much as you might think. Swing carders and stock (bench) carders also improve production quantities. Every handspinner's dream, a "real" carding machine, speeds things up even more.

A hand-turned drum carder will about double your carding output. That is, in eight hours you can pick, scour, and drum-card enough fleece to net 2 pounds of ready-to-go fiber. If you use a swing picker, you will shave off another hour, bringing your production up to 2 pounds in seven hours.

But there are other considerations. Bear in mind the old saying, "Machines can make you faster, but they cannot make you better." Partially scoured, poorly picked wool and indifferent carding do not count as progress.

That brings us to the spinning part. How long will it take you to spin up that pound of wool rolags? Well, the task will take as long as it needs to, and not a moment longer. However, we are surrounded by people who take comfort from numeric values and petty superlatives. It will promote our cause to speak their jargon and will aid us in fitting the timeless and the timed together while navigating our clock-dominated world.[7]

To satisfy those who must resolve the "how long" question *now*, here it is: you can spin up that pound of rolags in four hours, if you are (1) using a stock Ashford Traditional single-drive wheel, (2) spinning the yarn to a grist of 600 YPP with a twist component of 3 turns per inch,

---

[7] *An excellent review of this topic was given by Kate Peck Kent in* Prehistoric Textiles of the Southwest *(Chapter 1): "In such [pre-industrial] societies, time is not a commodity to be 'saved' or 'spent:' days are not divided into so many hours for work, so many for play, so many for the pursuit of art. . . . The finished product is an exquisitely delicate fabric that holds value and meaning within the weaver's culture, but not by the standards of judgment used in an industrialized society, where the number of hours of work is given a cash value. In pre-industrial society, the process of making the textile, regardless of how long it takes, is simply a part of the artist's life."*

and (3) able to maintain a drafting rate of 3¼ yards per minute.

Sounds formidable, doesn't it? Like something a production spinner would say.

We often hear the terms *production wheel, production spinner,* and *production spinning.* Some confusion exists about their meanings. In the context of this discussion, read the word *productive* in place of *production* and you will have cleared the air.

We handspinners (and hand workers in general) tend to be optimistic and jolly about where the time goes. Perhaps that is as it should be. Still, saving a little time and effort might be worthwhile.

Under the best of circumstances, a handspinner's hour is 48 minutes long. Under adverse conditions (sadly enough, the typical condition), the handspinner may achieve 20 minutes of spinning per hour. The other 40 minutes are consumed in locating things, winding yarn, preparing fiber, rethreading the wheel, finding the broken end, answering the telephone, going to the loo, and so forth. If we reduce the non-spinning part of the hour, we increase spinning time. It takes no great leap of imagination to realize that more spinning per hour = more yarn per hour, or more productive spinning.

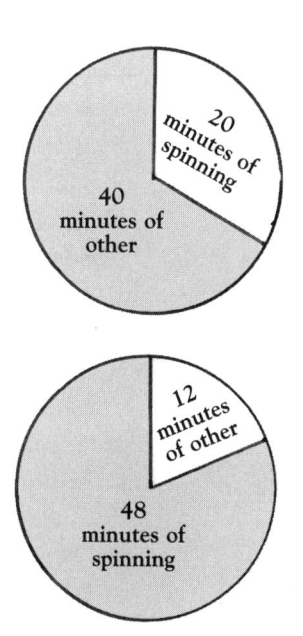

The spinner's hour: worst variant (top) and best (bottom).

RAW OR COMMERCIALLY PREPARED FIBER?

Fiber preparation is the primary bottleneck of handspinning. The more we understand the problem, the better we can deal with it. At least, that's the theory.

A handspinner's raw material is fiber. That statement appears simplistic, obvious to all . . . so why make it? It is a way of drawing your attention to an analogy. This analogy features a woodturner—a person who roughs out bowls, turns candlesticks, makes a few baby rattles for craft fairs. The woodturner's raw material is wood. Our turner could go out and chop down a tree, buck it into lengths, and then split, stack, and season the billets. Not all woodturners do this; a majority do not. They buy their stock with most of the preparations done. No muss, no fuss, no extra work, and much saving of time. This pretty good situation has a distinct limitation: woodturners who obtain their material this way must be happy with what they can get. Overall, they have three choices: take what is available, do without, or prepare their own stock.

How does this relate to handspinners? We are in a similar situation: we take what is available, we do without, or we prepare our own stock or "raw material."

Doing without does not interest us.

When we take what is available, we speak of "raw" fibers (grease wool, cotton in the boll, and so forth) or "prepared" fibers (rolags, batts, sliver, and so on). The preparation may range from minimal to advanced, and we need to understand preparation to know whether we will benefit from further preparatory work.

To carry this a step further, we need to be able to determine whether the fiber preparation in question suits the project and techniques we have in mind. Not just the choice of fiber, but the preparation and form.

Before beginning to examine that question, consider that most commercial fiber preps available to handspinners represent either mill remnants (off-grade or excess) or are fiber preps that manufacturers hope will have the widest market appeal at the greatest possible mark-up. Also, not one of the commercial put-ups is intended for handspinning. Actually, few of them are intended to be spun from at all, even in the mill environment. They are assembled as an intermediate processing step, with more treatments to come before the actual spinning. The fact that handspinners produce excellent yarns from such "partial" preparations testifies to the adaptability and superiority of the human spinning machine.

Fiber preparation methods vary from fiber to fiber, yet the principles are common to all fibers. You will remember (we hope!) that fiber preparation consists of three steps: gathering the fiber, cleaning it, and arranging it in a predictable manner.

Of course, it is possible to spin fiber with no preparation at all, and some people make much of this. Contemporary examples include stunts like spinning directly from the rabbit, from cotton bolls, or from occupied cocoons. One might argue that some preparation has been done—the boll is not on the plant, out in some dismal field; the cocoon is not lashed to a twig; and the rabbit is usually clean, content, and in someone's lap, not lurking beneath a log.

To the author's knowledge, no one is in the habit of crowding a Columbia ram into a corner and spinning his wool direct, or setting up the wheel in a flax patch and spinning the material "nature's way." These fibers demand some level of preparation (gathering, at least).

What of the second and third steps? Handspinners like the notion of avoiding work, especially in fiber preparation. In truth, the more time and appropriate effort taken in fiber preparation, the better the yarn. In our heart of hearts, we know this. Still, we pursue snake-oil cleansing potions; new, effortless methods of work; and magical equipment that will solve our problems.

Some methods, equipment, and assists do make life easier. The use of these aids depends on a sound knowledge of the options, and the results to be gained. This knowledge requires an understanding of the principles and goals of fiber-preparation. We want to get rid of the fiber conditions that hinder us and to establish and maintain the fiber conditions that aid us in spinning the yarns we need.

In this context, two fiber conditions hinder us: (1) the physical arrangement (or derangement) of the fiber and (2) the presence of contaminants.

CONTAMINANTS AND CHEMICAL DAMAGE

Fiber contaminants are of two sorts, natural and induced. Natural contaminants come with the territory. Induced contaminants exist because the seller benefits from their presence. Most of the time, you deal with contaminants when you are working with raw fibers. With a few exceptions, prepared fiber stocks do not involve contaminants.

Contaminants in wool. We have discussed natural contaminants in wool. They consist mostly of grease, along with varying amounts of sand, grit, mud, manure, and so forth, generally amounting to between 30 and 40 percent of the fleece weight. In processed wool, induced contaminants can include carding oil, perhaps dyestuff . . . or how about another fiber? Would you class a 50/50 blend of wool/silk as contaminated wool? Or contaminated silk? Blending is actually a form of induced contamination.

Contaminants in silk. Silk is unique in many ways, and not just for its luxury. Its contaminants are exotic. In cocoons, the primary natural contaminant is the builder's carcass. In broken (vacant) cocoons, as well as in flakes, mawata, schappe, and the like, the chief contaminant is sericin, which may constitute as much as 30 percent by weight. Silk has always been subject to induced contaminants, especially when dyed.

Contaminants in cotton. Ginned cotton of handspinning quality is basically free of contaminants. It may contain small amounts of *pepper trash* (bits of seed and leaf), dust, neps, and other debris amounting to 1 or 2 percent. Unginned seed or boll cotton will be full of all sorts of stuff, primarily the seeds, plant parts, moisture, dust, and trash. Machine-picked cotton contains a higher percentage of junk than hand-picked, so your homegrown and hand-picked cotton is very high-class fiber.

Contaminants in flax. Contaminants in flax generally fall into the realm of dust, boon, shives, and moisture. If you grow and process your own, guess who is to blame?

Flax is offered at retail in various stages of preparation. That which has not been taken to the hackle stage is full of everything you can imagine. It is not spinnable as is, but certainly worthwhile as study and practice material. Commercial flax in spinning form varies in quality, based on degree of preparation. The chief contaminants, if there are any, are moisture and dyestuff.

Line flax is clean, in the normal sense of the word. All but the very finest grades of flax benefit from being re-hackled. Tow, the short broken product of the hackles, contains a portion of junk (boon and shives) and benefits from being re-hackled, willowed, and carded.

Dyestuffs and dye-related damage. Dyestuffs and mordants add weight to all fibers, but seldom more than 1 percent. Exceptions are very bright colors (strong yellows, in particular), very dark colors (navy blue and black), and weighted silks. Black-dyed silk may, by law, have as much as 15 percent added weight and still be called pure silk.

While on the subject of dyeing-related degradation: wool is sometimes dyed in sliver form and may become felted as a result.

Flax is offered as bleached or dyed; approach these forms with caution. Flax is troublesome to dye, for the same reasons that it tends to shed dirt and wear well. Common commercial practice is to bleach flax before dyeing, and therein lies the trouble. Bleaching always weakens the fiber somewhat, even when carefully done. When done without care, it weakens the fiber a lot. Dyed flax has almost surely been bleached. You fill in the rest.[8]

Wool is mordanted to prepare it for dye application, or when undyed stock must share wet-processing schedules with dyed material. The undyed material receives mordanting to insure that both dyed and undyed stock have the same take-up, shrinkage, and fulling action. Wool is sometimes over-mordanted by mistake, and this can cause damage. The fiber becomes sticky, harsh, brittle, unpleasant to handle, and difficult to spin.

Now that we have brought up the subject, suppose we wish to blend similar fibers, say the same fiber in two colors. We have red wool and blue wool, and we want purple wool. Semantics aside, the best way to color-blend fibers is during the earliest practical stage of their mechanical preparation. In other words, when we hackle our flax or when we comb or card our cotton, wool, silk, or tow.

You already have some experience with carding, or should have . . . in any case, in this chapter we are going to discuss woolcombing and hackling. Let's start with woolcombing.

An overview of types of wool combing

Woolcombing predates carding by thousands of years, although it has not been practiced much in the past 100 years. As with other resurrected crafts, the old version may have little in common with the new. Woolcombing is not only for worsted preparation, but for other forms of

---

[8] *Flax is not easy to dye or bleach. Traditionally, it has always been bleached, rather than dyed—snow-white linens and all that. The old-time ways of bleaching involved green, park-like meadows; young maidens; warm, clear, sunny mornings; buttermilk; romance . . . and a lot of time and work. Basically an ozone/ultraviolet/oxygen sort of thing. Where a fast natural dye for flax is concerned, woad or indigo works pretty well.*

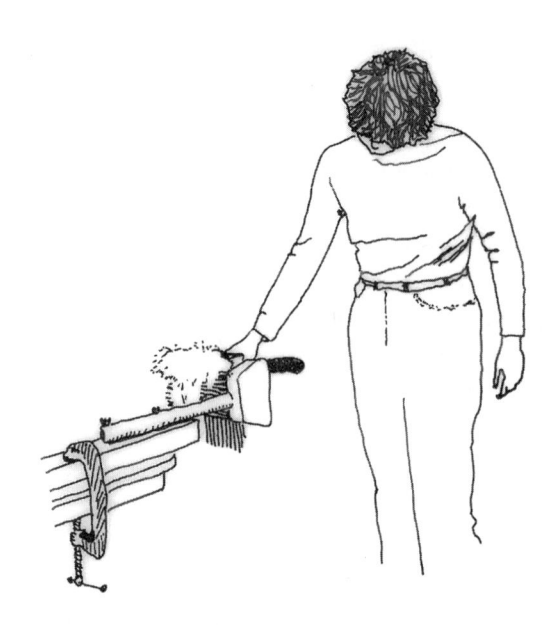

Wool combing comes in several varieties and can prepare wool for general spinning as well as worsted procedures.

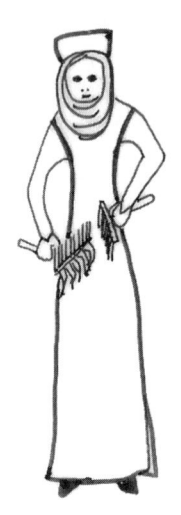

Combing, one of the oldest wool-processing techniques, has evolved through history. So has the design of wool combs.

preparation as well. Wool combing allows the handspinner to prepare long-staple wools and hairs that are unsuited to carding. As a practical matter, anything with a staple over about 3 inches will work better combed than carded. Wool combing, like carding, removes great amounts of junk, twigs, seeds, and so forth, and if carried to its extreme (*full worsted combing*) will remove all short and broken fibers.

The presence of grease and dirt make combing difficult, if not downright impossible. Still, some lubrication and moisture must be present to control static electricity and to reduce noils. Because uniformity is the name of the game in fiber preparation, we remove the random amounts of "natural" lubricants (the infamous grease) by scouring, and replace them with a known quantity of another lubricant. The result? A more uniform product.

There are two basic schools of combing: (1) *woolcombing* (one word), which denotes the preparation of *top* for worsted spinning, and (2) *wool combing* (two words), which is combing for preparations other than top. To reduce confusion, we use the terms *worsted combing*, rather than woolcombing, and *roughcombing*, rather than wool combing.

Combing is the oldest "formal" method of wool preparation. Any worker in wood, bone, or metal could come up with a passable comb. Forging or drawing wire for card clothing requires higher technical skills.[9] Old pictures and illustrations indicate that there was considerable latitude in how one handled the combs, and they show great differences in what combs were like.

The objective of worsted combing is to produce a *top* (or *tops*). The term has several specific meanings. We mean a combed preparation of uniform staple, arranged for spinning on the worsted system. A commercially combed top will be a *sliver* composed of uniform-length fibers, all parallel.

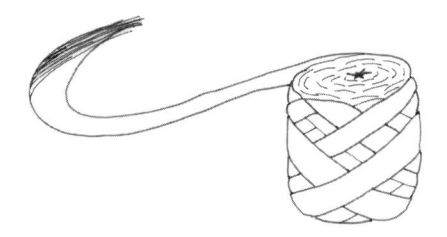

Commercially combed sliver consists of fibers of even length, arranged parallel to each other.

The amount (density) of wool in commercial top runs about 4 to 9 ounces of wool per 10-yard length of sliver. Hand-combed tops are less dense, running perhaps 2 ounces per 10-yard length of sliver. The linear density of slivers is of some interest, especially with respect to draft amounts required to spin a given grist.

For example, let us say that we have a sliver with a density of ½ ounce per yard. If we treat that as a yarn, how many yards weigh 1 pound? Because there are 32 half-ounces per pound, we need 32 yards of sliver to weigh 1 pound and the grist of our sliver is 32 YPP. Let's say we want to draft out this sliver to a yarn with a grist of 3,200 YPP. We want to figure out how many times we have to extend the 32 YPP sliver to reach 3,200 YPP. It turns out that we have to extend it to 100 times its original length. Suppose we have the same sliver, but want a yarn that measures 1,600 YPP. What is our draft? The answer is 50, of course.

In commercial practice, a goal is to accomplish as much of the drawing as possible before spinning occurs. In general, commercial wool spinners avoid drafts greater than 10 or 20. Therefore worsted is drawn

---

[9] *Hackling probably predates combing, and rough-combing has been practiced since the dawn of civilization. Hand carding, as we practice it today, had to wait until technical advances made it practical to draw large amounts of fine, hard, iron wire that would make good teeth for card clothing. This event seems to have taken place in Nuremberg (Bavaria) circa A.D. 1350. The carding machine is a product of the eighteenth century, and the first "powered" carding machine in America was built circa 1793.*

(drafted) without twist all the way to an approximation of finished grist. Woolen slivers are drawn down into mini-slivers, then drafted against twist. Some wool (and cotton) is processed as *condenser yarn*, going directly from card to condenser to spinning frame, and all drafting takes place during spinning. With worsted spinning, the final (spinning) draft is 1-to-1; final spinning draft for woolen yarns is on the order of 6-to-1.

But that draft assumes mini-sliver, not a fiber source at ½ ounce per yard. Mini-sliver or cheese roving (jack roving) will have a "grist" of 300 to 600 yards per pound. To draw 300 YPP sliver down to 1,600 YPP requires a final or spinning draft of about 5.3-to-1. The handspinner navigates spinning drafts of 200-, 500-, or 1000-to-1 without fanfare. Because of this high draft capability, handspinners are not concerned with sliver density unless the fiber source becomes too large to hold or too flimsy to manipulate.

Sliver is a word like "bundle" or "stack." It describes a package form or shape, not the contents. A sliver is a sort of band, round ribbon, or non-twisted rope of fiber.

A sliver composed of combed, uniform, parallel fibers is called a *top*, or *tops*. If composed of random, non-uniform, non-parallel fibers, it is called a *roving*. Let us hope that settles the matter—at least for a while. Worsted combing results in a top. Rough-combing results in roving, roves, rolls, wads, and locks.

Rough-combing is not much publicized these days, which is too bad. As it has served humankind well over the past 5,000 or 6,000 years, it is hard to understand why it seems out of favor.

Rough-combing

As a technique, rough-combing includes the use of wool combs, paddle combs, Viking combs, Icelandic combs, rake combs, bench combs, flat combs, dog combs, curry combs, hair combs, and just about everything else except hand cards and flickers.

To rough-comb wool, we need equipment to rough-comb with: two C-clamps, a sturdy table, and a set of *simple combs* (Chapter 12), or a *simple hackle* (Chapter 12) and a sturdy metal grooming comb (from the local feed-and-grain or pet store). We also need a small funnel or a *diz* (Chapter 12), some *carding/combing mix* (Chapter 13), and clean wool.

Basic equipment for rough-combing.

It is difficult, if not impossible, to comb decently unless the wool is in proper condition. The wool needs to be clean, open, warm (70°F), and about 16 percent moisture content. It also needs to be lubricated. A typical by-weight addition of lubricant amounts to between 5 and 10 percent.

For the past 5,000 years, the premier lubricant for wool processing has been olive oil. The oil is applied in various ways.[10] Workers may dip their hands in oil, then manipulate masses of wool in taffy-pull style. The neat oil may be sprinkled directly over the wool, as in the old-fashioned method of dampening family ironing. The wool can also be

---

[10] *Here's a related set of questions pertaining to the economic and other costs of lubricants for fibers. Question: how many people could earn their living working at a refinery that produces 5,000 barrels of synthetic carding oil per year? Answer: 6. Question: how many people could earn their living working at an olive orchard and press that produces 5,000 barrels of olive oil a year? Answer: about 40. Other questions in this sequence concern where these two outfits get their power, where their raw materials come from, whether they generate toxic wastes or by-products, whether you can eat the stuff . . . you know. For those of you who know of and support modern substitutes, my apology: our avoidance of the topic of synthetics includes ersatz olive oil derived from petrochemicals.*

sprayed on as an emulsion. Spraying the lubricant as an emulsion allows the spinner to add controlled, uniform amounts of lubricant while adjusting moisture content. We will use this method.

First select a couple of ounces of clean, dry wool. Spray the whole works with generous spritzes of the carding/combing mix, then seal the wool in a plastic bag, a big burper-ware container, or a close-fitting can. Set the container in a warm place for a few hours. This conditions the wool and allows the mix to mellow, or distribute itself more evenly.

Before starting to comb, lubricate the fibers.

While waiting, set up the comb array. Use the two C-clamps to fasten the fixed or bench comb to the table. Use protective cardboard pads or strips as required. Check to see that there's nothing on the table that can fall off.

If you must use a grooming comb instead of the bench comb, you will have to change your body and hand positions to be effective. But read through the how-to before you do anything.

After a few hours (not more than twenty-four), open the bag or container and extract a handful of wool. Close the container and set it aside. Dump the handful of wool on the table and pick it over. Open up lumps and knots; pick out sticks and twigs; get rid of all the chaff, straw, bits, and pieces that you run into.

Now we are going to talk you through a rough-combing session in which you will produce some sliver.

Grasp a bit of wool between your thumb and the side of your forefinger. Use about the same grip you would employ when using a pencil as a drumstick. Now drag the wool through the fixed comb numerous times. Don't hang on tight, but allow the comb to take some wool on each pass. The idea is to load the

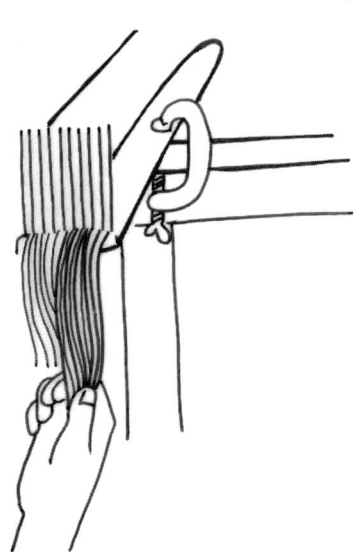

Lash on: load the comb with wool.

156   The Alden Amos Big Book of Handspinning

comb with wool without sticking yourself. This is called *lashing on*.

Once you have a nice handful of wool lashed onto the fixed comb, wipe your hands and pick up the working comb. Choke up on the handle—you want the center of your grasp to be a few inches behind the head, with the comb teeth pointing down and the comb handle below and roughly parallel to your forearm(s). It is somewhat clumsy to grasp the comb handle with both hands, but it is certainly okay to do so. Still, the alternate and preferred grip (once you're used to it) is one-handed. Let's start that way, at least until you have mastered the combing motions.

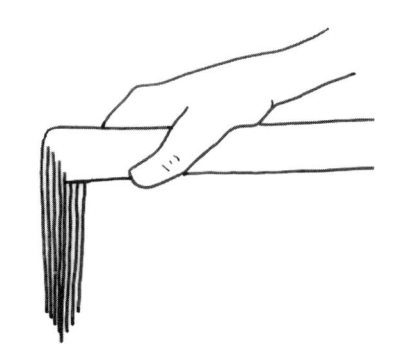

When you hold the comb, choke up on its handle.

Here's the combing sequence from the comber's point of view.

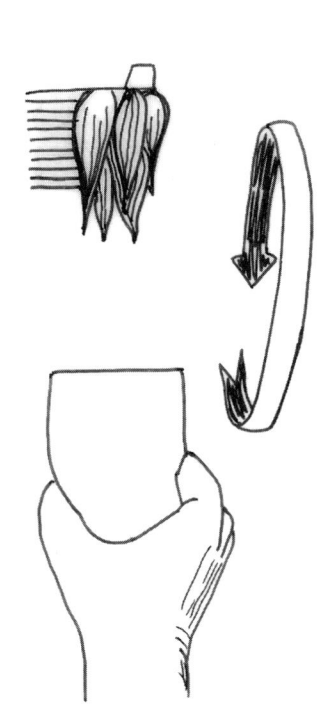

The comb moves in a circle.

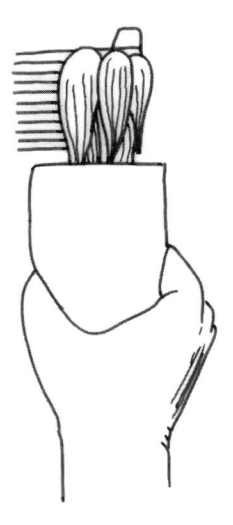

Engage the tips of the locks first.

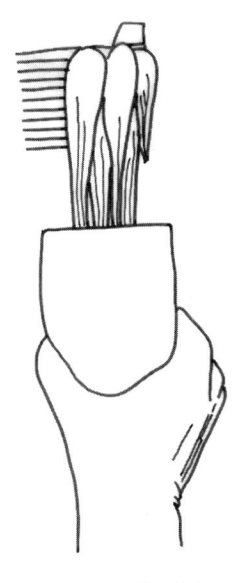

Draw the teeth of the comb through the locks.

If you have ever rowed a boat, you have an idea of the comb movement. It is the same as one-handed rowing, except that you do not need to put your back into the motion. Pretend that you are rowing with your combing hand. Instead of an oar, which points across your body, you are holding the comb, which is pointed fore and aft. The comb head is in front of your hand, the comb teeth point down, and the comb handle points back toward your elbow. As you row, the head and handle of the comb remain parallel to the ground, and the comb describes a circle about a foot in diameter. The top of the circle occurs as the comb moves forward, away from you. The bottom of the circle occurs as the comb moves toward you. Practice once or twice to get the feel.

Now for a little refinement: keep your circle about the same size, but change it into a round-cornered square, with the two sides straight up and down and the top and bottom parallel to the floor. Give your circular path four corners and you will have the shape. Try this a few times.

Here's the combing sequence from the bystander's point of view.

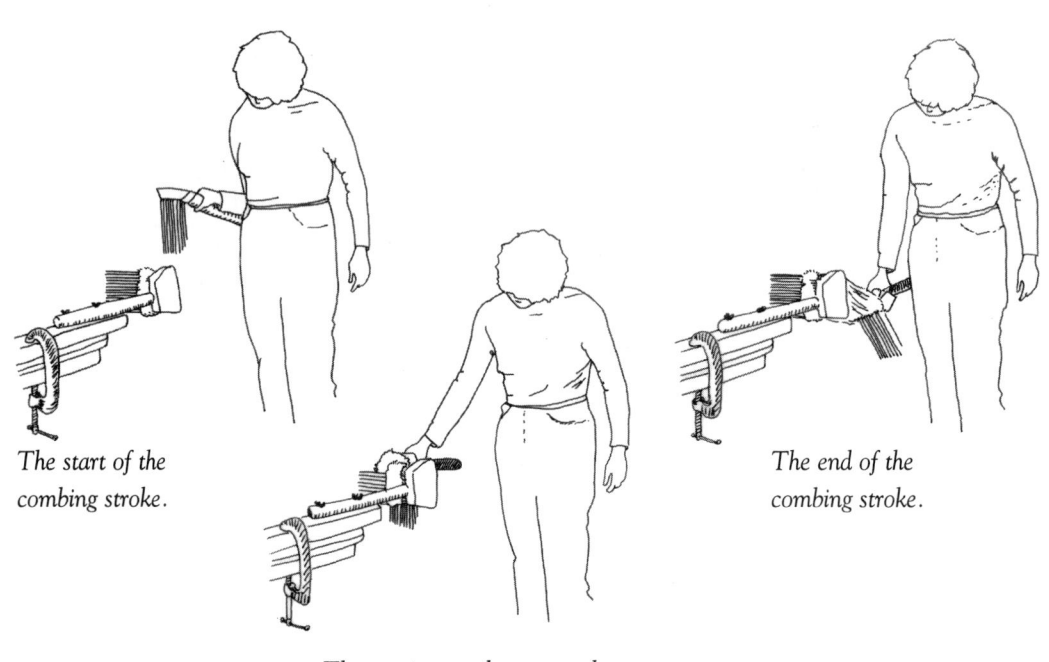

The start of the combing stroke.

The moving comb engages the fiber on the stationary comb.

The end of the combing stroke.

158   The Alden Amos Big Book of Handspinning

Let's do some combing. With comb in hand, stand directly in front of the fixed or bench comb. Do not stand too close; start about 2 feet away. Begin the combing motion, making sure that you do not hit the bench comb or ram the comb's teeth into your table. Go slowly.

When the working comb (in your hand) comes forward and down, its teeth just pass through the wool fringe hanging out of the fixed comb. Keep rowing. Each time you pass the teeth through the fringe, you pick up a little more wool. Go slowly, picking up a little wool each time.

Don't bury the teeth of the working comb into the fringe, just tease the wool. Each time a bit more fiber will be picked up on the working comb. After a number of passes, most of the wool will be on the moving comb and very little will be on the fixed comb. Stop. Take a look at the fixed comb. If all went well, the fiber still stuck there is pretty much trash. Pull it off and save it for felting, stuffing, or as a gift to handspinners upon whom you seek revenge.

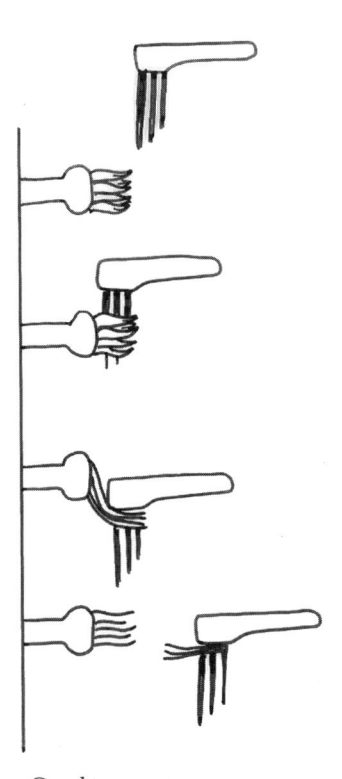

Now turn to the wool on the working comb. Carefully pull it up and off of the teeth. The block of fiber will have a fringe end and a pin end. Slip the pin end onto the fixed comb, keeping the fringe end hanging out toward you. Be careful not to stir things up more than necessary.

Combing motions.

Tweak out a few fibers in the middle of the fringe, then poke or pull them through the hole in the diz. A fine wire hook can be useful for accomplishing this. The cup of the diz faces the comb, and its bottom faces you. Hold onto those few fibers, and gently but firmly push the diz toward the fixed comb. Start pulling on the few fibers . . . pinch them and pull, gently but firmly, rather like removing a sticky-label from a new book. Keep pressing the diz toward the bench comb. Pinch, pull, and push. Keep changing the position of your pinch-finger so it stays close to the diz, and keep the diz crowded up against the wool. Lo and behold, the fiber will start to travel from the comb through the diz, magically turning itself into a sliver as it does.

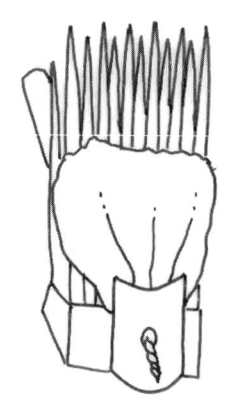

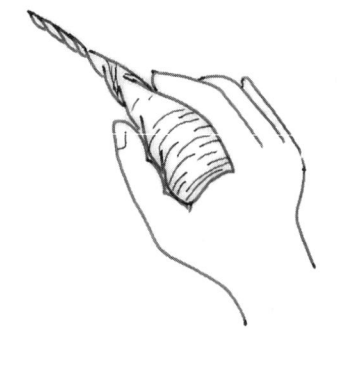

Starting the draw-off.

Spinning over the knuckle.

Each inch of sliver that you draw off is worth 100 words of text. Everybody's first try is shaped like a football, so don't worry.

Keep drawing off until you run out of fiber or patience, or until junk and trash start to draw from the comb. With a little practice, you will draw off yards of sliver at a time. The length of the sliver is determined by (1) the amount of wool on the comb, (2) the diameter of the sliver, and (3) your expertise.

Item 2, diameter of the sliver, is mostly related to the size of the hole in your diz. A good size to start with is ⅛ inch. Don't let this apparently tiny hole fool you; it will produce a fairly robust sliver. Of course, your skill in pinching, pushing, and pulling might have something to do with your end results.

Once you have drawn off several lengths of sliver, what do you do with them? As you draw each one off, lay it gently across the table top. You have gone through a lot of trouble to straighten out the wool, so don't disarrange it.

You may spin directly from each length. Or you may gently break off lengths about as long as the wool staple. Fold a few of these over your knuckle and spin away.

Or take three drawn-off lengths of sliver of roughly similar dimensions and lay them in a pile. Gently but steadily roll and rub back and forth across the pile, mashing them together to make a larger sliver. You can draw out this plumper sliver to considerable length. By drawing out while rolling and rubbing the fiber back and forth on

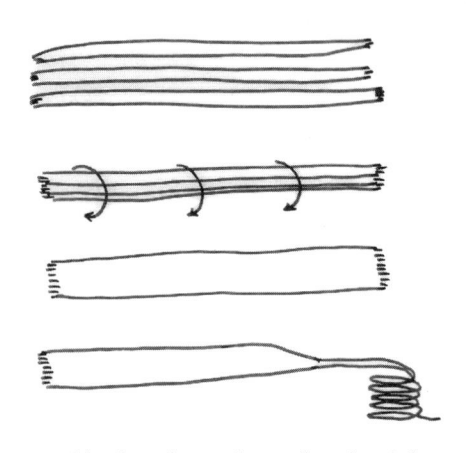

You can blend top by combining lengths of sliver: roll them together and draw them out together.

160   The Alden Amos Big Book of Handspinning

your knee, you can make what is called a *pencil roving* (although *sliver* is the better word).

A number of procedures work, some better than others. Your imagination places the only limits on what you can do. For the pleasure of handspinning, though, the first form you produced—fresh sliver, straight off the combs—is about as good as it gets. Most of the rest of the manipulations take place for the sake of appearance.

Lock combing

Lock combing is a variation on the above. You will need a fixed *comb block* or *utility hackle* (Chapter 12). This works best for preparing wools with staple lengths of 5 inches or more which have coherent, discrete locks. To maintain the integrity of the locks, you will have to take care during preparation. You will not be able to pick or open the wool much, and it will take longer to dry. The actual scouring will be no particular problem.

Let's imagine that you have a quantity of clean, coherent locks, and you have clamped the comb block or utility hackle to the working edge of your table. Grasp a lock as if it was a bundle of fiber, which it is, of course. Hold firmly and act as if you were lashing on, but don't let go of the fiber. You don't want the combs to take the fiber away from you, but to open the ends of the lock you are continuing to hold. Don't stick yourself on the pins, either. Lash on and pull through. Tease or comb out a little more than half the fiber's length. When you have one half opened up, reverse the lock and grasp the combed ends. Repeat the teasing and combing process, changing your grip as necessary, until you have opened the lock completely and it is ready to spin.

You can use a hackle, most often associated with flax, to open out wool locks. Open the tip first (left) and then the butt (right).

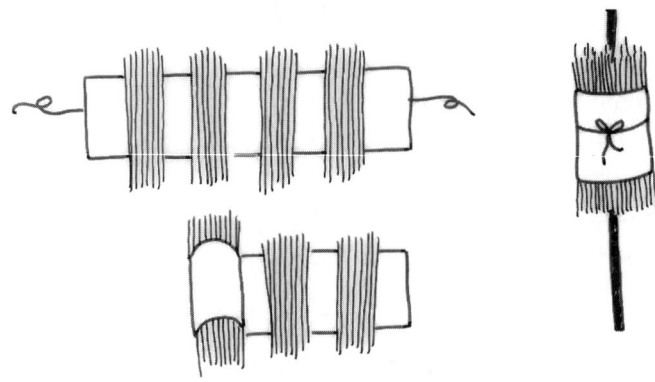

Here's how to dress a distaff with prepared locks of wool.

Locks are best spun folded over your knuckle, in the same manner as short sections of sliver.

To keep a group of locks handy while you spin on either a wheel or a spindle, you can lay out the locks side by side on a band, and then carefully wrap the band and locks around a distaff. Secure them with ribbons. This authentic and archaic method perfectly suits handspinners of Renaissance persuasion.

The locks may also be treated as short sections of a worsted sliver, which is what they are, and spun from the end in full-worsted style.

Which brings us to a discussion of full-worsted combing.

Full-worsted combing

According to devoted practitioners of the art, worsted combing and spinning are the highest, most exquisite, and perfect form of string art known to humankind. In some ways, worsted combing is akin to the practice of spinning in the grease: those who advocate it do so with vigor. Others consider it a waste of time.

Maybe. It is best to consider it as a technique, a series of procedures that achieve a particular product. That product is worsted yarn, which can be appropriate for a project.

A true worsted yarn has several distinct features. It is spun (1) from long fibers that are (2) in a combed preparation and (3) drafted without twist. Worsted processing results in dense yarns that have clear outlines, resist abrasion, possess more-than-average tensile strength, and usually show luster well. Worsted yarns do not full or felt easily compared to woolen yarns.

These features determine appropriate use. For example, stockings are often knitted from worsted yarns, while blankets are seldom woven from them. Stockings benefit from being sleek, lean, strong, and abrasion-resistant, and knitted structures show decorative elements (such as cabling) best when made of worsted yarns. Blankets need to be soft, full, and lofty—a set of parameters that calls for woolen yarns.

Full-worsted yarns, and the fabrics made from them, are rather like white bread. In days of old, only the rich could afford them.[11]

Aside from the mystique and amazement that surrounds full-worsted work, there are good, technical reasons to learn this practice. The reproduction of an archaic or historical item may demand use of full-worsted yarns for authenticity; or the physical details of a project may best be served by the lean, strong character of a proper worsted yarn.

Let us do some full-worsted combing. First, we need a pair of *worsted combs* (Chapter 12). Worsted combs are rated by *pitch*, a word which describes the number of rows of teeth they have. A 4-pitch comb has four rows of teeth; a 6-pitch six rows, and so forth. The teeth are graduated in length, diameter, and number. Obviously, as the pitch increases, so does the weight of each comb. For practical purposes, a set of 4- or maybe 5-pitch combs will do anything you care to.

Tradition has it that the finer the wool, the greater the pitch of the comb. In practice, you will find that a better rule goes "the finer the wool, the greater the number of teeth engaged."

Tradition also has it that the combs must be heated. Experience shows that if the work area, the wool, and the combs are above 65°F, there is no reason to heat them. If the temperatures drop below 65°F, then heat the workplace, the wool, and the combs. All together.

Begin with clean wool. Open it up, spread it out, and give it a few blasts with your spritz bottle of carding/combing mix. Roll it around a little, then stuff it into a bag or a can to condition and mellow.

Meanwhile, set up the combs. The device or fixture that holds one of the combs to the table is called the *pad*. Fasten the pad firmly to the table. For your own safety and that of others, do not mount a comb in the pad until you are ready to use it.

---

[11] *Until the combing process was satisfactorily mechanized in the 1850s, worsted was expensive stuff. After 1860, the cost of worsted goods dropped to the point that cheap ready-to-wear suits could be made from them. Some of us are old enough to remember blue gabardine suits with shiny seats.*

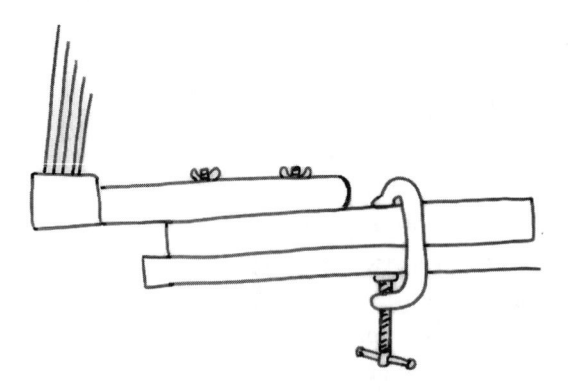

When you are ready to use a pair of combs, mount one securely in a clamp pad with its teeth facing up.

When ready to lash on, mount one of the combs securely in the pad, teeth up. Check again to be sure nothing will fall over or off the table as you work. Bring out the conditioned wool, and lash onto the fixed comb. Between 1 and 1½ ounces will do. Pay attention. Do not get careless or arrogant, and do not allow anyone to distract you.

Once you have loaded the fixed comb, loosen the mounting arrangement that holds the comb to the pad. Turn the comb on its side and re-fasten it to the pad. At this stage, it does not matter which way the teeth point (right or left).

Wipe your hands and pick up the empty comb. Start combing the fringe of wool, with the same rowing action you used in the rough-combing exercise. Keep up the rowing motion, or *jigging*, until the moving comb has picked up most of the fiber from the fixed comb. Keep going as long as you can, then put down the moving comb.

Take a look at the fixed comb. The remaining wool usually is not worth combing. Remove it and put it in your spinner's surprise bag.

Back to work. At this point you have two options. You may transfer the wool back to the fixed comb by passing the moving comb back and forth, sideways, as if you were spraying the lawn, or you can simply change combs. Let's just change combs.

Release the fixed comb from the pad and replace it with the loaded one. Fasten the comb with the teeth pointing either right or left, your choice. Repeat the rowing exercise until all the worthwhile wool is on the new moving comb.

Repeat this procedure two more times: comb most of the wool onto the moving comb, clean off the fixed comb, then swap combs. On the third round, stop combing when you have about half of the fiber on one comb, half on the other. Set the moving comb down out of the way and get your diz.

Safety note: If your combs do not have a guard or shield to cover the

164   The Alden Amos Big Book of Handspinning

points of the teeth when you are not working, *make one yourself*. A rolled-up bundle of corrugated cardboard or a coffee can will do. Anything. Do not just put those combs down, teeth all gleaming, sharp and hungry for human flesh. In particular, don't abandon them with their points up.

Shape the "beard" that hangs out of the fixed comb into a neat goatee and pull the tip of the goatee through the diz. Draw off, keeping the sliver fairly dense and uniform. You will be able to draw off at least several yards.

Break this sliver into 1-yard pieces and lay the pieces on the table, side by side. This is called *planking*, and it gives a way to manage the sliver while you continue working. Devotees feel that planking allows you to keep all the fiber flowing in the same direction; experience indicates that any end-product improvement is spiritual in nature.

When you finish drawing off one comb, replace it with the other. Draw off as before.

When you have combed, drawn, and planked all of your prepared, mellowed wool, you are ready for the next step. Tidy up: clean both combs, and pick up all the trash and swarf lying about.

If you cannot finish in one session, protect your planked sliver or every child, pet, grown-up, and critter within miles will sample it with great joy and glee. The quickest way to protect sliver is to lay something on top of it. The "something" could be a large bread board or a folding table. The most surefire way to protect sliver is to put it into boxes or tubs with lids. Cardboard cartons are your first choice. Old GI footlockers work well. A toy chest can be pressed into service. If you must leave the job for over a day, large plastic storage/utility tubs are best.

The principle is to prevent mechanical derangement, contamination, and loss of condition. You don't want the sliver to dry out or get dusty, dirty, or wetter. Your container must have a lid. Without a lid, this excellent wool represents the ultimate nest to creatures great and small.

All right, break is over. Expose your protected goods. Re-mount one of the combs on the pad, placing it in lash-on mode. Pick up three or four of the slivers, all in a bundle. Gently tear off 6-inch sections of the bundle and lash them onto the fixed comb.

Release the filled comb from the pad and turn the comb so the teeth point to the side. Re-mount and fasten firmly. Start combing again. If you want to impress someone with your dedication, comb and swap combs twice. In practice, there is no discernible improvement from re-combing more than once.

When you have had enough, stop with about half of the combed wool on each comb. Draw off the bench comb, then replace it with the other comb and draw off the rest.

That is worsted combing. Seems like a lot of work, doesn't it? Well historically, worsted spinning involved about four times as much work as woolen. You still have not spun your true worsted yarn, which requires that you use a spinning technique known as the *inchworm*. There is no other way to make a true worsted yarn. If that is what you need, that is how you get it.[12]

Spinning semi-worsted yarn

What happens if you want the technical advantages of a worsted-type yarn (lean, strong, firm, lustrous), but want to avoid the extra work involved in a true worsted?

Simple . . . you prepare and spin semi-worsted yarn. By folding combed locks or sections of sliver over your knuckle and spinning out of the fold, you can make a remarkably worsted-like yarn. Hardly a new idea, this technique allows you to spin a functionally "worsted" yarn, at speed, on the driven spindle (the great wheel and its ilk).

In fact, a slight variation on this method permits you to spin strong and lean flax yarns from fiber normally classed as tow. Well, the fiber still qualifies as tow, but you can turn it into a superior yarn through rough-combing and semi-worsted spinning.

---

[12] *What you require is true draft-without-twist, discussed in Chapter 2. This tedious yet necessary procedure has acquired other descriptive names, like "push'n pull," "the fuddly-duddly," and (the author's favorite) the "orifice crawl." Worsted spinning is slow. If we remember that a handspinner's hour is only 48 minutes long, a production rate of 125 yards an hour would be finger-wigglin' good.*

Flax

Which brings us to flax. You already know that you can grow flax in the window box, right? If you have any yard at all, you can grow it there. Here's an anecdote to illustrate the point. A few years back, Lee Raven, a past editor of *Spin-Off* magazine and the author of *Hands-On Spinning*, planted her entire front yard in flax. Here are notable observations about her project: very few people knew what the stuff was; it was the first flax crop ever grown in a posh Berkeley neighborhood; and the flax thrived.

The flax plant (a renewable resource) produces fuel, liquid manure, oil for paints and varnishes, feed cake for animals (like sheep!), foodstuff for humans, and premier fiber. It does take a lot of work. Flax passes through several stages of abuse before it becomes a useful textile fiber. But the numerous rewards and your personal sense of satisfaction will give new meaning to the word *smug*.

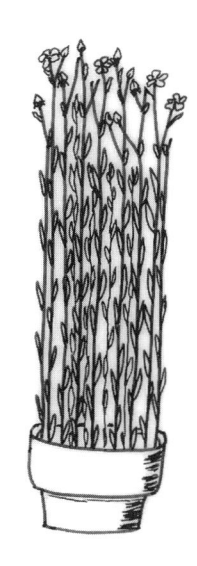

Flax: grow and process your own to acquire a major sense of spinner's satisfaction.

Processing flax

Aside from the retting and drying, the flax straw must first be *rippled*, an old term that means "rip the seeds off." A flax ripple is a coarse, comb-like block or bar, held in a stationary position while in use. A ripple can be clamped to a table or trestle, secured between foot and hand, built into a bench or seat as a permanent fixture, and so on. Chapter 12 contains working plans for a simple flax ripple. The rippling motions closely resemble the actions used to comb locks. You lash the seed heads down through the ripple teeth and then pull the plant toward yourself, stripping off the seed pods, or bolls, in the process.

If you want to save the seeds from your flax, before you begin to ripple you need to arrange

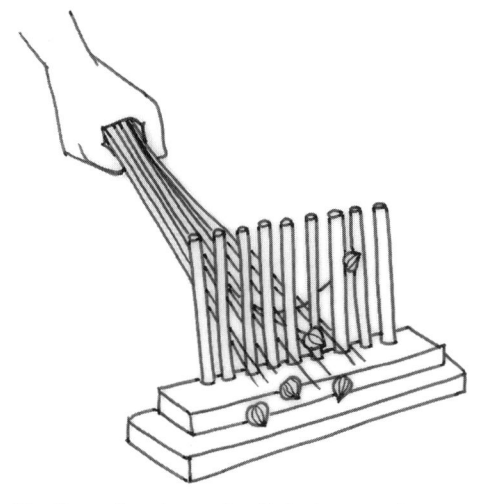

Rippling takes the seeds off the harvested flax stalks.

The Alden Amos Big Book of Handspinning

a bedsheet or large tablecloth beneath the ripple block to catch them as they fall out. If the flax is ready and dry, it will *shatter*, or drop its seed easily, as you drag the heads through the ripple teeth. You will need to separate the seeds from the pods. You can gently roll the seed pods to break them up, then winnow the seeds from the chaff. Do this outside on a nice breezy day over bedsheets. Or you can slowly pour the seeds (and chaff) from one large bucket to another, through the blast of a large fan. The lighter parts will go downwind and the seed will fall into the lower bucket.

The seeds must be kept dry unless you are going to plant them within a few hours. Flax seeds (linseed) qualify as good food, and not just for humans. Miguel Raton and his kin enjoy them, so store as you would any edible seed.[13]

Several authorities state that the finest fiber comes from immature plants. If you are new to growing flax, we advise you to aim for a good seed crop along with good fiber. This means you want mature plants with fully developed seeds. Experiment only after you have developed a frame of reference.

After the rippling comes *retting*, or high-class rotting. Retting renders brittle all parts of the flax plant except the fiber bundles. In general, all the necessary ingredients for retting exist on or in the plant. Simply submerge bundles of the whole plant in stagnant water and let nature take its course, although not too far.

First word of caution: some municipal water contains enough chlorine to affect retting. If you are using a kids' plastic wading pool as a retting tank (the contemporary default), fill it with city water a few days in advance and the chlorine will have time to gas off.

Second word of caution: retting develops interesting stenches. The effluent is good for your lawn or garden and will not harm the sewer or septic tank. But it stinks.

Retting proceeds rapidly in warm weather, slowly in cool. Therefore we can offer no fixed schedule of soaking times. Instead, check stem fracture. If you can break a stem in half and can also peel continuous

---

[13] *By the way, flax-seed recipes and preparations are in Chapter 13.*

bands of fiber along the break, retting has gone far enough.

If you are using the kids'-pool approach, be advised that retting may proceed at an alarming pace during hot weather—so rapidly that going a few hours over the "ready" stage as indicated by the fracture check attacks the fibers themselves. Weak, *frow* (crumbly) fiber will result. Check the stems frequently once the process starts working. When the flax is ready, get it out of there.

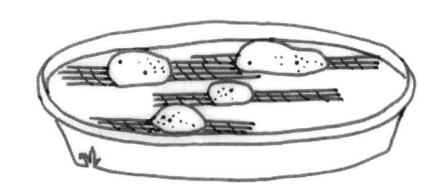

Retting breaks down all parts of the flax plant other than the fiber bundles. You can do it in your back yard in a kids' wading pool.

Dry the flax bundles without great delay. When dry clear through, they will be brittle, easily crushed, and ready for the next step, *breaking*. This "crunching" process breaks up all the brittle, woody, and pithy parts of the stems. Properly done, it has no effect on the fiber. Breaking can be accomplished with a variety of implements, but the idea remains the same: crush the pith, bark, and stem, and leave the fiber.

Scutching finishes separating the boon and shives (miscellaneous bits) from the fiber. The scutcher holds a bundle of broken straw so that part of it hangs down the face of a vertical board. Using a dull-edged wooden sword or blade, the scutcher strikes and scrapes the fiber bundle with downward-slicing, hacking strokes, frequently repositioning the fiber bundle so that all parts receive the same treatment and are cleared of woody junk.

Finally, we are ready to *hackle*. Hackles come in various degrees of fineness. The finer a hackle is, the more teeth it has per square inch and the sharper they are. Traditional flax-hackle teeth have square, diamond-shaped, or triangular cross sections, on the theory that they are designed to create "split ends." By and large, they are also easier to forge that way. Round

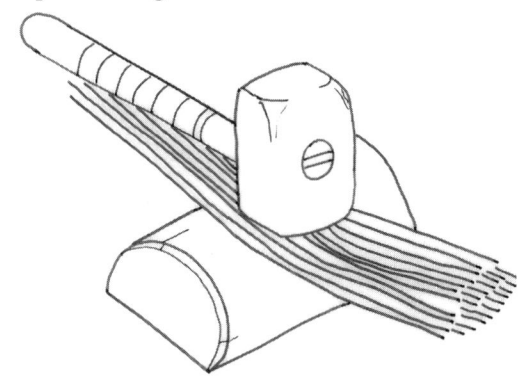

Breaking crushes the stems, making it easier to scutch.

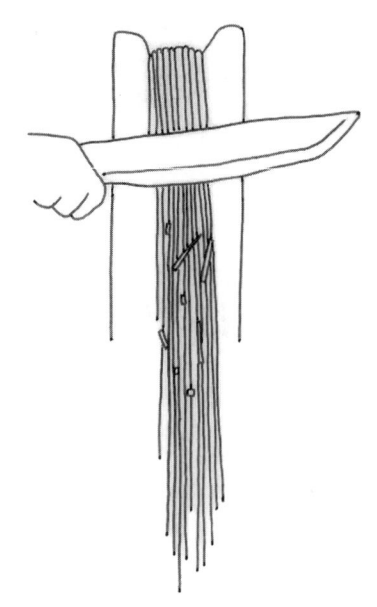

Scutching separates the fiber from the other plant parts.

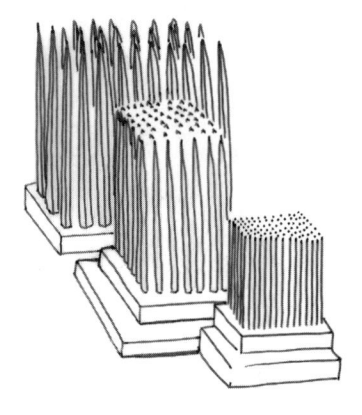

Hackles come in various sizes, with teeth that differ in quantity and fineness.

pins, found on most modern hackles, seem to work well enough if they have sharp points.

Start with the biggest, coarsest hackle you have. Fasten it down firmly. Grasp a handful of the straw and start dragging it through the hackle. Reposition your grasp so that you drag all parts of the bundle through the teeth. You will probably start by trying to work too big a bundle. No problem; adjust the amount and thwack away. After processing a quantity of straw through your coarsest hackle, clean all the stuff out of the tool, dismount it, and put it safely away. The short, broken stuff you clean out is barely tow-quality. Save it for future play-arounds of your own invention, or compost it.[14]

Mount your next hackle, a slightly finer one, firmly and securely. Repeat the process. This time, save the tow that comes off the hackle. This is usable fiber.

If you have a finer hackle, hackle it all again. By now you are getting pretty nice fiber. It also represents about half the quantity you started with. Such is life.

The tow, which you have been pulling off the hackles between and after sessions, can be carded or rough-combed and spun. **Do not use any oil** on flax, no matter what you are doing. A little moisture may help, when the atmosphere is very dry. But *never use oil on flax.*

Spinning flax

In the old days, tow was sometimes carded or rough-combed and drawn into a sliver. This sliver was then

---

[14] *It really was used as authentic tinder for starting fires. During the 1940s, the really short, busted stuff went into linoleum and those pressed phony-leather chair seats, and it filled cheap mattresses and cushions.*

wound in a figure-eight around the prongs of a fork or tow distaff. More often than not, a big wad of tow was simply stuffed into a suitable basket distaff. Tow spinning goes a little more slowly than woolen spinning, if only because tow will not draft as consistently.

Spinning from line flax is even slower. Line spinning takes about the same amount of time as worsted spinning, although the techniques are different. Line is spun with a variation of drafting-without-twist. With line, (1) you allow a tiny bit of twist into the drafting zone, (2) the drafting zone measures between 12 and 24 inches long, and (3) spinning proceeds most smoothly when the line flax is damp.[15]

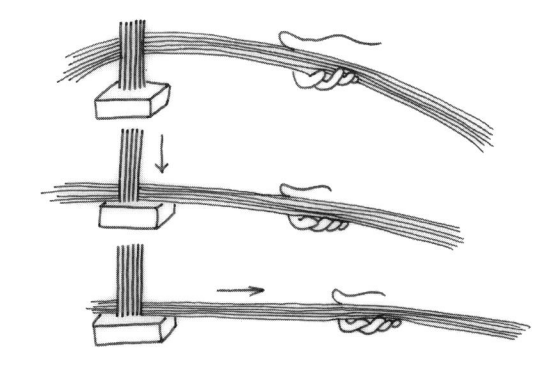

Hackling involves drawing bundles of fiber through the teeth of the hackle.

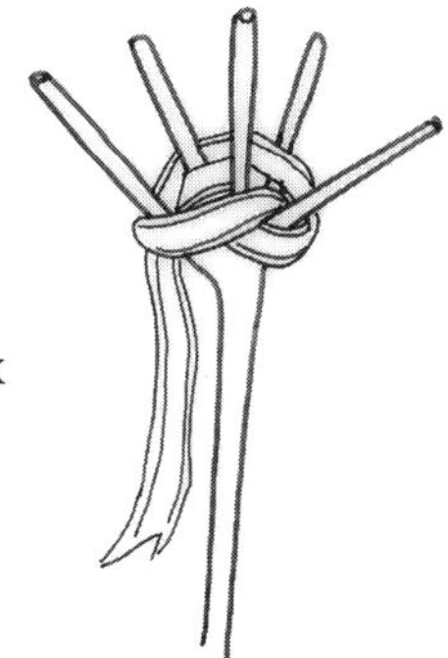

Line flax consists of the long fibers resulting from the hackling process.

Tow, the short flax fibers, can be rough-combed, drawn into a sliver, and wrapped around the prongs of a fork distaff.

---

[15] *If we have two yarns of the same grist, say 3,000 YPP, and one is worsted wool and the other is line flax, they will have almost identical numbers of twists per inch (about 10 twists per inch for a warp yarn). While the flax theoretically needs slightly less twist than the wool, the two come out about the same in practice, for various obscure reasons. Overly simplified, this depends on the following facts: (1) flax is spun wet (at least 30 percent moisture) and wool is not; (2) a given quantity of worsted wool has greater rigidity (resistance to twisting) than an equivalent quantity of wet line flax; (3) flax is inelastic and wool is quite elastic; (4) equal amounts of these two fibers do not foreshorten the same distance per unit of twist; and (5) line flax has such a long staple it doesn't need a whole lot of twist.*

How fast can a person spin?

To close this chapter, we will explore the question of "How fast can a person spin?" In general, your author recognizes three speed determinants: (1) drafting rate, (2) spinning rate, and (3) production rate.

Drafting rate refers to how much of a given yarn an individual can draft and spin in three minutes. It measures only drafting and twisting speed. The spinner does not have to procure and prepare fiber and normally is not concerned with yarn handling.

Spinning rate measures similar factors on a longer sample—typically ten minutes. It allows more time for things to go wrong, and also checks out operational details like how long it takes to change a bobbin or to wind-off a niddy-full of yarn.

Production rate involves a 48-minute test and includes everything that a handspinner does *except* fiber processing. Everything else that can happen gets counted: misfortune, yarn handling, broken yarns, dropped spindles, going to the bathroom . . . the works. If you are obtaining ready-to-spin fiber, production rate closely approximates how much yarn you can produce through sustained effort. Production rate always turns out to be about half of the drafting rate.

Here's a question. If you raise and process your own fibers, how many hours do you invest in the fiber to get one hour of spinning? We had some fun with this one. Answers: for wool, about twelve hours; for flax, about four hours; for cotton, about three hours; for silk, about forty hours.

The answers depend on qualifiers, of course, and the question is not fair, for reasons that should become clear. In any case, we established the following conditions. (1) During the golden hour, the spinner would spin as much as 4 ounces of wool, 2 ounces of flax, or 1½ ounces of cotton or silk. (2) The turf on which the flax or cotton fiber was raised would be a backyard plot of 8 by 20 feet. (3) For wool, the minimum number of sheep (one) would be raised, because it is not possible to raise 4 ounces of wool. (4) Our calculations for silk involve wild, although conservative, guesses. It takes something like seven to eight weeks for a silkworm to progress from egg to cocoon, and the little buggers get more demanding each instar.

We then calculated times on the basis of "portions." Although the types of investment varied, we ran through the same process for each fiber.

For example, the flax patch represents rototilling (two hours), chicken manoo patrol (one hour), sowing (one hour), raking (one hour), weed patrol (two hours), watering and general weeding and admiration (three hours), pulling/stacking (two hours), rippling (two hours), tanking and stacking (four hours), breaking (two hours), scutching (three hours), and hackling (seven hours).

Yield was about 20 ounces of usable fiber, composed of 12 ounces of line and 8 ounces of tow. The spinner's portion was 2 ounces of flax, but we raised and prepared 20 ounces of flax in thirty hours, or one-and-a-half hours per ounce. For 2 ounces, the portion is three hours.

So what? It's just time. Here's another opinion about time: "It does not show how much time it took: but it will show how good the work is."[16]

---

[16] *Quote attributed to Inga Krook's grandmother, from* Handspinning Flax *by Olive and Harry Linder.*

Chapter 7

Spinners' tools and savvy: Types of distaves, spindles, and wheels; hiring out fiber preparation; issues with storage and critters; making rope from leftovers; and disassembling yarn

Most handspinners begin with a manual spindle of some sort. Many people continue with the spindle, as either main course or side dish. Yet there are those among us who have (1) forgotten the use and protocol of the spindle or (2) never were comfortable with a spindle in the first place.

If you use a spindle at all—whether in your persona (as a public demonstrator), for portability, because you like it, because you need the yarn, or whatever—use it well. Be professional with it. Use appropriate techniques and fiber preparations, and spin an appropriate yarn. "An appropriate yarn" means one you expect to use for something other than tethering your cow. Put on a show, if only for yourself.

Distaves

For example, use a distaff. You do not have to be spinning flax to use a 'staff. You can authentically dress a distaff with wool sliver (look at pictures on Greek vases), and the fiber lends itself to drop-spindling. If you move around while spinning, use a wrist, hand, or waist distaff.

Distaves (plural of *distaff*; not distaffs) are fascinating in their own right. Like textiles, they reflect historical and agricultural advances. For example, Bette Hochberg showed that as improved agricultural practices produced longer flax fibers, distaves increased in length. The longer the flax, the longer the distaff to work it.

The primary purpose of a distaff is to keep the prepared fiber in good order for spinning. Distaves often have romantic and ceremonial purposes beyond spinning, but they are practical objects. All distaves, for all fibers, share certain characteristics. They come in three types (freestanding, waist, and hand); they are designed to maintain a deliberate fiber arrangement throughout the spinning process; and they are of as many configurations as the spinners who use(d) them.

Handheld distaves include the wrist distaff and distaves with short shafts. Once the shaft becomes long enough to be usefully supported by a waist band, sash, or belt, the device becomes a waist distaff. The waist distaff is almost always used while walking. While handheld distaves may also used by mobile spinners, they are more often employed by seated spinsters. Both types may be used while walking or sitting, although it is a little awkward to use a waist distaff (often 40 to 50 inches long) while seated on the ground. Waist distaves are adaptable, becoming freestanding distaves when mounted on a suitable support.

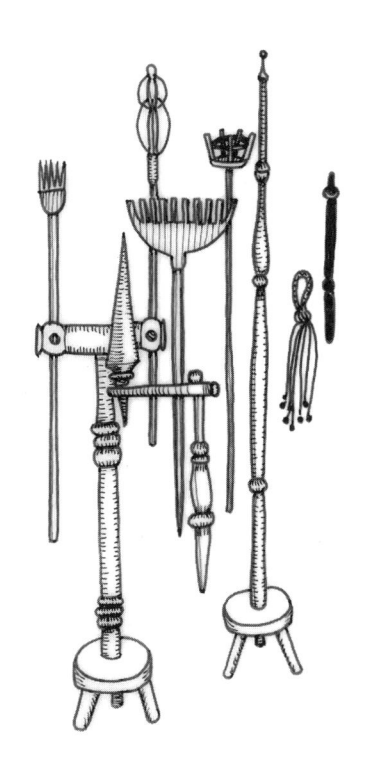

Various types of distaff: wrist, waist, several styles of freestanding. Waist distaves can also be freestanding when placed on a base.

The freestanding distaff takes two forms. It can be supported by a wheel's bench or framework, or it can be a separate entity with its own bench and legs.

All forms of distaff can be used with a manual spindle. For wheel use, a freestanding 'staff is the primary choice. The wrist distaff is used with the tahkli, the Thai-style spindle, and the various bead-whorl spindles.

In any case, the use of a distaff in concert with a drop spindle is as natural and authentic as sitting down to treadle your Wee Dinkus spinning wheel. Get and use a distaff. Treat your spindle as what it is: a favorite and faithful tool. Practice with it and with the use of the 'staff. Get good.

A wrist distaff.

A waist distaff.

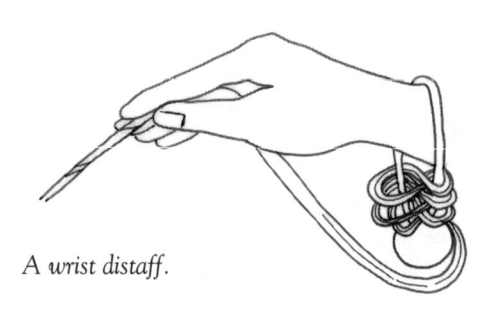

REFINING YOUR SPINDLE SKILLS

Other, more gifted authors have written about teaching yourself to spin with manual spindles. That means you are not going to get a spindle-spinning lesson here. What you will find are selected helpful hints and stunts—routines, if you like—that will enhance your use of this ancient and honorable tool.

Don't use too heavy a spindle, or attempt to spin exceptionally fine or thick yarn. Be conservative. When spinning wool on a spindle, aim for

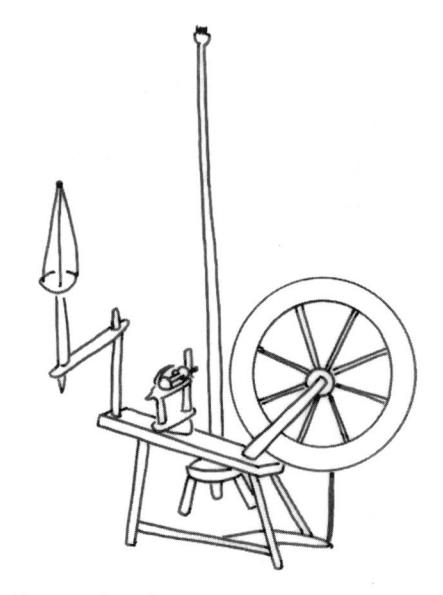

Freestanding distaves.

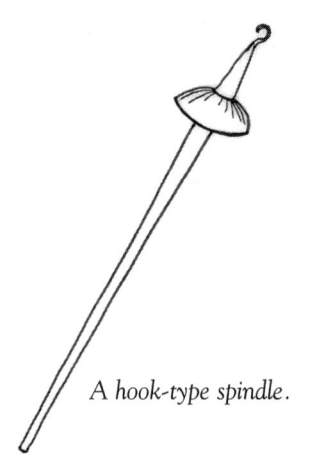

A hook-type spindle.

176   The Alden Amos Big Book of Handspinning

a general-purpose single at 1,600 YPP and 6 twists per inch, which will be easy to handle while walking. To spin the above yarn requires the appropriate spindle. A suitable general-purpose, single-whorl, "wool" spindle will have about a 10-inch shaft with a shaft diameter between ⅜ and ½ inch and will weigh less than 3 ounces. If it is a hook-style spindle, the hook needs to be sturdy, smooth, and of a workable profile. *Sturdy* means sturdy enough to stand being dropped.

Princess Twinkle versus the Egyptians

You can use either a top- or bottom-whorl spindle. People don't expect to see you spinning in the top-whorl, or Egyptian, mode.[1] They have seen too much spinning in the Fairy Godmother and Princess Twinkle manner. The top-whorl or Egyptian mode is more efficient because you can introduce lots of twist quickly. For optimum productivity, it won't hurt if the spindle has a slightly longer shaft, say between 12 and 14 inches.

Princess Twinkle mode #1.

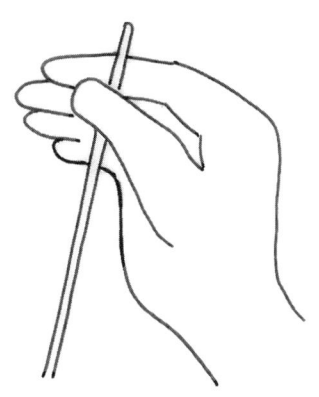

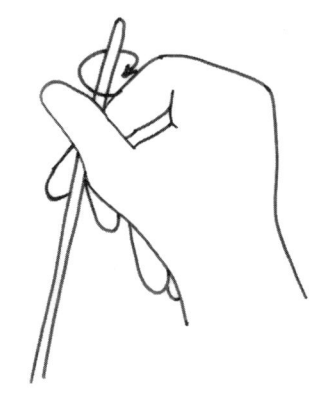

Hold spindle between thumb and index finger.   *Put twist in with snapping motion.*

---

[1] *Top-whorl mode is called* Egyptian *because the earliest pictures (and spindles) showing the technique come from Egyptian tombs circa 2000* B.C. *However, this spindle type was ubiquitous throughout the ancient and classical world. It could be called the Mesopotamian spindle, or the Persian spindle, or the Anatolian. For convenience, we will follow common usage.*

Princess Twinkle mode #2.

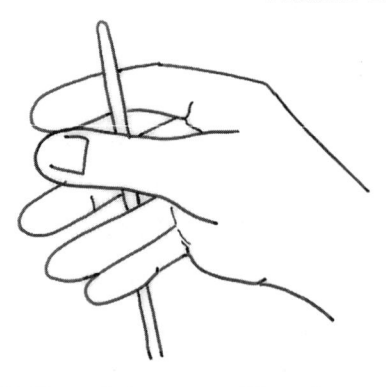

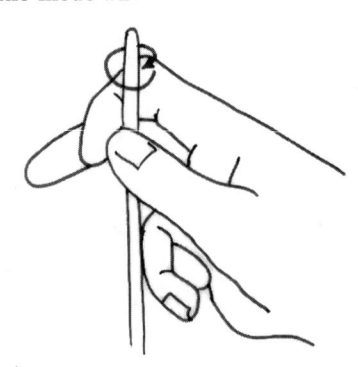

Hold spindle between middle and ring finger.

Put twist in with index and thumb.

In Princess Twinkle mode, you twirl the spindle shaft between your thumb and forefinger. Even a brisk *snap!* from this position doesn't produce anything like the torque and twist you get from rolling the shaft of a top-whorl spindle up (Z) or down (S) your thigh. The Princess Twinkle mode suits small supported spindles, such as the tahkli. It works with the "conventional" drop spindle well enough to be perpetuated (it's easy to do), but it is not efficient with a spindle shaft bigger in diameter than a wire, or about 3/32 inch.

A few years back we did strobe-and-photo studies of rotational speed. In Princess Twinkle mode, Jane Q. Spinner can put an average of 400 RPMs' worth of spin onto a 3-inch whorl with a 3/8-inch-diameter shaft. Some people got more speed, some got less. Rolling the same spindle on the thigh gave average speeds in the realm of 2,050 RPM, with no trouble on anyone's part (everybody who tried it accomplished these speeds). In other words, the top-whorl mode is four or five times as twist-efficient as the bottom-whorl mode.

Spindle proficiency

Build your copp on the Egyptian spindle with some care, rather like the copp on a great wheel. When ready to wind-off, hang the spindle by its hook overhead. Then route the yarn down and under the top rail of a chair, thence to your skeining or bobbin-winding setup.

Most handspindles today are built to look pretty, fashionable, exotic, or . . . you supply the line. Few are made with spinning in mind, and even fewer, if any, take winding-off seriously. This probably occurs because most handspinners don't take winding-off seriously. Dare to be different.

Small supported spindles, the tahkli type, are best wound off in side-delivery mode. Because all tahklis have hooks of sorts, it is seldom practical to wind them off in end-delivery style. For side-delivery position, you want to trap the spindle, end-to-end, between two supports. Traditionally, the supports have been made from a split reed, and the spindle rests horizontally. When the spindle shaft does not have two sharp ends, the spindle can be trapped "standing up," with its point (whorl end) down and resting in a shallow depression and its upper shaft in a slotted support rail.

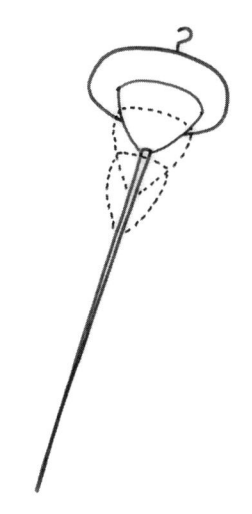

Unwinding your spindle can go easily if you build your copp as a series of stacked cones.

To remove the yarn from an Egyptian spindle, secure the spindle above a chair, bring the yarn under the chair's back, and wind.

Build charkha and great-wheel copps as end-feed packages, cone upon cone.

Traditionally, a split reed has been used to hold a tahkli spindle horizontally for unwinding.

The Alden Amos Big Book of Handspinning

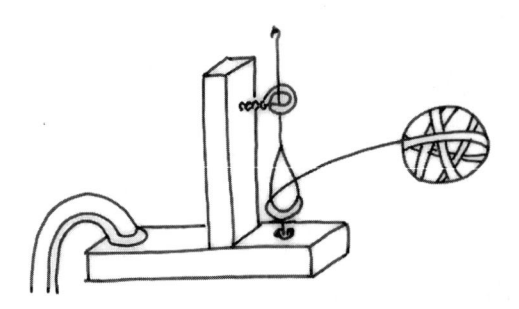

Unwinding a small spindle without using a split reed.

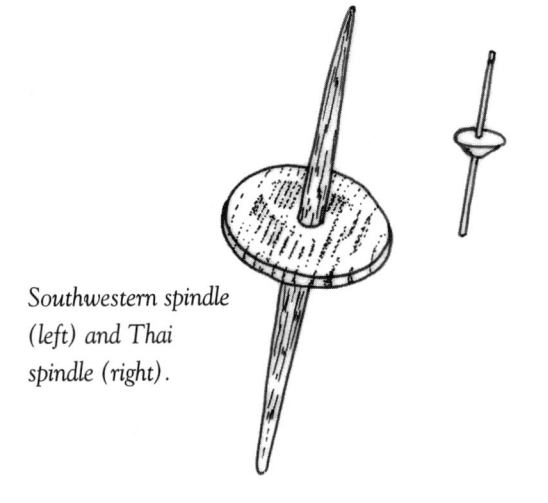

Southwestern spindle (left) and Thai spindle (right).

Not all supported spindles are small. The "Navajo" spindle is an example of a large supported spindle.[2] A good "Southwestern"-style spindle should have a shaft between 14 and 16 inches long, double-tapered from ⅜ inch in the middle to about ³⁄₁₆ inch at each end. Its whorl, placed at about the middle of the shaft, should be ⁵⁄₁₆ inch thick and about 4 inches in diameter.

A half-scale version of this is known as the Thai spindle. Thai spindles are used the same way as bead-whorl spindles. That is, the yarn supports one end of the spindle and the hand supports the other end. Keep the spindle shaft parallel to the ground while working, and put twist into the shaft almost as a flick of the wrist.

Two specialty spindles that are not as well known as they should be are the "Turkish" and the "Balkan" spindles, both used as drop spindles.

The Turkish spindle could be called the Alexander the Great spindle. Its eastward movement seems to coincide with move-

---

[2] So are the "tossed" Salish spindle and the Hopi spindle. In this context, the term supported *means that the spindle never dangles freely from the yarn, as in the drop-spindle mode. Instead, most or all of its weight is supported by the ground, the spinner's thigh, a table, the spinner's hand, or another object. Here's an anecdote about support spindles. Back in the 1970s, an order came to Straw into Gold for some "Navajo" spindles to be used in a school project. Either AA (yours truly) or the Bros. Schacht ended up making the spindles. They were big, with 30-inch shafts and 6- to 7-inch whorls. Off they went. In due time we received a nice letter from the teacher, along with pictures of the third-graders. Everyone had lots of fun, she wrote, but could we maybe come up with a smaller spindle? The pictures showed why she asked: the whole class was lined up with their spindles in, you guessed it, drop-spindle mode.*

ments of Alexander's camp followers, showing up as far east (from Greece) as Tibet. The Turkish spindle consists of a spindle shaft with two or more cross-arms, which are mortised together so the spindle shaft locks them in place. In both structure and method of employment, the Turkish spindle lends itself to the making of coarse, hair-based yarns. The yarn is spun in top-whorl or, more commonly, low-whorl fashion. The spinner wraps the newly spun yarn around the spindle cross-arms, forming a ball. When the ball becomes big enough, the spindle shaft is pulled out, the arms are slipped apart, and *hey, presto!*, there it is.[3]

The Balkan takes an entirely different approach. The contemporary Balkan or double-whorl spindle first came into our workshop in the late 1970s, when a visitor commissioned a replica of a family keepsake (her mother's or grandmother's spindle) brought from the vicinity of Yugoslavia and Albania. Thus the name.

The Balkan spindle is a double-whorl affair, with both whorls removable, a hook top, and a 10- to12-inch shaft. According to the owner of the original, the spindle was used in hook-top mode, á la Egyptian. When the spindle is full of yarn, the whorls are slipped off and the shaft is used directly as a shuttle. It does work that way, although it is more efficient to remove the bottom whorl and then wind off onto a more appropriate bobbin or quill.

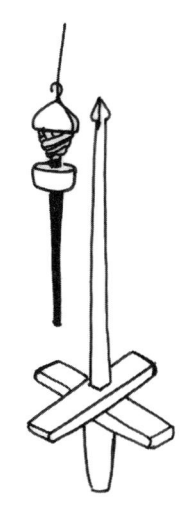

Balkan spindle (left) and Turkish spindle (right).

SPINNING WHEELS

Enough on handspindles. Let's talk about spinning wheels. Where do we begin? First we need to make sense of the types of wheels.

Joan Cummer's *A Book of Spinning Wheels* lists more than 100 different wheels. They are not all different styles, but in fact there are almost as many styles of wheel as there are makers. It is not possible to list her types here. And, to what purpose? The only reason for the

---

[3] *These coarser yarns are used to make ropes and cords. When enough yarn has been accumulated, the rope-making process begins. In the author's experience, the Turkish spindle seems ideal for this work. Maybe those old timers knew a thing or two.*

terminology is to give another person an idea of what you are talking about.

Judith Buxton also considered the classification of spinning wheel types. She came up with a precise discipline including fourteen overall groups, eleven major categories with twelve additional qualifiers, and twelve supplemental and descriptive parameters. Her useful system is somewhat more than adequate for our purposes.[4]

What kind of wheel is it?

For several reasons, our system, devised by Stephenie Gaustad for use in her classes, can be simpler than Joan Cummer's or Judith Buxton's. (1) We need not satisfy the demands of academic publishing. (2) In our experience, handspinners (as opposed to general or scholarly readers) are quick studies and don't need a lot of prodding. (3) We are not covering the same ground.

We first describe a spinning wheel in terms of its **class,** of which there are two: (1) *driven spindle* and its derivatives, and (2) *flyer/bobbin* and its derivatives.

Then we describe it by **type**: is it treadled, motorized, hand-turned, accelerated, direct-drive, friction-drive . . . ? A single wheel can belong to one or more types. For example, it can be hand-turned and accelerated.

The third description category is **style,** and here is where the arguments begin. "Style" is what most people mean when they want to know what "kind" of wheel they have. For example, what is the difference between a Saxony and a Dutch wheel? Between a castle wheel and a Shetland? An Orkney and a Bohemian?

Basically, nothing. These evocative names are imprecise. A Saxony and a Dutch wheel are both sloping-bench, three-legged, double-drive, bobbin-lead, treadled wheels, often of the similar physical sizes. About the only difference is that the rim on the drive wheel of the "Dutch"

---

[4] *In her monumental work,* Selected Canadian Spinning Wheels in Perspective: An Analytical Approach *(Ottawa: National Museums of Canada, 1980); original edition listed for Judith Buxton-Keenlyside). The book was reissued in 1992 by the Canadian Museum of Civilization as part of their Mercury Series (History Division, Paper 30).*

tool is quite wide—so wide that the spokes may be very short.

If the same wheel that we just called "Dutch" were fitted with a hand crank instead of or in addition to its treadle, and had a single-drive, flyer-lead (variation) arrangement known as a Picardy flyer, we could call it a Belgian flax wheel.

All of the wheels we just described fall into a generic style known as *Saxon* or *Saxony wheels*.

What about the differences between the castle wheel and the Shetland? There are none. A Shetland qualifies as a type of castle wheel, *castle* in this case meaning that each wheel has a central, castle post that supports its working parts. Same with the Orkney and the Bohemian: a three-legged base, two castle posts (wheel posts), and the mother-of-all hung on top.

The generic style for the above group is *upright wheels*.

But some wheels will not quite fit into any scheme. Sometimes a given wheel generates its own category. The perfect example is the Ashford Traditional wheel—known, loved, and hated by handspinners all over the world.

Rather like Comet, Kleenex, Brillo pads and Crisco, *Ashford* is becoming a generic term. We have received invitations to spinning events that ask us to "bring lunch, bring the kids, bring your Ashford, and we'll all have fun. . . ."

Is an Ashford a Saxony? Where's the bench? Because the wheel fits down between the rear legs, couldn't we call it a frame wheel? And what kind of tensioning is that, anyway?

The Ashford is enough of an original that we consider it a style of its own. So we'll call it an

Dutch wheel/Saxony wheel.

Castle wheel/Shetland wheel.

Ashford-style framed Saxony with straight-line hinge-plate (toggle) tensioning, fitted with a single-drive, flyer-lead array.

Any other wheel so arranged is also an Ashford-style wheel. At least four Ashford-style wheels are being made or are in common use.[5]

Another unique wheel style is the Irish castle wheel. Unlike most wheels, it also seems to have a definite nationality. Apparently isolated in Ireland for some time, this distinctive design made the trip to North America by the 1830s.

Occasionally a manufacturer markets a single "signature" design long enough for its marketing or brand name to become synonymous with a particular style. Examples include the Pirtle, the Yeadon Wishbone, the Schacht, and the Indian Valley. These are not what you would call "traditional" styles or designs, which brings us to another brief digression. What is the traditional design for a microwave oven? A traditional airplane? A traditional laser?

Right.

Anyway, these wheels have their own shape and "style," and only time will tell if they are "traditional." Some of these wheels have already disappeared. In the meantime, the most convenient way to describe them is by the most commonly used denominator.

Then there are chair wheels, and low-bench accelerated wheels (sometimes called Macedonian or Turkish wheels), and great wheels (also called wool, muckle, long, cottage,

Ashford Traditional wheel.

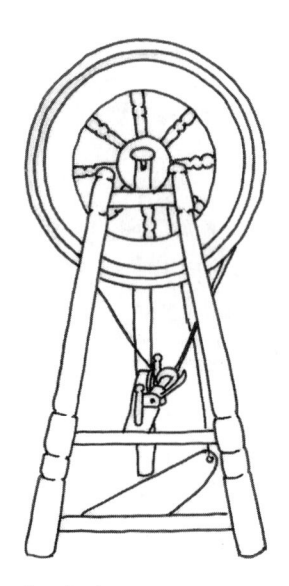

Irish castle wheel.

---

[5] These include the Ashford itself, the U-Bild, the Ashram Teak, and the Herring Gordon. Doubtless there are others.

Turkish wheel.

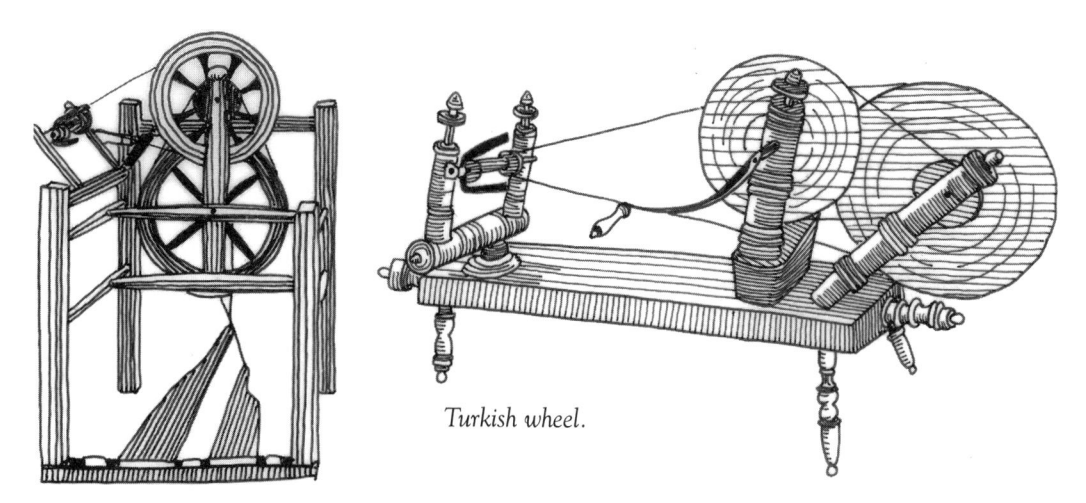

Chair wheel.

big, and other names), and so forth. Plus there are barge wheels, parlor wheels, girdle wheels, Swiss wheels, Shaker wheels, Canadian wheels, Acadian wheels, Brunswick wheels, Tyrolean wheels, French frame wheels, German frame wheels, Ding-dong wheels, Whoopee wheels, and L-frame wheels, and. . . . Most fit into the **class** plus **type** plus **style** system.

Saxony subtypes. Several subtypes of treadled Saxony wheels are in common use. The Scandinavian (also Swedish, Norwegian) has a split-level bench and wheel-alignment rods. The Canadian uses a simple rotating mother-of-all arrangement to adjust drive-band tension and often includes a cast-iron or cast-aluminum treadle plate.[6] The steep bench on a South German model is slotted at the wheel end to allow short wheel posts. And the (ahem!) American Saxony Production Wheel features double-guide and slide-block screw tensioning for the mother-of-all.[7]

Upright subtypes. Uprights have several variations. Some have frames and some don't. The flyer/bobbin array can be positioned either above or below the wheel. Some have benches, some don't. Some have three legs,

---

[6] *The aluminum type appears on contemporary wheels.*

[7] Editor's note: *This wheel design originated in Alden's workshop.*

Great wheel.

Scandinavian wheel.

some four. Some fold up, some fold up into travel cases, and some won't fold under any circumstances.

When we speak of frames, we mean joiner's work as opposed to turner's work. A vertical-frame Swiss is a framed upright in which the lathe may have played little part beyond spokes and bobbins. A Farnham or Owego wheel is framed, yet has turned legs and details.

South German wheel.

Farnham wheel.

On the other hand, . . . while a chair wheel may be a framed wheel, it doesn't really fit into the upright category. Many chair wheels are accelerated, as are some Saxony-style wheels. Some uprights have double flyers. . . .

Tensioning systems

If a wheel tensions the drive-band at all, it can be set up to accomplish this feat in several different ways.

Rubber-band drive, no tensioning adjustment. Wheels like the Louët or the old Ashford Country spinner use what we call "rubber-band" drive. Since they are bobbin-lead, single-drive arrangements, the makers felt there would be no need to change drive-band tension. The factory-furnished drive-band consists of a length of end-welded string-trimmer cord, or a generously sized industrial O-ring or packing seal. The rubber-band drive is standard practice for keeping costs down. No tension adjustments and all that.

The two basic types of drive-band tensioning, and their variations. The majority of wheels, double- or single-drive, use some form of drive-band tensioning. There are two basic types: Type A, where the entire flyer assembly moves away from or toward the drive wheel, and Type B, where only one end of the flyer shaft moves away from or toward the drive wheel.

The A type, called a *straight-line tensioning* system, is superior. It maintains the bias alignment between the flyer shaft and the wheel axle, prevents extreme end-thrust problems with regard to the flyer shaft and its supports, and solves bearing-alignment problems. Straight-line tensioners are found on all wheel styles.

Accelerated Saxony wheel.

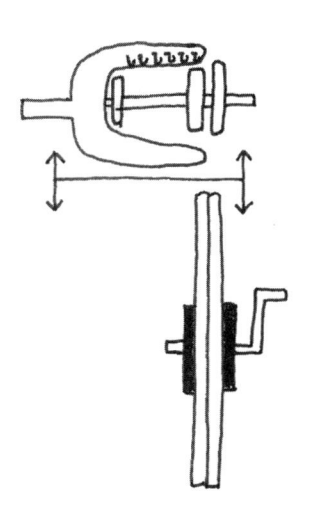

Type A: straight-line tensioning system.

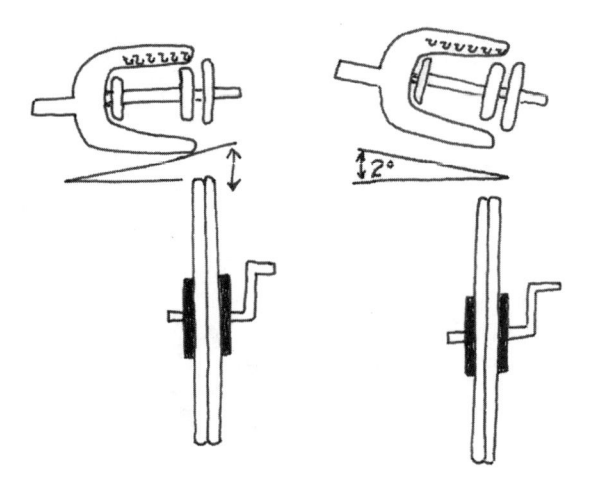

Type B: single-end tensioning system.

Bias is the angle of divergence between the drive-wheel axle and the flyer shaft.

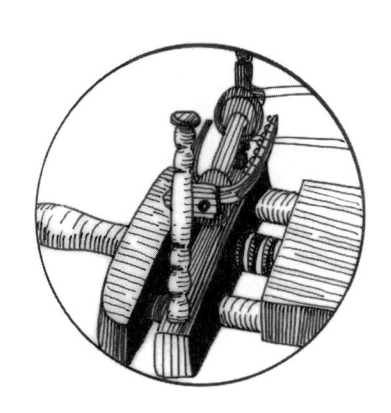

Tensioning system on an American Saxony wheel.

The B type, called a *single-end tensioning system*, presents no advantage to the handspinner. Rather, it is the source of several problems related to drive-bands, tracking, and alignment. No bias or float adjustments are practical. It is considerably cheaper for the manufacturer. Single-end tensioners are found on upright wheels.

Single-end tensioners all work pretty much the same: a bearing block is slip-fit into the rear maiden or flyer support, and a screw adjustment moves it toward or away from the wheel. The barrel end of the flyer doesn't move.

Straight-line tensioners have three basic variations: (1) those that move the entire mother-of-all away from or toward the wheel; (2) those that rotate the mother-of-all about its own axis, parallel to the wheel axis (or its bias angle); and (3) those that tilt the mother-of-all away from or toward the wheel.

The traditional standard arrangement falls into the first group, because the mother-of-all slides back and forth, controlled by a screw arrangement. The screw threads may be visible, as in the various uprights, the "horned" Saxonies, and the Tyrolean/French styles. In most Saxonies, the screw arrangement is contained in the bench proper.[8]

---

[8] Editor's note: A horned Saxony is a wheel like Alden's American Saxony Production Wheel. He says that no contemporary builder that he knows of is using the system ("except old Ahem! himself"). This is how spinning wheels evolve. See the process in action. . . .

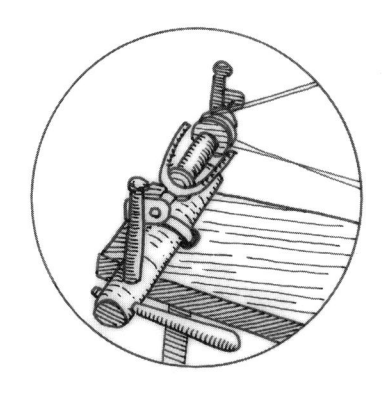

Canadian tensioning system.

The second sort, where the mother-of-all rotates, is common in Canadian Saxonies, and thus is called the Canadian tensioning system. It has three basic variations: (1) those that have an elaborate support clamp, above bench; (2) those that use a simple retaining strap and a bench notch; and (3) those that use a through-bolt and tab system. Of the three, the second sort is the most common and the third sort is the least common.

The final type—the tilting, hinge-plate, or toggle system—is used on the Ashford Traditional wheel. Toggle or hinge-plate systems have been used on uprights as well as Saxony wheels.

If you have a choice, remember that the straight-line system is superior, from the handspinner's point of view.

Using the classification information

No matter what wheel is being discussed, ask or state the basic questions. What is its *class*—spindle or flyer? What is its *type*—treadle? motor? hand? direct drive? What is its *style*—upright? Saxony? L-frame? "Modern"?

In the appendix, we have included wheel silhouette charts so that you can practice wheel spotting. Use your common sense. First impressions are right more often than wrong.

Does it matter which class, type, and style of wheel you use? Yes, and no. Let's simplify matters and give you some advice.

Straight-line tensioners.

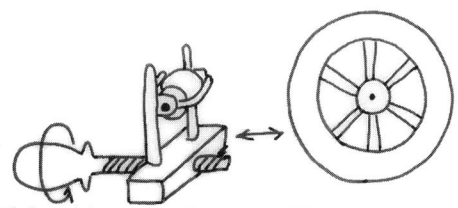

Sliding (American Saxony style).

Pivoting (Canadian style).

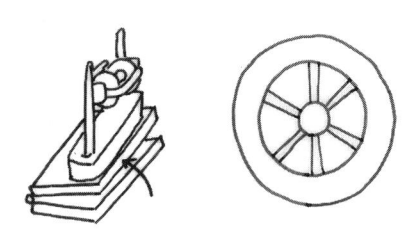

Hinged (á la Ashford Traditional style).

The Alden Amos Big Book of Handspinning 189

Vertical-frame Swiss wheel.

For spinning flax: the double-drive, bobbin-lead, vertical-frame Swiss wheel is specifically designed for spinning flax from a freestanding distaff.

For spinning wool: the great wheel is designed for spinning wool yarns on the woolen system. The double-drive Saxony is excellent at spinning worsted.

For spinning silk: look to the great wheel, the charkhas, and Saxony wheels, in that order.

For spinning cotton: the larger charkhas are ideal. On a treadled wheel, the single-drive, flyer-lead system is the most forgiving.

A good flyer/bobbin wheel will do a pretty fair job with any useful fiber over a wide range of grists and twists, although there are almost surely better ways to deal with individual requirements. That means that you don't have to have a great wheel to spin wool, or a charkha to spin cotton. Do the best you can with what you have, and you will find that it is better than you thought.

The only times when you will wish for a different tool is when you spin flax on a driven spindle, try to make a good three-ply on a drop spindle, or try to spin fine yarn on your Kountry Kanyon wheel.

For plying yarn: the motor spinner has no worthy rival.

Don't bother with a double-treadle wheel unless (1) there is something wrong with your legs, (2) the wheel design is such that you cannot manually turn the wheel in order to start it, (3) you are operating at extremely high drive ratios, (4) there is great rigidity (resistance to twisting) in the yarn, (5) you are such a klutz that you cannot keep the wheel going with one foot, and/or (6) you like to sit there, squeezed-in, hunched-over, and head-on with your knees together. Most double-treadles allow you to work twice as hard for the same amount of yarn. There are justifications for double treadle setups, to be sure, but they are few and far between.

Unless you have a soft spot for little twinkie wheels, leave the "uprights" and castle wheels for the turistas. Although they are advertised as portable (a relative term), the trade-off may not be worthwhile. Little wheels do not spin as well as big ones, simple as that.

Tensioning notes

If you are operating a single-drive wheel, you should not make frequent adjustments to anything. Normally you will adjust the take-up on a Scotch-tension wheel two or three times per bobbin. Once the drive-band tension has been set, you don't need to do anything about it.

On a single-drive, German-tension wheel, you may have to tweak the take-up a few times—that is, you may increase drive-band tension to increase flyer drag. Even minor changes of this type will make a big difference in treadle effort, so use this adjustment as a last resort.

A double-drive system may require frequent tweaking of drive-band tension to get just what you want in the way of twist and take-up. If "just what you want" falls outside the efficient range of the *differential rotational speed* (DRS) established by the whorl diameters, you will do more than tweaking. You might change flyer whorls, if alternatives are available, or change drive-bands. Drive-band diameter and material can have a dramatic effect on performance of any system, not just flyer/bobbin arrangements.

Here's some good stuff to remember.

To increase take-up with a double-drive system, (1) increase drive-band tension or (2) increase DRS by increasing the difference between whorl diameters.

To increase take-up on a single-drive, Scotch-tension wheel increase brake-band tension. Make small changes. You may also have to increase drive-band tension to reduce slippage produced by the increased drag.

To increase take-up on a single-drive, German-tension wheel increase flyer drag. Make minor increases by increasing drive-band tension; make major increases by introducing more flyer drag via the brake band. Always try increasing drive-band tension first.

Don't overfill your bobbins. Roughly two-thirds full is about right. Never fill a bobbin over disk-to-disk (beyond the diameter of the spool ends) and expect it to be trouble-free during spinning or winding-off.

Remember that flyer-lead bobbins fill in the opposite direction with respect to bobbin-lead systems. Thus if you change systems in midstream (as any double-drive system can do on demand) to demonstrate a point, for your own amazement, or whatever, be sure and anchor the yarn down until there are a few wraps on board, heading in the new direction. A good way to do this is to strip a yard or so off the bobbin, out of (through) the iron, and then deliberately create a backlash.[9] Even more practical is a little dab of masking tape.

Remember that the spinning direction (S or Z) has not changed, just the winding-on direction. And don't forget that you changed directions when you go to wind off. Otherwise, you will be winding off, all neat and tidy, until *snap!* the yarn comes to the reversed winding. Then and there it breaks and buries itself.

Here's a way to prevent that problem. Break the yarn to start with, let it ply itself for a few inches, and then wrap it onto the bobbin core. Using a new leader, wrap on a few turns in the appropriate wind-on direction. Then, when you wind off, no problem.

Do not build monster copps on your great wheel's or your charkha's spindle blade. Take that yarn off frequently and get it out of harm's way. If you do not, sooner or later you will make a mess that includes snags, self-plying, and kinks, which are all unpleasant to encounter during winding-off.

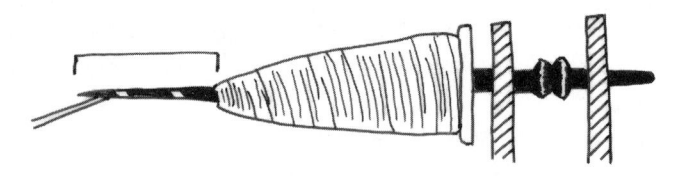

Keep the spindle blade clear.

Motor spinners

Motor spinners come in various configurations. Obviously, Studio Gaustad's is the best, although the other makers would certainly argue the point. Be that as it may, all motor spinners share certain characteristics.

Use a ground-fault interrupter (GFI) circuit when operating electrically-powered textile equipment, especially outside or in damp locations.

---

[9] Editor's note: *Alden explains his use of "through the iron" as opposed to "out back through the orifice:" the former is a cord-makers' and rope-makers' term relating to the use of cores in certain constructions, such as steerage ropes. It means to reverse the flow of components through the existing setup.*

If the appropriate circuitry is not available, don't run your motor spinner at pool-side, on the museum lawn, or in the garden. By the same token, do not be foolish with supplemental lighting setups.

Dealing with electricity is like dealing with firearms. Do not take anything for granted. Never take chances. Never assume anything, unless you wish to assume the toes-up, lily-grasping, crossed-hand position, with all of your friends gazing down upon you as they file sadly past.

Even if carelessness doesn't zap you, it can zap your equipment, especially nowadays, with electronic chips and all. A simple polarity reversal can cook your Whiz-Tech's control circuits.[10]

In all fairness, it should be said that the typical modern reaction to a blinking red failure light is "What's that light blinking for?" Few people read manuals or follow instructions. We just plug in our equipment and turn it on, and if it doesn't work we flick the switch a few times.

We handspinners are above that, right? We do check out what's going wrong with the machine, after unplugging it, of course.

HIRING OUT YOUR FIBER PREPARATION

Fiber preparation causes the handspinner's primary bottleneck. Some spinners may imply that "this method of spinning" or "that way of scouring" eliminates all that messy fiber-prep stuff. If you believe them, you will be shocked when I tell you that Howdy Doody has strings.

The more time and effort put into fiber preparation, the faster and better the spinning goes. No exceptions.

Certain yarns can *only* be produced from well-prepared fibers. No exceptions.

You can't spin yarns without fiber preparation, except for yarns that look exactly like what went into them. No exceptions.

Since there seems to be no way to avoid fiber preparation, do everything you can to be efficient at it. For example, you save no time by scouring a few locks of wool. Invest a bit more time up front, scour a few pounds of wool, and save time in the long run. Don't card up a couple of

---

[10] *A certain not-to-be-named plastic motor spinner of recent years gave many people fried electronic surprises.*

rolags; card up a bunch. Do the same with combing, hackling, picking, or cleaning cotton.

Do not hesitate to purchase prepared fiber if its price and degree of preparation suit your purposes.

Do not hesitate to use someone else's services as long as you like their work, their price, and their speed. Of course, if you have high standards, people like this may not be easy to find.

Let's talk about that. Carding and scouring services are available at more or less reasonable prices. The problem areas are more personal in nature.

We (Amos & Gaustad) used to do a fair quantity of carding and scouring for hire. We no longer provide these services for other people. We only do them for ourselves. The reasons were simple and many—competition, water supply, too tired, and so on—but only one is important here: the customer's expectations.

Very few customers have any idea of what the process entails, how it proceeds, what is necessary . . . and what the final results are. Their experience tends to be limited to a few hours of work with a pair of hand cards, or a guild session with a drum carder while color-blending dyed fleece. When these people call you, it is like you have been asked to overhaul a transmission on the living room floor. The customer summons you, you explain what's going to happen, they say "not to worry, we understand, just fix it," and you set to work. In good time, you are done, the transmission is in good order, runs fine . . . and the customer is in shock because there is grease on the carpet. When trouble arises in these transactions, in most cases this occurs because the customer's expectations bear no relationship to real life.

Once we prepared 7 pounds of batts from a nice blend of kid mohair and Romney. The customer was completely turned off because the fiber "had some sort of oil on it." There was no way she would believe that the oil was necessary, since she had no experience with carding.[11]

---

[11] *No one machine-cards wool without carding oil. Not for long, anyway. On top of that, not everybody uses the same stuff, and some formulations don't smell so sweet.*

Another time a customer supplied some fleece from a Colorado friend, saying she liked the color, would we card it up so she could get someone to spin it, blah, blah. This was a pound-and-a-half lot, pretty small to start with, but okay. When we scoured it, the first tub looked like tomato soup. Arable, oh yes. Got it clean, ran it through the carder, beautiful stuff! She didn't like it, didn't take it, didn't pay for it . . . we did "something" to it that ruined that "nice reddish color."

Speaking of color, we used to do color blending: How about this one? A customer had a gray fleece dyed, half of it pink-over-gray, the other half blue-over-gray. She liked that just fine, but wanted them blended. We did. She walked on the order because it was "too much gray."

For another person, we did several batches of carding. Then she sent a fleece from "Jimmy," or "Nancy," or whatever. We scoured it, carded it, and sent it back. She refused it, saying that even though it was a fine job, it wasn't "Jimmy, Nancy, or any sheep she knew," and her customers would never stand for that.

Well, fleece mix-ups do occur, especially at larger establishments, since no one there is of any mind to first-name a !#@$* sheep. That's not what happened with us, but that's not the point.

The point is, don't send your 3-pound fleece in a white plastic garbage bag, with an old envelope inside that says "Othello spring 96," to an outfit that handles a thousand pounds a week and expect to get Othello back. Well, you can "expect" to get him back, but that does not mean that you will. True, some outfits perform personalized operations, but only if you make prior arrangements. Don't assume otherwise. In fact, it might be better to take care of Othello yourself, if you care that much.

You should expect your dirty fleece to look different when it comes back, but you need to have an educated idea of what that means. In other words, don't judge anyone else's carding and scouring unless you judge it with respect to your own.

This does not mean that you have to be a blind, trusting, amateur fool. If you send out a sound, well-picked, clear, shive-free fleece with few or no second-cuts, and you get back a sorry, neppy, noil-loaded felter's stock that smells like a freeze-dried goat and drafts like an old zipper . . . you have every right to go on the warpath.

A legitimate outfit doesn't handle small or premium lots unless they get premium prices for their efforts, and most of them won't do it even then. They are not set up to do so. They can't. Even a modest commercial card, say 36 to 48 inches wide, takes about a pound of wool just to get loaded up for work. That makes it hard to guarantee that you will get all of "Blanche" back. A big card set may need between 3 and 5 pounds before fiber shows on the last doffer comb.

Whether you process the wool yourself or send it out, spin the stuff up when it is ready. It really is not a good idea to let the fiber sit around, all carded but unspun, if only because of moths, beetles, dogs, cats, cats, cats, kids. . . .

STORAGE, AND CONTENDING WITH CRITTERS

If you want to store wool, store it clean (scoured) and picked, or store it as spun, clean yarn. Keep it dry, too. Store it greasy/dirty? Sure, if you can put it in cold storage. Otherwise, you are asking for trouble.

Store it clean and dry. Plastic bags are convenient, cheap, and ready-made. Probably more wool has been ruined by plastic garbage bags than any other storage medium. One of the problems with plastic is our attitude about it. Put something in a garbage bag and everybody, yourself included, leaves it alone. Out of sight, out of mind.

The moths love this. They consider the bagged fiber their little ecosystem and live out generation after generation, always with plenty of food and plenty of sex. Who cares about the view?[12]

Far better are big muslin or sheeting bags. They allow ventilation, don't trap moisture, and are easy to handle. For a closure that keeps wool in and moths out, throttle the bag's opening and put a choker tie on it. To be extra sure, slip a plastic food baggy over the neck after the choker is in place and secure it with twist-ties, freezer tape, whatever.

---

[12] *An acquaintance put 15 pounds of Masham fleece up in small (wastebasket-sized) lots, carefully sealed and packed away. Time passed. A need arose for Masham fleece. Sad to relate, each bag contained some recognizable Masham, a large portion of past and present moth population, and the remainder—composed of whatever fleece becomes after passing through a moth. Moths can live many, many life cycles without seeing daylight.*

Don't store your wool away for years and years, either. Rotate your stock, as they say in the trade. The same goes for other fibers. Mohair, wool/silk blends, wool/anything blends, hairs, exotics, and feathers should be treated the same way. Clean, dry.

Silk is a little different if it is loaded with weight-increasing additives. Then I have no advice for you. If it is pure, or mostly so, store it like wool.

Moths and carpet beetles: How they work

When contending with moths, you need to know who your opponents are and how they operate.

First, moths seek out the sulfur component peculiar to hair, feathers, wool, and down. While they are not really after the sulfur itself, it tells them the kitchen is open. If a substance doesn't have the sulfur, that doesn't mean moths can't or won't eat it, it just means they are not attracted to it.

Second, the larva, not the moth, does the eating. The larvae of two main types of moths do the most damage: the webbing moth, *Tineola biselliella Hummel,* and the case-bearing moth, *Tinea pellionella.*

Third, damage to hangings, tapestry, upholstery, and rugs is usually the work of carpet-beetle larvae, of which there are four main villains: *Anthrenus scrophulariae,* the common carpet beetle or buffalo moth; *A. flavipes* or *A. vorax,* the furniture carpet beetle; *A. verbasci,* the varied carpet beetle; and *Attagenus piceus* or *A. unicolor,* the black carpet beetle.

Fourth, without complete biological and microscopic studies, it is impossible to determine whether damage has been caused by beetle or moth. Not that it matters much.

There are a couple of ways to reduce or control the free-lunch program (to invoke "moth-proofing"). One method is to apply a substance that makes the fiber unattractive or unpalatable to the larvae. Another is to treat the fiber so that it is

Carpet beetle and larva.

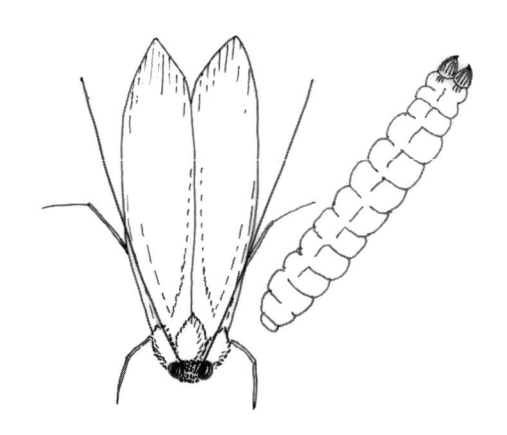

Webbing moth and larva.

specifically toxic to the critters. A third method makes the fiber useless as food for the grubs because they can't digest it, yet nontoxic to humans. The little buggers munch along for a while, then die of starvation.

A common, low-impact method—passive, so to speak—involves storing fiber and fabrics in an atmosphere that is inimical to moths and beetles. For example, you can pack them in an airtight container along with moth balls (paradichlorobenzene, naphthalene), or in a container or display case with a maintained positive pressure of a non-life-supporting gas, such as carbon dioxide or nitrogen. This is how museum displays solve the problem. We wish we could tell you that if you wrap it in old brown paper bags with thyme and rosemary, moths will never harm it. In fact, nothing—repeat, nothing—works like that.

Getting rid of bugs

If you think you have critters in your yarn, woven goods, a sweater, or your sock collection, you can do a few things about it.

Method 1: Get a 5-pound chunk of dry ice and a clean, large trash or garbage can with a good lid. Put half of a Sunday paper in the bottom, place the dry ice on top of the paper, lay the other half of the paper on top of the dry ice, and set the goods on top of that. You can fill the can to just below its top edge. Put the lid on, but don't try to seal the container. Go away for a week or two.

Method 2: Same as above, without the dry ice and the Sunday paper. Use a carbon dioxide cylinder, like the ones for carbonating soda water or pressurizing your Cornelius for home brew. Stick the hose down in the wool, and just crack the valve. Lay the lid in place and go away for fifteen minutes. When you come back, strike a match, lift the lid on the can, and stick the match down inside, just below the rim. If it doesn't go out, put the lid back in place and go away for another fifteen minutes.

Check again. When the match goes out (it just sort of snuffs out), shut off the CO_2, remove the hose, close up the can, and come back in a week or two.

Both of these methods inject carbon dioxide gas. The second method puts the gas in place directly, and the first method derives it from the dry ice. The carbon dioxide, which is heavier than air, displaces the air in the can. Although it is not toxic, carbon dioxide will not sustain life. As long as the can remains undisturbed, it will be full of carbon dioxide and wool. And dead critters.

The problem with this method is that you are never quite sure that it has completed the vermin-killing job. It takes care of the grubs, and pretty quickly at that. The eggs are a different matter. Unless they hatch while the carbon dioxide is still there, too bad.

You know what does work to get rid of bugs? Hot water, soap, sunshine, and fresh air. Real simple stuff. No magic potions.

Although maybe hot, soapy water is a magic potion after all. Look what it does to dirty wool, dirty hands, and dirty faces. . . .

If you do have an item infested with critters, the best plan is to give them, and it, a Viking funeral. Torch it. If you want to save the object, immerse it in soapy water and bring it to a simmer—over 180°F. If you can't get the fabric wet (why not?), try the carbon dioxide treatment, above, or get the thing dry cleaned; dry-cleaning chemicals kill everything.

Keeping stuff in the freezer works, in the sense that nothing happens until spring thaw. . . . You can freeze the grubs solid, but cold doesn't do much to the eggs: that's why they have moths in Minnesota.

We don't know anything about the microwave oven as an insect control device, but it should have the same effect on moths as it did on gremlins. While on the subject, don't put bobbins in the microwave. As for the rest of it (casserole dyeing, setting, and so forth): we have no experience and thus no advice. If you stick your yarn in there, you are on your own.

SETTING TWIST AND STORING YARN

For a quick set on wool and wool-blend yarns, nothing beats steam. If you work often with yarn as an entity (a product), get yourself a portable steam source. If you work with woolens in the dressmaker or tailor sense, you should already have what you need. Used or unwanted garment or drapery steamers show up at flea markets, and one of those little travel steamers that you find for $9.99 at the local StuffLess-Mart will work.

The cellulosics are another matter. Boil them. Wind them onto boiling cores and boil them. Or ply them, wind and tie them into compact skeins, and boil them. But boil them. Add a little soap, if you are using soft water, or a little washing soda, and boil them until the cores or skeins sink, or for a half an hour, whichever takes longer. Once boiled, wind the yarn onto a blocking reel, under "moderate" tension, and allow it to air-dry.

Plied wool yarns can be simmered, as they are when dyed. If you are going to dye yarns as soon as they are plied, fine. Wind off from the primary package (wheel bobbin or spindle copp) to storage bobbins; then ply, wind, and secure in skeins; then into the dye liquor with them. When done with the dye work, scour, rinse, wuzz, and wind the yarn onto a blocker (under "gentle" tension) to air-dry.

Silk will need to be boiled to remove the gum. If the yarns are very fine singles, leave the gum on the fiber until you have woven, knitted, plied, or otherwise combined the singles into larger units. If the yarns are plied, especially if you intend to dye the stuff, get the gum off.

There is considerable pride and self-satisfaction in handling goods of your own making, and that is as it should be. Making yarn is a major accomplishment, and those who debase the task have never done it.

In certain parts of the country, it is worth your while to stop up all your bobbin cores, orifices, holes in general, because of various types of bugs. Wasps, mostly, consider an open hole as an invite to build a house. They don't do real damage, but they do make a mess. So when you put storage bobbins away, plug them or hope for the best. Simply storing your bobbins on a suitable rack, with well-fitting shafts, can do the trick. Pipe cleaners, folded into thirds, can be stuck into the ends of the bobbins and partially bent over to close the openings.

Don't store bobbins away for years and years with yarn in them, unless you really have no choice. The yarn will suffer, and so will the bobbin.

It is not good to store wet or damp-spun yarn (read *flax*) on your wheel bobbin, or any bobbin, for that matter. Bobbins can be, and are, made from damp-proof materials, but the yarn suffers mostly from mold and mildew. Get the yarn out of there and get it dry.[13]

RECORDS

Keep usable records of what you do. You don't need sheets with the name of the sheep, the state of the weather, and all that detail, but you do need information that will let you continue the project if you get sidetracked. *Diverted,* we call it around here.

Every time we get diverted and haven't made project notes, the project gets redesigned. That's not so bad, but the original idea may have been better. We'll never know, will we?

You can continue on your original course if you know: (1) what you need, (2) how much of it you have, and (3) how much more you have to produce. You need to know what the yarn is (grist, twist, and material); any treatments, and if so, what they will be; and what you have planned for the yarn to become.

Make it easy on yourself by deciding on numbers at the start. For example, if you need lebenty-thousand yards of yarn, which is the equivalent of ten storage bobbins, then put ten empty storage bobbins in a nice box. Every time you fill a bobbin, put it in the box and take out one of the emp-

A project sheet helps you keep track.

---

[13] *The very wide arms on early flax flyers gave the yarn a little more chance to dry before being wound onto the bobbin. As far as possibilities of mold and mildew, well, what was the yarn wetted with? Another good reason to boil it. Here's how to damp-proof a bobbin for wet-spinning, if you want to. Heat the bobbin gently until comfortably hot to touch (with a heat lamp, hair dryer, or other controllable heat source). At the same time, carefully (flammable!) melt paraffin (wax) in a double boiler. Paint the inside disks and core of the hot bobbin with the melted wax. Let it cool and there you are. With luck, the bobbin will not warp when full of sloppy, damp yarn. It's still not a good idea to leave wet yarn sitting on a bobbin.*

ties. As long as there are empty storage bobbins in the box, all you have to do is to keep producing the same yarn. Simple, no? Nothing to worry about until you have loaded ten bobbins. Then you turn the page and see what comes next.

Of course, the easiest way to stay on track is to not get off. For some of us staying on track means that at 4 P.M. we have our tea and then we spin for 1 hour and 20 minutes. At 5:30, we start dinner. Some of us get into a project and when it is done we come back to planet Earth. Most of the rest of us just muddle through, depending on our project notes to keep us in line.

THE LUXURY OF HANDSPUN ROPE

There are always times when you have leftover yarns: not enough to do this or that, but too much to throw away. Especially since the resource consists of expensive, hard-to-come-by handspun.

About twice a year we have a thing called "kids' college," which always incorporates a couple of rope/cord classes in which the kids make friendship bracelets and such. We use leftovers for that, the more varied the better.

And we make ropes and cords out of leftovers, for our own use . . . ropes and cords from which we fashion fancy knots, button knots, braiding . . . all sorts of things.

You know, ropes (and the related cords, hawsers, cables, lines, and other bindings and joiners) have held the world together since time out of hand. Rope making is, indeed, an ancient and productive craft.

Rope consists of three or more strands twisted around a common axis. Each strand is made up, or formed, of two or more threads. The threads themselves may be singles or plied yarns. Fibers include flax, hemp, silk, nylon, cotton, jute, abaca, or whatever else comes within reach. Plus rags, raffia, paper, hay, bark, wool, hop vines, rawhide, horsehair. . . .

Rope consists of three or more strands twisted around a common axis. Each strand contains two or more threads.

Making rope

You need several pieces of equipment to make rope, although you can make do pretty well with plenty of helping hands. A *rope jack* or multiple-hook twisting head is almost a must. You need a *top*, or strand divider/controller, as well as something to serve as *tail-hook*. And you will need a linear space; in the old days, this type of space was called a *rope walk*.

A practical rope for a first effort is 12 feet long, with 3 strands, 4 threads per strand.

Step 1: Walk or thread the strands. Components for each strand are strung from jack-hook to tail-hook. Space the jack and the tail-hook 12 feet apart, and allow side clearance for a person to walk back and forth.

Tie the beginning end to the tail-hook. Now, walk down to the jack, and loop your yarn over one of the jack-hooks.

Walk back to the tail-hook, loop over it, and walk back to the jack. Loop over the middle hook, and go back to the tail-hook.

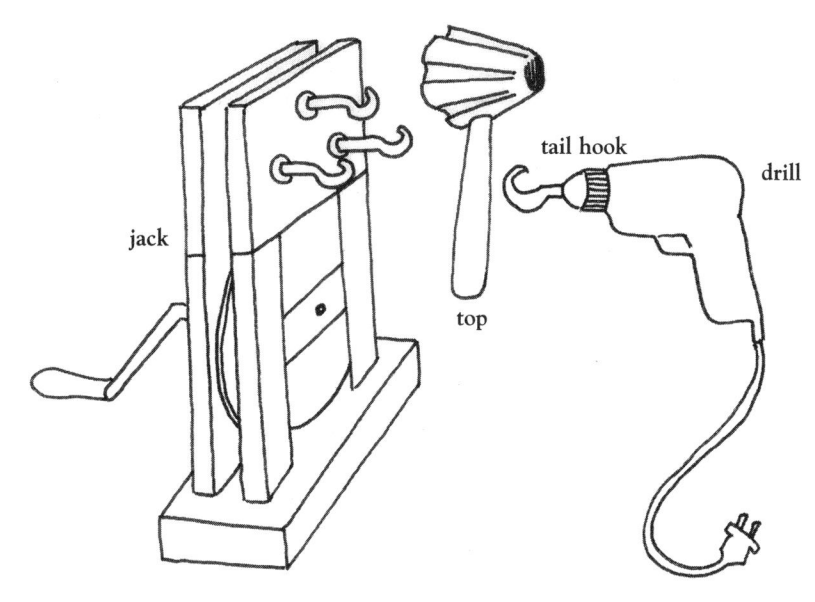

Ropemaking equipment

Loop over it, back to the third hook on the jack, then back to the tail-hook. You now have 2 threads in 3 strands.

Repeat the procedure, so that you have 4 threads on each of 3 jack-hooks. All threads go over the single tail-hook.

Step 2: Form the strands by placing them under tension and twisting them, as appropriate to the end product.

Hold the tail-hook (or have it held) so that it cannot turn. Now, start cranking the jack, rotating it up-twist of the twist direction in the component threads. If your threads are Z, twist in the Z direction. If S, twist S.

Begin a rope by walking the strands.

Keep enough tension between the tail-hook and the jack so that no kinks develop. If they do, stop instantly, down-twist the jack, and remove them. Do not attempt to remove kinks by pulling harder on the jack.

In a "real," or hard-laid, rope, you use enough twist at this stage to shorten the strands by almost a third. In this case, we will settle for about 2 feet, or a sixth. Keep cranking the jack until the tail-hook, even though under tension, is about 2 feet closer to the jack than it was. At all times, prevent the strands from tangling with each other. They will certainly try to, and the solution is to stop, untwist until the mess is cleared up, and then proceed with due caution.

Step 3: Lay the rope. To do this, you will place a top (a spacer or a guide) between the strands at the tail-hook end and advance it toward the jack, while turning the tail-hook to lay up the rope.

Throughout this, the jack continues to up-twist the strands.

Then form the strands by twisting them.

204   The Alden Amos Big Book of Handspinning

Keeping tension on the strands, put the top in place. This keeps the individual strands under control and properly spaced as the rope is laid up.

Slowly move the top toward the jack end, while slowly rotating the tail-hook *in the same direction* as the jack-hooks. The tail-hook will turn at about one-third the speed of the jack-hooks.

Continue to move the top, twist the tail-hook, and twist the jack-hooks. Remove the top as you close in on the jack-hooks.

Finish by laying the rope.

If you do this process evenly and at the right speeds (relative to each other), you will produce a perfect rope. If not, no problem. You can take the rope completely apart and try again.

Step 4: Pack or tender the rope. Put all the strands at the jack end on one of the jack-hooks. Put tension between the jack and the tail-hook, then up-twist with either the jack or the tail hook.

Give the rope a good pull. Whip the ends, trim them, and your rope is ready!

Using rope

What do you do with a handmade rope or cord?

Lots of things: loom cords, basket elements, shade pulls, curtain cuffs, couching, passementeries of all sorts, pet leashes, fair leads, jump ropes, bellpulls, belts, fancy knots, mats, warps, wrappings, fish lines, whitework, fancy braids, sinnets, buttons, laces, net bags, clothes ties, upholstery cording, stool and chair seatings, doormats, trivets, cats' cradles, magic tricks, kid leads, swing ropes, adult fun, sack ties, clotheslines, bolt ropes, latch strings, jewelry, lanyards, string ties, braces, fringes, hammocks, pump packing, tump lines, towropes, plant hangers, button knots . . . . in short, you can make just about any rope you need. Plus you are in a position to control color, fiber, size—all design aspects, really. How can you go wrong?

And you are not limited to handspun yarn, you know. Commercial yarns are often to be had for nothing or a song, and they can be reconstructed in various ways. Let's talk about that a little.

Disassembling Yarn

To reconstruct yarn, or, more exactly, to disassemble existing yarns, you need a blocking reel, a skirder, and a flyer-lead, single-drive spinning wheel. Why flyer-lead? You will see.

Try this initially with two-ply yarn. Begin by loading a few bobbins with yarn. Partial down-twisting, or unplying, occurs as part of the loading process. Thread the two-ply as if for spinning, then merrily unspin it while winding-on. Don't remove all the ply twist, just most of it. Do a neat and tidy job, changing hooks frequently. After preparing a few bobbins this way, you are ready for the next step.

With the yarn coming from the bobbin and through the iron, separate the plies and tie each end onto a common blocking reel. Space the ends 4 to 6 inches apart. Position a skirder so it separates the strands.

Now reduce your take-up (bobbin brake-band tension) to just over zilch, and slowly begin to wind the blocking reel. At the same time, slowly begin treadling in the direction that removes twist. You are reeling the yarn out of the orifice onto the blocking reel, while taking out the remaining twist with the wheel.

If all is going well, your yarn will come apart like magic somewhere between the orifice and the skirder. Stop and rest frequently, and admire your handiwork.

Change bobbin hooks often, especially if there is an increase in effort required to wind-off. Keep going until the bobbin is empty or something is wrong. If something is wrong, STOP! instantly. You cannot treadle your way out of trouble.

Three things can go wrong.

First, you can get ahead of yourself with the treadling. This is the most likely problem and

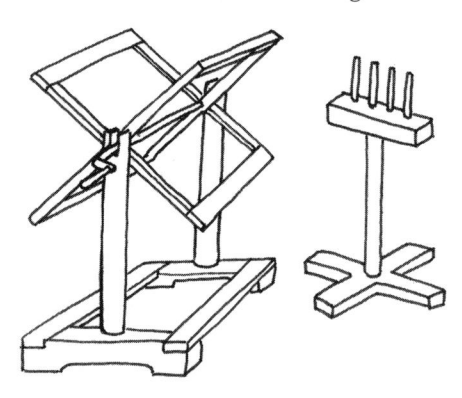

Here's equipment for disassembling yarn: blocking reel (left) and skirder (right).

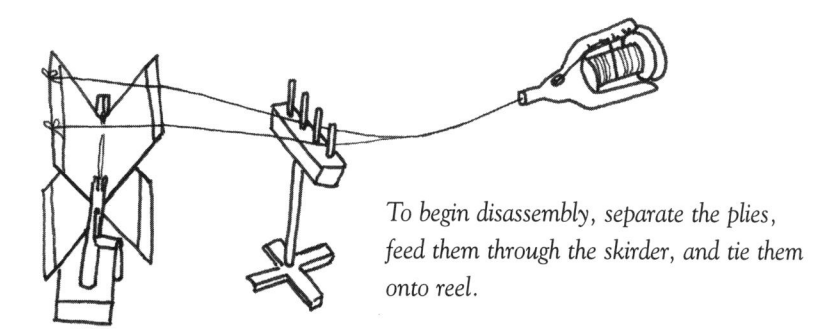

To begin disassembly, separate the plies, feed them through the skirder, and tie them onto reel.

causes the yarn to ply in the opposite direction, so no way is it going to keep on coming apart. Stop treadling. If you think about it, you will see why it is not practical to treadle the other way to straighten this out, but feel free to try.

At a time like this, a helper can be handy. Drag out enough yarn so the amounts of twist cancel each other out. Keep tension on the unplied yarn or it will kink up on you. Wind the extra length onto the reel, and start the normal procedure again.

Second, a sort of horrid little fur collar may form around the "unplying zone." This has a simple solution. Cut the collar with a pair of sharp embroidery scissors or a razor blade, clear away the mess, and press on. Do not try to break the collar loose. The yarns will break first, which brings us to the least likely problem.

Third, you break an end. Simple, tie a knot. The only difficulty will be lost twist, which you can put back in by finger twiddling. However, the broken strand will be shorter than the unbroken one, so you either have to piece in a length of similar yarn. . . . Or break both yarns and tie them at the same time.

Once the yarn has been unplied and the ends have been wound onto the reel, you treat these strands exactly as you would any other lively, high-twist singles. And you know what to do with those, right? See, you can make yarns and not know a lick about spinning.

Chapter 8

Wheel Mechanics: In which are disclosed an astounding number of things, some of which will make you a faster spinner

A spinning wheel is a machine, a contrivance, which serves as an interface between the handspinner and the twisting/spinning device. For our present purposes, that spinning device is either a driven spindle or a flyer-and-bobbin arrangement.

It may seem simplistic to state that driven spindles and flyer arrays are not alike. In that respect, they resemble spinning and plying. At first glance, the concepts seem much the same. In reality and in most ways, the only "alike" part is the context in which they are employed, which is to spin yarns. We shall get to plying in due time.

Now, for some review.

To spin a yarn, we first attenuate a mass of fiber. We strengthen the attenuated fiber strand by rotating it around its own long axis. We call this axial rotation *twisting*, and it can take place during the drafting or after drafting—in short, according to the two spinning systems, woolen and worsted.

Drafting and twisting occur somewhere between fiber supply and twisting device; the locations of these operations are determined by the spinning system being used. Virtually all drafting takes place between the handspinner's hands, despite such stunts as "one-handed" spinning (working against system take-up).

> **USEFUL ABBREVIATIONS FOR THIS CHAPTER IN PARTICULAR**
>
> | | |
> |---|---|
> | DRS | differential rotational speed |
> | EPI | ends per inch |
> | PTPI | plying twists (or turns) per inch |
> | RPM | revolutions per minute |
> | TPI | twists (or turns) per inch |
> | YPP | yards per pound |

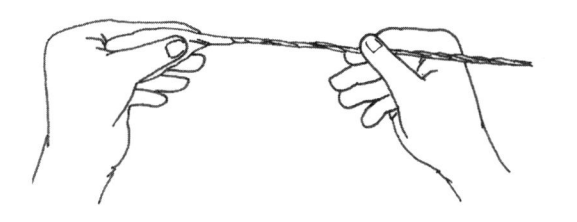

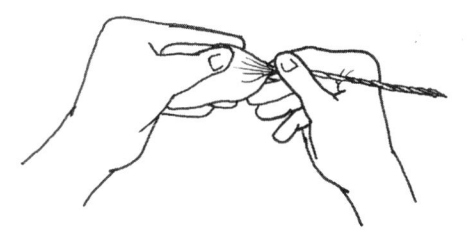

Woolen draft, drafting-against-twist.   *Worsted draft, drafting-without-twist.*

If we are spinning using the woolen system, twist is allowed to enter the drafting zone during drafting, thus the concept of drafting-against-twist.

When we use the worsted system, we prevent twist from entering the drafting zone until we have completed drafting each section, thus drafting-without-twist.

CONTINUOUS AND DISCONTINUOUS SPINNING DEVICES

A flyer-and-bobbin system involves continuous spinning. Whenever the system rotates, twist is being produced and accumulated. In addition, winding-on takes place without any interruption of the twisting process. This means that a flyer system produces twist 100 percent of the time, whether winding-on or not.

A spindle system involves discontinuous spinning. During winding-on, twist production is greatly reduced or even halted. In other words, twist accumulation occurs less than 100 percent of the time—in practice, less than 60 percent of the time.

If you compare the efficiencies of a flyer system and a spindle system, both turning at the same speed, the spindle system is 60 percent as efficient as the flyer system simply because it has to stop twisting while winding-on. This does not mean that spindles are "bad" and flyers are "good." It simply demonstrates that they operate differently. As far as spinning is concerned, they're both pretty good. In fact, for certain yarns and grists, the spindle has no equal—a topic we will discuss later.

Plying is another story. Spindles are flaming bad news for plying. So bad, in fact, that before A.D. 1475 people used flyer-and-bobbin wheels for plying, not for spinning. Leonardo da Vinci worked on the idea of the flyer-and-bobbin mechanism (he did not invent it) and came up with such items as gear-driven hecks (level winders) and broken-end stop-motions. It should be noted that these refinements are necessary for plying multiple yarn ends; they are not needed for single-end handspinning.[1]

Of course, before long someone decided to spin on the flying plying device (a little joke, ha, ha) and found that it worked especially well with flax. Well enough that flyer wheels dominated linen yarn production by the last half of the seventeenth century.[2] Of course, by then everyone had taken a shot at designing the perfect flyer-and-bobbin system. Some strange specimens resulted. Eventually the dust settled and the major types we know today survived.

The flyer-and-bobbin assembly

The flyer-and-bobbin assembly is arguably the most critical group component of a flyer-fitted spinning machine. You can attach a high-class flyer array to a shabby table and wheel and still accomplish good spinning. But if you fit a shabby flyer array onto even the finest of wheels, the best you can hope for are frustration and mediocre performance.

All flyer-and-bobbin systems work upon the principle of differential rotational speed, called DRS for short. That is, winding-on occurs only

---

[1] *For a spinning machine, on the other hand, you need some form of mechanical drafting. Leo never got around to that.*

[2] *Until recent times, a flyer wheel has been more expensive than a great wheel. A flyer wheel has always cost a great deal more than a drop spindle. Why then, the success of the flyer wheel? Simple: for line flax, the great wheel is not much faster than the drop spindle, whereas the flyer system lends itself to the "two-handed" spinning of line flax. The spindle, while slow in production, can be used while you also perform another task, such as herding goats, walking to market, carrying firewood, or minding the geese. As for the flyer wheel . . . well, three flyer wheels fit in the space of one great wheel. It takes minimal expertise to get a flyer wheel to produce yarn (not necessarily good yarn), and you can sit while you work. In short, you can hire the elderly, the feeble, and the very young to operate flyer wheels. Perfect for the factory system. Lots of machinery under one roof and plenty of low-wage, easily replaced, unskilled labor to run the machinery.*

when the flyer rotates faster or slower than the bobbin (conversely, the bobbin rotates faster or slower than the flyer). If both elements turn at the same speed, twisting takes place but winding-on does not.

The three main flyer-and-bobbin systems primarily differ in how they establish and control DRS. Each system has a peculiar "feel" or character in operation, and each system has enthusiastic, even lunatic, fans. The options include (1) those in which both flyer and bobbin are driven, commonly called *double-drive*, (2) those in which only the flyer is driven, called *single-drive, flyer-lead* or *Scotch tension*, and (3) those in which only the bobbin is driven, called *single-drive, bobbin-lead* or *German tension*.

The double-drive system is most often arranged as double-drive, bobbin-lead, although you'll occasionally encounter a double-drive, flyer-lead setup.[3] Any double-drive system can be operated as single-drive, bobbin-lead or as single-drive, flyer-lead. The opposite is not always possible. That is, a single-drive system of either type may not be adaptable to any other configuration.

All flyer systems share three common characteristics of operation, as follows: (1) a steady pull or drag against the working yarn, (2) a specific (restricted) range of production,[4] and (3) limitations on rotational speed, which in turn limit twist accumulation and, ultimately, yarn production.

The first two items—drag and range of production—are interrelated, because they are caused by the same thing: the method used to establish

---

[3] *There is no reason, other than whim, to set up a double-drive as double-drive, flyer-lead. Why expend energy in making the flyer the faster element? It wants to lag. Oh, well. No accounting for tastes. Sometimes an old double-drive flyer array comes across the bench set up as an apparent flyer-lead. This means that someone has swapped whorls, bobbins, or both. According to the owner, the wheel is set up as flyer-lead because "that was the way it was done." Right. If you repair wheels long enough, someone will certainly bring you Priscilla Mullins' original Shaker wheel—the only wheel to come around Cape Horn as deck cargo on the Mayflower.*

[4] *The range, unique to each individual flyer-and-bobbin array, determines which twist and grist relationships it produces effectively.*

The Alden Amos Big Book of Handspinning

Variations on flyer-and-bobbin systems.

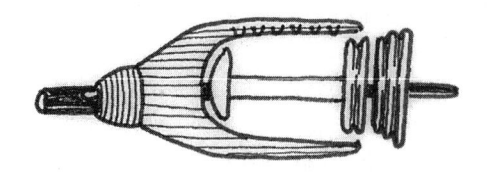

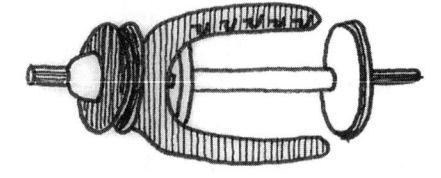

Double-drive.

Single-drive, flyer-lead.

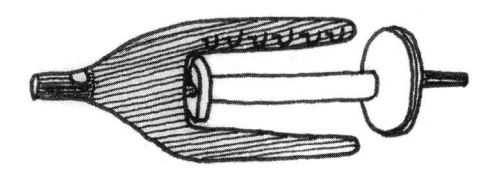

Single-drive, bobbin-lead.

and adjust DRS, and thus yarn take-up (or wind-on). The third item—limitation on rotational speed—is a direct result of all of the above plus friction, wind resistance, centrifugal forces, dynamic imbalance, fiber form, operator technique, dimension and design of the several parts, and the alignment and conjunction of assorted heavenly bodies.

Single-drive, bobbin-lead wheels

The simplest flyer-and-bobbin arrangement is single-drive, bobbin-lead. There is only one drive-band, which drives the bobbin whorl (pulley). The system is called *bobbin-lead* because the bobbin turns faster than the flyer during take-up.

In operation, the driven bobbin tows or drags the flyer along with it, the two being linked together by the yarn. As long as the yarn is held back and cannot wind on, the bobbin and flyer rotate at the same speed, or *in phase*. This state of affairs exists when the handspinner has finished a make and is waiting for twist to build up.

When enough twist has accumulated, the handspinner relaxes tension against the new yarn (called *breaking yarn lock*) and allows it to wind-on. At that moment, the flyer slows down and goes out of phase with the bobbin. The bobbin, being driven, continues to rotate, pretty much at a constant velocity. As a net result, the bobbin winches in a length of yarn, the length being determined by the handspinner's judgment. Once satisfied with the amount wound-on, the handspinner places enough tension on the yarn to prevent further wind-on, thus re-establishing yarn lock. The flyer has no choice but to speed up to match the rotation of the bobbin.

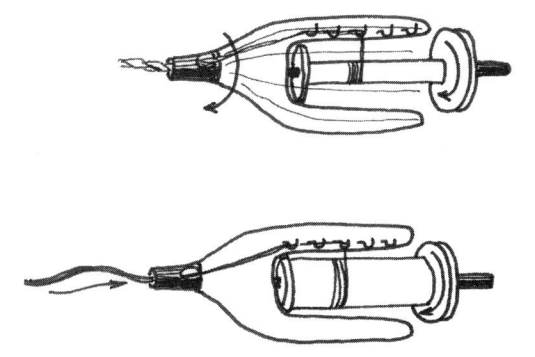

This cycle repeats as necessary. As long as the handspinner maintains yarn lock, the bobbin pulls the flyer around with it. When the handspinner breaks yarn lock to enable winding-on, the bobbin continues to rotate at a constant velocity and the flyer attempts to stall.

Single-drive, bobbin-lead system. During twisting, the bobbin drags the flyer with it, rotating in phase (top). When the spinner breaks yarn lock, the flyer slows down (bottom) and the bobbin reels in the yarn.

The natural take-up characteristic of the system is, in a word, considerable.

The driven element, the bobbin, has little resistance to rotation. The flyer has considerable resistance to rotation and it attempts to slow down, or stall, whenever possible. At the moment the yarn slackens because the handspinner breaks yarn lock, the flyer stalls.[5] Whenever the elements turn at different speeds, winding-on takes place.

You can adjust the take-up on a single-drive, bobbin-lead system in several ways. However, you will usually want the minimum take-up that the system offers. You can make minor increases in take-up by increasing drive-band tension: this increases the support-bearing loads, and thus the flyer drag. You can produce major changes in take-up by introducing friction to the flyer shaft. Most often you do this by (1) adjusting the front support bearing (which supports the orifice barrel) or (2) increasing the

---

[5] *The basic force which causes the flyer to stall is its drag, or resistance to turning. Drag results from the combination of friction (from the flyer support bearings) and wind resistance (of the flyer arms).*

tension on a friction band that crosses a special whorl or the flyer barrel itself.

Spinning high-grist, high-twist yarns on a single-drive, bobbin-lead wheel. Many traditional single-drive, bobbin-lead systems have large, flat, paddle-like flyer arms. These arms have significant windage, or air resistance, which increases dramatically as the flyer turns faster. Because take-up increases as the flyer speed increases (more air resistance, remember?), it makes it impractical to spin fine, high-twist yarns on such a system.

You can increase the flyer speed by (1) by treadling faster or (2) raising the drive ratio between the bobbin whorl and the wheel. No problem there: anyone can treadle a little faster, right? And with a single-drive, bobbin-lead system, you just change the bobbin to change the drive ratio. The smaller the bobbin whorl's diameter, the higher the drive ratio; the larger the whorl, the lower the drive ratio.

However, the problem with these wheels and fine, high-twist yarns does not derive from the drive ratio or your treadling speed. It comes from the design of the flyer. No matter how high the drive ratio is, a flyer that gives you adequate take-up at low speed will give you an intolerable amount of take-up at high speed. And there is not much you can do about that. On the single-drive, bobbin-lead arrangement more than any other flyer system, the physical size of the flyer array determines how fine a yarn can be spun.

Here's a sort of circular catch that shows how hard it is to adjust a single-drive, bobbin-lead wheel for the spinning of fine yarns. The bigger the flyer, the greater the windage and the greater the drag. The greater the drag, the more drive-band tension you need to reduce drag-induced slippage. The more drive-band tension, the greater the bearing load. The greater the bearing load, the greater the drag; the greater the drag, the greater the take-up. . . . You get the idea. Take-up from H"lle, which is the last thing you need when working fine yarns.

It is possible to reduce the amount of take-up that the *handspinner perceives*. You do this by crossing the yarn over several hooks or by winding it once around the flyer arm—that sort of thing. As far as the yarn is concerned, however, the take-up has not been reduced. Even if you don't feel a pull, the yarn does.

Therein lies a major weakness of the system: the yarn must always be strong enough to haul that flyer around. All of the flyer drag must be overcome by the yarn. Even worse, the yarn must be strong enough to bring the flyer up to operating speed from a dead stop. With an underspun yarn, that is impossible. While the yarn may have sufficient twist and strength to maintain the system at speed, it may not have enough to bring it up to tempo.

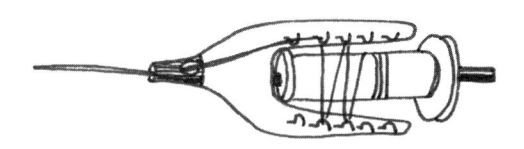

When spinning fine yarns on a single-drive, bobbin-lead system, you can reduce the perceived take-up by crossing the yarn over several hooks.

In order to spin a fine yarn using a single-drive, bobbin-lead system, the flyer itself must be designed accordingly. It must be small, lightweight, balanced, streamlined, and precise. With a bobbin to fit. If the parts are appropriate, very fine yarns may be spun. How fine? 23,000 yards per pound, cotton sliver; 19,000 yards per pound, carded Targhee wool (58's count).

The flyer used was 4½ inches long with an arm spread of 3 inches. The inside dimensions of the bobbin were 2⅜ inches long by 1¾ inches in diameter, with a core ¾-inch in diameter. Drive ratio was 16½-to-1. This particular flyer is capable of spinning much finer yarns, although no one hereabouts has had a reason to test its limits. The yarns needed were for odd projects, and the system was at hand. . . .

That's a small flyer. Most flyers on single-drive, bobbin-lead wheels measure between 5 and 8 inches in length, between 3 and 4 inches in internal diameter, with bobbins to match.

Advantages of the single-drive, bobbin-lead system. As a class, these wheels have several superior points. This is the most efficient flyer-and-bobbin system because it is rarely necessary to introduce additional friction to increase take-up and because these wheels do not require drive-band slippage for operation.

The system is mechanically simple. Other than concentricity and balance, the component fits, dimensions, and parameters are not critical.

It is a flexible and versatile system, second only to the single-drive, flyer-lead system. Any fiber may be spun on it with good results. Some advanced techniques (yarn disassembly and yarn reconstruction) do not

Single-drive, flyer-lead system. The flyer drags the bobbin with it (top), rotating in phase. When the spinner breaks yarn lock, the bobbin slows down (bottom) and the flyer wraps the yarn around it.

work on it, but all conventional plying procedures are satisfactory.

For the beginning wheel-builder, this system is the easiest to fabricate, and for the occasional handspinner of wool, it is an excellent choice.

Historically speaking, this is the oldest of the three systems, having been in continuous use since the last half of the fifteenth century. Even so, it is probably the least common flyer-and-bobbin system in use today.

Single-drive, flyer-lead wheels

Among contemporary wheels, the most frequently encountered flyer system is the single-drive, flyer-lead. Its operation reverses that of the previous system: the flyer is driven at a fairly constant velocity while the bobbin is pulled around behind it. A single drive-band leads over a whorl (pulley) which is attached to the flyer shaft. Only the flyer is driven.

Note that the position of the flyer drive whorl may vary. The whorl may be a permanent part of the flyer arm structure[6] or it may be a separate element, attached at the rear of the flyer shaft.

The bobbin, trapped on the flyer shaft in one of several ways, is free to rotate independently. In addition, one end of the bobbin is equipped with a shallow-grooved brake whorl.[7] When the bobbin is in operating

---

[6] *Located at the end closer to the orifice, that is, at the front of the wheel.*

[7] *Many contemporary wheel makers are offering "double-ended" bobbins — bobbins with drive or brake cord grooves at both ends. The various grooves are of assorted diameters, and the intent is to increase the options available to the spinner. The idea is of some value, except that the groove profiles are seldom suited for their intended use. A good drive-band groove profile is not a good brake-band groove profile. A good bobbin-lead single-drive groove profile is not good for double-drive, bobbin-lead set-ups, and so on. Much of the hoopla surrounding the subject is just that... hoopla. So much so that in some cases, the manufacturer's new and improved will not fit his product. As they say in computerese... not "downwardly compatible". It should be noted that systems set up to operate as single-drive, flyer-lead have no need to change "brake" ratios.*

position, the brake groove is at the rear, or the end farther from the orifice. An adjustable brake-band goes over and around the bobbin's brake groove. This brake-band usually attaches to the mother-of-all or to the flyer-and-bobbin support structure. One end of the brake-band is fastened to an adjusting device, such as a rotating peg, and the other end is attached to the structure by an elastic band, spring, or equivalent arrangement.

During spinning, newly spun yarn goes through the orifice, barrel, and eyes to the flyer arms and heck array (yarn guides), then to the bobbin. As long as the spinner maintains yarn lock, the flyer and the bobbin turn in phase. The driven flyer pulls the bobbin around behind it.

The moment that the spinner breaks yarn lock, the bobbin attempts to stall. The flyer, being driven, continues merrily and wraps yarn around the bobbin core.

The bobbin attempts to stall because of the drag introduced by the adjustable brake, the so-called Scotch tension. The degree of take-up is determined by the eagerness of the bobbin to stall, and that eagerness relates directly to the tension on the bobbin brake-band. The more brake tension, the greater the tendency to stall the bobbin. The greater the stall, the greater the take-up.

By now the astute reader has picked up this system's chief drawback. It requires extra, introduced friction to work. Extra friction means greater treadling effort.[8] Without introduced friction, there is no reason for the bobbin to stall, no change in relative speeds, and no wind-on.

The restraining friction is adjusted by increasing tension on the brake-band via a screw, peg, or winding device. Most modern wheels use a tuning-peg arrangement. Some other setups can be so elaborate that they are hard to figure out.

The single-drive, flyer-lead system has strong points. It is the most

---

[8] *That is why the single-drive, bobbin-lead system is more efficient. Additional friction is rarely required. The inherent flyer friction and drag suffice. For the flyer-lead system, the wheel must overcome built-in drag and must also introduce more friction to enable winding-on. Well, eventually all flyer-and-bobbin systems have to overcome the flyer drag.*

versatile, widest-range configuration of the three main types of flyer-and-bobbin systems. It is forgiving, and tolerant of casual operation—it is not "cranky" or "touchy."

It will also spin very fine yarns, because the take-up can be adjusted to apparent zero. Even though the yarn must be strong enough to pull the bobbin around, the bobbin offers almost no resistance to rotation. The only tense moments (no pun intended) occur while bringing the system up to speed. In fact, the system's greatest efficiency is with spinning of garment-weight yarns (1,200–12,000 YPP). Performance drops off only when excessive friction must be introduced, or when element size and windage prevent appropriate rotational speeds.[9]

The single-drive, flyer-lead system's greatest benefit also presents its greatest weakness. Because the system is able to spin anything (within reason), it will do just that: if you are not paying attention, grist and twist (to a lesser degree) tend to wander around. This is not the system's fault. The tool does exactly what you make it do, or rather whatever you allow it to do.

Neither of the single-drive systems self-regulates. That does not mean that they do bad work; they do what the operator lets them do.

Double-drive wheels

In contrast, the double-drive, bobbin-lead system does tend to self-regulate. For brevity, we will call this simply the double-drive system.

Double-drives have been and can be set up to be double-drive, flyer-lead systems, but are seldom so arranged. Why drive the flyer as the lead element if we don't have a profound reason to do so? Because both elements are driven, there is no reason—profound or trivial—to make the flyer lead.

The double-drive system is arguably the most complex system in use today. It presents several unique characteristics. (1) It is "semi-automatic" in operation, at least where the twist of a particular yarn is

---

[9] It's not just speed: if there were no limitations on the system input power, there would be no problem. If we are speaking of treadled wheels there is a definite problem, and it becomes severe as yarns become thicker (grist drops) and yarn rigidity rises. That statement is true of all systems suited for handspinners. When you apply outside power, you move into an entirely different game that is beyond the scope of this discussion.

concerned, (2) it is precise and "stubborn," relatively speaking, and (3) of the three systems, it is capable of producing the finest yarn.

A double-drive system may be set up to produce a very specific (narrow) range of twists and grists and can virtually force you to stay consistently within the design parameters.

The two single-drive systems may be set up to allow you to produce a very specific (narrow) range of twists and grists, but neither system will force you to be consistent. That is up to you.

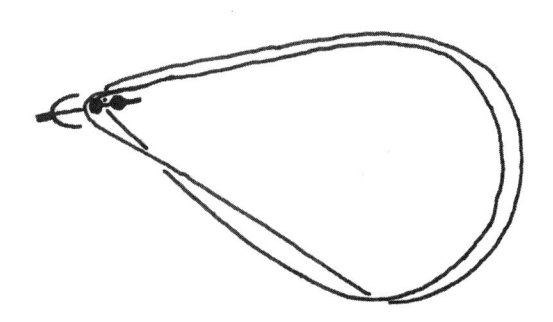

On a double-drive wheel, the drive-band goes around both the flyer and the bobbin. This drive-band is set up for Z spinning.

In the typical double-drive arrangement, a double-length cord is led around the drive wheel, around one of the whorls (bobbin or flyer), over and around the wheel again, and over the other whorl. The two ends of the cord are joined at the drive wheel. When the cord has been properly installed, both strands of the doubled drive-band will run in the groove of the drive wheel and a single strand of the cord will run in the groove of each whorl.

With all adjusted, each rotation of the drive wheel will cause the flyer, and the bobbin, to rotate a certain number of times—let us say 10 revolutions for the flyer and 12 for the bobbin. These are realistic amounts.

Notice that both elements are driven. The flyer is driven, and rotates 10 times, and the bobbin is driven, rotating 12 times, for 1 revolution of a common drive source. These different rotational amounts occur because of the differences in the whorl diameters of the two parts, or elements.

The bobbin whorl, cut into the rear disk, is an integral part of the bobbin. The bobbin itself is supported on the flyer shaft, as in the single-drive systems. If the drive-band has not been installed and no yarn is present, the bobbin can rotate without restriction.

The flyer whorl is attached to the flyer shaft so that it stays rigidly in place while the machine operates but can be removed when necessary.

600 RPM   **600 RPM**

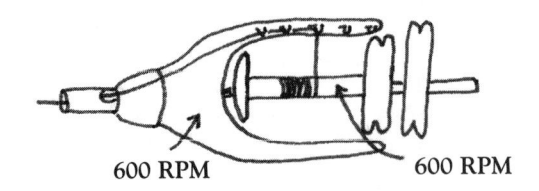

Double-drive wheel. The flyer and the bobbin rotate in phase until yarn lock is broken, at which time the whorl's diameters determine the faster rotating element.

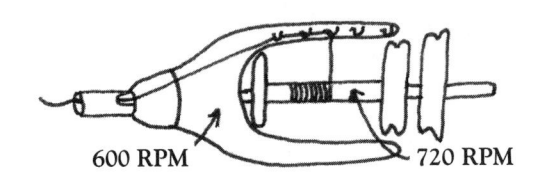

600 RPM   **720 RPM**

During winding-on, the bobbin rotates faster than the flyer, reeling in the yarn.

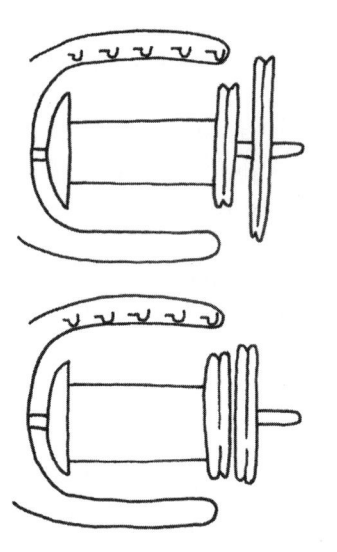

On a double-drive system, you can change to a different flyer whorl to produce more (top) or less (bottom) take-up.

Both whorls (flyer and bobbin) are at the rear of the flyer shaft—at the end opposite the orifice. Once a drive-band has been led over both whorls and the drive wheel, the bobbin is no longer able to turn freely but must respond to its "own" drive-band and drive whorl. The same goes for the flyer. Although the flyer turns "independently" of the bobbin, it responds to its own drive arrangement. All other things being equal, if the bobbin turns 12 times, the flyer turns 10 times.

This differential rotational speed (DRS) relationship between the flyer and the bobbin establishes the major feature of flyer systems, that of continuous take-up. Increase the DRS, increase the take-up. Reduce the DRS, reduce the take-up. Simple, yet subtle.

The two single-drive systems have no proportional mechanism to establish DRS. The double-drive system does: it is the relationship between the diameters of the whorls. Logically, it follows that various diameters of whorls will produce different take-up characteristics. True, but the results are not always what we expect.

Mathematical excursion concerning double-drive wheel mechanics. Before we launch into a discussion of "take-up-ratios" or whatever, let's look further into system operation. While you don't have to do much math with the other two systems, you do have to do some with the double-drive.

Imagine we are spinning away, using a double-drive system with the parameters given in the example—for each revolution of the common drive wheel, the flyer turns 10 times and the bobbin turns 12 times. We will also fit our mathematical spinning device with a wheel diameter, a treadle, and some whorl dimensions. Our drive wheel has an effective diameter of 20 inches, our flyer whorl has an effective diameter of 2 inches, and our bobbin whorl has an effective diameter of $1^{21}/_{32}$ (1.656) inches. We won't work through all the math this time. Take it on faith that the wheel/flyer ratio is 10-to-1 and the wheel/bobbin ratio is 12-to-1.

Let's imagine that we are treadling at 60 treads a minute, or 60 RPM. The flyer turns at 600 RPM. The bobbin, if unhindered, turns at 720 RPM, or 120 RPM faster than the flyer. Let us assume that the bobbin-core diameter is .955 inch; we do this because .955 times pi is 3 inches, so the bobbin-core circumference is a handy number. Thus each additional revolution (relative to the flyer) winds on 3 inches of yarn. [10] In 120 revolutions it winds on 120 times 3 inches, or 360 inches. At the same time, it puts in 720 turns of twist. If we put 720 twists into 360 inches of yarn, that works out as 2 TPI.

No problem at all. Suppose we want to increase the amount of twist in our yarn, say to 3 TPI, or 1,080 twists in 360 inches. We need to figure out what to change.

We can make the bobbin whorl smaller in diameter, which will make it turn faster even though we keep our treadling rate the same. Let's try that. If we need 1,080 twists in one minute from a 20-inch wheel at 60 RPM, we need a wheel/bobbin ratio of 18-to-1, which comes from a bobbin whorl about $1^{1}/_{16}$ inch in diameter. . . . Wait a minute. That whorl will put in 1,080 twists, all right, but it will wind on more than 120 times 3 inches, won't it?

---

[10] *Watch out, though. The circumference increases with each layer of yarn. This will complicate future calculations. For now, though, you can forget this factor.*

Hmm. It will wind on 1,080 minus 600, or 480 turns per minute. [11] Because each turns is worth 3 inches of yarn, that's 1,440 inches. With 1,080 turns, we can only be putting in ¾ TPI.

That can't be it, let's try something else.

What if we treadle faster while keeping the drafting rate the same? At 90 treads per minute and a bobbin ratio of 12-to-1 (the one we started with), we come up with 1,080 turns in one minute. If the yarn pulls onto the bobbin at the same rate as in our first scenario, 360 inches per minute, we will achieve our 3 TPI. Let's take a look at the rest.

The flyer is going at 900 RPM (90 times 10) and the bobbin at 1,080 RPM (90 times 12). The difference between the two indicates that the wheel will wind on at the rate of 180 revolutions per minute. Each revolution puts 3 inches of yarn on the bobbin. There are 180 times 3 inches of yarn going onto the bobbin every minute, or 540 inches. Looks good, and 1,080 turns divided by 540 inches equals . . . wait a minute. 2 TPI?

This is not working. Increasing the treadling speed doesn't solve our problem. And it can't, unless something else changes.

You have probably guessed the answer by now. If we reduce the DRS, or differential rotational speed, we increase the twist per unit of length, and if we increase the DRS, we decrease the twist per unit of length.

Let's see if we can get this system to do what we want. We'll start by reviewing our parameters. We want the DRS to be 120 RPM (because we want to wind on 120 x 3 inches, or 360 inches) and we need 1,080 RPM on the bobbin (so we can put 3 TPI in that 360 inches of yarn).

This means we need a flyer speed of 1,080 RPM minus 120 RPM, or 960 RPM, to get a DRS of 120 RPM and a twist rate of 1,080 RPM.

Remember that we have a 20-inch wheel. Let's assume we are treadling it 90 times a minute. What whorl-to-wheel ratios do we need now?

The bobbin/wheel ratio of 12-to-1 seems to be working. It is giving us the twist rate that we want (12 × 90 = 1,080), so let's leave it alone.

---

[11] *The treadling rate remains at 60. The 1,080 comes from 18 × 60 (18-to-1 ratio of bobbin whorl) and the 600 comes from the established flyer-whorl ratio of 10-to-1. The difference between the two gives the wind-on rate of 480 turns per minute.*

To reduce that DRS, we do have to speed up the flyer, to reduce that DRS. In fact, we want the flyer to turn at 960 RPM. The treadle speed is 90 RPM. How many times do we have to multiply that to get 960 RPM? The answer is 10.6666+, so we will round it off to 10.7. The flyer/wheel ratio is 10.7-to-1.

Because we have a 20-inch wheel, we calculate the effective flyer-whorl diameter by dividing the drive-wheel effective diameter by the flyer/wheel ratio. Okay, 20 divided by 10.7 = 1.87 inches. Our flyer whorl needs to be about 1⅞ inch in diameter.

All right, let's put it all together. We are treadling at 90 treads per minute, so the drive wheel is turning at 90 RPM.

Because this is a bobbin-lead system, the bobbin is the lead element and the flyer is the lag (as in *lags behind*) element. Remember that; it will save a lot of ink later on.

The flyer whorl-to-wheel ratio is 10.7-to-1, so the flyer turns at 90 × 10.7 = 963 RPM. Forget the 3 RPM, which represent a negligible 3 twists in 360 inches. Call it 960 RPM.

The bobbin whorl-to-wheel ratio is 12-to-1, so the bobbin turns at 90 × 12 = 1,080 RPM.

The DRS equals lead RPM (1,080) minus lag RPM (960), or 120 RPM.

If the bobbin winds on 3 inches of yarn per relative rotation, then it winds 120 × 3 inches per minute, or 360 inches.

If, in the same minute, we put 1,080 twists into that 360 inches of yarn, the average TPI must be 1,080 divided by 360, or 3 TPI.

Talking DRS. The abbreviation DRS (differential rotational speed) can be stated in a couple of different ways: (1) as we just did, you can use it in the context of a mathematical example, stated as the number of revolutions relative to the opposite element, or (2) as a numerical value—one of those "take-up ratios" that spice up a workshop conversation. For those of you who want to wade through the math and concepts for establishing DRS, we have stuck the heavy stuff into Chapter 13 ("Noils, linters, and thrums"). In order to proceed without the digression, you need to simply accept that changes in bobbin-core diameter can be significant.

Slippage saves the day

Now that we have settled that, the next question is how to deal with it. The long, big bobbin idea works, and is used by industry. As we've pointed out, it is impractical for contemporary handspinning.[12]

We cannot prevent the bobbin core from changing diameter, but we can establish a DRS so high that the effects of the changes become irrelevant. Take it on faith that a DRS ratio of 1.5, which means the bobbin turns 1½ times faster than the flyer, is substantial. When the flyer is at 1,000 RPM, the bobbin is at 1,500 RPM.

With a bobbin-core diameter of .955 inches (empty), 1,500 inches of yarn will be wound on per minute. With a bobbin-core diameter of 2½ inches (full), 3,926 inches will be wound on in the same amount of time.

Of course, that is far too fast a wind-on to allow any twist build-up. In the first example, 1,500 inches of yarn wind on with only 500 turns, and in the second almost 4,000 inches of yarn wind on, still with only 500 turns. What to do?

Slippage one. Simple. Slippage. We let the bobbin stay in phase longer, thereby reducing the effective DRS, and we do this by maintaining yarn lock. Until we break yarn lock again, the bobbin has no choice but to pull the flyer around behind it in phase. So the wheel behaves as a single-drive, bobbin-lead system, except that the terrible inherent drag of the single-drive system has been conquered. Most of the work in pulling the flyer around is being done by the double-drive arrangement, in particular by the flyer drive whorl.

To visualize this, imagine two systems side by side. One is our double-drive, bobbin-lead example and the other is single-drive, bobbin-lead. Other than that, they are identical: same size, same bearings, same cross-section to the flyer, spinning the same yarn at the same speed.

We have been using a model yarn of 3,600 YPP with 4 TPI. In real life, that yarn would not have enough twist. It would drift and it would be difficult, if not impossible, to spin on a single-drive, bobbin-lead system

---

[12] *In drawing down rovings, an adaptation of the flyer-and-bobbin array is used. The device actually changes DRS for each complete layer placed on the bobbin core. This is necessary because the drawn sliver has no twist and no strength and can only endure winding-on as a passive element.*

because a self-drafting yarn cannot pull the flyer around. The flyer wants to stall and the yarn does not have enough strength to prevent it.

Because yarn strength has little to do with the operation of a double-drive system, soft, low-twist yarns are practical.

There is a paradox, however. Because a high DRS is necessary to reduce twist amounts per unit length, take-up is thereby increased. Thus, increased pull on the yarn. And if we increase the pull on the yarn, the yarn needs to be stronger to take the pull, right?

Slippage two. Absolutely right. We don't really resolve or eliminate the paradox, but there is a sort of work-around: slippage, again. In a practical double-drive system, both elements slip. The object with the smaller diameter, the bobbin whorl, slips more than the object with the larger diameter, the flyer whorl. But they both slip.

Which introduces yet another paradox. To increase efficiency in any twisting system, we need to reduce slippage; to make *this* system work, we *introduce* slippage.

En debrouillage d'un paradoxe, il faut un autre invoquer. Every spinning book needs a little French to give it some class. Especially when speaking of flyer-and-bobbin systems.[13]

The necessary (introduced) slippage can be closely controlled through four factors: (1) the *physical size of the whorls* themselves, a factor which includes the drive ratio as well as the *swept area*, or effective friction area, (2) the widths and cross-section profiles of *the whorl groove(s)*, (3) the system's design *differential rotational speed (DRS)*, and (4) the *amount of slippage*.

Let's look at each of these in turn.

Physical size of the whorls, including drive ratio and swept area. The larger in diameter a driven whorl is, the greater its swept area. A quick example: say we have a 20-inch wheel and a 2-inch whorl. The drive ratio is 10-to-1, and the whorl swept area equals about 45 percent of its

---

[13] *This translates approximately as "In the unraveling of a paradox, it is necessary to invoke another," a quote from the Greatest Lady of Spinning, Stephenie Gaustad, who made this remark during a discussion on flyer-and-bobbin mechanics.*

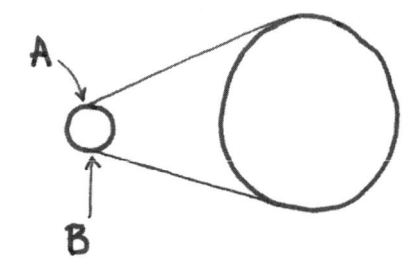

The swept area is the portion of a whorl in contact with the drive-band.

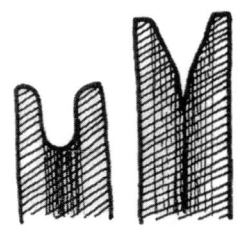

Here are classic groove profiles for the bobbin (left) and the flyer (right), in relation to the grist of the drive-band.

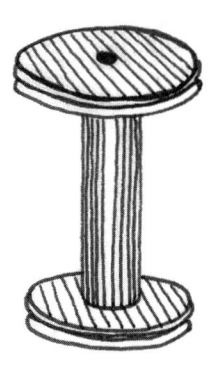

On a double-ended bobbin, you change whorls by reversing the bobbin on the flyer shaft.

circumference. Its full circumference is 2 inches (diameter) x 3.1415 or 6.283 inches; 45 percent of that is the swept area, 2.827 inches.

Now imagine that we have a 30-inch wheel. With a 10-to-1 drive ratio, the whorl diameter must be 3 inches. The circumference is 3 inches x 3.1415, or 9.424 inches; 45 percent of that is 4.241 inches.

And the greater the swept area, the lower the drive-band tension needs to be, resulting in less load on the bearings and less drag.

Width and cross section of the whorl groove. This factor has more effect upon system character than any other item.

Generally, bobbin-whorl grooves should be fairly wide and round-bottomed, while flyer-whorl grooves should be fairly narrow and v-bottomed. Both types of groove should be between 10 and 15 diameters deep, the diameter in question being that of an appropriate drive-band. The flyer-whorl grooves should be about ½ diameter wide at the bottom of the groove; the bobbin-whorl groove should be 1 diameter wide.

Differential rotational speed. The designed DRS is, of course, determined by the physical sizes of the two whorls, and the differential between them.

It is not uncommon for a flyer whorl to have more than one groove: two is the norm, and occasionally you will find three. More than three is showmanship, more than anything else. Some wheels come with additional flyer whorls, although they usually cost extra.

Contemporary bobbins often feature multiple whorl grooves, with the "double-ended bobbin" being currently in favor. The idea is to give the spinner "more options."

Slippage. Those first three factors are built into the system and cannot be adjusted during a spinning session. The real adjustment opportunities involve the fourth factor. The slippage may be adjusted at any time by increasing or decreasing drive-band tension.

An increase in drive-band tension reduces slippage and forces the system behavior to become more in line with the designed DRS. All things being equal, that means take-up increases and twist-per-unit length drops.

A decrease in drive-band tension increases slippage, which allows the system behavior to diverge from the designed DRS. Again, all things being equal, the take-up decreases and twist-per-unit length increases.

Let's imagine that we are spinning away with a typical double-drive system. We are at a point in the cycle where we have just started winding-on. Because we have broken yarn lock, the bobbin and flyer are going out of phase.

In a "model" system, the bobbin accelerates to the maximum allowed by the DRS, while the flyer speed remains constant. At the end of wind-on, yarn tension again rises, forcing the system into phase. The bobbin slows down to match the constant flyer speed.

Not in real life. In fact, whenever yarn block is broken, the bobbin speeds up and the flyer slows down. Whenever yarn lock is established, the bobbin slows down and the flyer speeds up.

They don't speed up or slow down in equal measure. The whorl with the greatest swept area (larger diameter) changes speed less than the other, and the whorl with the least swept area (smaller diameter) changes speed more than the other. In addition, increases in drive-band tension have greater effect on a V-groove configuration than on a U-groove one.

The net result is that whenever yarn lock is established (or when the two elements are in phase as a result of yarn lock), the flyer speeds up "a little" and the bobbin slows down "a little more."

Digression on effective drive ratio of the array as a whole. How do you calculate the effective drive ratio of the double-drive flyer-and-bobbin array as a whole? Answer: The effective drive ratio is approximately 6 percent less than the average of the two ratios. This is based on the premise that the system must have slippage, and in an ideal system that slippage is at least 6 percent.

Example: the flyer whorl is at 10-to-1 and the bobbin whorl is at 12-to-1. 10 + 12 = 22; 22 divided by 2 = 11; 11 x 6% = .6; 11–.6 = 10.4. The effective drive ratio is about 10.4-to-1.

Another one: the flyer whorl is 12.5-to-1 and the bobbin whorl 18-to-1. 12.5 + 18 = 30.5; 30.5 divided by 2 = 15.25; 15.25 x 6% = .915; 15.25–.915 = 14.34. The effective drive ratio is 14.34-to-1.

Slippage continued. Back to our story. About 4 to 5 percent of that slippage takes place on the bobbin whorl. The remaining 1 to 2 percent is lost somewhere between the wheel surface and the flyer whorl.[14]

In a well-designed and properly adjusted system, our friend "creep" amounts to about 1 percent loss. Notice *well-designed* and *properly adjusted*. Sad but true, far too many wheel-builders (and users) know little about flyer-and-bobbin function or design. As a wheel user, you can't do much about the well-designed part, but you can do something about the properly adjusted part, beginning with your own attitude.

Do not expect the flyer-and-bobbin array to be able to spin something that it cannot spin. Further, do not expect the flyer-and-bobbin array to furnish expertise, or to enhance your own skill, through mere possession.

---

[14] *In real life, spinning wheels show an overall slippage loss of between 8 and 50 percent, measured by comparing the number of actual flyer-and-bobbin turns during a test run with the number of theoretical flyer-and-bobbin turns during a calculated run. For example, with a single-drive, flyer-lead system having a flyer whorl-to-wheel ratio of 10-to-1, the flyer should rotate 10 times for each revolution of the drive wheel. It may do so during a slow tabletop demonstration. Under spinning conditions, it does not. At a rate of 60 treadles per minute, the flyer-and-bobbin array should accumulate 600 turns per minute. In practice, it will accumulate at most 540 or 560 turns. The difference between 600 and 560 may be expressed in various ways. Normally it is stated as a percentage loss with respect to the theoretical amount: 600 minus 560 = 40, and 40 divided by 600 = about 6.7 percent. Now, as drive ratios increase and swept area decreases, both operational speeds and slippage increase. In double-drive systems, where slippage must be present for the system to work, the lowest possible amount of slippage is something like 6 percent. The single-drive, bobbin-lead system shows the least slippage loss in operation. Unfortunately, this is often offset by the typical single-drive, bobbin-lead flyer's deplorable aerodynamics and monster drag.*

It will not do so. *L'avoir n'est pas savoir.* A little more for the Francophiles.[15]

Double-drive wheel adjustments

A study of flyer-and-bobbin adjustments is a study of "just enoughs," or minimums. The correct amount is just enough to accomplish the desired effect, and almost all adjustments will involve trade-offs.

For example, we want to reduce slippage so there is no lost motion. To do so, we must increase drive-band tension. Increasing the drive-band tension increases the effective take-up (DRS, but let's keep this simple) and increases the drag on the system (bearing loads), making the wheel harder to treadle.

You get the idea. The double-drive, bobbin-lead system is anything but simple. Still, you do not have to know much about it to do good work, as long as things are going well. When things are *not* going well, it behooves you to understand more about the system and its operation.

Testing the drive-band tension. Here's an easy, preliminary check for the correct amount of drive-band tension. It involves the reverse of spinning. If you can strip the yarn (that you are spinning) off of the bobbin, by way of the heck, eyes, and orifice, you've got the tension right. To do this test, first stop spinning. Manually rotate the wheel and the flyer-and-bobbin array to an at-rest condition. Pull the yarn out through the orifice, slowly and carefully. If the bobbin slips "just enough" to allow this, without the flyer rotating, then drive-band tension is about right.

This test works as long as all is in order: the bearings are clear, properly lubricated, and aligned; the bobbin is reasonably well (uniformly) wound; the yarn has sufficient twist for its intended use; there is no binding or interference with the bobbin or the flyer arms; and the yarn path is clear, with no snags or rough spots.

---

[15] Roughly, *"Just because you have it doesn't mean you know anything about it."* Literally, "to have it is not to know it." Ah, the French. Attributed to Erik Satie, after learning that a student had bought an old saxophone at a Paris secondhand shop (circa 1912).

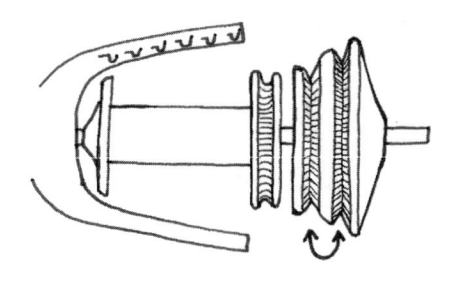

To change the default range of yarns spun by a double-drive, bobbin-lead system start by selecting a different groove on the flyer whorl.

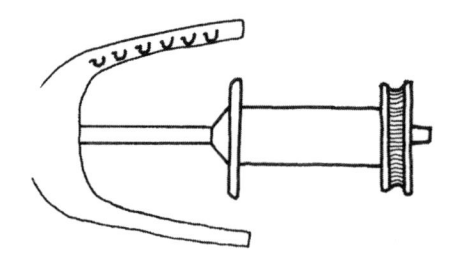

Then select a different bobbin-whorl size.

As you can see, that test covers a lot of territory. If you get by that one, then comes the biggie. This test is the definitive one.

In this test, you sit at your wheel, treadle at your natural rate, spin exactly the yarn you are after, as fast or as slow as you want to go, bobbin after bobbin, with no fanfare, no hoopla, whenever you like, and as often as you like. The wheel just puts in twist and takes the yarn away, smoothly, with so little hassle that you take it for granted.

When that happens, you probably have everything adjusted right.

Adjusting to spin a different range of yarns. To change the default range of yarns spun by a double-drive, bobbin-lead system, you change the DRS. Usually you start by selecting another groove on the flyer whorl. Remember that the farther apart in diameter the bobbin and flyer whorls are, the greater the DRS; the closer together they are, the lower the DRS.[16] The next option involves changing the bobbin-whorl size. Again, the farther apart the effective diameters are, the greater the DRS; the closer together, the lower the DRS.

The third option with a double-drive system is to change it into one of the single-drive configurations. This is not as uncommon as you might think. The change is usually to the single-drive, flyer-lead mode. In a single-drive system, you don't have quite the same situation as with a double-drive. That should seem pretty obvious. The point is not *that* the wheel is different, but *how* it is different. And it is a whole lot different.

---

[16] *Don't confuse that with drive ratio. As we noted a page or so ago, on a double-drive system, the drive ratio equals ½ the sum of the two (effective) groove diameters, minus 6 percent.*

Solving a double-drive equation by operating the wheel as single-drive, flyer-lead

Let's say we have a spinning situation with a single-drive, flyer-lead system. The current flyer speed is 1,500 RPM, and the bobbin is in phase.

Now, let's break yarn lock. Instantly, the bobbin attempts to stall. If we ran enough yarn in, fast enough, the bobbin would stall—stop completely—while the flyer continued at 1,500 RPM.

Normally, DRS equals lead speed divided by lag speed, which in this case is 1,500 RPM divided by 0, or 0. We cannot have a DRS of 0, since the mathematical model requires that both flyer and bobbin have to be turning. To cut this digression short, we will say that the minimum number of rotations of the lag element is 1. Thus, the theoretical DRS will work out as 1,500 RPM.

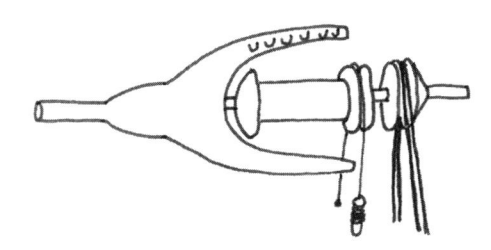

To get what you want from a double-drive wheel, you can also convert it to single drive, flyer-lead operation. This is a big change.

Wow! That is a lot of take-up! In a practical system, we need much lower differential speeds, and in the single-drive system we really make the DRS dependent upon how fast we run the yarn in during wind-on. The faster the run-in, the higher the DRS; the slower the run-in, the lower the DRS.

The double-drive is a little different. With the double-drive, you can run in yarn (or wind on) only as fast as the two whorls will let you. In other words, the DRS is limited by the fixed mechanical ratio of the two whorls. In a double-drive system, it is no stunt at all to set up a DRS ratio of whatever you want, within reason. Want no take-up? A DRS ratio of 1-to-1 will do the trick. Want moderate take-up? Use a ratio of 1.25-to-1. Want a real winch effect? Go to a DRS ratio of 2-to-1. We do this by adjusting the diameter of the several whorls.

Not so easy with the single-drive systems, because there is only one whorl: as a result, the DRS is in direct proportion to bobbin-core diameter, to the linear speed of wind-on, and to the rotational speed of the leading element.

It's still DRS or differential rotational speed, but there is only one whorl: so we will come at it in a different way. Get your yellow pads and

#3 pencils. Let us imagine that it is a single-drive, flyer-lead system, with a flyer whorl-to-wheel ratio of 12-to-1.

Let's further say we are operating the flyer at 600 RPM, and that the bobbin-core diameter is our convenient .955 inches. Say we have decided we want to produce a yarn that has 3 TPI. The question is, how frequently and for how long must we break yarn lock to get what we want?

Each relative rotation of flyer and bobbin will wind on 3 inches of yarn. Because we want 3 TPI, we need 9 turns of the bobbin for each 10 turns of the flyer. So we divide lead by lag to find our DRS. 10/9 = 1.11+. This 1.11-to-1 DRS only holds true as long as we have a bobbin-core diameter of .955 inches. Or. . . .

Or we run in 3 inches of yarn for every 10 turns of the flyer, and to hell with the bobbin-core diameter, or DRS, or anything like that. And the easiest way to do that is to wind-on 30 inches of yarn for every 100 turns of the flyer, or 180 inches of yarn for every 600 rotations of the flyer.

While you're thinking on that one, here's something else to think about. The twist incumbent in a length of newly spun yarn is determined by how many times the beginning end of the yarn has rotated with respect to the working (drafting) end of the yarn. Because the beginning end of the yarn is attached to a bobbin, by logical extension we can say the twist in a length of yarn is determined by how many times the bobbin has rotated with respect to the working end of the yarn.

Now, in a flyer-lead system, the bobbin slows down or stalls to enable wind-on. The first thing to consider is whether the bobbin rotations per minute equal those of the flyer. Answer: No, they do not. They cannot. The bobbin must lag to enable winding-on. Next question: If the bobbin is accumulating fewer RPMs than the flyer, how is drive ratio calculated? Answer: It ain't easy. The effective drive ratio constantly increases as the bobbin-core diameter builds up.

We can avoid going through another tedious arithmetic lesson if you will take the following figures on faith.

Single-drive, flyer-lead systems have an effective drive ratio of 82 percent of the flyer whorl-to-wheel ratio at the beginning of a session—that is, with a bobbin core of 1 inch in diameter (or less). The same unit will have an effective drive ratio of 95 percent of the flyer whorl-to-wheel ratio at the close of a session—that is, when the bobbin core is at a diameter of at least 2½ inches.

The amounts vary somewhat. Core diameters less than 1 inch result in lower beginning ratios. The normal core diameter for an extremely well-known wheel from New Zealand ranges between ⅝ inch and the metric equivalent of ⅞ inch.[17] Going the other way doesn't work miracles. By the time bobbin-core diameter exceeds 2½ or 3 inches, overall system efficiency is such that a percent or two of gain is a moral victory, at best.

In sum, single-drive, flyer-lead systems become more efficient at putting in twist as the bobbin-core diameter increases. About 15 percent more efficient, overall. The reason is simple. The fuller the bobbin, the less time it spends in stall, or lagging behind.

Why? More yarn wraps around in each relative rotation, so the system spends more time turning and less time stalling. As a result, the bobbin turns "faster." Well, it racks up more turns per unit of time, which amounts to the same thing. And the more the bobbin turns, the more twist it puts in.

Changes in twist amounts during winding-off

That opens a can of worms—the whole mystique about whether twist amounts increase or decrease during winding-off. Several authorities have made some amazing statements about this topic.

There is no question that you can adjust (raise or lower) the amount of twist in a yarn, depending upon how you wind off the bobbins. However, the *amount* of adjustment is small, one might say insignificant.

Here is what we determined by actual measurement, using bobbins from a well-advertised Colorado wheel. We carefully filled the bobbins with a commercial two-ply yarn of 750 YPP, 2 PTPI. When filled "disk-to-disk," they contained about 404 yards. We side-wound the

---

[17] *Ashford has slightly shifted the diameters of their bobbin cores over the years, and ultimately converted to entirely metric measurements.*

bobbins using a bobbin winder, taking the yarn from another side-delivery package (skeins on a swift). We then wound off the bobbins from their ends, as one would a yarn cone, and ran 1-yard twist samples on perhaps eight or ten lengths. The change in twist amounted to 6.3 turns per yard, which equals .175 TPI, or just over 1/6 TPI.

Using the same procedure on an ubiquitous New Zealand wheel netted similar results. With the same yarn and "old-style" bobbins, disk-to-disk capacity was about 266 yards. The change in twist amounted to 7.66 turns per yard, or .213 TPI, just under 1/5 TPI.[18]

Well, what if you wind it off through the flyer barrel and orifice? If you wind off through the orifice, allowing the bobbin to turn, you are winding off as a side-delivery package. If you wind off through the orifice, holding the bobbin and allowing the flyer to turn, you are winding off as an end-delivery package. (If the bobbin is from a bobbin-lead system, you are increasing twist. If it is from a flyer-lead system, you are reducing twist.)

Frankly, if you wind off through the orifice for any reason, you need to share this fact with your fellow spinners . . . maybe we can help you.

---

[18] *The twist amount available to play with is equal to the number of turns it takes to load the bobbin with a given length of the subject yarn. That in turn is determined by the yarn diameter, the bobbin's bare core diameter, and the distance, in yarn diameters, between disks. In essence, the smaller the bare core, the more turns it takes to load that bobbin with a given amount of yarn. The yarn diameter matters as well. The finer the yarn, the more turns required to wind it on. On the other hand, the twist component of fine yarns is normally so high that any gain or loss in twist due to winding-off is lost in the woodwork. For example, identical tests with two types of New Zealand bobbins (the only difference involved the core diameters) and a 3,600 YPP, 8.5 TPI yarn ended up as follows. The small-core bobbin (.625 diameter) took 34 wraps (layers) to load 780 yards of yarn. The large-core bobbin (.875 diameter) took 30 wraps (layers) to load 782 yards. Potential twist change for the small-core lot was about .26 TPI; for the large-core lot it was about .23 TPI. Let's round that off to .25, or ¼ TPI. That amount of change would make a difference if our incumbent twist was 1½ TPI, because it represents about 17 percent of the total twist per inch. In the case of our 8½ TPI, it represents less than 3 percent of the total twist per inch. The topic resembles drive-band slippage—nobody pays any attention until troubles begin. The textile industries use an item called a two-for-one twister to exploit the concept, but it is not a burning issue in handspinning. Or is it?*

To wind off a bobbin without changing the incumbent twist, wind it off as a side-delivery package.

To wind off a bobbin while changing the incumbent twist, wind it off as an end-delivery package.

To re-wind yarn for the sole purpose of increasing its twist count is hardly worthwhile. When done in conjunction with other procedures, fine . . . press on. But where twist is concerned, it is far better to run the yarn through the wheel a second time. This is an operation known as up-twisting or down-twisting, depending on which way you go.

Winding the yarn off a bobbin or cone from either end changes its twist.

Additional notes on flyer-and-bobbin wheels

Scotch tension (single-drive, flyer-lead). Single-drive, flyer-lead systems are equipped with what is commonly called *Scotch tension*. In most applications the arrangement consists of a brake-band, attached at one end to an adjusting device at the other end to a flexible connection. This flexible connection can be a rubber band, an extension spring, a doubled length of yarn, or a simple weight. In any case, the brake-band should be routed so that the flexible connection yields in the direction of bobbin rotation. That is, the bobbin (on the brake-band) should pull or drag against the solidly anchored end of the cord, not against the flexible connection.[19]

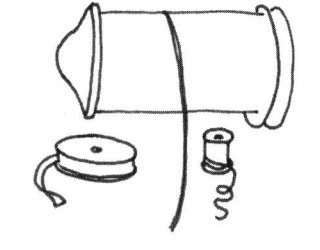

Winding the yarn off any package from the side does not change its twist.

German tension (single-drive, bobbin-lead). On a single-drive, bobbin-lead system, the equivalent arrangement is called *German tension*. It needs about as little adjustment as you can give it. The default take-up is most often "somewhat more than adequate," at least for garment-weight yarns. (For our present purpose, a garment-weight yarn is any single yarn that would sett square at 12 EPI. Say about 1,200 YPP, with between 4 and 6 TPI.)

The single-drive, bobbin-lead system is unique because it feels "sponge-like." There is often a hesitation, or soft spot, as the handspin-

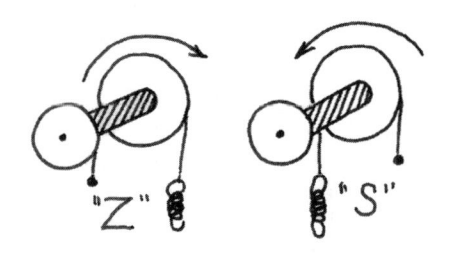

The flexible connection at one end of a brake-band should be in the direction of bobbin rotation. This means that its ideal position changes depending on direction of twist.

ner breaks yarn lock. This can be followed by a rapid increase in take-up. It may also be followed by a period of "not enough" or "mushy" take-up, and a sudden jerk as yarn lock is re-established.

The thing to remember on this system is that while the take-up is relentless, it is quite variable and will require getting used to.

Variations on the three flyer-and-bobbin types. There are a vast number of variations on the three flyer-and-bobbin types, including those with no orifice, no hooks, no bobbin, no flyer, no flyer arms—and we are not talking about spindle systems, but variations on bobbin-and-flyer arrangements.

DRIVEN SPINDLES

Now let us consider a set of systems with no take-up at all: the driven spindles.

A driven spindle receives rotary motion from an intermediate mechanical device, such as a drive wheel, and not directly from the operator's hand or foot. This requires that the spindle be supported between fixed bearing points. A *great wheel* is an example of a driven spindle.

Spindle spinning is discontinuous. The spindle turns in a given direction during winding-on, drafting, and twisting, then is stopped and turned in the other direction to clear the spindle blade. Rotation in the original direction then resumes, beginning the next cycle of winding-on, drafting, and twisting.

In spite of their stop-and-go operation, driven spindles have advantages over flyer-and-bobbin systems. For example, flyer systems cannot

---

[19] *The flexible connection (spring, rubber band, weight, whatever) maintains only a minimum amount of tension on the brake-band, thus establishing "default" friction. Hook it up the other way and you will have nothing but trouble, sprung springs, flying bands, all sorts of lurid stuff. Don't argue, just do it right.*

Discontinuous spinning consists of three steps: drafting and twisting (a), clearing the spindle tip (b), and winding-on (c).

attain the rotational speeds of spindles—driven spindles can put in twist much faster.

Consequently, driven spindles work well for fine, high-twist yarns, which require large amounts of twist. In addition, practical flyer-and-bobbin systems impose a relentless and often frustrating pull on the yarn. Driven spindles never do this, which gives even neophytes a sporting chance of finishing a make.

Still, under some circumstances the driven spindle is a poor choice. For example, sometimes drafting tension against the spindle tip is great enough to stall the spindle or to lift it out of place. This occurs when attempting to draft too thick a yarn, or when drafting from a "sticky," or overly cohesive, fiber mass.

Another "poor choice" area concerns drive ratios. Driven spindles have such high ratios that they are unsuited for producing soft-twisted yarns. The condition involves rapidly escalating operator frustration, not mechanical impossibility.

Sometimes the necessities of spindle operation impede the task at hand—for example, plying. Driven spindles will and do ply yarns. People also cross bodies of water in bathtubs, when a boat would be a better conveyance. Consistent plying owes much to uniform, jerk-free yarn movement and to high, constant yarn tension. These are impossible on a discontinuous device. Rapid, dependable, productive plying requires two hands on the yarn(s). Rapid, dependable, productive spindle work demands one hand on the yarn, one on the wheel.

The intermittent nature of driven spindle operation forces certain design features. The device must start, stop, and reverse easily. It must attain and endure high spindle speeds. Adjustments must be positive,

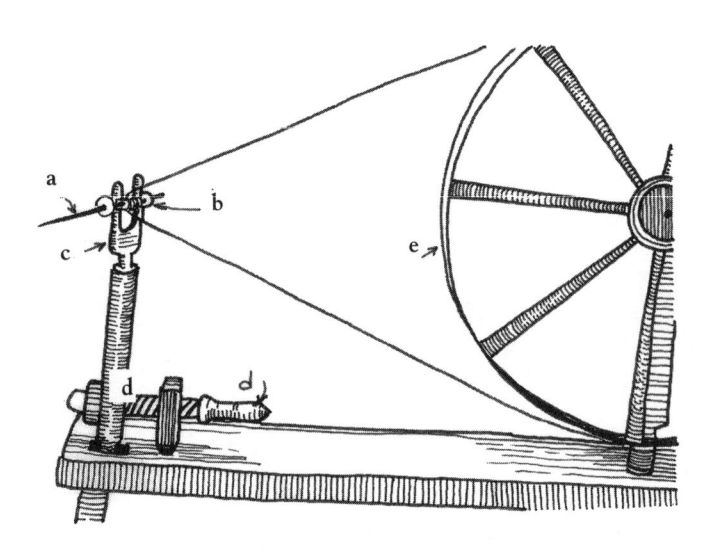

These are the parts of a driven spindle: spindle blade (a), bearings (b), mother-of-all (c), tensioning device (d), and drive wheel (e).

reliable, and simple. This does not imply that the tool must be unsophisticated, simplistic, or fitted only with a stop-and-go switch. It does mean that all features and adjustments must do something useful.

A certain safety factor is involved. Driven spindles, especially the smaller ones, tend to be stiff, hard, obtrusive, and almost invisible. Thus, there needs to be a safe at-rest or storage provision built into the machine, or a simple, obvious procedure to provide a margin of safety when the wheel is not in use. The foolproof method of removing the spindle point from harm's way is to dismount the spinning head. On most wheels, this is possible. A secondary approach involves a huge caution sign, with fluorescent plastic foam balls on it. This guarantees that 96 percent of the human race will attempt to discover why the sign exists.[20]

A direct-drive spindle is a simple device. It consists of a spindle shaft or blade, two spindle bearings and supports, a substructure roughly akin to the mother-of-all, a tensioning device, a drive wheel, and the structure which supports the drive wheel.

Accelerating or multiplying heads are devices that compound primary wheel input, usually (but not always) by means of pulley arrangements.

The primary wheel (the great wheel) drives an input pulley, or whorl, mounted on a common shaft with an accelerating pulley.[21]

A typical multiplying head of American make has an input-pulley effective whorl diameter of 1.25 inches. If we assume a great (primary) wheel diameter of 40 inches, the theoretical ratio between input pulley and drive wheel is 32-to-1. Thus the input whorl rotates 32 times for each revolution of the primary wheel.

Attached to the input whorl, mounted on the same shaft, is the secondary accelerating wheel. A typical diameter for this secondary wheel is 5 inches, and of course it rotates in phase with the input whorl. The secondary wheel has an effective whorl diameter of about 4½ inches. It drives a spindle whorl about ½ to ¾ inch in diameter, which we will round off to ⅝ inch (the decimal equivalent is .625 inch). This produces a "secondary" drive ratio of 4.5 divided by .625, or about 7.2-to-1.

The primary drive ratio times the secondary drive ratio gives us the "final" drive ratio, or the number of times the spindle rotates for one revolution of the primary wheel. In this case, about 230 times (7.2 × 32 = 230.4). As a drive ratio, this is 230-to-1.

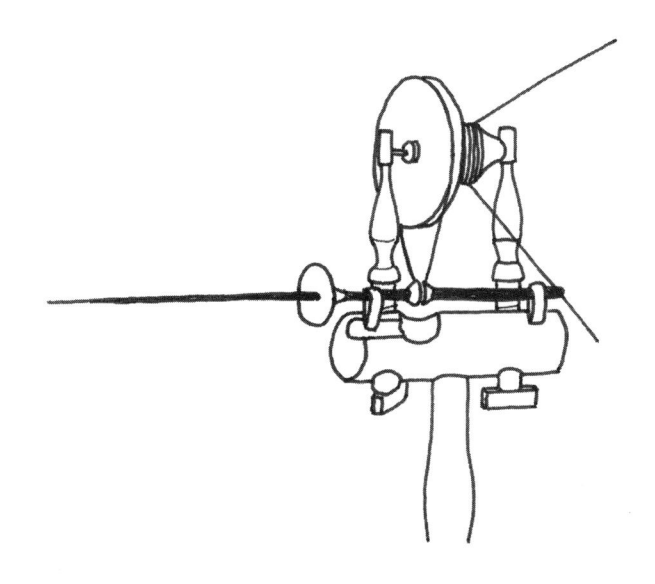

A Miner's head multiplies the speed at which the spindle turns in relation to the drive wheel.

---

[20] *Incidentally, Sleeping Beauty did not prick her finger on a spindle. We deal with that story in the glossary, under the topic of* boon.

[21] *By the way, it is an advantage if the primary and accelerating wheels are light in weight (low in inertia). This makes them easier to start, stop, and reverse, all things considered. It is one of the main reasons for open-spoke, bentwood rims and thin, disk-like whorls.*

That is a high drive ratio. A skilled long-draw practitioner, working a great wheel and spinning semi-worsted yarn, will make about 6 draws a minute. Each make will be about 50 inches long, for a total of 300 inches per minute. Let's say that the yarn is 2,400 YPP, with 7½ TPI.

The spinner will turn the wheel about twice per make, minus a little for wind-on, so the average speed of the wheel is 2.25 turns times 6 makes, or 13.5 turns per minute. The spindle speed is another matter.

Spinning 300 inches per minute at 7½ TPI means that the spindle must be accumulating twist at more than 2,200 RPM. That's not so much, except that it occurs in six segments, each only a few seconds long.

Any time the operator "twists-at-the-tip," the primary-wheel rotation speed is at least 50 or 60 RPM.[22] The spindle is operating at a drive ratio of 230-to-1, which amounts to a spindle speed of 10,000 or 12,000 RPM.

Agreed, it only runs at those speeds for a few seconds. But you can see that the driven spindle has no equal when it comes to putting in twist. No practical flyer-and-bobbin array can even approach those speeds.

By garment standards, a yarn that measures 3,600 YPP and 7½ TPI is not a fine, high-twist yarn. Accelerating heads were designed to turn wool into yarns at 5,400 YPP with between 12 and 16 TPI.

A great wheel is an extremely efficient device for inserting twist in fine yarns.

---

[22] *Twisting-at-the-tip occurs after drafting and before winding on: the yarn is held at the length of the make while the spindle rotates and the spinner adds enough twist to strengthen the yarn. Then the make is wound onto the spindle and another draft begins.*

Because we are in a mathematical vein, let's consider the lowly direct-driven spindle, as in the "common" great wheel. The typical drive ratio is on the order of 40-to-1. The question is, what sort of performance can one expect?

Pretty good, as a matter of fact. A reasonably active spinner can manage three 50-inch makes per minute, or about 150 inches (4⅛ yards) of yarn, and put in 20 turns on the wheel. That works out as 800 turns for 150 inches, or 5.3 TPI.

In round figures, that's 255 yards of yarn per hour. Not too bad.

Chapter 9

The purposeful yarn: Projects and calculations, and yarn for all reasons

Once upon a time, handspinning was a commonplace activity and handspinners were the only source of yarn. Nowadays, yarn may be obtained from all sorts of places.

That is all to the good. Still, to obtain handspun yarn, should you want or need such a thing, you must approach a handspinner; and if you want good yarn within a reasonable amount of time, it is worthwhile to approach a skilled and productive handspinner.

That brings up a question: why should you want to bother with handspun yarn? That question has many right answers, starting with something as simple as "doing it yourself."

Another consideration, which has not been stressed publicly, concerns the fact that commercial yarns are produced to gain the maker maximum profit. This means that something about the yarn involves a compromise—usually several things. In short, because of economics, the yarn is not as good as it might be.

While it may be very "good" yarn, it is not likely to be available in the colors, grists, and twist amounts that you want. Nor your choice of fiber, or method of treatment. How about twist direction? Hmmm. For example, try to buy a 3,000 YPP single semi-worsted in a natural silver-brown marl, at 5 twists per inch. Or how about a red/red-orange silk three-ply that will sett at exactly 32 ends per inch in a balanced 2/1 twill? Ever find a bargain on high-twist 8's singles in natural brown cotton? Ever find them for sale at all?

Mills are capable of spinning these yarns, but they don't. And if they did, the first thing they would have to do to stay in business would be to cut costs by using less costly fibers, less twist, more synthetic staple, cheaper dyes, whatever. Almost always, they would use less twist.

As a handspinner, you may produce a yarn where cost is no object, with exactly the twist, grist, and fiber that you wish, and with any amount of costly "hand labor" that you deem necessary.

FIBER THROUGH HISTORY

Today, hand textile workers tend to think about a narrow range of possible projects—things like yarn to knit a sweater or the warp to weave a baby blanket. Here's a different viewpoint.

There is no question that handspinners and handweavers have clothed the human race, since time out of mind. In fact, without spinning and weaving most of us would be buck nekkid. Today we have a tendency to equate spinning with weaving, and weaving with the wearable arts, or clothing. To a lesser degree, we think of shelter—as in a yurt or a tent. With a little imagination, we can also see the relationship between fibers and food; after all, mutton has been a staple foodstuff for a long, long time.

This brings us to an awareness of the tie-ins (no pun intended) between the so-called basic needs of humankind—Food, Clothing, and Shelter. For practical purposes, Clothing and Shelter may be the same thing. Clothing is a sort of ultra-portable shelter, and the family Shelter (home) may be seen as extremely heavy clothing. In any case, Shelter, Clothing, and Food all depend strongly upon fibers and textiles.

Begin by considering items as easy as a bowstring, or a fishing line, a rabbit snare, a bird net. From there proceed to mats for sleeping, baskets for storage, and cords to lash together timber or to assemble tools and weapons. Then look at sailcloth, ropes, and cables; bands, straps, sacks, wrappers, bolting cloth, sieves, cheesecloth, jelly bags, pudding sacks, sheeting, tarpaulins, papermakers' felts, mops, polishing cloths, belting, and wagon covers.

An agricultural society uses vast quantities of rope, twine, and bag material; a maritime society uses huge amounts of rope, cord, net, and sailcloth; a mining society consumes rope, cable, and bagging. And the people who live in these societies must have ropes, cords, nets, straps, and other useful objects in addition to the things we normally think of, like clothes, blankets, rugs, dishtowels, washrags, curtains. . . .

Every bit of this, woven or knitted or not, starts with a handful of fiber and a spinner. True, basketmakers don't always need spinners, and you can make a coat from fur and sinew, and yurts are felt. But what of the rest?

Virtually all of the threads, cords, ropes, straps, bags, nets, canvas, sailcloth, and so forth that have held this old world together for so many years have been (and still are) based on the four major fibers, plus one.[1] How are we able to produce these incredibly varied textiles from only five primary fiber sources? Or rather, how do we make these fabrics and items so different from each other when we have so few fibers to choose from?

The answer is threefold. We carefully control (1) the method of fabric construction, (2) the method of yarn construction, and (3) the fibers used.

THE RELATIONSHIP BETWEEN THE YARN AND THE TEXTILE TECHNIQUE

As a handspinner, you may never take up weaving or tatting. You may, however, want to spin yarns appropriate for these uses. For example, your Auntie wants to knit a sweater, has touted your worth to the skies, and puts the bee on you for the yarn. There is no graceful way out.

This brings us to a discussion of what are called project-specific yarns. A project-specific yarn is designed to fit a specific need or set of parameters. For example, knitting yarns are quite different from warp yarns. This does not mean that you cannot weave with a knitting yarn, and you can certainly knit with a warp yarn. However, yarns for different purposes have different design parameters, or factors, built into them.

In order of importance, these design factors are (1) grist, (2) twist,

---

[1] *That plus-one fiber is true hemp, or* Cannabis sativa. *True hemp has always been a premier fiber for making sailcloth, ropes, cords, wool sacks, bale wrappers, hammocks, heavy clothing, straps, harnesses, nets, and so forth—what we would call "industrial textiles" today. Hemp was grown and used during WWII to produce U.S. Army web gear. In Japan it is still used for clothing. If we consider the historical usage of hemp, we should be talking about the Big Five fibers, but that would not be PC (politically correct), would it?*

(3) spinning method, (4) ply, and (5) fiber. There are other considerations, such as twist and ply directions, treatments, color, and so forth. But before we get too involved, we need to consider the methods by which yarn is converted into fabric and what those techniques require from our yarns.

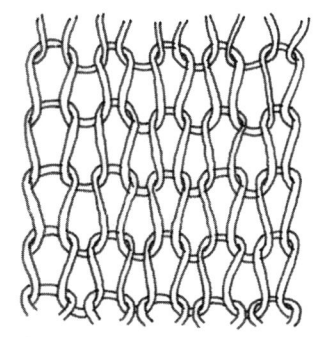

Knitting yarns. Knitting proceeds through the formation of interlocked loops. Normally the yarns do not undergo much strain during knitting, and the finished fabric has a great capacity for elastic movement. This means that relatively weak or soft, low-twist yarns may give reasonable service. As an example, Kiwi knitting is done with a roving that has no twist. The built-in elasticity of the knitted structure does much to ensure the survival of the component yarns. As a result, some pretty strange stuff passes as yarn suitable for knitting.

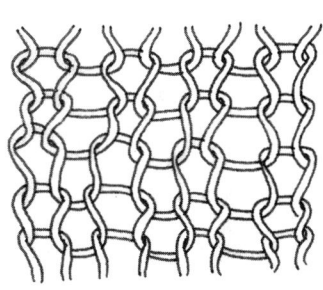

The knit structure consists of interlocking loops. Yarns are not normally stressed a great deal during construction.

In most cases, knitting yarns need to be elastic (extendable), of uniform diameter and twist, not prone to felting, and of medium or better luster. These yarns are almost always plied. Fibers are often medium to long staple, spun low-twist in the single and high-twist in the ply, with attention to making the yarn as twist-stable as possible. Yarns used for intricate or extensive cabling should be three-ply. Yarns for intarsia and color pattern work must match ground yarns in grist and construction.

Knitted fabric stretches, regardless of the elasticity or strength of the component yarns.

Weaving yarns. Weaving, as we all know, is simply an interlacement of two sets of yarns, the warp and the weft. The weft yarn needs enough twist to hold together during the shuttle's passage. Warp yarns must function under more rigorous conditions. They are under constant tensile strain and are exposed to a remarkable level of abrasion caused by the shedding motion, the reed, and the shuttle. Thus weaving yarns, and especially warp yarns, have certain requirements.

Warp yarns need to be abrasion-resistant, have relatively high tensile strength, be uniform in twist with few thick-and-thin areas, and, depending upon the weave structure, appropriate to the projected

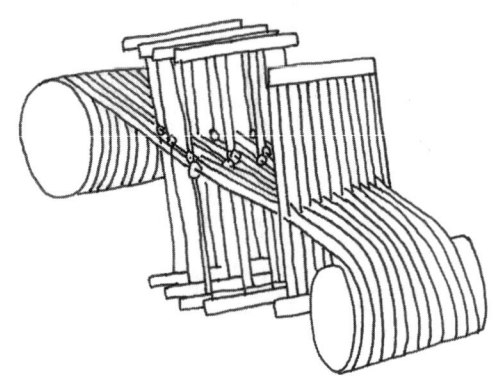

Here's an elementary loom. The warp yarns—those that run lengthwise through the fabric—must endure both tensile strain and abrasion.

Relative to knitting, the woven structure is inelastic.

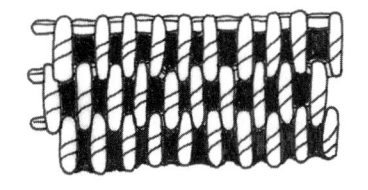

Crochet is significantly less elastic than knitting and requires more durable yarns.

demands for surface wear and/or fulling powers.

Historically, warps are singles. If singles are used for warp, they must be made twist-stable through blocking and/or sizing. Mohair makes an almost indestructible warp, although the weaver needs to size or dress a mohair warp carefully.

Weft yarns may be identical to the warp, or may be entirely different. Weft yarns need enough strength and twist to survive the winding, weaving, and finishing processes. Weft yarns need to be twist-stable, either because the ply is balanced or because the singles have been blocked.

Crochet yarns. Crochet involves the formation of a series of knots. While knitting is composed of more or less two-dimensional loops, each crochet stitch is, at heart, a three-dimensional knot. Each stitch acts as a hard, focused point of wear, with little ability to move out of harm's way. As a result, crochet is not elastic in the sense that knitting is. Each stitch contains a relatively fixed amount of yarn. Under stress, the textile itself changes shape, or deforms. Crochet is not (nor was it ever) a substitute for knitting.

Crochet yarns should be hard. Only a firm, strong yarn will survive long in a crocheted stitch. Elasticity is not required, although the ability to felt may be valuable.

An ability to resist surface abrasion is desirable. Semiworsted yarns are appropriate, spun from medium- to long-staple luster wools. Uniform diameter is important. Twist does not need to be as consistent as for knitting yarns, as long as there is plenty of it.

Needlework yarns. We use *needlework* as a generic term that includes embroidery, bobbin or pillow lace, tatting, and the like, as well as other techniques.

Needlework yarns are almost invariably selected on the basis of color and surface appearance. All other considerations seem to be less important (except for lace), with the possible exception of the brand name or whether the threads or yarns have been imported.

For practical purposes, needlework is composed of knots or knot-like arrangements and the yarns are exposed either entirely, as in lace, or partially, as in embroidery. Knotted pile and Russian punch-needle techniques expose the yarns differently from embroidery, but the yarns for this variety of techniques require three common qualities.

(1) Resistance to abrasion. During needlework, the yarn is handled and passed through backings, itself, knots, and so forth, and must therefore be firm and smooth.

(2) Inelasticity. An elastic yarn (one that stretches and collapses) makes needlework very difficult. By way of an example, consider tying a uniform pattern in bobbin lace with a yarn that stretches.

(3) Uniformity of color. The fiber for needlework yarn should be chosen with this in mind. In other words, uniform color must be planned from the start, before spinning, dyeing, and all other processing, so that the finished yarn in the completed project will be uniform in color.

In general, wool needlework yarns should be long-stapled, combed, and spun on the worsted system. Woolen-spun yarns are not generally suited to needlework, because their strength and abrasion resistance are low.

Silk yarns for embroidery, couching, and so forth should be spun on the worsted system, as they need to be as smooth as possible.

Flax is (was) much used. Its chief limitation has been its limited color palette. Line flax, wet-spun, makes an excellent, smooth, strong yarn.

Cotton is commonly used today but must be spun to high counts, plied, and slack mercerized before it is dyed.

Ropes. Ropes (and the related cords, lines, and so on) are a study in their own right. Ropes (three or more strands) and cords (two strands only) are composed of multiple elements twisted about their common longitudinal axis. Each strand is made up of two or more threads.

The threads themselves may be singles or plied yarns. The fibers used include flax, hemp, silk, nylon, cotton, jute, and abaca, plus rags, raffia, paper, hay, bark, wool, hop vines, rawhide, horsehair. . . .

There are differences between rope-making and plying. In plying, for example, the incumbent twist of each component is relatively low and cannot be adjusted once the process begins. In rope-making, each component begins with a considerable amount of twist. Although twist amounts in the original threads are fixed, the twist amounts of all other components can be adjusted continuously.

It is possible to make decorative rope from junk yarns, but it is impossible to make durable, serviceable rope or cord from trash. Yarns used in rope must be strong, firm, elastic, and relatively uniform in grist.

Substantial weights of yarn are needed for even modest projects (a hammock, for example). If there is any possibility that the rope or cord will become wet, do not use silk, wool, or hair fibers. Use only those fibers which become stronger when wet. Not all cellulosic fibers get stronger when wet. Some, like jute, get positively puny. Your best bets are cotton, hemp, flax, and ramie. There are others, but bear in mind some reasonable degree of availability.

GENERAL CONSIDERATIONS FOR ALL YARNS

Here are some general considerations for all yarns, bearing in mind the desired end result.

It is a good idea to spin knitting yarns with the plying process in mind, which is to say that you spin "fine," put a little more twist than you think you need into the single, and try to ply to the twist-stable point. It is worthwhile to substitute a three-ply for a two-ply, especially when you plan to do much cabling.

For weaving purposes, weft does not have to be strange, soft, low-twist stuff. Consider the finishing process that will be used. Do you want less collapse (take-up of various sorts) or more? Lots of fulling? None?

All else being equal, including grist, a plied yarn is stronger, more uniform, more twist-stable, and less prone to felting than an equivalent single. It is also more elastic (extendable) and lofty (bulky). Plied yarns take longer to make, and you must spin finer singles. When wet, skeins of plied yarns are easier to handle and less fragile than skeins of singles.

In short, give some thought to how the yarn will be used, what its service conditions are, how you want to finish the fabric or textile, and so forth. Then spin away!

How much yarn?

How do you know how much yarn you need for a given project? Let's start with the activity that consumes the greatest amount of yarn, bar none: the weaving of cloth.

Imagine that you are 5 feet 6 inches tall and weigh less than 160 pounds (ahem!). In round figures (that's not a pun), you can make yourself a nice Kinsale (Celtic) cloak, with full hood and collar, from 8 yards of wool material, 27 inches wide. (You will actually have a little left over, for mittens, bags, repairs, or a hat for him. Better to have leftovers than not quite enough.)

Those measurements represent the finished cloth size, after being

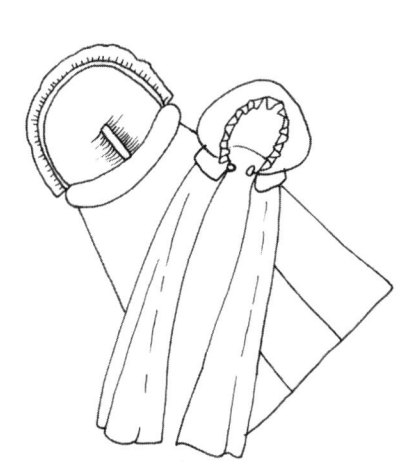

With a full hood and collar, a Kinsale cloak can require about 8 yards of finished fabric, 27 inches wide, although you'll have enough left over for accessories.

A Kinsale cloak consumes a great deal of material. How much? How would you plan for a project of this size?

washed and dried. Of course, wool cloth shrinks in washing and the weaving process condenses (pulls in, takes up) the material. We need to put enough extra on the loom to provide for this shrinkage. How much extra? Let's figure it out.

The following discussion gets very basic. It is not our intent to insult your intelligence; it is likely that you are familiar with weaving, warp, weft, and all that. But if you are not, then it would be unfair to leave this out. After all, this is a book for handspinners, not weavers. Bear with us, or skip along to another section.

If you look at a piece of woven material, you notice that there are threads running lengthwise (called *warp threads*) and threads running across it (called *weft threads*).

Length calculations. We can expect take-up in the warp to run between 15 and 20 percent, because the warp gets shorter as we weave and the cloth shrinks in length when washed. To play it safe, let's allow 20 percent. That means that 8 yards is 80 percent of something or 20 percent less than something else.

This is one of those problems that haunt you from grade school. It's done thusly: X (8 yards) divided by Y (80 percent) = Z (.1). Multiply Z (.1) by 100 (percent) and the answer ("something") is 10 yards. We must put on at least 10 yards of warp.

In addition, however, each loom has a sort of operating loss, called *loom waste*. Loom waste is warp that cannot be converted to cloth because it is used up in the knots that attach it to the beams and/or it cannot get through the heddle stack to be woven. Loom waste varies from loom to loom, but as a good average runs 1 yard. Adding the loom waste (1 yard) to our 10 yards of warp, we have a total of 11 yards. That takes care of the length.

Width calculations. Now we need to figure width. We know we want our finished cloth to be 27 inches wide. The width is determined by two main things: how many warp threads there are, and how close together they are. You can guess by now that we have to set up our cloth to be wider than 27 inches because of shrinkage, take-up, and so forth. If we do our part, that width loss will amount to between 10 and 15 percent—of what? Of the width we need to put on the loom so that we end up with 27 inches when we are through.

Let's be generous and assume 15 percent loss. That means our 27 inches is 85 percent of something or 15 percent less than something else, just like before. X (27 inches) divided by Y (85 percent) = Z (.3176 . . .). Multiply Z (.3176) by 100 (percent) and the answer is 31.76 inches. Now we know how wide to make the cloth on the loom.

How many warp ends, and how much warp yarn? On to the next steps. Each piece of cloth has so many warp threads and so many weft threads per inch. When we set up a project to weave, we start by determining the number of warp threads, or *ends*. Until we do that, the weft threads can wait.

We know we want the warp 31.76 inches wide, also called *in the reed* or *as drawn in*. But how many threads do we use? The number of threads, or *sett*, depends on the diameter of the yarns and on the weave structure. For our example, we are using plain weave, sometimes called *tabby*. The diameter of a yarn is found by direct measurement, as described previously (wraps). Because this is a Kinsale cloak, we are using wool. To save time and to keep you from having to swallow all this weaving calculation stuff at one shot, take it on faith that a plain weave will be workable if sett at 16 ends per inch with a 2,000 YPP woolen single.

Because we want 16 ends per inch and we are threading the loom 31.76 inches wide, we need 16 times 31.76 ends = 508.16 ends, rounded off to 508. Each of those 508 ends has to be 12 yards long (the warp length, remember?), so we need 508 times 11 yards = 5,588 yards of warp.

In weaving and spinning, it is better to have a little more than you need as opposed to a little less. Add a little for the mythical Grandma, about 10 percent, and 5,588 plus 559 = about 6,147 yards of warp yarn.

Figuring weft density and quantity. We want this cloak material to be a good, sturdy cloth. The most durable material is usually plain weave, woven square. *Woven square* means that it has the same number of weft threads per square inch as it does warp threads. A square plain weave requires that the warp and weft yarns be about the same grist, although they need not be identical (we'll talk about twist in a moment).

Weave structures that have equal or square warp/weft threads are called *balanced weaves*, and they contain almost as much weft as they do warp. With weft, you don't have to allow for loom waste so we need about

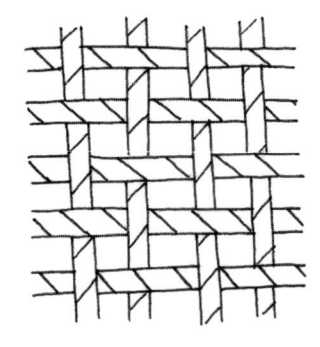

If warp and weft are twisted in the same direction, the threads will bed together during weaving.

95 percent as much weft as we have warp. Since we have 6,147 yards of warp, 95 percent of that is 5,840 yards.

Twist direction, amounts of twist, finished weights of yarn, and raw wool. For this project the weft does not have to carry as much twist as the warp, even though they are both 2,000 YPP. How much less? For this project, the warp will have about 8 turns per inch, and the weft about 5 turns per inch.[2]

If the warp and weft have the same twist direction, the threads will bed together better during the weaving. All else being equal, they will also full more because of this. If the warp and weft have opposing twists, the individual yarns will be plainer or clearer in outline, the cloth will not be quite as dense, and the fabric will not full as well. If that is what we want, the weft should have more twist, say 7 turns per inch instead of 5.

But we do want a soft, strong, well-fulled material, and so we choose the values that will produce those results: same twist direction, slightly different amounts of twist.[3] For the warp, we need 6,147 yards of Z-twist

---

[2] *This information comes from the charts and tables in the back of this book. Here's how to make similar calculations yourself. (1) Establish the yarn you wish to use—one you like to spin a lot of. Determine its grist, diameter, and twist requirements. To determine twist, find the square root of the grist in YPP, then multiply the square root by the appropriate factor. Factors used here: for warp twist, .165; for weft, .115. (2) Decide on a weave structure or construction. (3) Determine how much finished cloth you need for the project. (4) Calculate additional warp length and width to allow for loom waste, shrinkage, and take-up. (5) To calculate sett, apply Ashenhurst's formula (an educated guess; see next section). (6) Multiply warp length by total number of ends to determine how much warp yarn is needed. (7) Allow about the same amount of yarn for weft, or possibly a little less. Say 95 percent. Add all of this together, and start spinning.*

[3] *We worked this one off, and the obtained cloth that was about 8½ yards long and 27¼ inches wide weighed about 13 ounces per square yard (about 6½ square yards) and counted 18.6 ends and 17.5 picks per square inch. What was the cloth like? Similar in weight to a medium-heavy wool shirt material. We fulled it pretty well, and raised the nap with a dog brush. All in all, pretty nice. Not as heavy as I wanted, but okay.*

yarn, 2,000 YPP, 8 turns per inch. That's about 3 pounds 1 ounce of finished yarn. For the weft, we need 5,840 yards of Z-twist yarn, 2,000 YPP, 5 turns per inch. That's about 2 pounds 15 ounces of finished yarn.

Total for both warp and weft is 6 pounds. You already know that you will need to start with at least twice that much grease fleece. We could calculate the yields and percentages, but if you figure that 2 pounds of grease fleece equal 1 pound of clean wool yarn, you will seldom be wrong.

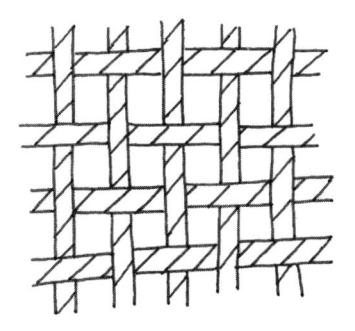

If warp and weft are twisted in opposite directions, weave structure can be seen more clearly.

How long will it take to spin? Without a sermon, here's the answer: about 65 "spinner's hours," if your wheel has a drive ratio of 10-to-1, you maintain a treadle rate of 90 RPM, and you draft about 3 yards per minute.[4]

Here's a breakdown of the figures. They include spinning only, not fiber preparation or yarn handling. At 10-to-1, the flyer speed is 10 times the treadle rate (90), or 900 RPM. That's 900 turns per minute.

Warp: At 8 turns per inch for the warp, we put in 288 turns per yard. 6,147 yards × 288 turns = 1,770,336 turns.

Weft: At 5 turns per inch for the weft, we put in 180 turns per yard. 5,840 yards × 180 turns = 1,051,200 turns.

The whole job: Add the total warp turns and the total weft turns (1,770,336 plus 1,051,200 turns) and we have 2,821,536 turns. At an average speed of 900 twists per minute, it takes about 3,135 minutes to build up that twist. If we used 60-minute hours, it would only take us 52 hours and 15 minutes to do the task.

---

[4] *The astute reader has spotted a family resemblance in this calculation. The values are based on the nominal performance of the ubiquitous Ashford Traditional single-drive . . . about as close to a generic spinning wheel as we are likely to see.*

The problem is that our hour is only 48 minutes long. So 3,135 minutes divided by 48 gives us 65 "spinner's hours."

Wasn't that fun?

Educated guesses

The handspinner's secret for calculating how much yarn to plan on for weaving is called Ashenhurst's formula, or *the educated guess*.

There are several methods used to determine how many warp ends per inch are needed for a particular cloth. The simplest way is to follow published advice or copy an existing example. Another practice involves wrapping both warp and weft yarns, side by side, around a ruler. There are also mathematical methods, bristling with square roots.

Use the math method of estimating. We will use a simple method based on work done by a Victorian-era gentleman, Thomas R. Ashenhurst. Mr. Ashenhurst was the Headmaster of the Textile Department, Bradford Technical College in Huddersfield (England), circa 1880. His procedure accurately calculates basic weave setts "on the squares."

Here's the plain, original formula: *The number of diameters per inch TIMES the ends in one repeat, DIVIDED by: the number of ends PLUS the number of intersections in one repeat*. The result is in ends (and picks) per inch, and gives the basic sett. In practice, the answer represents the *theoretical maximum* number of ends or picks per square inch for a given yarn diameter.

$$\frac{D \times R}{R+I}$$

D is the number of diameters per inch, R is the number of ends in one repeat, and I is the number of intersections in one repeat.

For a number of reasons (yarn hardness, softness, twist, and so on), we use a modified formula, to wit: *Yarn diameter in inches times factor (.8, for example) TIMES ends in one repeat, DIVIDED by: the number of ends PLUS the number of intersections in one repeat*. This formula gives us the *practical maximum* number of ends or picks per square inch, assuming that warp and weft are the same diameter.

$$\frac{DF \times R}{R+I}$$

D is the number of diameters per inch, F is the factor (varies with yarn), R is the number of ends in one repeat, and I is the number of intersections in one repeat.

As a matter of convenience to us English-system (inch/pound) folks, it happens that a quick and fairly accurate way to find a yarn's diameter is to determine the square root of its grist in yards per pound. For a yarn with a grist of 900 YPP, what is its diameter? The square root of 900, or 30. A 900 YPP yarn is about 1/30 inch in diameter. How handy. How about a yarn at 1,600 YPP? 1/40 inch?

Okay, now for a sample problem. Let us use the 900 YPP yarn and figure a plain-weave sett, using a factor of .8—about right for a firm woolen single. We begin calculating: (30 x .8) x 2 (number of ends in plain-weave repeat); divided by 2 (number of ends in repeat) + 2 (number of intersections per repeat), or:

$$\frac{(30 \times .8)2}{2+2} = \frac{24 \times 2}{4} = \frac{48}{4} = 12$$

We know that the cloth will take up and shrink a bit when done, so we can expect the finished cloth to be, say, 14 ends/picks per square inch.

How about our 2,000 YPP yarn? The factor will be about the same, .8. The square root of 2,000 (which gives us approximate grist) is 44.72 . . . . We'll round off to 44.7. Here's the calculation: (44.7 x .8) x 2 (number of ends in plain-weave repeat); divided by 2 (number of ends in repeat) + 2 (number of intersections per repeat), or:

$$\frac{(44.7 \times .8)2}{2+2} = \frac{35.8 \times 2}{4} = \frac{71.6}{44} = 17.9$$

That rounds off to 18 ends/picks per square inch. For practical reasons of reed spacing, a weaver always rounds off to a convenient and easily divided number of ends per inch.

But when we began calculations for the cloak, we asked you to take it on faith that plain weave in a 2,000 YPP single woolen yarn would work well at 16 ends/picks per inch. Why the difference between this calculation and our previous suggestion for the same yarn? This answer, 18 ends per inch, represents the *practical maximum* number of ends/picks per inch at which we can sett this yarn, and the other figure, 16 ends per inch, represents what we *actually did* with it.

We threaded the loom at 16 ends per inch, 31.76 inches wide, and wove it off at about 15 picks per inch. The material came off the loom about 29⅛ inches wide and about 9 yards 8 inches long. Out of the suds and dry, it was 8 yards 19 inches long and 27¼ inches wide. Thread count was 17.5 ends and 18.6 picks per inch.

The calculation lets you make a pretty close guess. But what if you do not wish to tackle all that number work?

Work from a similar fabric. Here's the first "easy" solution. Find a like item, weigh it, and add 10 percent for "whatever." That will give you the amount of yarn, by weight.

You still need to figure the grist and twist. Count the number of warp and weft threads in one square inch. The ideal device for this work is called a *pick glass*. Lacking one, a good, strong reading glass (think Sherlock Holmes), plenty of light, and a small ruler will do. It is easier to count along a cut edge (at a hem, perhaps).

Imagine that the sample appears to have a total of 36 threads—that is, warp threads plus weft threads equals 36. The amounts may not be equal (18 and 18); they probably are not. As long as they are not more than 20 percent off, we can disregard the difference. If they are more than 20 percent off, this system won't work and you need to try the method for "uncountable ends/picks," coming up in a moment.

With that information in hand, here's another way to figure yarn diameter in fractions of an inch. Multiply the total number of threads by 1.1. The result equals the yarn diameter in fractions of an inch. 36 × 1.1 = 39.6, which we round off to 40. The diameter of the yarn(s) equals ¹⁄₄₀ inch. This means it would wrap 40 turns to the inch. That number squared gives you the approximate number of yards per pound: 40 × 40 = 1,600 yards per pound.

This method will not work if you cannot count threads—for example, in a complex weave or in heavily fulled goods. If you can obtain a few square inches and pick the fabric apart for analysis, good. If not, once again we must demonstrate our right to have the initials D.I.G. after our name.[5]

In this case, we need an average thickness for the material, which we measure any way we can. If you have a micrometer, perfect. A "mike" will read out in at least three decimal places, more than enough for our needs. To measure cloth thickness with a mike, get two quarters or similar coins. Sandwich the material between the coins and measure combined thickness. Try to measure at a consistent place on each coin, say from Washington's ear on one coin to Washington's ear on the other, with the fabric sandwiched between them. Then measure the coin sandwich without any filling, maintaining your consistent places. Subtract coin-coin measurement from coin-fabric-coin measurement. What remains is fabric thickness. It may be necessary to double the fabric for measuring. This stunt allows you to disregard seams, lapels, and (with a little juggling) linings and interfacings.

If you cannot lay your mitts on a micrometer, use calipers. If you cannot obtain calipers (see Chapter 15), then skip to another part of the book.

Say that the fabric in question is about $31/100$ inch thick in micrometer terms, which translates to $1/32$ inch, or about the same thickness as 6 or 7 sheets of standard three-hole notebook paper. State the thickness as a whole number (in this case, 32, because it is one 32nd part of an inch). Multiply that by 1.3 and you have an approximation of yarn diameter in wraps per inch: $32 \times 1.3 = 41.6$. Round off to 42.

Remember, we're not trying to find the sett. We are after the yarn diameter, and therefore the grist. Here the diameter is estimated at $1/42$ inch, so its grist is approximately 42×42, or 1,764 YPP. Call it 1,760 YPP.

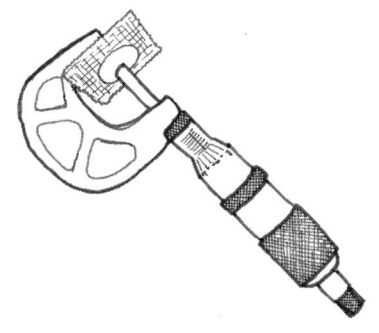

To measure cloth thickness with a micrometer, sandwich the fabric between two coins and measure combined thickness.

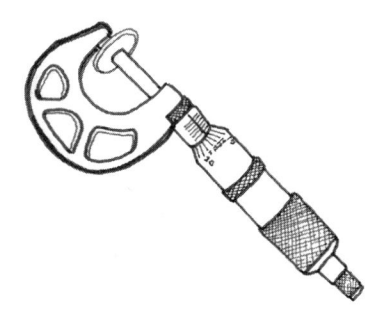

Then measure the coins without the fabric and subtract this from the combined total.

---

5 No, not "damn, I'm good," although that is true. In this case, the letters mean "Doctor of Informed Guessology."

Here's another one. Let's say the fabric is the same thickness as a U.S. dime, funny-munny series. That's about 42 thousandths of an inch, or .042. To find the fraction, divide 1 by .042. That gives us 23.8, or round off to 24. The fabric is about ¹⁄₂₄ inch thick. As above: 24 × 1.3 = 31.2, round off to 31. The yarn diameter is equal to ¹⁄₃₁ inch, same as 31 wraps. If it wraps 31, then its grist is about 31 × 31 = 960 YPP.

Let's review this method.

(1) Weigh the total project and add 10 percent. This gives the total weight of yarn needed. That's *clean, dry yarn.*

(2) Determine the required grist by one of two methods, as follows. (a) Count total threads in one square inch. Multiply that number by 1.1. The answer (rounded off) is the yarn diameter, in fractions of an inch. (b) Measure thickness of cloth in fractions of an inch. Multiply the fraction (as a whole number) by 1.3. The answer (rounded off) is the yarn diameter, in fractions of an inch.

(2, continued) Square the yarn diameter (multiply it by itself) to find the grist in YPP.

Now you have the grist of the yarn, and a total weight required. Use math (!) to calculate twist requirements, or peek in the back of the book, or wing it.

But do not miss this opportunity to improve on the yarns. You can use better materials, spin more carefully, put in more twist . . . always put in more twist.

Follow project instructions. You can always follow project instructions of the sort found in fine publications like *Handwoven, Spin-Off,* knitting magazines, and many well-known weaving texts. They supply instructions and materials lists. The weaving texts even mention grist, something that was unheard-of in knitting circles until recently.

Knitters, bless their hearts, have had to deal with evocative pulchritudes or verbal passementeries when discussing grist. The situation has been grim. Instead of honest statements that a particular two-ply yarn has a grist of 2,400 YPP, the knitter is told that the yarn is a "sportweight," whatever that is, or "fingering-weight," or "bulky," without a clue as to the grist or number of plies. One manufacturer's fingering may be another's sport. One sportweight yarn has a grist of 1,072 YPP and another sportweight yarn has a grist of 1,660 YPP; that is a difference of 588 YPP.

To a handspinner, the phrase *yarn weight* should mean how much the yarn weighs, nothing else. We all use the term *heavyweight* when we mean thick yarn, and *lightweight* when we mean thin yarn. We should stop, right?

Some mills do label knitting yarns with "grist" information, but you still have to translate. The skein band will say something like "Spindulu Pompyfluf Babycakes, 38 gm, 137 m." I'll figure it out for you: 2,774 MPK =1,376 YPP.

Calculations for knitting. So we need to give handspinning knitters a bit of extra help. The yarn companies don't. There are various ways to calculate yarn requirements for knitting projects that will give you the information you need: how much? what grist?

The easiest method is to exploit the instructions. If the magazine says "get 14 balls of Bloopie GummyGlitz," your mission is to find out what 14 balls (of BGG) weigh and what length of yarn is in each ball and thence what length is in 14 balls. In short, figure the grist. You start with the weight, you calculate the grist, and then you know how much and what kind of yarn to spin.

Here's the next easiest (and probably best) method. Spin up some 20-yard samples of yarn that you like, plied and everything, keeping track of grist and such as you go along. Have the knitter (yourself or someone else) make up swatches, at least 4 inches square or whatever the quantity of yarn allows. Choose your favorite swatch. When you do so, you have selected your intended fabric and you already know how you made the yarn: grist, twist, everything.

It is time to determine quantity: how much of this yarn do you need? If you can estimate the weight of a similar project, add 10 percent and proceed. If you cannot find a similar item you will have to do more calculating.

Examine your swatch. How many stitches does it have per inch? How many rows? How many stitches total? How many square inches is it? How many yards per square inch (divide 20 yards by the number of square inches)? Your sample yarn measured 20 yards, right?

If not, all is not lost. Carefully measure the gauge swatch (you did wash and dry it?) and record the dimensions. Then figure out the swatch size in square inches. Let's imagine that the sample was $3\frac{3}{4}$ inches by

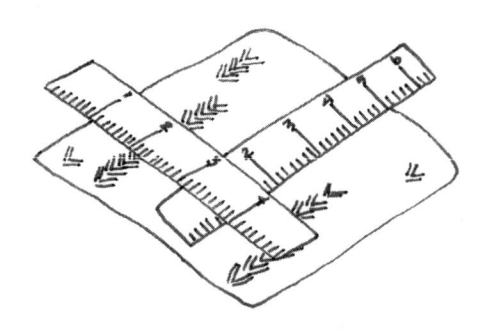

On a knitting sample, you need to measure the number of stitches and rows in an inch.

4½ inches, which gives us 16⅞ square inches; round it off to 17 square inches. Clip the bind-off and unravel the whole thing. Measure the length of yarn actually contained in the sample. Let us suppose that it measures 18 yards 3 inches. If 18$\frac{1}{12}$ yards gives us 17 square inches, how many yards per square inch? Divide 18.08 by 17; the answer is 1.07, or about 1 yard 2½ inches. Call it 39 inches of yarn for every square inch of knitting.

Now to figure how many square inches you need. Quickest way is to select or obtain an equivalent garment, lay it flat, and measure it. Be generous rather than thrifty. Because it is unlikely that the garment will be square, some stratagem must be employed to adjust for shaping, such as finding the closest approximation using rectangles and squares. Calculate the area of each part, then add all together.

Let's suppose that we have done that and come up with 1,176 square inches. Multiply the amount of our yarn it takes to knit 1 square inch by 1,176 to determine how much yarn we need for this project: 1,176 × 1.07 = 1,258 yards.

The same system of rectangles and squares may be used to map out a pattern where there is no pattern. Use the subject's own body and block out back, front, sleeves and so on.

Knitting stitches, other than extremes such as laces or all-over cabling, are pretty consistent with regard to the amount of yarn used.

Calculations for crochet. Calculating yarn amounts for crochet works much in the same way, except that the various crochet stitches use quite different amounts of yarn. Slipstitch and half-crochet do not use the same yarn per unit as double-crochet, and so forth. For that reason alone it is best to allow 25 percent extra for yarn amounts. Swatches are necessary and should incorporate a fair sampling of all stitches or combinations to be used.[6]

Calculations for other techniques. No attempt has been made to tell you how much yarn is needed for special techniques, such as Tunisian crochet or the afghan stitch, or, in knitting, the "weaving" procedure or double-knit work. You can swatch with a measured length of yarn, as above, and do a small amount of math.

Netting calculations are simple, as long as the mesh is symmetrical. Use the distance between meshes, times the number of meshes in a course, times the number of courses, times 1.4. Always allow a little for Grandma.

Here's a short course in net design. Say we want a net bag 1 foot in diameter and 3 feet deep—just the thing to haul a small watermelon. We want the meshes to be 2 inches square, which gives us a 3-inch diagonal, for practical purposes. This is, after all, a flexible textile event.

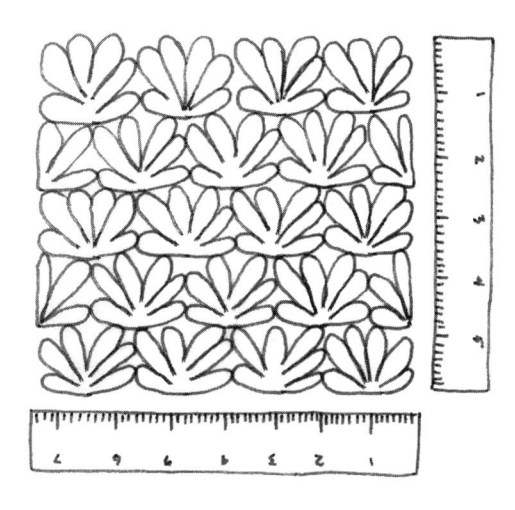

Various crochet stitches use radically different amounts of yarn. Make a generous sample using the stitches you plan to include, and be ready to make more yarn than you think you will need.

The meshes will be tied on the header, which is about 3 feet long, spaced on the diagonal distance of 3 inches. It will take 12½ meshes to complete one course.

Thus the amount of material needed per course is 12.5 meshes × 3 inches × 1.4, or 52.5 inches per course. That is 1.46+ yards per course, round it off to 1.5 yards, or about 54 inches of yarn.

---

6 *The combined information and procedures here have been drawn from numerous sources. It seems strange, but for the last 75 years, no one cared much about knitting calculations, at least not at the hobby or craft level. The best advice you got was "always purchase enough yarn to complete the project." Because the projects, the advice, and the yarn were usually proprietary, few questioned the situation. Nowadays, things are different. Priscilla Gibson-Roberts, in* Knitting in the Old Way, *states the situation clearly. She feels that today a "once simple and delightful craft has become shrouded in elaborate line-by-line instructions, enough to daunt the most skillful knitter while thoroughly intimidating the novice. But, armed with a general overview of sweater construction and some basic sweater formulas, today's knitter can once again be in control of the craft, knitting in the old way." But even Priscilla in her pioneering work avoided the thorny entanglement of grist.*

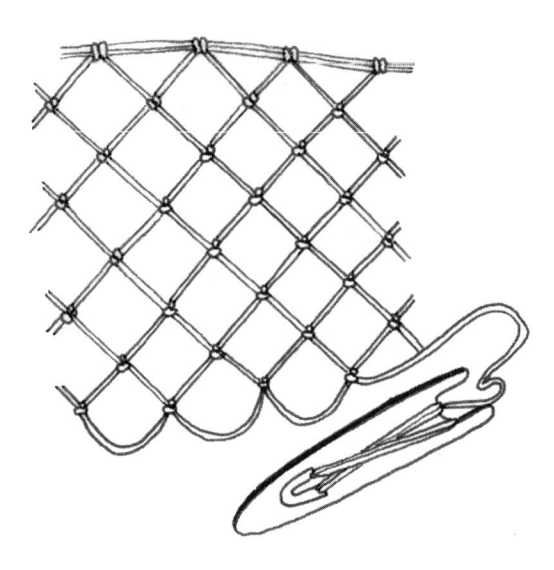

Each course makes the net ½ diagonal deeper, or 1½ inches in this case. If the bag is to be 2 feet (24 inches) deep, the depth will require 24 divided by 1½, or 16, courses. 16 courses × 1.5 yards = 24 yards. Always, for Grandma, add some extra, say 10 percent. Figure about 27 yards.

Rope- and cord-making are straightforward in their requirements. Figure 1½ times the length of the rope or cord, times the number of threads or yarns in each strand, times the number of strands.

Using a 20-foot, 6-thread, 3-strand rope as an example, we need 1.5 × 20 = 30 feet × 6 (threads) × 3 (strands), or 30 × 6 = 180 × 3 = 540 feet = 180 yards of yarn.

Cord is the same, except that cords are 2-stranded and the strands seldom contain more than 3 or 4 threads. Let's work through a 50-foot cord, made with 3 threads per strand. Each thread is 50 feet × 1.5, or 75 feet long, and we must have 3 threads (225 feet total) times 2 strands. The grand total is 450 feet of thread.

Not that you have to figure everything out beforehand, but there are advantages if you do invest in a little planning. . . .

Netting is as much a part of our craft as are knitting, crochet, weaving, etc.

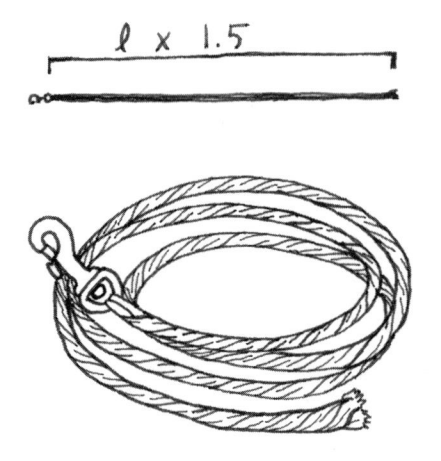

For rope- and cord-making, figure 1½ times the length of the finished cord or rope, then multiply that by the total number of threads in all component strands.

Chapter 10

YARN HANDLING AND PROCESSING FROM BOBBIN TO HANK: IN WHICH WE LEARN TO MANAGE SKEINS WITH SPEED AND ACCURACY WHILE REMAINING PERSONALLY UNSNARLED

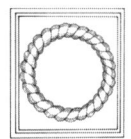

Once you have spun a yarn, you have to decide what to do next. You could leave the yarn where it is and consider it an artistic statement, perhaps titled "Spiral Expression #25." Most of the time, you intend the yarn for further conversion. This means that you need to remove the yarn from the bobbin or spindle, and do "something" with it. Removing yarn from the bobbin or spindle constitutes the first stage of what is called *yarn handling*. Overall, yarn handling consists of nothing more or less than those tasks necessary for transferring your yarn from one "yarn package" to another "yarn package." Yarn handling requires time, the amount of which will depend on your methods and equipment.

During yarn handling, you also have opportunities to modify and improve your yarn. For instance, simply winding from the bobbin to a skein will (1) let you examine every inch of the yarn, (2) aid in leveling the twist, (3) test the yarn for tensile strength, and (4) allow you to repair or remove major faults. Because you are going to handle the yarn anyway, why not take advantage of the situation?

The generic phrase *yarn package* means whatever form a yarn is stored in. For instance, yarn stored on a bobbin is in a package, which happens to be in the form of a bobbin or spool. If we wind the yarn into center-pull balls, then the yarn package is the center-pull ball.

The universal yarn package, at least for handspinners, is the *skein*. A properly constructed skein is durable, compact, difficult to derange, and convenient. It provides for easy scouring, dyeing, and related "wet" activities; it lends itself to moth control; it dries quickly; and it permits quick yet comprehensive examination of the yarn.

Obviously, there are other package forms. Package form is, or should be, determined by the specific nature of the task or series of tasks we are about to embark upon. For example, if we intend to ply the yarn, we wind from wheel bobbin to storage bobbin, reserving the skein form until after the plying has been completed.

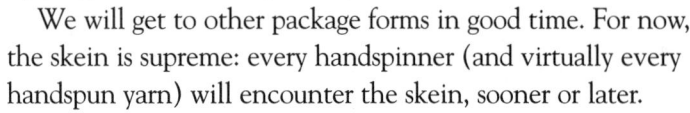

We will get to other package forms in good time. For now, the skein is supreme: every handspinner (and virtually every handspun yarn) will encounter the skein, sooner or later.

Here is an illustrative everyday scenario. Imagine that you have filled your wheel bobbin and now wish to skein it off in order to wash the yarn. Winding the yarn from bobbin to skein is basic yarn handling: you transfer yarn from one package (the bobbin) to another package (the skein).

Anyone can wind a skein. Not everyone winds skeins that are useful. To be useful, a skein must at least be unwindable. We begin with a brief look at equipment used for winding and unwinding skeins.

Familiar yarn packages include the spool, the ball, and the skein.

Equipment for winding skeins

Elbow. The human arm forms an elemental skein-winder. The arm is bent, and yarn is wound around the forearm, its terminal points composed of a Y formed by thumb and forefinger at one end and the elbow at the other end. Skeins wound in this manner are called *elbow skeins*, for obvious reasons. While convenient to produce, elbow skeins have serious limitations. They have small overall diameters and they vary widely in length, both turn-for-turn and from skein-to-skein. Although every handspinner owns the equipment for making them, elbow skeins have never obtained serious use.

Niddy-noddy. Some very early, unsung genius came up with the three-stick arrangement that we know today as the *niddy*, *niddy-noddy*, *kniddy knoddy*, or simply *nid*. The typical niddy consists of a handle crossed by two arms. The arms are

Elbow skeins can be handy, but they are small and do not have consistent diameters.

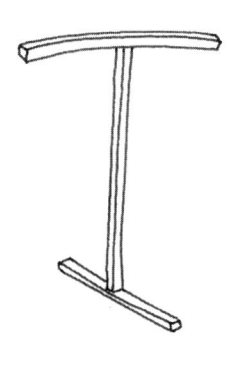

arranged at right angles to the handle, and at right angles to each other. A niddy looks rather like the letter H, turned on its side, with the top cross-arm twisted ¼ turn in relation to the bottom cross-arm.

In use, one hand holds the niddy by the central bar or handle while the other hand guides and wraps yarn in a precise pattern around the two cross-arms. An operating nid moves in a twisting, bobbing motion, giving rise to the old rhyme "Niddy-noddy, niddy-noddy, two heads and one body." This bobbing motion and the peculiar cross-arm arrangement allow the nid to achieve an amazing feat: it will wind a skein that is twice as long as itself.

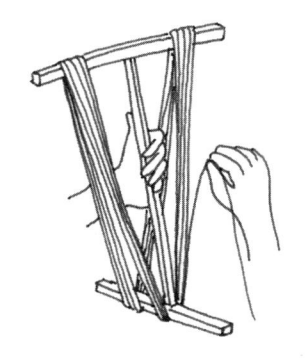

A niddy-noddy allows you to wind a skein that is four times the tool's arm-to-arm length.

To use a niddy-noddy, hold its handle or central bar in one hand and, using the other hand, wrap the yarn around and about the two cross-arms.

Where skein-winding is concerned, the niddy is a great improvement over the elbow. And, like the elbow (almost), a niddy is portable, inexpensive, and simple to use, once you get the hang of it. On the minus side: it is inherently slow in operation.[1] The niddy's relative slowness may not matter, and practice will make one adept. Still, when large quantities of

---

[1] *Surprisingly, many handspinners are mystified, even terrified, by the nid. Good niddy use requires a certain amount of faith and a lot of practice. It also requires a solid, well-designed niddy. In skilled hands, the niddy has a lot going for it, and it is startling in performance considering its simplicity. Yet you will find it well-nigh impossible to wind more than 120 yards per minute. This limitation arises because of the oscillating nature of niddy operation.*

Any good reel (clock or otherwise) will wind several hundred yards per minute. A counting reel will also track the number of turns, which a nid does not. So a proper reel is not only faster, it puts you ahead in the grist-determination department. The reel is also more accurate with regard to skein diameter. (The nid was enough of a problem in this area to force legal regulation about its use.) Last but not least, the author has yet to see a handspinner who had any problems operating a clock reel; yet scarcely a spinning class goes by without student hints about seeing "an expert" use the niddy. And some modern interpretations of the niddy need—nay, cry out!—for explanation and demonstration.

yarn need to be processed, some form of reel becomes highly desirable, almost mandatory.

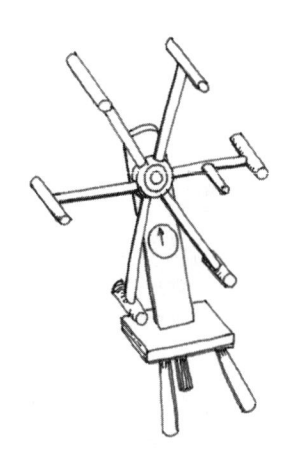

Clock reel or click reel. Reels come in wide variety. A popular, traditional form is the *clock reel*, so called because it has a clock-like dial that reads out in turns, yardage, or another useful increment. In addition, many such reels incorporate a "clicker" or "popper," a mechanical device that audibly signals when a predetermined number of turns has been made, thus the alternate name of *click reel*.

The traditional clock reel consists of a 4- or 6-armed reel mounted on the front of a box containing the works (wooden gears and worms). The box itself is attached to the top of an upright (made from a post or plank), which in turn is fixed to a sturdy 3-legged bench. The reel ranges from 1½ to 2½ yards in circumference, and the reel hub is about waist-high.

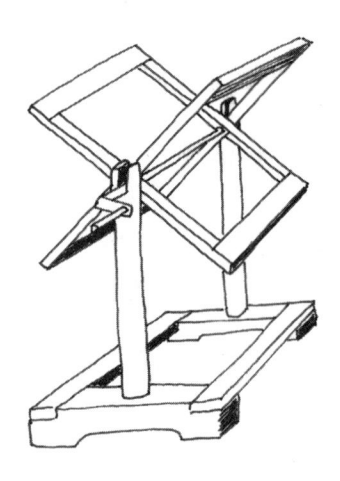

A common variation of the "traditional" pattern does away with the enclosed clockwork and places the reel assembly between two end supports, rather like an electric spit or rotisserie. The reel must be removed from the supports to release a skein. A contemporary example of this arrangement is found in the several "yarn blocker" designs.

A clock or click reel is much faster and better than a niddy.

Yarn blockers can be used to make skeins as well.

Equipment for unwinding skeins

Imagine that the skein produced in our opening scenario has now been washed and dried. Further imagine that we wish to wind it into balls for knitting convenience. This transition to the next packaging form brings us to our second consideration, unwinding skeins.

Other Person. The classic "skein unwinder" is any Other Person. This Other Person extends both arms forward, elbows gently bent, palms facing each other yet with a slight upward tilt. The body position is similar to that assumed by individuals explaining to the officer why they were slowly backing the wrong direction up a one-way street.

The winding-operative (love it!) installs the skein around Other Person's arms and hands. Other Person is charged with keeping mild tension on the yarn, no matter what happens. The winding-operative takes up a station facing Other Person, yet several feet removed, and proceeds to wind the yarn into one or more balls. Other Person stands there, shifting body weight from foot to foot, moving arms and hands gently so the yarn unskeins in orderly fashion.

This system, generally available at no direct cost, has several drawbacks. First, it is not always available. Second, it requires cooperation from some Other Person. Third, it is slow and often temperamental, because Other Person may draw the line at handling certain types and conditions of yarn.

Mechanical unwinders in general. As a result, we have mechanical skein unwinders. There is a major difference between a skein-winder and a skein unwinder: the winder has a precise and fixed diameter, and the unwinder accommodates skeins of different diameters. It adjusts, for a simple reason. It is difficult to stretch a skein of yarn enough to get it back around what it was originally skeined on. If the yarn is cellulosic (cotton, hemp, flax, ramie, and their relatives), this stretching becomes impossible.

The skein unwinder can be reduced in diameter, making it easy to install a skein, no matter how inextensible the fiber is or how much the skein has shrunken. The skein unwinder may also be expanded so that it places appropriate working tension on the yarn.

Skein-unwinding devices bear the general name of *swift*. Of the several types, three interest handspinners: (1) the umbrella swift, (2) the lampshade or lantern swift, and (3) the squirrel-cage swift.[2]

Umbrella swift. The umbrella swift consists of a series of loosely joined slats arranged around a pair of central hubs. The hubs themselves

---

[2] *Because the word* swift *has a broader meaning when applied to textile and fiber appliances, not all swifts are yarn unwinders. In general,* swift *means the main rotating cylinder or working surface of a machine or device—for example, the swift of a carding machine. Of course, in carding terminology this swift goes by another name, the cylinder. But not to worry. To handspinners, the word* swift *means a yarn unwinder. In other words, a* rice.

are mounted upon a center shaft in such a way that the hubs rotate freely. In addition, one or both hubs may slide independently up or down the central shaft, producing changes in the angles of the joined slats and thus adjusting the swift diameter. The basic adjustment action is similar to that of old-fashioned "lazy tongs," or, if you will, an umbrella. Well, not exactly like an umbrella, but, as with the umbrella, movement of a hub along the central shaft causes the device to expand or contract.

In use, the umbrella swift is mounted on a table or other convenient surface. The user opens the swift to some experimental diameter, places a skein of yarn over it, then further expands the swift to working diameter and desired yarn tension.

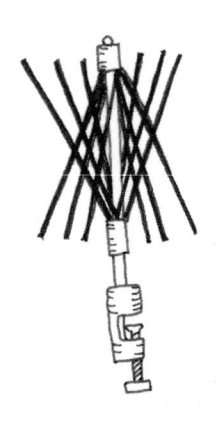

An umbrella swift changes diameter to accommodate different diameters of skeins.

This is a good place to advise you that swifts (and reels, too!) benefit from plenty of working space. Actually, the swift needs more "clear" space than the reel because during active use you will work at a distance from the swift and will not be able to keep an eye on local conditions. A swift in action stirs up breeze, dust, and loose yarn ends. It snags coffee cups and scissors. Always clear an operational space. You plan to proceed at a rapid pace, right? Make this possible by clearing the way.

Umbrella swifts are primarily a knitter's and needleworker's appliance. By nature and design, the umbrella swift is complex (many parts and joints), picturesque, and fragile. In general, the device is too fragile for serious or extended use by handspinners and weavers.[3]

---

[3] *A typical modern umbrella swift has perhaps 30 moving parts. Until the late 1800s, an umbrella swift was the gift of choice for a sweetheart or mother. A labor of love, it required many hours of painstaking hand labor, using the best of materials. Thus, in spite of the delicate design, ancient ones were considerably more durable and serviceable than their modern counterparts. Nowadays, umbrella swifts are made with as little skilled labor as can be arranged, using indifferent material, to be sold at a low price. So how do you get a good one? You build it, and you take your time. We have included plans, of course, later in this book. Some interesting reading on swifts and related items is found in Gertrude Whiting's Old-Time Tools and Toys of Needlework. Technical accuracy was not Ms. Whiting's long suit.*

Lampshade or lantern swift. The lampshade or lantern swift, unlike the umbrella swift, is sturdy and plain and has but one moving part. There are no adjustments to make. In appearance, the device looks like its namesakes: a lampshade or a large, old lantern. Essentially it consists of a tapered frame, square at top and bottom. The taper occurs because the top square is smaller than the bottom square, and arms or rails connect the two squares. A typical lantern swift is perhaps 14 inches square at the top, 19 inches square at the bottom, with side rails 24 inches long. This tapered frame is mounted freely upon a central post, which in turn is fixed into a massive base.

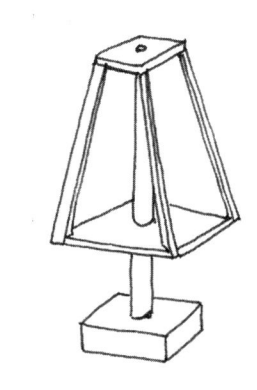

A skein of yarn is opened and simply dropped over the top of the frame. The skein slides down to the portion of the frame which matches its diameter and it can then be unwound.

A lantern swift is durable and simple.

Lantern swifts have several distinct characteristics. Because they are not adjustable, they can handle only a limited range of skein diameters. The skein diameter must match the swift diameter somewhere along the tapered arms. If the skein is too small, it cannot be installed. If the skein is too large, it will fall down past the swift frame.

If you plan to handle a wide range of skein diameters, you need more than one swift frame. In times past, this was not a problem. Skeins were produced "in-house" and the local swift was fitted to the local reel.

Squirrel-cage swift. Probably as a result of specialization, weavers of two centuries ago found themselves dealing with a wider range of skein diameters. Spinner and weaver no longer worked in the same household, or even the same village. Yarn for weaving might come from a new factory, a faraway city, or even distant and mysterious India. Skein diameters lost their predictability.

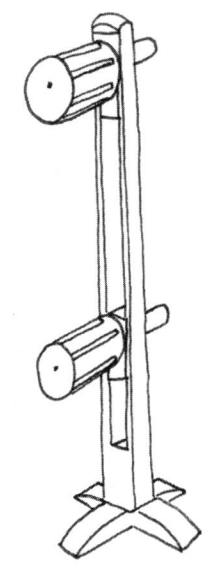

So people who handled large quantities of yarn needed something more durable than the umbrella swift and more adjustable than a lantern swift. Someone invented what is known today as a *squirrel-cage swift* or a *roller-cage swift*. This

Most versatile of the unwinders is the squirrel-cage swift.

The Alden Amos Big Book of Handspinning   269

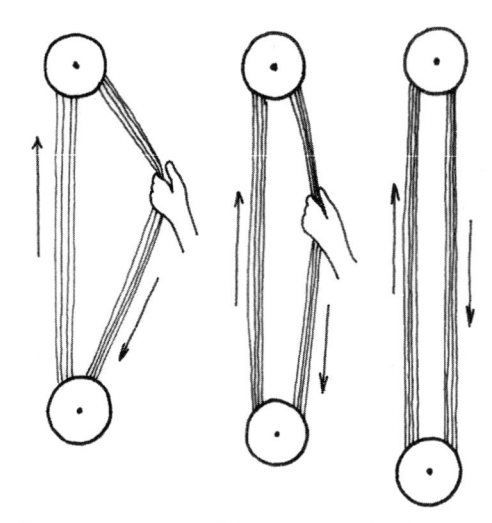

The squirrel-cage swift lets you round a skein. Rotate the skein while exerting pressure against it with your hands.

"modern" invention seems to date back no earlier than the middle of the eighteenth century. Although it originated in northern Europe, within 50 years its use spread to America's shore.[4]

A typical squirrel-cage swift has two flanged rollers, or *cages*, end-mounted on a central support plank. The cages are arranged to allow adjustment of their center-to-center distance. Once the vertical support plank has been attached to a suitable base, the entire affair stands perhaps 60 inches tall. The cages, usually 6 to 8 inches in diameter and 6 to 10 inches long, freely rotate on their center pins or axles.

To prepare the swift for use, raise and temporarily position the lower cage. Drape a skein over the upper cage, then arrange it between the flanges of the upper and lower cages. Adjust the lower cage downward, placing appropriate tension upon the skein. Locate the working end of the yarn, lead it to the next winding device you plan to use, and begin unwinding.

Unlike the other two types of swift (umbrella and lantern), the squirrel cage accommodates a technique called "rounding the skein"—a helpful stunt when you need to handle badly arranged or miswound skeins. Rounding begins by installing a skein on the swift in usual fashion, except with slightly less than normal tension. The operator braces the swift with foot or knee, then passes the skein around the cages repeatedly while exerting considerable pressure against the skein with the hands.

---

[4] *For practical purposes, historical dating of textile appliances is done by looking at pictures. No matter what literary references are at hand, the only acceptable proof seems to be a graphic representation—a picture. When you are dealing with a committee, the situation becomes worse: you need two or more pictures, from different sources. In any case, the squirrel-cage or roller-cage swift, sometimes called a* rice, *appears to be a product of continental Europe. There is reason to believe that it is a French invention.*

After a number of passes, the skein will have stretched. The operator increases tension on the skein and repeats the process, as many times as seem necessary.

What rounding does, of course, is even out the lengths of the individual turns in the skein. Too little pressure won't accomplish anything useful. Too much pressure, applied too quickly, will rupture the skein in various places. Bad day. It is not a good idea to use rounding on weak yarns.

The squirrel cage swift has some negative qualities. It has a tendency to "throw" large, bulky skeins unless considerable tension is applied. It is not charitable toward poorly wound skeins. Unless the swift is clean, well-oiled, and properly adjusted, it can make an unbelievable mess with a skein of fine yarn.

Squirrel-cage swifts are the "quickest" unwinder available to handspinners. The rotating parts reach considerable speed. As a result, they move with a lot of energy. Moral: don't get careless or casual with them.

SKEIN CONSTRUCTION

If a skein was not wound with care, it will not unwind well, no matter what sort of swift is used. And, because skeins represent the closest we have to an all-purpose yarn package, it is worthwhile to examine the fine points of skein construction.

It should come as no surprise that good skeins get their start during the spinning. If yarn has inconsistent twist, weak spots, and large variations in diameter, it will not wind quickly and easily. In addition, the way that yarn is distributed in the bobbin or on the spindle makes a big difference in the amount of time and trouble required to get the stuff off. Evenly filled bobbins and carefully built spindle copps unwind easily. Carelessly filled bobbins and sloppy copps do not. In hard truth, sometimes they do not unwind at all.[5]

---

[5] *Proper handspinners sneer at the word* unwind, *and rightly so. For example, suppose you are in a spinning class, and the leader says something like "All right, everyone, unwind your yarn." The correct and universally recognized term is* wind off. *To wind-off is to wind the yarn from one package to another package, as in the imaginary scenario where we wound off from the bobbin to a skein.*

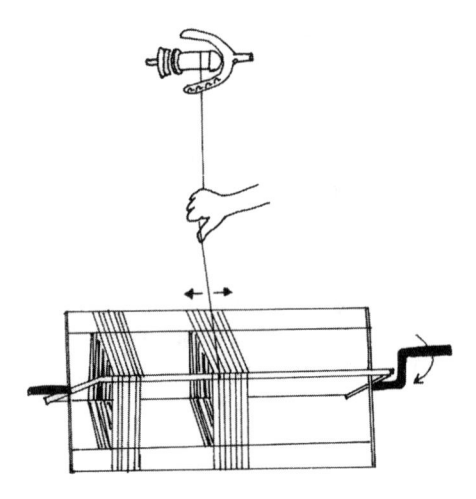

When winding to a reel, traverse the yarn back and forth. Wind to a space several inches wide.

Badly wound bobbins and copps affect the skein, if for no other reason than that your attention is divided. If the winding-off is going well, you can concentrate on building the skein. If the winding-off is not going well, you have to pay attention to something else.

Winding-off from a wheel bobbin to a skein begins with letting the yarn run in through the orifice, just as it does when you break the yarn. You do not want to wind-off through the orifice but from the bobbin alone.

Arrange things so that the bobbin has some braking tension against it and the flyer arms stay out of the way. Locate the yarn end and lead it to the skein-winder (reel or niddy). Attach the yarn end to the skein-winder in such fashion that you will be able to find and release the yarn easily. You will need the end when the skein is finished.

Decide which hand will guide and tension the yarn and which hand will turn and/or control the skein-winder. Made up your mind? Send your hands to work. One hand grasps, guides, and tensions the yarn between bobbin and skein-winder while the other hand is charged with turning the reel (or nodding the nid, as it were).

When winding-off to a reel, build the skein in crisscross fashion. To do so, traverse the yarn back and forth while winding, across a space about 2 or 3 inches wide for a small skein and about 4 or 5 inches wide for a big skein. Your traverse frequency should be less than the turning speed: say once across and once back for six turns of the reel.

Continue winding, maintaining uniform tension against the yarn, and keeping your attention on what is going on. If you see or feel something that you don't like, stop! A snarl, kink, or dropped turn may wind on just fine, but it will not wind off as sweetly.

Uniform, consistent tension is more important than the relative degree of tension, high or low. Actually, if the skein is not going to be wet-processed while still in place on the winding device, high tension is better than low tension, if only because high tension makes it easier to maintain uniformity. Winding a wet skein onto a yarn blocker is another matter, which we will discuss very soon.

Winding skeins offers a perfect opportunity to measure yarn length. If you are using a clock or other counting reel, this detail has been taken care of for you. If you are using a non-counting reel, or a nid, it is still fairly easy to obtain an accurate yardage figure. Something else to remember: checking yardage is important and you should do it whenever the occasion allows.

To determine yarn length when your winder doesn't do it for you, physically count the number of strands across any span and multiply this number by the winder circumference. For example, you have a niddy that makes a skein two yards around, and you count the strands spanning any two arms. You come up with 57 strands. Multiply the number of strands (57) by the skein diameter (2 yards). Your skein contains 114 yards. Suppose your reel is 1½ yards around and you count 112 strands. Proceed as above: number of strands (112) times skein diameter (1.5 yards). Answer? 168 yards.

You could simply count turns as you wind. The drawback to this plan is that you will lose track if you are distracted, as when you stop to repair a broken end, to reduce a snarl, or to look about for a pencil and paper to write something down. You will probably end up counting across the skein

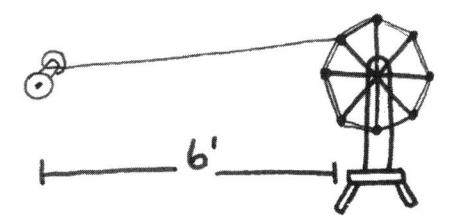

Winding off over a distance helps equalize the twist in your yarn.

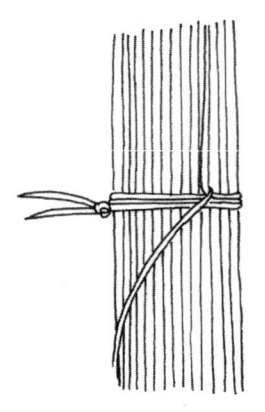

At the end of your skein, tie the original and final ends of the yarn together, leaving long tails. Wrap the tails loosely across the skein and tie them together again.

to verify your count anyway. Make life easier: don't worry about counting as you wind.

Winding-off to skeins also helps equalize the twist in your yarn. To take advantage of this feature, wind off with a fair distance between the bobbin and the hand that guides the yarn onto the skein-winder. As a guideline, try locating your guide hand about 6 feet from the wheel bobbin.[6]

Winding-off provides a second chance to fix bad joins, really gross slubs, and other weak or undesirable features in the yarn. (The first chance was while you were spinning.) The entire length passes through your hands and under your eye. If you see or feel something you are not pleased with, stop and make repairs.

When you have finished winding-off, you need to secure the skein so that it may be removed from the winder, handled in various ways, and eventually wound off into another yarn package. Find the end of the yarn that you originally attached to the skein-winder. Bring this end around and up to the outside of the skein. Tie it and the other end together, leaving long tails. Wrap the tails loosely across the skein, one above and one below, and tie them together again. This makes it easy to find the ends when you need them.

You will often wind a skein and find that there isn't enough yarn to bring the ends together. What to do? Some folks patch in a piece of

---

[6] *In general, the greater the distance, the better. On the other hand, as the distance increases, so does the required amount of tension. This is arranged by having the wind-off package (the wheel bobbin, in this example) braked in some manner. The procedure can be carried to extremes. Keep increasing the distance and tension and sooner or later you reach a point of negative return: the stupid thing is too hard to wind-off or the yarn keeps breaking. Note that the tension applied by the guide hand has little effect on equalizing twist, since there isn't much distance between hand and skein-winder. Tension applied here only serves to build neat and tidy skeins. The distance between the source package and the guide hand does the trick. In any case, distance between the source package and the guide hand should be at least twice the length of your make. You don't know what a make is? Go back to Chapter 2. The "right" amount of tension keeps the yarn straight (without sagging) over the package-to-package distance. Remember that as you wind off a bobbin, it speeds up as it empties; you must pay attention and adjust the brake accordingly.*

scrap yarn, but this is not a good idea. Better to back up a turn, break off the excess, and proceed as above. It will be easier to remember that you have 34 yards of the real yarn, rather than 34¾ yards plus a little bit of scrap.

Once you have secured the ends, you must install *lease-ties* (also called *leases, leashes,* or *safeties*). They keep the skein coherent during further handling, by preserving both order and direction of winding. No matter how tangled or distorted the package becomes, lease-ties save the day—but only if they are installed, and only if they are installed before you release the skein from the winder.

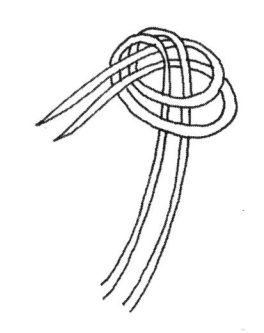

Here's a close-up of the knot.

A common question is "How many lease-ties should I use?" The answer is "Better too many than not enough!" As a rule of thumb, tie at least three for each yard of skein diameter. Thus a 2-yard skein requires 6 lease-ties, a 1½-yard skein needs at least 4, and so on. Use more rather than less, especially with large skeins of fine yarn.

Lease-ties should be made from yarn different in material and color from that in the body of the skein—at least different in appearance so they are easy to find. This is especially important when the skeins are later dyed. A good, all-purpose lease-tie material is a two- or three-ply cotton. Commercial pearl cotton offers a good alternative to cotton of your own.

There are several ways to tie leases, and all will give good results. Even though a good lease is better than a bad lease, a bad lease is a lot better than no lease. Here is how to tie a good, basic lease on a 2-yard skein. Divide the skein width into 3 equal parts. This means that you divide the solid, 3- to 5-inch–wide skein into sections between 1 and 1½ inches wide. Separate the sections by gently pushing the yarn apart. The sections don't need to be very far apart; a gap of ⅛ inch is plenty. Now follow around the skein, continuing the separations. When the skein has been sectioned, cut 6 pieces of lease-tie material, each about 24 inches long. Fold one tie in half, making a doubled piece of material about a foot long. Using the doubled end rather like the point of a needle, guide your tie down through the first skein separation, up through the second skein separation, down, around, and under the outside edge of the skein, back up through the second separation, down through the first separa-

The Alden Amos Big Book of Handspinning

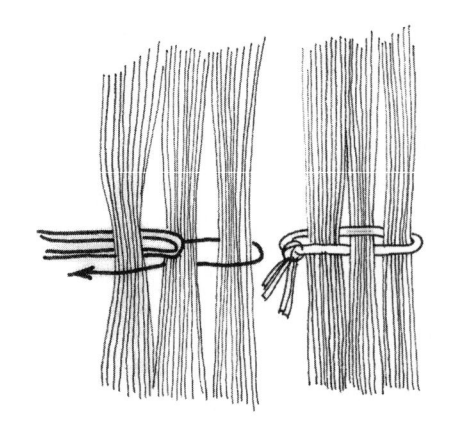

Leases keep the strands in a skein organized. Divide the skein into three equal parts, and separate the sections with ties that loop around both sides of each section.

tion, then under the first skein section, and out to you. Even up the ends of the lease material and knot them together. The best knot for the job is the common overhand, tied in all ends at once: treat all the ends as one piece of string and tie an overhand knot.

Allow plenty of slack in the lease, which is to say don't choke the skein sections. If you do not allow for generous movement, the lease-tie will act as a sort of resist during scouring or dyeing. Better too much slack than too tight.

Install the rest of the ties in the same manner. Exactly the same manner. Not that this style of lease-tie is superior (it is pretty good).

The principle is to tie all leases exactly the same, no matter what style you use. Uniformity matters because the lease-ties serve as a sort of road map to your skein. There is a weavers' saying, "trust your leases," which is just as true for handspinners.

You have no time or need to deal with a tangled skein, one with sloppy and indifferent lease-ties. Make the ties the same and space them the same. You will never regret it. Lease-ties are spaced equally around the skein. It is a good plan to locate one lease-tie right next to the starting-and-ending tie—the knotted ends and loop that show you where the beginning and end of the skein are.

Once you have installed the lease-ties, you can release the skein. Surprisingly, a skein is quite a durable package. More so than a cone, a ball, or even a storage spool. About the only thing that can derange a well-constructed skein is for it to get snagged on something that pulls one or more strands free from the skein body. This will have the effect of changing the skein diameter, or rather (and worse!) changing part of the skein diameter. It is a bother when you are ready to wind-off the skein into another package (although "rounding" the skein will usually set matters right). The free or extended strands tend to snarl, tangle, wrap around, and get mixed up with everything available. The big danger is that these free ends will get themselves broken, in which case you will be dealing with a "broken" skein and you have my sympathy.

Skein handling

Wet skeins. Now we will imagine that you have washed this skein and you want to set the yarn. Setting the yarn can certainly be done in the skein, but you will get better results by winding-off to a blocking reel. This means that you will be winding-off a wet skein. In the interest of keeping the terminology and jargon straight, you will be winding off the skein and winding on a blocking reel. Once again, moving the yarn from one package to another—in this case, from a skein package to a reel package.[7]

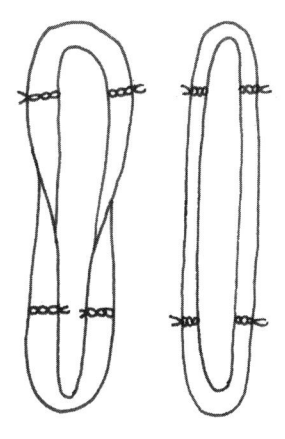

Before you install a skein on a swift and begin to unwind it, make sure it is straight.

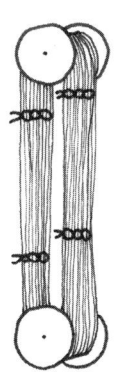

Winding-off skeins demands a certain protocol. You must first install the skein on a swift of some sort, or, lacking that, an Other Person. We will continue on the assumption that you have a swift.

Before you install the skein, look it over. Do the lease-ties all look alike? Do the strands of the skein pass through those ties in a logical and visible order? Does anything look out of place? If so, correct these things before going further.

Once everything is in order, install the skein on the swift and adjust to a comfortable tension. On a lantern swift, adjusting tension means pushing the

Then arrange the skein on the swift and adjust it to a comfortable tension.

---

[7] *Generally speaking, a blocking reel is a large form of bobbin, which makes it a side-delivery package. This is discussed at length in the chapter on plying. Just to tweak your curiosity, given the right design and circumstances a blocking reel may also be an end-delivery package. A skein is always a side-delivery package, except when it is being wound off with the aid of some Other Person. Then the Other Person and the skein form a side-delivery package. To tweak you further: side-delivery packages are always core-stabilized and end-delivery packages may not be. Does that make sense? Do you care?*

After you have located and separated the two ends, use the outside one to start unwinding.

skein farther up or down on the frame. Mess, fiddle, and fuss around with the skein until it is as neat and tidy as you can manage. Then, and only then, remove and discard all lease-ties.

Find the skein yarn-end tie, cut the loop, and break the two ends apart. With luck (and good preparation!) you will have located the inside and outside ends of the skein. The one you want is the outside end. Lead the outside end to the next winding device, fasten it to the device, and you are ready to go.

Or you will be, as soon as you check to see that everything is out of the way, that the swift is stable and securely mounted, that water drops and spray are not going to hurt anything, and that you have a workable plan for instant shut-down (stopping everything) should the need arise. The need will arise the moment the yarn breaks or snags, when the swift collapses, when the phone rings, or for any number of other reasons.

Because this skein is wet, special rules apply. If your yarn is cotton or another cellulosic fiber, wind as fast and as heartily as you please; these fibers are stronger when wet. If your yarn is wool, or even silk, take more care, especially in the tension department, because wool and wool-like fibers are weaker when wet. Winding a wet woolen or worsted yarn onto a blocking reel calls for "mild" or "moderate" tension. Unless you have a specific reason to stretch the yarn, use only enough tension to keep the yarn from sagging between the reel slats or arms.

When winding onto a blocking reel, traverse widely. Make your traverses from side to side of the reel, instead of using the 2- to 5-inch traverse you employed when winding skeins. A typical blocking reel is from 12 to 20 or more inches wide, so traverse accordingly, with about two turns of the reel for each trip across the surface. The idea is to space the yarn so that it will dry quickly. If the skein has been treated with sizing (a process often involved in preparing warps), close winding will let the strands glue together and the yarn will be tedious, if not impossible, to wind-off.

When winding a wet skein onto a blocking reel, traverse widely so the yarn will dry quickly. If you have sized your yarn, this will also minimize the tendency of the strands to stick together.

Preparation for plying. *Another sort of winding-off precedes plying.* While you can ply from hand-wound balls, the process qualifies as an act of desperation rather than a productive technique.[8] You can ply from skeins, although that is fairly involved because you need to have two (or more) swifts, and it is difficult to adjust their rotation so that you maintain proper plying tension. You may also ply in "traditional" fashion. As you fill each bobbin, you remove it from the wheel, place it on a rack, and continue spinning on a new bobbin. You continue this until you have spun an appropriate amount of yarn or you run out of bobbins. Then you begin to ply.

For reasons discussed in Chapter 11, these are not the best ways to ply. A better job of plying results when you wind off from the wheel bobbins to storage bobbins, and then ply from the storage bobbins. For

---

[8] *Here is one of the few existing "clean" spinning jokes, a two-parter which illustrates the point. Part one: How do handspinners know when they are in Heaven? Answer: they are greeted with "Welcome to Heaven, here's your reel, swift, and bobbin winder." Part two: How do handspinners know when they are in the other place? Answer: they are greeted with "Welcome to Hell, here's your niddy and your coffee cans."*

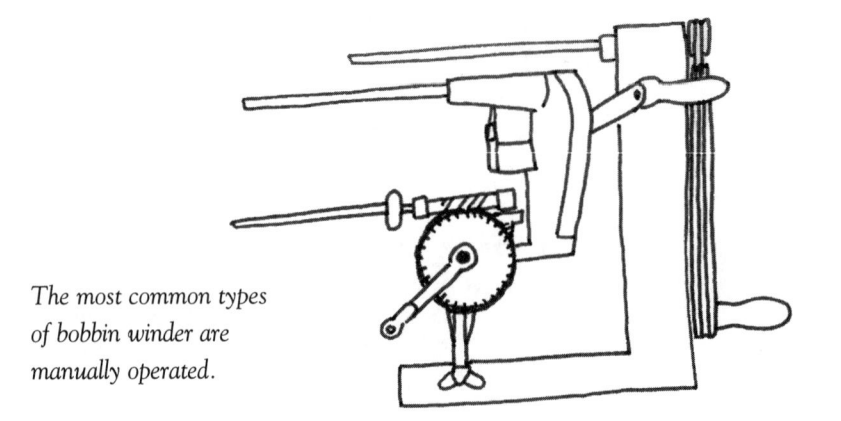

The most common types of bobbin winder are manually operated.

this reason, you need to know something about winding-on to storage bobbins.

("Wait a minute," you say, "what are storage bobbins?" For practical purposes, a storage bobbin is any bobbin not being used in the spinning wheel.[9])

In order to wind yarn onto a bobbin, you need to be able to rotate that bobbin rapidly. The device that accomplishes this is called a *bobbin winder*. A bobbin winder can be as simple as a rod stuck in a hand drill, or as complex as an automatic affair that loads, winds, and spits out bobbins without any interference on your part. The most common and useful form consists of a drive wheel, a drive cord, and a spindle, all mounted on a convenient base.

The drive wheel, usually about 6 inches in diameter, is fitted with a knob or crank-handle. The spindle is between 3 and 6 inches long,

---

[9] *There is room for improvement in the terminology. The author makes a distinction between bobbins for spinning and bobbins for yarn storage by calling the storage item a spool. Technically, these two types of bobbins can be constructed differently. The "spinning bobbin" must meet requirements not demanded of the "storage bobbin." Storage bobbins don't have to be precise, well-balanced, and fitted the way wheel bobbins do. Storage bobbins can be less expensive than wheel bobbins, and their size is not limited by flyer dimensions. You can obtain bobbins built specifically for storage (worthwhile if you ply lots of yarn), but for general and moderate service, standard Ashford bobbins make pretty good storage bobbins. See the bobbin plans later in this book for more specific information on our ideas.*

roughly ¼ inch in diameter, and very often split for the greater portion of its length. This spindle, fitted with a drive pulley, is mounted above the drive wheel. A drive cord, routed over the spindle pulley and around the wheel, typically turns the spindle 8 to 10 times for each rotation of the drive wheel.

A frequent variation replaces the drive wheel with a gear and the spindle pulley with a matching, smaller gear or, in one case, with a worm section. You can easily recognize this type of bobbin winder by its all-metal construction and by its solid, tapered spindle shaft.

Most bobbin winders are designed to wind shuttle bobbins, but with a little adaptation they will wind storage bobbins quite well. The adaptation consists of making the spindle shaft fit snugly in your storage bobbin cores. If your bobbin winder has a split spindle, making it fit your storage bobbins is usually a matter of spreading or narrowing the spindle slightly. If you have a bobbin winder with a solid shaft, then you have to stuff a little wool into the bobbin core, or wind tape or string onto the spindle shaft, or fill the gap with a combination of tape, wool, string, rubber bands, and whatnot. Don't lose sight of the fact that you want to remove and replace the bobbin without a lot of trouble.

Once you have fitted the bobbin to the winder, you are almost ready to wind-on. As before, check your setup and arrangements, making sure that everything runs freely, that nothing is going to get snagged, and that you will be able to stop without heroic gyrations.

Winding-on to a storage bobbin is much like winding-on to a skein. One hand turns and controls the winder while the other guides and tensions the yarn. There is one big difference. With the skein, you want to develop a crisscross package. With the storage bobbin, you want to lay in the turns smoothly and firmly, side by side, layer after layer. The main idea is to keep the bobbin diameter as even and uniform as possible, because any sudden change in package diameter will cause trouble when you ply.

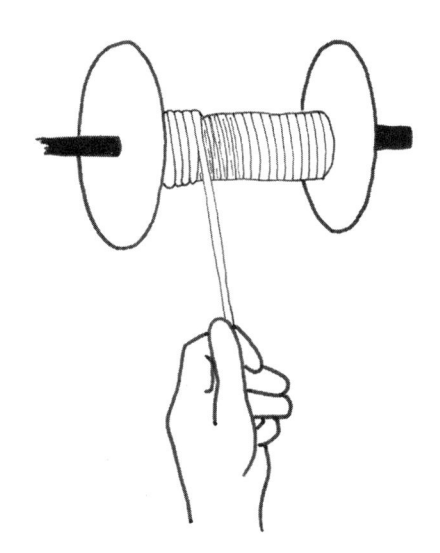

Wind a bobbin so that its diameter stays uniform.

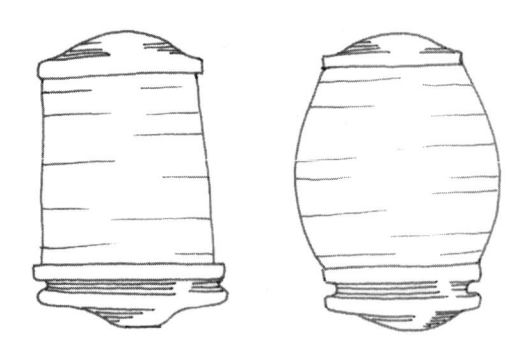

Do not overfill storage bobbins. The bobbin on the left looks good. The fiber football on the right will cause problems later.

Do not overfill storage bobbins. If your storage bobbins are large, each will hold the yarn from several wheel bobbins. Use that as an increment—say, two wheel bobbins per storage bobbin. If you are using reassigned wheel bobbins as storage packages, fill them disk-to-disk, or level across. Don't make them look like fiber footballs.

Use moderate tension. You need enough tension to pack the yarn in firmly and smoothly, but not so much that the yarn is stretched or under obvious strain. If you are winding a lean, hard-twist yarn, you will know you are using too much tension when the ends of the bobbin pop off the core. Moderation in all things.

As in all yarn-handling operations, winding-off to storage bobbins presents you with an opportunity to review, upgrade, and refine the yarn. Because none of us is perfect, it is not likely that we spin a perfect yarn. It is also not likely that we will catch every fault the first time we wind off, or the second time, or even the third. But we can try. So hit it a lick every chance you get. The results will be worth it.

Making balls of yarn. Let us imagine that you have spun a yarn, wound off to storage bobbins, plied the yarn, wound off to skeins, washed the yarn, wound off to blocking reels, and now are ready to wind-off once more, this time to balls for knitting.

Ball winders come in quite a variety of types, all more complex than they look. What you need to pay attention to is correct threading, and keeping the yarn out of the gears and works. Other than that, you crank. You will tend to make your first few balls too large, but that will pass.

Most available ball winders are designed to wind-off from commercially coned yarn. This means a handspinner often needs to wind-off twice in order to form useful balls of yarn. Because ball winders are very sensitive to the yarn tension, a ball wound at speed from a swift will be too compact, too dense, and too hard to be comfortable in use. The simplest way to take care of this is to wind the ball twice.

This is not as bad as it sounds. It goes pretty quickly. Start by winding-off to the ball winder, making as many balls as are required. Then line them up and wind off each one to the ball winder again. This time, the balls will be much softer and pleasanter to use.

Yarn to be used for machine knitting should be waxed. The only reason we mention that now is that the time and place to take this action is during the great ball wind-off. All you do is keep a cake of paraffin wax in gentle contact with the yarn as it zips through your guide hand. You only have to wax once, and you don't use very much wax: if you have cut a couple of minor notches in the cake by the time you're done, you have used plenty.

That is about all there is to yarn handling. To be sure, there are refinements and special operations, and they are discussed in their proper place. But for now, you should know more than enough to make sense of the next chapter.

When winding balls from a swift or reel, always rewind the ball into yet another ball. This reduces tension in the yarn.

Chapter 11

Plying: An introduction to a high-level skill, often taken for granted

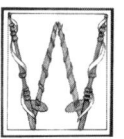

We tend to take plying for granted. The general attitude is that if you are able to spin yarn in the first place, anything as easy as plying comes with the territory. That would be nice, but it isn't so. Plying calls for as much skill as spinning singles. By now you know that there is more to spinning singles than "just twisting and drafting," and so it is with plying.

Because plying looks so easy, many handspinners see no reason to study the art. This is too bad, because the plying process contains so many inherent design possibilities. Plying provides the means for producing novelty yarns, crochet yarns, knitting yarns, and any other yarns that might benefit from twist stability, high tensile strength, wear resistance, unusual color effects, and/or true softness with strength and elasticity.

There are good reasons to ply yarns, and good reasons not to ply them. To make sense of these reasons, you must begin by understanding that spinning and plying differ in fundamental ways. In truth, their only common ground involves the presence of yarn and the use of a twisting device, such as a spinning wheel.[1]

Read the next two statements carefully.

Useful abbreviations for this chapter in particular

PTPI	plying twists (or turns) per inch
TPI	twists (or turns) per inch
YPP	yards per pound

---

[1] *Certain irreverent persons of the author's acquaintance have remarked that the similarities involve "the presence of yarn and a nut."*

Spinning is a process of attenuation, with a fiber mass being drafted and drawn out while twist is introduced, either concurrently or as a following step. The working material of spinning is a *fiber mass*, and the immediate product is a *single strand*, or *end*, of *twist-active* yarn.

Plying is a process of twisting multiple yarn ends about a shared longitudinal axis. The working material is *two or more strands* of yarn, and the immediate product is a *plied (multi-element) yarn*, which *may or may not be twist-active*. No attenuation takes place.

The differences are more than theoretical. Plying goes faster than spinning singles. One reason for this is because the typical plied yarn requires less twist than the singles that go into it. Because there is no need to draft, plying seems simpler than spinning singles. Also, the great fear of many handspinners, that of breaking the yarn, is removed. (Yarns do break during plying, yet for some reason not fathomed by the author, no handspinner engaged in plying seems concerned.)

The point to be made is that to do plying justice, you must make mental room for some things that are quite different from what you know about handspinning. Actually, to be good at plying you don't have to know a lick about spinning. You don't even have to spin the yarn that you ply. In fact, an excellent way to learn about plying as well as yarn structure and design is to ply, twist, de-ply, and re-assemble commercial yarns in various ways. Such activities are known as *yarn reconstruction*, the relatively simple process of taking a yarn apart and then putting it back together in a different way.

This raises the question of why you would want to do such a thing, or, more germane to our discussion, why, how, and when yarns are plied?

WHY PLY?

Yarns are plied to develop qualities available through no other procedure. These specific ply-related qualities may be demanded by the design and/or structure of the end fabric or textile. For example, most sweaters of all types are knitted from plied yarns.

Why? Could it be because people who knit tend to be traditional and conservative and are aghast at the notion of knitting singles?

Well, there is a little more to it than that.[2] Tradition aside, a plied yarn is stronger than an equivalent single and, unlike the single, can be twist-stable. All else being equal, the plied yarn is more elastic and more resilient than an equivalent single, and it will withstand more wear before failing. The plied yarn has more loft, more warmth, and a better *hand*.

If these statements are true, why aren't plied yarns used for everything? Because "everything" does not require or even benefit from their use. By and large, knitted articles benefit from use of plied yarns, while woven fabrics, especially of garment weight, may not.

The conventional two-ply yarn, a simple thing, consists of two single yarns twisted around their common center, in a direction opposite to their original direction of twist. With a proper amount of ply twist, the yarn ends up *balanced* or *twist-stable*, which means that the yarn has no tendency to twist or untwist itself. The opposite of twist-stable is *twist-active*. A twist-active yarn tends to twist or untwist itself, given an opportunity. Single yarns are always considered twist-active. Plied yarns may or may not be twist-stable, depending upon their construction and their incumbent twist amounts.

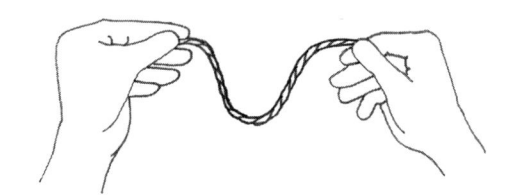

A twist-stable yarn has little or no tendency to twist or untwist itself.

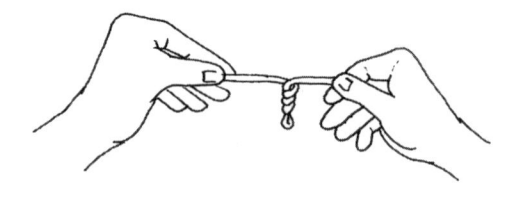

A twist-active yarn tends to twist or untwist itself.

---

[2] *In the author's experience, knitters are more opinionated than spinners, probably because the knitter tends to be the spinner's mother. Someone's mother, anyway. And you know how mothers are. Knitters seem to own uncanny skill in diversion: that is, they can divert a conversation away from topics they are not familiar with (such as spinning) toward topics you are not familiar with, such as obscure knitting techniques. All knitters possess the ability to spout authentic gibberish (a typical offering being the "left-handed single-needle Swibbonian two-color invisible cast-on"), and they are quick to do so when cornered. Of course, knitters do not have an exclusive right to the use of authentic gibberish. Take spinning wheel makers, for example. . . .*

Twist-stability is a relative condition. Insert a toothpick crossways through a balanced two-ply yarn. Stretch the yarn and then release it. The toothpick will rotate.

Here's an experiment which demonstrates the *twist-active* status of single yarns. Obtain a yard-long sample of a single yarn. Tie one end to a ceiling hook and suspend a fishing weight from the other end. Allow the weighted end to hang freely. Depending upon local conditions—humidity, amount of weight, and so on—you have a sporting chance of getting out of the room before the sinker hits the floor. No, the yarn does not break. It untwists and drafts itself until it drifts apart.

Plied yarns, on the other hand, may approach the definition of *twist-stable*, although the term is, at best, relative. Here's your next experiment. Obtain or make a 3-foot length of balanced, mild-mannered, two-ply yarn. Tie a knot in each end. Stick a toothpick or matchstick crossways through the yarn, a few inches away from one of the knits and roughly centered between the strands. Now hold a knotted end in each hand, and slowly stretch the yarn taut. Watch the matchstick or toothpick rotate as you stretch the yarn, and then again as you relax it.

You started with a balanced, or twist-stable yarn, and yet this rotation occurs. So you can see that a truly twist-stable yarn is more a theoretical ideal than a real-live critter.

Remember your fundamentals? When you place end-to-end tension on a yarn (single or plied), it increases in length, reduces in diameter, and redistributes or equalizes twist along the stretched length. A given length of the yarn has slightly less twist when stretched: it has "unwound itself," and thus fits the description of twist-active.

It is not particularly important that the yarn has less twist. What matters is that the yarn rotates around its own axis, a twist-active

Suspend a weight from a single yarn and let it hang. It will untwist. All single yarns are twist-active.

The Alden Amos Big Book of Handspinning

characteristic that doesn't matter much to knitters but is of considerable interest to weavers.[3]

But we handspinners cannot thrive on theory alone. Take hope: plied yarns may be twist-stable, or at least twist-stable enough for most practical purposes.

The first benefit of a twist-stable yarn is in ease of yarn handling: the stuff doesn't kink up every time you relax yarn tension. For knitting, the main advantage in using twist-stable yarn is that it reduces or eliminates the form of knit-fabric distortion called *leaning* or *biasing*.

Yarns may be made twist-stable in other ways. Several yarn treatments (setting, blocking, and sizing) can establish transitory forms of twist-stability, and are of considerable value for ease in yarn-handling and conversion techniques. These treatments are reversible—which can be a strength or a weakness, depending upon your intent. Plying remains the only practical way to achieve permanent twist-stability.

SIMPLE, COMPLEX, AND THE MATTER OF STRENGTH

Plied yarns may be simple or complex. The two-ply we mentioned earlier is an example of a simple yarn. A complex yarn involves multiple strands, with each strand composed of two or more yarns. The basic two-ply yarn can be constructed by plying in the opposite direction of spinning twist. On the other hand, a complex yarn might be built from three strands of two-ply, each of which has been ply-twisted in the same direction as its singles were spun.

That is one example of a complex yarn. There are a surprising number of variations, considering that we have only two choices of twist direction.

---

[3] *The astute reader will observe that the plied yarn doesn't really untwist itself, but that a given amount of twist ends up being distributed over a greater length. So what? In some cases it might be less frustrating if the yarn did "untwist" itself and part company, giving you an idea of what to fix, and where. Instead, plied yarn tends to rotate and gyrate in response to changes in tension, grabbing the neighbors by the short hairs, shaking hands, and snarling everything up. This little feature alone once turned a perfectly serviceable mohair warp into an incredible, matted mess, in which a shed could be opened only with the aid of a shovel handle. That particular warp ended up in the circular file.*

The study of plying concerns the application of twist.

In spinning singles, you add twist to something that is not twisted. You will remember that yarn tensile strength is affected by the amount of twist more than by any other factor.

As you would expect, plying is different. The amount of ply twist doesn't make a great deal of difference in the tensile strength of the components. The yarns that are being twisted together either are strong or are not strong. The ply twist has little further effect on their strength. Notice that we said "little further effect": changing the incumbent twist amount always affects yarn strength, and whenever you ply a yarn you change the amount of twist in the individual strands.

During plying, twist is added to or taken away from each component yarns. In the case of the "simple" two-ply, plying takes twist away from each of the single yarns. Unless you put a slight "excess" of twist into each single before plying, this will reduce the tensile strength of each strand. Is that important? Yes, and no. Sometimes.

Yarn is not always plied simply to enhance tensile strength, which is not always important. Instead, you may be plying in order to develop such yarn qualities as loft, softness, elasticity, or to produce combinations of colors or fibers.

However, it is important to remember that the twist in the original single pretty much determines what the plied yarn is going to be.[4] To restate the obvious (and the important!): plying begins at the spinning stage. If you intend to ply the yarn you are spinning, put in a little more twist than you think you need. You will see why presently.[5]

---

[4] *This reiterates our major theme: the fabric or textile depends upon the yarn that goes into it, the yarn depends upon the spinning, the spinning depends upon the fiber, the fiber depends upon the preparation, and this is the warp that Jane built. You cannot make a silk purse out of a pig's ear, and all that. Put in a little more twist than you think you need.*

[5] *What about yarns spun by someone else? Can anything be done about them? Yes. If the yarn is a single, ram it back through the wheel, adjusting twist as you see fit. If the yarn has already been plied, you can still do something about it. However, the process requires numerous steps and we are not yet ready to get involved with it.*

TWIST: S AND Z, UP AND DOWN

Handspinners have various ways of describing twist direction. There are S twist and Z twist, of course; right-hand and left-hand twist; and clockwise and counterclockwise twist. Less frequently you'll encounter open-band and closed-band twist, and once in a while you will spot a reference in popular spinning literature to sun-wise twist.

For clarity, we use S twist and Z twist (explained in Chapter 5), supplemented with the terms *up-twist* and *down-twist* when we consider plying and yarn reconstruction. *Up-twist* means that your current operation adds to the twist introduced during the previous operation. *Down-twist* means that you are reducing, or taking away from, the twist introduced during the previous operation. Down-twist is the opposite of up-twist.

As an example, let's return to our simple two-ply. Suppose that the single yarns were spun as Z-twist, which is the "normal" direction for woolen yarns. For our simple two-ply, these singles are plied in the opposite direction, or S-twist.

Now suppose that this is linen, not wool. Tradition decrees that linen singles be spun S-twist. If they are plied in the opposite direction, then the plying is Z-twist.

But no matter in which direction the single has been spun, "normal" plying is in the opposite direction. In both cases, our simple two-ply example is plied *down-twist*. The

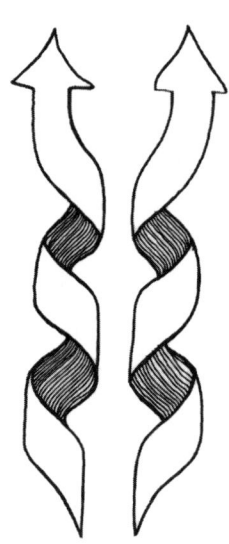

S twist (left) and Z twist (right).

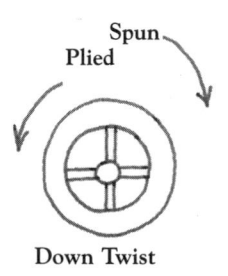

If you spin singles Z and ply them S, then you are plying down-twist.

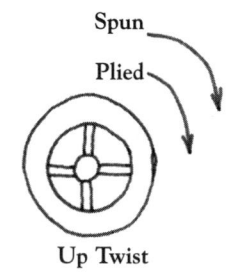

If you spin singles Z and ply them in the same direction, then you are plying up-twist.

ply-twist direction reduces twist introduced during the previous twisting operation.

Just for fun, let's look a little more closely at the previous example of a complex yarn, "three strands of two-ply, each of which has been ply-twisted in the same direction as its singles were spun." Further imagine that we want to construct such a yarn, which will make an excellent warp for a flat-woven rug.

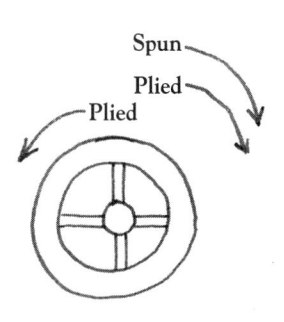

The construction known as *hawser* will serve our purpose very well. A hawser is made by assembling strands in which two or more singles are plied up-twist, and then plying two or more of the resulting strands down-twist.

To make a hawser, begin by assembling strands in which two or more singles are plied up-twist. Then ply two or more of those strands down-twist.

Stated in S and Z notation, that means that the plan of a hawser looks like this: Z-Z-S or S-S-Z. For Z-Z-S, the singles are spun Z, then two or more singles are plied Z, then two or more of these really strange two-plies are plied S. S-S-Z is just the reverse: the singles are spun S, then plied S, and the results are plied Z.

When we talk in terms of up-twist and down-twist, we do not need to mention a specific spinning direction. Regardless of initial twist direction, you produce a hawser by plying two or more ends up-twist, and then plying two or more resulting strands down-twist.

When singles are plied up-twist, the resulting strand may be described as twist-active. Actually, twist-active is too mild a label, so we use the term *twist-lively*. In fact, if they are not kept under control, singles plied up-twist are quite ill-behaved. Keeping them under control usually means keeping them under tension.

THE FOUR GREAT PRINCIPLES OF PLYING

First principle: Tension

This brings us to one of the four great principles of good plying: *keep all of your working yarns under tension*. This applies whether the working yarns are twist-lively, simply twist-active, twist-stable, or as limp and pacific as a boiled noodle.

The first principle of plying: keep the working yarns under tension.

And just what is a *working yarn*? It is any yarn you have not finished with yet: yarn on storage or wheel bobbins, yarn coming to your hands, yarn leaving your hands, yarn winding onto a blocking reel or other yarn package, all yarn that has not reached its final destination.

Second principle: Distance

The second great principle of good plying involves *distance*. Keep plenty of distance between your hands and the wheel, and keep plenty of distance between the yarn sources and your hands.

Distance during plying accomplishes all of the wonderful things for which it has received credit in previous chapters, and then some. As in spinning, distance allows you space and time in which to catch and correct mistakes.

As in yarn handling, the distance aids greatly in leveling the twist. It also prevents you from getting those embarrassing, greasy, orifice tracks all over your fingers, and does wonders for your back. Being 2 feet away is not enough. A fair number of spinners work very closely to the flyer, using a technique called "The Orifice Crawl." We have all seen it: the spinner, head bent, sits hunched over the wheel, busy fingers crowding the flyer, grimly handing in little 2- and 3-inch makes.

The second principle of plying: keep plenty of distance between the yarn sources and your hands and the wheel.

That is a ridiculous way to ply. It is a ridiculous way to do anything, but especially ridiculous for plying.

How much distance do you need? As a guideline, about 4 feet from the storage bobbins to you, about 1½ to 2 feet between your two hands, and 2 or 3 feet from your hands to the wheel. That works out to

292   The Alden Amos Big Book of Handspinning

about 8 feet between the yarn source (storage bobbins) and the wheel, with you more or less in the middle.

A little more distance won't hurt. The author's normal plying distance measures about 10 feet from yarn source to wheel. While a 20-foot plying array works and is interesting to watch, you then encounter concerns about blocking traffic and tripping innocent passersby.

Distance and tension. Keep these two in mind.

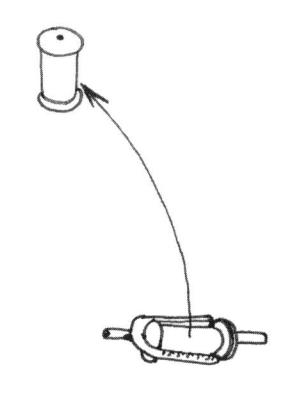

Third principle: Ply from re-wound bobbins

The third principle is to *ply from re-wound bobbins*. Wind off the wheel bobbin (or spindle) to storage bobbins, and use the storage bobbins as yarn sources during plying. The storage bobbin will be a better yarn package than the wheel bobbin because you have the opportunity to manually wind a tight and uniform bobbin. Consequently, re-winding improves yarn tension and produces more consistent layer-for-layer diameter.

The third principle of plying: re-wind to storage bobbins before you ply.

These qualities greatly enhance fast and faultless plying. The uniform-layer diameter means that the bobbin rotates at a steady speed, with no speed-ups or slow-downs caused by sudden changes in bobbin diameter. The firm winding ensures that (1) the bobbin holds more yarn and, (2) the working end is not so eager to bury itself below the surface and ruin your day.

For greatest consistency, spin the entire lot of yarn on the same bobbin.

As a secondary benefit, re-winding releases the wheel bobbin for more spinning. Because no two bobbins perform in exactly the same way, you will achieve the greatest yarn consistency by using the same wheel bobbin to spin all the yarn in a given lot.[6] In addition,

---

[6] Most handspinners agree with this last item in practice, even while decrying the theory at full volume. Every spinner has a favorite bobbin, and nine times out of ten it is the one in the flyer. At the very least, winding off the wheel bobbin lets you keep using your favorite. That in itself will help you produce a superior yarn, if for no other reason than you feel good about it. In addition, if you wind off from the flyer, you have a ready-made holder for the bobbin during that process.

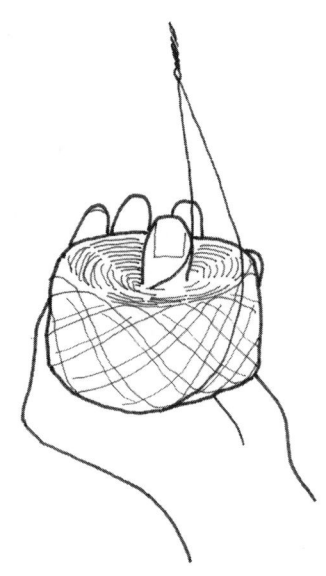

Plying from a center-pull ball works for short samples or as a demonstration. The technique has limitations for serious work.

Plying from surface-fed balls gives rise to madness.

winding-off (as always) affords you an opportunity to refine and improve your yarn. And it is a demonstrable fact that the best all-around yarn package for hand workers to ply from is a firmly and evenly wound storage bobbin or spool.

Digression on yarn packages

This brings us to a consideration of yarn packages. To begin, there are primary packages and secondary packages. A *primary package* is the form into which the yarn is wound as it is spun. Examples include the supply on a wheel bobbin or the copp built on a spindle. Because we are considering plying, the only thing you need to remember is that primary packages are not good to ply from. The yarn needs to be wound-off into a secondary package.

Secondary packages include all those forms that yarn is wound to after spinning: skeins, balls, cones, other bobbins, and so forth. A secondary package has been rewound. Not all secondary yarn packages are suited to plying. The best packages for plying make it easy to keep all working yarns under tension. For example, skeins are not good to ply from unless specialized yarn-handling equipment is available. Center-pull balls are not good, either, except for short samples and as an amazing demonstration for pilgrims. For a variety of reasons, the center-pull trick is less than adequate in serious work.

Spinners often resort to plying from surface-fed balls (the old-fashioned granny balls), although this practice gives rise to madness. If it does not produce madness on the part of the operator, it invokes madness in any pet able to view and participate in the operation.

As in yarn handling, the best package form is the one which best serves the next step. In this case, we want the package form that best suits plying.

Yarn storage packages are classed as either *side delivery* or *end delivery*, depending on how they best unwind. Notice the key word *best*. End-delivery packages can often be unwound in side-delivery fashion, although side-delivery packages usually won't unwind in end-delivery mode.

In a side-delivery package, the package rotates while yarn is removed. Side-delivery packages include the bobbin in your wheel, a storage bobbin or spool on a lazy kate, standard shuttle bobbins, and a skein mounted upon a swift.

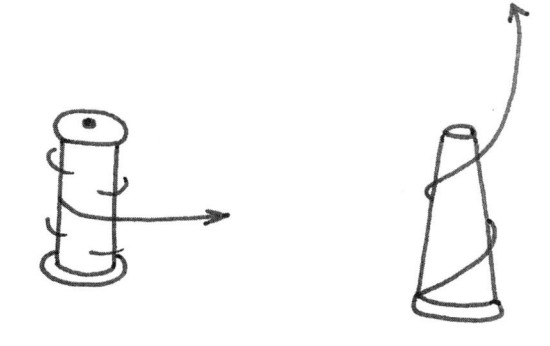

Yarn storage packages can be unwound in either side-delivery or end-delivery fashion.

An end-delivery package does not need to rotate during unwinding. Some end-delivery packages are yarn cones, the tapered copps on great wheels, center-pull balls, the pirns in fly shuttles, or Another Person who supports a skein (normally a side-delivery package) around poor, aching, outstretched hands and arms.

Side-delivery and end-delivery packages have advantages and disadvantages.

End-delivery packages feature high-speed unwinding and excellent start-and-stop capacities because there is no significant rotating mass to deal with. On the negative side, end-delivery packages must be carefully built to work at speed, and they are relatively fragile. They are cranky about what yarns they will feed. In addition, end-delivery packages cannot maintain or control tension on the yarn as it is delivered.

For this reason alone, the end-delivery package is less than ideal for plying, especially when twist-lively yarns are involved. Twist-lively yarns seem to jump off the package, find a companion yarn, and snarl together, instantly and without any effort on the spinner's part.

Side-delivery packages can handle any yarns, at any time, in any place, and are forgiving as to construction. They don't have to be wound "perfectly" to work, although the more carefully they are wound, the better they work. From the plyer's point of view, side-delivery packages have the great advantage of allowing direct and simple yarn tensioning.

The main difficulty with side-delivery packages is that they must rotate to deliver yarn.

Therein lies a problem: the package wants to remain at rest when you need it to get turning, and then it wants to keep turning when you need it to stop. In the first instance, the yarn may break because you have pulled a little too hard or too fast, particularly if the yarn is fine. In the second instance, the bobbin coasts merrily along, dispensing extra and unwanted yarn. The bobbin then re-winds itself the wrong way, generating a nasty tangle called a *backlash*.

Even so, side-delivery packages are well suited to hand plying. Their inherent problems can be pretty well controlled, if not eliminated, by using good techniques and proper equipment.

Fourth principle: Constant motion

The fourth principle of plying is *constant motion*—specifically, you need to keep all yarns in constant motion.

The yarn passing through your hands never stops moving; the yarn winding onto the wheel bobbin never stops going through the orifice; the storage bobbins or packages never stop turning; and your hands never stop.

It may sound involved although it is not. There are several ways to accomplish constant motion, but first we need to explain why it is important.

A twist-active yarn will attempt to ply itself. Sometimes it succeeds. Most often it only produces snarls and kinks. It cannot do these obnoxious things as long as it is under tension.

When you keep the yarn moving, always traveling, it must necessarily be under tension for you to wind-off the storage bobbin. Result? No kinks, snarls, pigtails, or other nuisances. All of which make for a

The fourth principle of plying: keep everything in constant motion.

superior yarn. Even if you do not seek to make a superior yarn, controlling snarls and kinks allows you to produce mediocre yarn at greater speed, since you won't waste time trying to ignore snarls, kinks, and other clutter.

When you are plying, you actually wind off one yarn package (storage bobbin, whatever) and wind onto another yarn package (the wheel bobbin), by way of the orifice and the flyer arms. Of course, you are twisting the yarns during the process. Nonetheless, you wind off and wind on.

Consequently all the principles, procedures, and stunts for yarn handling outlined in Chapter 10 pertain here, right? Yes, indeed. Plying is a glorified form of yarn handling, with a little twist, ha, ha. A little joke.

PLYING METHODS

Along with the joke comes a diversion. It is certainly possible to ply yarns with a handspindle or a driven spindle (like a great wheel). If this were not the case, plied yarns would not have existed until the High Renaissance.[7] That is silly as plied yarns existed well before then, but the observation contains an interesting point about efficiency. For hand plying, flyer-and-bobbin systems are far superior to any spindle.

You can ply on a spindle for reasons of historical and technical authenticity, or for research, or because you do not have access to more suitable equipment. Or perhaps you just choose to work that way. No argument there. Still, when productivity and quality of the finished yarn are of concern, the flyer-and-bobbin systems have the field to themselves.

---

[7] *It is a widely known fact that Leonardo da Vinci did not invent the flyer and bobbin. It is also known that he engaged in design work involving a power-driven, level-winding, flyer-and-bobbin mechanism. It is the author's contention that Leonardo was investigating plying equipment, and that he had neither the intent nor the desire to develop spinning equipment. Then, as now, the flyer and bobbin represented an immense improvement over the spindle with respect to plying, and the technology to make Leo's plying device existed in his time. The technology that supports machine carding, sliver, and "cheese" production did not. Nor does it appear that Leo was ever involved with the mechanics of drafting fibers, and no work along those lines became public until the early eighteenth century—centuries after his death.*

This does not mean that you cannot ply yarn with simple implements. You can. However, plying is much easier and more productive when you have the right equipment and techniques. You can drive a nail with a rock, but a hammer makes the task a bit easier and if you intend to drive a lot of nails over an extended period of time, you might want to invest in a hammer.

Jerk-it and tromp-and-hope plying

Now, you would imagine that handspinners everywhere know that a twist-active yarn tries to kink when the tension is off. They probably do. Still, they seem to care nothing about this fact when plying, an observation which brings us to a discussion of the most commonly used modern plying method, the jerk-it approach.[8]

Jerk-it plying, also known as *jerk-and-curse plying,* proceeds thus: the operator, seated before a spinning wheel, jerks lengths of yarn from an indifferent assortment of yarn packages. When twisted together, the several strands run into the orifice. This cycle repeats, with frequent pauses to correct broken ends, snarls, tangles, and related faults. In all fairness, jerk-and-curse works. A great deal of yarn gets plied with this technique. However, there are better ways.

All you need to know about jerk-it plying is contained in the preceding paragraph. The lack of rules, guidelines, and performance criteria probably accounts for the system's widespread popularity. In case you are wondering, the "curse" part in the alternate appellation refers to the

---

[8] *Handspinning enjoys a colorful vocabulary. There are the "traditional" terms, such as* mother-of-all, retting, lazy kate, scour, rolag. *Then there are the contemporary phrases, some no doubt destined for use and argument in the next century. By "contemporary" we mean phrases that are instantly recognized by today's handspinner, yet would have required explanation to a Victorian counterpart. Consider* SOAR, Spin-Off, charkha, production wheel, Schacht, 30-weight, Ashford, cashgora, SS&D, Convergence, sheep-to-shawl, motor spinner, long draw, tahkli . . . *the list goes on. Modern writers in the field (present company included) are responsible for introduction of many items, of course . . . but you, the handspinner, either adopt or reject each usage. Handspinners today are far better read than at any previous time in history, and today's handspinner communicates with other handspinners almost instantly. As a result, our handspinning vocabulary is growing and changing, and you, gentle reader, are the final authority on definition and usage.*

interjection of colorful words and phrases by the operator at appropriate intervals.[9]

A less popular, yet still fashionable, system of plying is called *tromp-and-hope*. Tromp-and-hope plying borders on good plying technique, except that too much attention must be devoted to keeping it going. Consequently, not enough attention is paid to degree and uniformity of tension or to consistent twist distribution.

Tromp-and-hope plying proceeds as follows: the operator sets up assorted freely rotating bobbins close to hand, leads the several strands through the orifice, and attaches them to the bobbin. As soon as the wheel has been adjusted for maximum winch, the operator holds the separate strands loosely, depending entirely upon wheel take-up to pull yarn from the storage bobbins, through the hands, and into the orifice. It is necessary to treadle desperately to accomplish this end—thus the name.

With this method, it is impossible to place sufficient tension on the yarns being plied and it is virtually impossible to maintain an even rate of twist insertion. The technique requires inordinate amounts of physical effort, at least when using a conventional treadled wheel, and practitioners must be more concerned with keeping the operation up to tempo than with controlling yarn characteristics. The same imbalance applies to oarsmen in racing shells: they must concentrate on pulling, and cannot in all fairness be expected to steer.

All in all, tromp-and-hope plying is full of sound and fury, and is thus fascinating to watch. It is not particularly productive, and results in yarns that have considerable variation in twist.

---

[9] *An ongoing survey (The Spinning/Weaving Joke Project) has produced interesting related information concerning spinner curses, "bad" words, and interjections. Because this book is striving for a PG rating, we shall be suitably obscure. The one word favored above all others for use in dynamic situations is the well-known Anglo-Saxon S-word, delivered in standard military form. Regional differences affect pronunciation and speed of delivery. For static tragedies and unpleasant discoveries, the S-word is prefaced by the word OH and ended invariably with the exclamatory, according to the formula prefatory word, S-word, exclamatory. Example: OH, S-word! The F-word is also used, with greater frequency than one might think, often accompanied by implausible verbiage. Space does not permit further elaboration, but it may be seen that the handspinner's vocabulary is, indeed, colorful.*

Neither of the two preceding plying methods includes all four of the plying principles.

Hand-over-hand plying

A method that does include all four principles is called *hand-over-hand plying*. It is a little more involved than the other methods. It requires more attention to detail, and usually more working space.

Hand-over-hand plying begins with the physical arrangements. Storage bobbins, set up at some distance from the operator, are tensioned or braked so that they stop rotating the moment the yarn stops moving. The yarn ends are then led to the wheel, threaded through the orifice, and attached to the bobbin. The wheel is adjusted for moderate to strong take-up. The operator assumes a working position between the wheel and the storage bobbins.

The operator's position is determined by three factors: comfort and ease of treadling, ability to reach and manipulate the yarn on the flyer guides or hooks, and maintenance of a straight line from storage bobbins to orifice. The yarns need to pass from the storage bobbins, through the

Plying begins with physical arrangements, which will vary depending upon your preferences in handedness and the design of your wheel.

You may find it convenient to have the yarn coming across your body, as in this left-handed setup.

Alternatively, you can set up with the bobbins behind you, as in this right-handed arrangement.

operator's hands, and into the orifice with little or no deflection. Ideally, the operator (that's you), the wheel, and the distant storage bobbins are positioned so that when the operator releases the yarn, it maintains a straight line from orifice to storage bobbin.

When all of the furniture-moving has been taken care of, plying begins. For literary convenience, the description assumes right-handed procedure. The author, being right-handed, is poorly qualified to advise left-handed persons as to which hand best performs serial manipulative activities.[10] The operator grasps the working yarns with both hands. The right hand is farther from the wheel, and is henceforth referred to as the *supply-side hand*. The left hand is closer to the orifice, and is henceforth referred to as the *wheel-side hand*.

Be warned that this is the sort of task where one minute spent seeing the technique does more good than reading any amount of prose. However, you are there and we are here, so prose must carry the day.

Both hands are at a comfortable height, perhaps 6 or 8 inches above

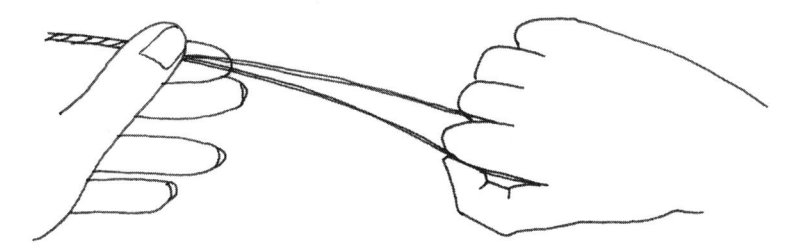

Here are the hand positions for hand-over-hand plying. The supply-side hand is shown on the right, with the incoming yarns routed between the curled fingers. The wheel-side hand, shown on the left, faces inward and grasps the yarn between the ball of the thumb and the side of the forefinger.

---

[10] *This is not entirely a true statement. The author will tell anyone, right- or left-handed, how to run their entire life, when the occasion warrants. In this case he wishes to spare you the confusion resulting from such gratuitous remarks as "for left-handed readers, simply reverse," which is just the sort of thing you need after wading through eleven paragraphs of detailed instructions. Anyway, once you southpaws get past the very paragraph to which this note is attached, the terms* wheel-side hand *and* supply-side hand *apply to you as well as they do to less perfect creatures.*

the operator's lap—generally located about where one would hold a paperback book. The palm of the wheel-side hand faces inward, and that hand pinches or grasps the yarn between the ball of the thumb and the side of the forefinger. The palm of the supply-side hand faces down in a soft fist, as if to rap discreetly upon a table, and the incoming yarns are routed from below the palm to go up between the curled fingers. For a two-ply yarn, the strands on the supply-side hand are arranged so that one incoming yarn passes between thumb and thumb-side of the forefinger and the other passes between the inside of the forefinger and the facing side of the middle finger.

In hand-over-hand plying, both hands move. The purpose of keeping the hands in motion is to keep the yarn in motion. Even though the operator's hands never actually go hand-over-hand, the yarn continues

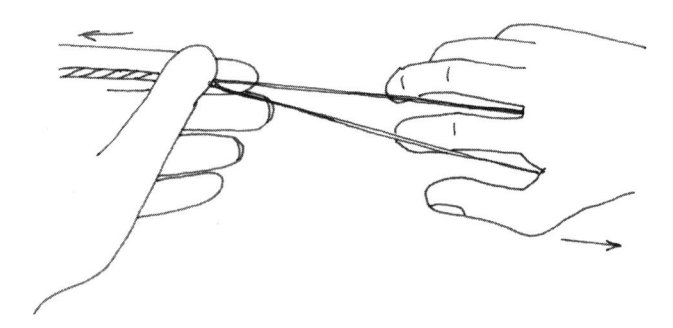

To obtain a fresh supply of yarn, the wheel-side hand moves toward the wheel and the supply-side hand moves quickly back and grasps another length.

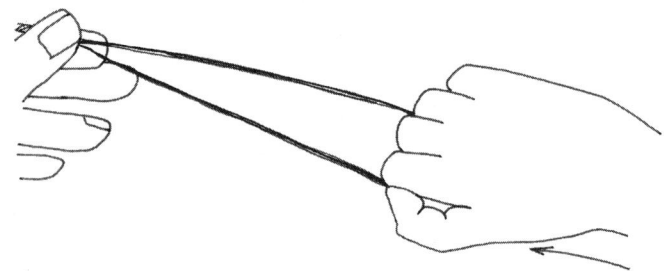

To feed the newly plied yarn onto the bobbin, the supply-side hand moves toward the wheel as the wheel-side hand moves quickly back to its original position.

to move as if this were the case. One hand or the other always moves toward the wheel. First the wheel-side hand moves toward the wheel as the supply-side hand moves quickly back to grasp another length. When the supply-side hand has a fresh supply of yarn, it begins moving toward the wheel as the wheel-side hand moves quickly back toward its original position.

The cycle repeats, and the yarn never pauses on its way to the wheel. A casual observer would note that the operator's hands move first toward each other and then apart. The observer might also note that the storage bobbins rotate slowly and steadily, with no pauses or starts.

Visualize this manual process by imagining that the yarn is an endless wire rod and your job is to stand in one place and push the rod, slowly and without pause, into a pipe, a rat hole, or some such. In the case of a rod, you might well go hand-over-hand, but if for some reason you can't, what do you do? First one hand pushes while the other takes a fresh grasp, then the other pushes while the first finds a new hold.

Those are the basic hand movements of hand-over-hand plying. There are a few other details, of course. After all, we are not really pushing anything into a rat hole and the yarn is not a wire rod.

Actually, the wheel pulls the yarn in and we control the rate at which it does so. We also control the ply twist, direct our hands through a careful and curious set of movements, and maintain tension on all working yarns. The control of ply twist involves the same techniques by which we control twist when spinning singles, and we need not discuss them again. Both hand movements and tensioning require further explanation.

The wheel-side hand performs three basic plying movements, which we will label the *re-grasping* motion, the *wheel-ways* motion, and the *rolling release*. The supply-side hand performs only two basic movements: the *wheel-ways* motion, and the *recovery* motion. Both hands have some minor motions, but we'll let those go for now.

You will remember that a casual observer would have noted that the operator's hands seem to move toward each other, and then apart.

When the hands move toward each other, the supply-side hand is performing the wheel-ways motion and the wheel-side hand is engaged in the re-grasping motion.

When the hands move apart, the supply-side hand is performing the recovery motion and the wheel-side hand is engaged in the wheel-ways motion. At the end of that wheel-ways motion, the wheel-side hand performs the rolling release.

Wheel-side hand, in detail. Let's take each hand by itself. Imagine that the wheel-side hand is moving in the wheel-ways motion. The hand clamps or pinches the yarn, to prevent twist from traveling into the separate yarns between the two hands. It also keeps tension on these separate yarns, tension that helps the other hand finish its recovery motion. We'll get to that in a moment.

At the end of its wheel-ways motion, the wheel-side hand performs the rolling release: the thumb and forefinger roll the clamped yarn in the ply direction, as the fingers release the clamping pressure. The rolling release keeps all elements in order as the twist rushes in; this becomes very important when you ply three or more strands. The technique also promotes superior two-ply, because it reduces or eliminates the tendency for one yarn to wrap around the other, instead of plying evenly around a common center.

That last statement provides the main reason for this detailed description of physical considerations and movements. We don't want the

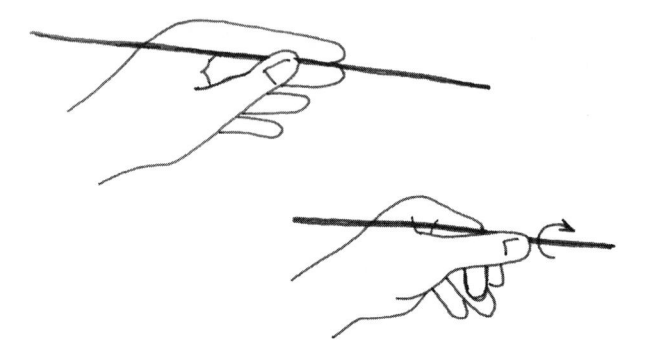

The rolling release, performed by the wheel-side hand, keeps all elements in order as they are twisted. It improves any yarn, but becomes very important when you ply three or more strands.

yarns to wrap around anything, including each other. We want them to *ply*, which means that they are wound about a shared longitudinal axis. Now, back to the motions.

Once the wheel-side hand has performed the rolling release, it begins the re-grasping motion. To do so, it moves quickly toward the approaching supply-side hand and grasps the yarn just at the end of the plied section. It then begins the wheel-ways motion.

Supply-side hand, in detail. When the wheel-side hand performs the rolling release, the supply-side hand has just finished the recovery motion and is beginning its wheel-ways motion.

During its wheel-ways motion, the supply-side hand does nothing except keep a grip on the several yarns and keep moving toward the wheel. The end of its wheel-ways motion coincides with the re-grasping motion of the other hand. The wheel-side hand grasps the yarn and begins moving wheel-ways. The supply-side hand relaxes (but does not release!) its grip on the yarns, and moves away from the wheel toward the storage bobbins. When it completes this recovery motion, it grips fresh lengths of the yarn coming from the storage bobbins.

Once this is done, the supply-side hand begins its wheel-ways motion; at the same time, the wheel-side hand performs the rolling release and begins its re-grasping motion.

The cycles continue until you are out of supply yarn, out of room in the wheel bobbin, or just want to stop.

Maintaining tension. Hand-over-hand plying involves three areas and degrees of yarn tension.

The first area is *between the storage bobbins and your supply-side hand*. The degree of tension in this area is fairly constant, and pretty much determined by the amount of braking applied to the storage bobbins.

The second area of concern is the tension *between your two hands*. During the cycle of hand movements, there is a point when the hands are as far apart as they are going to be. At this time the wheel-side hand performs the rolling release. During the moment of release, yarn tension between the two hands should be at its highest degree.

The third area of concern is *between the operator's hands and the wheel*. Yarn tension in this area is governed by the take-up adjustments of the wheel, which should be sufficient to ensure a firm wind on the bobbin, but no more. Mighty winching action on the part of the wheel is seldom needed. Remember, too, that any increase in wheel take-up comes at the cost of increased treadling effort.

Additional minor motions. The supply-side hand may need to swing right or left slightly, to make small adjustments in the tension on individual elements. When this motion occurs, it is done just prior to the other hand's rolling release.

The wheel-side hand sometimes uses a quick release and re-grasp motion, similar to that used in spinning. This accommodates small adjustments in element tension before the entire complement of twist is installed in the make.

IMPERFECT YARNS, IMPROVED YARNS, AND NOVELTY YARNS

The application of the four plying principles will greatly enhance your productivity, and will certainly offer you opportunities to improve the quality of your yarn. Plying has the reputation for improving poorly constructed yarns. In some ways this is true, but it is not sufficient justification for assembling mediocre yarns in the belief that plying will disguise or remedy an initial lack of care.

Unless you choose to apply the principles with forethought and understanding, unless you choose to exploit those opportunities, unless you choose to repair the bad join, remove the unwanted slub, reject the substandard section, then any improvements gained through plying will be marginal. Yarn faults don't fix themselves.

Plying is the primary method of producing novelty yarns. Now a technical description of a novelty yarn includes a statement, direct or implied, that such a yarn is imperfect: imperfectly spun, imperfectly plied, imperfectly set, whatever.

Imperfect or not, a good novelty yarn is not easy to construct. To be attractive and useful, a yarn must not only be consistent or uniform in its "imperfections," it must also be strong and stable in spite of them. It follows that you need skill in "straight" plying (the basics) before you can produce good novelties. In short, you must walk before you run.

Uniformity is the name of the game. Most handspinners are aware that plying results in a "more consistent" yarn, that is, a compilation which is more consistent than its several parts. This supports plying's reputation for making bad yarns better.

Handspun or machine-made? While on the subject of uniformity, let's look at the old adage about how it's a bad thing to spin and ply so well that (horror of horrors), "people think the yarn is machine-made." In the first place, your yarn *is* machine-made, unless you used nothing but your fingers. In the second place, so what? Third, do you cater to people who are agog over superficial appearance? Fourth, does handwork have to be sloppy, and is mediocrity a hallmark of handspinning skill?

Last but not least, good handspun has a lot more going for it than uniformity alone, which is more than can be said for numerous commercial yarns. After all, you select your fiber; scour it; dye it; comb, card, or otherwise prepare it for spinning; spin it to just the right grist and twist for the project at hand; carefully ply it . . . in short, put a lot of time, effort, and yourself into it.

And someone suggests that you shouldn't do a good job because another someone will think that you are using mass-produced yarn? That's ludicrous.

Uniformity, and figuring the grist of a future plied yarn. Plying promotes uniformity because a plied yarn is more uniform than the individual strands that go into it (with the exception of some novelty-yarn variations).

One way to explain why is to look at plying as a simple mathematical operation. Imagine, if you will, that each strand of a plied yarn has a numerical value. Through the plying process, these numerical values are added together so that the plied yarn represents the sum of the parts, or an average combined value.

Suppose you have two bobbins of singles. Let's say you spun one bobbin when you were on top of the world, everything was swell, and the wind was right in your hair. The yarn is even, consistent, beautiful! The other bobbin did not have a happy childhood. You found bits of time for spinning over 10 days, the weather changed for the worse, other people messed with the wheel, and you had occasion to use those colorful words mentioned in the footnotes. The yarn is beautiful, perhaps, but not as even or consistent as the other stuff. Imagine that yarn from the first bobbin has a grist of 3,000 YPP (yards per pound) and that the yarn from the second bobbin has an average grist of 2,500 YPP.

When you ply these two yarns together, the resulting two-ply will have a grist of about 1,375 YPP. How did we arrive at that figure?

Method 1 for determining the grist of a plied yarn. There are several ways to calculate the answer, and here is one of them.[11] *Find an average grist value for the yarns being plied.* Do this by adding the grists together, then dividing by the number of grists involved. In this case, we have two grists, 3,000 YPP and 2,500 YPP. Added together they total 5,500, which, divided by 2 (the number of grists added together) equals 2,750. Our average grist value for these yarns is 2,750 YPP.

$$\frac{G1 + G2 + G3 \ldots}{N} = A$$

$$\frac{3,000 + 2,500}{2} = \frac{5,500}{2} = 2,750 \text{ YPP}$$

G1, G2, G3, and so on are the grists of the elements, N is the number of grists, and A is the average grist.

Divide this value by the number of elements in the yarn.[12] The two-ply grist will be 2,750 divided by 2, or 1,375 YPP.

$$\frac{A}{E} = P$$

$$\frac{2,750}{2} = 1,375 \text{ YPP}$$

---

[11] *While calculations are useful, even necessary, there is no substitute for physical testing—for example, winding-off to a skein, measuring the length, and weighing the yarn.*

[12] *By the way, each of these yarns is called an* element. *In plying, elements are always the elemental building block. In short, the element is the original singles yarn. Where complex structures are concerned, the word* strand *is used, but the strand is composed of elements. For simple plying, such as our example two-ply,* strand *and* element *are taken to mean the same thing.*

A is the average grist, E is the number of elements in the yarn, and P is the grist of the plied yarn.

Suppose the average grist value of two singles works out as 2,500 YPP. What will the two-ply grist be? It will be the average element grist (2,500 YPP) divided by the number of elements in the finished yarn (2), or 1,250 YPP.

Let's look at a three-ply yarn. The singles grists are 3,000, 4,000, and 2,600 YPP, which add up to 9,600. Divide 9,600 by three and you get 3,200 YPP, our average element grist. Divide the average element grist by the number of elements, or 3, and you get about 1,067. A three-ply made from those singles will have a grist of 1,067 YPP.

Method 2 for determining the grist of a plied yarn. Another way is to *add up all element grists, then divide this sum by the number of elements squared* (times themselves). For example, we have a four-ply and the element grists are 4,000, 3,600, 4,200, and 4,400 YPP. These total 16,200. There are four elements, and 4 times 4 equals 16. Divide 16,200 by 16, which gives us the four-ply grist of 1,012.5 YPP.

$$\frac{G1 + G2 + G3 \ldots}{E^2} = P$$

$$\frac{4,000 + 3,600 + 4,200 + 4,400}{4^2} = \frac{16,200}{16} = 1,012.5 \text{ YPP}$$

G1, G2, G3, and so on are the grists of the elements, E is the number of elements in the yarn, and P is the grist of the plied yarn.

Same problem, both methods. Wanna do another one? Assume a five-ply, with all elements measuring 6,000 YPP. What is the grist of the plied yarn?

Using the first method, we add 6,000 five times (total 30,000), divide by the number of grists (5), then divide again by the number of elements in the yarn (5 again). The answer is 1,200 YPP.

Using the second method, we add up all element grists (total 30,000) and divide by 5 squared, which is the number of elements times themselves, or 25, to end up with 1,200 YPP.

Well, how about that?

Here's a problem for you to work on during the next break.

You have constructed a three-strand hawser, with two elements in two of the strands and three elements in the third strand. Grist of all singles but one is 5,200 YPP; the odd single is 6,105 YPP. What is the grist of the hawser?

The question is not as hard as it looks. There are 7 elements, and 6 of them are the same. Don't let the strands fool you. The 6 strands at 5,200 YPP give you 31,200 plus one strand at 6,105 produces 37,305. Divide by the square of 7 (the number of elements) and the answer is 761 YPP.

We can see, on paper at least, that plying results in a yarn that is more uniform than its least consistent part. We can also see, if we look a little more closely, that the more elements there are, the more uniform the plied yarn will be.

Non-functional plied yarns. Because plying changes the twist of the elements, it is possible to produce non-functional plied yarns. This often occurs when attempting supersoft, low-grist items.

Suppose you assemble a conventional two-ply from singles that contained a bare minimum of twist—only enough to keep them from further drafting. What happens when they are down-twisted? Plying down-twist removes some twist from the singles, and these don't have any to spare. They no longer have any practical strength and will draft or "drift" apart under minor tensile stress. The resulting two-ply has the same character, and in an extreme case will not survive the trip from hands to wheel, or from wheel to reel. In this case, plying makes bad yarns worse.

How to avoid this problem? When spinning the singles, put in a little more twist than you think you need. You have seen that comment before, and you will see it again.

Plying and twist

That brings us to the subject of ply twist: how much, when, why, and what happens to it?

When plying two elements down-twist, as in our example just above, you remove twist from the strands. Let us imagine that each strand has 4 TPI, Z direction.

Further imagine that we ply these two using 4 TPI down-twist (S direction). Have we removed all the twist from the singles?

If we ply them with 8 TPI down-twist, how much twist do the singles have, and in which direction?

Or if we ply them with 4 TPI up-twist, how much twist is now present in the elements?

To carry these questions a step further, remember that complex yarn we did, for rug warps? How do we determine the twist amounts required to make it a balanced yarn, one that is twist-stable?

The following discussion will remove all mystery.

Self-plying tests. As you know, a newly spun length of yarn tends to double back on itself whenever it can. It endeavors to self-ply. Now, suppose this newly spun yarn has a convenient amount of twist, say 6 TPI.

If we take a short length of this yarn, hold the two ends together, and allow the loop to hang free, the yarn will quickly and neatly self-ply into a balanced (twist-stable) two-ply. This is very convenient. One simple test tells us exactly the amount of ply twist required to assemble a given single into twist-stable two-ply yarn. In this particular case, the two-ply will have half the twist of the single, or 3 TPI. (It will also have half the grist value, but that is not our present concern.)

Let's make a sample length of three-ply. Stretch three strands side by side, tie them together at one end, hang a small weight on the knot, and allow the weighted ends to hang free. The combined strands will self-produce a balanced three-ply yarn. Using our 6 TPI single as a basis, the three-element yarn will have a balanced ply twist of 2 TPI.

Any self-ply test has an important limitation: *the single used must be newly spun*, fresh from the spinner's hand. If not, the results will not be accurate. The "older" the yarn, the more misleading the results. This is because the moment any yarn is spun, it begins to "set" itself, or to become less twist-active. The degree of set is essentially time-dependent. The longer the yarn is stored, the greater the degree of set.

Protein fiber yarns (wool, silk, etc.) set themselves quickly, often within a weekend. Cellulosics take much longer. In fact, it can be argued that cellulosics never become fully set the way wool or silk does, certainly not without energetic external treatment.

Superior balanced yarns. To produce a superior balanced yarn, you have to use every trick in the book. You must start with the mechanics, which means using the appropriate amount of ply twist. You introduce this twist through good plying techniques, and you finish by scouring and setting the completed yarn. With cellulosic yarns, boiling is included, usually during the scour.

To use the appropriate ply twist, you must know or determine the twist amount of the single elements. The time and place to measure the twist is during spinning, obviously, because that is when you get accurate results from the simple self-ply test.

Suppose you spin up a large quantity of yarn over an extended period of time. If you make self-ply tests (and recorded them) while spinning, the results will be valid even after prolonged storage.

When such yarns are plied, the *mechanically correct* amount of ply twist will seem excessive, until the moment that the yarn enters a tub full of hot scouring suds—at which time the spinning fairy pops into view, shakes her magic distaff, and the yarn promptly "remembers" what it is supposed to do in the twist department. It may not "remember" all that it is supposed to right away, but then no one is perfect.

The point is that you don't have to ply a yarn right away. You can store the singles until you need them and still achieve the superior plied yarn. On the other hand, don't store yarn for five years, tightly wound on storage bobbins, and expect it to act as it did in its youth. It might, but that will be what we call a pleasant surprise.

We stress the importance of determining and recording the singles twist during spinning, because this is the most practical time to do so. There are other procedures for determining the twist component of a yarn, and you must use them whenever the self-ply test is inappropriate. Unfortunately, these other methods are harder.

Twist in a plied structure is easy to see and evaluate, but determining the twist of a worsted or semi-worsted monochrome single is another matter. But no matter how you go about it, you need to determine the twist component of the element yarns.[13]

Approaching the "ideal" plied yarn

Now, let's look at some answers for the questions posed a few pages back.

If we have two elements and we ply down-twist, we remove twist from them. If we install enough ply twist, we will remove all of the original twist and begin twisting them in the opposite direction. A discussion of why you might do this is coming soon. But first, why doesn't the yarn self-destruct when we take out all the element twist? Under certain circumstances, it does. Most of the time it does not, if you have done a reasonable job of spinning. If you put in a little more twist than you think you need, it never will. But that's a statement, not an explanation.

Here is the explanation. The friction between fibers is what holds yarn together. Twisting the yarn is one method of pressing the fibers together. Increasing the twist increases the fiber-to-fiber pressure, and thus increases the fiber-to-fiber friction. A convenient name for this fiber/pressure/friction relationship is *nip*. Increasing the twist increases the nip. Because plying also twists the fiber, it follows that the ply twist also induces nip. Plying down-twist will remove twist (then, if you go far enough, it will put it back in), but it replaces the twist-induced nip of the element with the twist-induced nip of the plied structure. Even though the twist in the elements may be reduced or removed entirely, the nip remains.

Numbers of plies. The "ideal" plied yarn is a three-ply, plied down-twist to stabilization, from uniform, moderate-to-high twist singles. Such a yarn approaches a circular cross section, certainly more so than a two- or four-ply. A three-ply yarn assumes a rounded triangular cross section. If the yarn is soft, the cross section may look almost like a pie, divided into three equal slices. Five-ply yarns have traditional currency, but they are tricky to ply, and hard to keep "round."

No matter what you do to a two-ply yarn, the cross section is a squashed figure 8 or, if you prefer, the infinity symbol—in other words, two strands lying side by side. The form has limitations when you come

---

[13] *If you find yourself unfamiliar with twist-related concepts or confused by the terminology, it will be worth your while to review the discussion of twist measurement, principles, and procedures in Chapter 5.*

Two-ply yarn, longitudinal view and cross section.

Three-ply yarn, longitudinal view and cross section.

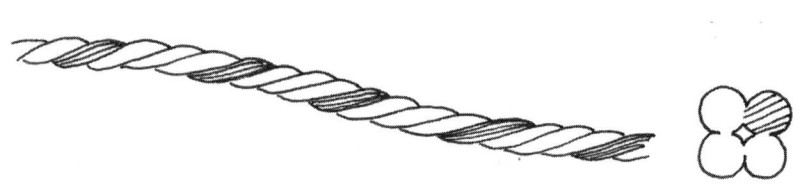

Four-ply yarn, longitudinal view and cross section.

to make fabric from it, and under some circumstances loses visual coherence. For example, a two-ply may not be the best choice when you want to establish a line of color in a fabric. To illustrate the point, crochet or knit a multicolor two-ply yarn into a beret or cap. The resulting color effect may resemble an amorphous, homogenized pudding. If you intend to make pudding, all is well. If not, use a three-ply yarn, or perhaps a cable construction.

Two-ply yarns are suitable for weaving; they are less than ideal for knitting, crochet, and the like. That doesn't mean they won't work, because they do, however three-ply is better. By the same token, three-ply yarns, while ideal for knitting, are somewhat "overqualified" for weaving.

Nothing inherent in the weaving process demands three-ply yarn. A plied yarn, perhaps, but not specifically a three-ply. Of course, you might want the enhanced cross-sectional stability for cord weaves or other surface designs and effects.

How much ply twist produces twist-stability? Stage one: the basics. Now let us take a look at some practical theory: how to calculate the amount of ply twist required to produce twist-stable yarns. Remember that these calculations are hinged on the premise that you really and truly know what the twist component is in the elements.

Here's the first method of calculating. For a simple plied yarn, where the elements are equal in character: *divide an element-twist amount by the number of elements in the yarn.* The result is the twist component of the plied yarn.

That looks easy enough, as these things go. But suppose that not all elements are equal in material, twist, or grist? This is not uncommon, usually being a deliberate procedure, as when you want to combine different-colored yarns, to introduce metallics such as Lurex,[14] or to construct certain types of novelty yarns. The preceding formula won't give us a right answer, at least not directly. Still, we will use it as a springboard.

For a yarn that will contain diverse elements, we need to find the average twist component of all elements. Add up the element twists, then divide by the number of elements.

Imagine that we want to make a twist-stable four-ply of three handspun elements (of 9 TPI Z) and one Lurex element of 0 TPI. Zero is right. Lurex has no incumbent twist. Add $9 + 9 + 9 + 0 = 27$ and then divide by 4, for a result of 6.75 TPI as the average twist component of each element.

Now apply the above formula. Divide the average twist component by the number of elements, and the answer is the ply twist of the yarn. In this case, 6.75 divided by 4 gives 1.6875 TPI. While this answer is correct on paper, in practical terms that will not be enough ply twist to produce a twist-stable yarn. How did we go wrong?

We have two more things to consider. First, we did not allow for what is called yarn (or fiber) rigidity, although in this case what we didn't allow for was the lack of it. *Rigidity* describes the force required to twist a yarn in the first place, and while we are untwisting three of the elements, we are twisting the Lurex. The force used to twist the Lurex is in opposition to the forces presented by the other elements.

---

[14] *Trademark for Lurex is held by The Dobeckmun Company, Cleveland, Ohio.*

The second thing to consider is *torsional reaction*, the force that makes a yarn want to untwist itself. Torsional reaction is closely related to twist amount and fiber rigidity. Basically, the more twist you have, the more torsional reaction there will be, or the greater tendency for the yarn to untwist itself.[15]

Torsional reaction is the result of overcoming rigidity. We force the yarn to twist against its desire to do so, and if we give it a chance, the yarn will try to untwist itself, to release that "stored" energy. Essentially, the greater the yarn (and fiber) rigidity, the greater the torsional reaction to introduced twist.

In even simpler terms: the more fiber present (the thicker the yarn), the greater the rigidity, or resistance to twist, in the first place. The more twist present, the greater the rigidity, or resistance to additional twist.

Result? Yarns with a lot of resistance to more twist (rigidity) want to untwist themselves, in proportion to their rigidity. Thick yarns are quite public about the matter.

Why not let a couple of yarns try to untwist against each other, to torsionally react against each other? In short, let each element's desire to untwist be opposed, somehow, by every other element's desire to do the same thing.

---

[15] *As mentioned, rigidity describes the quality of fibers that resists twisting. Rigidity also describes the resistance to up-twisting exhibited by all yarns—single, plied, or complex. We will avoid getting heavily involved with the entire, complex subject of rigidity and torsion reaction. You may do likewise. Note, however, that fiber rigidity (1) increases dramatically as twist accumulates and (2) is about fifteen times as great in dry wool as it is in damp wool. The author has no specific figures as to rigidity of the other Big Four fibers, although they obviously do not behave in the same way under humid conditions as when bone dry. However, changes most obvious to the handspinner from increase in moisture usually include static control and the reduction of dust, fly-away, and the like. In the shadow of these greater changes, reductions in rigidity pass unnoticed. In industrial applications, rigidity is energy-related, and thus economic. In a single-end application (as with the handspinner), fiber and yarn rigidity is of theoretical interest and minor practical consideration. For a mill spinning 30,000 ends at once, three shifts daily, reductions in rigidity (and/or twist amounts) produce substantial reductions in energy costs. Thus we have another reason why mills put in less twist than is ideal, and why the handspinner can, and should, put in more twist—in short, why handspinners can produce better yarn.*

That is exactly what twist-stable plying is all about. When the torsional forces balance each other out, the yarn becomes twist-stable. That is why a single spun yarn always has the twist-active label. It has no internal and opposing forces to keep it from untwisting. While only plied yarns stand a chance of being twist-stable, a plied yarn is not, by definition, twist-stable.[16]

In an ideal twist-stable plied yarn, all torsional reactions balance each other out. The total yarn has zero torsional reaction. It resists twisting and untwisting, and in the normal course of events will behave very nicely, indeed. To achieve this wonder, we have to arrange the twist amounts so that each torsional reaction is balanced by an opposite and equal reaction. Which is interesting, if you stop and think about it.

Once again, let's use our simple two-ply example. Just how do two like-twisted yarns become balanced by opposite and equal reactions? Where does this opposing torsional reaction come from?

It comes from nothing more than the rigidity (resistance to twisting) of the plied structure. When we allow the several elements or strands to self-ply in the normal way (down-twist), each loses some twist and some rigidity. At the same time, they are being distorted into a spiral around a common axis. That is, they are re-forming into another twisted structure—the plied yarn.

The energy stored in the twisted elements is spent in "work," which consists primarily of up-twisting the plied yarn. When the decreasing stored energy of the elements is equally opposed by the increasing rigidity of the plied structure, the yarn is said to be twist-stable.

---

[16] *There are times when no plied yarn is really twist-stable. By way of example, review the twirling toothpick demonstration earlier in the chapter (see page 287). An illustration with more practical appeal comes from the author's younger days, when he aspired to be a commercial fisherman. Fishing nets are fitted with paired right-laid and left-laid ropes for the head-lines. This prevents the whole net (often 1,000 feet long) from rolling up like damp underwear when you haul it in. The principle used in stabilizing fishing nets may interest all who study selvedges. Of course, there are other ways to assemble yarn into twist-stable structures, as in braiding and plaiting. See* The Ashley Book of Knots *for a considerable discussion of same. You would not believe that there are so many possibilities for plaiting beyond pigtail braid.*

That's all informative, but what of the problems outlined in our novelty yarn? Those remain to be dealt with. Everyone back to the Lurex.

We can disregard rigidity or torsional reaction as far as the Lurex itself is concerned. At the stated twist amounts, Lurex has no significant effect twist-wise. Thus this particular yarn needs to be plied as if the Lurex were not there—that is, as a simple three-ply. The correct amount of ply twist is therefore 3 TPI. If we were dealing with much higher twist amounts (finer yarns), say 15 TPI in the elements, then the rigidity and torsional reaction of Lurex would become significant.

How much ply twist produces twist-stability? Stage two: a complicated yarn. Leaving Lurex behind, let's look at another application of the plyer's art, one that might be used to salvage an odd or leftover yarn of attractive color yet opposite twist. This procedure results in a twist-stable, three-ply yarn containing two elements of like twist direction and one of opposite twist.[17] We will imagine that the two similar elements are 9 TPI Z and the color element is 9 TPI S.

It is simple enough to calculate a stable ply twist for this yarn as long as we make certain assumptions: that (1) the elements are similar in material and grist and (2) yarn rigidity remains constant over the range of twist that we propose. That's not true in this case, but read on.

Since we want our finished yarn to be twist-stable, we will ply down-twist with respect to the greatest amount of twist. That means we will be plying in the S direction. The two Z elements will lose twist, and the S element will gain twist.

Now comes the tricky part. How much twist do the Z elements have to lose and how much does the S element have to gain in order to produce a twist-stable yarn?

The S element is being up-twisted, which it is going to resist (because

---

[17] *The author wishes to advise you that this particular yarn is not pretty. It is an example and a warning. Example: the procedure does indeed produce a twist-stable yarn as described. Warning: the yarn is weird-looking, as are most yarns that include opposite-twist elements. The moral, if there is one, is that opposite-twist yarns never look quite "right" as yarn, even when their technical parameters are correct. Of course, once these yarns have been further converted—knitted, woven, or whatever—they appear entirely different.*

of rigidity). The Z elements want to down-twist, and that is torsional reaction. While all of this is going on, the plied structure increases its rigidity.

Thus we have two strands wanting to ply themselves, and one strand (plus the ply structure) that must up-twist to allow those two strands to approach equilibrium. The two like-twist strands must overcome not only the rigidity of the ply structure, but that of the odd strand as well.

A little reflection may suggest that if we treat the twist amounts as positive and negative numbers, we might be able to apply the simple ply-twist formula after all. Because the elements differ from each other, we need to find the "average" element twist. We add up the twists, 9 + 9–9, which equals 9 (9 + 9 = 18; 18–9 = 9), and then divide by the number of elements, 3, to end up with 3 TPI. Hard to believe, but the average element twist is only 3 TPI. Divide the average element twist by the number of elements and you have the twist-stable ply-twist amount: 3 divided by 3 = 1.

Neat, huh? Well, our formula is "almost" right: the "paper" result of 1 PTPI (plying twists per inch) is only correct when our assumptions about element character are in force. In real life, any change in yarn twist produces changes in yarn rigidity *and* in torsional reaction. As the Z elements down-twist, they rapidly reduce their torsional reaction forces, and as the S element up-twists, it rapidly (very rapidly) gains rigidity. It gains rigidity, while the other two elements lose rigidity. Let's not forget the increasing rigidity of the forming plied structure.

By now you have guessed that the calculated value of 1 PTPI is suspect. That is correct. With the reader's edification in mind, the author spent the better part of an afternoon performing calculations that allowed for rigidity, torsional reaction, and all that. Eventually he came up with an answer (.67 PTPI), and then in about two minutes checked out his results by running a sample. The sample agreed with the calculated result.

Enormously pleased with himself, the author ran another sample—just for the record, you understand. Uh-oh. Not the same. Well, no problem to run a third, ha, ha. Should do so anyway, shouldn't we, ha, ha. Uh-oh again.

By the tenth sample, a strong trend had developed: that an average of all samples and calculations (yeah, we did more) seemed more or less related.[18]

For us handspinners, the mathematical gyrations necessary to forecast changes in yarn rigidity and torsional reaction are not worth the effort. So they have been excluded from this work, and the author is relieved not to have to attempt their explanation.

As a result, our calculations for yarns with dissimilar elements will give ballpark answers at best. Sometimes our answers will not be in the ballpark at all, but can be located wandering around the parking lot.

In a situation where all yarn elements and values are symmetrical, calculated answers come quite close to reality. But once an odd element enters, well, ... Which brings us to the subject of checking the answers, of proving or disproving any calculated values.

Simple: make a sample. This is the preferred procedure for yarns with unusual or dissimilar components.

"Well, how nice," you say, after having trudged through all this stuff. "Why don't we just do that in the first place?"

That is a good point. Samples are the best way to arrive at a working answer for any yarn, not just odd ones, and to verify or overrule calculations. At the same time, comparing calculations with "real" results significantly increases your understanding of what is going on within your yarns.

In addition, no matter how much you like obscure math or how faithfully you perform calculations, you should always run empirical tests. We repeat: Always Run Samples.

---

[18] *Average actual value for ten samples was .77 PTPI. To make these samples, we used our twist-checking board to twist cheese rovings in the appropriate directions to the appropriate TPI. Half of the samples were allowed to self-ply to stability via a suspended, free-turning spindle arrangement. The other half were grimly plied up to calculated ply-stable amounts, using the twist checker. These were checked for twist stability through the self-ply method, then allowed to arrive at ply stability through the free-turning spindle routine. Actual twist amounts were discovered and verified through linear incremental methods (we laid a ruler next to them and counted humps), and by use of our twist-checker array, in accordance with procedures outlined in the American Society for Testing and Materials, ASTM designations D 1285–58 T and D 180–57 T.*

So why bother with calculations? Because calculations can be of considerable aid. At the very least, they reduce the amount of time spent in cut-and-try efforts. They also make your guesses more educated. The differences between calculations and actual results indicate trends, showing you when to treadle more or to treadle less; or what to correct when the grist falls off; or when to change the length of your make; or when to change anything about your plying procedure. Calculations provide one form of quality control.

The calculations nudge you into keeping track of what you have done, are doing, and intend to do. They serve as a reference source, because they require that you obtain specific information about your yarn. You will be pushed to keep some sort of records. And that can be convenient, indeed, if you ever need to reproduce a yarn.

Back to theory. Earlier we posed questions about what changes occur in element twist as a result of plying, both up-twist and down-twist. As you remember, we were plying two strands (elements), each strand being a Z-spun single with 4 TPI.

The first example asked what happens to the element twist when we ply these items, down-twist, to 4 PTPI. The second asked what happens to the element twist if we ply down-twist to 8 PTPI. The third wanted to know about element-twist amounts if we ply the same construction up-twist to 4 PTPI.

This appears to be a complex, number-filled series of questions, with trick answers. Take hope, they are easier than they look. In each case we apply another simple formula, a variation of what we have been using. This time it will work—no ifs, ands, or buts.[19]

The formula variation is as follows. (1) *Determine the ply-twist amount.* (Glance at Chapter 5 if you are hazy on twist measurement.) (2) *Assign this number a negative value if the ply direction is down-twist (the usual) and a positive value if the ply direction is up-twist (the not-so-usual).* (3) This number is then *added to (positive value) or subtracted from (negative value) the individual element-twist amounts.*

---

[19] *This time it works because we do not have to introduce mystery factors and obscure values. We have all the necessary information and must simply do a little math.*

In the first example (two strands, each 4 TPI, plied down-twist to 4 PTPI), the ply twist is given as 4 PTPI. It is a negative number because the ply twist is down-twist with respect to the element twist. So we subtract it from the individual element-twist amount: 4 - 4 = 0, the amount of twist present in each element after plying.

What??! Zero twist in the single? How can such a yarn survive? Good question—one that was answered a little while ago.

However, a properly designed plied yarn should always strive to have a little twist remaining in the elements. This is best accomplished during the spinning by (you guessed it!) always putting in a little more twist than you think you need. Or by selection of twist amounts and direction during the design stage. After all, if *you* are making the yarn, you can have any twist amount and direction that you want.

The second example consists of two Z-spun elements of 4 TPI, plied down-twist to 8 PTPI. What is the twist amount (and direction) present in each element after plying?

Once again, determine the ply-twist amount and direction, and assign the appropriate negative or positive values. Add or subtract the value from the element amounts. In this example we subtract 8 from 4, which gives us -4. Not to worry. When you get a negative number in this sort of calculation, it means the plying operation has removed all element twist and then proceeded to twist the elements in the opposite direction. In other words, it has reversed the element-twist direction. Each element now contains 4 TPI in the S direction. [20]

In the third example, we had two elements, each Z-spun to 4 TPI,

---

[20] *It is easy to check these results via mechanical testing. The ASTM (American Society for Testing and Materials) method may be taken as practical and proceeds as follows, more or less. Prepare a sample of the subject plied yarn by fixing both ends in the twist-checking device (for more detail, see "Checking the Twist," by John Gickie, Spin-Off 11, no. 1 (Spring 1987), page 27). Secure the device so that it cannot rotate without your permission. With a pair of sharp little scissors, cut away all elements except the one you want to check. When all the others have been removed, check the survivor for twist in the ordinary way. Nothing to it. ASTM's published standards are available through your local library. Not that your local library has the ASTM publications on hand, on the shelf (they might!)... but they can get them through interlibrary exchange programs and the like. Isn't that what a library is for?*

which were plied up-twist to 4 PTPI. What is the twist amount of each element after plying?

Here the ply direction is the same as the element twist, which gives it a positive value. Thus we add the ply-twist amount (4) to the element-twist amounts. Each element, after plying, has 8 TPI in the Z direction.

Using the calculations in producing complex yarns. None of these examples results in a twist-stable yarn. The samples do, however, represent intermediate stages in the production of complex yarns, and to find the twist components required for stabilization, you apply the first formula after you assemble the components.

Let's illustrate with the last example above.

We produced a twist-active plied structure, which we now call a *strand*. This strand is composed of two elements, plied up-twist to 4 PTPI. The individual elements, up-twisted during plying, now have 8 TPI as incumbent twist.

Imagine that we take three of these strands and ply them to a twist-stable condition. How much ply twist do we need this second time around?

Apply the first formula for a twist-stable yarn: for a simple plied yarn, where the elements are equal in character, divide an element-twist amount by the number of elements in the yarn. The result is the twist component of the plied yarn.

The only change we make in the preceding is to replace the word *element* with the word *strand*. Thus, we divide the strand-twist amount by the number of strands. The strand-twist amount is 4 and we are using three strands. Correct ply twist in this case is 4 divided by 3, or 1.33 PTPI. It should go without saying that the ply-twist direction is down-twist.

To carry our calculations a step further, how much twist is there in each strand after plying? Well, we "used up" 1.33 turns in the plying, so each strand contains 4 turns minus 1.33 turns, or 2.67 TPI.

What about the elements? What is their twist content after plying? After plying, each strand of two elements has 2.67 TPI. We can add this amount to the beginning single twist of 4 TPI. That works out as 6.67 TPI now incumbent in the singles.

We can work our numbers the other way, too. We "used" 1.33 TPI in the final plying, and subtracting that amount from 8 TPI (element twist before second plying) gives us 6.67 TPI. Isn't that amazing?

Generalizations about all this math. Now we need a break from ply calculations and formulas. But before we leave them to gather dust on a high shelf, here are several general observations about the math used to determine the construction of twist-stable yarn.

(1) The twist amounts in the elements or strands are found from the twist amounts of the twist-stable plied yarn through simple addition, subtraction, and division.

(2) The final twist amounts required for a twist-stable plied yarn are found from the twist amounts of the elements or strands in the same way—through simple addition, subtraction, and division.

No matter how complex a complex yarn may be, the above observations hold true.

As long as elements or strands are roughly similar in grist and material, yarn rigidity values need not enter the calculations. Which is nice, since we haven't discussed such values or any algorithms for applying them.

There is no substitute for a sample. Calculations are never enough. An old saying about samples goes like this: if the first sample comes out right, be alarmed and do another one. If the second sample comes out right, be very alarmed, and do a third. If the third comes out right, congratulate yourself but proceed with caution.

Common sense and experience are your best guides. You don't really need to know all this stuff to do a good job of plying, but it can help, and it will surely astonish your friends.

The study of ply twist is something like the study of astrology. There always seems to be an absolute answer somewhere, if we only had all the necessary information. You might say that twist calculations resemble forecasts, because only after the thing has happened, or the yarn has been assembled, are we in a position to whittle our prognostications to fit.

A flirtation with novelty yarns

It is time to examine novelty yarns. Every handspinner, at some time or place, has a flirtation with novelty yarns. Some of these flirtations grow into life-long affairs, and the handspinner so committed becomes noted—a specialist, as it were—in the field of novel and unusual yarns.

The novelty yarn business has attractive aspects. First, a great many observers will evaluate your work solely upon surface effect and appearance, and will neither understand nor care about structure. Second, as a novelty-yarn producer, you set your own standards. These two factors make novelty yarns seem the sure path to fame and glory. Perhaps.

Novelty yarns fall into two broad classes: those that are cheap and dirty, and those that are not. It is an editorial premise that you are not concerned with the first sort. We move immediately to the second.

There are four basic methods used to produce a novelty yarn. (1) You include unusual (novel) elements in an otherwise uniform yarn. (2) You introduce a repetitive fault during the plying process. (3) You combine the methods 1 and 2, introducing novelty elements or strands while making repetitive derangements of the plying process. (4) This, broadly speaking is a form of yarn finishing, involving brushing, felting, and otherwise mechanically or chemically affecting a yarn produced either by conventional plying or by any of the methods mentioned above.

Since other authors treat the glitter-and-glory aspects of novelty-yarn production, we will limit our discussion to basic structure, keeping in mind such qualities as yarn strength, abrasion resistance, and twist stability.[21]

A method-one novelty yarn. A simple yet useful first-method novelty yarn results by plying a soft, low-twist element and a finer, high-twist element down-twist to the twist-stable point.

To do the job right, arrange things so that the low-twist element retains some incumbent twist after plying. We include some guideline values. Soft, low-twist element = 800–1,000 YPP, Z, 3 TPI. Fine, high-twist element = 3,000–4,000 YPP, Z, 13 TPI. These yarns will ply-stabilize at about 4 PTPI, with about -1 TPI in the soft element and about 8–9 TPI in the fine element.

You can make a simple novelty yarn by plying a soft, low-twist element with a finer, high-twist element.

---

[21] *Works of interest for the novelty-minded include Diane Varney's* Spinning Designer Yarns, *Eliza Leadbeater's* Handspinning, *and Elsie Davenport's* Your Handspinning.

During plying, place high tension on the fine element. The soft element should be worked with only enough tension to prevent visible sagging. This is best arranged by having strong braking on the fine element's storage bobbin and allowing the soft-element bobbin to run easily. You can (and should) check for correct ply twist during plying: use the simple self-ply test.

Variations on this yarn include using two fine, high-twist elements; adjusting the element twists and grists; and using a plied yarn as the novelty element.

A method-two novelty yarn. A basic second-method yarn is constructed by abruptly, alternately, and drastically changing the angle at which the working yarns come together in the plying zone. During normal hand-over-hand plying, this angle remains acute, being around 10 to 15 degrees, and the supply-side hand keeps all elements under control.

For the purpose of second-method novelty plying, hold the working strands in separate hands. First one hand moves quickly forward, changing the angle between strands to 90 degrees or more. This causes the yarn controlled by the leading or forward hand to wrap around the other element, forming a cylindrical wad.

The forward hand then returns to its original position. The other hand moves quickly forward and repeats the motion, with the same result. As the hands alternate this action, element A wraps around element B, then element B wraps around element A, and so forth. This yields what is called a *knop yarn*.

It is not practical to calculate a twist-stable ply amount for this sort of yarn; there are too many variables. Still, it is not difficult to find the values through samples and, once done, follow a procedure that produces the necessary twist amount.

A method-three novelty yarn. The third-method novelties combine procedures from the first and second methods. A typical yarn may be constructed by plying two fine, high-twist

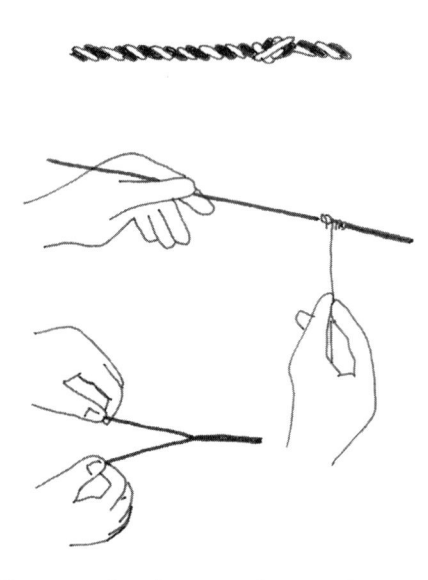

You can make a knop yarn by wrapping two strands around each other alternately while you are plying.

You can make a bouclé or loop yarn by plying two fine, high-twist elements with a heavier third element, which you manipulate at frequent intervals to form loops.

elements with a third element of novel character and low to moderate twist.

During plying, the two finer elements are controlled by one hand and kept under high tension. The other hand controls the novelty element, which it frequently and abruptly jogs forward and back, as in the second method.

With a little practice, this routine makes a pretty fair *bouclé*. Depending upon twist amounts, rate of jogging, and constitution of the novelty element, it may also result in a *loop yarn*.

Moving to the fourth method. Let's imagine that we have produced a yarn according to the third method and want to further modify it by mechanical abuse, as in the fourth method. Assume that our yarn is a sort of loop, with the novelty element being kid mohair.

Suppose we were to wind this yarn around something large, solid and cylindrical—a metal storage can, a garbage pail, a length of duct pipe, or perhaps a portable propane tank (empty and disconnected, of course). Now, suppose we use a clean, new, wire brush (the kind used by welders and other metal workers) to gently and carefully brush the entire wrapped surface.

First we brush along the yarns. Then we brush across the yarns. Well, well. Look at that—we have made a brushed mohair yarn.

Here are several things to keep in mind. Unless the yarn is well constructed, it will not tolerate the treatment. It will get fuzzy, but it may remain serviceable as yarn. And unless the cylindrical device is firmly and stoutly arranged, both you and it are going to quit early on, giving the whole thing up as a bad job.

The value, varieties, and treatment of novelty yarns. The variety of novelty yarns possible is considerable, although not without limit. It is not a tour de force to produce a novelty that is attractive, unusual, and unique, yet impractical or even useless for any conventional conversion process. In weaving, for example, it is generally deemed desirable that yarn be able to pass through a reed, or at least to survive being wound into shuttle packages.

Thus the intended use of the yarn will establish its parameters, and it helps if you know something about how the yarn is to be used. The opposite view is also valid: the characteristics of the yarn establish how it may be used. Just avoid producing yarns designed for yet-to-be-invented purposes, unless you intend to do something about that as well.

Novelties may be constructed using complex yarns, high-twist yarns, or existing novelty yarns as elements. Interesting and durable novelties of various sorts are based upon high-twist elements and strands, plied in ways that encourage collapse and kinking. In a way, crepe yarns used in weaving are novelty yarns, although their structural and visual effects do not become apparent until the cloth is finished.

As with all yarns, novelties need to be scoured in hot, soapy water, well rinsed, and then dried. In general, novelties should be blocked under moderate to firm tension. Yarns to be converted through knitting are an exception, and should be dried under low tension. Some novelty

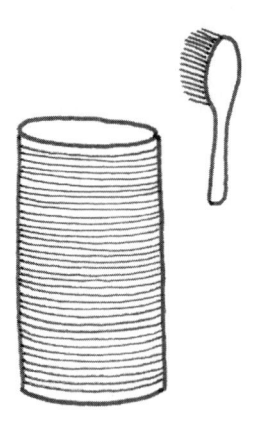

Wrap a mohair yarn around a firm, large cylinder and brush it with a clean wire brush. Brushed mohair yarn!

elements will not withstand the rigors of a good scour: avoid them. If you anticipate using such items as feathers, loose fibers, and dyed yarns of unknown character in your creations, you are on your own.[22]

It is generally worthwhile to examine commercial yarns as examples of construction. In conventional (plain) yarns, the mechanical production procedures are similar to the techniques used by the handspinner and plyer. The same is true of older commercial novelty yarns. But, sad to relate, many modern commercial novelties are made through nonspinning methods, or in conjunction with stunts and tricks that are simply not practical for the hand worker. Current industrial practice includes heat-setting and distortion of synthetic fibers (most modern novelties depend upon synthetics); chemical modification; punch-needle assembly; heat or adhesive bonding; and the like. These processes cannot be easily done at home. So you are often better off to invent your own novelties than to attempt to copy a high-tech plastic wonder.

Complex yarns

Complex yarns span the gap between simple, "straight" plying and the novelties. Complex yarns resemble novelties because they often include unusual or novel elements, although complex yarns are always constructed and plied with as much symmetry and consistency as possible. You have already been exposed to one version of a complex yarn, the hawser construction mentioned earlier in the chapter (see page 291). Another construction of interest, especially for knitting purposes, is called *cable*.

---

[22] *Some strange things show up as novelty items. The author has seen bones, plastic tubing filled with metal-lathe cutting curls, real straw, cellophane Easter-egg straw, shredded computer paper, sausage casings, dry-cleaners' plastic bags, aluminum foil, silk cocoons, chopped-up fast-food wrappers, soda straws, raw fleece, lumber string, red rubber inner-tube strips, flowers and stems . . . the list goes on. Please note that the author has seen these, not used them. Although it is true that a class participant once asked if Amos could spin any type of wool, and Amos remarked, "Sure!," whereupon the participant produced a wad of steel wool. Double 0, as I recollect, "in the soap." Any wool is especially hard to draft when you leave the soap in. However, the blue steel-wool pads are a little easier to draft than the red ones, if you dampen them first. . . .*

Cable yarns. "Novelty" cable is produced according to the plan Z–S–Z, as follows. (1) Two similar single yarns are plied down-twist beyond the twist-stable point, forming a twist-active strand. (2) Two of these twist-active strands are then plied down-twist, just to the twist-stable point. The resulting four-element, two-ply yarn is then scoured, rinsed, and dried under low tension.

Here is a sample. The single elements are 4,000 YPP, Z, 8 TPI. (1) Ply two singles down-twist to 8 PTPI (S). This forms a strand. (2) Ply two strands down-twist to the twist-stable point, about 4 PTPI. Scour, rinse, block under mild tension. This will result in a medium-soft (whatever that means) knitting yarn of about 1,000 YPP.

Here are several interesting things we have noted from constructing yarns of this type. Their texture has been described as "fine granular," and if color or luster is present the yarn appears to be braided.

This "braided look" is the chief *visual characteristic* obtained through cable construction. A *mechanical advantage* of cable construction is the yarn's reduced tendency to untwist as it passes through the knitter's hands. It appears "rounder" and more consistent in the finished work than an equivalent yarn of different construction.

Cable construction is not limited to four-element two-ply yarn. The number of elements per strand and the number of strands may be increased, with varying effects. Two strands of two elements each may be plied with two single elements, each a thick, soft single . . . and so forth.

However, be sure that all elements and strands are symmetrical—for this type of yarn, there should be no odd elements or strands. If it is a three-strand yarn, do not have two elements in one strand, one in another, and three in the third. Do not mix and match: if one strand is composed of two Z elements of 2,000 YPP each, it must be paired with an identical strand. In a three- or five-strand construction, all elements/strands must be equal. Beyond 5 strands, you are exploring new horizons and must make up your own rules.

A cable yarn contains four elements and two plies, combined in sequence according to the plan Z–S–Z.

Spinners, to your wheels! For those of you who have trudged this far, what is left? The whole subject of plying, really. You are going to perform your own trials, make and evaluate your own samples, apply your own remedies and corrections, develop your own techniques and procedures. Discard those things that do not work for you, embrace those that do, and remember the four principles: tension, distance, motion, and rewound packages. Your plied yarns will be advanced thereby.

Chapter 12

Tools and Equipment

Every book of this sort needs working drawings for equipment. We have a number of things in mind, but it's only fair to warn you that we assume you know something about woodworking, metalwork, and the allied arts.

The projects range from extremely simple to fairly complex, all the way from a spindle shaft to a blocking reel. In most cases, we will only make general remarks concerning finishing, stock preparation, assembly, and allowable dimensions. If there is a difficult or tricky part, we'll talk you through that.

With regard to finish coatings, our only criterion is that they be functional.

And about metalworking: several projects require metal components, and possibly a special tool or two, which may have to be of your own making. Not to worry, you or someone you know can handle it.

The projects are as follows, more or less in order of complexity:
(1) Scutching sword and base
(2) Beetling mallet and log
(3) Nøstepinne (ball winder)
(4) Hooked stick (twisty-stick) and crochet hook
(5) Niddy-noddy, two forms
(6) Coin spindle
(7) Drop spindles: low- and high-whorl
(8) Thai spindle
(9) Southwestern spindle
(10) Storage bobbins and rack
(11) Simple combs, ripples, and hackles
(12) Distaves: handheld, belt, and freestanding
(13) Skirders
(14) Blocking reels and stand

A few general observations are in order, and these observations apply to *all* plans, not just those that follow.

First, review the statements concerning equipment in the preface of this book.

Second, bear in mind that every piece of the included equipment represents a proven, sturdy design that has served both modern and old-time spinners well. Make no changes just because you have a chance to do so.

Third, if the plan calls for a specific item or procedure, think twice before substituting other materials or methods. Nothing here is arbitrary. If a project calls for hickory or a certain type of joint or stainless-steel screws, those specifications exist for a reason.

Fourth, and this is important, every procedure mentioned here involves certain hazards. You are your own supervisor, your own shop steward, your own safety inspector. Before you do anything with power, sharp tools, heat, or hammers, sit down and think it through.

Fifth, and most important, *protect your eyes*. If you wear glasses, get the type with safety lenses. If you don't wear glasses, put another barrier in front of your eyes: safety glasses, goggles, a face shield. I've been an artificer for at least 50 years, and have saved my eyes many, many times because of goggles, masks, or glasses. Do not be a stupid, arrogant fool. Wear eye protection.

1: SCUTCHING SWORD AND BASE

This pair of items is used for removing the boon from retted, broken flax, hemp, and nettle stems.

Both sword and upright are best made from hard, tough, fine-grained wood, such as sugar maple, hop hornbeam, or beech. Oak, pine, or whatever is fine for the base. A good-sized split of firewood will do, say a split half of a log about 8 inches in diameter and 18 inches long. The heavier, the better.

Clean up and flatten the bottom of the split log, and peel the bark. Round over the edges. Find top center and lay out the mortise lines. Drill and chop the mortise about ¾ inch wide, 3 inches deep, and 2 inches long. The mortise doesn't need squared corners.

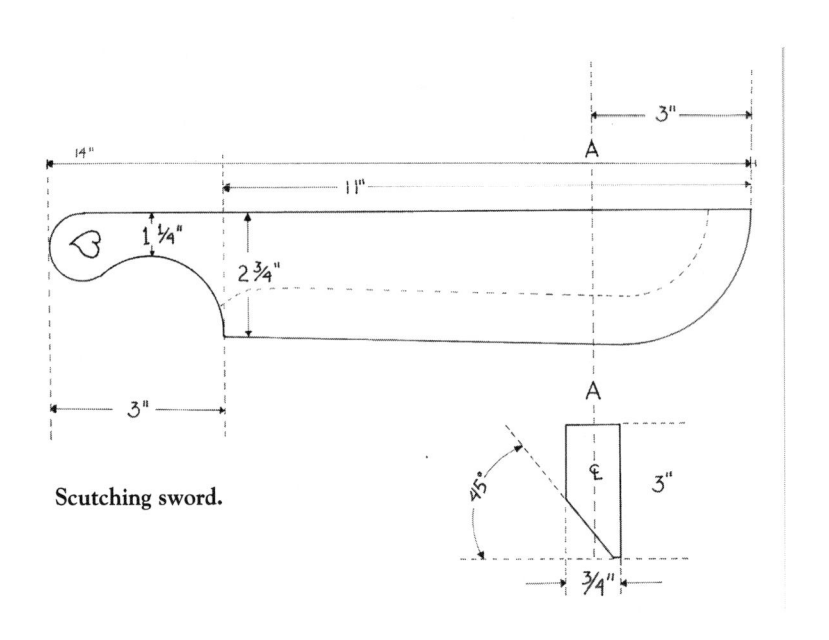

Scutching sword.

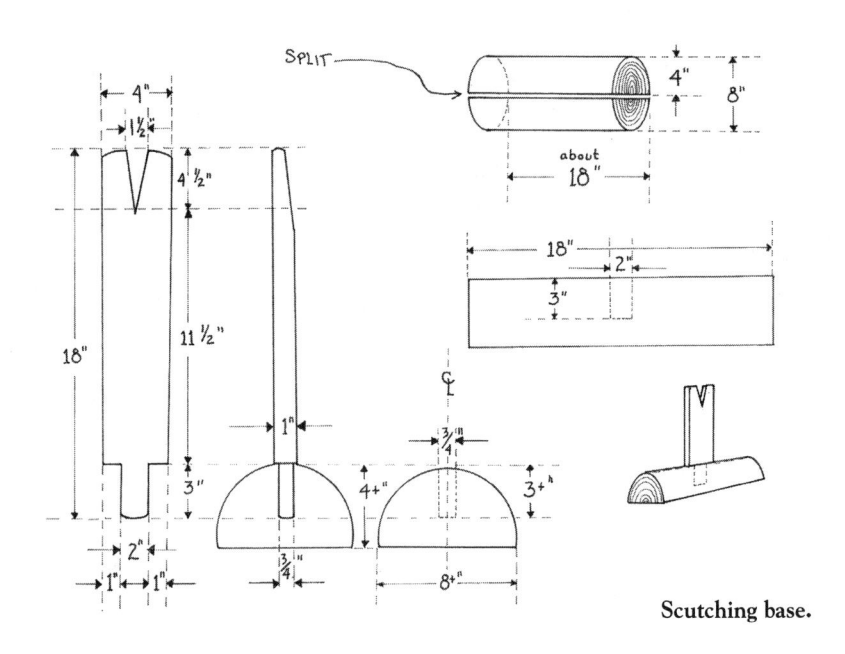

Scutching base.

334   The Alden Amos Big Book of Handspinning

Cut the upright from 1-inch stock, making it about 12 inches long and 3 inches wide. First cut a tenon to fit the log base; then cut the scutching notch as a narrow V shape about 3 inches deep and 1½ inches wide at the top.

Plane or re-saw the top ⅓ of the upright to a gentle taper, say from 1 inch to ⅜ inch thick. Leave one side of the board flat; remove all stock from the other surface. Then round off all edges and the top.

For a permanent installation, cut blind wedges and slots to fit. Apply a little glue, slip the upright into the mortise, and knock it home with a suitable binky. Set it aside, and move on to the sword.

Cut the sword from 1-inch stock. Lay it out and cut to shape. With the sword flat on the table before you, mark out the edge bevel and decorative fretwork or carving on the same side of the blank. If the sword will be used by a right-hander, lay out with the handle to your left. If it will be used by a left-hander, lay out with the handle to your right. The plan shows a "right-handed" sword.

Shaping the bevel is the last step. Clamp the sword down and plane, shave, or file away extra stock. There is no need for a razor-edge; about ¹⁄₁₆ inch thick at the edge is fine. Leave the back flat.

In general, scutching swords are expendable, so traditional finish for the project is nothing. Sometimes an old sword has been painted, but that's probably because it was used to stir paint. A "courting" (fancy) sword may have highlighted carving, pyrography, fretwork, or even tole painting. One for service is seldom so finished.

Historical and geographic occurrence: Neolithic to present. Europe, Mediterranean region, North America.

2: BEETLING MALLET AND LOG

This item is used to pound or beetle textiles woven from flax, hemp, nettle, and other bast fibers. A beetling mallet is also used to break retted fiber stems, prior to scutching.

Several versions are shown here. The *club* is so simple it merits little explanation, except to say that it is more for breaking flax and hemp straw than for beetling textiles. For practical purposes, a short section of baseball bat makes a good breaking club.

Beetling mallets and log.

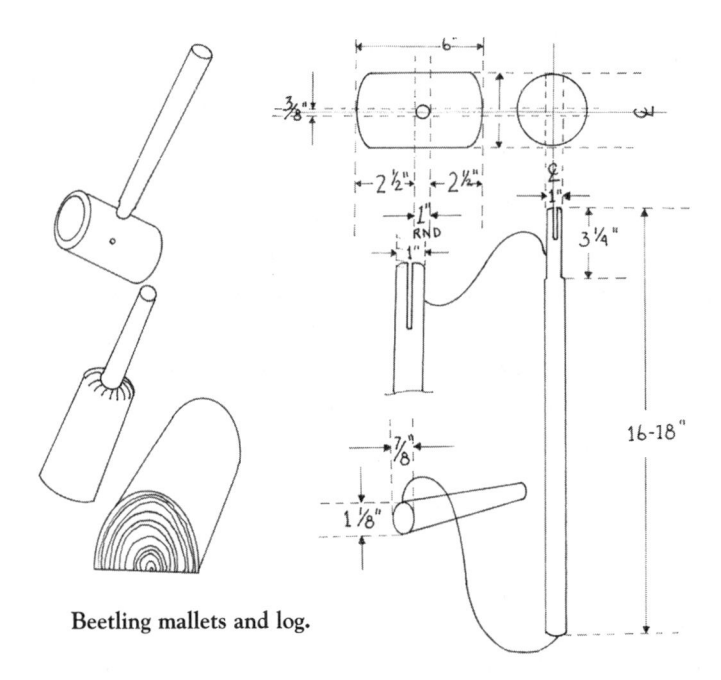

The beetling mallet is mainly used on woven cloth, instead of for breaking straw. It is a two-piece construction, although sometimes a mallet is cut in a single piece from a suitably shaped root or branch formation.

Do not make the head too heavy because it will wear the user out before any work gets accomplished. A pound and a half is plenty.

Start with a limb about 3 inches in diameter and cut the head block 4 to 6 inches long. Maple, beech, and birch are best, but oak will work. Gently round the ends. Peel the bark if there is any.

Using hickory, ash, pecan, maple, or a similar wood, cut the handle from 1¼-inch square stock or a suitable small limb. Turn or trim to comfort, and cut it to between 16 and 18 inches in length. A large, commercial framing hammer or hatchet handle will serve, if you wish to save yourself some extra work. The extra length of handle improves the tool's balance. Remember that she-hands are mostly smaller than he-hands, but don't make the handle too small. An oval about 1⅛ inches on the long side is about right.

Find and mark the center of the head. Bore a ⅞-inch hole through the blank. Use a V-block or jig to make boring easier. Turn, whittle, or shave one end of the handle to a snug fit, full depth.

Knock the handle into place, then drive a cross-wedge in the top. Best that the wedge be crossways of the head. An alternative method is to cross-drill both head and handle and drive a snug pin across.

Once the handle has been seated, "bake" each face (or end) of the head over a stove-burner or similar flame source. Brown it like toast, don't set it on fire. Move quickly. If you take too long, the wood is bound to crack. When the wood has cooled off, scrub each end with 80-grit garnet paper to remove any carbon or ragged edges. Repeat the process of "toasting" and scrubbing at least one more time.

Scrape and shave the handle to finished size and shape. Give the handle a coat or two of linseed oil. If you used a commercial hammer handle, remove the factory lacquer finish. Give the beetle faces a coat of paste wax.

Condition the beetle faces by tap-tap-tapping them against a hard, smooth surface, such as an anvil or a bowling ball. Touch up the wax job from time to time. Make any changes (refinements, if you are speaking to a customer) in the handle shape, length, and so forth after you have conditioned the beetle faces.

You will also need a log to beetle or break against. The half-log left over from making the scutching base will work if you remove the bark and plane the rounded surface slick and smooth. Flatten off the lower surface so that it sits without wobbling. Break the sharp edges, give it a coat of wax, then mount it on a chunk of old carpet.

Historical and geographic occurrence: Neolithic to present. Europe, Nile region, North America.

3: NØSTEPINNE OR WINDING STICK (BALL WINDER)

This amounts to a variation of the kite-string winders of our youth. It is used to wind center-pull balls of yarn and cord. Also used to rap uppity children on the top of the head.

Two versions are described here, one lathe-turned and the other a draw-knife project. Stock for either needs to be large enough for you to net a finished length of 8 or 9 inches and diameter of about $\frac{3}{4}$ to $\frac{7}{8}$ inch.

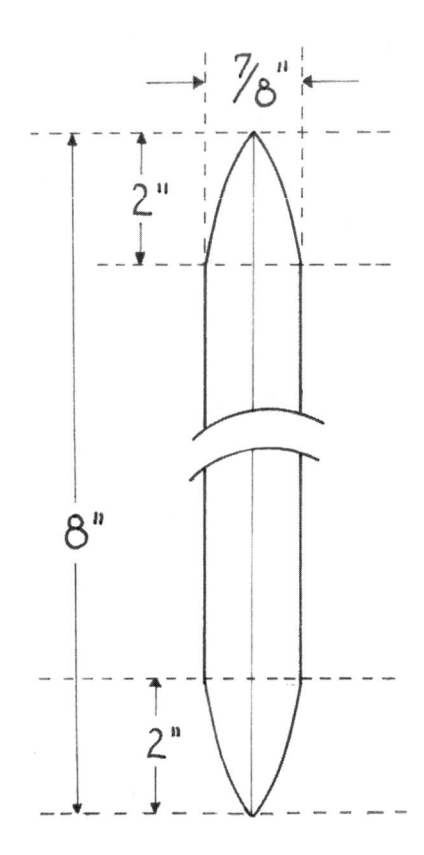

Nøstepinne.

Avoid the use of exotic woods. Most of them generate toxic and/or allergy-triggering dust, while some are more or less endangered. Besides, you don't need to endorse or justify the stripping of another country's forestland and watershed. Use sugar maple, beech, or birch for starters, or well-seasoned orchard cuttings. Pear, apple, plum, peach, olive, and cherry prunings represent a few possibilities.

Shave or shape both ends symmetrically to a smoothly tapered Gothic-arch outline. Each taper should be about 2 inches long. Avoid any major changes (grooves or carvings) in the body diameter, except as the two ends taper to points. Remember that the yarn has to slide off when you are through winding.

No matter how you shape the nøstepinne, it's a good idea to "raise the hair" by dampening the work and allowing it to dry. If you turn the form in a lathe, burnish with chips, going in both directions. If you cut and scrape the form by hand, use fine garnet paper (150 grit or finer) to finish up.

Once smoothed up, finish with wax and elbow grease. This item needs a pretty good polish, no matter how it was made.

Historical and geographic occurrence: Neolithic to present. Europe, Scandinavia, North America.

4: Hooked stick (twisty-stick) and crochet hook

We list these together only for convenience. The hooked stick or twisty-stick is a simple metal wire production, while the crochet hook is a little more involved.

The hooked stick. This spinning and sampling aid is easily as useful as the wheel-threading hook. Suitable material can be found in any old-fashioned wire coat hanger. Cut a straight piece about 7 or 8 inches long. You can obtain at least three good lengths from the typical wire hanger.

With a fine file, round off one end and point the other. Bend the pointed end as shown, and scrub off any rough spots with emery cloth or abrasive paper.

If you anticipate making a number of these, for guild events or a spinning class, use a jig, made as follows. Cut the head off a 40-penny nail. Bend the remaining nail shaft double, making a short, stout staple. Clamp this in a metalworking vise, with the two ends down and about ½-inch of the U sticking up. The two legs should be about ⅛ inch apart, or slightly more than the diameter of the wire you are using to make the twisty-sticks.

When you are making multiple twisty-sticks, begin by cutting numerous 7- or 8-inch lengths of coat-hanger wire. Work over the ends. When all are ready, start bending. In the name of uniformity, it is best to make Bend A on all items, then Bend B.

Two crochet hooks are shown. One is iron and the other is wood.

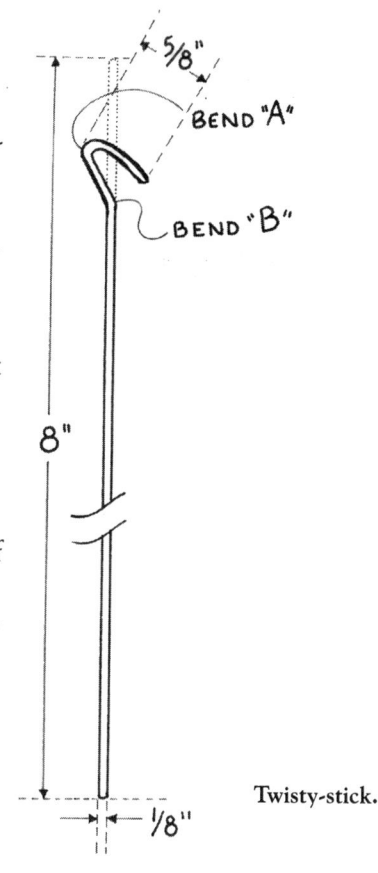

Twisty-stick.

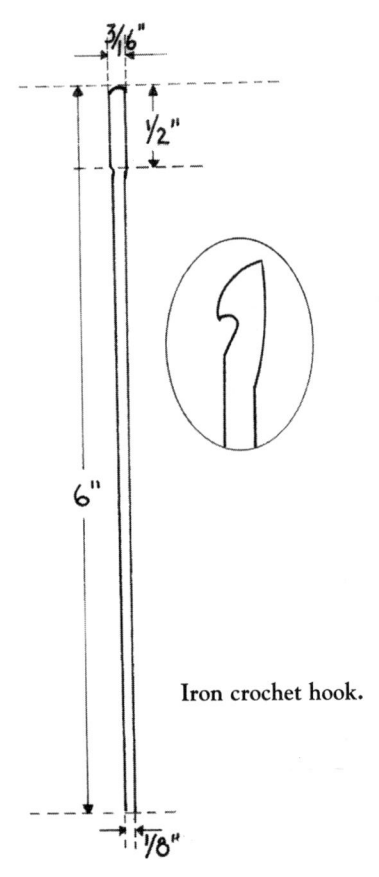

Iron crochet hook. First, the iron one. Cut a piece of coat-hanger wire about 6 inches long. File one end square across and round off the other one.

Using all due caution, heat the square end to a visible red-hot, then quickly give it a gentle hammer-smack while holding it on a suitable surface, such as a steel plate or an anvil. Before you heat or smack the metal, think about what will happen if you hit it "wrong" and it flies out of your hands, off into some inaccessible place, and lies there in the dust and stuff, still red-hot.

Back to work. You want to flatten the square end slightly, for about ½ inch. Red heat keeps it from cracking. Let the metal cool off before you proceed. You can speed up the cooling: wait until you no longer see any color, then quench the metal.

Using fine files, shape the end as shown. Take a little time and care at this. When shaped, re-heat to red and plunge the hook into a quart or more of cold water (or super-quench; see Chapter 13). Remove the metal and wipe it dry.

Next, lay the other end of the metal piece on a block and, using a chain-saw file and piece of wood, roll-knurl the handle. This makes the handle easier to grip. Clean up the metal, wipe with an oily rag, and it's done.

Wooden crochet hook. The primary use for big crochet hooks is the production of mud rugs, door throws, and bath mats from monster yarns, skinny rag strips, or cotton mop rope.

Secure a piece of tough, hard-to-split wood such as hickory, pecan, elm, or sugar maple. Cut it about 10 inches long and shave, plane, and scrape it down to about ⅝ inch in diameter.

Shape a blunt bullet-point at one end. About 1¼ diameters back from the point, start to whittle a notch. You want the smallest possible notch that will do the job. To be durable, the notch in a wooden hook needs to be about ⅓ diameter deep and about ½ diameter wide. Slightly undercut the notch for the best results.

The depth of the notch determines how big a yarn you can work

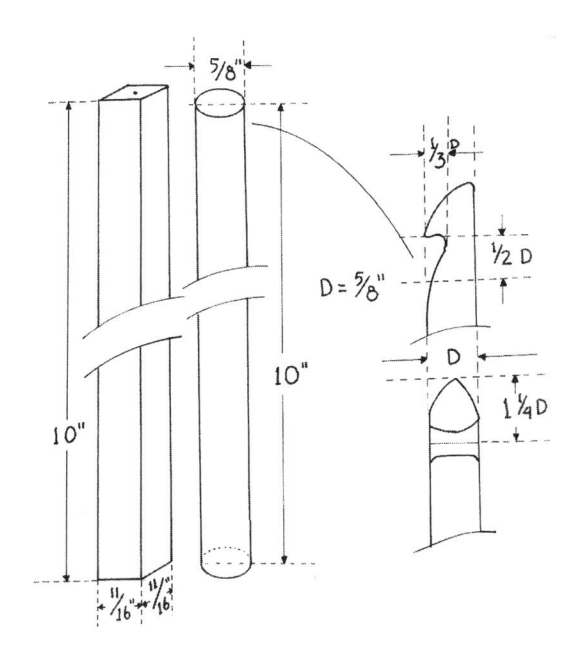

Wooden crochet hook.

with. The bigger the yarn, the bigger the hook shaft needs to be, because the hook depth should always be about ⅓ diameter deep and ½ diameter wide.

Historical and geographic occurrence for twisty-stick: Prehistory to present. Europe and Scandinavia.

Historical and geographic occurrence for crochet hook: Unknown beginnings. In use from medieval Europe (A.D. 1200) to present time. Name is from ME and OFr. Middle-Eastern, Arabic in origin. Post-Columbian in Americas.

5: NIDDY-NODDY, TWO FORMS

Beginners and young people find the handled version considerably easier to use. For both styles, the woods to use are maple, beech, ash, and birch.

Old-style niddy-noddy. With a gentle curve on the limbs, there is no need to have the niddy jointed or arranged to collapse.

Old-style niddy-noddy.

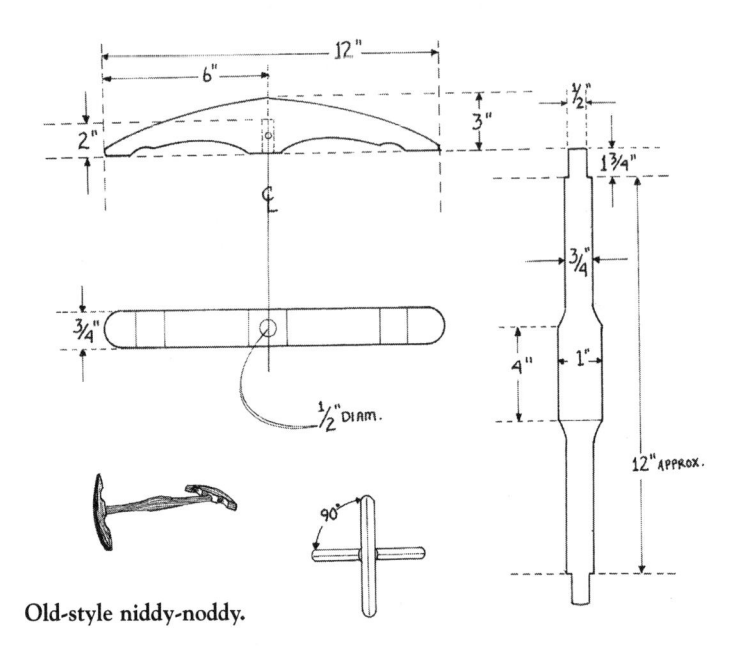

Lay out the arm patterns parallel to the grain. Rip arm stock to width, bore each mortise hole, then fretsaw or bandsaw arms to shape. Round and shape upper surfaces, then do decorative carving and so on.

Cut handle stock to length. The dimensions given result in a nominal 1½-yard skein. Cut tenons to be a tight fit.

If using adhesives, cut air-relief notches in tenons, apply glue, and assemble. Ensure that limbs are at right angles. Bump together with a dead-blow mallet or padded binky.

If cross-pinning is used, assemble niddy as above except both limbs should be flat. Drill and pin one head. Then rotate the other head 90 degrees and drill and pin it.

Break all sharp edges and slick up all rough spots. Raise the grain, then slick again. The correct finish during all ages has consisted of rubbed-in coats of linseed oil, scrubbed and allowed to dry. Add a coat of wax polish.

Handled niddy-noddy. Start by cutting the central shaft. Form tenons on each end. Allow extra length because it is easier to shorten wood

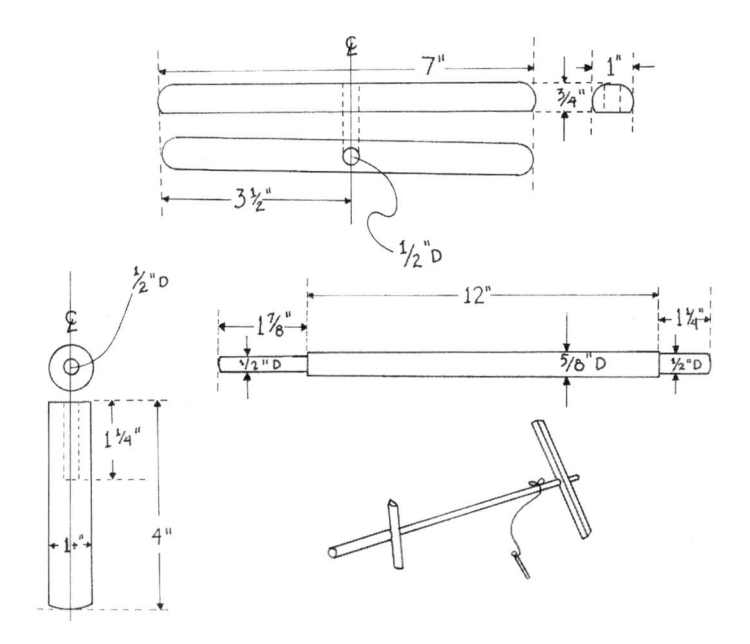

Handled niddy-noddy.

than to stretch it. Do not make the center shaft big and beefy; its weakest part is the tenon diameter. Cut and shape both limbs, and bore center holes. The lower limb (at the handle end) will be permanent. The upper limb needs to rotate, so fit the tighter tenon through the lower limb. Scrape the upper tenon to slip-fit the upper limb.

Cut, bore, and shape the handle. Bore for a snug fit on the stub tenon from the bottom limb. Try a dry fit. When the fit works, apply glue and assemble the shaft, lower limb, and handle for real. Allow the glue to set while you take a break.

Round off the top of the upper tenon and fit the upper limb. Rotate to 90 degrees with respect to the lower limb and carefully cross-drill, using backing scrap. The hole should be about ⅓ of the tenon diameter. Prepare a tapered cross-pin, attach a retaining string or thong, and give the niddy a test wind.

To release the skein from this handled niddy, pull the pin and rotate the upper limb until it is parallel to the lower limb, then slide the skein off. Return the upper limb to right-angle position and reinstall the pin.

The finish for this niddy is the same as for the other.

Both nids are set up for a nominal 1½-yard (54-inch) skein. You will be tempted to change the dimensions of the niddies. If you do, you are on your own.

Historical and geographic occurrence: Old-style niddy-noddy—unknown origin, with no pictorial evidence earlier than the fourteenth century. Handled niddy-noddy—fifteenth century.

6: COIN SPINDLE OR TAHKLI

This small spindle, commonly called a *tahkli*, has become popular in this country for spinning fine yarns from cotton and exotic fibers.

Imported models use brass or steel whorls and metal shafts. For this one, we depend on a coin and a dirt-bike spoke.

The spoke is hardened steel. If you cannot cut it with heavy-duty diagonals, grind and break off a section about 7 inches long. Clean up the cut end and grind a long, smooth taper. Take your time.

Grind a short taper on the threaded end. It needs to be about ⅓ of the threaded length. Then point the end, about sharp enough to draw blood. Water-dip the work to cool it. Often.

The thread is a fine metric series. This is no problem, because we will use the shaft itself to tap the hole threads. Well, not tap so much as flow or swage the threads.

Find and mark the center of the coin, and drill a hole a few thousandths smaller than the thread diameter. Note! The thread diameter is always larger than the spoke-shaft diameter, so measure diameter across the threads, not the smooth portion of the spoke. Chuck up or clamp the shaft with just the thread sticking out of the jaws. Be sure everything is braced and firm.

Now press the coin down on the point. Press hard, and screw it on. Be sure you are going the right way (it is a "normal" right-hand thread). This may take a try or two to get the hang of it, but it does work. Screw the coin onto the spindle shaft until about ½ inch of spindle sticks out the bottom. Do not go too far, because the unthreaded body of the spoke is almost always smaller than the threaded portion. Be careful, and do not impale yourself in the effort. That point is SHARP!

With the coin in place, give the spindle a try. If it wobbles much, rotate the spindle slowly, eyeballing it to see where the trouble lies. If the coin is not at right angles to the shaft, apply a little force and make it so, but do not bend the shaft.

Once you have a passable spindle, pay attention to the top or hook end. You should already have the top 1½ inches or so filed or ground down; if not, do that now.

Then, with pliers in hand, heat the top to red-hot. While still at red heat, quickly shape a hook of sorts, and then let everything cool off. Do not quench it. Let it cool slowly. It won't take long.

Refine the hook shape as necessary. Close it in a little more than you think you need. When satisfied, lay it on a suitable hard, smooth, steel or iron surface and give it a mild smack with a smooth-face hammer. Don't do this more than a few times. If you do, it will work-harden and may crack. If you do need to pound on it a bit more or do more bending, best anneal it. That means to reheat the hook to a dull red and then allow it to cool slowly.

When happy with the shape and so forth, polish up the shaft with emery cloth. Give the spindle a test spin.

A little wobble is acceptable. If the spindle wobbles so much that it can't reach the necessary speed, balance it as follows. Put a center-pop in a suitable block of wood. Stand the tahkli with its point in the center-pop, shaft straight up and down. Tape a working felt-tip pen to another block and arrange it so that the pen tip just touches the outer edge of the tahkli whorl. Rotate the spindle carefully, so that the felt-tip just touches the high spots, marking them. Carefully file or grind the pen marks from the coin rim. Try again. Continue to trim and check until you have a working spindle.

Historical and geographic occurrence: In India, in use from at least the tenth century on. In Europe and North America, has been evident post-1970. Until recently, almost exclusively used for cotton spinning.

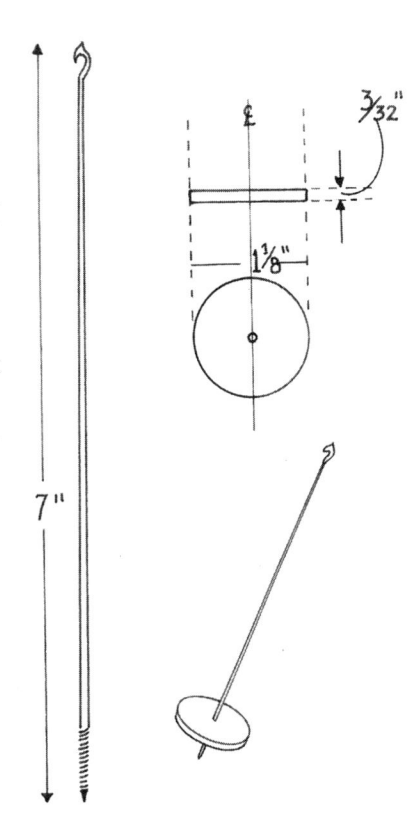

Coin spindle.

7: Drop spindles: low- and high-whorl

The simple low-whorl spindle is the easiest, and lends itself to young-person activities. The high-whorl is a high-performance device.

Simple low-whorl drop spindle. Select the plainest, least-figured piece of wood you can find. This will make balancing the whorl easier.

Strike a center mark and bore a 7/16-inch diameter center hole from the "wrong side," or bottom. Rough-cut the round.

Clamp the whorl to a suitable surface, as in workbench. Using a sharp paring chisel and some care, rotate and trim the whorl to size. Turn the whorl over and carefully re-trim the edge. Remove from the jig and gently round over and refine cut surfaces.

Any pyrography or stamp/punch work should be done now. Give the decorated surfaces a coat of linseed oil; rub in, wipe down, and set aside.

You can make the shaft from a ½-inch diameter dowel rod or from suitable stock. In either case, the wood needs to be at least 12 inches long, straight, and about ½ inch in diameter. If you are using the stock, split out several pieces and pick the most likely candidate. Plane, shave, and scrape the dowel or split section of wood to a uniform taper. This split-and-shave procedure on a section of wood results in a superior spindle shaft—very authentic. Either way, the 12-inch shaft will taper from about a ½ inch diameter at the lower end to ⅜ inch at the upper end.

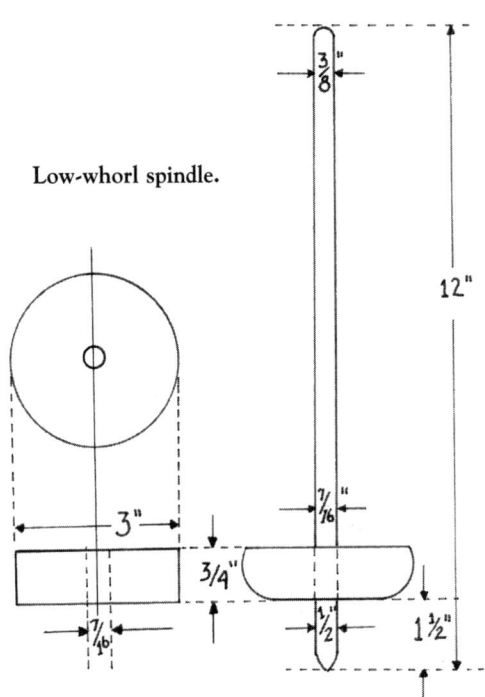

Low-whorl spindle.

Continue to scrape and shave the shaft until the whorl, "wrong side" down, slides down to a firm fit about 2 to 3 inches above the bottom point. Put a blunt point on the bottom of the shaft and round off its top. Avoid putting hooks, notches, and other stuff on the shaft.

Give the spindle a test whirl. Check for obvious wobble, out of round, and so on, and make corrections.

When satisfied, touch up the oil finish on whorl. Put nothing on the shaft.

High-whorl drop spindle. The high-whorl or Egyptian spindle has to withstand high rotational speeds, and thus requires careful balancing.

Start by selecting the shaft material. Split out a suitable 14-inch section, then trim, shave, scrape, and shape to a gentle taper. The end result should measure no less than ½ inch in diameter at one end and about ⅜ inch in diameter at the other. The last 2 inches of the ½-inch end require no taper. Take some care in shaping the shaft. Dowel rods may be used as an alternate source of material.

Select plain stock for the whorl. Strike and mark the center and lay out the whorl. Bore the center hole to a nominal ½-inch diameter. Rough-cut the whorl to shape. Again, using a sharp paring chisel, trim and refine the whorl.

Scrape and file the shaft so the ½-inch end fits snugly into the hole in the whorl. The fit should be such that it is not easy to put the shaft into

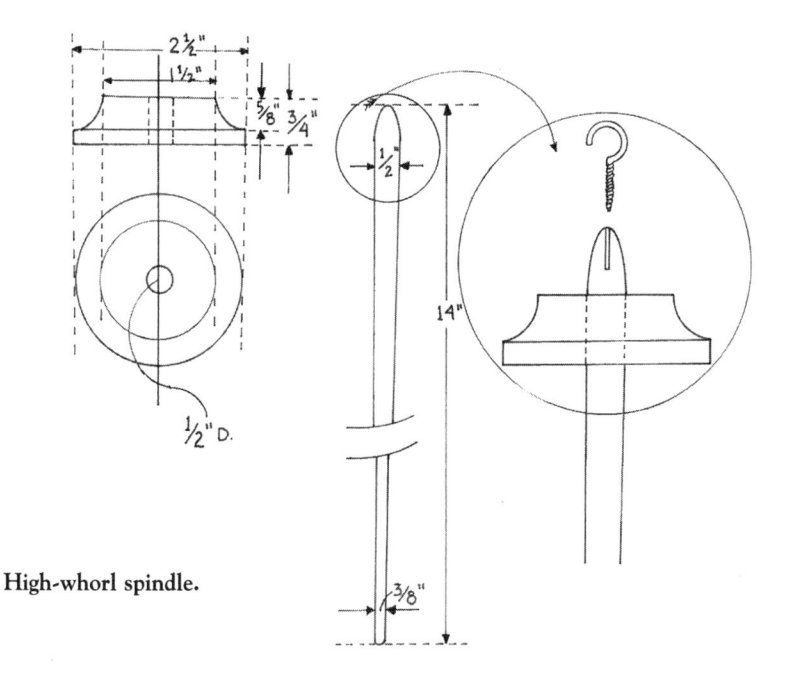

High-whorl spindle.

the whorl. A gentle tap may be in order, but be careful and do not split the whorl.

Find and mark the center at both ends of the shaft. Supporting the shaft on two brad points, balance by marking and trimming. Do not install the hook until you have achieved a reasonable balance.

An appropriate finish for either spindle is nothing except use.

Historical and geographic occurrence, both types: Stone Age to present. Ancient Egypt and throughout the world..

8: THAI SPINDLE

This is a sort of miniature Southwestern spindle, but it's used in the double-supported or bead-whorl mode.[1] The construction involves no particular difficulties other than the delicacy of the elements.

Traditional materials include coconut shell for the whorl and palm rib or split bamboo for the shaft. Contemporary materials include thin sections from vegetable boxes for the whorls and shaved chopsticks for the shafts.

Don't fool around with dimensions on this one. For the shaft, ³⁄₁₆ inch is too big and ⅛ inch is too small. The whorl needs to be lightweight but fairly large (between 2 and 3 inches in diameter), ergo thin. The "hook" notch is necessary, but do not make it too large.

Historical and geographic occurrence: Unknown. Has been around for a while.

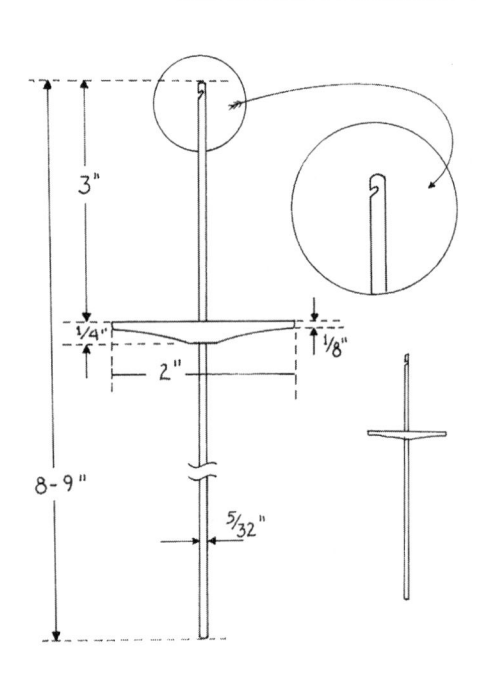

Thai spindle.

---

[1] Typical of Andean bead-whorl and akha spindles, the spindle is supported during use by both the hand and the yarn.

9: Southwestern Spindle

Some people would call this a small Navajo spindle, or perhaps a Hopi spindle. Without getting into an argument: the big differences between these types of spindles involve where the whorl is positioned on the shaft and their methods of employment.

Make the shaft first. From straight, dry wood, split out sections between 14 and 18 inches long. Pine, spruce, poplar, cottonwood, and cedar all make good shafts. Split out a few extras, just for practice.

Using a small block plane, spokeshave, and scraper, carefully shave, trim, and scrape the shafts to a nice double taper. The shafts will end up about ⅜ inch in diameter in the center, tapered to 3/16 inch in diameter at the ends.

Scrape smooth, or use a sanding block and scrub them down. Using pine, cedar, cottonwood, or similar wood, split out thin, shingle-like sections for the whorls. Make them about ¼ inch thick, and big enough to net a 3½- or 4-inch whorl diameter.

Strike and mark the center, then bore a hole just slightly smaller than the thickest part of the shaft. Carefully trim the whorl to shape. Scrape down the edges and flat surfaces.

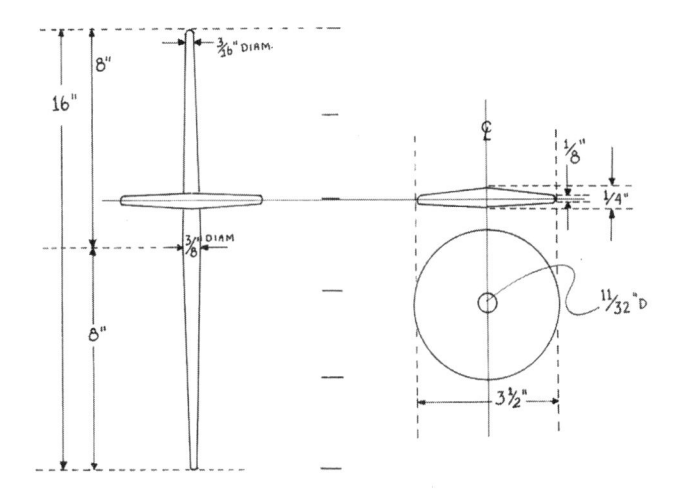

Southwestern spindle.

Apply decorative work, then fit the whorl to the shaft. The whorl should be positioned just off the midpoint of the shaft. There will be about ⅗ of the shaft on one side, ⅖ on the other. The working drawing shows fifth-interval spacing.

The appropriate finish comes with usage.

Historical and geographic occurrence: Ubiquitous, really. In context, the Southwestern United States, from pre-Columbian times to the present.

10: Storage bobbins and rack

Everybody who plies yarn needs these items.

Storage bobbins. Make the cores first. Rip suitable stock, say 1 inch square. Cut to rough length (slightly too long), bore center holes, and then rough-round the cores. Best to make more than enough.

Then prepare the flange (disk) rounds. Lay them out, strike centers, mark, and bore the rounds. Rough-cut them to diameter. Cut enough to have spares.

Trim the cores to a standard length, then chuck them between stub arbors or mount them on a suitable mandrel. Cut core tenons for a snug fit in bobbin-disk mortices (round center holes). Dry fit a disk on each end. When happy with the fit, disassemble disks and core, then reassemble using waterproof glue. Allow to set overnight.

When dry, bore or ream the core to its finished internal diameter. Mount on suitable arbor(s) and trim core and flanges to the indicated profile. Reverse and rough-sand (80-grit).

Weigh each bobbin and mark its weight on one or both bobbin disks (this step is not really necessary). Coat the bobbins with lacquer or water-resistant varnish, and allow them to dry completely. When dry, coat the inside surfaces with paste wax, well rubbed in.

Bobbin rack. This is simplicity itself. Select a large, heavy scrap or plank stub. The heavier the better. Lay out and bore a handle hole and rod holes. Clean up the base, trim the handle end to fit the center hole in the base, and drive the handle into place. Install "feet" (rug squares and carpet tacks).

Cut rod stock to length, round the ends, and drive the rods into place. Use a sledge or anvil for bucking.

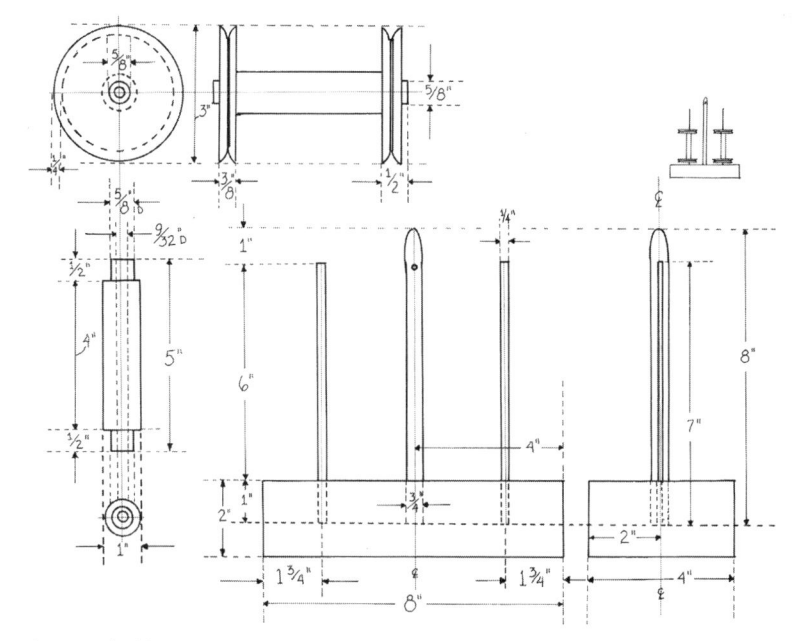

Storage bobbins and rack.

Cross-drill the handle, chamfer the hole, and install a thong or cord. Punch out washers and install them on the rods. Check rods for rough spots and remove irregularities as required. Clean and wipe the rods with an oily rag.

Check each bobbin for smooth fit. Ream as required so you end up with a good, smooth, not sloppy fit on the rods. Lubricate rods. Punch out and install buffer washers. Always make extra—these fit over the shafts and form a friction surface between the bobbin core and the base.

Historical and geographic occurrence: Known from late medieval times to present era. Europe, North America.

11: Simple Combs, ripples, and hackles

The ripple is the simplest of these tools, and uses ready-made (wire) nails. Hackles are constructed using masonry nails, with the points improved by grinding. Combs require pins with forged points.

Ripple. Cut the block to length, then lay out and drill the

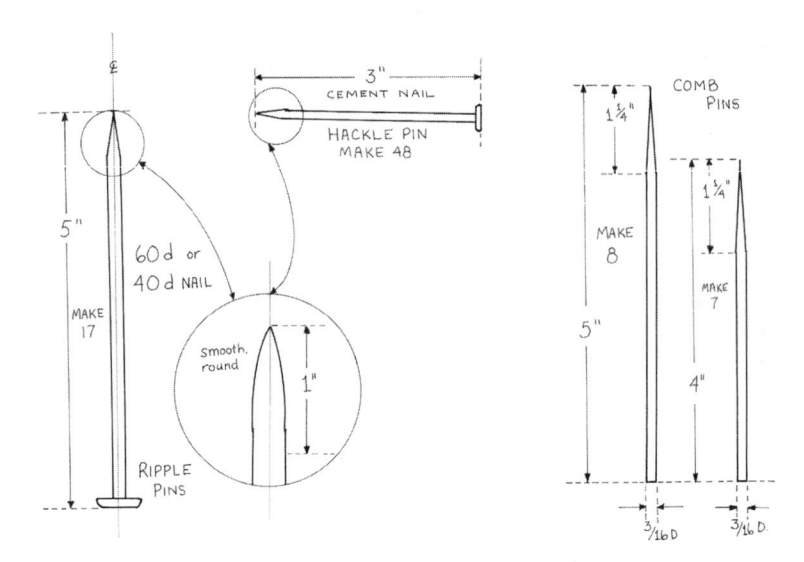

Pins and teeth.

counterbores, making them about $1/64$ inch deeper than the thickness of the nail heads.

Drill the nail holes, centered in the counterbores. The nail holes need to be about $1/64$ inch smaller than the nail diameter.

Use a backing piece to prevent tear-out. Clean up the counterbores and slightly countersink the nail holes on the top side.

Select and prepare the nails. With a file, break off any oversized flanges or forging flash. Wear eye protection. Don't use nails that have partial or misshapen heads. Tidy up the points.

Obtain an 8- or 10-inch section of 1-inch black iron pipe. Secure the pipe in a solid vise. Clean off and touch up the pipe end to reduce marring. This is now your "bucking" aid.

Keeping the ripple face firmly against the bucking pipe, drive each nail through and flush with the back of the block. Seat down the nails with a stub set. Drive the end nails first; then, if you split the block, you haven't wasted all that work. Each time you drive a nail, reposition the ripple on the bucking pipe. Never drive a nail without using the buck.

Cut the backing plate to size. Mix up a thick paste from some glue and fine sawdust. Paint the nail heads and the back of the nail block

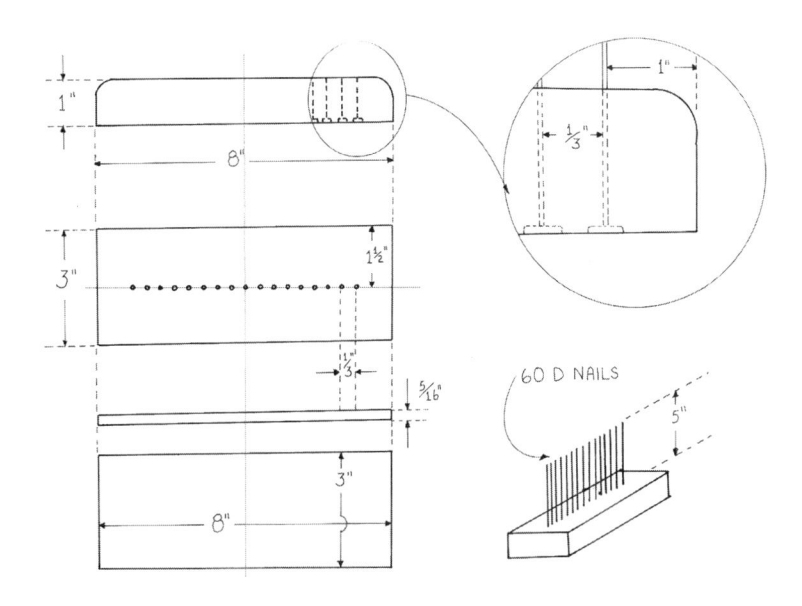

Ripple block.

with a thin coat of plain glue. Wait a few minutes, then spread the sawdust/glue mixture over the same area. Spread glue on the face of the backing plate, then clamp in place using rubber bands, weights, whatever. Set aside to dry overnight.

When dry, give the wood several coats of oil paint. It won't hurt the pins to have paint on them.

Hackles. Hackles are similar in construction and are assembled in much the same way. They have a lot more teeth, which are more closely set. Hickory, pecan, and elm are good choices for the block material.

These teeth are based on concrete nails because of their hardness and strength. Have all the pins prepared before you cut the block. The points need to be refined and the most effective way to do the job is by grinding.

ALWAYS WEAR EYE AND BREATHING PROTECTION WHEN GRINDING. ALWAYS.

It is not necessary to make long, thin needle points. Just refine the tips a little and round off the 4-bang effect. While you are at the grinder, check each nail and nail head for rough or ragged spots, and touch up these spots as and if required.

The block is laid out on concentric lines. Mark out and divide each ring as suggested. Lay out the whole block before you drill any holes. Take your time and work carefully. There are a lot of holes.

Counterbore all of the holes, and then drill the undersize pin holes. Holes that are $2/1000$ to $3/1000$ undersize will do fine.

Use the bucking aid while driving the pins: it will be a little tricky, but you must back it up while driving. Use a stub set (nail set) to seat each nail head below surface. These nails will be harder to drive than the ripple nails, and there are more of them. Do not be in a hurry, and take breaks when you are tired.

The pins will be tight enough so that no back-board is required. Give the block a couple of coats of linseed oil, rubbed in and then rubbed off between coats.

Combs. The combs can be made with nails for pins, but you'll get much better results when you forge the pins to points. The material used is plain (no flux) mild steel, $3/16$-inch-diameter gas welding rod. Auto parts stores and welding supply houses have this in stock. If it is

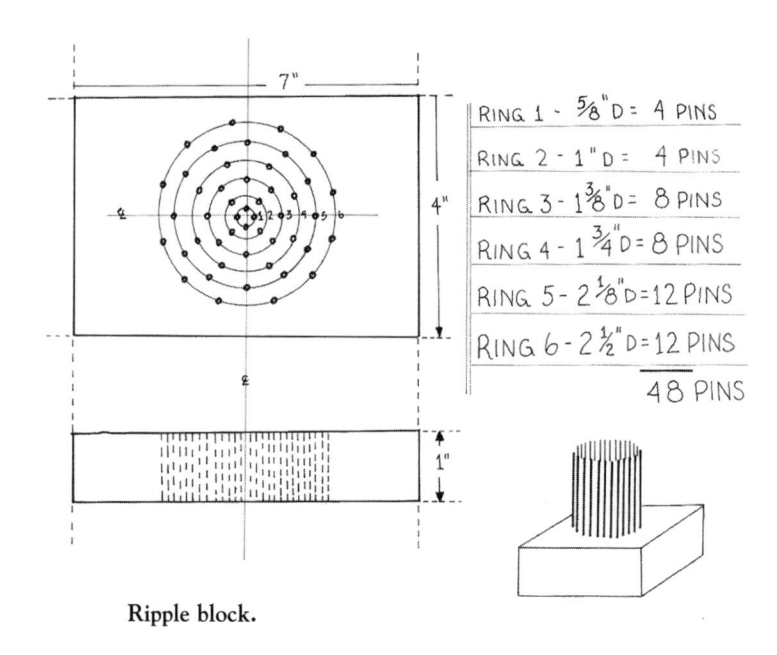

RING 1 - $5/8$" D = 4 PINS
RING 2 - 1" D = 4 PINS
RING 3 - $1 3/8$" D = 8 PINS
RING 4 - $1 3/4$" D = 8 PINS
RING 5 - $2 1/8$" D = 12 PINS
RING 6 - $2 1/2$" D = 12 PINS
48 PINS

Ripple block.

copper-plated, no problem. Get 36-inch sticks or rods, and cut each in half. What you are doing is giving yourself enough stock to keep from burning your hands; you will cut off pairs of pins as you go along.

Arrange your forge and anvil close together; 3/16ths will not stay red for long. Even at a bright red, you will not have time for more than eight or ten licks. Do not try to have "too many irons in the fire." Now you know what that means.

Don't work the steel cold. It is possible to do so, but (1) it is bad practice and (2) sooner or later you will get a cracked point. Points with cracks are worthless.

Bang 'em square, taper 'em, bang 'em round. With a 2-pound hammer and a little practice, you will be able to get a decent point in three heats or less. With a little more practice, you'll get good points in two heats. Yes, you can get a good point in one heat, but this is not a 'smithing contest.

When both ends of a rod have been pointed, measure to the middle of the rod and mark it. Clamp each rod in the vise and cut it on the mark, using a hacksaw.

Now forge and point the newly cut ends. Always make too many pins. Once all have been worked, secure the forge (put the fire OUT) in a safe and appropriate manner.

Each point must be dressed. To save extra wear and tear on your files, it is best to grind or sand the scale from the points, because the forge scale is very hard on files. Then proceed as follows. Clamp in a vise as shown. Using a handled file, clean up and refine each point. Turn the stock several times. Work all pins to the same degree before going to the next step. It is easier to work and handle them before you cut them to finished length.

This may seem stupid, but try not to stab or impale yourself. NEVER LEAVE A POINTED ROD OR PIN IN THE VISE.

Eventually, you will have all points in order. Once they are all done, you are going to harden them using the technique called super-quench (see Chapter 13).

Heat about 1 inch of each pointed tip to a bright cherry red. Then immediately plunge it into the bucket of super-quench. Swirl the point around, then lay the point aside. When all points are done, cover the bucket securely and set it aside for future use.

Dry each tip carefully, and wipe down with an oily rag. Because you are using mild steel welding rods, there will be no reason for further heat treatment.

Mark each pin to length, using the point as reference. Then clamp up and saw off. Until you are ready to drive the pins into the comb stocks, store them (point down) in a tin can.

The comb stocks are cut from elm, hickory, pecan, walnut, sugar maple . . . anything, really, as long as it doesn't easily split. Elm is about the best because of its interlocking grain, but many other woods will do the job.

You need hardwood lumber, at least 1 inch thick and 4 inches wide, long enough for two handles. Lay out the stocks, strike and mark centers, and rough-cut to shape. There is no difference between right and left, other than the countersunk bolt hole in one handle (either one). Bore and chamfer spacer-bolt holes and countersink one of them.

Carefully lay out and mark each row of pins. Mark all before boring any. The layout is made on the point side of the stock; the pins will be driven through from the other side.

Using a new $3/16$ brad-point drill bit, carefully bore each hole. Be careful, and avoid swarf (chip) build-up on the down-side of the stock. Cut a slight countersink in each pin hole, on both sides of the stocks.

Give each stock a coat of thinned lacquer, and be sure to get lacquer into the holes and the end grain. Set aside to dry for a few hours.

Have a drive-pin (large nail set) handy. Buck the stock against an anvil or the bucking pipe you used before, and drive the end pins through. Use the drive-pin to make minor adjustments. If a pin seems too loose, drive it completely through with the drive pin. Lay the pin across the anvil and deform the pin shaft with a judicious hammer blow. Pins should be too tight to push through by hand, but should not have to be driven through with great force.

Once all pins are in place, check for length. If the pins are within $1/8$ inch of even, leave them alone. If greater, drive the short pins through the stock to match them up. Do not attempt to drive the pins backward. If one pin is too far through, drive it through completely and reinstall it.

When the pin length is satisfactory, give the stocks another coat of thinned lacquer. Soak it in, especially on the end grain and around the bases of the pins. Allow to dry overnight.

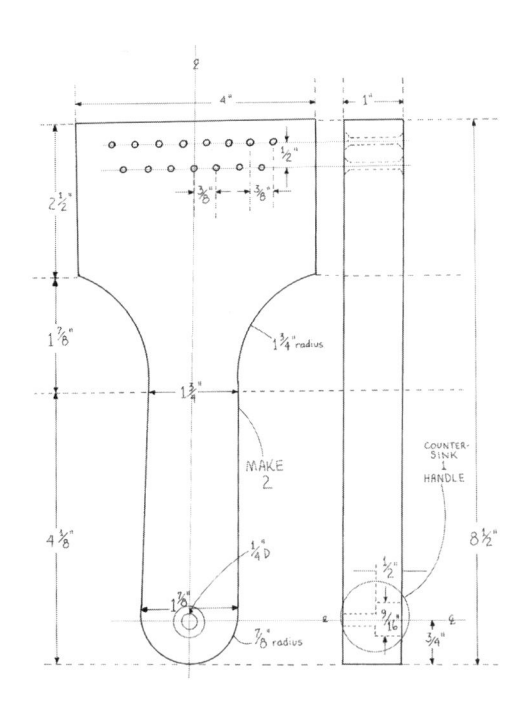

Combs.

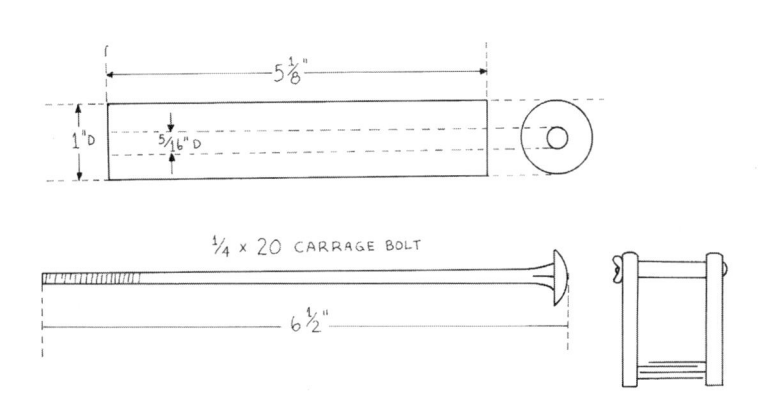

Comb carry handle.

The Alden Amos Big Book of Handspinning

Shape the handles to a comfortable configuration. Coarse garnet paper wrapped around a stick will shape the finger grooves and shoulder details. Finish up, re-lacquer as required, and let the assembly dry. Give the combs a coat of wax. To carry or store the combs safely, install the spacer core, long bolt, washers, and wing nut.

Historical and geographic occurrence: Wool combs were in use before the Iron Age, although the wing nut is probably medieval and later. Appropriate to all wool cultures, from prehistory to the present.

12: DISTAVES: HANDHELD, BELT, AND FREESTANDING

A freestanding distaff is essentially a belt distaff stuck in a base, and that's how we'll treat this device. A handheld distaff is another creature.

Handheld distaff. Split out or cut some stock between 18 and 24 inches long. Turn, plane, shave, and/or scrape until it is about ⅝ inch in diameter. Do not make it club-like.

Select one end to be the handle. Mark out about 8 inches, and put a slight taper from the mark to the upper end (top) of the 'staff. Now lay out marks 3 inches and 9 inches from the top of the 'staff.

Choose disk stock of ½-inch thickness. Mark and bore a hole that will allow the stock to slide down the 'staff to the 9-inch mark. Cut stock to rough dimension. Prepare the top disk in the same way, boring it with a smaller drill. Cut to dimension.

It is not necessary for the disks to be concentric, so eyeball-correct is plenty good.

Remove disks and decorate them as desired. Refine handle of 'staff. Carve a rudimentary knob at the top.

Reassemble with a drop of glue on each disk location.

Finish is a matter of personal preference. Stains and painted designs have both been used

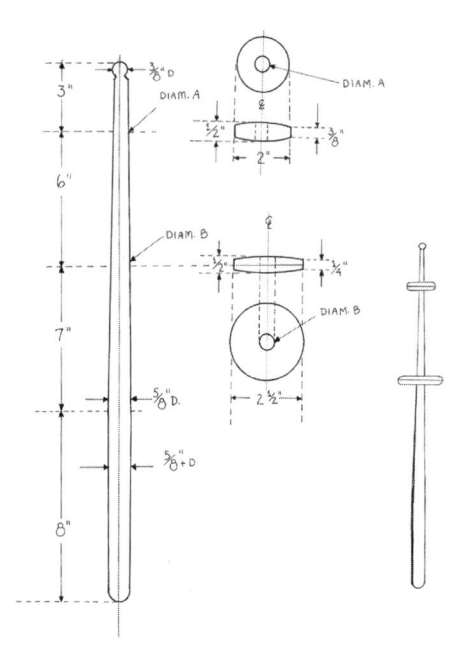

Handheld distaff.

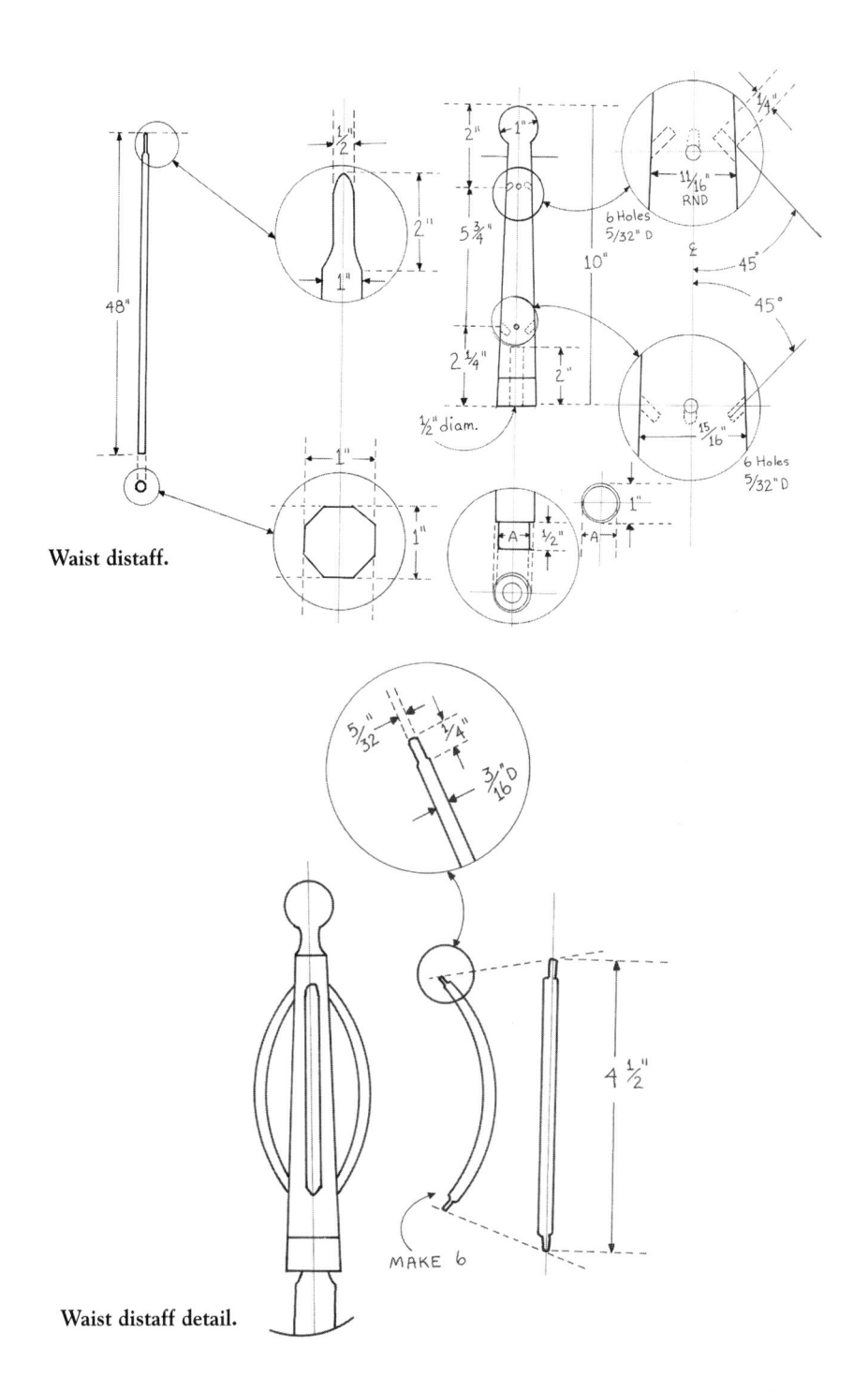

Waist distaff.

Waist distaff detail.

The Alden Amos Big Book of Handspinning 359

traditionally. Still, the handheld 'staff was seldom as fancy as the waist or bench (freestanding) type.

Waist distaff. For the belt or waist 'staff, first select and prepare a shaft. Rip 1-inch-square stock about 48 inches long. Clamp in a vise, and form to an octagonal section with plane, 'shave, and drawknife. Work slowly, checking frequently. A sloppy octagon is a sloppy octagon; a proper octagon is a thing of beauty. When almost finished, lay shaft aside.

Select head stock from clear 1¼-inch-square stock. Carefully bore the shaft mortise in one end. Prepare ferrule and head stock, and fit them together firmly.

Turn or round the headstock to approximate profile. Lay out reed positions and mark with center pops. Carefully bore the reed holes. Do not bore too deep.

Scrape, sand, and burnish the headstock. Cut reed sections to length, then dry-fit them to the headstock.

When all reeds have been cut and fitted, remove the reeds and then install them one at a time, using a drop of glue at each end. Set aside and allow to dry.

Finish up the distaff by scraping or shaving a round tenon to fit the head (socket). Give all parts a coat or two of proprietary Danish oil finish. Do not install the head on the shaft until completely dry (overnight).

Freestanding distaff. See above for the head. The base is a simple slab arrangement. Please note: this base will also work well with the skirder project, coming up. After selecting an appropriate plank or slab, decide which is to be the "top" surface. On the bottom, find and mark the center; strike and mark the first division line. Lay out two division lines at 120 degrees from the first line.

Mark out approximate diameter; mark out a second diameter 2 inches within. Center-pop where inner diameter crosses division lines.

Working carefully, bore the leg sockets to the indicated depth and at a 45-degree angle. Rough-cut the base to outline shape, then scrape and clean up the bottom. Bore the center hole halfway through the bench, using a ⅝-inch bit.

Change to a 3/32-inch bit and bore the center guide hole the rest of the way through the bench (in center). Turn the bench over and, with a ¾-inch bit, bore about halfway through the bench block. Do not attempt this with a spade bit.

Finish up the bench by scraping, turning, and sanding it to shape. Select leg stock (⅝ material) and cut to ⅝ square and 8 inches long.

Strike and mark centers. Turn the legs between centers on a lathe, or shave the legs to shape and profile them. Cut tenons to fit bench snugly. Round the leg bottoms. Tap the tenons into place in the bench.

Grind an old file edge to make long taper (about 3 degrees) reamer. Chuck up the file in a brace and bit, and ream out the center hole of the bench. Try the shaft of the distaff in the hole: it should fit comfortably, but not jam or wobble.

Appropriate finish would be red or brown stain, linseed oil, and usage.

Historical and geographic occurrence: Distaves have been used worldwide, since the dawn of history.

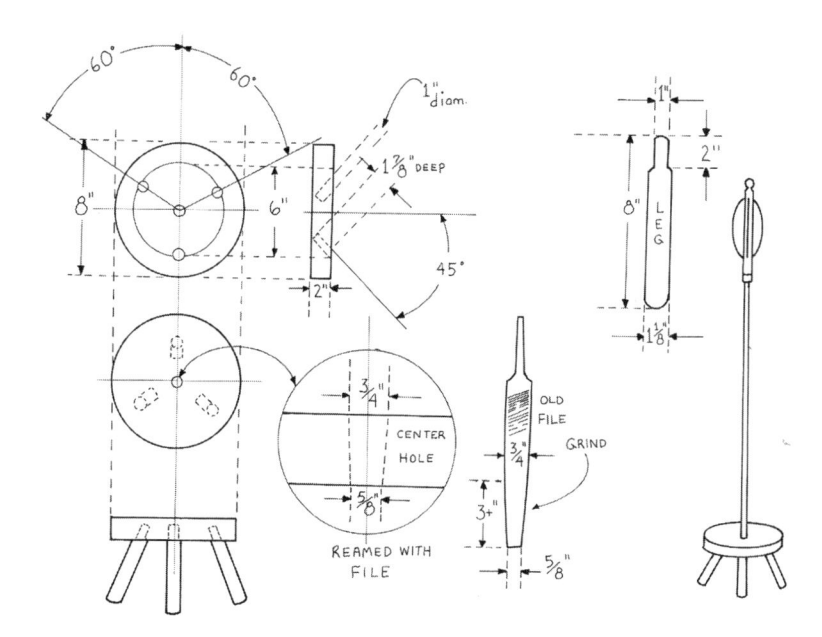

Distaff base.

13: SKIRDERS

Skirders are plying and rope-making aids. They support yarns and strands stretched out over a distance. Two sorts are shown, freestanding and handheld.

Handheld skirder. The handheld item is used for "work party" situations, like extemporaneous rope-making at shows and conferences. It is nothing but a suitable piece of stock, say 30 inches long, 1 inch thick, and 2 inches wide. If you make one, might as well make three or four—four will allow you to make a 50-foot rope.

Bore sockets for the upright pegs, which are cut from ½-inch or 7/16-inch dowels. Cut the pegs to length, touch them with glue, and knock them into position.

No finish is required, although a coat of lacquer or varnish will not hurt.

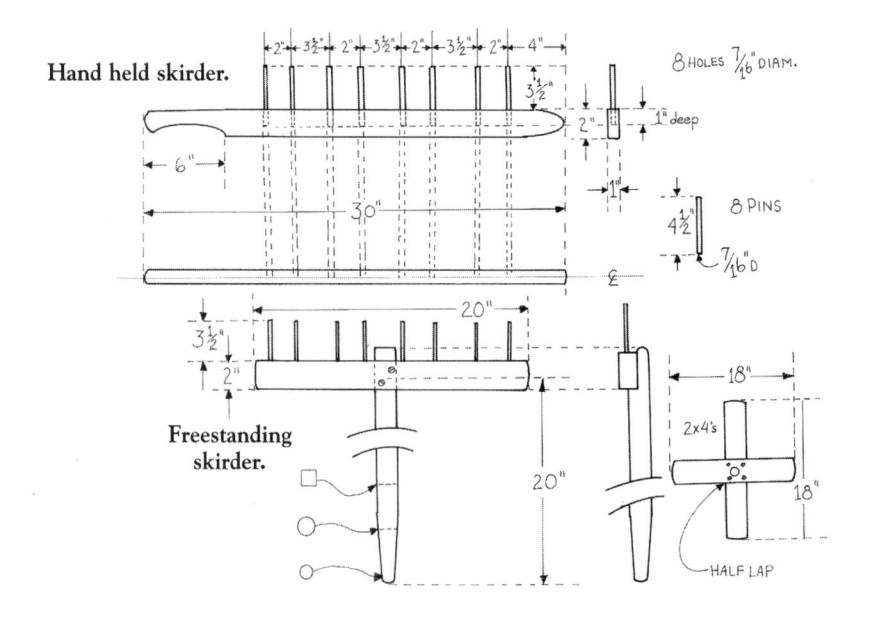

Freestanding skirder. This is the same as the handheld version, except the top stock is screwed to an upright. The upright can be the same material as the top stock. The bottom end of the upright is arranged to fit an appropriate base.

For plying, you can use the base you made for the freestanding distaff. For outside work, flat X-style bases with center holes will do the job. To make the flat X-style base, cut some 18-inch lengths of 2x4. Cut centered half-laps, and nail them together. Bore center hole as required. This is similar to the common Christmas tree stand.

Historical and geographic occurrence: Known since classical times, wherever rope has been made. Europe, Mediterranean region.

14: BLOCKING REEL AND STAND

These become invaluable for any wet processing of yarn. This equipment doubles as a skein-winder, and allows easy counting to determine skein length.

The best all-round size is 1½ yards. The dimensions here will result in a 56-inch-diameter skein, 2 inches over the 1½ yards. That allows for a certain amount of yarn stretch. It is a good idea to make at least two reels, and to make more reels as you require them. One stand and one crank-and-shaft usually serve the needs of three or four reels.

As with several other projects, this one seems to invite builder interpretation. Don't alter the plans unless you have built and used this sort of thing before.

From 2-inch-thick, clear, knot-free lumber, lay out and rip all the end slats to width and length. Then cut rebates at the ends. Do all of the slats exactly the same.

Next, carefully lay out and mark the center of each one. The punch mark must be centered both from end to end and from side to side.

Carefully bore a ⅝-inch hole at the center of each slat. Using stub ⅝-inch dowels as center pins, arrange each pair of end slats as shown. Notice that the rebates and round-overs are all heading the same way.

From this point on, keep the slat pairs matched up; mark them as you deem appropriate. Carefully mark half-lap lines at right angles on each slat. Separate a pair and cut the half-laps to full depth. Fit the stub dowel back in the center and check the lap for fit. Make corrections as required. When satisfied, separate the halves and remove the stub dowel. Coat each joint face with glue, and reclose the joint. Keep the glue away from the center (axle) hole, if you can; a little won't hurt, but a lot is not good. Clamp the joints, and set aside until dry.

Prepare the remaining end-slat pairs in the same manner. Allow them all to set and cure at least overnight.

Half of the end-slat assemblies will be used as is. The other half need to have square center holes. Lay out the holes (about ¾ inch square), clamp, and cut with coping saw or jigsaw. Use the prepared section of square stock as a go/no-go gauge. Finish up with a paring chisel and file, then clean up and finish-ream the round-hole slats.

Select and cut the cross-slats for the reels. Make all cuts in series: rip all, end-cut all, and so forth.

With all slats worked then select the best edge of each for the rounding chamfer. Shave, plane, and scrape to profile. Finish all slats before moving on to the next step.

With the aid of a helper and small clamps, assemble the end and cross-slats. Square all away, drill pilot holes for the screws, then replace clamps with screws (I recommend number 8 × 1½ FH stainless-steel wood screws). Until it has been completely assembled, the reel is quite fragile, so be gentle and work slowly. Glue may be used at this step, but it is better to wait until all is fitted, then follow around with glue, joint by joint. Note: If you glue, use waterproof glue.

With all reels assembled, fabricate the shaft and crank. Cut to length, then shave, plane, and scrape round end to dimension. Use reels as go/no-go gauges. The ideal is a snug fit on the round end, with about 4 inches of stub, and a good but not tight fit on the squares.

Mark shaft 1 and 3 inches from crank-end; carve or turn rounds on shaft. Scrape everything down, fit the crank and the handle together, and try the combination in each reel for fit, in all positions. Scrape, file, plane, and chop until right.

Now for the base. Bore and rebate the two ends, then turn and fit the two post tenons. Leave the posts square until the axle holes have been bored. Lay out the top slots, but do not cut them until you have completed all the rounding. Allow ⅛ inch clearance for the axle retainer pins.

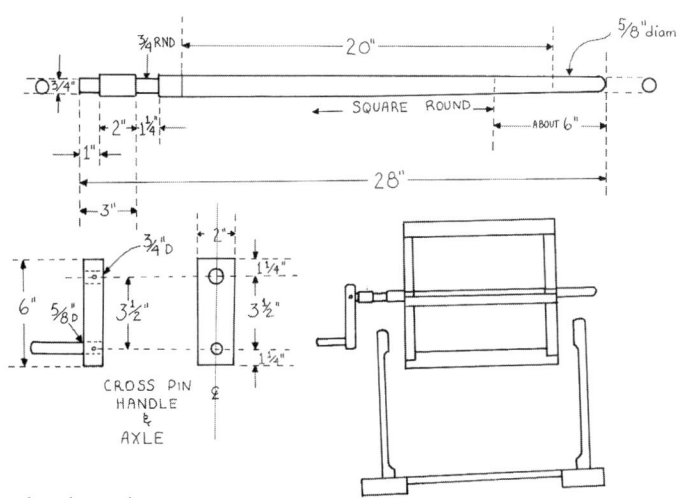

Reel and stand.

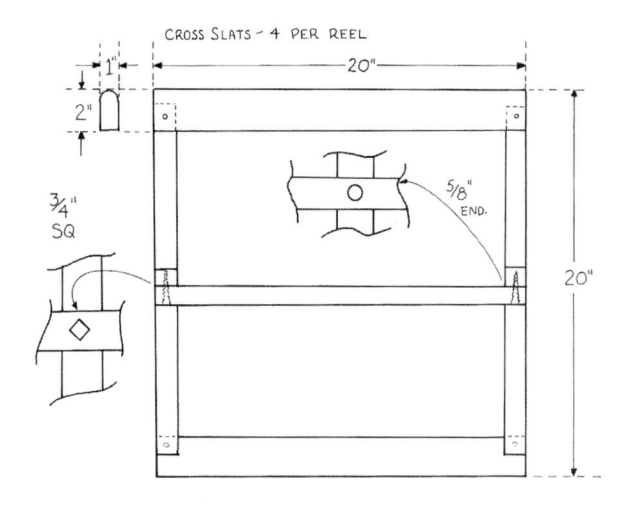

Reel and stand.

The Alden Amos Big Book of Handspinning

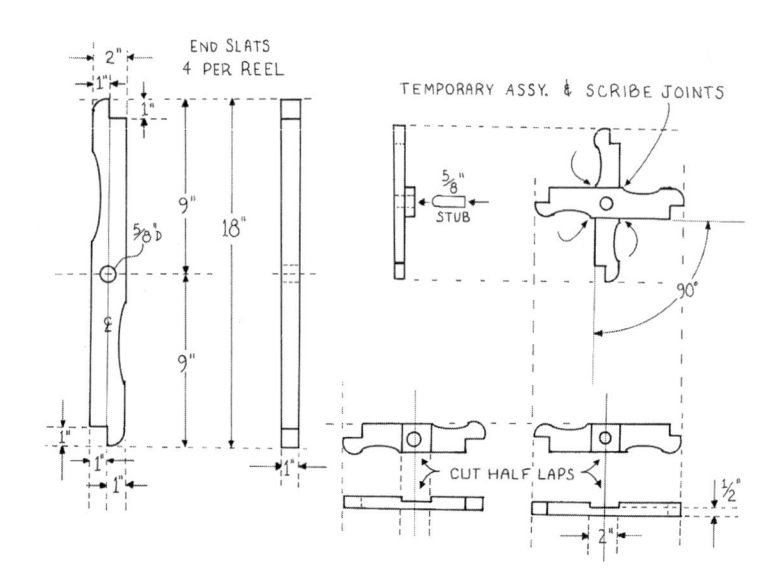

Reel and stand.

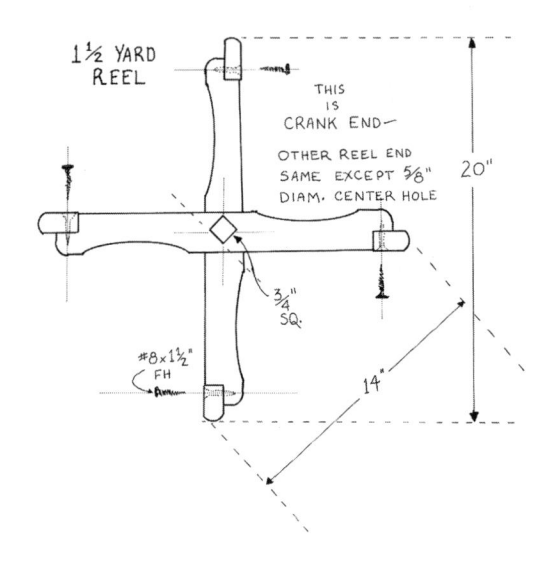

Reel and stand.

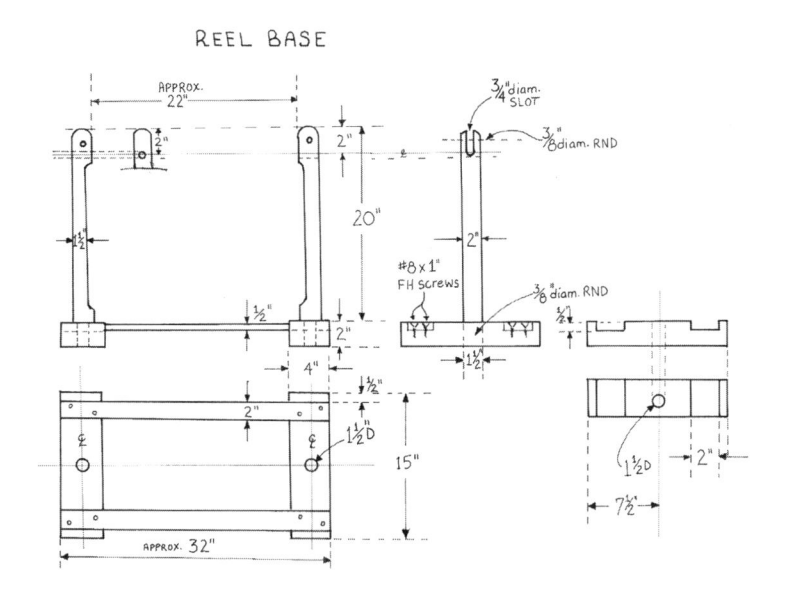

REEL BASE

Reel and stand.

Cut the posts to profile; this provides clearance for the reel and keeps it from hitting the posts. Then cut the top clearances and the axle slots. Knock the posts into the base pieces. Ensure that the axle holes are aligned at right angles to the base.

Clamp the base stretchers into place. Adjust their length and square them; use a reel and the axle to check fits. You want an inch or so of clearance on each end of the reel. Mark and cut the stretchers if necessary. Drill the stretchers and screw them in place. Then (and only then), mark and drill the cross-peg holes in the posts. Check the fit again; if it is correct, drive the post pegs into place.

Knock down all rough edges and splinters. The base requires no particular finish. The reel(s) are best given several coats of lacquer, followed by wax on the reel slats.

Historical and geographic occurrence: Pictorial evidence as early as ninth century A.D. Probably much older.

Additional comments on building equipment

Possibly you are now enthusiastic, ready to build anything! Good! Excellent! Press on, and Godspeed. . . .

The bibliography lists several books that contain plans for various other equipment, so finding plans is not a real problem. But building good tools involves more than simply finding plans, and in the author's opinion anyone who builds the equipment should be experienced in its use. In other words, learn to spin before building that wheel; give weaving a try before undertaking a 12-shaft loom. You don't have to be an "expert," whatever that is. However, if you understand the basics it does, and will, make a difference.

The reasons are complex, but may be simply stated: not every set of plans works. Most of the stuff you build will work, after a fashion, and a lot of it can be made to work better. Some of the stuff works very well, indeed.

But how do you know which is which? You need a frame of reference, a standard of performance, and unless you understand the fundamental movements, procedures, and products of the craft, you will be working without objective guidelines.

There is plenty of room out here for more good wheel and loom builders.

Chapter 13

Noils, linters, and thrums: Recipes, tips, charts, calculations, and miscellanea

This chapter is named in honor of a gone but remembered part of the old *Textile Artists Newsletter*, or *TAN*, as we called it. *Noils, linters,* and *thrums* refers to bits and pieces—textile process leftovers.

Noils, of course, are little broken wads of fiber. *Linters* are what is left on the cotton seed after ginning. And *thrums* are the little warp ends left when a finished cloth is cut from the loom.

This chapter contains all those little scraps that are too good to throw away but don't seem to fit elsewhere. Without further ado....

MIXTURES

Carding-and-spinning oil emulsion

This wonder of household alchemy can facilitate combing, carding, blending, and spinning. If you're working with your good homemade soap (see page 372), using it in this combination will give you a great jolt of confidence in its grease-cutting abilities.

You need:
2 tablespoons of grated dry soap (your own, if at all possible)

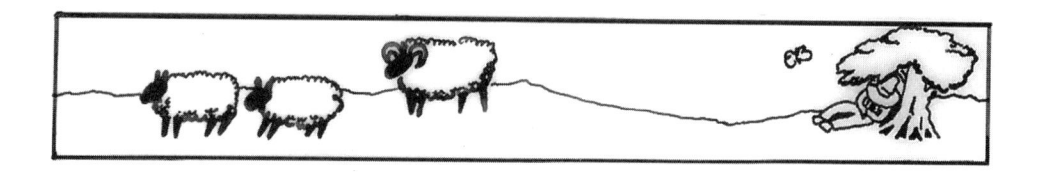

¼ teaspoon of washing soda
2 cups of hot, soft water[1]

Put these three ingredients in a 2-quart canning jar, close the jar with its normal cap and ring, and shake the jar until all the soap and soda have dissolved. Open the jar and add

2 cups of olive oil[2]

Close the jar again and shake it for a while. Shake it occasionally over the next 24 to 48 hours. It will become emulsified and "stable."

This makes up to about ¾ gallon of carding spray, enough to dose between 10 and 15 pounds of clean fleece. Local conditions vary; some fleeces need more, others less.

To use the mixture, cut it 2-to-1 with warm soft water (2 parts water, 1 part goo) and spray or sprinkle it on the stock to be worked. Allow to mellow—to sit for a short while on the fiber—before you start processing. But do work the wool without much delay. It's not good practice to oil up wool and then store it for great lengths of time. Spin the wool soon, and scour the yarn soon. Do not leave the assist on the fiber for weeks and weeks.

Drive-band dressing

Great for single-drives and the occasional troublesome double-drive. This stuff is tacky. It also works on bobbin-winder belts and sewing machine bands.

You need:
a couple of ounces of crude beeswax
¼ cup of athletic (powdered) rosin
¼ ounce of gum turpentine (about a tablespoon)

---

[1] Remember that soap plus wool plus hard water spells MESS.

[2] Olive oil is not cheap, but it is a proven performer. Other vegetable oils work okay, but once they have been sprayed on the wool they may go sticky and weird in just a few days.

Shred the beeswax into an old tin can, and set the can over boiling water (in a double-boiler) to melt. *Note:* Don't heat beeswax over direct flame. The wax will degrade, and there is always the danger of fire.

In another disposable container (an old cat food can?), paste up the rosin and turps. When mixed, dump the combination into the melted beeswax. Stir well.

Put muffin papers into a muffin pan, or use candy cups. Pour the molten wax goo into them. Discard the cans. Clean up the mess. Wait a while for the molds to cool.

To use, touch a cake lightly to the moving drive-band for a 5- to 10-second period: a thin coating will do.

Special wheel polish

Everybody needs a "special" polish for spinning wheels. This recipe produces a polish which is organic, authentic, and non-petroleum-based. It contains no harsh chemicals or additives except beeswax and turps. In fact, that's all it contains, unless you want it to have a fancy aroma.

Step 1: Get a disposable container of suitable size, like a big tin can. Never melt or process beeswax in your favorite pot. It's impossible to clean up.

Step 2: Half-fill the container with tap water. Set it on the stove to simmer. Introduce about ½ pound of raw beeswax, as broken supers, as combs, or as cap scraps. That will be a wad about the size of a hardball. What you are going to do is to "refine" it, a process similar to the way you clean fats and greases when making soap. Stir it around with a disposable stick.

Step 3: Repeat step 2 as necessary to get all the bug parts, trash, honey, and dirt out of the wax. Pour off the old water, put in some fresh, and heat again. When the wax seems clean enough, let the mass in the can cool to a solid and then skim the slush off the bottom of the cake of beeswax.

Step 4: Shred or grate the cooled, clean wax into another, smaller, clean can. If you started with ½ pound of raw wax, you will have about ⅗ of that now, or between 4 and 5 ounces. For every ounce of wax, add 1 tablespoon of gum turpentine. Real turpentine.

Step 5: Gently heat the combination over water (in a double-boiler) tending and poking it continuously. **DO NOT LEAVE IT UNTENDED UNLESS THE HEAT OR FLAME IS OFF.** Eventually the mixture will be all melted and creamy.

Transfer the mass to a good, solid container. Good possibilities include cold-cream jars or old, large-sized, shoe-polish cans. Short, wide-mouth, canning jars work, but the rubber gasket on the lid may go all soft and gooey. Better to replace the standard canning lid with a disk cut from plastic milk-jug material. Your wax polish does need to be sealed up when not in use.

Step 6 (optional): If you want the polish to have a pleasant scent (in addition to the turps), stir in a *small* amount (a drop or two) of appropriate essential oil before you remove it from the heat. Cinnamon or spruce is a good choice.

Step 7: Dispose of the disposable utensils. Don't bother to clean them up. Well, you may if you wish, but it is rather like cleaning all the burned lasagna out of the disposable aluminum pan before you throw it into the recycle container. Beeswax is tenacious to a fault.

Step 8: Let the polish mellow a week or two before you use it—several weeks, if you can wait.

To apply it, use an old wool sock, or part of one, and go after the woodwork as if you were polishing shoes. Caution: use thin coats and rub them in well. The wax is the polish, but to get it to gleam, you must apply elbow grease.

A good soap recipe

All textile persons have use for good soap. You can buy good soap, and you can make good soap. If you buy it, you have to take it on faith. If you make it, you know what went into it. Besides, soap making is rather like brewing, or spinning, or scratch baking—quite magical. Simple, but magical.

Warning: This is potentially dangerous because of the lye. Don't make soap when you are dealing with distractions or are tired.

You will have to commit yourself and a helper to an unbroken 3-hour chunk of time. You will get about 9-plus pounds of very good soap—soap with all of the glycerin still in it.

You need:
7 pounds of clean, salt-free fat (lard, bacon fat) [3]
1 pound of commercial caustic soda (sodium hydroxide, also known as lye) [4]
3 pints of soft water
. . . and a helper.

In a large pot, NOT MADE OF ALUMINUM, carefully dissolve the caustic soda in the 3 pints of water. Use good ventilation, eye protection, an apron, and rubber gloves. Have plenty of water handy in case something goes wrong. The solution will generate a good deal of heat.

Gently melt the fat in a large bowl or pot, also NOT MADE OF ALUMINUM. Add the warm caustic soda solution to the melted fat slowly, in small quantities, stirring continuously. Don't dump the lye in; drip it down the side of the bowl or onto another spoon: and keep stirring.

After adding all the lye, continue stirring until you obtain an even, creamy mass, about the consistency of thick cream gravy.

Pour the soap into a prepared mold (for example a shallow box, 2½ inches deep, 12 inches long, and 8 inches wide, lined with cotton cloth) and leave it to set for several days. A week is better. Protect it from rapid changes of temperature, drafts, and so forth. Otherwise cover it up and forget it for a while.

When the soap is good and firm (this could take as long as 10 to 15 days), dump it out and cut it into bars. The older it gets, the better it is.

Essential oils and other scents can be added, but it's best not to experiment at this stage. There are plenty of books on the formulation and manufacture of soap. This is not one of them.

---

[3] *This recipe also works with vegetable shortening, although you will need to be more patient. It will not thicken up as quickly or dramatically.*

[4] *A technical point: this recipe is based on 1 pound of caustic soda. The standard Red Devil Lye can contains 13 ounces (about $8/10$ pound) and their can-side soap recipe is based on 13 ounces, not 1 pound.*

Saxon blue, oleum, or acid indigo

According to one source, this dye procedure was much favored by the Norwegians around and prior to the turn from the nineteenth century to the twentieth. This is a method of applying a good blue to wool, using indigo.

The basic procedure, using natural indigo, produces a beautiful blue shot with smoky traces of red, gold, and brown. The process is simple, but requires the use of smoking sulfuric acid (also called *fuming*, full-strength stuff). With that in mind, the reader proceeds at their own risk. Disclaimer, disclaimer, blah.

Mix about ½ ounce of powdered indigo with about 5 ounces of strong sulfuric acid. Proceeding carefully, place a small amount of the acid in a strong glass jar or bottle, one that can be well stoppered. Add a small amount of the powdered indigo. Using a glass rod or wooden stick, "paste" or stir the mix thoroughly. Metal appliances must not be used. Continue adding acid and indigo in small amounts, stirring thoroughly with each addition. When entire amounts of both ingredients have been mixed together, seal the bottle carefully (no metal), and allow to stand for at least 24 hours. Once the oleum has been prepared, it will keep for a long, long time in an airtight bottle or jar with good closure.

If the acid used is not strong enough, the dye will perform badly or not at all. To check to strength of the mixture, add a few drops of the prepared dye (now called *oleum*) to a small quantity of water and filter the liquid through paper. If the filtered dye is still blue, then the indigo has been properly dissolved and is ready for use.

The oleum is used at your discretion. Start by adding a small amount, say a few drops, to a quart of lukewarm water. Observe the liquor color. If it is weak and "puny"-looking, add a little more oleum. Keep track of what you are doing, as you will be generating your own dye data as you go along. Now add an ounce or so of previously scoured, still-damp, wool yarn to the lukewarm bath.

The tricky (not really!) part: stirring gently but constantly, bring the bath up to a boil. Unless you used a lot of oleum and not much yarn, the dye will all be taken up by the goods, or, in dyer's jargon, the vat will exhaust. If the color in the goods is not dark enough, you must allow the whole thing to cool back down to lukewarm. Then remove the goods, allow them to drain, and discard some of the liquor. Add cool water to make back up to your desired quantity and then add more oleum, stirring carefully. Gently re-enter the goods and repeat the stir/boil step.

Once you are satisfied with the dye job, cool, drain, wash, and rinse the yarn. Dry under "appropriate" tension, then take the skein out into the sunlight and be dazzled!

It is a lot easier on you and the yarn to "sneak up" on the depth of color you want. Oleum doesn't strip or bleach well, and it is very hard on the yarn.

A most important point: When dyeing with oleum, the dye liquor must be lukewarm as the goods are entered—never cold, and never hot. Lukewarm, say about 100°F. And keep the goods constantly in motion during the rise in temperature.

Another important point: Oleum was normally prepared using natural indigo, not the highly alkaline paste and liquid forms found today. Natural indigo is still available through several suppliers. Although the synthetic indigo works, you must use extra sulfuric acid to "kill" the strong alkali.

Older recipes often call for other ingredients—for example, pre-mordanting the yarns with alum was a common procedure. Madder is featured in several recipes. Oleum was also much used in overdyeing.

All in all, it is a pretty satisfactory way to get a true indigo palette on wools. As far as washfastness? Old texts mention that "pale hues (pastels) should not be washed in strong soda water," which is not something you normally do to your woolen goods. As far as lightfastness? About like indigo. Pretty good.

The thing about it is that the area is open to experimentation. Rediscovery, if you like, of a process from our not-so-distant olden days. There are few contemporary recipes around, and there should be more.

Rob Gunter's soap quench, or super-quench

This is a magic potion to use for quenching/hardening/cooling those hot iron or steel parts, such as crochet hooks, coin-spindle hooks, comb and hackle teeth, and the like. It was developed by Rob Gunter, a well-known 'smith, while he was working at the Sandia (NM) Labs. The stuff is commonly called *super-quench*.

Mix the following, and stir before each use:
4½ gallons water
5 pounds salt
32 ounces Dawn dish soap (blue)
8 ounces Shaklee Basic I

Comments by Rob Gunter: "We all know that mild steel is not supposed to harden because of low carbon content. A cold chisel made out of mild steel heated to a dull red and quenched in the soap solution will cut a piece from the same stock you made it from. Don't get me wrong, it will not make tool steel from mild steel, but in those cases where you don't want to use tool steel and wish mild steel was just a little harder, it works fine."

Observations by Amos: The stuff works, making the steel seem a little "stiffer." As far as harder? Maybe. Do not use this on any high-carbon steel, as it will surely crack. Always wear eye protection, work safely, and cover the super-quench when not in use—keeps the bugs and critters out of it.

Sizing recipes

Sizing is used to prepare warps for weaving. As a spinner, it may be helpful for you to be aware of such things, especially if you are going to weave your own handspun yarn.

Boiled Flour–This is a thick, multi-purpose size. It works as well on wool as it does on cotton. It is slow to dry, but has little tendency to drip. To make: ½ cup all-purpose (not self-rising) flour plus 2 cups of water.

Make a paste of the flour and some of the water. When smooth, add about a cup of the remaining water and heat slowly while stirring. Bring to the boil. Continue stirring until the mixture becomes "pearly" and translucent. Be careful, as it scorches easily. Add remaining water, remove from heat, and stir until smooth. It is ready for use.

Gelatin–This size is runny, so watch for pooling. It does dry quickly. To make: 2 tablespoons or two individual packets of unflavored gelatin; ¼ cup cold water; 1 cup boiling water; ¾ cup cold water.

Soak gelatin powder in ¼ cup cold water until it swells. Stir in 1 cup of boiling water until gelatin dissolves. Add remaining ¾ cup cold water and stir well. Size is ready for use.

Milk–This is also a runny size, so beware of drips and pooling. It does not dry as quickly as the gelatin. Do not use whole milk as the butterfat may be hard to scour out. To make: 1 packet (for 1 quart) instant non-fat milk; 2 cups cool water. Stir powdered milk into water until well mixed. Size is ready for use.

THE ART OF THE DRIVE-BAND

Bumpless drive-bands

These come in handy for bobbin winders, charkhas, accelerating heads, treadled spinning wheels—even sewing machines. This isn't just a knot-tying technique. You will construct a custom-fitted drive-band. Before starting the process, you need to decide whether a bumpless drive-band will be a good idea for your equipment.

Wheel considerations. These drive-bands earn their keep on single-drive flyer wheels and are almost mandatory for charkhas, Miner's heads, and bobbin winders. Although they work well on all wheels, bumpless drive-bands are probably not worth the effort for double-drive systems, which require pretty long bands that need to wear out (see Chapter 8).

Bear in mind that unless you make your final join while installing the drive-band, you will have to unship the drive wheel, or remove it from its axle, to get the band in place. Some drive wheels (on Ashfords and Schachts, for example) don't unship easily. And keep records so you do not have to re-define this every time you want to put a new string on the Wee Dinkums.

Preliminary comments. Before you make a drive-band, you will have to decide which yarns to use in constructing it. Your choices will be determined by how large or small you want the drive-band to be. In general, a 6-stranded bumpless drive-band with a finished grist of about 900 YPP is appropriate for a single-drive setup, such as the Ashford Traditional. A similar bumpless cord for a double-drive band would be well served by 4 or 6 strands with a finished grist of about 1,200 YPP.

It follows that your beginning material needs to be $\frac{1}{14}$ or $\frac{1}{16}$ as large as the intended band. Around here, we use a two-ply #8 cotton twine as a base material (the yarn consists of two strands of cotton, each an 8-count or 6,720 YPP). The only way to be sure which grist is best is to try different combinations on *your* wheel.

The length of raw stock you must begin with to produce the finished results you need is subject to local conditions and procedures. Don't expect a perfect fit the first time out.

Make notes and keep records, though, so your second and later drive-bands will be easy to construct and of the correct length.

Materials and procedures.

You will need:
yarn
2 pins or pegs that can be driven into the ground, or otherwise secured
rotating hook
holding hook

Step 1: The basic rule for finding drive-band length is to add the wheel and whorl diameters together, take half of that, multiply the result by 3.142, and then add twice the distance from wheel center (the axle) to whorl center (flyer shaft).

Wheels using *in-line tension adjustments* have an adjustment excursion of about 1½ to 2½ inches. If it is a single-drive arrangement, your drive-band length allowances have to be pretty accurate. If it is a double-drive setup, you have a little more latitude, but not much. Measure carefully and plan ahead.

Wheels with *single-end tension devices* are another matter. The alignment of the flyer shaft quickly becomes critical, with a practical limit on excursion of about 1 or 1½ inches. Again, your measurements must be accurate, more so than for the in-line tension setups.

Here's an example of a single-drive setup, based on a 22-inch diameter wheel and a 2-inch whorl. The center-to-center distance we will imagine is 24 inches. Add the two diameters together: 22 + 2 = 24. Divide this number (24) by 2, getting 12 as a result. Multiply this number (12) by pi (3.1416), getting 37.7 as a product. Add 37.7 to twice the center distance, or 48). 48 + 37.7 = 85.7 inches, the calculated length of the drive-band. If the installation is for a double-drive, the calculated length is 85.7 times 2, or 171.4 inches.

Considering the amount of work that goes into making a bumpless drive-band, it is wise to check your calculations by doing a sample. Cut a dummy drive-band to fit.

Also, if you do not want to calculate the required length, fine. But don't cut a cord based on a guess about how long the drive-band should be. It will not fit. Either cut the existing drive-band or install a new string cord, then cut it. Stretch out the cut cord. Measure its full length. Mark down the number.

Step 2: Position two pins or spikes: the distance between them will be *twice* the full-length distance (above) plus 25 percent. Example: If the full length is 4 feet, the pins will be 8 feet + 2 feet = 10 feet apart.

Step 3: Select appropriate yarn. Wrap the yarn around the pins until there are two yarns on each side—a minimal skein, as it were. Tie the ends together using a water knot, drive-band hitch, or parcel bend. Cut off the surplus. Rotate the skein around the pins until the knot lies about ⅓ of the distance from one pin or the other.

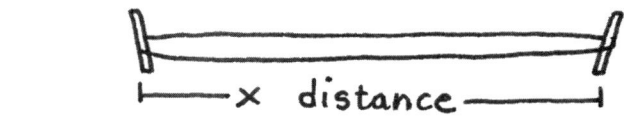

Bumpless drive-band, step 3

Step 4: Lift the skein from one pin and install a rotating hook. Up-twist until the skein has shortened by about ⅓ of the total distance.

Step 5: Keep everything under tension and install a holding hook in

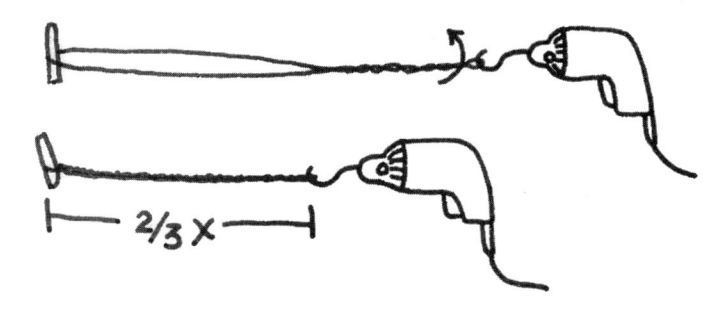

Bumpless drive-band, step 4

Bumpless drive-band, step 6

Bumpless drive-band, step 7

Bumpless drive-band, step 8

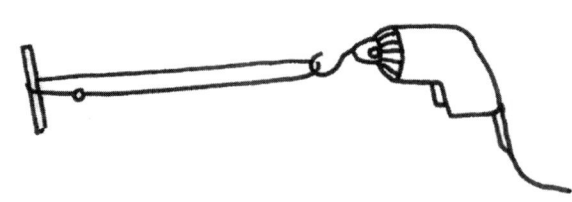

Bumpless drive-band, step 9

place of your rotating hook. Preserve that loop! Hand your rotating hook off to your helper.

Step 6: Have your helper install the rotating hook in the approximate center of the twisted strand. Now both you and the helper move in such a way that tension is maintained on the strand while you move your end of it next to the static pin.

Step 7: Have your helper down-twist the double strand, temporarily. This will relax the considerable tension and make your next task easier.

Step 8: Lace the two loops together, nose to nose, using a couple of turns of the same yarn used for the rest of the project. Tie a single overhand on one side of the loop; take an extra wind on the other side. Rub a dab of glue on the upper knot; using a tapestry needle, bury the ends back for about 1 inch. Leave a bit sticking out of each.

Step 9: Install the cord back over the fixed pin: have your helper untwist the band completely. Keeping the band under tension, slide the entire skein (band) around the rotating hook and pin so that the original knot and this new splice are located equidistant from the ends.

Step 10: Lay it up again. Overtwist it, then back to relaxation. Check the cord for length. You want it to be close to your original measured length, although slight adjustments can be made by adjusting the final twist.

Step 11: Butt-join and cord-splice the end loops just as you did in step 8, except use more turns and more overhand knots. Bury the ends several inches. Allow any glue or cement to set up. Roll the final join between your hands, and trim off projecting ends.

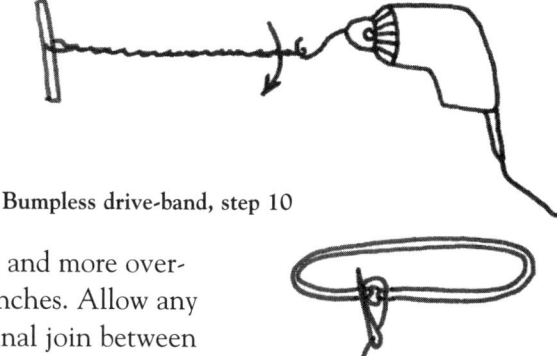

Bumpless drive-band, step 10

Bumpless drive-band, step 11

Double-drive drive-bands: "Why are they saying those terrible things about my drive-band crossing, and how do I fix it?"

Note: your physical point of view for this is as if you had been spinning in conventional spinning fashion, and then decided to stand up—the flyer is to your left, the drive wheel is to your right, and you are looking down at the top of the spinning wheel.

Rule 1: If the crossing is correct for spinning in the Z direction, the drive-band will be routed from the flyer whorl at rear left, will cross to front right on the wheel, and will pass over the other cord.

Rule 2: If the crossing is correct for spinning in the S direction, the drive-band will be routed from the bobbin whorl at front left, will cross to rear right on the wheel, and will pass over the other cord.

Rule 3: If the drive-band consistently rubs against itself as it crosses from side to side, the crossing is wrong for the spinning direction being used.

Rule 4: To change the crossing arrangement, the drive-band must be removed from both the drive wheel and the flyer, and the crossing itself must be reversed.

How to put on a plain old drive-band

Here's how to install a new Saxony drive-band from scratch.

Place the wheel at a comfortable level (perhaps on a table), with the wheel to the right and the flyer to the left (you face it in standard spinning orientation).

Wind down the tension adjustment to its lowest level. Place a supply of drive-band material (on a cone, in a ball, whatever) on the floor just below the drive wheel. Make sure the cord will be able to run free.

To install for Z-direction spinning: Take the working end of the drive-band material and lead it up to the wheel bench, under the wheel, to the left and under the bobbin whorl, over the bobbin whorl, to the right and over the top of the drive wheel, and down around the drive wheel; PASS IT UNDER THE EXISTING drive-band, to the left again, under and around and over the flyer whorl, then to the right and over the drive wheel again.

The working end of the drive-band is now hanging down the back of the wheel, just waiting to be tied to the other end. Snug up the cord, join the ends with a blood knot or fisherman's bend, and trim the ends.

To install for S-direction spinning: Follow the same procedure, EXCEPT that you will lead the drive-band under, around, and over the flyer whorl first; then over and around and under the wheel and first pass of the cord, then under and around and over the bobbin whorl. Finish up as before.

To install a new upright double-drive, bobbin-lead drive-band from scratch: Simply imagine that *up* equals *left* and *down* equals *right*. In other words, imagine that the wheel is fixed to a tilting base and can be tilted to one side without falling over. Imagine that it has been tilted so that the flyer/bobbin array is on your left and the drive wheel is on your right. Thread as described above.

To install bands on other types of wheels: Some wheels will not seem to fit any known or published description, but not to worry. You can get proper cords on them eventually.

Double-flyer wheels are something of a problem, because best results and control result from having two separate drive-bands, one for each flyer. Otherwise, it is well-nigh impossible to adjust one flyer without changing the other. Of course that may not be important, but there are other considerations. Unless you are spinning on both flyers, it is a lot simpler to run just one. Sometimes the wheel builder intended that one drive-band be routed, in order, over all four whorls and the wheel—in short, as a quadruple-drive, not a double-drive.

If you think that normal drive-band crossings are problematical, further adventures await you with the quadruple-drive. I cannot give you much help on this, but I will tell you that these systems are very sensitive about the crossing(s) and the spinning direction.

FACTORS AND CALCULATIONS: YARNS AND FABRICS

Here is a bunch of handy numbers. Some of them repeat, in shorthand form, information presented in earlier chapters. Some are new, although we've mentioned them and told you to find the details here.

Twist factors

To find the approximate twist required for a yarn, in twists per inch (TPI), multiply the square root of the sample yarn's grist (in yards per pound, or YPP) by the appropriate factor from the chart below. You can't just multiply the grist by some magic number; you have to do the square-root thing.

For most of the fibers, yarns spun to the "very soft" and "soft" levels will drift. If you intend to ply, spin to the "firm" level. Linen and hemp yarns are not spun "soft." For most linen and hemp yarns, the "firm" level is appropriate. Spin tow like coarse, broken wool.

Type of yarn	very soft	soft	medium	firm	hard	very hard
Woolen yarns	.061	.0884	.115	.166	.190	.210
Worsted yarns	.0581	.0708	.0965	.130	.1785	.205
Cotton yarns	.090	.110	.124	.138	.185	.2164
Silk yarns	.091	.111	.1245	.135	.181	.2206
Line-spun linen or hemp yarns[5]	—	—	.081	.1097	.131	—

[5] Linen and hemp yarns are not spun "soft." The "medium, firm" and "hard" notations are approximate. For most uses, the "firm" range is appropriate. Tow is spun like coarse, broken wool.

A method for estimating yarn grist from the thread count of a plain-weave cloth

Rule: Count the total number of threads in 1 square inch, and multiply that number by 1.1. The result approximates yarn diameter, in wraps per inch. Square the yarn diameter to achieve a close approximation of yarn grist in YPP.

Step 1: With a pick glass or other suitable magnifier, count the total number of threads in 1 square inch. That means both warp and weft. Disregard any stitching, odd floats, or other extraneous factors. The cloth you are counting is *plain weave*. Example: a piece of linen cloth shows 29 threads one way, 27 the other. Add the two together: 29 + 27 = 56.

Step 2: Multiply the sum from step 1 by 1.1. Example continued: 1.1 times 56 equals 61.6, which we round off to the closest whole number, or 62.

Step 3: The yarn diameter squared gives an approximation of the yarn grist in YPP. Example continued: 62 squared = 62 × 62 = 3,844 YPP.

A method for estimating yarn grist from the thickness of a textile

This comes in handy when the thread count is obscured or cannot otherwise be obtained.

Rule: Multiply the cloth thickness, as a whole number, by 1.3. The result approximates yarn diameter in wraps per inch. Yarn diameter squared approximates grist in YPP.

Step 1: Measure the thickness of the material. Take several readings and average them out. If you are measuring garment fabric, be sure that you do not include seams, facings, interfacing, linings, and other complications, although the most accurate results come from folding the material into multiple thicknesses for sampling (and dividing by the number of layers). Readings need to be to at least 3 decimal places.

If using press plates, subtract the total plate thickness from your measurements.

If using a micrometer, convert the mike reading to a fraction as follows: divide 1 by the reading. Example: the reading is .029; 1 divided by .029 = 34.48. Round off to closest whole number—in this case, 34.

If using dial-reading calipers, proceed as above. If using non-dial calipers, use a magnifier to get a reading.

Step 2: To find the yarn diameter, multiply the thickness of a single layer by 1.3. Example continued: Using 34 as the thickness, 34 × 1.3 = 44.2, which we will round off to 44.

Step 3: The yarn diameter squared gives an approximation of the yarn grist in YPP. Example continued: 44 squared = 44 × 44 = 1,936 YPP.

Wraps-to-Grist Conversion Table

Wraps are per inch; grist is in yards-per-pound. No correction has been made for fiber, or yarn construction.

Wraps	Grist	Wraps	Grist
4	16	6	36
8	64	10	100
12	144	14	196
16	256	18	324
20	400	22	484
24	576	26	676
28	784	30	900
32	1024	34	1156
36	1295	38	1443
40	1599	42	1763
44	1935	46	2115
48	2303	50	2499
52	2703	54	2915
56	3135	58	3363
60	3599	62	3842
64	4094	66	4354
68	4622	70	4898
72	5182	74	5474
76	5774	78	6082
80	6397	82	6721
84	7053	86	7393
88	7741	90	8097
92	8461	94	8832
96	9212	98	9600
100			9996

Fiber Burn Chart

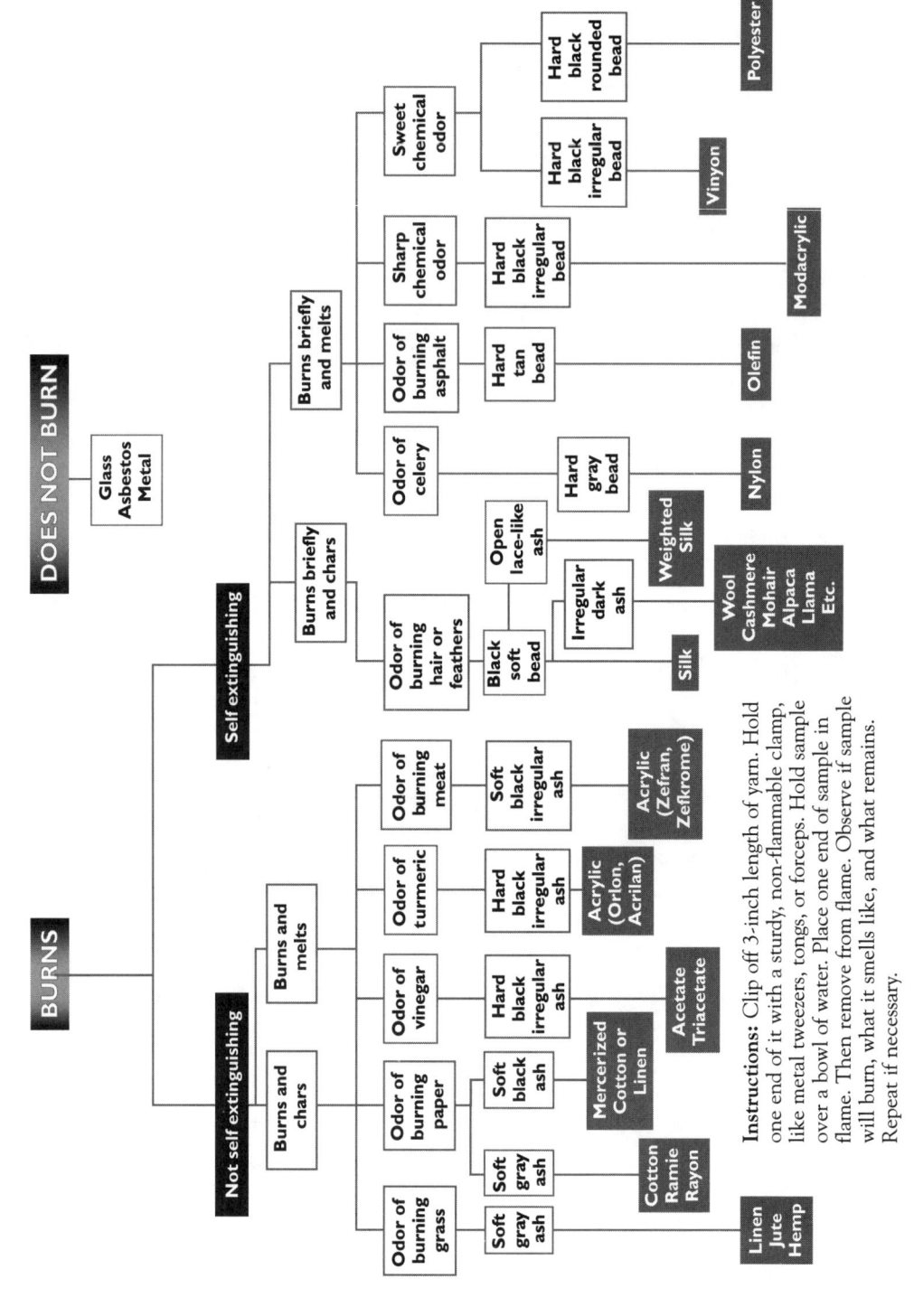

BURNS

Not self extinguishing

Burns and chars
- Odor of burning grass → Soft gray ash → **Linen, Jute, Hemp**
- Odor of burning paper →
  - Soft gray ash → **Cotton, Ramie, Rayon**
  - Soft black ash → **Mercerized Cotton or Linen**

Burns and melts
- Odor of vinegar → Hard black irregular ash → **Acetate, Triacetate**
- Odor of turmeric → Hard black irregular ash → **Acrylic (Orlon, Acrilan)**
- Odor of burning meat → Soft black irregular ash → **Acrylic (Zefran, Zefkrome)**

Self extinguishing

Burns briefly and chars
- Odor of burning hair or feathers →
  - Black soft bead →
    - Open lace-like ash → **Weighted Silk**
    - Irregular dark ash → **Wool, Cashmere, Mohair, Alpaca, Llama, Etc.**
    - (Black soft bead) → **Silk**

Burns briefly and melts
- Odor of celery → Hard gray bead → **Nylon**
- Odor of burning asphalt → Hard tan bead → **Olefin**
- Sharp chemical odor → Hard black irregular bead → **Modacrylic**
- Sweet chemical odor →
  - Hard black irregular bead → **Vinyon**
  - Hard black rounded bead → **Polyester**

DOES NOT BURN
- Glass
- Asbestos
- Metal

Instructions: Clip off 3-inch length of yarn. Hold one end of it with a sturdy, non-flammable clamp, like metal tweezers, tongs, or forceps. Hold sample over a bowl of water. Place one end of sample in flame. Then remove from flame. Observe if sample will burn, what it smells like, and what remains. Repeat if necessary.

The Alden Amos Big Book of Handspinning

L length	CD core diameter	FD front diameter	RD rear diameter	CAP capacity (yards)
3	⅝	2	2½	176
3¼	⅝	2½	3	279
3½	⅝	2¼	3⅛	280
3¾	⅝	2¾	3¼	368
4⅞	⅞	2½	3½	417
4⅛	⅞	2¾	3¾	502
4½	⅞	3	4	633
4¾	⅞	3¼	4	705
5	1	3½	4⅛	842
5½	1	4	4½	1,120
6	1	4½	5	1,511
7	1	5	5	1,979

SD	CD	CL	CSY
.093	.625	2.875	21
.093	.875	3.25	48
.093	1.0	3.5	60
.125	.875	3.25	46
.125	1.0	3.5	65
.125	1.125	3.75	89
.25	1.0	5.75	112
.25	1.25	6.25	196
.25	1.5	6.5	272

SD	CD	CL	CSY
.093	.625	2.875	57
.093	.875	3.25	112
.093	1.0	3.5	159

Maximum yarn capacities for common bobbin sizes

Here's a great little item for those among us who thrive on the obscure, arcane, and trivial. The bobbins were filled disk-to-disk, wound smoothly and evenly, as in re-winding or cross-reeling, not as in a spinning situation. All measurements, other than bobbin capacity, are in inches.

L = the inside bobbin length
CD = core diameter
FD = front (smaller) disk diameter

RD = rear (larger) disk diameter
CAP = capacity, in yards, of the standard yarn

The standard yarn in this chart is a 1-run woolen single of moderate twist, which means 1,600 YPP at 4 TPI.

Standard yarn capacity of various spindle copps

Here are some related obscurities. All measurements, other than copp capacity, are in inches. Copp build is presumed to be cylindrical, with a 30-degree cone at the working end and the beginning end flush at 90 degrees. Note: Good spinning practice requires that the spindle blade be bare at its tip by at least one copp diameter.

SD = spindle diameter
CD = copp diameter
CL = copp length
CSY = capacity (yards)

The yarn standard for the first chart is a 2-run woolen of firm twist, which means 3,200 YPP at 9 TPI.

The yarn standard for the second chart is a 10's cotton single of firm twist, which means 8,400 YPP at 12–14 TPI. These are typical charkha copps.

How to calculate requirements for making ropes and cords

One of the things to do with leftover and odd-lot yarn is to make rope out of it (see pages 203–205 for construction notes).

Basic rule: the amount of yarn required to make a cord equals the desired final length times 1½, multiplied by the number of threads or yarns in each strand, multiplied in turn by the number of strands.

Example: a stanchion rope, 24 feet long, is required for a wedding. The rope will be made of 3 strands, and each strand will contain 36 threads.

Step 1: Multiply required length by 1½. Example continued: 24 × 1.5 = 36 feet.

Step 2: Multiply the length by the number of threads in each strand. Example continued: 36 (feet) × 36 (strands) = 1,296 (feet).

Step 3: Multiply the thread/length product (1,296, above) by the number of strands in the rope. Example continued: 1,296 × 3 (strands) = 3,888 (feet).

This rope requires 3,888 *feet* (1,296 yards) of yarn.

By the way, we can take a rough guess at the physical size of the rope, if we know what the yarn grist is. Suppose we use some of that 1,600 YPP stuff from the bobbin-capacity project.

There are a total of 108 threads in the rope (3 strands of 36 threads each = 3 × 36 = 108). Each thread has a grist of 1,600 YPP. By dividing the grist of one yarn by the total number of similar yarns, we get the grist of the total assembly: 1,600 YPP divided by 108 threads = 14.8 YPP. This rope will have a grist of about 15 yards per pound, which works out with this construction method to a diameter of roughly $5/16$ inch.

CALCULATING DRIVE RATIOS AND TAKE-UP

How to calculate single-drive ratios

Slippage plays no necessary part in operation of either single-drive, bobbin-lead or single-drive, flyer-lead systems. In a single-drive system, the basic drive ratio can be determined if you divide the drive-wheel diameter by the drive-whorl diameter.

Single-drive, flyer-lead ratios. On this system, the drive ratio increases as the bobbin fills.

Step 1: Measure the drive-wheel diameter and the drive-whorl diameter.

Step 2: Divide the drive-wheel diameter by the drive-whorl diameter. This is the base drive ratio.

Step 3: If the bobbin is less than half full, the drive ratio is about 85 percent of the base drive ratio. If the bobbin is more than half full, the drive ratio is about 95 percent of the base drive ratio.

Single-drive, bobbin-lead ratios. On this system, the drive ratio does not change as the bobbin fills.

Step 1: Measure the drive-wheel diameter and the drive-whorl diameter.

Step 2: Divide the drive-wheel diameter by the drive-whorl diameter.

How to calculate double-drive, bobbin-lead ratios

In double-drive, bobbin-lead systems, slippage *is* required to adjust and control take-up. Therefore, the effective drive ratio is approximately 6 percent less than the average of both drive ratios.

Step 1: Find the ratio between the drive-wheel and the flyer-whorl. (Measure the drive-wheel diameter and the flyer-whorl diameter. Divide the drive-wheel diameter by the flyer-whorl diameter. This is the drive-wheel/flyer-whorl ratio.) Example: the drive-wheel/flyer-whorl ratio is 10-to-1, or just 10 for our purposes.

Step 2: Find the ratio between the drive-wheel and the bobbin-whorl. (Measure the drive-wheel diameter and the bobbin-whorl diameter. Divide the drive-wheel diameter by the bobbin-whorl diameter. This is the drive-wheel/bobbin-whorl ratio.) Example continued: the drive-wheel/bobbin-whorl ratio is 12-to-1, or just 12.

Step 3: Add these two ratios together, and divide by two. (This averages the two ratios.) Example: 10 + 12 = 22 ÷ 2 = 11 (average ratio).

Step 4: Multiply the average by .06 and subtract that amount from the average. Example continued: 11 × .06 = .66. Then 11 (average) −.66 = 10.34. The effective drive ratio for this wheel is about 10.34-to-1.

Differential rotational speed (DRS)

Here's a little digression for the flyer-bobbin designer. It was decided that the following information might impede the narrative flow a bit much for the general readership, and there is too much of it to make a graceful footnote. Enough jabbering.

DRS is short for *differential rotational speed,* and it is nothing more than the difference in speed between the flyer and the bobbin, in a conventional spinning wheel array. The DRS is the "math" approach to take-up, or wind-on. How much, how fast, how little . . . and why.

DRS can be described in RPM or as a ratio. As RPM, it consists of the leading element speed in RPM less the lagging element speed in RPM. As a ratio, it is found by dividing the larger whorl diameter (lagging element) by the smaller whorl diameter (leading element) in several ways. Here's an example. Say we have a flyer-whorl diameter of 2 inches and a bobbin-whorl diameter of 1.5 inches. 2 divided by 1.5 = 1.33. This means that the bobbin turns 1.33 times as fast as the flyer. Another way to state this is to say that for every 100 turns of the flyer, the bobbin turns 133 times. For convenience, we say that the DRS is based upon a ratio of 1.33-to-1.

Let's carry it a step further and imagine that we are designing a flyer-and-bobbin array. We have decided to use a DRS ratio of 1.25-to-1, and we know that we have a flyer drive whorl with an effective diameter of 2½ inches. Now we want to know how big a bobbin whorl we need in order to achieve the DRS ratio.

More of that stuff you just hated in high school. Well, some people love these problems . . . solve 'em in their heads. I need several pencils, a couple of pads of yellow legal paper, and lots of time. Anyway, back to business.

What is the effective diameter of the bobbin whorl? Simple. Treat it as a drive-ratio solution, which it is. Divide the greater diameter by the drive "ratio" (the DRS ratio, in this case) and the answer is the lesser whorl diameter.

Because the bobbin "drive ratio" is 1.25-to-1, we divide the flyer-whorl diameter of 2½ inches by 1.25; we get an effective bobbin-whorl diameter of 2 inches.

Just to check it out, we will put those parts onto an imaginary 20-inch wheel and bring everything up to a nominal operating tempo—90 treads a minute is about right for the wheel. Now let's calculate the other speeds.

On a 20-inch wheel, a 2½-inch flyer whorl gives us an 8-to-1 ratio; a 2-inch bobbin whorl equals a 10-to-1 ratio. At 90 RPM on the wheel, we have the flyer going at 8 × 90 = 720 RPM and the bobbin going at 10 × 90 = 900 RPM.

That gives us a DRS of 900–720 = 180 RPM. Notice that the DRS is the same as the lead element speed minus the lag element speed., and is stated in RPM. All right, our bobbin has a ¾-inch core. Let's say it wraps on 2.36 inches of yarn per turn—that's what we'd get with a bobbin core of ¾ inch—and in 180 turns it will wrap on 424.80 inches of yarn.

It will also put in 900 twists. 900 divided by 424.80 equals 2.12 turns per inch, or about 2⅛ TPI.

Simple enough. Now let's work it the other way. Going to another imaginary wheel, we find a DRS of 1.1-to-1 and an effective bobbin-whorl diameter of 1.25 inches. We need to find the flyer-whorl diameter. Well, we know that the bobbin-whorl diameter represents the flyer-whorl diameter divided by the DRS ratio, so the bobbin-whorl diameter times the DRS ratio will give us the flyer-whorl diameter. 1.25 inches times 1.1 = 1.375 inches, or 1⅜ inch. We can check it the other way. We have a DRS ratio of 1.1-to-1 and a flyer-whorl diameter of 1.375 inches. The bobbin whorl diameter must then be the flyer-whorl diameter divided by the DRS ratio. 1.375 divided by 1.1 = 1.25. Isn't that amazing?

Just for the fun of it, let's see what sort of twist is in order for a system with a 1-inch bobbin core and a DRS ratio of 1.1-to-1. To keep things realistic, we will treadle our theoretical 20-inch wheel at 60 RPM.

The bobbin-to-wheel ratio is 20 divided by 1.25, or 16-to-1; the flyer-to-wheel ratio is 20 divided by 1.375, or 14.55-to-1. At 60 RPM on the wheel, flyer speed is 873 RPM and bobbin speed is 960 RPM. That gives us a DRS of 960 minus 873, or 87 RPM. Once again, note that the DRS is stated in RPM, and that the DRS and the DRS ratio are not the same thing.

For this example, let's imagine that our bobbin has a 1-inch core. At 87 turns per minute, and with a core diameter of 1 inch, the bobbin will wind on 273.31 inches of yarn. How so? Because the bobbin turns 87 times more than the flyer, and at each turn it wraps on 1 inch × 3.1415 of yarn. 3.1415 inches of yarn times 87 turns equals 273.31 inches of yarn.

At the same time, 960 turns of twist will be introduced. 960 turns divided by 273.31 inches equals 3.51 TPI, about 3½ turns per inch. So far, so good?

The partially filled bobbin. Suppose the bobbin core is not 1 inch in diameter, but 1½ inches, perhaps because it is partially filled. Will that make a difference?

Oh, yes. In a real-life spinning scenario, the bobbin-core diameter is always increasing. Let's use our above example, but simply change the bobbin-core diameter. We get new values. Take a look.

At the same DRS (87 RPM) the 1½-inch bobbin now winds on 4.71

inches of yarn per rotation (1.5 × 3.1415 = 4.71 inches), and in 87 turns wraps on about 410 inches. The twist introduced remains the same, 960 turns, but now must be spread out over the additional length. 960 turns divided by 410 inches (we rounded it off) equals 2.34 TPI, or about 2⅓ turns per inch. Just by changing the bobbin-core diameter, we changed the twist of our yarn from 3.5 TPI to 2.34 TPI.

That is a significant change in twist component. So much so that we need to allow for it. There are a couple of ways to go about this.

The hypothetical long bobbin. First, set it up so that bobbin-core diameters don't change—or at least they don't change much. The only practical way to do this is to make the bobbins very long, with large cores to start with. If we make the bobbin core 10 inches long and 3 inches in diameter, we can wind on a substantial amount of yarn before the core diameter changes more than a few yarn diameters.

Suppose that we are spinning a yarn of 3,600 YPP grist. It has a yarn diameter of 1/60 inch. Because the bobbin core is 10 inches long, just one layer of this yarn on the core will contain 600 wraps. Each wrap is 3 × 3.1415 = 9.42 inches long. That's a total of 5,652 inches (157 yards) per layer, which will increase the diameter of the core by only 1/30 inch (.0333 inch).

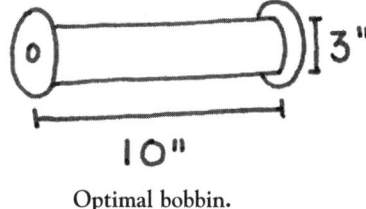

Optimal bobbin.

Each wrap in the second layer is 3.0333 × 3.1415 = 9.53 inches long. 600 turns = 5,718 inches more, and the core diameter has increased another 1/30 inch. Each wrap in the third layer is 3.0666 × 3.1415 = 9.63 inches long. 600 turns × 9.635 = 5,778 inches more . . . a total of 17,148 inches (476.33 yards) with only a 126-inch increase in wind-on per layer—about 7/10 of 1 percent change.

For further illustration, let's imagine that our "long-bob" system has been putting in twist at 4 TPI and the bobbin speed is 2,000 RPM. What we need to find is the DRS, and the various whorl diameters appropriate to our 20-inch wheel, which, for this example, is being treadled at 100 treads per minute.

First, it is putting in 2,000 twists per minute, which means that it must have a bobbin whorl-to-wheel ratio of 20-to-1. It is also putting twist into the yarn at 4 TPI. That means it must be winding on 500 inches per minute.

We will suppose that the bobbin-core diameter is the average diameter of the core after three wraps—that is, 3.033 inches. Therefore, each rotation of the core will wind on 3.033 × 3.1415 = 9.53 inches of yarn.

Since we need to wind on 500 inches per minute, that means we must have a DRS of 500 divided by 9.53 = 52.4659 turns, round that off to 52.5 turns.

Now we know that the flyer must turn 52.5 RPM more slowly than the bobbin, so 2,000 RPM minus 52.5 RPM = 1,948 RPM. A flyer whorl-to-wheel ratio of 19.48-to-1 will take care of that, because we have a wheel going 100 RPM as a drive.

Since we know the wheel diameter, we can calculate the actual diameters of the whorls. The 20-to-1 is easy: 1 inch. The 19.48-to-1 equals 20 divided by 19.48, or 1.0267 inches in diameter. We would round that off to 1.03, except when doing complex calculations.

Now let's find the DRS ratio. Remember, it is the lead element speed divided by the lag element speed: 2,000 RPM divided by 1,948 RPM = 1.0267, stated as 1.0267-to-1.

Having gone this far, let's check out the question concerning the increase in bobbin diameter and the twists per inch. The first complete end-to-end wrap puts on 600 wraps, at 9.42 inches per wrap. That's a total of 5,652 inches of yarn.

We know the bobbin is turning 1.0267 times faster than the flyer. What we are after is how many times the flyer turns to get the bobbin to advance one complete turn, relative to the flyer.

Since the bobbin "gains" or leads the flyer by a ratio of 1.0267-to-1, we can say that for each turn of the flyer, the bobbin gains on it by .0267 of a turn. So, we find how many times .0267 goes into 1 whole turn. 1 divided by .0267 = 37.45.

It means that the flyer has to turn 37.45 turns for the bobbin to gain 1 complete turn, which also means the bobbin has turned a total of 38.45 turns. At the same time, the bobbin has wound on one complete wrap around the core.

And that amount is equal to the bobbin diameter multiplied by the value of pi, or 3 inches × 3.1415, or 9.4245 inches. Now, if we wind on

9.4245 inches of yarn, and put in 38.45 turns at the same time, if follows that the yarn's twist component is about 4 TPI.

The actual calculator number is 4.079792031 TPI. Close enough to qualify as 4 TPI.

The values change for the second wrap layer: the bobbin-core diameter has increased by twice the yarn's diameter.

Because the yarn diameter is about equal to the square root of the TYPP grist (3,600 YPP, and see the glossary for TYPP count system), the yarn is $1/60$ inch in diameter. Two diameters equal $1/30$ inch, or .033+.

Add this to the bobbin-core diameter, and it is now equal to 3.033+ inches, so for each relative rotation, the bobbin winds on 3.033 × 3.1415 = 9.528 inches of yarn.

It still puts in 38.45 turns while doing so, making the twist component of the yarn equal to 38.45 divided by 9.528 inches, or 4.035 TPI. Still close enough to be 4 TPI.

Let's do the third wrap. The bobbin core is now larger by 4 yarn diameters. That's about $1/15$ inch ($1/60$ divided by 4 = 15), so the core is now 3.066+ in diameter, which we will round off to 3.067.

Each relative rotation now winds on 3.067 × 3.1415 = 9.635 inches of yarn, again, with 38.45 twists being introduced. 38.45 divided by 9.635 = 3.99 TPI, still close enough to qualify as 4 TPI.

Of course, by now we have wound on a total of 17,148 inches of yarn. Divide that by 36, and it amounts to about 476 yards. 476 yards of yarn, with less than $1/10$ of 1 percent variation in twist component. Not bad.

That is a pretty good-sized bobbin, though—10 inches long by 3 inches in diameter. What about the flyer that is around the bobbin? It will not fit on anybody's Wee Twinkie spinning wheel, that's for sure. Let's look at something smaller, something more realistic.

A more realistic bobbin. Let us suppose that we have a bobbin with a ¾-inch core diameter and an effective length of 3 inches. We will use the same yarn as an example—i.e., 4 TPI, 3,600 YPP, with a diameter of $1/60$ inch. Incidentally, this is a soft-twist yarn, with barely enough twist for weft.

Because the bobbin core is 3 inches long and our yarn $1/60$ inch in diameter, it will take 60 wraps to cover one inch of the core, and 180 wraps of our sample yarn to go from end to end. With the bobbin core as

¾ inch in diameter, each wrap will be .75 (decimal ¾) × 3.1415 = 2.356 inches long.

Now for the hard parts. To introduce 4 TPI, the bobbin is going to have to turn 4 times for each inch of yarn, or 9.424 times for each 2.356 inches wound-on.

And to wind-on that 2.356 inches of yarn, the bobbin has to gain one turn relative to the flyer. In other words, it has to turn 9.424 times for each 8.424 times the flyer turns.

That means the bobbin must turn faster at a ratio of 9.424 divided by 8.424, or 1.1187 times faster than the flyer. Let's round that off to 1.12. That's our DRS ratio, by the way—1.12-to-1.

Check it out. Say we are still using our 20-inch wheel and treadling at 60 treads per minute. We can make the flyer whorl any diameter we want, as long as we make the bobbin whorl in proportion, according to the DRS ratio.

We'll make the flyer whorl-to-wheel ratio a 10-to-1. We know the bobbin-to-wheel ratio has to be higher than that, 1.129 times higher, to be exact. 1.12 × 10 = 11.2-to-1. So the bobbin-to-wheel ratio is 11.2-to-1.

Let's give those whorls some physical dimensions: 10-to-1 is easy, because it is a 20-inch drive wheel. The flyer whorl is 2 inches in diameter. The bobbin whorl is 20 divided by 11.2, or 1.786 inches in diameter. As a fraction, that's just over 1¾ inches. Fine and dandy. Let's bring the system up to speed, just for the fun of it.

With a flyer whorl-to-wheel ratio of 10-to-1, and us treadling at 60 treads a minute, the flyer is coasting along at 600 RPM. With a DRS ratio of 1.12-to-1, the bobbin is turning at 672 RPM. 672 RPM minus 600 RPM gives us a DRS of 72 RPM. 72 differential rotations winds on 72 × 2.356 inches = 169.6 inches of yarn, at the same time the bobbin turns a total of 672 times. 672 turns divided by 169.6 inches of yarn equals 3.96 TPI . . . close enough to be 4.

It will take 180 wraps of 2.356 inches each to fill one layer in the bobbin. That's about 11.78 yards of yarn.

Just out of curiosity, let's figure how long it will take to put on one full layer of yarn. We already know that there are 72 relative rotations per minute, which winds on 169.6 inches of yarn. We need 180 wraps total for one layer, so 180 divided by 72 will give us the time. It works out as 2 minutes and 30 seconds (180 divided by 72 equals 2.5) for this layer (later layers will take longer).

Time for the second layer. The bobbin core is now 1/30 inch larger in diameter. Now its diameter measures .750 + .033, or .783 inch. Multiply .783 × 3.1415 and you get 2.46 inches of yarn per wrap. Nothing else has changed: we are still treadling at 60 treads per minute, and so on. The DRS is still 1.12-to-1, the flyer is still at 600 RPM, the bobbin still at 672 RPM . . . except now we wind on 2.46 inches of yarn per relative rotation.

That is, in one minute, we wind on 72 wraps at 2.46 inches a wrap, or 177.1 inches. At the same time, the bobbin turns a total of 672 times, putting in 672 twists. 672 twists divided by 177.1 inches equals 3.79 TPI.

Still close, but clearly losing ground. Let's do the third layer.

Again, nothing has changed except the bobbin-core diameter. We have a second layer of yarn on it (about 12.3 yards) and the diameter is up to .75 + .066+, or .816 inch. For each relative rotation, the wind-on length is now 2.6 inches. And for 72 relative rotations, it winds on 187.2 inches of yarn, but still with a total of 672 twists: 672 divided by 187.2 = 3.59 TPI.

With the third layer of yarn (about 12.8 yards) on board, the core diameter is now .849 inch. That means each wrap is .849 × 3.1415 = 2.67 inches long. At 2.67 inches per wrap, times 72 relative turns, we are winding on 192.2 inches of yarn, containing 672 total twists. 672 divided by 192.2 equals 3.496 TPI.

The fourth layer of yarn contains about 13.34 yards, and increases the core diameter another .033, making the diameter .882. For each relative turn, it wraps on 2.77 inches. In 72 relative turns it winds on 199.4 inches, still with 672 total turns of twist.

That is an average of 3.37 turns per inch. We have lost over 1/2 twist per inch, and we are still losing ground.

I won't inflict any more of this on you if you will agree that changes in bobbin-core diameter can be significant.

How to solve the problem. Now that we have settled that, the next question is how to deal with it. The long, big bobbin idea works, and is one method used by the industry—but, as pointed out, it is impractical for contemporary handspinning. The most practical methods to deal with DRS are those found in the three primary flyer-and-bobbin systems: slippage for double-drive arrangements, and introduced/inherent friction for the single-drive systems. All that is necessary is to establish a design DRS ratio high enough to guarantee take-up during any practical scenario.

Special treats

Punis, and how to make them

Here's a small mystery revealed. Punis are the little, compact cotton rolls used by all the really "top-drawer" cotton spinners. If you prepare your own cotton and have lint at hand, experiment with puni-making. Bear in mind that punis don't do well when made from long-staple cotton.

Step 1: Card a small amount of lint, making a filmy layer on the card surface. Put the card down, and gently lift the filmy web away from the card. Lay the web of cotton flat on a smooth, hard-surfaced table or slab.

Step 2: Card another web and lay it on top of the first one. Press these layers together firmly. Tear the small batt into two equal pieces. Lay one piece aside.

Step 3: Obtain an 8-inch length of smooth coat-hanger wire. Moisten it as you would an envelope flap, and lay it on the edge of one section of the cotton batt, parallel to the long edge of the original card web.

Step 4: Pressing firmly and working slowly, roll the wire up in the cotton. When all rolled up, roll it back and forth a few times to firm it up. Pull the wire out of the center. You now have a puni.

Step 5: Try out your first puni (spin with it) before you make any more. Play around with the amount of cotton in each batt, how firmly you roll the puni, the size of the core, and so on. Experiment. The combination of actions which produce the best results will vary from cotton to cotton, as well.

Step 6: If the punis work well for you and you make a bunch, roll them carefully in paper and put the rolls in a box. This will keep them all fresh and tidy. It takes about .22 second for a cat to discover how fun a puni can be.

A short discussion of fine spinning

The topic of fine spinning always turns to consideration of how fine a yarn can be spun. In a word, fine.

The following is an extract from *The Art Journal Illustrated Catalog of the Industry of All Nations, 1851*, more commonly known as the Crystal Palace Exhibition (pages iii and iv): "The yarns, exhibited as the basis of other products, show to what an extent the ingenuity of man can be carried, when employed in a given direction. There we have specimens of yarn spun by machinery, which is of so delicate a character, that the fibres of cotton can only be discovered in the fabric by the aid of the microscope; and so delicate is it that it falls to pieces by handling. This curiosity of manufacture is exhibited by Messrs. Thomas Houldsworth & Co., of Manchester, and is the result of the energy and enterprise of Henry Houldsworth, Esq. of that firm. In the contributions of this establishment we find specimens of cotton yarn ranging from No. 100 to No. 700, in single yarn; and No. 100 to No. 670, in double yarn, or lace thread. These figures express the number of hanks to a pound weight, each hank being 840 yards; and the last named number of 700 in single, and 670 in double yarn, is the triumph of cotton spinning for all practical purposes, since we find that a pound weight of cotton is elongated, in the first instance, to a length of 338 miles; and, in the other, to a double thread 324 miles, at a cost of £28, as the price of a single pound weight. The most remarkable example, however, is the specimen shown as No. 900, both of yarn and thread, as a curiosity, by which a single pound of cotton is extended to 430 miles. As late as 1840, 350 was the finest yarn attempted. In 1841, Messrs. Houldsworth spun 450, which was then considered as the limit. Another still more astounding specimen exhibited by Messrs. Houldsworth is that of 2150 yarn, in which we may fairly presume that they have reached the limit at which the fibre will at all cohere. A single pound of this yarn would yield the extraordinary length of 1,020 miles!"

Over a thousand miles per pound. . . . Pretty fine stuff. As one point of reference, Amos cannot even *see* a yarn finer than about a 50's cotton, which is 42,000 YPP or about 24 miles to the pound.

In case you are curious, to determine a yarn's grist in miles per pound, find the grist in YPP, then divide by 1,760 (the number of yards in one mile). Let's say you have a yarn that owns a grist of 3,400 YPP; what is the grist in miles per pound? The answer is just over 1.93 MPP.

Good to know this stuff. You never can tell when it might come in handy.

Real homemade ginger beer
Since we are in a recipe vein in this chapter, here's a concoction that has been a hit at numerous class lunches. Every time we serve it, someone wants the recipe. Read the whole thing through before you give it a try.

You need:
3 ounces fresh ginger root (chopped, shredded, thin-sliced, mashed)
2 pounds white-death sugar
4 fresh medium barkeep's lemons
1 ounce cream of tartar
2 gallons fresh, soft water (total)
1–2 envelopes dry active yeast
containers, crocks, graters, grinders, and so on. . . .

Step 1: Using all the lemons, pare or grate the LEMON ZEST into a suitable container. "Suitable" means large and heat-proof (enamel, glass, stainless, or crockery). Squeeze the LEMON JUICE into a different container, and set it aside for later.

Step 2: To the large container with the zest, add the prepared GINGER ROOT, the SUGAR, and the CREAM OF TARTAR.

Step 3: Add boiling WATER to cover the ingredients in the heat-proof container (about 2 quarts). Stir until SUGAR is dissolved. Let the mixture stand a few minutes, then add remaining cold WATER to make 2 gallons total liquid.

Mix gently and leave the stirring spoon in the container. Note 1: do not use a wooden spoon; stainless steel is okay. Note 2: the liquid is now what brewers call *wort* (rhymes with *flirt*).

Step 4: Prove the YEAST: that is, empty the YEAST into ¼ cup of lukewarm water. Add a dash of orange juice or a pinch of sugar. Stir well, cover, and set aside in a warm (not hot) place. In about 15 minutes, you will know if yours works or not. It will look bubbly and quite a bit different from when you first mixed it. That's what you want.

Step 5: When the wort is below blood heat (just cool to the touch), add the LEMON JUICE and your PROOFED YEAST. Stir gently but well. Remove the stirring spoon.

Step 6: Cover the container with clean muslin or cheesecloth; keep in a warm place (60–75°F) until the WORT has had active bubbles for a full 3 days.

Step 7: Arrange a siphon draw, avoiding the bottom layer of spent fruit, roots, and yeast. Or pour off the liquid through a suitable, sanitized strainer into a clean spigot tub. Leave the dregs behind and discard the strainer contents. Either way, you will lose about 1 pint of wort.

Step 8: Rack the ginger beer into clean, strong bottles (see note on bottles below). Allow 2 inches of headspace. Cap, and age 3–5 days at room temperature. Move the bottles to a cooler place for longer storage (possibilities include a cellar, basement, springhouse, or refrigerator).

Step 9: Hold at 45°F for at least six hours before serving. The beverage will be sweet, with nice condition (carbonation) at this stage. The alcohol will be less than 1 percent, and a hit with most kids.

If you let the mix bubble for 5 full days during step 6, it will be better suited to adult palates: dry (barely sweet), sharp, stronger (about 2½ percent alcohol), full condition, more gingery . . . delicious.

Adjustments for taste: DO NOT CHANGE THE SUGAR PROPORTIONS.

To remove part of the "bitter" component, reduce the amount of ZEST a little. To increase the ginger bite, add a little white pepper (¼ teaspoon per gallon). To increase the citrus tones, add a little LEMON EXTRACT (¼ teaspoon per gallon). For a "fuller, rounder" taste, add a small amount of common salt (¼ teaspoon per gallon).

However, most people favor the straight recipe.

Bottles: We're traditionalists. We use glass. Old-fashioned soda-pop bottles work great. The flip-top German beer bottles are good, and those indestructible plastic, liter-size soda containers will work for all you moderns. Recap them with the screw-off caps they came with.

In any case, you will need enough bottles to contain about 15 pints. That amounts to fifteen 1-pint bottles, about seven 1-liter plastics, or about twenty-one 12-ounce bottles. American champagne bottles work very well, and they take standard crown caps.; you will need about ten of the 750-mil size.

Clean-up: The chickens are not real fond of the rinds, roots, and yeast leftovers, but the stuff seems to do well in the compost.

Sanitation: Clean is everything. As long as the wort is boiling hot, nothing can harm it. But if it is then bottled in non-clean containers or allowed to sit around, uncovered, or the work place is dirty, or something else interferes with sanitation . . . then you will have trouble. Keep the entire process clean, use plenty of boiling water and suds, don't be careless . . . and remember that household bleach is a good sanitizer.

Safety: Don't store the finished product for more than a few days unless you can store it cold, for example in the fridge. The yeast will keep on working and building up pressure as long as it has nutrients and a benign environment. Enough pressure = explosion.

All home brewers note: this beverage is not fermented out. It still has sugar available, much like soda pop. A good chill will drop the yeast for a while, but not for all time.

So make the beverage in small batches. You can easily cut the recipe to 1 gallon by using half of everything. And drink it up "pretty soon."

Thanks to Ben Turner and others for this recipe.

Flax Crackers

Here is a yummy accompaniment for summer salads or winter soups. We brought thousands of crackers to the Amador Farmers Market, and have none to take home for us, they were so popular. The real secret to the process is the use of a pasta machine to do the tough work.

2 c flour
1 T sugar
½ tsp salt
1 T onion powder
2 tsp garlic powder
¼ tsp cayenne pepper
2 T olive oil
¾ c flaxseed
⅔ c water

Mix flour, sugar, salt, onion and garlic powders, and cayenne in a bowl. Add oil and mix until crumbly. Add flax seed and water and mix until dough forms ball. Divide dough into quarters. Run dough through pasta machine until it is satiny and thin. Or knead, then roll and fold dough until satiny. Place ⅛ inch (or thinner) dough on oiled foil-covered cookie sheets and score cracker shapes.

Bake at 400°F for 7–9 minutes. Turn over, remove foil and bake another 5 minutes or until light brown.

Cool on rack. Break apart into crackers.

An Idiosyncratic Glossary

Aalborg. City/seaport in Northern Denmark; once a well-known center for marine textiles (canvas, ropes), circa 1450. Also makes this glossary start before abaca, a fact that should set the tone for what follows.

Abaca. *Musa textilis*. A strong, coarse-leaf fiber, used for rope, cord, twine, mats, straps. Primarily a non-garment fiber. Also styled "manila hemp," although not related to *Cannabis* spp. Is actually a type of plantain. Sometimes confused with banana fiber, which comes from related *Musa* spp. *See also* Cellulosics.

Absorb. Take up, as a sponge sucks up liquids. The major natural textile fibers such as wool, silk, flax, and most of the cellulosics, have good absorbency, one of the characteristics that makes them comfortable to wear. *See also* Adsorb.

Abaca, or manila hemp.

Accelerated. In spinning, the term is applied to devices that have an intermediate gearing or pulley system, resulting in great mechanical advantage at the spindle or flyer-and-bobbin array. A typical accelerated system will have a primary drive wheel with a mechanical advantage (or drive ratio) from 5-to-1 to as high as 30-to-1; that primary wheel drives a secondary wheel which then drives the spindle or flyer with an additional advantage of perhaps 10-to-1; the overall ratio will be on the order of 300-to-1. *See also* Charkha; Miner's head.

Acid. It is difficult to accurately define just what an acid is. Technically, a substance with a pH of less than 7. Old-fashioned methods identified acids by their sharp, sour taste; by their ability to dissolve or corrode many metals; and by their ability to react with alkalis to form salts. Those most used in hand work are the relatively weak acetic, citric, and tannic acids. Hand workers seldom use the strong sulfuric acid. Acids are used to acidify acid dye baths and in after-rinses that adjust and control pH. *See also* Alkali; pH; Sour; Sweeten.

Acid dyes. Acid dyes are salts of organic acids, being mostly sodium, or occasionally calcium, ammonium, or potassium, chiefly sulfonic acid. They are the primary dyes used on wools. Goods are entered to an acidified dye/water solution, typically ¼ to 3 pounds of dyestuff to 100 pounds of wool. Glauber's salt is added to ensure that the color takes evenly. The bath is brought to simmer (185°F) until dyestuff is exhausted. *See also* On Weight of Goods; Direct dyes; Vat dyes.

Add-ons. Any substance, such as soap, dye, mordant, or reactive material, added as a portion of the total reactive material in a timed or structured sequence. The main reason to assist in scouring, dyeing, applying mordants or reactive materials. *See also* Adjuvants; Assists.

Adjective dyes. Dyestuffs that require use of a mordant, such as alum, iron, tin, etc. Most of the classic natural vegetable dyes are adjective dyes. *See also* Acid dyes; Alkaline dyes; Vat dyes.

Adjuvants. Supplemental ingredients used to adjust or modify an operation or process without being changed themselves. Adjuvants are catalytic: they do not really bond into a reaction, merely speed it up, slow it down, allow it to take place at an ideal temperature, adjust or modify pH, and so forth. *See also* Assists; Add-ons.

Adjustment. Changes in either a temporary sense, as in adjusting take-up or drive-band tension, or a permanent sense, as in adjusting drive ratio or footman length. The temporary sense is most often meant. Such adjustments are easily reversed, whereas "permanent" adjustments require the changing of parts, re-tying of bands or cords, disassembly and rearranging of an assemblage—such permanent adjustments cannot be made on the fly, as it were. *See also* Tweak.

Adsorb. Take up and hold by adhesion to the surface of a solid or liquid. Said of a thin film of gas or liquid. Adsorption of wetting agents to a fiber allows a dye solution to wet it. *See also* Absorb.

Agave. *Agave* spp. Generally, sisal (*Agave sisalana*) is what textile people mean by *agave*. It is considered a hard-leaf fiber; primary use is in twine, cords, straps, bags and rope. A cellulosic fiber. *See also* Century plant; Sisal.

Ai. From the Japanese, means *indigo*.

Akha spindle. Spindle type from Burma and Thailand. Similar to a small "Hopi"-style spindle, except used in double-

Agave.

supported mode. Sizes from 1½-inch whorl with 8-inch shaft up to 3-inch whorl with 12-inch shaft. Akha spindles are often fitted with a thread notch at one end; some are fitted with fine, hard-wire hooks. *See also* Thai spindle.

Alizarin. A classic mordant dye, the red pigment of madder roots, in use for centuries. Alizarin was first synthesized in the last quarter of the nineteenth century. The synthetic form is not often used alone as a dyestuff but is still used in the making of other synthetic dyes. *See also* Madder.

Akha spindle.

Alkali. Also called a base. Any of various compounds that when dissolved in water, have a pH greater than 7 and react with acids to form a salt. Strongly alkaline salts include sodium and potassium hydroxides (lye), sodium carbonate (washing soda), and potassium carbonate (potash). Weakly alkaline salts include sodium bicarbonate (baking soda) and ammonium hydroxide. *See also* Acid.

Alpaca. Most important fiber-producing member of Andean Camelidae, *Lama pacos*. Two distinct types occur: Huacaya (*bacaya*, in local usage) and Suri. Best fleece (typically 6+ pounds) from Suri; Huacaya fleece (typically 5+ pounds) is more llama-like. Animals are sheared November/December annually. Fiber is classed as a Specialty Hair Fiber. In the past few years, the number of alpacas and llamas in the U. S. has increased remarkably. Alpacas are primarily fiber animals; the llama also serves as a pack animal. *See also* Llama; Guanaco; Vicuña; Camelid.

Alpaca.

Alum. Any of various aluminum sulfate compounds used as mordants. The classic and most used mordant of ancient and medieval industry. According to K. Ponting, madder was mordanted with alum as far back as 2000 B.C. Typically, potassium aluminum sulfate, $KAl(SO_4)_2 \cdot 2H_2O$. *See also* Mordant.

Ammonia. Ammonia in the form of ammonium hydroxide, a mildly alkaline solution that may be obtained from natural fermentation of urine. It was/is the premier substance for indigo dyeing of woolen goods using the vat method. Household ammonia, diluted will not harm or harshen the woolen goods. The alkaline scouring liquor of choice, until quite recent times; now washing soda is added to the soap bath. *See also* Urine; Sweeten; Sour.

Angora goat. *Capra hircus hircus angora.* Source of mohair. Most U.S. mohair is from Texas (commercial); small flocks found in many western states. Earliest records of the breed seem to be from ancient Persia. *See also* Mohair.

Angora rabbit. Long-haired variety of domestic rabbit (*Oryctolagus cuniculus*), grown for fur (also called *angora*), used in effect yarns. Current domestic strains from France, Germany, Belgium, and Great Britain. Best spun as blend with fine wools; not durable or economical as 100 percent angora. Despite rantings and pifflings on the part of avid supporters, some people have significant allergic reactions to the animal, its fur, and its effluents. In this writer's experience, about 1 of every 7 humans shows some reaction to the bunnies' products.

Angora goat.

Angora rabbit.

Anthrax. Sometimes called wool sorter's disease. Flaming bad news. Caused by a spore-forming bacterium, *Bacillus anthracis.* Primarily a disease of herbivores but transmissible to other warm-blooded animal, including humans who handle infected wool. Can be fatal. If infected, seek medical attention. Rare in U.S. but not impossible.

Anti-stat. Substance used to control or eliminate the buildup of static electricity, especially in fibers and textiles. Most commonly used is an emulsion of water mixed with soap, lecithin, alcohol, etc. Anti-stats are not generally required if relative humidity is above 60 percent, but oil/water emulsions may be applied for other reasons, such as lubricating fibers and protecting the card clothing. *See also* Carding Oil; Steam.

Apocynum. Dogbane. Indian hemp. *Apocynum androsaemifolium* (spreading dogbane or bitterroot), *A. cannabinum* (Indian hemp),

Apocynum.

much used in the American prehistoric Southwest as fiber source. A bast or stem fiber. Not a true hemp (*C. sativa*). Called *dogbane* as is purported to be repellent to *Canis* spp. Has considerable herbal usage.

Arable. Literally, ready for the plow. Loaded with crud. Low-grade. Old-fashioned grading phrase that means you could plant potatoes in it, there is so much sandy soil present. Was originally a wool-grading term, but by usage may apply to any item as a relative grade or condition. *See also* Cotton grades.

Assists. Supplemental substances added to improve performance of a scouring bath, dye vat, or any operation, wet or dry. Beeswax for a drive cord is an example of the last type. Technically, anything that adds to the weight of the goods being processed, but general usage leans towards the meaning of "assistance." *See also* Add-ons; Adjuvants; Glauber's salt.

Backlash. Snarl or tangle caused by sudden release of linear tension, as in a reel or winding mechanism; also caused by breakage of line being wound or reeled in. Usually denotes temporary reversal of winding direction. A mess. Common complaint of fishermen and impatient yarn handlers.

Balanced yarn. A yarn that has no residual twist, or rather a yarn that shows no tendency to kink or fold back on itself when slackened. Normal usage refers to a yarn that has equal and opposing amounts of twist, as when ply twist balances twist of individual elements.

Band. Cord. Belt. As in drive band, drive cord, drive belt. *Band* is the preferred word, when speaking of brake-bands and drive-bands. Strictly speaking, a band is flat, like a shoelace, although usage has sweetened the pot, somewhat. Most modern drive-bands are made of round cord, a few are made of an elastic polymer (plastic) originally intended for gaskets and seals, or large industrial O-rings. Creep with an elastic band can be considerable, although friction-related slippage is quite low. *See also* Double-drive.

Barrel. The tubular nose of a flyer shaft; the part that goes through the front bearing. Serves as shaft extension for flyer shaft proper, and provides tunnel, or passage for yarn through support bearing. The barrel has the orifice in one end and orifice eyes in the other end. Also a foundation cylinder, as in a carding machine cylinder, or bare roller. A generous container of the flax spinner's favorite beverage.

Bast fiber. Any fiber extracted from the stem of a growing plant, vine, shrub, or tree. The bast fibers are not exclusively for textile use, although that is the chief use of flax and ramie. Nettle, jute, hemp, sunn, kenaf, *Apocynum* spp., and others have been used more for cords, bags, straps, rope, and so forth. Bark from various trees (linden, basswood, hickory) is technically a bast fiber.

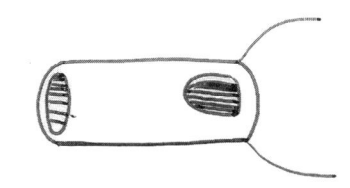

Barrel.

Bat-head. Spindle support assembly for a great wheel. Shaped like a paddle or bat, thus the name. Sometimes called a palm head. A flat, paddle-like arrangement with leather or husk bearing-stubs; the spindle is mounted transversely and the paddle handle plugs into a suitable socket in the top of the spindle support post (common) or the cross-bar of a dual-post arrangement (rare). Typical drive ratios on the order of 30- or 40-to-1. A direct-drive arrangement.

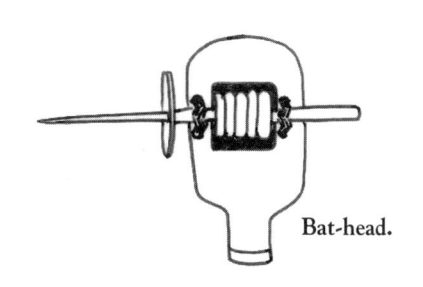

Bat-head.

Batt. A carding term. Intermediate fiber form. Thick, soft "blanket" arrangement of carded fibers, usually formed by winding card web around beam; when layers are thick enough, card is stopped, web layers are cut width-wise across the beam and batt is removed; "rainbow" batts are made this way. Batts can also be made by use of batt-former or lapping-feed device for the production of industrial felts.

Beetle. Literally, a cudgel or club. A heavy wooden mallet used in the process of beetling. To beetle woven cloth is to pound it with a club or mallet, giving it a smooth, semi-glossy finish. Beetling is a form of finishing for linen, ramie, hemp, and some cotton. Similar to (but not the same as) calendering, or passing between hot press rolls. Various stamp-mill mechanisms have been used for the process; now only done by hand workers, the industry having gone to calender rolls. *See also* Carpet beetle.

Beetle.

Bias. Angle of divergence between going-part shaft and driving-element shaft. In a model system, the flyer-and-bobbin system shaft is parallel with the axle shaft of the wheel. In an actual system, it is beneficial to have the two diverge at an angle of 2, possibly 3, degrees. The intent is to have the flyer array pull to the back (to float to the rear), in order to counter the pull (of spinning) toward the front. The ideal is to have the flyer array float free between the maidens, with no end thrust.

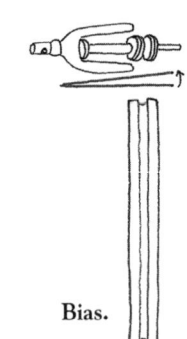

Bias.

Binky. Slang name for a large, lurid, or crude hand tool, one preferably with all those qualities. A tool that is somewhat more than adequate for the job at hand; by usage generally a striking instrument. Joking name for a flax beetle; also called a BFH.

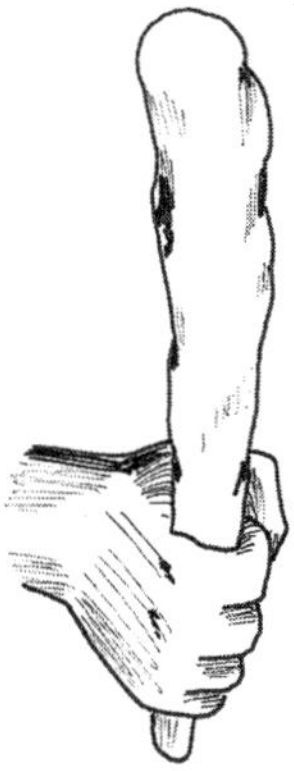

Blade. Synonymous with the spindle shaft of a driven spindle. Applies to great wheels, the various charkhas, the jenny, and so forth, but seldom to manual spindles. Also, a single wire or partition in a weaving reed, and the doctor-blade or scraper in roller-type gins.

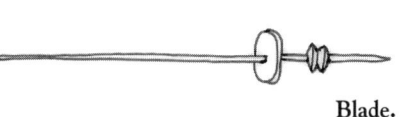

Blade.

Binky.

Bleach. As a verb, to remove color from, whiten. As a noun, an agent so used. Sodium hypochlorite, chloride of lime, sodium perborate, and hydrogen peroxide are examples of oxidizing bleaches. Reducing bleaches include sulfur dioxide gas, sodium thiosulfate ("hypo"), and sodium hyposulfite, familiar to indigo dyers. The safest but slowest bleach is sunlight in combination with dew and grass—old-fashioned stuff. The perborates, when used with care, are probably the safest modern bleaches.

Blivot. Two cups of coffee in a one-cup container; a quantity that exceeds the current capacity, as in trying to get 6 ounces of yarn into a 5-ounce bobbin. Too much, in the name of convenience. A deliberate, careless overload. An accident, looking for a place to happen.

Blocking reel. Sturdy rotating framework, in the shape of a skeleton box or barrel, used to hold yarn under tension during steaming, sizing, drying, or other processing. A necessary piece of equipment.

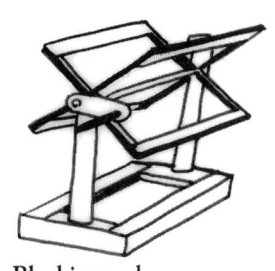

Blocking reel.

Blood count. System of nomenclature used to describe market grades or "fineness" (fiber diameter) of wools. The blood count is a statement of amount or proportion of Merino represented by the individual fleece or lot of wool. Grades include Fine (64's–80's+), Half-blood (58's–62's), Three-eighths–blood (52's–56's), Quarter-blood (48's–50's), Low quarter-blood (46's), Common (44's), and Braid (30's–40's). The enclosed numbers represent the equivalent English count values.

Bobbin-lead. A flyer-and-bobbin system in which the bobbin turns faster than the flyer during wind-on. The bobbin is continually driven; the flyer may be pulled around by the newly spun yarn. Bobbin-lead arrays are usually single-drive systems, and almost any double-drive arrangement may be set up to operate in bobbin-lead, single-drive mode.

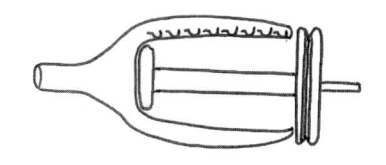

Bobbin-lead.

The arrangement is characterized by the strong take-up and a limited ability to produce fine yarns. The system is best suited to medium-heavy singles and plying. *See also* Scotch tension.

Boiling-off. Generally refers to degumming of raw silk, or the removal of the sericin. Boiling of the empty cocoons or the spun yarn(s) in a strong soap and water solution until gum is removed. May take several treatments. The term also applies to soap-boils of other fibers, as with fiber-reactive dyes (to ensure complete dye reaction) or with twist-lively yarns (to ensure set when yarns are dried). A good idea after any dye work is done, to prevent later problems. Also used the same way as *scour*.

Boon. Bits of woody matter adhering to the flax fiber after retting and breaking. Because the woody matter is broken down by microbacterial action, we probably have the real reason Sleeping Beauty went into allergic coma—she did not prick her finger on the spindle, but rather got a bit of moldy boon under a fingernail. A massive allergic reaction took place, she passed out, and stayed that way until Prince Whozis came and tumbled her about, thereby removing the bit of boon. The rest is history. *See also* Shive; Scutching.

Bouclé. French for *loops*. Also called *curl yarn*. Multi-ply, may have four or more elements. Made with one element (the decorative) of low, opposing twist, and much thicker than the ground element(s).

Bouclé.

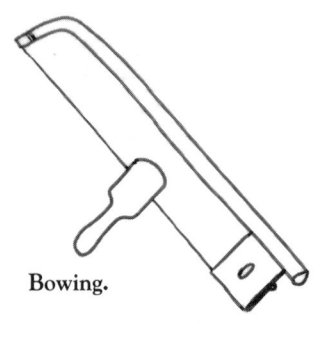

Bowing.

Bowstring hemp.

Bowl.

The yarn is assembled by slack-plying the decorative and ground elements up-twist of the ground element twist, then plying down-twist with a fine binder yarn, having twist the same as decorative element. In S–Z form, thus: A Z-twist effect yarn is slack-plied S with elements spun S; this is then plied Z with a fine Z-twist element.

Bowing. A method of cleaning and opening cotton fibers in preparation for spinning. Bowed cotton is usually converted to puni form for spinning. The cotton fiber is spread over a tabletop or shallow, large box; a taut bowstring is suspended above and touching the fibers. The bowstring is then "strummed" and individual cotton fibers clump about the string, shaking dirt and dust free as they do so. The clumped fibers are brushed off from time to time and go to the hand of the puni maker.

Bowl. As a textile term means *tub*. A scouring bowl is a wash tub. A *scouring train* for fleece consists of three, four, five, or more bowls. Typically, each rectangular bowl is 48 inches wide, 21 feet long, and roughly 4 feet deep, with a hopper-style bottom. In dye work, the bowl may be called a *kier* or *beck*. Old cast-iron bathtubs make pretty good bowls for home scouring; if the tub is set up on cinder blocks, external heat can be easily applied via a pan fire, old gas log, or other source.

Bowstring hemp. *Sansevieria* spp., usually *S. trifasciata*. Also known as *snake plant* and *mother-in-law's tongue*. Not a true hemp, more like New Zealand "flax" (*Phorium tenax*), in that it is a leaf fiber. Fiber is in tough bundles, running lengthwise of the leaves, and is harvested by manual, green decortication. Similar to yucca work. (Out of curiosity, mother-in-law's tongue also refers to *Dieffenbachia picta*.)

Bradford count system. A fixed-weight system for determining yarn grist. Also called worsted count system. The unit is 1 pound, and count number is the number of 560-yard skeins of yarn contained in a pound. Thus, a single skein of 560 yards in length, weighing 1 pound, has a Bradford count of 1 and a grist of 560 YPP. A 10's count means that ten skeins, each 560 yards long, weigh 1 pound, for a grist of 5,600 YPP.

Brake-band. Just what it sounds like. A cord, band, strap, et cetera, that serves to retard something through applied or increased friction, as in a bearing. Both Scotch and German ("Irish") tensioning systems establish and control take-up by means of brake-bands. Brake-bands are also used to tension or retard bobbin or spool rotation on devices such as lazy kates, storage bobbin racks, and blocking reels. Such arrangements establish and maintain a resistance to unwinding or reeling-off. *See also* Scotch tension; Single.

Brake-band for reel.

Break. Weak spot in staple locks, uniform across entire fleece. Caused by period of stress such as temporary lack of feed or water, shipment, lambing, and so forth. Wool grown during such times is significantly weaker than wool grown under no stress. To check: grasp staple lock by both ends, give sharp tug or pull. If break is present, fiber will "pop" apart. Check another lock; if it does the same, the fleece is damaged. A prolonged period of stress (malnutrition, illness) can result in a tender fleece, one that shows widespread weak spots.

Breaker card. Hand card(s) fitted with breaker clothing (clothing with coarse, long, widely spaced teeth) for the purpose of *breaking* or opening matted, tangled, or densely packed fibers (wool). Roughly akin to picking. Also, in large-scale mechanical carding operations, the first card in a two- or three-card set (breaker, scribbler, finisher card).

Britch. Also *breech*. Term describing wool that you do not wish in your home. A sheep's least fun part. Britch wool is seldom used for anything except organic fertilizer, for which purpose it is good.

Brushed. Means that yarn or fabric has been thoroughly brushed in order to raise the nap, or to form the effect known in knitting circles as *halo* or *nimbus*. Also means a fulled cloth with the nap deliberately brushed to make patterns or textures. A step in napping. In cotton fabrics, done with abrasives rather than brushes. *See also* Gigging.

Bucking. Bleaching of cotton and linen yardage by alternately soaking them in an alkaline solution (typically weak lye, often derived from wood ashes), then laying out the scoured goods on the grass (crofting). Finally, the goods were soaked in sour milk or buttermilk to neutralize the lye, scoured again, and laid out to dry.

Building motion. Mechanical arrangement that furnishes the movement that distributes yarn evenly over the bobbin length, thereby replacing the requirement to "change hooks." Three common motions used on contemporary spinning wheels are the geared Archimedean traverse, the bobbin traverse with manual movement, and the bobbin traverse with cam action.

Bulked yarn. A yarn that has been altered to make it fluff, plump, or otherwise appear to be something it is not. Where synthetic fibers are concerned, the possibilities appear endless; for handspinners, the technique known as *overply* is about the only game in town. *See also* Overply.

Bump. The package in which sliver leaves the mill; a cylindrical cross-wrapped package, perhaps 24 inches long and 16 inches in diameter, containing between 10 and 30 pounds of fiber. Commercial sectional warps are sometimes prepared in groups also called *bumps,* with each bump containing several hundred yards of warp consisting of several hundred ends, complete with lease crosses and safety ties. Recently, "home" carding machines have been able to produce mini-bumps.

Bump.

Cable. A thread, cord, yarn, or rope construction in which each successive twist goes in the opposite direction of the preceding twist; a ply construction where each twisting step is down-twist to the preceding twist, according to the notation S–Z–S or Z–S–Z. The process may continue through several levels, but for the handspinner, four is the practical limit (S–Z–S–Z or Z–S–Z–S). By definition, a cabled yarn has a minimum of four elements (strands). Thus, the normal two-ply yarn is not a true cable. *See also* Common ply; Hawser.

Cable.

Calcium. A metallic element of concern to the spinner mainly because of its role in water hardness. Calcium ions are the chief culprit in

414   The Alden Amos Big Book of Handspinning

forming insoluble soap-like scums and curds on washed wool that are nearly impossible to remove. If you have hard water (high in calcium) do not use natural soaps for scouring. No question of the importance of calcium in a well-balanced diet; but not in the normal scour or dye vat. *See also* Hardness; Soap.

Camel. *Camelus bactrianus*. The camel-hair coats of the good life are spun/woven from the fine undercoat (down) of the two-humped bactrian camel. The hair itself is strong and coarse: it resembles goat hair and is used for much the same purposes. The down is much like super-fine wool or cashmere, although not so slippery. Its staple length varies from ¾ inch to perhaps 3½ inches. *See also* Llama; Alpaca; Hair.

Camel.

Camelid. Denotes members of the camel family, including the one-humped camel or dromedary; the two-humped or Bactrian camel; and the several New World animals, like the llama and the alpaca. Interesting to note is that the Camelidae originated in the New World. The guanaco and the vicuña are not domesticated; the alpaca, the llama, and the two camels of the Old World have been domesticated for many centuries. *See also* Llama; Alpaca; Camel; Guanaco; Vicuña.

Camelids.

Candle. Candle denotes a fleece condition, indicative of high fleece quality—at least to showmen and grower. It is not a condition admired by the handspinner. Candle is the caking or stiffening of wool staple due to the heavy deposits of wool fat.

Carbonizing. Removing cellulosic trash (burrs, seeds, etc.) from wool by treating it with dilute (about a 6-percent by weight sulphuric acid/water liquor) sulfuric acid. Based on wool's resistance to acid, and cellulose's quick destruction by same. After a time, the treated wool is baked to concentrate the acid and turn all cellulose into frangible charcoal. The fiber is then beaten or dusted and the residue sucked out. The wool is sweetened in a weak alkaline solution to neutralize any remaining acid, then rinsed.

Card clothing. Fabric or material that covers the faces of hand cards. The combination of backing material and bent wire that makes up the working surface of a card. For hand cards, the card clothing is a sheet of material, punched and threaded through with lengths of doubled, fine wire. Carding machines have sheet clothing (as described for hand cards), fitted, or filet clothing—narrow strips of card clothing, except wound continuously around the cylinders. Card clothing comes in various tooth configurations.

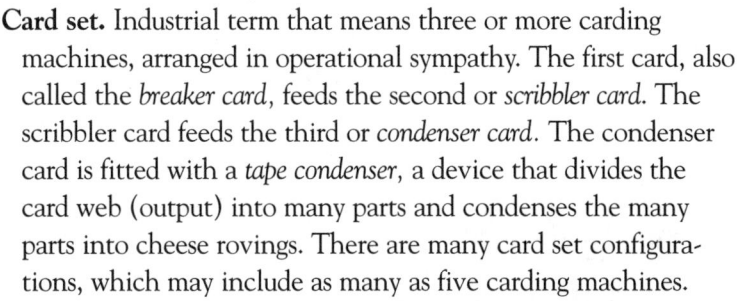

Card set. Industrial term that means three or more carding machines, arranged in operational sympathy. The first card, also called the *breaker card*, feeds the second or *scribbler card*. The scribbler card feeds the third or *condenser card*. The condenser card is fitted with a *tape condenser*, a device that divides the card web (output) into many parts and condenses the many parts into cheese rovings. There are many card set configurations, which may include as many as five carding machines.

Card set.

Carding. The separation and partial cleaning of a matted mass of fibers, and conversion of the fiber to a filmy web by working the fibers between two closely spaced, relatively moving surfaces, clothed with sharp points.

Carding oil. Oil applied to wool (or specialty hair fibers or blends) to increase inter-fiber lubricity, reducing friction. In addition, a proper carding oil protects the card clothing—or rather contains nothing that will harm the clothing. The oil is normally applied as an oil/water emulsion, and also raises moisture content, thereby increasing the plasticity of the fibers, which, to a point, reduces development of noils. Moisture also reduces or eliminates problems relating to static electricity. *See also* Add-ons; Assists; Anti-stat.

Carpet beetle. Wool-eating insects (beetles) which are also known as buffalo moths due to their fondness for heavy fur items such as cowhides, tiger skins, and buffalo robes. *Anthrenus scrophulariae*, *A. vorax.*, *A verbasci*, and *Attagenus piceus* are the common, furniture, varied, and black carpet beetles, respectively. They respond to the same treatment as clothes moths, although the beetles are tougher. The larvae (grubs) do the damage, and their work is often mistaken for that of the common *Tineola* and *Tinea* moth grubs. Bad news.

Cashmere. In general, the undercoat of the cashmere goat. Cashmere goats crossbred with Angora goats (source of mohair) results in what is marketed as cashgora. Cashmere is a luxury fiber, rare and expensive.

Castle. An upright beam or post. As a weaving term, applies to loom construction. By association, on a castle wheel the going parts (drive wheel, flyer-and-bobbin assembly) are supported by upright posts or beams. In general, denotes any upright spinning wheel with a three-legged base, two uprights or castles, with the drive wheel and flyer array supported by the same posts as the wheel. There are exceptions, of course—the Irish castle wheel being a prime example.

Cat. The fur of *Felis* spp. Some people do spin cat fur, but the endeavor is not practical. *See also* Dog; Novelty yarn; Practical.

Carpet beetle.

Castle wheel.

Caustic. Capable of destroying or eating away by chemical action. Corrosive.

Cellulosics. Generally refers to all vegetable-derived fibers: i.e. cotton, hemp, flax, abaca, jute et cetera including but not limited to tree bark and coconut coir.

Century plant. This is one of the plants you see in the best Westerns. It has stark, jagged, sword-like leaves and a scraggly center stem reaching to the sky. It is also a source (various spp.) for hard-leaf fiber, such as sisal. The century plant (*Agave americana*) gets large and mean; in about ten or twenty years, it blossoms with a stem up to 40 feet high, then dies back. *See also* Agave; Sisal.

Century plant.

The Alden Amos Big Book of Handspinning 417

Chair wheel.

Chair wheel. Unique type of wheel supposedly built into a chair frame, or a frame that looks like a chair. An accelerated arrangement with primary and secondary drive wheels; wheels may be solid (disk) construction. Typically, chair wheels of this type are double-treadle arrangement. Drive ratios of 30-to-1 are not unusual. Considered to be an American invention, if that matters. *See also* Saxony wheel; Irish castle wheel; Frame wheel.

Charkha. The word seems to mean *wheel* or *disk* (Sanskrit), although I have not been able to pin it down. In any case, don't say "charkha wheel." Current and common usage is that of a small, somewhat exotic appearing, driven-spindle setup with an accelerating system. The whole assemblage may fold into a small case, or it may look like a sort of miniature great wheel without legs. Less common are the banjo and bull-pup versions.

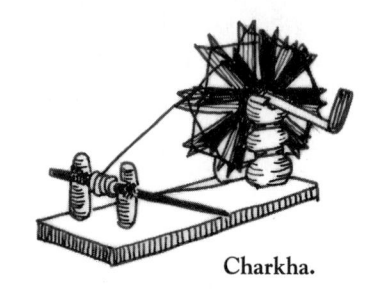

Charkha.

Cheese roving. Also called just *cheese* or *pencil roving*. A machine put-up of fiber, the product of a condenser card. Consists of a miniature roving (linear density runs about 25 yards per ounce) wound into a flat, cheese-like shape—thus the name. Fiber is usually wool, although blends are available now and again. Also sold as "twistless" yarn; used for certain soft, novelty knit structures. *See also* Sliver; Roving.

Cheese roving.

Chenille. Means *caterpillar* in French. A woven "yarn." Cannot be made by spinning; instead, it is something you make from your yarn, and then use like yarn. Essentially, a gauze weave structure with widely spaced warp-end groupings; the material is woven as weft-faced and then slit warpwise between the warp groupings. Strips of double-sided fringe result, and these are used in turn as weft in a normal weaving situation. Pseudo-chenille is produce by variations on novelty twisting or by overlock work.

Clock reel. Upright skein-winding reel, usually with four or six arms, 2 yards in circumference. Fitted with a gear train that drives a pointer.

The pointer is centered in a dial, thus the name *clock reel*. Clock reels are normally fitted with clickers that sound every so many turns: 40 turns (80 yards) is typical. Knot or string lease-ties are installed at each pop to keep track of the yardage. Reel dimension and pop frequency vary according to local usage. Also called a *click reel*, for obvious reasons.

Clothes moth. *Tineola biselliella* Hummel and *Tinea pellionella*, the webbing moth and the case-bearing moth. Their larvae do the damage. They cannot abide hot (simmering) soapy water, sunshine, and fresh air. They love dark, enclosed, undisturbed places, like plastic bags.

Coats. Sheep coats. A sort of a duster stuck on a sheep to keep dirt, feed shive, weed seeds, and such out of the fleece. A sheep so outfitted is said to be *rigged*. The idea dates back to at least Imperial Roman times. It is done only when premium fiber and prices are in order. Modern coats are plastic.

Cocoon. Silkworm's final effort, at least for most. A few go on to glory, the quest, and sex.

Coin spindle. A small metal spindle, traditionally made from a piece of stiff wire for the shaft and a small coin for the whorl. Used in the supported mode. The popular tahkli spindle, made famous by Bette Hochberg, Celia Quinn, et al., is made from hard-drawn spring (music) wire and a brass or iron disk whorl. Typical dimensions involve an 8-inch shaft and a $7/8$-inch–diameter whorl. Much smaller ones are found in use, made from small coins and bicycle spokes or slivers of bamboo.

Coir. Coconut fiber. *Cocos nucifera*. Could be considered a seed-covering fiber, if that matters. Actually is classed as a *nut-husk fiber*. Hard, red-brown, used for rope, cords, mats, and as brush fiber. The lashings holding King Kamehameha's canoe together. Not normally considered usable for garments, better suited to straps, hangers, lashings, and the like.

Colchis. Home of the Golden Fleece. The Eastern shore of the Black Sea, north of Turkey: Transcaucasia. Present-day European Georgian area; some feel the city of Sukhumi was close to the sacred grove holding the Golden Fleece, guarded by a fierce, ever-vigilant dragon—if you are into such things. Historical fact: The locals were into placing sheep pelts in streams for the purpose of cleaning them and of collecting gold dust in the greasy fleece. Much placer gold has been found in hills to the north. *See also* Jason and the Argonauts.

Collapse yarn. Any single or multi-element yarn structure that has had unusually high amounts of twist introduced for the purpose of causing collapse (significant foreshortening) when converted into fabric. It is the basis of old-fashioned seersuckers and crepes. The yarns must be stabilized through sizing and/or tensioning until conversion is complete, at which time the constraints are removed and the yarns are allowed to collapse, or relax. *See also* Twist-active.

Color blending. Process of mixing colored fibers, treating them as pigments. Blending takes place mechanically, through picking, carding, combing, and occasionally the conversion processes themselves (spinning, weaving, and so on). The intent is not always to gain a level color, and this must be taken into account. The further the material is processed, the more level the color effect will be.

Combing. As a wool grade, this term refers to any wool long enough and strong enough to benefit from the combing process. In general, any clean, fine, kemp-free, luster wool with a staple of 3 inches or more. As a verb, combing is the alternative to carding. It arranges fibers in parallel fashion, removes noils and trash, and prepares the fiber for worsted spinning.

Common ply. Common ply yarns are assembled, or plied together, using a ply-twist direction that is opposite to the twist direction of the individual elements or strands. Number of strands (plies) seldom exceeds five, with two being the overwhelming favorite. In practice, common ply is two-thirds of the cable process, and is constructed according to the plan S–Z, or Z–S. Those mean, respectively, *spin* S, *ply* Z and *spin* Z, *ply* S. With careful work, a balanced (twist-stable) yarn results. *See also* Cable; Hawser.

Condition. Strictly speaking, the moisture content of a fiber mass. Directly related to ambient relative humidity and fiber regain. In a broader sense, denotes overall features or faults with an item or fiber. As a verb, *condition* means to bring an item (fiber mass or the like) to a specific moisture content, or state of oiliness, or warmth, or other condition. Establishments that do this sort of work are called *conditioning houses*.

Cone. Classic shape of solid geometry—tapered cylinder form—used as basis of yarn storage package. Cardboard, plastic, or metal form for winding yarn, using a *cone winder*. Metal and plastic ones make good cores for boiling cotton. A secondary yarn package. By general usage, includes core tubes of cylindrical shape as well as the cone.

Copp. Disk mounted on a spindle blade, to keep yarn out of the bearings and to serve as a base for building the *copp*, which is the cone-like package of yarn built upon a spindle blade. Also spelled *cop*, although in U.S. that word means something else. A copp is a primary yarn package. Copps are sometimes built upon quills, then removed from the spindle blade for winding-off.

Cord. A miniature, two-stranded rope. The strands, formed up-twist of their elements, may contain multiple threads. The cord is laid-up rope style, that is, on the plan S (twist of threads)–S (forming twist of strands)–Z (laying-up direction), or Z–Z–S, depending upon spinning twist direction. Laying-up the strands is quite different from plying yarn, and requires a rope jack and an extra pair of hands. *See also* Rope; Hawser.

Core yarn. Used in novelty constructions. Any yarn used as a foundation for various amazements that are wrapped, plied, stuck, threaded, or otherwise arranged to look like something they are not. In general, a relatively strong and stable yarn, wound with some wondrous soft and lofty item.

Cotton count system. A fixed-weight system. The count value is based upon the number of 840-yard-long hanks (skeins) of yarn per pound. Thus, a single skein 840 yards long that weighs 1 pound is a 1's cotton. If ten 840-yard skeins weigh 1 pound total, the count would be a 10's, or 8,400 yards per pound. The same standard is used for spun silk, so 840 YPP is the same as a 1's count of spun silk. Compare with *Spinning counts*, which do not work quite the same way.

Cotton grades. The old Uplands grading system, where the distinctions were once differentiated by name but now are kept apart by number. There were originally nine grades, but the best, Middling Fair, no longer exists because we no longer have hand-picked cotton. Here are the remaining names and their equivalent numbers: 1 = Good Middling, 2 = Strict Middling, 3 = Middling, 4 = Strict Low Middling,

5 = Low Middling, 6 = Strict Good Ordinary, 7 = Good Ordinary, 8 = Below Grade. A second number is added to indicate color, as follows 0 = plus, 1 = white, 2 = light spotted, 3 = spotted, 4 = tinged, 5 = yellow stain, 6 = light gray, 7 = gray. A white Strict Low Middling would be a 4-1. *Plus* is white, white, white, twinkle, twinkle.

Cotty. Fleece wool matted together at the cut, or butt, end. Partially felted, while still on the animal, the wool is called *cotted*. A defect, whether on or off the sheep. Heavily cotted wool is no bargain, even when it is free. *See also* Nep; Second-cuts; Break.

Cover. Density or closeness of surface threads or yarns. In spinning, *cover* means how closely yarns are spaced across a reel or frame as a result of cross-winding, or how closely an effect yarn is wrapped around a core element. In weaving, *cover* means the degree to which any underlying structure or object is concealed by the surface material. As a dye term, *cover* refers to the ability of a dyestuff to conceal or obscure minor faults in the fabric. Usually stated as *percent cover factor*, 100 percent being total coverage.

Creep. Creep is the actual lengthening of a drive-band under load, with the result that the drive-band becomes longer on one side than the other. Because of this, a marker on the drive belt will slowly regress against the rotational direction. In any system with an elastic belt, creep is commonplace. A well-regulated system will exhibit less than 2 percent loss through creep, but the newer "spaghetti" cords may increase creep losses significantly—perhaps as much as several percent.

Crepe. Specifically, a type of woven cloth; the crepe effect is won through the use of collapse yarn(s) in weft, warp, or both. Also refers to a yarn construction based on cable construction, a two-ply yarn of four elements. Sometimes used to describe the yarn used to achieve collapsed fabrics.

Crepe yarn. Highly twisted single or two-ply yarns, carrying from two to four times as much twist as the normal (balanced) yarns of equal grist. Such yarns must be maintained under tension at all times, or snarls and kinks will result. A challenge to spinner and weaver alike. *See also* Collapse yarn.

Crimp. Recurring corrugation in wool fiber. In general, the more crimp (more corrugations per unit of length), the "higher" the wool count, and the more uniform the crimp distribution, the higher the "quality" of the wool. Moderation in all things: in many cases the crimp numbers are just that—numbers waiting for a chance to be important. *See also* Crimp grade.

Crimp grade. A grading system, not breed-specific, based on number of crimps per inch of a wool fiber. Useful for a rough field-check of an individual fleece. The grades, with numbers indicating crimps per inch, are: Very Fine = 22–30, Fine = 14–22, 1/2 Blood = 10–14, 3/8 Blood = 8–10, 1/4 Blood = 5–8, Low 1/4 Blood = 2–5, Common = 0–2, Braid = 0–1.

Cross-reel. To wind from one yarn package to another, for the purpose of leveling twist, examining and repairing the yarn, re-building or building of uniform yarn packages, measuring length, preparing for special operations, et cetera. It is always good to cross-reel yarn from the wheel bobbin to storage spools.

Cross-reel.

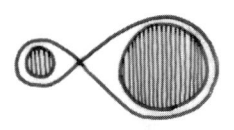

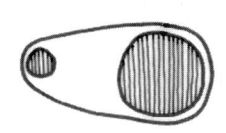

Cross-band. Archaic and colorful term for S-twist. It appears to be one of those obligatory entries in glossary-dom, because in over twenty years in the trade I have never known a human to use this word in any context, other than as an obscurity in verbal show-and-tell. The antonym is, of course, the Gowkonian phrase *uncrossed-band,* or, in modern English, *open-band*. *See also* Sunwise; Widdershins.

Cross-band.

Crossbreed. A designation of wool qualities, based upon presumed breed or mixed breed in fleece animal. Denotes a sheep of two-breed provenance, as in Suffolk/Hamp crossbred, Merino/Targhee crossbred, and so forth. Can also be used as a three-part litany, for example Welsh Mountain-Swaledale-Romney cross. Originally *crossbred* meant one parent was Merino, one wasn't.

Cut. A fixed-weight system of yarn measurement. In the U.S., the cut denotes the number of 300-yard hanks (skeins) of woolen yarn per pound weight. Thus a 5-cut woolen equals five 300-yard skeins per pound, for a grist of 1,500 YPP. Works on the same standard as the lea for linen, that is, 300-yard skeins.

Decorticate. Means to separate fiber from non-fiber by brute force. Word is from the Latin *decorticare,* to remove the husk, bark, or peel. For fibers that do not ret, decortication is done green. Some are given chemical treatments to decorticate them. As practiced for flax, hemp, and other fibers traditionally treated this way, decortication is accomplished by retting, breaking, and scutching.

Degras. Commercial term for crude, recovered wool grease.

Degum. To remove gums, glue, sticky ughs from fiber or yarn. Chiefly a silk term. Silk gum or sericin is removed by a process known as boiling-off, which describes the operation pretty well. Strong soap solutions are used. Silk gum is not, strictly speaking, water soluble. Hot water softens it but does not remove it in any practical sense of the word.

Denier. A fixed-length system of yarn grist measurement. The denier (sounds like *den-YEA*) is the weight, in grams, of 9,000 meters of yarn. A silk measurement, originally, but used for other filaments and fine yarns. Us older folks remember silk stockings being sold on the basis of denier; the lower the number, the finer the yarn, the more transparent the hose, and the higher the price. The system has been attributed to an anecdote concerning Louis the 14th.

Detergent. From the Latin *detergere,* to cleanse. Classically, soaps are detergents, but in modern usage natural soaps are excluded, the word being assumed to refer to alkyl sulfates, alkyl benzene sulfonates, and the like, rather than lye-and-fat products.

Direct Dyes. Synthetic dyestuffs requiring no mordant that are much used on cellulosics. In use since the late nineteenth century. One of the first major colors was styled as Congo Red. As important for cotton dyeing as acid dyes are for wool. *See also* Acid Dyes; Vat Dyes; Adjective Dyes.

Distaff. Device to hold fibers in a prearranged form in order to facilitate drafting and spinning from the arranged fiber mass. Distaves (plural of *distaff*) are of various constructions, as it is the purpose that counts. A distaff may be a nail on the wall, a hook, an old broom or rake. Often, a distaff is a purpose-built device, highly decorated, consisting of a shaft and some sort of arrangement to secure fiber in order. The distaff head may be cage-like, comb-shaped, scrolled and carved, bentwood, et cetera.

Distaff.

Diz. Traditionally a disk or curved plate made of horn, bone, or occasionally metal; has a central slot or hole; and is for the purpose of condensing and controlling fibers during the drawing-off step of combing. Nowadays a diz may be plastic, exotic wood, metal, ceramic material, or what-have-you. Natural horn works best. Dizzes are used in wool-combing, rough combing, and carding, as well as in reprocessing of other fiber forms, not necessarily wool. Essentially, it is a pre-drafter and sliver-forming aid. Sometimes spelled *dizz*. See also Sliver; Top.

Doff. To remove, or to empty from a working element, as to doff a copp from a spindle blade; to doff a bobbin is to remove it from the wheel and (by extension) to reel it off. You doff a reel by removing or winding-off the skein present. A *doffer* (mill term) is an operative who removes full bobbins, pirns, and other bits, and replaces them with empty ones. The doffer is also the last cylinder of a carding machine, fitted with doffer blades.

Dog. *Canis* spp. Some people make much out of spinning dog hair, particularly of certain breeds. There is an active cottage industry involved in spinning and converting (via knitting, weaving, and so on) the fiber supplied by dog breeders and fanciers, with sweaters being a mainstay. It is safe to bet that virtually all breeds have been spun; as to the success of such ventures, that remains in the eye of the beholder. Another problem area is that of inherent odors: people may notice nothing, but other dogs do. See also Cat.

Double-draft. Way of removing or reducing slubs or leveling diameter of yarns spun on the woolen system. Method consists of drafting relatively short, thick make of yarn, without sufficient twist to prevent further extension. While twist insertion is withheld, make is additionally drafted. Only minimum amounts of twist are allowed until "second" draft is complete. Yarn is finish-twisted in conventional manner. Method is a variant of "Navajo" spinning. Also called *extension drafting*.

Double-drive. Major bobbin-lead system for flyer-and-bobbin arrangements. Both bobbin and flyer are driven; bobbin-whorl diameter is less than that of flyer whorl; when driven from common drive surface, the two rotate at different speeds. System has semiautomatic

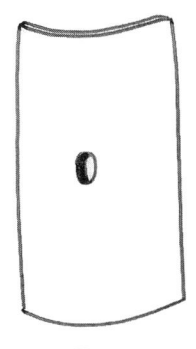

Diz.

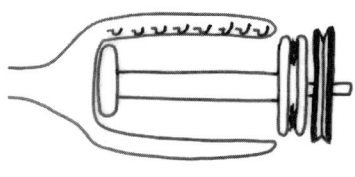

Double-drive.

tendencies and a narrow range of efficient yarn production. Slippage must be present for system to work. At one time, the "standard" for spinning flax. Much misinformation circulated about system, history, operation, and design. *See also* Welsh tension.

Double-supported. Describes technique peculiar to bead-whorl spindles, the Thai spindle, and others. Spindle is never allowed to hang free. Spindle shaft is supported by fingers at one end, by yarn at other. Total weight of spindle is divided between yarn and fingers. Also called *finger-spindle mode*.

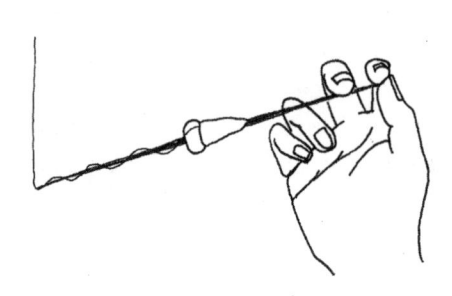

Double-supported.

Doubling. Winding two strands at the same time into a secondary yarn package. Adding or removing twist is not a concurrent activity. Doubling is a step in some complex yarn constructions. By usage, may also include the winding of paired ends concurrently, for example winding two, four, six, or possibly more ends at a time into a secondary package as a preparation for later twisting operations.

Down-twist. Introducing twist that is in opposition to that of the preceding twisting operation or that incumbent in a yarn, thread, strand, or element. Example: two strands of single yarn, both spun Z-twist, are then plied S-twist, that is down-twist or in the direction opposite to incumbent twist. In this case, the result will be a normally plied yarn.

Draft. In spinning, the attenuation and extension of a fiber mass, with or without concurrent introduction of twist. Drafting may take place in an untwisted strand (slubbing, sliver), or in a partially twisted strand (double drafting), or at any stage in-between. Drafting occurs during or before twisting; it is not practical to draft once twist reaches a certain point, because then the yarn will break, rather than extend. *See also* Make; Long draw; Double-draft.

Drafting zone. Area of operations in which a fiber mass is attenuated, or drawn down, to a linear density approaching that of the finished single yarn. The so-called *magic triangle*. Dynamic working area where the handspinner introduces twist to the drafted fibers, either as a concurrent act (drafting against twist) or as a subsequent activity (drafting without twist). The fiber area between the spinner's hands, bounded on one end by the untwisted fiber mass and on the other by newly twisted yarn.

Drag. In spinning wheels, the resistance to turning offered by the various going parts, especially the flyer-and-bobbin array or spindle arrangement. Always friction-related, although aerodynamics and fiber rigidity play a considerable part.

Drift. Separation failure of a yarn due to insufficient twist. The yarn does not break; the fibers have so little nip that the yarn simply slips apart. It drafts itself because there is not enough twist present. In so doing, it reduces grist, thereby requiring more twist, which is not forthcoming. The yarn just drifts apart. Underspun.

Drive ratio. Describes mechanical advantage of a wheel-to-whorl arrangement: the usual spinning situation is the relationship that exists between the driving wheel and the driven whorl. Drive ratio is stated as number of times the driven part rotates for each revolution of the driving part, for example, 10-to-1. Found directly by observation (turn the wheel and count the number of times the flyer or spindle turns) or calculated on basis of diameters. Drive systems may be multilevel, in which case the levels multiply each other.

Drop spindle. In the realm of manual or hand-operated spindles, this is the best-known type and mode of employment. The mode denotes that the spindle is suspended freely and totally from the forming yarn. Any spindle used in this fashion. Drop spindles are normally between 1 and 6 ounces in weight and have shafts between 6 and 20 inches long. They may have multiple whorls; be fitted with hooks, grooves, or other devices to hold or control the yarn during spinning; and be used in top-whorl or bottom-whorl position.

DRS. Differential rotational speed. Numerical description of the differential speed between elements in flyer-and-bobbin system. The lag element speed divided by the lead element speed: can be determined by observation or calculated using effective diameters. Example: For a system where the flyer whorl is 2 inches in diameter and the bobbin

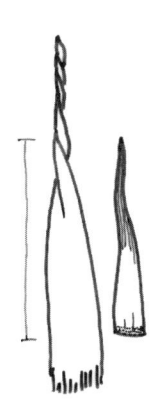

Drafting zone.

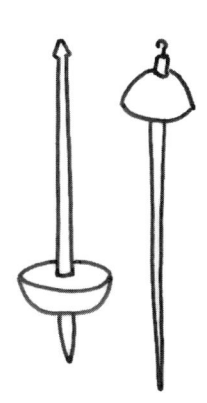

Drop spindle.

The Alden Amos Big Book of Handspinning   427

whorl is 1½ inches in diameter, 2 divided by 1½ = 1.33+. For each revolution of the flyer, the bobbin rotates 1.33+ times, and the DRS is 1.33+-to-1. A DRS of 1.25-to-1 is typical of modern wheels. *See also* Whorl; Take-up; Drive ratio.

Effective. Actual working values, as opposed to theoretical or "paper" values. Example: Effective drive ratios are always lower than the published data because an effective ratio includes band slippage, creep, drag, et cetera. The "paper" values are based on rounded (up) numbers. *See also* Practical.

Elastic. In spinning, *elastic* means a yarn or fiber will extend (increase in length) upon applying linear tension, and will return to original apparent length when tension is removed. Wool is elastic; flax is not. A plied yarn and/or a textile may in part be elastic due to construction—that is, not because of fiber character. Cotton is an inextensible fiber, yet elastic and extendable knit underwear is made from it.

Enter. To put into or to thread, as to *enter a warp* in the loom or to *enter skeins of yarn* into a dyepot.

Exhaust. Use up or react with all the available dyestuff, indicated by clearing of the dye bath. The dye bath may not actually be clear, but all useful color will have been absorbed by the fibers being dyed. The term applies to acid dyes and some natural dyes. Fiber-reactive dyes never exhaust, as they actually dye the water itself. (The fiber reactives actually bond to hydroxyl groups, of which there are many on cellulosics. Some of the dyestuff will react with the water's hydroxyl groups, thereby dyeing the water itself.)

Felt. A fabric of wool and/or wool-like fibers or fur, worked to coherence by heat, pressure, moisture, and movement. The fabric may have a woven or knit foundation. Certain industrial felts are based upon greatly hardened felts produced from double-, triple-, and quadruple-woven cloths. The fez of the Middle East is usually a knitted cap that has been heavily fulled (felted). Felt may be supplied in convenient sheets or strips, between 1/32 and 2 inches (or more) thick.

Fermentation Vat. The natural fermentation of sugars, glucosides, starches and yeasts in a vat has a strong reducing effect (removes oxygen). Make the vat liquor mildly alkaline, introduce indigo, and the result is indigo white, the water-soluble form of indigo. Dip the goods to desired hue, airing between dips to develop the blue indigo color. In the past, fermentation vats and the similar urine vats have been kept working for weeks at a time; nowadays the vats will be set and brought up to condition, then used for a session. *See also* Indigo; Woad; Vat Dyes.

Fettle. To fettle card clothing is to place it into *fine fettle*, or top-notch, first-class, freshly cleaned condition. *Fettling* is the removal of all waste, dirt, dead bugs, twigs, matted wool, and other debris from card clothing. In practice, it includes grinding the wires (carding-machine cylinders), checking and setting clearances, and making minor repairs.

Fid. A rope-working tool, used for making splices. Long, tapered cone or pin, often of wood, sometimes metal. Small ones of bone, ivory, and the like are used for knots. Typical fid for maritime usage is 10–18 inches long, 1–2 inches in diameter at the butt end, and $\frac{1}{8}$ inch or less at the tip. Used to work between the rope strands, to enlarge holes for sailmaking, et cetera.

Filament. A continuous strand or thread, extruded by machine or animal. Silk is a filament fiber; the silk may be from several sources. Synthetic fibers are filament fibers, but of no interest here.

Fid.

Flake yarn. A three-element yarn where flakes or patches of material (tufts of sliver, bits of matted silk) are twisted and bound into a two-ply ground yarn. Also called a *cloud yarn*. A novelty.

Flax. *Linum usitatissimum.* Sails to lace, baby clothes to ropes, flax does it all. You can grow it in the back yard. Space does not allow listing all virtues and features. Flax is an annual, planted from seed. Matures in 90 days. This year's flax is next year's linen, as one old saying puts it—which means it takes time to do the work. It is not necessary to take two years, but that's how it seems to work out after you raise a few crops. *See also* Linen; Hemp; Bast fiber; Tow.

Flake yarn.

Fleece. By itself, means sheared wool from one sheep, rolled and secured into a package or bundle. An individual unit: you may buy a fleece, or three fleeces, or a half of a fleece. Common usage allows you to buy

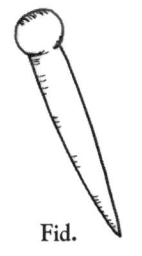

Flax.

Fleece.

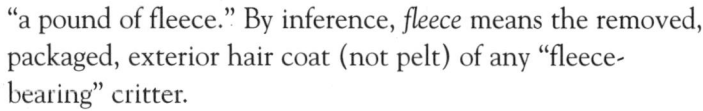

"a pound of fleece." By inference, *fleece* means the removed, packaged, exterior hair coat (not pelt) of any "fleece-bearing" critter.

Flicker. Also called *flick carder*. Narrow, specialized card, used as a rake or comb on selected, coherent bundles of fiber, such as locks of wool. A pad or protective plate is placed on worker's thigh; the staple is trapped between flicker and pad, while the worker's non-flicker-wielding hand keeps lock intact. Half of staple is worked between flicker and pad, then lock is reversed. Flickers are handy for samples and for fettling carding machines.

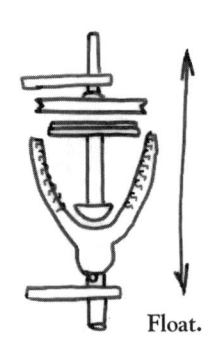

Flicker.

Float. Thrust (linear) clearances in a flyer-and-bobbin system, or in any trapped system. Space allowed, within the flyer, so that the bobbin can move back and forth on the flyer shaft. The space allowed, between the maidens, to allow the flyer assembly to move back and forth between the bearings and supports. End clearance, or play. The actual movement allowed by the float clearances.

Float.

Flyer. From archaic engineering use. Denotes extra-fast moving part or assembly, as in the American Flyer model train or Radio Flyer sled. In spinning, it is the extended heck assembly of the going part of a spinning wheel. Generally a composite assembly, shaped like horseshoe. The flyer shaft is central support for both bobbin and heck assembly. The bobbin is free to rotate; the heck assembly is fixed or locked to the flyer shaft. Entire arrangement is supported, fore and aft, by flyer-shaft bearings.

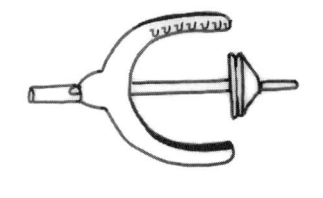

Flyer.

Flyer-lead. A flyer-and-bobbin system in which the flyer turns faster

430 The Alden Amos Big Book of Handspinning

than the bobbin during wind-on. Typically, the flyer is driven at a constant velocity, while the bobbin is pulled around by the yarn. Flyer-lead arrays are usually single-drive systems, although most double-drive arrangements may be set to operate in single-drive, flyer-lead mode. The arrangement is characterized by enhanced ability to produce fine yarns, beyond the default character of a given unit. The default flyer-and-bobbin system of the Ashford Traditional. *See also* Scotch tension.

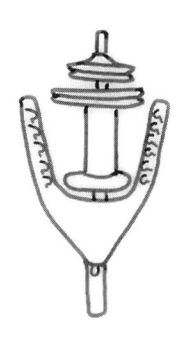

Folding. Generally used as synonym for *plying*. Specifically, it means to twist together two or more elements as an intermediate step. Direction of folding twist is not presumed, as in plying, and may be up-twist. A step in assembling complex plied structures. Same as doubling, except doubling does not presume twist at all. Thus the phrase "double and twist" to describe a plied yarn.

Flyer-lead.

Footman. British term is *pitman*. On spinning wheel, connecting rod which joins crank to treadle attachment point. Transmits treadle action to crank and crankshaft. Modern wheels have footmen of string, wire, leather, wood, aluminum, and so forth. A footman made of string or cord is a delusion and a dirty trick. As a handspinner, you should pay about as much attention to your footman as you do to tire pressure—which is not much, unless there is something wrong with it.

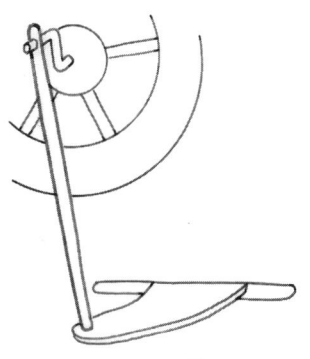

Frame wheel. The common form of frame wheel is that known as a Vertical-frame Swiss; less common forms include styles such as the Owego or Farnham wheel, as well as various wheels built using packing crates, boxes, ladders, and so forth. This is not to disparage such wheels—after all, the purpose of the frame is to hold the going parts in a practical and efficient relationship, and looks or traditional purity are eyewash or less when yarn production is the key objective. *See also* Irish castle wheel; Chair wheel; Saxony wheel.

Footman.

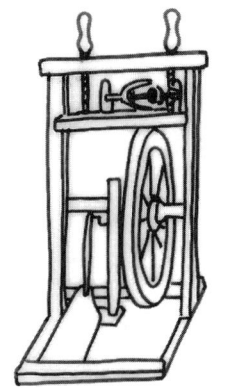

Frame wheel.

Frass. Adopted from trade jargon (out of carpentry and joinery) to iden-

The Alden Amos Big Book of Handspinning

tify fine, non-specific, granular waste of organic origin. The fall-out product of powder-post beetles, termites, wood-boring grubs, and the like. In general, insect-produced excrement or debris. What is left in a plastic bag once filled with wool after numerous life cycles of the clothes moth. *See also* Swarf; Shive; Boon; VM; Timber.

Fribs. Clumps of extra-short second- or third-cuts, a result of imperfect shearing practice. Also, small tags or dung-locks.

Frow. Old wool term, means dried-out, sun-baked, crumbly, frangible. Has degrees. Wool can be frow or, if really worthless, frow as a biscuit.

Fulling. The shrinking, felting, condensing, and thickening of a woolen material by treatment consisting of pressure, moisture, and movement. The process is aided by the application of soap, heat and cold water, music, and suitable beverages.

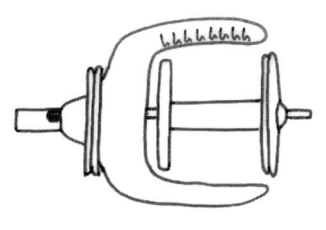

German tension. Same as single-drive, bobbin-lead system of flyer-and-bobbin spinning wheels. Refers to the brake-band on the flyer barrel or shaft, used to enhance DRS. System is commonly found on older wheels of German or Swiss origin: Richard Ashford (of Ashford wheels) states that he coined the term *Irish tension* a few years ago, but dropped it as "confusing" to the majority of wheel users and now uses the more precise *single-drive, bobbin-lead*. *See also* Irish tension; Scotch tension.

German tension.

Gigging. Brushing up the nap or piled cover on a piece of cloth, as a step in fulling or in finishing, usually woollen and seldom worsted fabrics. Can be done by hand, or by machine on a setup called a *gig mill*. Gigging is done to increase cover of fulled goods, for example blankets. Gigging increases fulling action, to obtain softness and "halo," to partially obscure (blend) colors, or to obliterate weave structure. Gigging is what teasels are used for, and the frames they are held in are called *teasel* or *gig frames*. Gigging by hand may also be done with fine, stiff brushes. The machine that does the same thing is called a *gig*. Gigging is done moist for majority of work; when the gig is fitted with wire teeth, wet gigging is done.

Gilling. Gilling is a sort of linear, continuous, combing-and-drafting operation applied to fibers, sometimes called *pin drafting*. Gilling is commonly used for color blending in fibers intended for worsted spinning; the handspinner sees the product as half-gilled (obvious color streaks). The pin drafter/gill box is sometimes used to upgrade a card sliver to semi-worsted status, without the expense of true combing. *See also* Sliver; Top; Roving.

Gin. *Gin* is a contraction of the word *engine*, and applies to any contrivance or mechanism that performs a specific action. In textile terminology, the word almost always refers to the cotton gin, of which there are several types.

Gingerline. A mohair equivalent of *moorit*, a reddish-brown natural color. Gingerline mohair seems to be a product of Turkey, and is seldom seen by the handspinner.

Glauber's Salt. Sodium sulfate decahydrate, $Na_2SO_4 \cdot 10H_2O$. Used for dyeing both vegetable and animal fibers; on wool, it slows the speed of dye strike, and on cotton, it increases it. Sodium sulphide is British dyehouse usage; generally applies to industrial grade (not entirely pure) of Glauber's salts. *See also* Assists; Add-ons.

Going part. The essential functional part of a device. The reason for the rest of the device. On great wheels, this means the spindle and on flyer wheels it means the flyer-and-bobbin array. Generalized usage for any and all parts that move during normal operation. Also indicates most important moving part of a mechanism, or the linkage between one motion and another.

Golden Fleece. Magical ram's fleece; major good-luck charm owned by the people of Colchis. Kept in a sacred grove, guarded by an ever-vigilant (24/7) dragon; "obtained" by Jason of Thessaly, aided by the enchantress Medea and the Argonauts. No one has any idea where it is today. *See also* Colchis; Jason and the Argonauts.

Grandrelle. Two or more differently colored ends plied together. Two-color two-ply. Also called jaspé yarn. A class called *fancy twist*.

Grassing. Spreading woven goods on special meadows or *greens* for the purpose of bleaching. Same as crofting. Grassing is a step in old-fashioned bleaching; not practiced nowadays.

Grex. Logical version of denier. A fixed-length system of yarn count: the weight, in grams, of 10,000 meters of the subject yarn. A filament measurement.

Grin. A textile flaw: filling (weft) may be displaced in the warp-wise direction by simple pressure, allowing whatever is behind the cloth to "grin" through. In hand work, caused by three major factors: (1) not a close-enough sett, (2) not enough weft picks, or (3) not close enough to the suds. Sleazy, slippery yarns add to the problem.

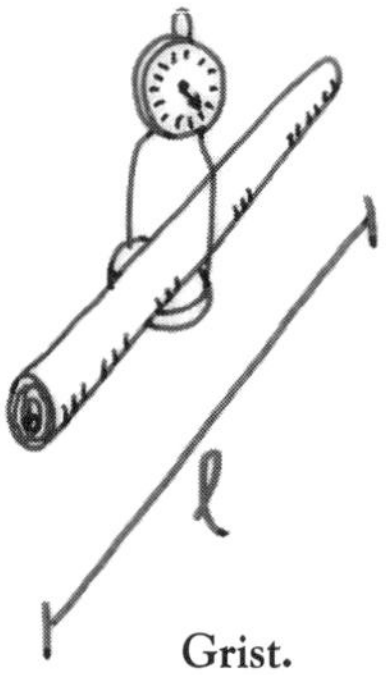

Grist. Describes a yarn's linear density, that is, its length-to-weight relationship, stated as a numerical value. Grist is measured by various means, and evaluated in numerous ways. Direct statements of grist value are best; no conversion is required. Example: a yarn has a grist of 2,000 yards per pound. Other systems are used; a few include direct systems (TYPP, metric) and indirect systems (lea, run, worsted). Systems are also classed as fixed-length (denier, grex) or fixed-weight (cotton, woolen, and so on).

Grist.

Grommet. A circular rope construction; a continuous circle or ring, made by laying-up a rope in a circle. Grommets are also made of brass, plastic, and other substances Their primary purpose is to reinforce a hole, as in a sail, tarpaulin, hammock, or other item. A sort of buttonhole. Also an imaginary handle, seized by extraordinary abilities or skill in some endeavor. A figure of speech. To do such a great work as to grab your observer "right by the grommet."

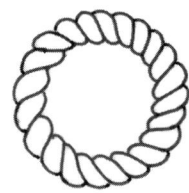

Grommet.

Guanaco. *Lama guanicoe.* Considered by some authorities to be the progenitor of the llama and the alpaca, the guanaco is the "lowland" version of the vicuña and is similarly considered wild, as opposed to domesticated. Whereas the vicuña lives at altitude, the guanaco ranges to sea level, especially in southern Chile, the Argentine, and Patagonia. *See also* Camelid; Llama; Vicuña.

Guanaco.

Hackle. A block or board fitted with sharp steel teeth, used to comb and straighten flax line. A hackle may have 60 or 70 teeth, between 3 and 10 inches long, spaced between ¼ and ¾ inch apart. Fiber is drawn through the hackle repeatedly, until all short parts (tow) have been removed and all long

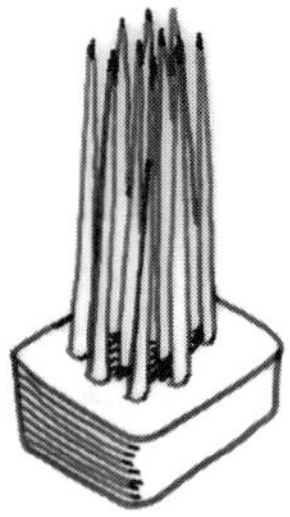

Hackle.

fibers are parallel. Fibers other than flax can be hackled. Also called *hetchel*.

Hair. In the textile sense, difficult to define clearly as the borders between wool, down, hair, and fur often consist of degree and point of view. Suffice it to say that the hairs used for violin bows (horsehair, and tail hair at that) differ considerably from Merino; cow hair differs from Angora rabbit; and so on. The degree of difference is often only in the eye of the beholder.

Hairy-seeded. Cotton varieties that have the lint firmly attached to the seed, also called *tight-seeded*. Upland and Acala (a major part of U.S. crops) are hairy-seeded, and hairy-seeded cottons require use of a saw gin for efficient harvesting. Roller-gins give mediocre to poor results.

Hand. Subjective quality of yarns, textiles, and fabrics, relating to how they feel. Two experts may agree that a given lot of stuff has "good hand," but getting them to agree what *hand* is seems beyond reach.

Hard fiber. Fibers from leaves or leaf stems; comparatively stiff, elongated strands. Abaca, sisal, henequen, phormium, and the like.

Hardness. We are speaking of water hardness, and hard water is bad news when it comes to scouring fiber or goods with natural soap. Measurement of calcium and magnesium cations in water; usually measured in parts per million (ppm) calculated as calcium carbonate, $CaCO_3$. In general, water with a hardness greater than 30 ppm is a candidate for softening. Another unit of measurement is grains per gallon; water hardness in grains per gallon is equivalent to ppm/17.1. *See also* Soap.

Hawser. Strictly speaking, a large rope used to moor a ship. In handspinning, a yarn construction that is based on the twist plan S–S–Z or Z–Z–S. In other words, the single- and first-ply twist are in the same direction (up-twist), and the second-ply twist is in the opposite direction (down-twist). Makes a hard, inelastic (inextensible) construction, suited for rug and tapestry warps, harness cords, and the like. *See also* Cable.

Heck. Fixed or movable guide for distribution of yarns, as in flyer pegs, hooks, or the sliding guide found on some flyers. A weaving term, with much the same meaning. A yarn guide.

Hemp. True hemp—*Cannabis sativa*—is a soft bast fiber. Similar to flax, except coarser and longer. Has great strength, much used in times past for clothes, sacking, sailcloth, rope, cord, twine. Great political stupidity, great public cupidity surround this plant. Not legal to raise it, although the strain cultivated for fiber does not contain enough of the psychoactive chemical to produce results for which other strains are noted.

Hesp. Ancient Scottish yarn-counting system. Not known if fixed-weight or fixed-length system. Also called *hasp*. Appears to be on the order of 3,600 yards in length. Obligatory entry for all glossaries of this sort.

Hogget. Borderland (Scottish/British) dialect, diminutive of hog; means a young sheep (12–18 months) that has not been shorn. That is, was not shorn as a lamb, and this is the first time out. Considered choice wool for various reasons.

Hops. *Humulus lupulus.* Provides a strong, tough bast fiber. Used in basket work, stem (vine) contains hemp-like fiber bundles. Fiber is stiff, gummy. We raise hops for beer and ales and for herbals.

Hunting the gowk. Fool's errand, Scottish version. Same as April Fool tricks; akin to the Southwesterner's snipe hunt, complete with bag, candles, and mosquitoes. A cup of lost. A slub stretcher.

Inchworm. Descriptive name given to extreme short-draw worsted technique, performed close-in to orifice (2 inches away), by grim folks with hunched-over shoulders and wrists resting on their knees.

Indigo. Classic blue dye, used on cotton, wool, hemp, flax, silk—virtually all of the natural fibers. Indigo was unknown in Europe until early in the fifteenth century, but was widespread throughout the Far East. Indigo is derived from leaves of plants of the genus *Indigofera*, which grow widely throughout tropical areas. Used mainly as a vat dye, indigo may also be applied to wool in a weak solution of oleum (Saxon blue): indigo dissolved in concentrated sulfuric acid. *See also* Woad; Dyer's Knotweed; Oleum; Saxon blue.

Ingrain. Dyed before weaving. Literally, dyed in the yarn or thread before further conversion. Ingrain goods are textiles and fabrics so produced, that is, dyed in the yarn before assembly.

Irish castle wheel. One of the few wheel designs that hails from a specific geographic location—Northern Ireland, principally Ulster. Probably based on the stool-maker's craft, has three legs arranged as a tripod. The drive wheel is at the top, with the wheel center (crank) being about 30 to 40 inches above ground. The flyer-and-bobbin array is supported below the drive wheel. Wheel traditionally used for flax, although any fiber may be spun on it. Stable and effective design. *See also* Saxony wheel; Chair wheel; Frame wheel.

Irish tension. Otherwise known as single-drive, bobbin-lead. Also called *German tension*, as it is the default system on many German/Bavarian wheels. The term *Irish tension* was first put forth by Richard Ashford, and was quoted by Anne Field in *The Ashford Book of Spinning*. Since then, Richard has discarded the phrase as he feels it causes confusion.

Irish castle wheel.

Jack. Lifting device. Thing used to raise car when changing tires. In weaving, it means a lever that transmits movement from treadle to harness frame, via lamms. Also a type of loom. In spinning wheels, refers to an intermediate lever (bell crank) sometimes used in complex treadle-and-crank arrangements. A lifting lever, most often with a 1-to-1 mechanical advantage.

Jargon. Specialized vocabulary; idioms of a particular trade, craft, or methodology. A dialect, unintelligible or incoherent to those not familiar with usage. The reason for glossaries. Authentic textile gibberish.

Jason and the Argonauts. According to legend, Jason was rightful heir to the kingdom of Iolcos, in Thessaly. His father's half-brother, Pelias, took over the kingdom. According to an oracle, a one-sandaled man would avenge Jason and take back the kingdom. Of course, Jason (clueless about the oracle) shows up in court one day wearing one shoe. Pelias sends Jason off on a Fleece Quest; Jason forms up the

Argonauts; they pirate around, eventually stealing the Golden Fleece from Aeetes, King-Priest of Colchis. *See also* Colchis; Golden Fleece.

Jaspé. More of a weave-effect than a yarn, producing faint stripes. A misnomer for grandrelle yarns. A plied yarn, with elements (strands) of the same grist and hue, but with slight differences of intensity, for example, pale blue and light blue, or deep rose-red and maroon red.

Jerk-and-curse. Standard plying method for beginner, or for professional know-it-all. Method consists of having supply yarns set up at a distance; plyer then jerks quantity forward, waits while ply-twist mounts, then runs finished plied make into wheel. Cycle repeats, except after first make (and ensuing tangle), cursing becomes component of performance. Very commonly done at affairs designed to illustrate joys of handspinning.

Join. Handspinner's splice between an unspun mass of fiber and a working yarn. Two things about joins: first, make as few as you can, and second, always draft them. Hard to believe, but good joins will happen, from time to time, in spite of all the things we do.

Jute. *Corchorus olitorius, C. capsularis.* A soft bast fiber. Weak, rough, rots quickly when damp. Not worth a handspinner's time. Burlap is made out of jute. Sometimes called *gunny*, as in gunnysack.

Kapok. *Ceiba pentandra.* Fiber comes from silky hairs on the fruits of this tree. Has staple length up to 1¼ inches, but is difficult if not impossible to spin and makes a pretty poor yarn anyway. Extremely light, buoyant. Used to stuff life jackets, as it does not wet-out or mat down. Hard to come by.

Kemp. Opaque, non-wool-like fibers included with wool. All wool contains kemp, to a greater or lesser degree. Kemp isn't hair. Kemp is coarse, inelastic, and won't take dye well, if at all. Not wanted or needed.

Kniddy-knoddy *see* Niddy-noddy.

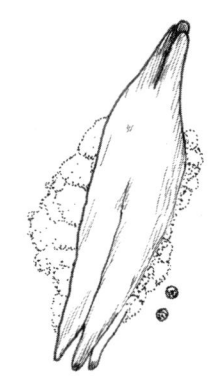

Jute.

Kapok.

Knit. Forming fabric by looping strands together, through the use of special pins or needles. Basic knitting is composed of stitches in rows; the stitches are slip loops, each looped through its neighbor and secured by the next row of stitches. Basic knitting is done with a continuous strand. Knits are characterized by their extreme elasticity.

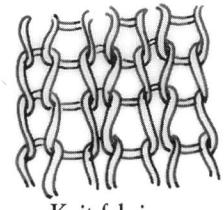

Knit fabric.

Knot. A fastening together of two or more ends of cord, rope, string, and so on by intertwining one or more of the ends in some orderly manner. A true knot is reducible—that is, it may be untied. Knots are also classed according to their usage, as binding knots, fastening knots, reefing knots, slip knots, adjustable knots. . . . *Knot* also means to tie an indicator or lease loop across a skein during winding, to show increments of length. The knot used to join drive-bands is the fisherman's bend.

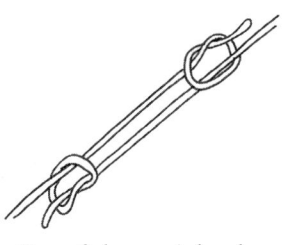

Knot: fisherman's bend.

Lant. Lant refers to old or stale urine, as opposed to fresh urine. Lant was a mainstay of the dyers and fullers crafts, being a source of a mild alkali (ammonia) solution, much used for scouring and several versions of vat dye application. The urea compounds in the urine break down into ammonia and carbon dioxide; the ammonia goes into solution as a weak ammonium hydroxide. Urine from certain people was highly prized; with red-headed pre-pubescent boys being an especial favorite. *See also* Urine; Vat dyes; Indigo; Fermentation.

Lantern swift. Simple, large framework, in shape an upright, truncated, four-sided cone, perhaps 2+ yards around at the base and less than 1½ yards around at the top, mounted on a robust base so that it rotates freely. A skein is dropped over the top and seeks its own level on the cone. It is then unwound in side-delivery fashion. Much used in working studio situations.

Laps. Another name for *card web*; intermediate form of batt. General usage means short, broken pieces of thick sliver, often packed and sold as laps. A carding-machine product, pretty much reserved for wool and hair-like fibers.

Lazy kate. Device for holding bobbins during wind-off of yarn. Most lazy kates consist of two uprights and several transverse

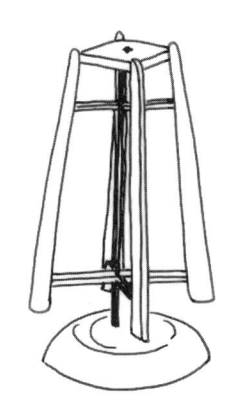

Lantern swift.

Lazy kate.

pins, mounted on some sort of base. The pins parallel the ground. Most lazy kates are unsuited for real use, including as bobbin storage.

Lea. A fixed-weight system of yarn measure, used for linen and other fibers. A lea equals one 300-yard hank (skein) of yarn, weighing one pound. In a 5-lea linen yarn, five 300-yard skeins weigh a total of 1 pound, for a grist of 1,500 YPP.

Leaf fiber. The largest category of vegetable fibers. A partial listing: abaca, mescat, zapupe, pineapple, sisal, infuscata, henequen, yucca—not many are attractive to the handspinner. Leaf fiber (also hard fiber) is mostly for rope, cordage, straps, bags, wrappers, matting, rug backing, and similar uses. Fiber is stripped or extracted from leaf stalks or leaf stems (not plant stems). Pineapple fiber has been used for remarkably fine work, but few of the others are used in the garment sense.

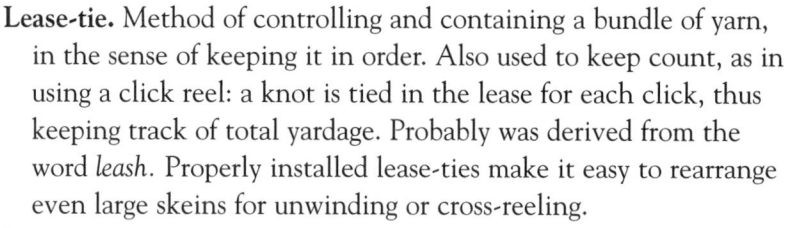

Lease-tie. Method of controlling and containing a bundle of yarn, in the sense of keeping it in order. Also used to keep count, as in using a click reel: a knot is tied in the lease for each click, thus keeping track of total yardage. Probably was derived from the word *leash*. Properly installed lease-ties make it easy to rearrange even large skeins for unwinding or cross-reeling.

Lease-tie.

Level. As an adjective, even, uniform. In a level dye job, the color is evenly taken up by the fiber, with no pale or dark spots. As a verb, spread evenly, as when transferring a skein or bobbin to a storage spool. Originally a dyeworker's term, but so useful that we all use it now. Really, this is on the level.

Level-wind. Name for a self-regulating heck, especially when fitted to the flyer-and-bobbin array of a spinning wheel. In many cases, the advantages are more imagined than real; they become practical when large amounts of plying are being done. More of a conversation piece for the occasional spinner. Leonardo da Vinci had a version of a level-wind for plying back in the 16th century.

Line flax. Fiber of *Linum usitatissimum* after it comes

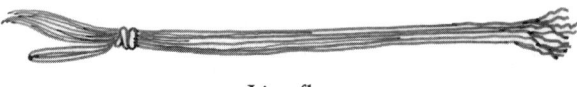

Line flax.

from the hand of the hackler. Long, parallel arrangement of fibers representing the flax worker's hand-full amount. A bundle of hackled flax. Further broken into smaller bundles called *stricks*. Current use of the term *line* indicates spinning is being done from full-length fibers as opposed to tow or broken fibers.

Lint. Trade name for cotton fiber as removed from the seed. Short, unspinnable cotton called *linters* is used in manufacture of explosives and man-made fibers.

Liquor. In textiles, liquor refers to water mixed with various active assists and other ingredients. Plain water is not liquor, yet.

Llama. *Lama glama.* The llama is the "flagship" of the American camelid family. It is the chief beast of burden in the Andes, and has been so used for perhaps thirty centuries. The llama and its close relative, the alpaca, yield similar fibers. The alpaca is kept mostly for its lustrous fleece, while the llama is also very much a pack animal. Both have been introduced to the continental U. S. *See also* Alpaca; Vicuña.

Loading. Addition of adulterants: sand in your fleece, an old transmission in the middle of the wool sack, dampened cotton, and so on. When done to silk, it is called dynamiting; tin and iron salts are used. By law, silk may contain up to 15 percent by weight of dyestuff and still be called pure silk. How nice for the silk merchant. For every 10 pounds of silk you buy, you could legally be getting 1½ pounds of metal salts. In the old days, 1 pound of silk could weigh 4 pounds after being dyed.

Llama.

Lock. Wool term: a coherent tuft or group of fibers, a natural division of fiber in the fleece. A bundle of fiber, sheared from a pelt or removed from a fleece. A form used when flicking and rough combing. Also for scouring experiments, and used by locker-hookers. A type of edging is made from locks of wool, using a technique known as *railroad sinnet*.

Long draw. The long draw is a woolen-system spinning technique. The term is attributed to Ted Carson; the technique is probably the most used for woolen spinning, that is, drafting-against-twist. The technique allows long makes, thereby enabling greater control and uniformity of twist in the yarn. The method works with all fibers, but not all fiber forms—for example, the long draw is not practical with flax strick. Yarns spun using the long draw are classed as woolen spun, or possibly semi-worsted. *See also* Woolen yarn; Worsted yarn.

Long draw.

Lye. Sodium hydroxide or potassium hydroxide. Industry sometimes uses potassium hydroxide for best results in mercerization, but more often uses sodium hydroxide because it works pretty well and is cheaper than potassium hydroxide. Lye is mainly used by the spinner in soap making. Sodium results in hard soap, potassium makes soft soap. Another common name for the two compounds is caustic soda. Handle lye with extreme care and caution. Small quantities may also be used (carefully) to adjust the PH of various liquors and dye vats (like indigo). *See also* Soda; Caustic; Soap.

Machine-combing. Machine-combing is the preparation of fibers for spinning on the worsted system, that is, drafting-without-twist. Basically, there are four types of machine comb: the nip motion (Lister); the square motion (Holden); the circular comb (Noble); and the rectilinear (Heilman or French) comb. Of the four, the Noble comb is the most comprehensive used in worsted service, followed by the Heilman or French comb. Space does not allow a description of their operation, but it is quite different from the motions of hand wool combing. *See also* Wool combing; Carding.

Madder. The herb *Rubia tinctorum*, whose roots are the source of one of the main red palettes of the natural dye world. Also the dye. Madder has been in use for at least 5,000 years. The plant is easily grown in the kitchen garden. Madder produces excellent reds and red-browns on wool, but aside from its use in dyeing military uniforms such as the British Redcoats, it was best known for its part in the famous Turkey Red hues produced on cottons. It was much used in calico printing. *See also* Alizarin; Adjective Dyes.

Madder.

Maidens. Traditional name of upright posts holding flyer-shaft bearing supports; from the German *madchen*. The French call them *puppets* or *dolls*. In conventional spinning wheels, the flyer-and-bobbin array or the spindle assembly is mounted through bearings, which in turn are mounted on or in maidens. Maidens and their support arrangement are collectively styled the *mother-of-all*. For driven-spindle arrangements such as the great wheel, the term *spindle supports* is more often used.

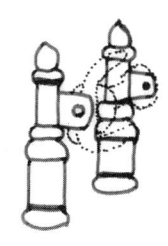

Maidens.

Make. Spinning term that describes length of yarn produced or manipulated at each complete cycle of an operation—i.e., spinning, twisting, or plying. Typical worsted make is about 1–2 inches; woolen make (treadled wheel) is 20–30 inches; charkha make (cotton) is 10–40 inches; great wheel make is 30–60 inches. In plying, makes may be 12–18 inches (jerk-and-curse); 18–30 inches (hand-over-hand); or continuous (tromp-and-hope).

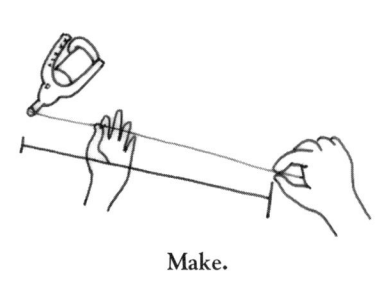

Make.

Mangle. Press rollers, as in old-fashioned wringer washing machine. The wringer is a mangle. Laundry press mangles may be obtained as a discrete item, not part or accessory to anything. When used heated, useful for pressing woolen goods.

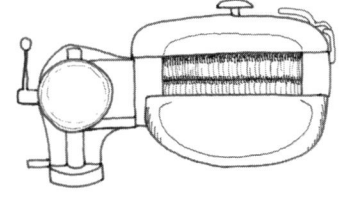

Mangle.

Marled yarn. Multicolor single produced by drafting and spinning two differently colored rovings as a single unit. Easily done by winding two rovings concurrently to a storage or jack spool, then combining the two ends and drafting and twisting as one in the spinning process. By general usage, a yarn spun of mixed colors.

Mawata. Japanese term: describes silk cocoons that have been opened out into sheets or small cloths, thin and felt-like. Mawata have considerable coherence; they may be pulled, with significant effort, into a sliver. Much imagination has been at work in the methods of using up mawata. The flakes or caps have been used as batting for clothing insulation. Will choke up your drum carder like you would not believe.

Mechanical advantage. The theoretical advantage gained by having driving and driven elements of different diameters, as in a spinning

The Alden Amos Big Book of Handspinning 443

wheel. Very simply stated, the greater the difference between diameters, the greater the mechanical advantage—however, there are practical limits. *See also* Drive ratio.

Mélange. A mixture, a hodgepodge. Denotes a single spun from blended colors and fibers. A formal version of OTF.

Mercerization. A process for cellulosics, named after John Mercer, nineteenth-century English calico printer, in which goods (usually cotton yarn) are entered into cold, strong solutions of lye (potassium hydroxide). In luster mercerization, tension is placed on the yarn by expanding the lye-soaked skein while flushing lye out. The pressure is relaxed when lye is gone. Produces perle cotton. In slack mercerization, the lye is flushed out without stretching.

Metric count system. A fixed-weight system to measure yarn grist. Weight unit is 1 kilo, and count reflects number of meters, expressed as a decimal or whole number. Thus a single skein of 1,000 meters in length, weighing one kilo, has a metric count of 1. A skein weighing one kilo and containing 2,000 meters has a metric count of 2; a skein with 3,500 meters, 3.5 metric count, and so on. It is nothing more than the grist in thousands of meters per kilo, expressed as a whole number or a decimal equivalent.

Micron count system. A grading system based on the average fiber diameter, specifically the diameter in microns (a micron equals a millionth of a meter, about .000039 inch). The micron grades as they relate to the blood grades are: Fine = 22.8 microns, Half-blood = 24.9 microns, Three-eighths-blood = 29.12 microns, Quarter-blood = 31.43 microns, Low quarter-blood = 33.05 microns, and Common/Braid = 36.71 microns. These are market wools, and not breed specific.

Miner's head. A spindle accelerating device, ascribed to Amos Miner circa 1803; in use well into the twentieth century. Not rare, as was widely copied (no patent). Miner's head consist of a jackshaft and whorl, mounted above the spindle proper, the entire assembly mounted on its own mother-of-all, ready

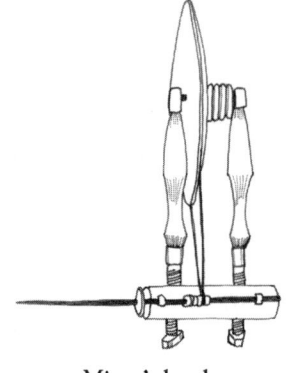

Miner's head.

to be plugged into the customer's wheel. Final drive ratios of about 8-to-1 are common; primary drive ratio depends on wheel diameter, with 30-to-1 typical, giving 240-to-1 overall. *See also* Accelerated.

Mohair. Specialty hair fiber from *Capra hircus hircus angora*, the Angora goat. There is much controversy regarding the systematics of the genus. Finest grade is kid mohair, average diameter less than 30 microns (the equivalent of a 56's wool); fiber has great luster, takes dyes well and brilliantly. Mohair is well suited to use in upholstery fabrics. As a garment fiber, it is best used as a blend. Mohair makes an almost indestructible rug warp.

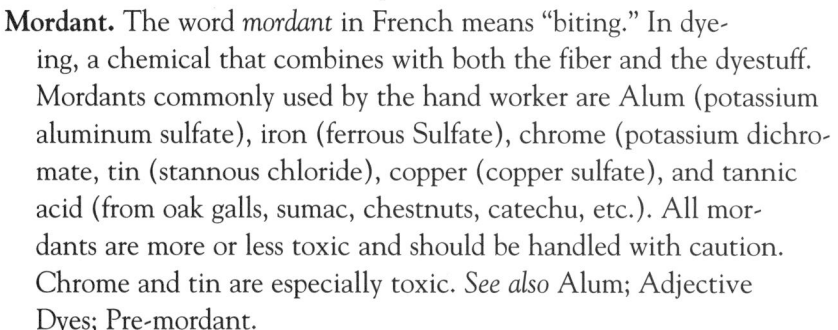

Mohair.

Mordant. The word *mordant* in French means "biting." In dyeing, a chemical that combines with both the fiber and the dyestuff. Mordants commonly used by the hand worker are Alum (potassium aluminum sulfate), iron (ferrous Sulfate), chrome (potassium dichromate, tin (stannous chloride), copper (copper sulfate), and tannic acid (from oak galls, sumac, chestnuts, catechu, etc.). All mordants are more or less toxic and should be handled with caution. Chrome and tin are especially toxic. *See also* Alum; Adjective Dyes; Pre-mordant.

Mother-of-all. The core unit that holds the flyer-and-bobbin array on a flyer wheel, or, by usage, the spindle array on a driven-spindle wheel. In the main, consists of three parts: two maidens and a support bar. In addition, may include the tensioning system.

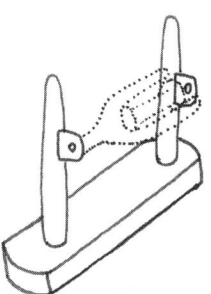

Mother-of-all.

Motor spinner. Spinning device powered by motor. Often a conventional flyer-and-bobbin array powered by a sewing-machine motor. Many variations and brand names. Computer-driven motors of various sorts are being used. The idea is not new. Leonardo da Vinci was known to be working on a motor plyer back in the sixteenth century; single-end motor spinners have been in use since the introduction of the small, domestic electric motor.

Motor spinner.

The Alden Amos Big Book of Handspinning

Mottled. Splotchy. Tortoise-shell effect. In yarn, done by painting or area dyeing either the yarn or the sliver/slubbing from which it is spun. Not precise as polka dots, nor so random as camouflage. Blotches of different tones or shades, more or less related.

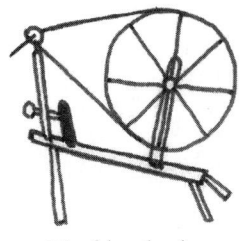

Mt. Mill-worker shorthand for empty: Mt = Empty.

Muckle. Scots for "a lot," as in "a big one." A muckle wheel is a great wheel or wool wheel.

Mungo. Mungo is recovered wool fiber, taken from shredded (garnetted) hard woolen rags, worsted fabrics, and tailors' clippings. Good grade wools but degraded/shortened by the garnetting or shredding operation. Considered less desirable than wool called *shoddy*. Used for filler yarns. *See also* Shoddy; Reworked wool.

Muckle wheel.

Nap. A raised, plush-like surface; fuzz. A downy, soft surface raised from a cloth substructure. Flannel has nap.

Navajo ply. Idiot's delight, twisted. A reversed idiot's delight slip loop is started in a single yarn, followed by another, and another, and another. . . . Twist is introduced, down-twist of the single's spinning direction. More of a stunt than a technique; very impressive when the operation is demonstrated to tourists.

Nep. Old word that means root vegetable. Turnips are neps. In spinning, a tangled knot of broken and disarranged fibers. Knobby little wads of knotted, tangled fiber forming chunks, lumps in yarn.

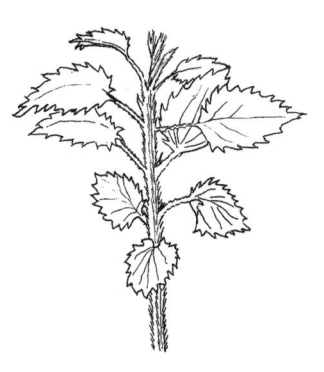

Nettle. *Urtica* spp. Common stinging or great nettle of Northern hemisphere. Used since prehistory as bast fiber. The Scandinavian folk tale of a young maiden making shirts from stinging nettle has a basis in truth. Nettle cloth is similar to coarse hemp and is used for cordage, sailcloth, and paper-making. Fibers are obtained through retting or by boiling and green decortication. The "sting" is removed by an alkali (soda) boil. Ramie (China grass) is a stingless tropical nettle. *See also* Ramie; Bast; Hemp.

Niddy-noddy. Winding device. A skein-winder, in simplest form a bowed stick. Usually composed of three members: a central shaft, or handle, and two arms. Arms are mounted at right angles to and centered upon the central shaft. Arms

Nettle.

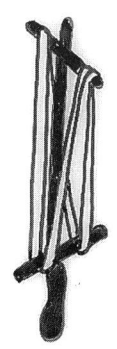

are further rotated 90 degrees with respect to each other. A niddy enables winding of large skeins. Also known as *nid* or *kniddy-knoddy*. Typical skein capacities include 1 yard (36 inches), 1½ yards (54 inches), 2 yards (72 inches), and one meter. Miniature niddies are available.

Nip. Localized pressure between fibers or bundles of fibers; the basic binder in a knot. Nip causes local friction, holding the knot or fiber bundle together. Some knots concentrate nip and will break before they slip; others will slip as long as sufficient pull is placed on the members. Knots tend to break right outside areas of greatest rigidity and nip. Increased twist in a yarn is reflected by increased nip. The more twist, the greater the nip. Also the nip, or pressure point, between two rollers, as in drafting.

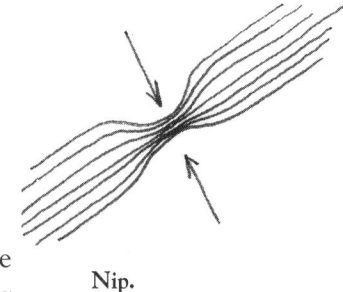

Niddy-noddy.

Nip.

Noils. Short, broken bits of fiber; scattered, short pieces, as in second cuts; the wool equivalent of tow. Most often caused by mechanical means—carding, combing, picking. Too much or too little moisture, the wrong lubricants, or dried, "set" grease (yolk) will increase noilment (the making of noils). Material carded for woolen cloths can tolerate some noils, although that makes spinning a uniform or consistent yarn more difficult. Noils may be in any combed or carded fiber, not just wool.

Noil silk. Type of silk yarn spun from short, broken staple. Sometimes has black flecks, which are dead critter parts. Called raw silk in fashion circles. Basically the silk equivalent of OTF with organic inclusions.

Nosegay. Fleece that has been urine/offal-soaked. Happens at livestock shows, fairs, et cetera, when system is overloaded. Sunday nights can be bad.

Nøstepinne. Short baton used for winding center-pull balls of yarn. Nominal dimensions: 1 inch diameter, between 8 and 10 inches long. Usually made of rare or exotic wood, highly polished. Scandinavian usage. Also called a *ball-stick*.

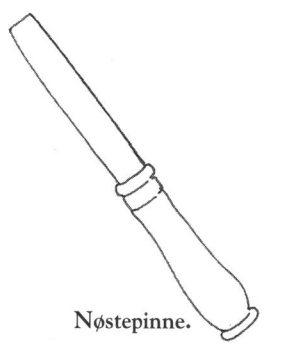

Nøstepinne.

Novelty yarn. Imperfectly spun or constructed yarn. Yarn of a class designed to have unusual appearance or character. Class of yarns formerly known as Fancy Twist Threads. Also, yarn spun from strange and novel fibers, such as aluminum shavings, steel wool, cat hair, and the like, where the chief merit of the yarn involves the odd stuff it was spun from. Dryer lint falls into this category. *See also* OTF; Cat; Dog.

Oleum. A woolen dyestuff prepared by dissolving indigo in concentrated sulfuric acid. The resultant liquid is then diluted with water and the goods entered into the dye bath, which is brought to a boil. The goods are then removed and scoured/fulled/dried in the normal manner. By the way, *oleum,* Latin for "oil," is the archaic term for a heavy oily strongly corrosive solution of sulfur trioxide in anhydrous sulfuric acid. *See also* Saxon Blue.

On-the-twist. Crooked. British euphemism. Not to be trusted. A bit warped or wingy. Merino top, from the back of a van, at $1 a pound. Too good to be true. Phony. Not right. You get the idea.

On weight of goods. Describing the weight of a substance being applied to a quantity of fiber, yarn, or textile as a percentage of the total weight (OWOG). Thus, a 1 percent add-on of dye to 100 pounds of wool is equal to 1 pound of dye. "½ percent Xanthu Crimson #2 (a rather common form of commercial dye) OWOG" means ½ pound of dye to each 100 pounds of dry fiber.

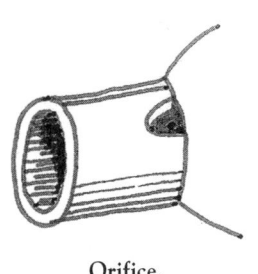

Orifice. A hole. In handspinning, it is the opening in the spinner's end of the flyer shaft, called the barrel. Freshly spun yarn enters the flyer barrel through the orifice. The barrel conducts the yarn through the front flyer bearing; yarn leaves the barrel through one of the eyes and is routed over the heck (flyer arms and hooks).

Orifice.

OTF. The term is short for "off the floor" and it denotes a project composed of materials at hand, with no selection criteria other than ready availability and low (no) cost.

Overply. Overplying is a technique often used to produce a lofty, soft yarn. Appropriate singles of given twist amounts are plied down-twist to a point well beyond twist-stability. The yarn is then steamed or otherwise set or stabilized. The result is a plump, lofty yarn with a high ply-twist component. The yarn should be classed as a novelty construction. *See also* Twist-active; Balanced yarn; Bulked yarn.

Overtwist. No such animal. Well, if you have to cram the yarn through the orifice with a pencil, you might have "excessive" twist. Undertwist is another matter. When there is not enough twist to allow the yarn to survive the next step, it is undertwisted.

Pepper trash. Bits of vegetable matter (leaf, stem flakes, bits) that remain in ginned cotton: not a good thing. Yarn spun from cotton with pepper trash will be scratchy, lumpy, rough. A commercial preparation that is contaminated with pepper trash is no bargain.

Period yarn. Effect or novelty yarn of such amazing and unusual color or construction, or of such unique and artistic conception, that when your friends see it they will just drop dead . . . period. Or scream, turn green, faint, whatever. Gauche, lurid stuff.

pH. pH is the term that describes the degree of acidity or alkalinity of a substance or solution. Neutral pH is given the value of 7.0; anything less than 7.0 is considered acidic, anything more than 7.0 is considered alkaline. Thus a pH of 5.5 is acidic; a pH of 9.5 is alkaline. The system is actually based on the ratio of hydrogen cations (+) to hydroxide anions (-). An increase in hydrogen cations results in a lower pH value, i.e. more acidic. An increase in hydroxide anions makes the solution more alkaline, with a higher pH value. *See also* Acid; Alkali.

Phase. Together, as "in phase"; separate parts moving together, where they belong. In spinning, *in phase* means to rotate at the same speed, as in flyer and bobbin. Out of phase means to be no longer operating or turning at the same speed, such as when winding-on. In a flyer-and-bobbin system, winding-on cannot take place unless the elements are "out of phase." In phase = same speed: Out of phase = different speeds.

Picardy flyer. Version of single-drive, flyer-lead flyer-and-bobbin array, in which both flyer-shaft supports are located at the rear of the flyer assembly. The main portion of the flyer, including the bobbin, is suspended cantilever-fashion. There is no bearing surface on the flyer barrel. System is so-called due

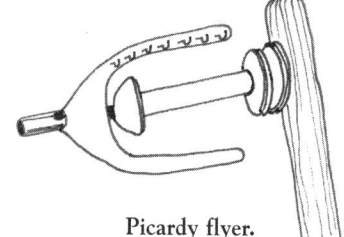

Picardy flyer.

to its apparent place of origin, the Picardy region of northern France (formerly Flanders). System was originally used for fine threads; has been adapted into all sorts of novel forms.

Pick. To rudely and roughly disassemble a fiber mass into its component parts. Preparatory step, precedes scouring, carding. There are mechanical aids in this task, known as *pickers* (see next entry). In weaving, a *pick* is the individual shot or passage of weft (filling) across the warp threads, through an appropriate shed, or opening.

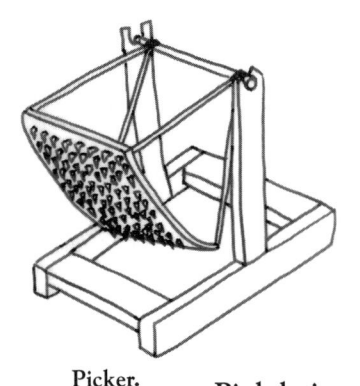

Picker. A device used to pick, or roughly open, locks of wool or other fiber. Pickers are of several types: hands (fingers); rakes or simple combs; comb blocks or heckles; swing pickers; sled pickers; and drum or roll pickers. Among hand workers, the swing picker is popular and several forms are in use. Commercial operations may use a device known as a *Fearnaught Willy*, a large, powerful, rotary device. Lacking all else, hands and fingers are probably the most often used form of picker. Fleece wool benefits from being picked prior to being carded.

Picker.

Pink lotion. Oil of Oompha. Secret scouring lotion passed down from the pharaohs of old. One teaspoonful in a pint of water will scour 10 pounds of wool with no effort on your part whatsoever. Further, makes you thrifty, rich, knowledgeable, beautiful, good at playing the Spanish guitar, able to make key lime pie, to barbecue without perspiring, and other swell things.

Pirn pin. Rod or pin, fitted with handle, used to hold a bobbin or spool for cross-winding purposes. A pirn pin may be improvised from a knitting needle. Pins may be double length, to accommodate two spools or bobbins on the same shaft. Spools can be set to contrarotate, thus reducing or eliminating backlash.

Pitman. On a spinning wheel, the connecting rod or rods found between the crankshaft and the treadle structure. British term, the same as our *footman*. One source states that the connecting rod is named for a British engineer. Also seen as *pittman* and *pitman rod*. In the technical sense, a connecting rod both pushes and pulls; many older and contemporary spinning wheels use pull rods that can only pull, not push. The extreme of this is a flexible cord. *See also* Footman.

Pirn pin.

Plying. Twisting together two or more single yarns or strands in a single operation. Synonymous with folding, except that plying twist direction is always assumed to be down-twist of the twist incumbent in single yarns or strands and the direction of folding twist is not assumed. Plying implies twist-stability in the plied yarn; folding (doubling, same thing) does not. Plying may be taken to be a finishing process in yarn construction; folding is an intermediate step. *See also* Throwing; Doubling; Folding.

Point of contact. Point of contact is one of many forms of long draw drafting and spinning; the procedure is attributed to Paula Simmons. *See also* Long draw; Push-pull.

Practical. Practical, for the purpose of this work, means something that is workable without undue effort, special procedures, additional movements, et cetera. In other words, if the item works "as advertised," with no ifs, ands, or buts, it is practical. A drive ratio of 12-to-1, for a traditional Ashford, is practical; a drive ratio of 30-to-1, applied to the same wheel, is not. We are not picking on Ashfords—just establishing a familiar example. *See also* Effective.

Pre-mordant. Mordants applied to fibers before dyeing as opposed to along with the dyestuff. The goods are first soaked/simmered in a mordant bath, "dyeing" the fiber with the mordant, then entered into the dye pot proper. *See also* Mordant; Adjective dyes.

Pulled wool. Wool removed from dead sheep. Generally, wool that has been removed from pelts of animals slaughtered by meat industries. Other names for the product: skin wool, slipe wool, tanner's wool, glover's wool, and fell wool. Dealers in the product are called fellmongers. Pulled wool has been used for centuries in textiles that are heavily fulled: Hudson's Bay "point" blankets are just one item.

Puni. A tightly-rolled cotton "rolag." A study on their own, traditionally the making of punis has been a special craft. Bowed or carded cotton is delivered to the puni-maker, who arranges a thick sheet of cotton lint and then rolls and compacts it on a core pin or wire. Finished items are slipped off, arranged in bundles, wrapped in paper. A typical, commercially made (India) puni is perhaps 5 inches in length, $3/8$ inch in diameter. U.S. spinners make their own.

Puni.

Push-pull. Also known as the *orifice crawl*. Approved method of worsted spinning, or drafting-without-twist. The spinner's hands are quite close to the orifice; twist is never allowed to enter the drafting zone, which is always shorter than the average staple length. The drafting zone length is also the make; thus, the makes are short and frequent. Production rates are rather limited—several hundred yards per hour would be a sterling performance. Unfortunately, about the only way to spin a true worsted yarn. *See also* Worsted yarn; Woolen yarn.

Qiviut. A down fiber, the undercoat of the musk ox (Bovidae, *Ovibos moschatus*). Like first-class camel down, although seems slippery. Rare, costly. Currently supplies are controlled and the fiber demands premium prices. Similar to cashmere. Browns, gray-browns. Also known and marketed under the name Qiviuq. Control situation seems to have relaxed since we started this project; the stuff's being grown commercially outside of the original reintroduced herds.

Qiviut.

Quill. Originally a section of goose, duck, or chicken feather, used as a core for winding yarn for weaving shuttles and also for plying from driven spindles. Nowadays plastic soda straws serve, but if you keep poultry, swear off the plastic and use the quills. English usage may spell it *queels*. Fit a quill over your spindle blade, and you can remove the loaded quill for direct use in a shuttle. No rewinding required—except that it is better to re-wind. Always.

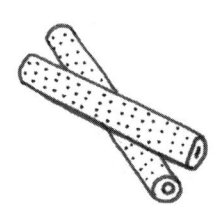

Quill.

Rainbow batt. Carded batt formed of layers of alternating colors, not always spaced evenly across the web or in linear fashion. Several schemes are possible. A batt of variegated colors, distributed in either graduated (gamp) manner or as random masses. Introduction of rainbow batts, and term *rainbow batt* itself, must be credited to the efforts of Susan Druding, possibly the greatest of the Great Ladies of Modern Fiberdom. She is also the life force behind

Rainbow batt.

Straw Into Gold and Crystal Palace Yarns, based in Berkeley, California.

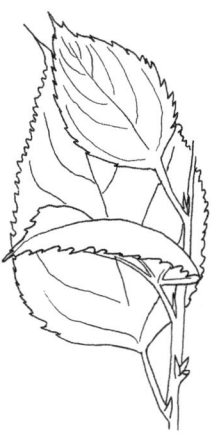

Ramie. *Boehmeria nivea.* A bast fiber, from a tropical nettle. Also called China grass. Grows in semitropics. Hard to separate stem material from valuable fiber. Decortication is a mechanical process and labor-intensive. Fiber is very strong, white, naturally dirt-shedding, and fine. Rot-resistant, used in tropical suitings, shirts, napkins, table coverings, and fire hoses. Legend has it that the white linen suits worn by Bogart, Laughton, Greenstreet, Saunders, and similar tropical bad dudes were made of ramie, not linen. *See also* Nettle.

Ramie.

Range. An array, such as a complete scouring setup or a dye works. A range may include several card sets, a scouring train, and a dye works as parts. The term most often refers to wet processing, and to dyeing in particular. *See also* Train.

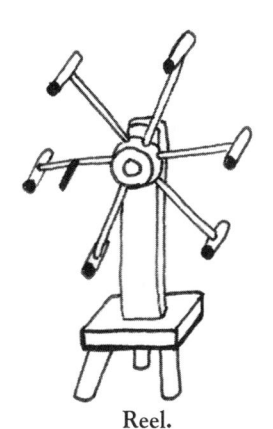

Reel.

Range wool. General usage indicates wool produced under range conditions in the American West and Southwest. Sometimes called Territory wool, if not classed as "Texas" or "California" wools.

Reel. A rice. Framework for winding and unwinding yarn, either into or from skeins. A rice has more of the sense of a *swift*. A reel may be of various sorts, such as clock reel, click reel, blocking reel, and so forth.

Rett. Archaic form of *rot*. Term specifically relates to damp or wet treatment of bundles of flax, for decortication, that is, the separation of fiber from stem material. Most retting today is tank retting: total immersion of fiber plant bundles in artificial ponds (concrete tanks or pools) and careful observation of progress. Process is halted by drying the bundles. Also used for hemp, nettle, and other soft bast fibers. For the craft worker, large plastic wading pools serve well as retting ponds.

Reworked wool. Recycled wool fiber. Taken from finished cloth, as in rags; tailor cuttings and scraps; knit goods; overruns on yarns; and card, combing, and processing waste. In many ways, the reworking applies to all fibers, not just wool. In some cases, the "recycling" has been carried to extremes—consider some of the silk "noil" blends. The stuff is little more that packaged floor sweepings.

Rigidity. Resistance to twisting shown by a bundle of fibers, as in spinning yarn. The thicker the yarn and the higher the twist, the greater the rigidity. Anyone who has spun hair into thick yarns has firsthand experience with it. Rigidity is a theoretical consideration for most handspinners; for a mill twisting several thousand ends at a time, it is a real item on the power consumption agenda.

Ripple. A device (comb or spike block) used to rake out and remove seed pods from dry, mature flax plants. An 8-inch–long bar with 6 nails, say 4 inches long, driven through. A small metal garden rake will do the job.

Ripple.

Rock. In English, *rock* means what stones are made of. Also, to gently sway to and fro, or to shake to a strong, regular beat, as in rock music. Means *distaff* in German—*die Rock*. Another word for distaff is *die Kunkel*. *Rock* also means rock. It does not mean *spindle*: in German a spindle is *die Spindel*.

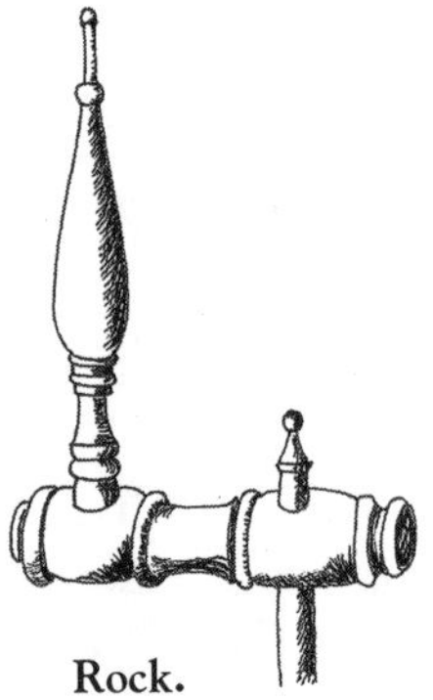

Rock.

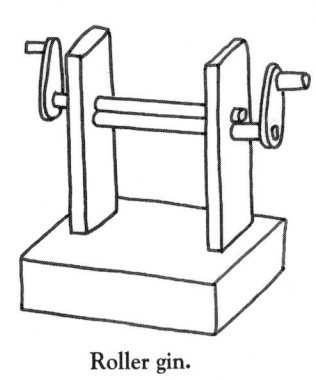

Roller gin. Roller-style cotton gin: *gin* is short for *engine*. Designed for removing lint from slick-seeded cotton. Action is the same as in the slab-and-pin method—seed cotton is laid on a flat slab, then tufts of the lint are pinched between the slab and a pin, or small roller. The seeds are "squeezed" away from the lint. A gin uses double rollers to do the same thing. Many small, hand-operated varieties in India, U.S., Japan, and similar places.

Roller gin.

Rooing. Plucking. Hold the critter down and rip the fuzz off by brute force. People who practice this say it doesn't hurt. Care to try it on a bobcat?

Rope. Thick, strong, cord-like structure: at least 3 strands, each strand having 2 or more threads; strands are formed up-twist, and the rope is laid down-twist of the strands. Rope cannot be made through normal yarn plying techniques. Also made through braiding and plaiting, although technically not rope at that point. Ropes may be made of a vast array of materials: wire, rags, plastic strips, straw, and so on. *See also* Cord.

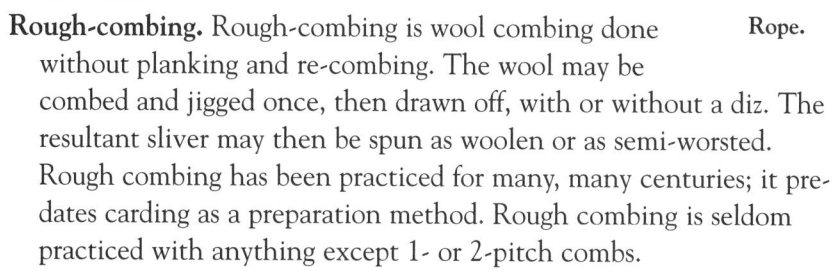

Rope.

Rough-combing. Rough-combing is wool combing done without planking and re-combing. The wool may be combed and jigged once, then drawn off, with or without a diz. The resultant sliver may then be spun as woolen or as semi-worsted. Rough combing has been practiced for many, many centuries; it pre-dates carding as a preparation method. Rough combing is seldom practiced with anything except 1- or 2-pitch combs.

Rounding. Manipulating a skein of yarn to equalize tensions; pulling a skein around a suitable roller, while placing considerable tension on the skein. Purpose of rounding is to make sure that each loop in the skein is the same length as the rest. Necessary for rapid and efficient yarn handling.

Roving. Rovings are slivers that have been drawn, redrawn, and run through a *rover,* or a sort of low-draft, low-twist, bulk spinner designed to prepare the fiber for worsted spinning. Common usage by the hand worker has made roving roughly the same as sliver. The form known as pencil roving denotes a slender, miniature sliver, usually the product of a tape condenser or a ring doffer with rubbing aprons. *See also* Sliver; Top.

RPM. Revolutions per minute: measure of rotational speed. In practice is the same as *turns per minute.* If a spindle turns at 2,000 RPM, the turns-per-minute count is the same—2,000 twists or turns per minute.

Run count system. A fixed-weight system for determining woolen yarn grist. Weight unit is 1 pound; count number is number of skeins, each 1,600 yards in length, that it takes to total 1 pound. Thus, a 1's count yarn has a grist of 1,600 YPP; a 2's equals 3,200 YPP; a 3's equals 4,800 YPP; and so forth. More used by weavers than spinners.

S twist. One of the two twist directions possible in spinning. If the twist angle runs in the same direction as the center stroke of the letter S, the yarn is said to be S-twist. Such a yarn is spun with the twisting

S twist.

The Alden Amos Big Book of Handspinning

device (spindle or flyer-and-bobbin) rotating in a counterclockwise direction with reference to the drafting zone and fiber mass. In general, the "default" spinning direction for cotton yarns. *See also* Z twist.

Saint Distaff. Patron Saint of Orderly Fibers of Long Staple. Feast day is day following Twelfth Night (twelfth day after Christmas), or 7 January. Traditional nonsense festival where handspinners went back to work after the Christmas and year-end activities. Any who have further to add, feel free to contact the author. This may be related to "hunting the gowk."

Saponification. Saponification is nothing more than the reaction of organic fats and oils with alkalis, forming soaps. The soaps so formed are more soluble in water than the fats and oils themselves. The soaps formed are also valued for their detergent action. In technical terms, it is the alkaline hydrolysis of an oil or fat, or the neutralization of a fatty acid to form a soap. *See also* Soap.

Saw gin. Saw-bladed cotton gin: *gin* is a contraction of *engine*. Designed for removing lint from hairy-seeded cotton. Was invented by Henry Ogden Holmes, 1787. A form of cotton gin is in use today. Saw-toothed circular blades fit partially through a screen or slotted guard. Seed lays against guard, saw teeth engage and remove lint from seed. A separate brush clears lint from saw teeth, and directs it to hopper. Seeds cannot pass through guard: when cleaned of lint, they are discharged to appropriate container.

Saint Distaff.

Saw gin.

Saxon Blue. Both a color and a dye process used on wool. The color is a deep, rich blue shot with traces of red and red-browns; the process is described above under Oleum. A recipe for Saxon Blue appears on page(s) 374–375. *See also* Oleum.

Saxony wheel. The treadle wheel most people see in their minds when they think about treadle wheels. Three legs; a sloping, plank bench; drive wheel located to the spinner's right-hand side; flyer-and-bobbin to the left. There are many variations—some with split benches, level benches, no benches (!), and so forth. Distinctions become blurred as one approaches the borderlands. The Saxony wheel supposedly began in the Saxony region of Germany, roughly the area between Berlin and Leipzig. *See also* Irish castle wheel; Chair wheel; Frame wheel.

Saxony wheel.

Schappe. Originally, waste silk degummed by natural fermentation or retting process, said to create horrific odors. Now means silk wasted or broken in reeling, throwing, and twisting operations. Also yarns spun from silk, as opposed to reeled, thrown, and so forth. The fiber is not necessarily degummed. Essentially, any commercially carded, combed form of silk for the handspinner. Not flakes or caps.

Scotch tension.

Scotch tension. Same as single-drive, flyer-lead. Refers to the brake-band on the bobbin, used to establish DRS. The flyer is actively driven; the bobbin is pulled around by the newly spun yarn and will remain in phase with the flyer until tension against the yarn is relaxed. At that point, the bobbin attempts to stop or slow down or stall; the flyer continues to rotate, wrapping yarn onto the bobbin. The brake-band is applied to the bobbin, and increases or decreases the stall tendency, dependent upon how tight or slack it is. *See also* Brake-band; Single.

Scour. A thorough cleansing or washing. Vigorous, strong washing of a fiber or a textile.

Scutch. To remove adherent particles, broken stem parts, dried and brittle plant matter. Applies to bast fibers, as a step in fiber extraction and preparation. A scutching blade or scutching sword is used. The material is presented over suitable surface; and through a series of scraping, slicing blows, the boon and shive are removed.

Scutching. The combined scraping and beating of bundles of bast fibers, for the purpose of removing boon, or the woody parts of the retted stems. Hand workers use a scutching post (a notched board), which supports the bundle of fiber, and a

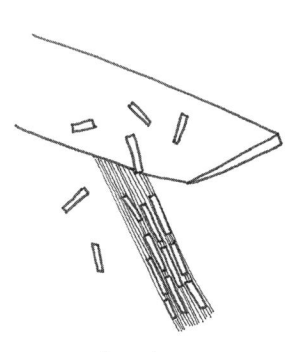

Scutching.

sword. They turn and twist the bundle of fiber while patting and scraping it with the sword. The scutched fiber will then be passed through sets of hackles, going from coarse to fine.

Second-cuts. Short nubs of staple wool, the result of the shearer making a second stroke with the shears or clippers. Undesirable, although will not be intolerable if material will be thoroughly carded. Best to avoid and remove. A fleece loaded with second-cuts can be used for general purposes, but it will not be possible to obtain a strong, lean, and uniform yarn from it. Workable for goods to be heavily fulled. *See also* Nep; Cotty; Break.

Seed fiber. Natural fibers derived from seeds; strictly speaking, seed-covering fibers. Cotton and kapok are seed fibers.

Sett. Weaving term; several meanings. First, the number of ends (individual strands) of warp, per inch, across a cloth width. Second, the number of spaces (open slots) per inch across the width of a reed. Third, the color progression and sequence of a tartan check or plaid across the width of the cloth (list-to-list).

Shaft. Mechanical term. A straight bar or rod of material. In a wheel, it denotes the flyer shaft or the crank shaft. For a loom, it is the word we should use whenever we say *harness*, as in "that is a nice 4-harness loom," which is better as "that is a nice 4-shaft loom."

Shearling. A pelt from a recently sheared sheep. Also applies to pulled wool from such sheep.

Shive. Also known as *boon*, this refers to the woody bits of retted stem material still adhering to bast fibers. The purpose of the scutching process is to remove them, preparing the fibers for hackles. *See also* Scutching.

Shoddy. Wool fibers recovered from "soft" woolen fabrics and textiles, such as blanket clippings, knit goods, and the like. A better (longer) grade of wool than mungo. In a general sense, all reworked wool used in woolen cloth manufacture. *See also* Mungo.

Single. One of something. In yarn, a single strand of twisted fibers. There is no such a thing as a single-ply yarn. For spinning wheels, as in *single-drive*, means that there is one drive-band, not folded, driving one element of a flyer-and-bobbin array.

Sinkage. Operational loss. A raw fleece that weighs 6 pounds on the

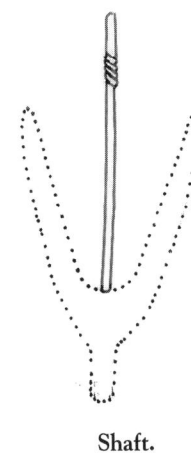

Shaft.

bench may result in 4 pounds of clean yarn and 3 pounds, 12 ounces of finished cloth. The loss in weight of goods overall is called *sinkage*, and includes scouring losses, dirt, waste, grease, weaving loss, fulling loss, and so forth.

Sisal. *Agave sisalana*. Hard-leaf fiber. Used for "native" hats, mats, cord, rope, rough bagging, et cetera. Takes dyes well. There are many agave species, not all of which yield usable fibers. *See also* Century plant.

Sizing. Substance applied to yarns, threads, or cloth to stiffen, strengthen, or otherwise enhance them. Typical sizings for protein fiber are glue or gelatine based; for cellulosics, starch and gum based. In spinning, sizing is applied by spinner as service for subsequent operators: i.e. the weaver or rope-maker. Sizing offers protection against manufacturing hazards, such as fraying or fuzzing of warp ends. Sizing applied to a warp that is already on the loom is called a dressing.

Sisal.

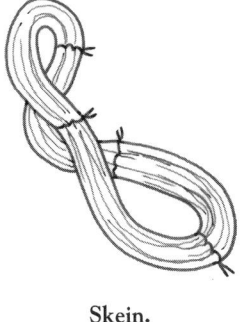

Skein. Similar to *hank*. Basic secondary package, consisting of large-circumference loops of yarn wound around a frame or support, as a skeiner or reel. Skeins are durable packages when properly constructed; they lend themselves to wet processing and handling, and can be made and converted with a minimum of equipment. Skeins are of various diameters, with 1½-yard or 2-yard skeins being most convenient. Also an archaic, rural term for a flock of wild geese or ducks, especially in flight.

Skein.

Skirder. Support frame used by rope-makers and yarn-plyers. Keeps strands and yarns from dragging in the dirt during formative stages and during working. Consists of a cross-arm fitted with heck pegs or pins, supported on a stand and base. A handheld skirder is simply a bar or length of wood, fitted with a series of pickets or pegs. Skirders are arranged along line of work at reasonable intervals: perhaps every 5 yards for rope work, every 3 feet for plying.

Skirt. To remove stained and dirty edges (belly, britch portions) of a

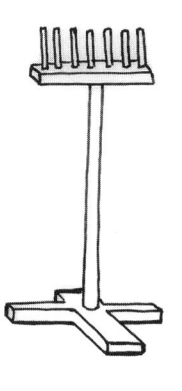

Skirder.

freshly sheared whole fleece, generally in the shearing shed or on the sorter's table. Practice is supposed to have originated in Australia, for what it is worth.

Sleazy. Just what it sounds like. Flimsy, thin, cheap in all senses of the word. Poor work, from lesser materials, pretending to have merit.

Sley. A weaving term, but applies in the technical sense to threading the yarn through the flyer hecks (hooks, usually) and orifice or equivalent "pigtail." In weaving, means to thread the reed and heddles according to a plan. The instrument used is called a *sley hook*.

Slick-seeded. Cotton seed from varieties with lint loosely attached to the seed. Sea Island, Egyptian, pima, many browns are slick-seeded, and slick-seeded cottons don't require the use of a saw gin to separate fibers from seeds. Roller gins work very well, as do simple arrangements such as pin-and-slab.

Sliver. A fiber form; untwisted "ribbon" or rope-like form of prepared fiber. *Card sliver* is made up of web output of a carding machine, condensed by slightly drafting through a tube or orifice, and winding the resultant untwisted rope up in a sort of ball, or *bump*. Slivers may be of any fiber. *See also* Roving; Top.

Sliver.

Soap. Metallic salt of a fatty acid. Soaps are of two types: synthetic and natural. Natural soap is produced by action of an alkali on fats or oils. If the alkali is sodium hydroxide, the result is "hard soap." If it is potassium hydroxide, the result is "soft soap." Soaps are detergents, although not all detergents are soaps. The best soap you can buy is one you make. Natural soaps are made with organic fats and oils. Natural soap doesn't work well in hard water: if the water is hard enough and acidic enough, it won't work at all.

Soda. Without further qualifiers, it is strongly alkaline washing soda, or sodium carbonate, that is meant. Caustic soda is sodium or potassium hydroxide, also strongly alkaline. Baking soda, sodium bicarbonate, is only weakly alkaline. Sodium hydroxide is used by the spinner only for making soap, slack-mercerizing yarns or woven goods, and removing paint. *See also* Assists; Adjuvants; Lye.

Sour. Rinse goods in weakly acidic solution to neutralize excess alkali or caustic left over from scouring or other processes. Some handspinners swear by an acid rinse after scouring wool; others swear at it. Caution: do not enter woolen goods into a sour rinse unless *all* soap has been removed. Acid and soap react to form an insoluble, sticky goo that will not rinse/wash off without great difficulty. *See also* Sweeten.

Spinning counts. System of grading relative fineness of fleece. Sometimes mistaken for Bradford count system. It uses Bradford skein or hank of 560 yards. The count number is the estimated number of 560-yard skeins that could be spun from 1 pound of wool. The finer the wool, the greater the number of possible skeins. Merino is rated from 60's on up; this means that the wool is fine enough to allow spinning 60+ of the 560-yard skeins per pound. That's a grist of 33,600 YPP. Compare to *Cotton count system*, which does not work quite the same way.

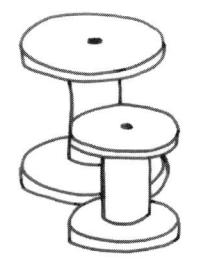

Spool. Secondary yarn package. The same as *bobbin*. *Spool* implies storage, whereas *bobbin* denotes production, as in spinning. Also a verb, meaning *to wind*.

Spool.

Squirrel-cage swift. Also known as *rice*, sometimes as *barrel swift*. A skein-unwinder. Designed to enable unwinding of skeins. Serves no other purpose, yet has no worthy rival. A necessary piece of equipment. It is essentially two rotating, barrel-like cages mounted on a vertical stand so the two rollers can be separated to any degree required by the skein lengths. Used to unwind both dry and wet skeins for winding into balls, onto spools, for conditioning, and so forth.

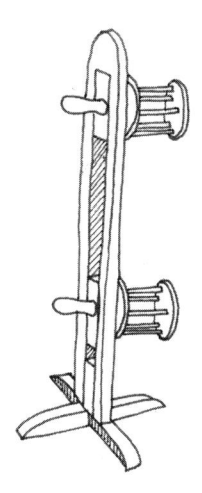

Stall. Stop, or try to. Balk, refuse to continue on.

Standard. A set of stated parameters. *Spinning to a standard* requires reproducing yarn with stated dimensions and values of twist, grist, material, diameter, color, length, et cetera. A gauge, or example. *Standard* is also taken to mean an upright, as the castles of a loom; the upright wheel standards of a "castle" wheel, and as the flag of an organization or entity—a symbol. *See also* Castle wheel.

Squirrel-cage swift.

Staple fiber. A fiber typical of its type; nominal in length. Means the same as *standard length* or *normal length*. Industrial meaning is that of synthetic or man-made fibers, cut or arranged to have a staple length similar to that of the natural fiber they are attempting to emulate.

Staple length. Average or nominal length of a natural fiber, based upon its maximum growth in a season. For animals, usually a year; for plant fibers, includes the normal growth from seed to mature fiber. Silk is not rated according to staple length, because it is a filament (continuous).

Stock card. Low-tech carding "machine." Consists of a bench with a raised, curved box at one end and a large, heavy, single hand card. Called a *stock card* because that's British for *bench*. The carder sits at one end of the stock; the other end has the card clothing, mounted on the raised, curved box. The large hand card is often hung from the ceiling via cords, in such a manner as to allow carding. Monster hand carding, actually. Effective, worthwhile, if you can get the card clothing.

Stock card.

Stuff. Old-fashioned term for material. More for verbal variety, although has more-or-less specific meanings in rope and cord work. A general textile term, denoting fabrics of specific types and styles—"a great-cloak of thick woolen stuffs."

Suint. Sheep sweat. Composed largely of potassium salts, suint combines with wool grease to form yolk. Commercial scouring firms use the potassium salts to make soap, but this is not worthwhile for just a few fleeces.

Sunn. *Crotalaria juncea.* Hard bast fiber from India used for cordage, rough mats, and bagging.

Sunn.

Sunwise. Clockwise. From the Northern hemisphere, facing south, the travel of the sun from east to west. Now, when one turns around and views the shadow of a sundial, it also travels "clockwise," which is how the term got started. When mechanical clocks started showing up, it was deemed appropriate to have them turn sunwise, as well. The Scots/Gaelic word for sun

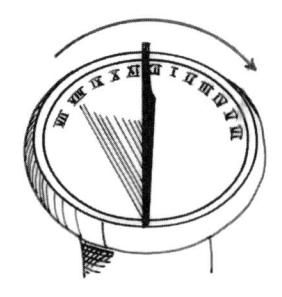

Sunwise.

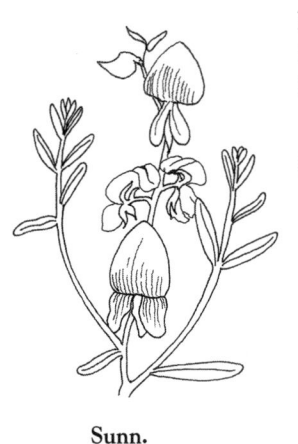

462   The Alden Amos Big Book of Handspinning

wise/clockwise is *deasil*. The antonym of sunwise is *widdershins*, an old German word meaning "contrary," among other things. *See also* Widdershins.

Supported spindle. Any spindle used in supported mode, which means the spindle weight is never supported fully by the newly spun yarn, as with a drop spindle. Supported spindles include the tahkli, the Navajo, the bead-whorls, the Thai, the Hopi, the Southwestern, and others. Primarily used for fine yarns. The bead-whorls and the Thai spindle (also called *finger spindles*) are sometimes used while the spinner moves, as in herding sheep, goats, chickens, and so on.

Swarf. Junk, trash showing up under a willy screen or frame; the stuff you get all over your lap when spinning "in the grease." Bits of vegetable matter, insect parts, leaf trash, boon, shive: all that stuff shed by the newly forming spun yarn. Happens with all fibers, but especially the wool/hair fibers. A generic term that is derived from carpenter's and joiner's jargon—"floor sweepings" from a file. Sawdust, sort of. *See also* Timber; Frass; Shive; VM.

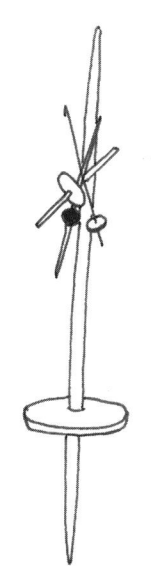

Supported spindle.

Sweeten. Neutralize acids with an alkaline rinse. Silk, for example, may be sweetened by rinsing in lant, weak ammonia water, or dilute soda solution. Sweetening as well as souring are always followed by a mild scour and rinse, or at least several rinses. In general, cellulosics are finished by sweetening, protein fibers by a mild souring. *See also* Sour; Soda; Acid; Alkali; Urine.

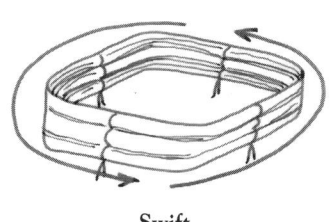

Swift.

Swift. Generally, a tool for unwinding skeins. In overall textile use, means the largest cylinder of a carding machine, or the largest quick-rotating part of a machine. Also holder for skeins during treatment. Common forms for hand workers are the umbrella swift, the lantern swift, the squirrel-cage swift, and the Bridport cross.

Tahkli. Urdu or Sanskrit word; a small, metal-whorl spindle, usually with a steel or iron wire shaft. Whorl may be a small coin or metal disk. Used in supported mode, for spinning high-count cottons. Also seen as *takli*.

Take-up. Take-up is the evident pulling of the yarn against the spinner's

Tahkli.

drafting or controlling hand. In a flyer-and-bobbin system, the pull is continuous. In spindle systems, the pull is discontinuous. Take-up is measured by strictly subjective means, and may be so great or strong (or so weak) as to prevent the spinning of a desired yarn. Take-up determines, in large part, the speed of winding-on. In a "perfect" system, take-up will be scarcely noticeable during spinning but will always wind on the new yarn quickly and easily. *See also* Wind-on; DRS.

Teasel. *Dipsacus fullonum.* Cultivated since prehistory, teasel has been used in gigging or nap-raising of woolen cloths. Has nothing to do with carding. Great for raising nap, brushing yarns, and the like.

Tender. Fleece condition where fiber is generally weak. Caused by extended or prolonged period of stress on the animal; less often by poor storage, chemical action, ultraviolet. Applies to fibers other than wool: cellulosics are tendered by weak acids and poor storage conditions (mildew, yeasts, and so on). All fibers are tendered by exposure to strong light (ultraviolet).

Tex. Another example of metric efficiency. A fixed-length system. The tex value is equal to weight in grams of 1,000 meters of the subject yarn. Thus, a yarn that weighs 200 grams per 1,000 meters has a value of 200 tex.

Thai spindle. Looks like a miniature "Navajo" or Southwestern spindle. Shaft is about 8–10 inches in length and $1/8$–$5/32$ inch in diameter. Whorl is about 1½ inches in diameter and $1/4$–$3/16$ inch thick, and is located about ⅔ of the way along the shaft. Spindle shaft is either notched at one end (the usual) or fitted with some form of wire hook. Spindle is used in "bead-whorl" or double-supported mode. *See also* Akha; Double-supported.

Thread. Same general meaning as *yarn.* Threads may be plied from several spun yarns. Everyday usage tends to equate thread with fine, firm, plied, mini-yarns, as in sewing thread. Excise Tax law denotes that if the strand has more than 400 turns per meter, it is thread; fewer than 400 turns per meter, it is yarn. As a verb, it means to feed each strand through something, as in threading a needle, threading a leader through the wheel orifice, or threading a loom. *See also* Yarn; Sley.

Threadbare. A fabric, textile or otherwise, so worn by usage as to show

Teasel.

the basic or primary structure threads or elements. The condition of being threadbare, that is, worn out, much used, shabby. Common today only on cuffs and hems. Also heavily worn carpets, upholstery, and so on.

Throwing. Originally a silk term, it means the plying together of filament yarns. *Thrown*, another silk term, means twisting together several reeled silk strands. A person engaged in the trade is called a *throwster*. A separate trade from spinning.

Timber. Sticks and twigs in a fleece. Unusual. Often caused by poor handling of fleece (after shearing), bad storage, mishap. Impossible to machine-card. Not burrs or seeds, but bits of bark, splinters, slivers, sawdust, broken twigs, and such. *See also* Swarf; Frass; VM.

Top. Fiber that has been combed, and from which all short or broken fibers, noilments, neps, and debris have been removed. Usually in sliver or roving form. May be any fiber, but if there is no other qualifier the term almost always means wool. *See also* Sliver; Roving.

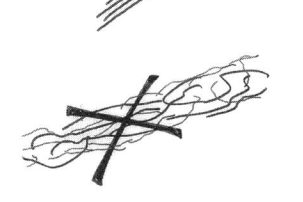

Top.

Tow. Tow is short, coarse, and broken strands of hemp or flax that result from the hackling process. Tow is traditionally used for coarse textiles such as tow sacks, straps, cords, and ropes. When thoroughly crushed and chopped, sometimes used as temper for brick-making, plaster, and so forth, although hair is preferred. Also makes good tinder for tinder boxes and such (reenactors take note). Hemp tow, braided or laid into a soft cord and then soaked in tar, is called *oakum*, and has been used for caulking plank seams in wooden boats. *See also* Flax; Hemp.

Tow.

TPI. Twist count: means turns per inch, or twists per inch.

TPM. Twist count: depending on context, means turns per meter or twists per minute.

Track. In the groove. The alignment and good order of a drive-band. Also means *traction*, or how little it slips. If a wheel is in track, everything pertaining to the drive-band is in order.

Train. Linear arrangement for a process, as in

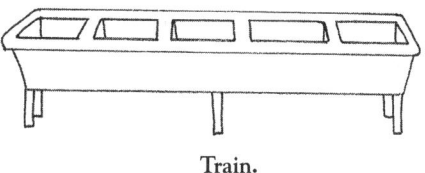

Train.

The Alden Amos Big Book of Handspinning 465

scouring train; similar to range. Scouring trains consist of bowls (rectangular tubs) arranged in a row.

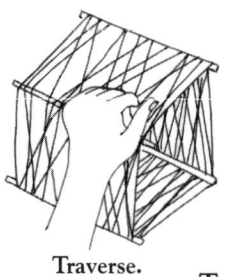

Traverse. Side-to-side or lateral distance between the points of reversal of the wind-on yarn package. Distance that a moving heck travels during one complete cycle of operation. In cross-reeling, the lateral distance an operator's yarn-guide hand moves during one turn of the reel. Also described as *excursion,* that is, the distance an item moves with respect to a fixed point, during one complete cycle. *See also* Building motion.

Traverse.

Treadle. Plate, bar, or board that transmits power from the foot to some other point. In a spinning wheel, the treadle transmits foot motion to the primary drive wheel; in a loom, the treadle transmits foot motion to the primary shedding mechanism; in a sewing machine, to the machine head; and so forth. There are many treadle-powered devices.

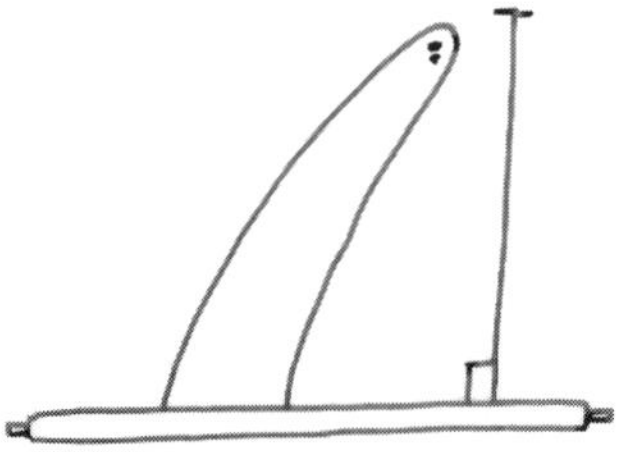

Treadle length. Also *effective treadle length.* Effective treadle length is the distance from the footman attaching point to the axis of the treadle pivot pins, measured at right angles to the pivot axis.

Treadle length.

Treadle ratio. Relationship between treadle length and the throw of the wheel crank. A comfortable wheel will have a treadle ratio of greater than 6-to-1. Treadle ratio is effective treadle length divided by crank throw.

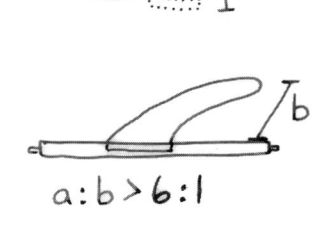

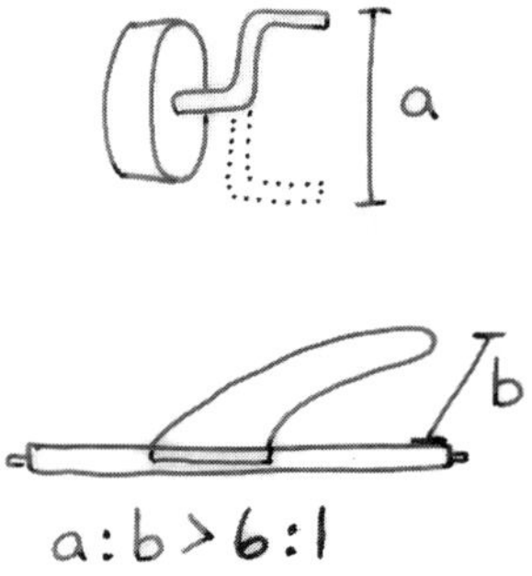

$a:b > 6:1$

Treadle ratio.

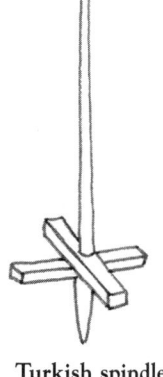

Turkish spindle. Spindle from the European/Asian interface; produces a ball of yarn as a package. Spindle is in three or more parts: a shaft and two or more sliding cross-arms. The cross-arms are slid down the tapered shaft where they form a whorl. A yarn is started and during winding-on the yarn is built into a ball around the arms. When finished, the spindle shaft is slid out, the arms are slipped apart, and the ball of yarn is released. The design is not especially Turkish, since it is found as far east as Tibet.

Turkish spindle.

Tweak. Fiddle with. Make small, fussy, or minor adjustments to any system. Minor changes that result in improved performance. In general, to fine-tune any system for maximum performance, under specific conditions that may (or may not!) change from moment to moment. *See also* Adjustment.

Tweed. Coined word from the 1840s (mid-1820s, one source), happy conjunction of the Scots word *tweel* and the River Tweed, which, for its last fifteen miles, forms a border between England and Scotland. Received further publicity as being worn by gentlemen fishing the river Tweed; exemplified by the Marquis of Lothian and Lord Polwarth. The cloth that is marketed today has little in common with the tweeds of the last century. Any cloth woven in common twill, using tight, natural fleece colors in single yarns may be styled *tweed*.

Twine. Stiff, hard-twisted cords made from vegetable leaf fiber, as in binder twine, bale twine, bagging twine. Sometimes made from paper, plastic.

Twist. Rotation about a common longitudinal axis. In practice of spinning, plying, and rope-making, one end of item being twisted is fixed, or non-rotating, relative to other, or *working*, end. The turns about its own axis, per unit of length, observed in a fiber, yarn, or cord. Expressed as turns per inch, or TPI; by turns per centimeter (TPCM); or by calculation, from the helix angle of surface elements with respect to the yarn axis, assuming a known diameter.

Twist-active. Containing residual, unbalanced twist. The yarn, cord, twine, or rope in question will kink, loop, snarl, or rotate on its own when slackened. The condition is usually caused by excessive twist, or rather, twist excessive to design; although complex structures will also be twist-lively as a result of twist insufficient to the design. In the case of crepe and such constructions, the yarn is deliberately designed to be twist-lively.

Twist direction. A single yarn has twist in one of two directions, defined as the S direction (S twist) or the Z direction (Z twist). S twist is any yarn that, when held vertically, has the same helix angle direction as center stroke of the letter S—that is, the surface helix is from upper left to lower right. Z twist is any yarn that, when held vertically, has the same helix angle direction as center stroke of the letter Z—from lower left to upper right.

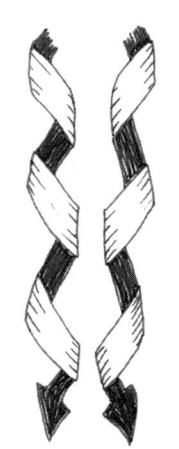

Twist direction.

Twist-stable. Shows no action due to excessive or insufficient twist. Applies to complex plied, laid constructions. A single twisted yarn is always considered twist-lively, or rather is never twist-stable.

TYPP count system. A fixed-weight system for measuring yarn grist. Weight unit is 1 pound, and the count number is the number of yards length, expressed as decimal or whole number. A single skein, 1,000 yards long, weighing 1 pound, has a TYPP count of 1. A skein weighing 1 pound and containing 2,000 yards has a TYPP count of 2. A skein with 3,500 yards, 3.5 TYPP count; and so on. Called American standard system. It is grist in *Thousands of Yards Per Pound*, expressed as a whole number and/or a decimal equivalent.

Up-twist. Twist component that is in the same direction as twist of the preceding operation. Also called *twist-on-twist*. Up-twisting will increase a yarn's strength and resistance to abrasion, and reduce its grist value—it will have fewer yards per pound. Up-twisting is used to modify an existing yarn, or as an assembly step in production of certain yarn constructions, such as hawser and crepe.

Urine. Waste matter secreted by the kidneys of vertebrates. It is rich in protein metabolism end products, salts, and pigments. Fresh urine is slightly acidic; as it ages, urea, the main solid component of mammalian urine, breaks down, and the urine becomes mildly alkaline. For textile purposes, human urine is best, because of its ready availability and the fact that the more protein in the diet, the more urea in the urine. *See also* Lant.

Vat Dyes. Remarkably wash- and light-fast water-insoluble dyes that are made soluble by reduction (treating to remove oxygen) in mildly alkaline solutions. Goods are entered, take up the dissolved dye, then are removed so that the dye may reoxidize and develop its final color. Greater depth of hue is developed by repeated dips. The classic vat dye is indigo. A very old procedure, vat dyeing was known to the ancients. *See also* Indigo; Woad; Fermentation Vat.

Vicuña. *Vicugna vicugna* is the more common scientific name, although sometimes appears as *Lama vicugna*. A wild (non-domesticated) cousin of the llama, has been hunted down to endangered species level. The brown-red fiber (primarily

Vicuna.

down) is considered finer and softer than cashmere. One source states that the fiber averages 13 microns in diameter, and 1½ to 3 inches in length. Lesser grades of vicuña are lighter in color. A rare fiber, partly because vicuña range is the high Andes (15,000–19,000 feet above sea level) and partly because the animal is killed to harvest the down. *See also* Llama; Alpaca; Camelid; Guanaco.

VM. Abbreviation for *Vegetable Matter*. A wool fleece term. Burrs, twigs, feed, bedding, et cetera. VM is a fault; excessive VM makes the fleece difficult to process. The industry removes VM through use of special "burr-works" on the carding machines and by the process known as carbonization—not something easily done by the hand worker. *See also* Frass; Timber; Swarf.

Water. Water is composed of one atom of oxygen, linked to two atoms of hydrogen. One could say that since hydrogen is a "metal," then water is an oxide of that metal. Water is considered to be the "Universal Solvent," and is the main portion of any "liquor" used in a textile process. Purity of the water is not so important as is the mineral content and the "hardness," or combination with calcium and magnesium cations (ions carrying a positive charge): "Hard" water is not well suited to textile scouring and dyeing. *See also* Soap; Calcium; Hardness.

Water pot. Pot, cup, or bowl to hold water or similar liquid while spinning flax, hemp et cetera. Water alone works pretty well, but a little bit of soap in the water acts as a wetting agent. Avoid synthetic detergent. Don't use beer or a soft drink: it contains acid. Do not wet-spin a bobbin-full and then walk off and leave it for days; it will mildew. Wind off to a blocking reel when you're done spinning for the day.

Waulk. Action of fulling, performed by singing characters on a patio, picnic table, or other suitable surface. Once accomplished by the same action as treading grapes, bare feet and all. Handcraft method of fulling cloth. Has odor of holiness about it. Ceremonial form of the bathtub or kid-pool stomp. Suitable for gatherings; thrives on potlucks, music, and good drink. Very effective method of fulling blankets, large piece goods, cloaks, capes, yurts, and similar projects. A group effort. *See also* Fulling; Scouring.

Waulking.

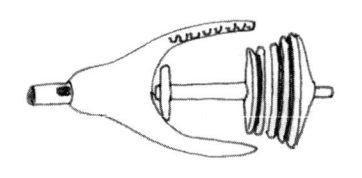

Welsh tension. Nickname for double-drive, bobbin-lead arrangements of flyer-and-bobbin setups. Name came about as result of Richard Ashford styling the single-drive, bobbin-lead arrangement as Irish tension; when in fact it would be better called German tension, as it is often found on wheels of Bavarian persuasion. Amos (a Welshman) felt that the Welsh deserved at least as much attention—thus Welsh tension came into being. *See also* Scotch tension; Irish tension.

Welsh tension.

Wether. Has-been or never-had-a-chance-to-be ram. Castrated ex-male sheep. A wooly capon. Supposed to grow superior fleece. Heavier, fuller.

Wetting-out. Pre-soaking goods (yarn, fiber, fabric) as a preparation for dyeing, bleaching, or other wet process. Purpose of wetting-out is to ensure even or level strike of the dye liquor or other processing fluid. Scouring is the normal wetting-out method for dyeing, mordanting, and so forth, since wetting-out is retarded by grease, wax, oil, dirt, and such that may be present. If fiber cannot be wetted-out evenly, it cannot be dyed evenly. Even with clean goods, the dye strike will be different, depending upon how wet or dry the goods are when entered.

Whorl. Disk, as a spindle whorl. Pulley, as a flyer whorl. Sometimes seen as *wharve*, *whirl*, et cetera. May also serve as a copp, especially on some great wheels. The "platform" and flywheel of manual spindles. A *bobbin whorl* is a driving or braking pulley, attached to or part of a bobbin. A *flyer whorl* is a pulley that drives a flyer array, the fork- or wishbone-shaped yarn distribution device found on flyer-and-bobbin wheels.

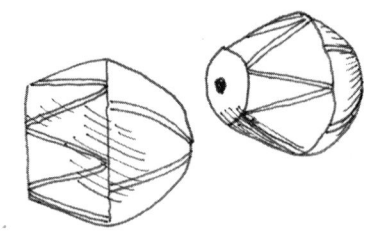

Whorls.

Widdershins. From an old German word which means, among other things, contrary. The antonym of sunwise. Thus, an archaic way of saying counterclockwise. This one should be worth something to the Scrabble player. *See also* Sunwise.

Willow. A device and an action. Device is used to open up and break up compressed fibers. To willow a mass of fiber is to whip, flog, open, and break it up. By hand, this is done by laying fiber (fleece) upon a screen platform and then walloping and whipping it for a while, using two long, whippy willow rods. Hence, the name. A commercial machine that performs this service is a *willy* or, if heavy-duty, a *Fearnaught Willy*. *See also*, Picker.

Windage. Air resistance in an operating spinning system, especially air resistance of the flyer arms. Also an old term for a sloppy or loose fit, as in "the shaft has plenty of windage," meaning clearances are on the generous side.

Windle. Archaic term for reel. From Danish/Icelandic *windas* or *vindass*, a winding-beam. Sometimes a general term for a wheel, in the textile senses. Possible source of "pop goes the weasel."

Wind-on. The taking in of newly spun yarn, as from the spinner's hand to the flyer-and-bobbin array or a spindle. The act of storing the newly spun make of yarn. More or less the same as take-up: wind-on is the action, and take-up describes how vigorous that action is. Wind-on and take-up are both related to the momentary value of differential rotational speed that exists between the flyer and the bobbin. This differential rotational speed, or DRS, is arranged in several ways, depending upon the type of drive system in use. *See also* Take-up; DRS.

Windle.

Woad. *Isatis tinctoria*. The stuff used by all the better Picts, Celts, and Britons as war paint, and the mainstay blue dye of Europe until at least the end of the fifteenth century. As an adjuvant to the indigo process, it continued in use until the early twentieth century. The coloring material of woad is the same as that of indigo but is only one-tenth as concentrated as that in indigo. The result was that indigo all but replaced woad, and was itself replaced by synthetic indigo in the 1900s. *See also* Indigo; Vat Dyes.

Wonder yarn. A form of OTF. A yarn you look at and wonder what to do with it, or wonder where it came from, or wonder what it is made of. Inconsequential, out-of-hand, availability being the primary concern, if there is any concern in the first place. Not to be confused with *period yarn*. *See also* OTF; Period yarn.

Wool combs. Multi-toothed hand combs for combing of wool. Combs are rated by pitch; the greater the pitch, the more teeth. Tradition has it that the finer the wool to comb, the greater the pitch. Typical

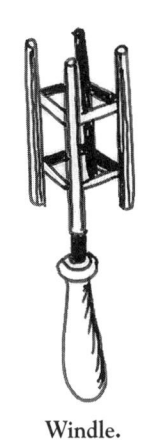

Woad.

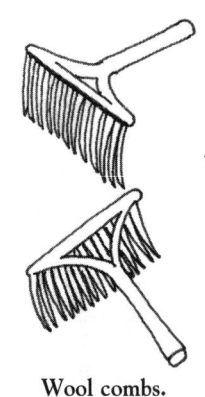

pitch is 4 rows of teeth (4-pitch combs); in the nineteenth century, 8-pitch combs were known. Nowadays, a variety of combs is available—not just "English," but "Russian paddle," "Viking," and so on. Combs are a necessary item if worsted spinning is anticipated.

Woolen count system. A fixed-weight system for measuring yarn grist. Weight unit is 1 pound; count is number of skeins of yarn, each 1,600 yards long, that weigh 1 pound. Thus a single skein, 1,600 yards long, weighing 1 pound, has a woolen count of 1 and a grist of 1,600 YPP. A 10's woolen count equals 10 skeins, each 1,600 yards long, weighing a total of 1 pound and a grist of 16,000 YPP. Also called Run system; American Woolen system; and Philadelphia Run system.

Woolen yarn. Yarn spun on the woolen system (drafting-against-twist), from carded wool. Characterized by bulk, softness, obscured outline ("fuzziness"), and propensity to felt in certain weaves. Linear tensile strength less than that of the equivalent grist of worsted yarn, assuming the same fiber and degree of twist. Without further qualifiers, the yarn is a single, typically Z-spun.

Worsted count system. A fixed-weight system for measuring yarn grist. Weight unit is 1 pound; count is the number of yarn skeins, each 560 yards long, that weigh 1 pound. Thus, a single skein 560 yards long, weighing 1 pound, has a worsted count of 1 and a grist of 560 YPP. A 10's worsted count equals ten skeins, each 560 yards long, weighing a total of 1 pound, for a grist of 5,600 YPP. Also called *Bradford count system*.

Worsted yarn. Yarn spun on the worsted system (drafting-without-twist), from combed fibers.

Wuzzing. Removal of water and other liquids from wool (and yarns) by means of centrifugal force. In the simplest form, goods are entered into a porous sack or bag, then swung

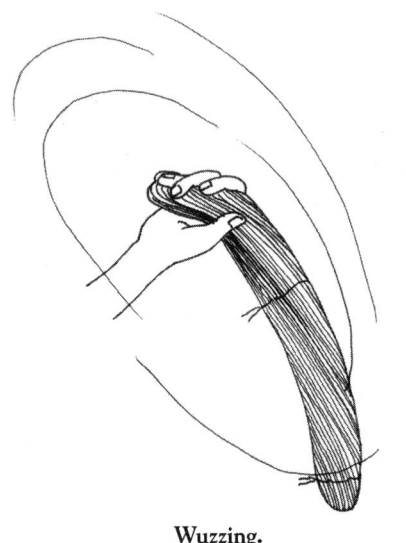

Wool combs.

Wuzzing.

about the head and shoulders with vigor and determination. Variations include the use of pantyhose, or a bucket with pierced bottom, swung about on a sturdy stick in various ways. The family washing machine can give good service, as long as the spin-cycle only is used, and carefully controlled. Commercial outfits use large hydroextractors for "wuzzing" wool.

Yarn. A main topic of this book; the twisted and drafted stuff of dreams, from which so much of this world is fabricated. The primary product of the spinning process.

Yarn lock. Maintaining a constant tension on a yarn during spinning, so that it neither draws in nor strips out of a flyer array.

Yolk. The infamous "grease" everyone speaks of. The term is used to describe the extraneous material of animal origin that adheres to the fleece. Mostly composed of suint and wool grease. The suint is primarily potassium salt complexes; the wool grease is mostly hydrous lanolin and related fats/waxes. *See also* Suint; Grease.

YPM. Yards per minute: a measure of yarn production or handling speed. By inference, YPH is yards per hour, another production term.

Z twist. One of the two twist directions possible in spinning. If the twist angle runs in the same direction as the center stroke of the letter Z, the yarn is said to be Z-twist. Such a yarn is spun with the twisting device (spindle or flyer-and-bobbin) rotating in a clockwise direction with reference to the drafting zone and fiber mass. In general, the "default" spinning direction for woolen yarns. *See also* S twist.

Z twist.

An Opinionated, Annotated Bibliography

Square brackets indicate dates of early editions.

Adrosko, Rita J. *Natural Dyes in the United States.* Washington, D.C.: Smithsonian Institution Press, 1968. *Also known as United States National Museum Bulletin 281. It's impressive. Many of the natural dye recipes popular today owe much to Ms. Adrosko's work, and to this book in particular. Well worth owning, and invaluable if you want to dye a skein or two. Light-years beyond onion skins and back yard weeds.*

Alexander, John D., Jr. *Make a Chair from a Tree: An Introduction to Working Green Wood.* Newtown, Connecticut: Taunton Press, 1978. *The best contemporary work on green-wood joinery. Not wheel-specific, but best info on use of shave, drawknife, bench, and scraper that you are likely to see. Anyway, if you make wheels, you need to make spinning stools and chairs, right?*

American Wool Council. *Spinning Your Own Wool Yarn.* Denver: American Wool Council, 1980. *Puff piece for the American Wool Council. Colonial overtones. Was designed to be furnished to schools and groups as cheapo handout plug. This contains good, fifth-grade level of instructions. Trivia bit: was written for the AWC by Bette Hochberg.*

Amos, Alden. *Spinning Wheel Primer.* Loveland, Colorado: Interweave Press, 1989. *Short and pompous. Has good description of basic operations of flyer-and-bobbin systems, driven spindles. Source of* production spinner, production wheel. *Current edition contains extracts from 101 Questions for Spinners. Intro by Bette Hochberg.*

Amos, A., S. Druding, L. Hanson, and B. Hochberg. *101 Questions For Spinners.* Berkeley: Straw Into Gold, 1978. *This goldmine of spinning information is mostly the work of Susan Druding, owner of Straw Into Gold. The info is not to be found anywhere else, and the style and presentation of the material is true genius. Has to be the only format where egos could ever agree to agree.*

Anderson, Enid. *The Spinner's Encyclopedia.* Newton Abbot, Devon, U.K.: David and Charles, 1987; New York: Sterling, 1987. *"Encyclopedia" is too strong a term. Still, a valuable reference text. Written in "British," and a few terms are strange to American eyes/ears. Work is a compendium of spinning fact, data, and technique; although eclectic, it is not comprehensive.*

Andrews, Jack. *New Edge of the Anvil: A Resource Book for the Blacksmith.* Drexel Hill, Pennsylvania: SkipJack Press, 1994 [1977]. *Contemporary work to ease you into* the blacksmith's frame of mind. If you build wheels, sooner or later you're gonna have to bang out them cranks, spindles, and flyer shafts. Jack eases you into the smith's work with a minimum of projects and furor.

Ashenhurst, Thos. R. *A Treatise on Textile Calculations and the Structure of Fabrics.* Second edition. Huddersfield and Bradford: J. Broadbent and Co., 1886 [1884]. This is probably the oldest still available work of this sort. Fascinating stuff, and part of the delight comes from making the creaky old calculations work again. Try some of these on a piece of contemporary handwoven. Know what? He was right.

Ashley, Clifford W., with amendments by Geoffrey Budsworth. *The Ashley Book of Knots.* Corrected edition. New York: Doubleday, 1993 [1944]. Best there is. Not just knots, but every conceivable application for string, yarn, cord, rope, hawser, cable, twine. And with the exception of the small part about wire rope, every bit of this is right down the handspinner's alley. Sections on fancy knots, plaiting, decorative work. Something for everyone.

Bacon, John Lord. *Forge-Practice (Elementary).* New York: Wiley, 1996 [1906]. Modern reprint of standard 1900s text. A different perspective. Was written for "beginning" students, but don't let that put you off—this is good stuff. Common fare in 1910, but stark amazement for today's custom-fitted, computer-driven, cellular dweeb.

Baines, Patricia. *Linen: Hand Spinning and Weaving.* London: B. T. Batsford, 1989. In spite of some remarkable statements about how things "were" in olden times, this is a pretty good book. Scholarly, in the style of her earlier work, Spinning Wheels, Spinners and Spinning, and loaded with good advice and useful tips. Another one in great British style; but they have gotten a lot better at speaking American.

———. *Spinning Wheels, Spinners and Spinning.* New York: Charles Scribner's Sons, 1978. Scholastic work on the spinning wheel. Much history and British trivia. Ms. Baines enjoyed research and museum connections that are the envy of us all—she also used her connections well. A great deal of historical background (otherwise unavailable) is there for the reading. There is even a section on how to spin.

Barber, E.J.W. *Prehistoric Textiles: The Development of Cloth in the Neolithic and Bronze Ages, with Specific Reference to the Aegean.* Princeton, New Jersey: Princeton University Press, 1991. Fascinating! This book is, to the lover of textiles, a truly monumental work. If you have the least interest in textile prehistory, you must get this. Book is of limited interest to those who don't work with yarns and fibers. Makes you humble and proud. No how-to, but how-was.

———. *Women's Work, The First 20,000 Years: Women, Cloth, and Society in Early Times.* New York: W. W. Norton, 1994. Textile and historical delight. Much like her previous work, Prehistoric Textiles, (I wonder why?), except transferred from third to second person. Lots of daily bits and scenarios, written for the nonscholar. Not so much a source as a sort of manifesto.

Bériau, O-A. [Oscar-Alphonse]. *Home Weaving*. Gardenvale, Quebec: Arts and Crafts of Gardenvale, 1947 [1939]. *The first 30 pages of this great old work are directed toward the spinner. Fibers, preparation, carding, spinning, skein winding and treatments, bleaching, spool winding—right up to the basics of weaving, which continues for the next 267 pages. Might as well pick up a little weaving smart as well.*

Beveridge, June H. *Warp/Weft/Sett: A Reference Manual for Handweavers*. New York: Van Nostrand Reinhold, 1980. *Big book: pictures of swatches, lots of yarn tables and stuff. Lets you see what your weave will look like without the work of samples. Bad point: there's not one of these that I consider useful for garments. Only two warps have been used (cotton and linen) and none of the samples have hit the suds. Great book for a guild library.*

Blumenthal, Betsy, and Kathryn Kreider. *Hands On Dyeing*. Loveland, Colorado: Interweave Press, 1988. *One of the justly famous "Hands On" books from Interweave Press, this one follows the tradition of being clear, logical, and comprehensive. Good graphic show of process and progress, great photos. Brief and good discussion of color theory.*

Born, Wolfgang. *The Spinning Wheel*. West Yorkshire, U.K.: Olicana Crafts, 1977. *This is a reprint for CIBA-Geigy, Ltd. W. Born published* this material in the now-defunct CIBA Review. Material is fascinating. Of course, historical research and experience have advanced since this. Accept the facts as such, but take along some salt for the opinions. If you build, fix, use, or study wheels as devices, this is invaluable.

Bowles, Ella Shannon. *Homespun Handicrafts*. Philadelphia and London: J. B. Lippincott Company, 1931. *Interesting narrative description of "Colonial days and Colonial ways." Much nostalgia and anecdote, second- and third-hand information. Still, she was not as far removed from the subject as we are, so her observations have some merit. Read between the lines. Sort of a Nancy Drew version of Alice Morse Earle.*

Bradbury, Fred. *Calculations in Yarns and Fabrics*. Twelfth edition. Manchester, U.K.: Emmott and Company, 1948. *For the serious spinner. This is boring. It's full of such goodies as all of the British and Continental count systems, blending of fibers, and the biggy—"Calculations involved in the analysis and reproduction of woven fabrics," with formulae and 47 exercises with answers. Work similar to Ashenhurst's (1880).*

Braudel, Fernand. *The Structures of Everyday Life: The Limits of the Possible*. New York: Harper and Row, 1985 [1981]. Volume 1 in a 3-volume set. *Translated from French and revised by Sian Reynolds. Wonderful, erudite time-machine that takes us back to the fifteenth century, then brings us forward. Not about spinning except that spinning was a commonplace part of life. The history of humankind is that of textiles, and all textiles begin with the spinner.*

Brown, Rachel. *The Weaving, Spinning, and Dyeing Book.* Second edition. New York: Alfred A. Knopf, 1983 [1978]. *Arguably the greatest spin-dye-weave book of the twentieth century. By one of the Great Ladies of our craft. If you spin, this will make you want to weave; if you weave, it will make you want to spin. In either case, it will make a dyer out of you. It's all here. You must have it.*

Bryant, David. *Wheels and Looms: Making Equipment for Spinning and Weaving.* London: B. T. Batsford, 1987. *Plans, plans, plans. Plans for drop spindles, for hand cards, for a Great wheel, for several types of treadled wheel, for small looms, jigs, floor loom. Working instructions, but look out for the metric jitters. Mr. Bryant assumes you know something of woodworking.*

Buxton, Judith. *Selected Canadian Spinning Wheels in Perspective: An Analytical Approach.* Hull, Quebec: Canadian Museum of Civilization, 1992 [1980]. *If you build or study wheels, this is a gotta-have reference. Ms. Judith is the first author other than Fannin and yours truly to treat the spinning wheel as a device, not some holy relic of the good old days. Fascinating variations and mechanical analysis; interesting postulations. Original publication appears in catalogs under Judith Buxton-Keenlyside, and was published in Ottawa, Ontario, by National Museums of Canada.*

Cartwright-Jones, Catherine. *The Prolific Knitting Machine.* Loveland, Colorado: Interweave Press, 1990. *You know, the knitting machine was made to work with handspun yarn. Why not? That's Catherine's attitude, and she has the expertise to make it stick. This is a book for machine knitters, but the section on handspinning for your knitting machine is well worth the price of the book.*

Catling, Harold. *The Spinning Mule.* Newton Abbot, Devon, U.K.: David and Charles, 1970. *The spinner/mechanic needs this. Lucid description and illustration of every aspect of driven spindle use, management, and so forth. Lots of mechanical stuff. A good read, as well. Jenny patterns, too. If you are a cottage-industry person, this is required reading.*

Channing, Marion L. *The Textile Tools of Colonial Homes: From Raw Materials to Finished Garments, Before Mass Production in the Factories.* Second edition. Marion, Massachusetts: Marion L. Channing, 1971. *Excellent illustrations. Not a "how to do it" book, more of a "how it was done" work. There are a few flights of fancy, but otherwise good stuff. Reads like a docent's lesson plan. You know, the one they give to Wednesday afternoon groups touring the Richepigge Estate.*

Clark, Hazel. *Fibres to Fabrics: Techniques and Projects for Hand Spinners.* North Pomfret, Vermont: Trafalgar Square, 1985. *I included this for several reasons. First, the author uses the phrase "treadle effortlessly" with no qualms whatsoever. Second, the color and cover photos are illustrations for a "Gidget does Stonehenge" give-away calendar. Third, some projects here are perfect for your next competitive event—*

sheep to shawl, whatever.

Coleman, Donald G. *Woodworking Factbook: Basic Information on Wood for Woodcarvers, Woodshop, Craftsmen, Tradesmen, and Instructors*. New York: Robert Speller and Sons, 1966. *Reference text for a non-technical person, by chief (1966) of the research division at the USDA Forest Products Labs, Madison, Wisconsin. What wood is, why it cracks, why it won't, finishes, species, hardness, odor, strength, stiffness, ease of cutting and working, stability, etc. Good reference.*

Crockett, Candace. *The Complete Spinning Book*. New York: Watson-Guptill, 1977. *A somewhat different approach. Good illustrations (not just because I'm in some of them, ahem) and some off-beat material. Like a set of plans for a "bulky" wheel. This book is a sort of trip down memory lane, in which you get to see "feet, arm, and torso" shots of a lot of famous handspinning personalities.*

Crowfoot, Grace M., and H. Ling Roth. *Hand Spinning and Woolcombing*. McMinnville, Oregon: Robin and Russ, 1974 [1931]. *Reprint of two excellent works: Ms. Crowfoot's* Methods of Hand Spinning in Egypt and the Sudan *(1931) and Mr. Roth's short* Hand Woolcombing *(n.d.). Both published by the Bankfield Museum in Halifax, England. Ms. Crowfoot's work is a must for handspinners. Mr. Roth's notes are the source for much lore about woolcombing.*

Cummer, Joan Whittaker. *A Book of Spinning Wheels*. Portsmouth, New Hampshire: Peter E. Randall, 1993. *Lots and lots of pictures. The text is vague but pleasant. The pictures are a labor of love, and the entire work is cut from heroic stuff.*

Davenport, Elsie G. *Your Handspinning, with 86 Diagrams and Plates*. Tarzana, California: Select Books, 1971 [1948]. *Reprint of 1948 publication. One of the older Great Books about handspinning. No-frills advice, straightforward and demonstrable. The illustrations are clear, the information is timeless. The book is too short, and Ms. D. takes it for granted that you know something of the topic.*

da Vinci, Leonardo. *Leonardo da Vinci: Drawings of Textile Machines*. Compiled and edited by Kenneth G. Ponting. Atlantic Highlands, New Jersey: Humanities Press, 1979 [simultaneously, Bradford-on-Avon, Wiltshire, U.K.: Moonraker Press]. *Mr. Ponting compiled and edited this collection of da Vinci's notes and drawings, material clearly and unmistakably textile-related. For builder and mechanic, this is fascinating. This should put to rest the notion that da Vinci invented the flyer and bobbin. He was way beyond that… well, see for yourself.*

Diderot, Denis. *Encyclopédie, ou Dictionnaire raisonné des sciences, des arts et des métiers, par une société des gens de lettres*. New York: Harry N. Abrams, 1978. *This is a half-size repro edition of the original illustrated quarto volumes. Outstanding collection of graphic images concerning eighteenth-century textile process and procedure. Of course,* L'encyclopédie *covers much more than the textile arts, but that is* our present focus. Carding, spinning, wheels, looms, dyeworks, fulling, raising, shearing—page after page of meticulous copperplate engravings. A wonderful window on the arts and sciences of times gone by.

Dixon, Margaret. *The Wool Book.* London and New York: Hamlyn, 1979. *Unchallenging, comfortable, but presents another view. The illustrations are new, yet "familiar." Excellent chart of wool classes and a version of oleum dyeing of wool with indigo. Natural dye stuff and a nice selection of project patterns. Rather well done.*

Earle, Alice Morse. *Home Life in Colonial Days.* Stockbridge, Massachusetts: Berkshire House, 1992 [1898]. *Well-known member of the how-it-was genre. Great read, and it does contain information on "Colonial" textile arts, plus other items. Good illustrations, what there are of them.*

Ensminger, M. Eugene. *Sheep and Wool Science.* Danville, Illinois: The Interstate, 1970 [1964]. *A sort of FFA version of Ryder's* Sheep and Man. *No archaeology, but everything you could possibly want to know about raising sheep, caring for them, breeding them, preventing disease, feed compositions, buying, selling, showing, shearing . . . all of it. A one-stop source.*

Fannin, Allen. *Handspinning Art and Technique.* New York: Van Nostrand Reinhold, 1981 [1970]. *Mr. Fannin uses four words where one is enough: you will become aware of that as you read this. And read it you must, because he knows whereof he speaks. Each time you read through it, you will be impressed by how much he learned since the last time you read the same words. The illustrations are excellent; the text is ponderous. Many facts.*

Field, Anne. *The Ashford Book of Spinning.* Second revised edition. Christchurch, New Zealand: Shoal Bay Press, 1995 [1986]. *Good book of the type, great to give someone along with their brand new in-a-box Ashford Kitset Spinning Wheel. Contains a discussion of Irish tension. If you're not from New Zealand, are not using an Ashford, and are a beginner, this is not the best beginning book. There are projects in the back.*

Forbes, R. J. *Studies in Ancient Technology.* Third edition. Leiden and New York: E. J. Brill, 1993 [1955]. *Early (1950s) comprehensive work on "ancient" textiles. In the multi-volume set from 1955 (Leiden: Brill), volume 4 is dedicated to textile crafts and related tasks. Heavily annotated. Much chatty material, cross-referenced to other sources. Textile archeology has come far since this was published, but the book remains a major favorite.*

Fournier, Nola, and Jane Fournier. *In Sheep's Clothing: A Handspinner's Guide to Wool.* Loveland, Colorado: Interweave Press, 1995. *The formidable team of Fournier & Fournier have come up with a gem of a book for the handspinner—a great deal of valuable information in a comfortable, chat-like format. All about wool, the major divisions and subdivisions of wool types, recommended usage by breed, photo illustrations of* individual locks, and even a little history. *If you process wool, this is a gotta-have reference and guide.*

Gaddum, P. W. *Silk: How and Where It is Produced.* Macclesfield, Cheshire, U.K.: H. T. Gaddum and Company, 1979. *Written by the current generation of a respected family of silk merchants in England. A lucid, knowledgeable account of silk, both historical and in the modern world. No silk worker should go without reading it.*

Gibson, Charles E. *Handbook of Knots and Splices and Other Work with Hempen and Wire Ropes.* New York: Barnes and Noble, 1995 [1961]. *This work covers about 1/100 of Ashley's book, but largely because of that it is not so scary. Handy, actually, and written in a different style. Has all the basic knots and splices, plus useful tables concerning rope strengths and so forth. Uses of ropes and cord, care of your rope, rope materials, and more.*

Gibson-Roberts, Priscilla A. *Knitting in the Old Way.* Loveland, Colorado: Interweave Press, 1985. *Famous knitting person, also known as a handspinner. Poo-poos the incomprehensibility of modern pop-mag knitting gibberish and shows in plain English how knitters can take command of the whole process, the "old" way. Champion of the "100-yard rule," she avoids the term grist, for unknown reasons.*

Grasett, K. *Complete Guide to Hand Spinning: Teasing, Carding, Spinning, Illustrated.* Pacific Grove, California: Craft and Hobby Book Service, 1971. *Reprint of a 1930 original. Short, pithy, and concise. Many hand-spinners have begun their career with this one. A good little book.*

Graumont, Raoul, and Elmer Wenstrom. *Square Knot Handicraft Guide.* New York: Random House, 1949. *Was one of my kidhood treasures. Learned lots and lots from it. Not a string-fun book, but was actually written for adults. The notion of what you do with handspun yarn is answered here, even if you don't knit, can't weave, don't want to crochet. You will not believe some of the stuff, the jewels, that you can make.*

Grierson, Su. *Whorl and Wheel: The Study of Handspinning in Scotland.* Perth, Scotland: Su Grierson, 1985. *Lot of whole cloth here, interspersed with nasty-nice bits of trivia, conjecture, and gowk-hunting. Her work on the Scottish dyes is better.*

Guadalupi, Gianni, and Laura Casalis, editors. *Cotton and Silk Making in Manchu China.* Translated from the Italian and the French by Michael Langley. New York: Rizzoli International, 1980. *Copies of watercolors (on cotton), colored engravings (on silk), originals circa eighteenth century. Housed in National Library, Paris; similar material in National Library, Florence. Plates are informative, text supplied from other sources.*

Hald, Margrethe. *Ancient Danish Textiles from Bogs and Burials: A Comparative Study of Costume and Iron Age Textiles.* Copenhagen: National Museum of Denmark, 1980. *Aside from historical material, there's much here for the hand spinner. The "twist patterned" cloths are both fascinating and an inspiration source for handspinners . . . plus remember, this was all made on drop spindles.*

Hayward, Charles H., editor. *Staining and Polishing: How to Finish Woodwork; Staining, French Wax, and Polishing; the Cellulose Finish; Varnishing; Lacquering.* New York: Drake, 1969. *Probably the best readily available text on French polishing. Covers other finishes, but those are not strong points. The chapters on Frog-polish make the book worthwhile. Not that a wheel-maker would finish a wheel that way, but. Anyway, it's a great finish for a dulcimer.*

Hayward, Charles H. *Woodwork Joints.* New York: Sterling, 1979 [1973]. *More basic training. All about joints. Mr. Hayward wrote many books on woodworking and allied trades. This is one of the good ones. Description, methods of work to produce most of the practical joints in common woodworking. Thing is, the standards applied here are the standards of yesteryear, and he does it all by hand. No machinery. You can, too.*

Heinrich, Linda. *The Magic of Linen Flax Seed to Woven Cloth.* Victoria, British Columbia: Orca Book Publishers, 1992. *Modern illustrated book about the !Magic! of linen. Big, has color photos, many illustrations. Interesting text. Book is too heavy, sharp, and fragile to read in bed. Information on cultivation, harvesting, processing.*

Hildreth, E. M., and W. Munn Rankin. *Textiles in the Home, Part II.* London: Allman and Son, 1966. *Wonderful little book. British home economics text. Has good set of tests for natural fibers, blends. Endearing feature is section on making and testing soaps. Sorry, no pink lotions here. Just hot, soft water and lots of soap. Speaks of soaps and water hardness, with respect to woolens and the wool industry.*

Hochberg, Bette. *Fibre Facts.* Santa Cruz, California: Bette Hochberg, 1981. *From the first sentence in the intro: "This is a basic guide for handweavers. It tells how fibers behave, how they are formed into yarns, how to use them in weaving, and how to care for them." The information applies to other yarncrafts as well. Bette is best known as a handspinner, and she knows her fibers and yarns.*

———. *Handspindles.* Santa Cruz, California: B. and B. Hochberg, 1977. *This is nothing less than the popular, definitive, twentieth-century work on handspindles. Nothing fancy, just what they are and how to use them. To date, there is nothing to compare with it. Non-pareil.*

———. *Handspinner's Handbook.* Santa Cruz, California: B. and B. Hochberg, 1976. *First book by the Hochbergs, and still one of the best: Warm, no-nonsense advice and practical how-to. A comfortable learning session with one of the handspinning Great Ladies. I recommend this little book to any person who wants to learn to spin. No fluff, no flights of fancy, no spare words, no math. A great work.*

———. *Spin Span Spun: Fact and Folklore for Spinners.* Santa Cruz, California: B. and B. Hochberg, 1979. *If you keep reading matter in the john (a lot of spinners do), be careful with this one. Guaranteed to* put your buns to sleep. Not arranged in conventional style, although it has an intro, a chapter, a bibliography and an index. Pick it up any time, anywhere, and read frontward, backward . . . amazing collection of spin-stuff.

Horne, Beverley. *Fleece in Your Hands*. Loveland, Colorado: Interweave Press, 1979. A revised handbook about selecting particular wools for particular projects. Not a how-to-spin book, rather a how-to-prepare-and-use book. A different point of view. Most projects are knitted. Last project is genre that gets shot during power failures on scary nights, so hang it against a chimney or brick wall.

Jones, Bernard E., editor. *The Complete Woodworker*. Berkeley, California: Ten Speed Press, 1980. Basic training manual. Material is dated, but then so are spinning wheels, right? This one contains good stuff on steam bending, cart wheels, curved work. Nothing "spinning-specific," but a lot of ancillary activity. Interesting enough to sidetrack you from the wheel project.

Kent, Kate Peck. *Prehistoric Textiles of the Southwest*. Santa Fe, New Mexico: School of American Research, 1983. Ms. Kent wove and spun: those facts are apparent in this work. A rich source of technique, material, design. A good read to boot. The diagrams of textile constructions are clear, and the textiles and artifacts are well illustrated, many in color. More of a weaver's book, but contains valuable insights and information on spinning and fibers.

Kent, Kate Peck. *Pueblo Indian Textiles: A Living Tradition*. Santa Fe, New Mexico: School of American Research Press, 1983. This is not a textile "how" book, but rather a textile "why" book. The reasons why Pueblo textile arts take the shape and form that they do are clearly explained. The section on tools and materials is reason enough to include this in the handspinner's library.

Knutson, Linda. *Synthetic Dyes for Natural Fibers*. Loveland, Colorado: Interweave Press, 1986 [1982]. Clear, concise, and logical. One of the few contemporary texts covering commercial dyes, and the only one specializing in natural fibers. Great glossary. Avoids becoming brand-name dependent, so discusses dyes as types: fiber reactive, acid, direct, and so forth. Methodology and safety, handling, skein tying(!).

Kolander, Cheryl. *A Silk Worker's Notebook*. Loveland, Colorado: Interweave Press, 1985. Much valuable and interesting information about silk—its sources, forms, morphology, historical usage, and background. Has a 19-page section on handspinning; info on boiling-off, weighting, all sorts of stuff. If you work silk as a contemporary craft person, you need this.

Leadbeater, Eliza. *Handspinning*. London: Studio Vista, 1976. Perpetuates the Jurgen–da Vinci story, and there are some remarks about teasels and carding. Still, this is written in plain old American (she was an expatriate Yank) and contains useful stuff about British sheep (what else?) and a great picture sequence of flax-working and distaff-dressing.

Ligon, Linda, editor. *Homespun, Handknit: Caps, Socks, Mittens and Gloves*. Loveland, Colorado: Interweave Press, 1987. *Majority of projects shown in this wonderful book are made from handspun yarn; my own mother did a piece, and the editor is a well-known spinner, weaver, publisher, and spaghetti cook who allows itinerant authors to repair old trucks and vans right there in her driveway.*

Liles, J. N. *The Art and Craft of Natural Dyeing: Traditional Recipes for Modern Use*. Knoxville, Tennessee: University of Tennessee Press, 1990. *Color on the back cover (his linen! shirt) and skeins on the front cover should tell it all. This is one of the best dye books to be seen in some time. No mysteries, no secrets: just how to do it and get color like the covers. The photos don't do the colors justice. Another must-have for the would-be or am-now natural dyer.*

Linder, Olive, and Harry Linder. *Handspinning Cotton*. Phoenix, Arizona: Cotton Squares, 1977. *Great info on preparing your cotton, carding, making punis, and so forth. One of the best contemporary books for handspinners, and certainly the first about cotton. The Linders spun, wove, and wore their stuff, so they practiced what they preached.*

———. *Handspinning Flax*. Phoenix, Arizona: Bizarre Butterfly Publishing, 1986. *Fact density for this little book is fifteen per page. Not that it is stuffy; it is as if Harry were giving you a class. Clear, concise, no footnotes: easy to read and remember. Refreshing remarks about growing flax, distaff methodology.*

Mack, Norman, editor. *Reader's Digest Back to Basics: How to Learn and Enjoy Traditional American Skills*. Pleasantville, New York: The Reader's Digest Association, 1992. *Big, Bold, Beautiful: a coffee table book, but has good stuff back in Section 5—the home industries part. Some natural dye info, basic spin/weave procedures, conversion, and related tasks. Some tool-making info, adaptable to fibers, wheels, looms, and so on.*

Manchester, H. H. (Herbert). *The Story of Silk and Cheney Silks*. South Manchester, Connecticut, and New York: Cheney Brothers, 1924. *Admittedly a puff piece for Cheney Mills, but fascinating none the less. From earliest history to the early twentieth century, all about silk. Lots of historical trivia, some startling name-dropping. Gets downright bullmoose-ish toward the end, but the dates and places are all there.*

Margon, Lester. *Construction of American Furniture Treasures: Measured Drawings of Selected Museum Pieces with Complete Information on their Construction and Reproduction*. New York: Dover, 1975 [1949]. *One of the few works available that has spinning wheel plans: this is the first wheel Amos built. I'm not going to say any more except that the flyer-and-bobbin information is from hunger. Of course, most published info available on flyer-and-bobbin units is from the same source. They all seem to shine it on.*

Montgomery, Florence M. *Textiles in America, 1650–1870: A Dictionary*

Based on Original Designs. New York: W. W. Norton, 1984. *The ultimate comeuppance to those who feel that to be handspun and handmade is to be funky purple cheesecloth. Majority of textiles pictured, described in/on the 100+ color plates, and in the dictionary listing are pre-1750, which means that it is mostly handspun, folks. Blow your mind, along with a $100-dollar bill.*

Morton, William Ernest, and G. R. Wray. *An Introduction to the Study of Spinning*. Metuchen, New Jersey: Textile Book Service, 1966 [1957]. *Industrial text, but the fiber information is good. In fact, it's all good; but not all about spinning. Not handspinning, anyway. Good reference for cottage-industry types.*

Pain, F. *The Practical Wood Turner*. Revised and expanded by James J. Jacobson. New York: Sterling, 1990 [1958]. *Best book on all-round wood turning in existence. Mr. Pain is both modest and practical. He deals matter-of-factly with items and procedures that today would be major books by Great Artistes. He will get you turning legs, posts, spokes, and all, and doing it better than any number of "experts."*

Pauli, Karen. *The Care and Feeding of Spinning Wheels: A Buyer's Guide and Owner's Manual*. Loveland, Colorado: Interweave Press, 1981. *Answers those pesky, everyday questions about wheels and are they all there and will they work and if not, why not. There are things here that I don't agree with, but so what? If you have doubts about a "found wheel," or this is good reading.*

Pennington, David P., and Michael B. Taylor. *A Pictorial Guide to American Spinning Wheels*. Sabbathday Lake, Maine: The Shaker Press, 1975. *Convenient pictorial reference and "guide" to American spinning wheel types, styles, and so forth. Much holiness about Shaker wheels.*

Pollak, E., and M. Pollak, editors. *Selections from the Chronicle: The Fascinating World of Early Tools and Trades*. Mendham, New Jersey: Astragal Press, 1991. *This work is a collection of articles from a historical group's newsletter. Fascinating reading for the historically inclined. It is included here because it contains an article on spinning wheels. It's not much, but it's one of the few such items we have.*

Ponting, Kenneth G. *A Dictionary of Dyes and Dyeing*. Richmond, U.K.: Mills and Boon, 1980. *Sort of like Hochberg's* Spin, Span, Spun, *except that it features alphabetical entries and the primary theme is dyeing. Another deadly book for the john. Fascinating stuff about dyeing and all related matters. Mr. Ponting spent his lifetime in a dyehouse, then became director of textile history at the Pasold Foundation.*

Pownall, Glen. *Spinning and Weaving*. New York: Drake, 1973. *If Golden Turkey awards were made for books, this is in the money. A "Glen Pownall's Creative Leisure series," a product of the editorial trash can. Trouble is, it has some textual merit.*

Quinn, Cecilia. *Yarn: A Resource Guide for Handweavers*. Loveland, Colorado: Interweave Press, 1985.

This sort of work is great. A source dries up; the material you need is N/A; can't get the brand any more, etc. So? This is valuable. Yarns are shown life-size, with all data for the spinner. Celia's remarks on fibers and yarns in general are well worth the price of the book. Enough info to reproduce any yarn you want.

Raven, Lee. *Hands On Spinning.* Loveland, Colorado: Interweave Press, 1987. *As the title suggests, this is hands-on teaching, not book-larnin'. Written for the beginner by an accomplished all-round Renaissance spinner. Good stuff, well presented. Should have been bigger. That's one of my wheels on the cover. Almost all of the hands are Deb Robson's. The other hands are Linda Ligon's.*

Riggs, C. L., and J. C. Sherrill. *Textile Laundering Technology.* Hallandale, Florida: Textile Rental Services of America, 1990 [1979]. *Answers questions about real soap, detergent, hard and soft water. An eye-opener, actually. Written in plain English.*

Righetti, Maggie. *Universal Yarn Finder.* New York: Prentice Hall, 1987. *You have to calculate grist from skein-band data of length/weight, but all the rest is here. Like the old* Northern Needleworks Blue Book, *which gave all vital data on popular yarns. This does the same, but vastly expanded. Plus, has nifty charts in the back on average sizes, and so forth. If you make or copy yarn, git it.*

Ross, Mabel. *Encyclopedia of Handspinning.* Loveland, Colorado: Interweave Press, 1988. *A disap-* pointment. *On opening page of entries, there are eight items: four tell you to look elsewhere. The next fifteen entries? Five tell you to go away. It can also be argued that many entries have nothing to do with handspinning. Lots of information here, sort of. Original U.K. edition published by B. T. Batsford, same year.*

———. *The Essentials of Handspinning.* Kinross, Scotland: M. Ross, 1984 [1980]. *Mabel's first book, probably her best. Short, terse, with flights of fancy in nomenclature. Material is parochial: Colonials must suffer. This is the work she refers to in her second book. Reminds you of Groucho and Chico in* Day at the Races.

———. *The Essentials of Yarn Design for Handspinners.* Kinross, Scotland: M. Ross, 1984 [1983]. *Problem with this work: Mabel hits you with her ** symbol, which means "Process fully described: Essentials of Handspinning." That's her first book. This is her second. About a dozen **'s. Much tabular data, much unfounded theory, avoids grist. Info on novelty yarns. Better run samples.*

Ryder, M. L. *Sheep and Man.* London: Duckworth, 1983. *Answers all the questions: where the first sheep came from, why shepherds do what they do, sheep products besides wool, why Italian sheep dogs are white: here it is. Expensive and contains only limited textile information, but the definitive work on how sheep and humans work together.*

Sanctuary, Anthony. *Rope, Twine and Net Making.* Aylesbury, Bucks., U.K.: Shire, 1996 [1980]. *Shire's little book number 51. Handy refer-*

ence on making rope, cord, and various sorts of nets. Not a how-to, really, but the illustrations are so clear and the text is so lucid that it's almost as good. Interesting pictures, too. A more detailed example is found in Diderot (if you have a copy, and speak French).

Scarlett, James D. *How to Weave Fine Cloth*. Reston, Virginia: Reston Publishing Company, 1981. *Virtually nothing about spinning here, although there is a good description of the yarns (from whatever source) required for weaving fine cloth. And I admire his general attitude. Plans in the back for a good, all-purpose loom with weight-box tensioning.*

Seagroatt, Margaret. *A Basic Textile Book*. New York: Van Nostrand Reinhold, 1975. *Overview of British "art" fiber and spinning from the 1970s. If you can get it for cheap$ then okay, otherwise.... Gives you an idea of where some of the old fogeys are coming from. Does have some nice pictures of stuff, and a shot of kids spinning with potatoes and stix. The good olde days.*

Simmons, Paula. *Spinning and Weaving with Wool*. Seattle: Pacific Search Press, 1977 [1925]. *Paula is one of those who have become a legend in their own time. Read this and you will see why. It's one of many books she has done, but I think it is the best. It's all here: breeds, scouring, carding, spinning, wheel plans, pictures, loom plans, projects, blocking reel plans, spindles, a great wheel; how can you go wrong?*

Small, Cassie Paine. *How to Know Textiles*. Boston: Ginn and Company, 1932 [1925]. *A great deal of textile information—a mini-course in how textiles come to pass. Easy-read, not technical but information-packed. It does not matter if you are a seasoned, old-hand, know-it-all or a rank, green beginner. You will learn useful stuff from this little work. A gem.*

Stavenow-Hidemark, Elisabet. *1700-Tals Textil: Anders Berchs Samling I Nordiska Museet (Eighteenth Century Textiles: The Anders Berch Collection)*. Stockholm: Nordiska Museets, 1990. *Another breathtaking collection of textile samples, swatches, yarns, and so forth, dating from the end of the handspinning era. Because most of the samples were in hand before 1760, it can be safely said that the bulk of them are handspun as well as handwoven. Look at this and be proud.*

Streeter, Donald. *Professional Smithing: Traditional Techniques for Decorative Ironwork, Whitesmithing, Hardware, Toolmaking, and Locksmithing*. Mendham, New Jersey: Astragal Press, 1995 [1980]. *Read Jack Andrews before you tackle this. Mr. Streeter doesn't talk much. He does things. He also figures you for basic skills, so he treats you accordingly. Nothing specific to spinning wheels, but plenty that can be adapted. A "classic" text. A lot of know-how and do-it. There is a lot of textile tool work out there to be done by a good smith.*

Sturt, George (George Bourne). *The Wheelwright's Shop*. Cambridge and New York: Cambridge University Press, 1993 [1923]. *Lots of information here, some about wheels, some* about tools, some about working of wood. This is also a window on the past, a man's view of the way things were (or could be) when hand labor and good work were still the norm and cost accounting had not yet grasped us all by the grommets.

Teal, Peter. *Hand Woolcombing and Spinning: A Guide to Worsted from the Spinning Wheel.* McMinnville, Oregon: Robin and Russ Handweavers, 1994 [1976]. *Magnificent modern-day rescue of the craft of woolcombing, and re-introduction to a popular audience. Contemporary woolcombing owes a great deal to this work. One-stop source for woolcombers, includes comb plans and some design material. Much easier to read than Fannin, but I like Allen's pictures better.*

Thompson, G. B., editor and curator. *Spinning Wheels: The John Horner Collection.* Belfast: Ulster Museum, 1973 [1952]. *Classic reference, a reissue of Bulletin, volume 1, no. 5 (1952). Bulk of the text was originally in catalog of the John Horner Collection (spinning wheels, ancillary items). Text describes individual entries. Illustrations are scaled, more or less. It helps if you know something of wheels. The original reference for most of us wheel-builders, or at least an inspiration.*

Varney, Diane. *Spinning Designer Yarns.* Loveland, Colorado: Interweave Press, 1987. *Title could be* Constructing Novelty Yarns. *Shows and tells all about getting super novelties out of your own stuff. Design factors, equipment capabilities, use of commercial yarns, spinning your own, warp size recipe, dye and color advice, novel and SHOCKING yarn treatments.*

Vinroot, Sally, and Jennie Crowder. *The New Dyer.* Loveland, Colorado: Interweave Press, 1986 [1981]. *First contemporary dye work that treats the subject as a procedure, rather than "misterie unveiled." Has excellent section on color theory and relationships; has gel sheets that may be used to design hues. It describes general procedures, lab details, and hazards. Three main "chemical" dye-types are shown.*

Von Bergen, Werner, and H. R. Mauersberger. *American Wool Handbook: A Practical Text and Reference Book for the American Woolen and Worsted Manufacturer and Allied Industries.* New York: Textile Book Publishers, 1948. *This is one of the seminal reference works on wool and wool processing. It is old enough that technology has not grasped us by the throat, and new enough that the information is usable. High fact density, approaches thirty facts a page. Twists, weaves, counts. All of it.*

Wakeling, Arthur, editor. *Home Workshop Manual.* New York: Popular Science, 1935. *Nothing about making a spinning wheel. Contains a great deal of material and many tips about making things in general, and lots of projects, great and small. Written back when they were not afraid to tell you to hit things with a hammer, for fear of liability lawsuits.*

Wakeman, T. J., and Vernon Lee McCoy. *The Farm Shop.* New York: Macmillan, 1960.

Straightforward, no-romance information on setting up a basic workshop, on tool maintenance, "cold" metalwork, blacksmithing, welding, soldering, sheet metalwork, woodworking, painting, glasswork, rope work . . . plus plumbing, masonry, and electrical basics.

Watson, Aldren A. *Country Furniture*. New York: Thomas Y. Crowell, 1974. *Nothing on spinning wheels. But the entire book is devoted to woodworking as it was done in rural USA circa 1750–1850. Superb drawings and sketches show joinery, tools, fixtures, methods of work. Illustrations of pre-plastickum construction should get the wheelmaker's juices flowing.*

———. *The Village Blacksmith*. New York: Thomas Y. Crowell, 1968. *Nothing about spinning wheels. A "method-of-work" book, one that shows working iron by hand. It won't show you how to make a wheel crank or flyer iron, but it does show you how such things may be made. Also numerous projects useful around the Colonial home, methods of work, the bellows, the forge . . . and an attitude.*

Watson, William. *Watson's Textile Design and Colour: Elementary Weaves and Figured Fabrics*. Seventh edition. Revised by Z. Grosicki. London: Newnes-Butterworths, 1975 [1931]. *Originally published in 1931 (London, New York, and Toronto: Longmans, Green and Company). Excellent discussion of yarn construction; a great deal about textile designing and methodology. Includes exhaustive treatment of weave structures, drafting systems and methods (draw-downs and all that), and much material on calculating yarn/weave/sett parameters.*

Weir, Shelagh. *Spinning and Weaving in Palestine*. London: British Museum, 1970. *Like Crowfoot's work, except thirty years later. Good contemporary shots of drop spindling, plus description of spindle technique and methods. Did you know that along the Gaza Strip in 1970, most yarns were still being spun on drop spindles? Good information on ground looms as used for kilims (flat-woven rugs).*

Whiting, Gertrude. *Old-Time Tools and Toys of Needlework*. New York: Dover, 1971. *Reprint of an original from Columbia University Press in 1928. Not much on spinning per se, and what there is should be taken with some salt. If you can disregard the air of condescension, this is fun to read. Good illustrations but off-handed descriptions. Reels, winders, swifts, pins, bobbins, etc.*

Wigginton, Eliot, editor. *The Foxfire Book: Hog Dressing; Log Cabin Building; Mountain Crafts and Foods; Planting by the Signs; Snake Lore, Hunting Tales, Faith Healing; Moonshining; and Other Affairs of Plain Living*. Garden City, New York: Doubleday, 1972. *The Foxfire series has many other books in it, but the original and 2 are about the best. "Down-home" stuff for your author. Anyway, Foxfire 1 has info on soap-making and green-wood joinery (also moonshine).*

———. *Foxfire 2: Ghost Stories, Spring Wild Plant Foods, Spinning and Weaving, Midwifing, Burial*

Customs, Corn Shuckin's, Wagon Making and More Affairs of Plain Living. Garden City, New York: Anchor/Doubleday, 1973. *Foxfire 2 is the one on spinning/weaving—includes plans for great wheels (plus how to build) and loom plans.*

Wily, John. *A Treatise on the Propagation of Sheep, the Manufacture of Wool, and the Cultivation and Manufacture of Flax, with Directions for Making Several Utensils for the Business.* Williamsburg, Virginia: Colonial Williamsburg Foundation, n.d. *Reprint from 1765. Straightforward advice for the textile types of the eighteenth century. Mr. Wily speaks with the voice of one who knows.*

Woolman, Mary Schenck, and Ellen Beers McGowan. *Textiles: A Handbook for Students and Consumers.* Second edition. New York: Macmillan, 1926 [1917]. *Old but valuable text, written for the student and the consumer. Woolman and McGowan took the position that since modern (1917!) people were so far removed from the textile processes, it was necessary to educate them as to what constitutes good cloth. Which they do. Interesting remarks about laundering.*

Worst, Edward F. *Foot-Power Loom Weaving.* Third edition. Milwaukee, Wisconsin: Bruce Publishing, 1924. *This is not a spinning text, but contains much information that is valuable to the handspinner, dyer, and hand worker in general. Includes an original recipe for oleum (Saxon blue), along with many variations. Great loom and gadget plans, as well. And if you spin, you might as well know something about weaving. Great place to start.*

———. *How to Weave Linens.* Milwaukee, Wisconsin: Bruce Publishing, 1926. *A classic weaving text, yet has more on flax and its workings than most spinning books. The illustrations of work and of tools are priceless, and he includes workable plans for all sorts of gear. I've built it. All of it. The stuff works.*

Yates, Raymond Francis. *Soldering and Brazing: A Handbook for Mechanics Giving Directions for Soft Soldering, Hard Soldering, and Brazing.* Bradley, Illinois: Lindsay, 1992. *Good, all-round text on soldering and brazing metals. Low-tech applications, common materials. You need this stuff for flyer shafts and cranks, that sort of thing. Also for many other textile tools and applications, cans, bobbin tubes, water cups. Plus, it's good to know.*

Young, Stella, Nonabah Bryan, and Charles Shirley. *Native Navajo Dyes: Their Preparation and Use.* New York: AMS Press, 1979 [1978]. *A seminal work on the subject, originally published by the Bureau of Indian Affairs (BIA) in 1940. S. Young was the home economics honcho at Fort Wingate Vocational High School in the late 1930s. She collaborated with Mrs. Bryan, the dyer, and Mr. Shirley, the illustrator. The recipes have all been tried and proven, or, as Ms. Young puts it, "definitely formulated."*

INDEX

Figures in **boldface** refer to illustrations. Footnotes and the glossary have not been indexed.

A

Acid indigo, 374–375
Acid rinse, scouring and, 60–61
Alkali,
 in saponification, 49
 preferred form of, 52
 scouring baths to test for, **53**, 54
 wool scouring and, 49–54
Almost-worsted yarn, 72
American Saxony Production wheel, 185, **188**
Arranging fibers. *See* Carding; Combing; Hackling; *specific fibers*.
Ashenhurst's formula, 254
Ashford Traditional wheel, 183–184, 189
Assists. *See* Scouring of wool.

B

Balanced ply. *See* Natural ply.
Balanced twist. *See* Natural ply.
Balanced weave, defined, 251
Ball winder. *See* Nøstepinne.
Balls of yarn, from skeins, 282–283
Bast fibers, defined, 33
Bathtub, use in scouring, 37, 51
Beetling mallet, construction plans for, 335–337, **336**
Belgian flax wheel, 183
Bias in yarn, 288
Bibliography, 474–489
Big Four Fibers
 described and compared, 29–35, 118–123, **119**, 136–137
 measurements of, 127–136
 physical properties and life requirements of, 136–138
 sources of, **120**
Bleach and flax, 151
Blocking of wool, 121
Blocking reel, 206–207, **206**, 277–278, **279**,
 and stand, construction plans for, 363–367, **365**, **366**, **367**
Bobbin. *See* Flyer-and-bobbin.
Bobbin, storage, 279–282, **280**, **281**, **282**, **283**,
 in plying, 300–301, 303, 305
 and rack, construction plans for, 350–351, **351**
 yarn capacity of, 387–388
Bobbin winder, 279–283, **280**
Bohemian wheel, 183
Boiling off silk, 33, 34, 200
Bombyx silk, 31, 33
Bouclé, 327, **327**
Bowing of cotton 38, **38**
Brake-band, 217, 235–236, **236**
Breaking of flax, 38. *See also* Flax, preparation of
Breaks in yarn, 116–117
Brixton, Judith, 182
Brushed yarn, 327

C

Cable, ply construction of, 330, **330**
Calcium, water hardness and, 49
Calculations
 clean yield of wool, 142, **142**
 drive-ratios and take-up, 389–398
 grist,
  by direct measurement of length and weight, 91, 93–94
  estimating from thickness of textile, 384
  estimating from thread count of plain-weave cloth, 384
  of plied yarn, 308–309
 moisture content of yarn, 134, 139
 moisture regain of yarn, 136, 141
 ropes and cords, yarn requirements of, 388–389
 twist-stability in plied yarns, 314–324
 twists per inch required for yarn, 383
 weaving, yarn quantity required for, 254–256
 wraps-to-grist conversion table, 385
 yarn capacities for common bobbin sizes, 387–388
 yarn capacity of various spindle copps, 388
Canadian spinning wheel, 186
Caps (of silk), 32

Card clothing, **64**, 65
Carding
 actions used in, 66–72, **70–71**
 of almost worsted yarns, 72, **72**
 blending action of, 67
 and card structure, 65–66
 hand cards and, 64–66, **64**, **65**, **66**
 lesson in, 68–71, **70**, **71**
 purposes of, 63, 67–68, **67**
 rolag and, 67–68, 70, **70**, 72, **72**
 stripping and, 66–67, **66**, 69–71, **70**, **71**
 time required to, 145–147
 value of, 143–145
 wool and, 63–72, 143–147
Carding oil
 purpose of, 144
 recipe for, 369–370
Carpet beetle, 197–199, **197**
Castle wheel, 183, **183**, **184**
Chair wheel, 184, **185**
Charging a card, defined, 69
Chlorine damage to flax, 168
Clean yield of wool, 142, **142**
Click reel. *See* Clock reel.
Clock reel, 266, **266**
Cocoons (of silkworm), 32, 39, **39**
Coin spindle (tahkli), 178–179, **179**
 construction plans for 344–345, **345**
 wrist distaff and, 175
Combing, 151–166
 action, 156–162, **152**, **156**, **157**, **158**, **159**, **160**
 purpose of, 63–64
 wool and, 63–64, 151–166, **152**, **156**, **157**, **158**, **159**, **160**
  full worsted, 162–166, **164**
  lock, 161–162, **161**, **162**
  rough, 154–161, **155**, **156**, **157**, **158**, **159**, **160**
  semi-worsted, 166
Combs, construction plans for, 354–358, **357**
Complex yarn, 288–289, 323, 329–331
Contaminants. *See* Cotton; Fiber; Flax; Silk; Wool.
Cord
 calculations for making, 388–389
 yarn for, 247–248, 262
Costs of fiber preparation and spinning,

measured in time, 145–147, 172–173
Cotton
　bowing of, 38, **38**
　carding of, 37
　characteristics of, 30–31, **30**, 118–122, **119**, 137
　cleaning of, by gin, 37
　combing of, 37–38
　contaminants in, 37, 150
　cultivation of, 138
　defined, 30
　grist of (count), 89, **89**
　introduction to, 30–31
　and needlework, 247
　picking of, 37
　preparation of, 37–38, 398
　source of, **120**
　staple length of, 30, **31**
Crackers, flax, recipe for, 402–403
Crochet hook, construction plans for, 340–341, **340**, **341**
Crochet yarns, 246, **246**, 260, **261**
Cummer, Joan, 181

D

Detergent, use in scouring, 52–59
Diameter of yarn
　and grist, 90–91, **91**, 93–98, **94**, **95**, **97**, 384
　and twist angle, 113–115
Differential rotational speed (DRS)
　adjusting, 79–86, **80**, 191
　calculating, 390–398
　flyer-and-bobbin assembly and, 191–192, 210–233
Discontinuous spinning, 76, 209, 237, **237**
Distaves, 162, **162**, 174–175, **175**, **176**
　construction plans for, 358–361, **358**, **359**, **361**
Diz, 154, 159–160
Double treadle wheel, 190
Draft, how to, 18–23, **18**, **20**, 78, 82–86, 89
Drafting hand, duties of, 84, **85**
Drafting rate, defined, 20, 172
Drafting zone, defined, 42
Drafting-against-twist. *See* Woolen spinning method.
Drafting-without-twist. *See* Worsted spinning method.
Drive band, 187–189, 213–214, 216, 219, **219**
　bumpless, plans for, 377–381, **379**, **380**, **381**

double, **219**, 381
　installing a, 381–383
　tension and slippage, 226–227, **226**
Drive-band dressing, recipe, 370–371
Drive ratios
　calculating, 389–398
　and double drive systems, 227–228
　and driven spindles, 237, **237**
　and single-drive, bobbin lead systems, 214–215
Driven spindle. *See* Spindles.
Drop spindles. *See* Spindles.
Drying scoured wool, 61–62
Dutch wheel, 182–183, **183**
Dyes, 374–375
　and microwave oven, 14
　and weight of fiber, 150–151

E

Elasticity in yarn, 120–122, 246–248, 286
Elbow skeins, 264, **264**
Emulsification, 47–48, **48**. *See also* Soap.
Equations. *See* Calculations.
Equipment for fiber preparation and spinning,
　construction of 15–16, 332–333, 368
　beetling mallet and log, 335–337, **336**
　blocking reel and stand, 363–367, **365**, **366**, **367**
　bobbin, storage, and reel, 350–351, **351**
　coin spindle (tahkli), 344–346, **345**
　combs, 354–358, **357**
　crochet hook, 340–341, **340**, **341**
　distaves
　　freestanding, 360–361, **361**
　　handheld, 358–360, **358**
　　waist, 359–360, **359**
　hackle, 353–354
　niddy-noddy, 341–344, **342**, **343**
　nøstepinne or winding stick, 337–339, **338**
　ripples, 351–353, **352**, **353**, **354**
　scutching sword and base, 333–335, **334**
　skirders, 362–363, **362**
Southwestern spindle, 349–350, **349**
　spindles, drop, 346–348, **346**, **347**
　storage bobbins and rack, 350–351, **351**
Thai spindle, 348, **348**
Twisty-stick, 19, **19**, 339, **339**

F

Farnham wheel, 186, **186**
Felting, 29–30, 37
Fiber
　animal sources of, 27–28, **28**. *See also* Silk; Wool.
　burn chart, 386
　characteristics of, 27–28, 118–123, 136–137
　commercial preparation of, 143–144, 147–149
　contaminants in, 149–151
　defined, 26–28
　elasticity, 120–122
　hiring out preparation of, 193–196
　history of, 243–244
　home production of, 137–138
　man-made vs. natural, 27
　obtaining, 23–24, 29, 43
　plant sources of, 27–28, **27**. *See also* Cotton; Flax.
　preparation of, 35–41
　raw, 26–30, 36–37, 44–47, 147–149
　resilience, 122
　See also Big Four Fibers; Cotton; Flax; Silk; Wool.
Fine spinning, 399–400
Finger-rolling (spinning method), 18–19
Fingers of flax, defined, 34–35
Flax
　and bleach, 151
　breaking, 38, **39**
　characteristics of, 33–35, 118–122, 137
　cleaning, 38
　combing, 39
　contaminants in, 150
　crackers, recipe for, 402–403
　cultivation of, 138, 167–168, **167**
　defined, 33–34
　and dyes, 151
　flammability of, 35
　fingers, defined, 34–35,
　hackling of, 39, **39**, 169–170, **169**, **170**, **171**
　introduction to, 33–35
　line type, 34, **34**, 39, 171, **171**
　linen compared to, 34
　and needlework, 247
　preparation of, 34, 38–39, **38**, 167–170
　retting of, 38, 168–169, **169**
　rippling of, 38, 167, **167**
　scutching of, 38, **39**, 169, **169**, **170**

semi-worsted yarn from, 166
spinning, 119–120, 170–172
strick, 34–35
tow type, 34–35, **34,** 39, 171, **171**
ultimates, 33–34
Flour, for sizing, 376
Flyer-and-bobbin-assembly, 77–86, 210–241
    double-drive, 211, **212,** 218–233, **219, 220, 226, 230, 231**
    and plying, 297–306
    single-drive, bobbin lead, 211–216, **212, 213,** 235–236
    single-drive, flyer lead, 211, 216–218, **212, 216,** 235–236
    winding off from, 233–235, **235**
Formulas. *See* Calculations.
Friction
    in single drive, flyer-lead wheels, 217–218
    in twist, 102–105
Full worsted combing, 162–166

G

Gaustad, Stephenie, 182, 192, 194
Gelatin, for sizing, 376–377
Ginger beer, recipe for, 400–402
Glossary of terms, 404–473
Grease wool, 36, 44–47
Great wheel, 184–185, **186,** 240, **240**
Grist
    calculating, 21–22, 91, 93–94, 98–100, **99,** 134–136, 384–385
    changing, 89–90, **90**
    defined, 21, 88, **88**
    factors affecting, 97–98
    McMorran Yarn Balance and, 98–100, **99,** 130–132
    metric system and, 92–93
    moisture and, 133–136, **133**
    plying and, 307–310
    stating directly, 89, **89,** 91, 93–94
    stating indirectly (as count), 89, **89**
    textile thickness and, 384
    thread count and, 384
    wraps to, conversion table, 385
    yarn diameter and, 90, **91,** 93–98, **94, 95, 97**
Gunter, Rob. Soap Quench of, 375–376

H

Hackle, 39, **39,** 161, **161**
    construction plans for, 353–354
Hackling, 39, **39,** 169–171, **169, 170.** *See also* Flax, preparation of.
Hand cards, 64–66, **64, 65**

Hand-over-hand method of plying, 300–306, **300, 301, 302, 304**
Handwoven (magazine), 258
Hard water. *See* Water, hard; Wool, scouring of.
Hawser (plying technique), 291, **291**
High-whorl spindle. *See* Spindles.
Hochberg, Bette, 174
Homogenization, emulsification and, 48
Hooked stick. *See* Twisty stick.

I

In the grease. *See* Grease wool.
Inch gauge, 94–97, **94, 95, 97**
Indian Valley wheel, 184
Indigo, 374–375
Irish castle wheel, 184, **184**

J

Jerk-it method of plying, 298–299

K

Keratin and wool, 29
Kinsale cloak, 249–254, **249**
Knitting yarns, 245, 248, 259–260, **260**
Knop yarn, 326
Knots in yarn, 102–103, 207

L

Lashing on, defined, 156–157, **156**
Lease ties, 275–277, **276**
Leonardo da Vinci, 210
Lemon juice, wool scouring and, 60–61
Line flax, 34, **34,** 171, **171**
Linters, 369
Liquor
    assists, 47–54
    defined, 50
    ratio in wool scouring, 50–51, **50,** 56–61
    temperature of 50, 52, 54, 56–59
Loading a card, defined, 69
Long-draw, 240
Lye, 49, 372–373

M

Macedonian wheel, 184, **185**
Mail ordering, yarn and, 43
Make, defined, 73
Master hand
    defined, 68
    use in carding, 68–70
Mawata (of silk fiber), defined, 32. *See also* Cocoons (of silkworm).
McMorran Yarn Balance
    grist and, 98–100, **99,** 130–133

Mercerization (of cotton and flax), 122
Milk, for sizing, 377
Miner's head, 238–239, **239**
Mohair, 324, 327–328, **328**
Moisture content
    cotton, 137
    flax, 137
    silk, 137
    wool, 133–137, 139–142, **140,** 144–145, 155–156
Moisture regain, 134–136, 139–142, 144
Mordants. *See* Dyes; *Specific fibers*.
Mother-of-all, 188–189, 217
Motor spinners, 192–193
Moths, 197–199, **198**

N

Natural ply, 106–111, 286
Natural soap, 49, 55
Needlework yarns, 246–247
Netting, 261–262, **262**
Niddy-noddy, 264–266, **265**
    construction plans for, 341–344, **342, 343**
Nip, 102–103, 313
Noils, 369
Nøstepinne, 337–339, **338**
Notes to readers, 14–15
Novelty yarns, 306, 324–329, **325, 326, 327, 328**

O

Oleum, 374–375
Olive oil as wool lubricant, 155, 369–370
Orkney wheel, 183
Owego wheel, 186

P

Phosphates, 55
Pirtle wheel, 184
Planking, defined, 165
Plying, 284–331
    cable yarn, 330, **330**
    complex yarn, 288–289, 323, 329–331
    defined, 285
    and grist, 307–310
    ideal yarn, 313–320
    methods of, 297–306
        hand-over-hand, 300–306, **300, 301, 302, 304**
        jerk-it, 298–299
        tromp and hope, 299
    non-functional yarns, 310

novelty yarns, 324–329, **327**
principles of, 291–294, **292, 293,** 296–297, **296**
    constant motion, 296–297, **296**
    distance, 292–293, **292**
    ply from re-wound bobbins, 293–294, **293**
    tension, 291–292, **292**
reasons for, 284–286
and rigidity, 315–320
simple, 288–289
superior balanced yarn, 312
and tensile strength, 289
and torsional reaction, 316–320
and twist, 285–291, **286, 287, 290, 291,** 310–324, **314**
and uniformity, 306–310
yarn storage packages and, 294–296, **294, 295**
Pull hand, duties of, 84, **85**
Punis, 398

R

Raven, Lee, 167
Recordkeeping, 201–202, **201**
Reflectiveness of fiber, 40–41, **40, 41**
Resilience of fiber, defined, 122
Retting (of flax), **38.** See also Flax, preparation of.
Rewards of spinning, 23–25
Ripples, construction plans for, 351–353, **353, 353, 354**
Rippling (of flax), 38. See also Flax, preparation of.
Rob Gunter's soap quench, 375–376
Rooing (of wool), 35
Rope making, 202–205, **202, 203, 204, 205**
    calculations for making, 388
    yarns for, 247–248
Roping, defined, 104
Rough-combing, 154–161, **155, 156, 157, 158, 159**
Roving, defined, 104
Rubber-band drive, 187
Rubbing, yarn and, 104

S

S-twist, 119–120, 290, 291, **290, 291.** See also, Twist, direction of; Twist-stable yarn.
Saponification, 47–49. See also Soap.
Saxon blue, 374–375
Saxony wheel, 182–183, **183**
Scales, 132–136, **132**
Scandinavian wheel, 186

Scarlett, James, 16
Schacht wheel, 184
Schappe, 32, 40
Scouring of wool, 36–37, 44–61, **44,** 143–145
    assists,
        alkalis, 50–54
        washing soda, 50–54
        defined, 52
        detergent, 52–54
        soap, 47–49, **49**
        defined, 45
    emulsification and, 47–48, **48**
    hard water and, 49, 54–55
    lemon juice and, 60–61
    liquor
        defined, 50
        ratios, 50–59, **50**
        temperature of, 50, 52, 54, 56–59
    saponification and, 47–49
    soft water and, 49, 54–55
    value of, 143–145
    vinegar and, 60–61
Scutching (of flax), 38
Sword and base for, construction plans for, 333–335, **334**
Sebaceous glands (of sheep), 47, **46**
Setting (in yarn), 109, 199–201, 311–312
Semi-worsted yarn, 166
Sericin, 33
Sheep, **29, 36,** 45, **120, 137,** 138, **369**
Sheep raising, 138
Shetland wheel, 183, **183**
Silk
    boiling off, 33, 40, 200
    bombyx compared with tussah, 31, 33
    caps, 32
    carding, 40–41
    characteristics of, 31–33, 40, 118–122, **119,** 137
    cleaning of, 33, 40
    cocoons, 32, 39–40, **39**
    combing, 40–41
    contaminants in, 33, 40, 150
    defined, 31
    dyeing of, 33, 150
    forms, **32**
    introduction to, 31–33
    mawata, 32
    moth, 39, **39,** 120, 137
    in needlework, 247
    preparation of from cocoons, 32, 39–41, 138

reeling of, 32, 39–40, **40**
reflectiveness of, 40–41, **41**
schappe of, 32, 40
seracin and, 33
staple length, 31
storing of, 197, 200
throwing, 32, 40
types of, 31
Silkworms, raising, 138
Sinkage, 143
Sizing, recipes for, 376–377
Skein tag, 23
Skeins. See Yarns, skeins.
Skirder, 206–207, **206**
    construction plans for, 362–363, **362**
Skirting of wool, 36
Slippage, double-drive system and, 224–229
Sliver, 35, 153–154, **153** 160, **160,** 165
Slubbing, defined, 104
Soap
    emulsification and, 47–48, **48,** 50
    natural, 49, 55
    protection of, 50
    recipe for, 372–373
    saponification and, 47–49, 50
    scouring with, 47–61
    and water hardness, 49, 54–55
    scum, wool scouring and, 49
Sodium carbonate. See Washing soda.
Soft water. See Water, soft; Wool, scouring of.
South German wheel, 186
Southwestern spindle, 180
    construction plans for, 349–350, **349**
Spindles
    Balkan, 180–181, **181**
    coin (tahkli), 178–179, **179**
        construction plans for, 344–346, **345**
        wrist distaff and, 175
    discontinuous spinning and, 76, 209, 237, **237**
    driven, 73–74, **75,** 236–241, **238, 239**
    drop, 73–74, 176–181, **177, 178,** 179
        construction plans for, 346–348, **346, 347**
    Egyptian method with, 177, **179**
    hook type, **176,** 177
    manual, 73–74
    plying and, 209–210
    Princess Twinkie method with,

177–178, **177, 178**
proficiency with, 178–181, **179**
refining skills with, 176–178, **178**
Southwestern, 180, **180**
    construction plans for, 349–350, **349**
spinning with, 74–75, **74, 75,** 176–181, **177, 178, 179,** 209
supported, 73–74, 179–180
Thai, 180, **180**
    construction plans for, 348, **348**
Turkish wheel, 180–181, **181**
    winding off from, 178–179, **179, 180**
    winding on to, 74, **74, 75**
Spinners, motor, 192–193
Spinning,
    as determinant of yarn character, 123–125
    first yarn, 77–86
    history of, 12, **12, 14,** 17–18, **17**
    methods. *See* Woolen spinning method; Worsted spinning method.
    rewards of, 23–25
Spinning oil, recipe for, 369–370
Spinning wheels
    classification by class, type, and style, 181–190. *See also specific names of wheels.*
    drafting with, 78, 82–86
    evaluation of, 190
    flyer-and-bobbin. *See* Flyer-and-bobbin.
    mechanics of. *See* Flyer-and-bobbin.
    polish for (recipe), 371–372
    spinning first yarn on, 77–86
    treadling, 80, 82–85, 108, 206–207, 214, 221–223, 229
    troubleshooting, 79–82
    See also Tensioning systems.
Spin-Off (magazine), 43, 167, 258
Staple
    defined, 30
    cotton and, 30–31
    wool and, 30–31, 102, 152
Storage bobbin. *See* Bobbin, storage.
Storage of fiber and yarn, 62, 192–197, 200–210
Strick (of flax), defined, 34–35
Stripping, 66–67, 69
Suint, defined, 47
See also Grease wool; Wool, scouring of.
Sulfuric acid, 374–375
Sunlight, drying wool in, 61–62
Super-quench, 375–376

Swifts
    lantern, 269, **269,** 277–278
    squirrel cage, 269–271, **269, 270**
    umbrella, 267–268, **268**
Swingling (of flax), 38. *See also* Flax, preparation of.
Swiss wheel, 185, **190**

T

Tagging (of wool), 36
Tahkli. *See* Coin spindle.
Take-up. *See* Flyer-and-bobbin assembly.
Tensioning systems, 187–189, **187, 188, 189**
    adjusting, 191–192
Textile technique, yarn and, 244–248
Thai spindle, 180
    construction plans for, 348, **348**
Thrums, 369
Time required to prepare and spin fiber, 13–14, 145–147, **147,** 172–173, 253–254
Tools (for spinning). *See* Equipment; *specific tools.*
Top, 152–154, 160, **160.** *See also* Worsted combing.
Tow flax, 34–35, **35,** 171, **171**
Treadles, double type, 190
Treadling, 80, 82–85, 108, 206–207, 214, 221–223, 299
Tromp-and-hope method of plying, 299
Turkish spinning wheel, 184, **185**
Turns per inch. *See* Twist, measurement of.
Tussah silk, 31, 33
Twist, amount of, 20–23, 101–117, **101,** 383
    abrasion and, 105
    breaks resulting from excessive, 116–117
    commercial yarns and, 285
    controlling while spinning, 106–108
    and diameter, 105
    effects of, 101–106, 252–253, **253**
    elasticity and, 105
    excessive, 116–117
    friction and, 102–105, 313
    loss of, 110
    measurement of, 20–22, 101–102, 106–111, 311–312
    counting humps, 107–109, **107**
    counting with tracer fibers, 106
    self-plying, 106–111, **106, 107,** 311–312
    untwisting, 111–112, **111**
    per inch required for yarn, chart, 383

plying and, 285–291, **286, 287, 290, 291,** 310–324, **314,** 383–385
reflectiveness and, 105
setting and, 109–110, 199–201, 311
tensile strength and, 22, 102, 105, 289
unplying and, 285
winding off and, 233–235, **235**
Twist-active yarn, 100, 110, 286–287, **286, 287**
Twist angle, 113–115, **113**
Twist count. *See* Twist amount.
Twist direction, 192, 252–253, 290–291, 310–325
    and drive band installation, 382
Twist factors, 382, **383**
Twist, learning to, 18–19, 23
Twist rate, defined, 20–21
Twist-stable yarn, 110, 286–287, **286, 287,** 311, 314–320
Twisty-stick, 19–20, **19, 20,** 41–42, construction plans for 339, **339**

U

Ultimates (in flax), 33–34
Unplying of yarn
    determining twist count and, 111, **111**

V

Vinegar, scouring and, 60–61

W

Washing soda, use in scouring, 50, 52, 54
Water
    hard, 49, 54–55
    soft, 49, 54–55
    wool scouring and, 45–62
Weaving, handspinning and, 18, 245–246, 248, **246**
Willowing of wool, **56,** 57, 68
Winding on. *See* Flyer-and-bobbin assembly.
Winding off. *See* Yarns, skeins.
Wool
    acid rinse of, 60–61
    blocking, 121
    carding of. *See* Carding.
    characteristics of, 29–30, 118–122, **119,** 136–137
    clean yield of, 142, **142**
    cleaning. *See* Wool, scouring of.
    combing. *See* Combing.
    commercial preparation of, 140–145
    contaminants in 36, 44–47, 68, 142, 149–150, 152, 156

defined, 29
drying, 61–62, 145
and dye, 150–151
elasticity of, 121–122
felting of 29–30, 37, 150
grading of, 36
grease, 36, 44–47
hair follicle, **46,** 47
introduction to, 29–30
lemon juice and, 61
and lubricants, 152, 155–156, **156**
moisture content of, 133–137, 139–142, **140,** 144–145, 155–156
in needlework, 247
obtaining, 23–24, 29, 43
olive oil and, 155, 369–370
picking of, 36, 145–146, 156
rinsing of, 60–61
rooing of, 35
scouring of, 36–37, 44–61, **44, 58,** 143–145
scouring temperature, 50, 52, 54, 56–59
shearing of, 35–36, **36**
skirting of, 36
sorting of, 36
staple length of, 30–31, **31,** 152
storage of, 62, 196–197, 200–201
stripping of, 66–67
suint, 47
sunlight and, 61–62
tagging of, 36
teasing. See Wool, picking.
vinegar and, 61
willowing of, 57, 68
wuzzing of, 59–60, **60**
yolk, 47
See also Sheep.
Wool combing. *See* Rough combing.
Woolcombing. *See* Worsted combing.
Woolen spinning method, 41–42, **42,** 123–125, **123,** 153–154, 208–209
Woolen-type yarn, characteristics of, 41, **41,** 63, 123–125, **123, 124**
Worsted combing, 63–64, 153–154, 162–166
Worsted spinning method, 41–42, **42,** 123–125, **123,** 153–154, 208–209, **208, 209**
almost-worsted, 72
Worsted-type yarn, characteristics of 41, **41,** 123–125, **123, 124,** 162–163
Wraps (per inch)-to-grist conversion table, 385
Wuzzing, 60–61, **60**

Y

Yarn
balanced, 312
balls, 282–283, **283**
beginners', what to do with, 86
breaks in, 116–117
capacity of various copps, 380
characteristics of, 126–128, 248, 286
complex, 288–289, 323, 329–331
conditioning, 133. *See also* Yarn, moisture regain of.
design factors, 244–245
diameter
determining, 90–91, **91,** 94–98, **94, 95, 97, 98,** 384
and twist angle, 113–115
disassembling, 206–207, **206, 207**
elasticity of, 120–122, 246–248, 286
grist. *See* Grist.
imperfect, 306
measurements, 127–136
length, 130–131, 273–274
for plying, 294–296, **294**
weight, 132–136, **132**
moisture content of, 133–137, 139–142, **140**
moisture regain of, 135–137, 140
novelty, 306, 324–329, **325, 326, 327, 328**
packages, 263–283, **264,** 294–296, **294, 296**
parameters of, defined, 127
plying. *See* Plying.
quantities needed for weaving, calculating
by following project instructions, 258–259
for Kinsale cloak, 249–254, **249**
length, 250–253
by making educated guesses, 254–256
twist, effects of, 252–253, **253**
weft density, 251–252
width, 250–253
by working from a similar fabric, 256–258, **257**
quantities needed for other crafts
crochet, 260, **261**
knitting, 259–260, **260**
netting, 261–262, **262**
rope and cord making, 262, **262**
reconstruction, 285
setting of, 109, 199–200
skeins, construction of, 271–277, **272, 273, 274**
lease ties and, 275–277, **275, 276**
and measurement of yarn length, 273
skeins, equipment for winding, 264–267
clock reel, 266, **266**
elbow, 264, **264**
niddy-noddy, 264–266, **265**
yarn blockers, 266, **266,**
skeins, equipment for unwinding, 266–271
person, 266–267
swifts
lantern, 269, **269,** 277–278
squirrel-cage, 269–271, **269, 270**
umbrella, 267–268, **268**
skeins, handling, 277–283
making balls from, 282–283, **283**
winding off to a blocking reel, 277–278, **279**
winding off to a storage bobbin, 279–282, **279, 280, 281, 282**
storage, 200–201
stored vs. newly spun, 109
tensile strength and, 118, 245, 289
tension in measuring length, 130–132
and textile technique, 244–248
crochet, 246, **246,** 260,
knitting, 245, **245,** 248, 258–260
needlework, 246–247
netting, 261–262
rope, 247–248
weaving, 245–246, **246,** 248
twist. *See* Twist.
without twist 103–105
twist-active, 100, 110, 286–288, **286, 287**
twist-stable, 110, 286–288, **286, 287,** 311, 314–320
uniformity in, 306–310
weight of, effect on moisture, 133–136
winding off and twist, 233–235, **235**
without twist, 103–105
Yarn gauge, 94–98
See also Fiber; Grist, Twist, Spinning methods.
Yeadon wishbone wheel, 184
Yolk of wool, defined, 47

Z

Z-twist, 119–120, 290–291, **290, 291.** *See also* Twist, direction of; Twist-stable yarn.

W hen you subscribe to SPIN·OFF, you get four project-packed issues a year, filled with:

- Beautifully photographed projects
- Instructions and know-how from experienced spinners
- Inspirational articles on the techniques and joys of spinning
- The latest product news

SPIN·OFF Magazine
1-800-767-9638
$24 (1 yr. U.S.) Dept: A1BS

Visit www.interweave.com, a great resou for finding local spinning groups, events, basic information, and to view our selec of spinning books. Titles include:

TOPS WITH A TWIST
A Special Publication from SPIN·OFF Magazine
Hats are what you'll find in this special publication developed from the collection of fabulous, inventive entries submitted to Spin·Off's hat contest. There are 17 fun and funky hats to knit and 1 to crochet with close-up photographs, accompanied by easy-to-understand instructions.
8½ x 9, paperbound, 80 pages,
color photos, line drawings, and charts.
ISBN: 1-883010-75-6
$14.95/$22.95 CAN

HANDS ON SPINNING
Lee Raven
Understanding how spinning works, building a simple spindle, spinning on a treadle wheel, choosing a wheel, preparing fibers, carding, twisting, and plying are explored in fully illustrated detail.
8½ x 10¾, paperbound, 120 pages,
color and b&w photos and illustrations.
ISBN: 0-934026-27-0
$16.95/$25.95 CAN

And coming Fall 200
THE SPINNER'S COMPANIO
ISBN: 1-883010-79-9 $19.95/$29.95 C/

Interweave Books are available at craft shops and bookstores
Or Call 1-800-272-2193